The Private Side of American History

READINGS IN EVERYDAY LIFE

Second Edition

II SINCE 1865

EDITED BY Thomas R. Frazier

THE BERNARD M. BARUCH COLLEGE
OF THE CITY UNIVERSITY OF NEW YORK

UNDER THE GENERAL EDITORSHIP OF

John Morton Blum

YALE UNIVERSITY

Harcourt Brace Jovanovich, Inc.

NEW YORK   SAN DIEGO   CHICAGO   SAN FRANCISCO   ATLANTA

ISBN: 0–15–571965–3

Library of Congress Catalog Card Number: 78–71873

Printed in the United States of America

Preface

Most studies of history concentrate on public figures and public affairs, the events and people that most historians consider important or influential. What is left out in these traditional presentations is the ordinary, day-to-day life of most of the members of the given society—that is, the "private side" of history. This phrase is meant to suggest not events hidden from public view, but, rather, personal incidents and the attitudes of ordinary people—especially their responses to the policies of the dominant power in their society.

This second edition of *The Private Side of American History* continues and expands on the themes of the first edition. The essays collected here present a sampling of the varied attitudes, life-styles, living arrangements, and cultural conflicts that have affected the American people. The selections deal both with the mainstream culture and with cultural groups considered deviant by the mainstream. Portrayed here are people—rich and poor, black and white, male and female, young and old—as they go about their daily tasks trying to provide for themselves a satisfactory way of life. New topics covered in this expanded second edition include the dilemma of the poor in the South during the late nineteenth century; the medical profession's treatment of female patients; labor strife in a New England mill town; Mexican-American workers; government welfare programs; the struggle of working-class families in modern America; and the problems of America's aged.

This portrayal is necessarily incomplete, for only an encyclopedic work could encompass the complexities of everyday life throughout American history. But it is hoped that the essays presented here will give the reader a taste of the manifold cultures found within American society today and in the past.

The sixteen selections, arranged in roughly chronological order, are grouped into four sections, each of which concludes with an annotated bibliography. The headnote accompanying each selection attempts to place the subject matter in its historical context. A brief introducion to the volume describes the major areas that should be considered in a historical survey of everyday life.

For assistance in the preparation of this revision I would like to thank most of all William J. Wisneski, my editor at Harcourt Brace Jovanovich, who, along with Thomas A. Williamson, my former editor, suggested the theme of the original edition and provided encouragement. For scholarly assistance I would like to express my appreciation to the following colleagues: Carol Berkin, the Bernard M. Baruch College of the City University of New York; Mary Beth Norton, Cornell University; John Morton Blum, Yale University; Gary Nash, University of California, Los Angeles; Michael Ebner, Lake Forest College; David Culbert, Louisiana State University; Daniel Walkowitz, Rutgers University; and Robert C. Ritchie, University of California, San Diego.

THOMAS R. FRAZIER

Contents

1930–1950
Depression and War

1950–1975
Contemporary Society

Topical Table of Contents

HEALTH, DISEASE, AND DEATH

VIOLENCE AND WAR

SOCIAL CONTROL

Introduction

In recent years the traditional presentation of American history in schools and colleges has come under criticism. The growth of various liberation movements in the 1960s has led to a rewriting of many history texts to include material on blacks, American Indians, white ethnic groups, and women, among others. New Left historiography has brought about a reconsideration of economic and class interests both domestically and in foreign policy. A third area in which the historical record has been remiss is the one represented by the essays reprinted in this volume—the realm of the everyday life of the American people, the private side of American history. The traditional emphasis on public events has resulted in an historical record that fails to provide sufficient insight into the role of ordinary people in the development of our culture and society. Their feelings, the ways in which they responded or reacted to public events, the hopes, desires, and needs that have been the basis of their response are now recognized by many American historians as a legitimate and important area of historical concern.

In attempting to understand and write about the everyday life of ordinary people, it has been necessary for historians to draw on the theoretical and methodological approaches of the social sciences. Several of the selections in this volume, in fact, have been written by professional sociologists and anthropologists. Historians are only just beginning to apply to recent American history the new historiographical approach so well represented in the second edition of Volume I of *The Private Side of American History*, which treats America's early growth.

This second volume is concerned not so much with a growing America as with the attempts to build a national culture based on "traditional American values" in the face of serious challenges by different groups who have little desire to participate in such a value system at the expense of their own culture and perceived past. The consensus on the national culture so sought has proved to be extremely fragile and ultimately incapable of being sustained. When history is viewed from the perspective of the "movers and shakers" of the nation, as it has been in the traditional textbooks, the consensus appears to have been established. When the everyday life of the American people is examined, however, the fragility of the consensus is clear. While the people may appear quietly to acquiesce in the dominant culture of the society, they go right on living their lives, often outside its stated values.

In this volume we will examine the attempts to establish a cultural consensus and will look at those who try to pattern their lives after its

1

perceived values. We will look more often, however, at those who live by a different set of norms, those whose continued existence challenges the dominant culture and who, ultimately, refuse to abide by the rules of what has been called "the American way of life." The groups dealt with in this volume fall, for the most part, then, into the category of those left out of, or briefly mentioned in, the traditional texts: women, poor people, ethnic minorities, the young, and the old, among others. But the focus here is not on the causes of their oppression or the conflicts in which they engage in their attempts to come to grips with the dominant power in our society. We concentrate, rather, on the effects of their oppression and the adaptations and adjustments they have made in their attempts to live as fully as possible under often difficult circumstances. Throughout the nation's history, the majority of the people in the United States have lived outside the dominant culture; so we are, in fact, exploring here the private lives of most Americans.

What we are concerned with, then, are the things that most Americans do most of the time—the day-to-day activities and experiences that concern and shape the individual and, thus, are factors in shaping American society. This "private side" of American history is revealed by studying those areas of concern common to the majority of people throughout history.

The quality of individual life is determined largely by such basic factors as work, education, family relationships, and stage in the life cycle. By examining what work people do, how they feel about what they do, what its effect is on them, and whether or not it does what they expect it to—to provide them with a living—we can see the effect employment, or lack of it, has on society as a whole. We need also to understand the impact that the various sources of education in our society—schools, mass media, advertising, family and peer group interaction, and religious institutions, among others—have on the total development of the individual. Because, traditionally, the family has been one of the major forces shaping an individual's life, we must look at the family structure in the United States and see how changes in the structure affect the lives of all of its members. We should also note the impact of changes in the society on the various members of the family in their relationships with each other.

Religion is another important part of American life. The religious institutions have been a major force in the establishing of societal norms, and religious ideas have often been influential in forming counter-norms and in providing emotional support for those outside the mainstream of American culture. So, an understanding of the roles religion has played in the cultural development of America is necessary to our study.

Also important are those areas of concern that, for the most part, are even less directly governed by the individual. Included here are such factors as health, disease, and death; violence and war; and social control. We can examine how the people of the United States have dealt with these crucial and, in some cases, ultimate questions. We will consider their responses to the improved quality of medical care over the past century; the myths and realities of medicine and how the people have perceived these issues; how death is handled; and the value placed on human life in general and on particular lives. We will explore both personal and institutional violence as well as the social function of war—war as an example of foreign policy is not considered; we are more concerned here with war as an integrative factor in society. And we will examine the means society uses to shape the individual's behavior to the desired norm. Here we will consider how the dominant society attempts to assimilate or govern the groups it considers deviant; the actions "deviant" groups take to maintain their distinctiveness—and the price they pay for their efforts; and, of particular importance, the way certain institutions such as schools and churches operate directly or indirectly as agents of social control. The areas of concern considered here by no means exhaust the possible categories for the study of everyday life, but they are at least suggestive of the kinds of experiences that must be covered in exploring the private side of American history.

In this volume, each section contains at least one selection that attempts to delineate the norms or activities of one segment of the dominant culture. The other selections describe behavior or attitudes that deviate from the traditional norms. The volume begins with an essay that thoroughly explores the values of small-town Midwestern society. The norms described there still operate, under the rubric "traditional American values," and serve as an appropriate place to begin our consideration of everyday life in America since the middle of the last century. Other essays in this section describe the distinctive way doctors dealt with the variety of disorders that afflicted middle-class women in the Victorian age, the impact of economic oppression on blacks and poor whites in the post-Reconstruction South, and the attempt by the traditional elite to escape from a changing society by withdrawing into restrictive enclaves where they need associate only with others of their own class.

In the next section, we see changes that are taking place in family life and sexual relations. Then come two selections dealing with new immigrants—the first having to do with childhood, adolescence, and young adulthood among the Jews of New York City's Lower East Side, and the second with the struggle of immigrant mill workers to achieve a decent standard of living in the face of oppressive working conditions. The next essay exposes the rather desperate and pathetic attempt by the Ku Klux Klan to perpetuate in a rapidly changing society the "traditional values" delineated in the opening section.

The first essay in the third section shows how the Great Depression brought into question many of the widely held attitudes about the promise of American life. Also, we see the way dominant society has dealt with two of its prominent nonwhite minorities, blacks and chicanos. The concluding essay in this section describes how massive governmental economic investment in social welfare during the war years changed the nature of the American economy and distorted the very meaning of welfare.

The last section opens with an analysis of the quality of suburban life, a mode of existence chosen by a majority of the American people at the present time. In contrast to the contentment expressed by the suburbanites, the powerful and persistent counter-culture movement that affected so many Americans, particularly the young, in the late 1960s is presented next. The concluding selections deal with problems facing two of the increasingly dissatisfied segments of the American population—the working-class family and the aged—whose adherence to the "American Dream" has trapped them in what may seem more like a nightmare.

This volume provides but a sampling of the enormous variety of life-styles and life experiences of the groups and individuals who make up what we call the American nation. The editor has attempted to acquaint the student with the possibility of better understanding the history of the United States through a study of the many different ways in which people have shaped their lives in order that they might live with as much of their essential humanity intact as possible. For many this has been an extremely difficult task because of the structural disorders in American society. Only if these disorders are seen for what they are, however, and seriously challenged, will the private lives of the American people improve in significant ways.

1865–1900
The Gilded Age

Morality on the Middle Border

LEWIS ATHERTON

In a recent attempt to find a term that could be used to describe the "traditional" American value system, politicians and their intellectual supporters have devised the phrase "middle America." Although it is recognized that the belief system expressed in the phrase may have Midwestern roots, "middle America" is not a geographical term. Middle Americans live in Suffolk County, New York, and Orange County, California, as well as in Peoria, Illinois.

It is important to point out that there really is a "middle America" that proclaims the values attributed to it. And, although the appellation is modern, the belief system is not. One finds in the values of "middle America" a restatement of a basic conflict of American life—the antagonism between the urban and rural (or small town) ways of life. This conflict is at least as old as the agrarian philosophy expressed by Thomas Jefferson in the late eighteenth century.

The phrase "middle America" is particularly apt because much of the intellectual and spiritual content of traditional American morality found its strongest advocates and clearest statements in the Midwest, or, as the area was called in the late nineteenth century, the Middle Border. Some of America's greatest creative writers of the late nineteenth and early twentieth centuries—Mark Twain, Hamlin Garland, and Sherwood Anderson among others—grew up on the Middle Border and have immortalized its culture in their works. These writers, whose works both celebrate and derogate Midwestern life, provide insight into the ethics and morality that pervaded the Midwestern culture.

Certainly one of the primary sources of Midwestern morality was Protestant Christianity. The East may have contained the intellectual giants of WASP (White Anglo-Saxon Protestant) culture, but the Midwest provided the substance both of revivalistic piety and popular ethical teaching. The Sunday school, not the academy, provided Midwestern Protestants with much of their understanding of religion and morals. The famous **McGuffey's Readers** used in the public schools and in home instruction became another major source of religious and ethical teaching, since most of those who learned to read on the Middle Border did so with the aid of McGuffey's books.

Lewis Atherton of the University of Missouri, a son of the Middle Border himself, describes in the selection reprinted below the substance of Midwestern morality as portrayed and propagandized by the **Readers.** He properly stresses the religious underpinnings of the moral world portrayed by McGuffey. Belief in the existence of God and belief in his ultimate judgment act as moral levers whereby the powerful urges of mankind can be turned from sinful pursuits and moved in a heavenward direction. Although it was true that less than half of the

Midwestern population were affiliated with churches, religious institutions had widespread influence in the community because most of the leaders in any town or village were active members. Protestant morality was also espoused in newspapers and the vast number of popular magazines whose existence was as ephemeral as their presence was ubiquitous.

Atherton deals here not only with the public and official morality but also with elements of actual practice that were often in conflict with it. He points out that the upper classes in the towns often operated on a different ethical wave length than did the mainstream. Rarely, however, did they publically challenge the official morality. There were, of course, others who defied the norms; most communities had their share of drunkards, village atheists, and other ne'er-do-wells, as well as those deviants by definition—Roman Catholics.

The structure of morality built up on the Middle Border still stands as a conservative judgment on the looser, more flexible morality developed in the cities. Its continued appeal has led to a recent attempt by groups of concerned citizens to restore the **McGuffey's Readers** as a learning tool in Midwestern schools in order to combat the godless, materialistic teaching they find there today.

CHURCH, SCHOOL, AND HOME

B etween 1850 and 1900 Americans bought one hundred million copies of William Holmes McGuffey's school readers.[1] Though well re-

---

[1] Richard D. Mosier, *Making the American Mind: Social and Moral Ideas in the McGuffey Readers* (New York, 1947), 168. I am indebted to this study and to Harvey C. Minnich, *William Holmes McGuffey and His Readers* (New York, 1936) for biographical detail concerning McGuffey and for suggestive leads. The material cited in this study comes from the 1857 edition of McGuffey Readers, the titles of which follow: *McGuffey's New First Eclectic Reader: For Young Learners* (Cincinnati, 1857); *McGuffey's New Second Eclectic Reader: For Young Learners* (Cincinnati, 1857); *McGuffey's New Third Eclectic Reader: For Young Learners* (Cincinnati, 1857); *McGuffey's New Fourth Eclectic Reader: Instructive Lessons for the Young* (Cincinnati, 1857); *McGuffey's New Fifth Eclectic Reader: Selected and Original Exercises for Schools* (Cincinnati, 1857); and *McGuffey's New Sixth Eclectic Reader: Exercises in Rhetorical Reading, with Introductory Rules and Examples* (Cincinnati, 1857). In the absence of graded schools the titles lacked the same significance that they would bear today. For instance, many pupils got no further than the third reader. Material in the sixth reader was very advanced in nature and would be read today not earlier than junior high school.

"Ethics, Folklore, and Morality on the Middle Border" (Editor's title: "Morality on the Middle Border"). Reprinted from *Main Street on the Middle Border* by Lewis Atherton, pp. 65–88, 95–100, copyright © 1954 by Indiana University Press, Bloomington. Reprinted by permission of the publisher.

ceived virtually everywhere, they appealed particularly to the Middle Border. As an apostle of religion, morality, and education, McGuffey wanted to bolster midwestern civilization against the dangers inherent in pioneering new frontiers. Since his Readers were directed to a supposedly classless society, they were all-inclusive in their appeal, and from them came a set of principles which remained unchallenged in the minds of common people until the turn of the century.

McGuffey worried so much about frontier dangers that he overlooked the revolutionary changes in transportation, manufacturing, and management which were then taking place. The 1857 revision of his Readers, which most Midwesterners studied, barely mentioned steamboats, and railroads received no attention at all. Pupils learned about horse-drawn transportation, about merchant rather than manufacturer, about artisan in place of factory laborer, of the outdoors, of birds and farm animals, of gossipy barbers, of Longfellow's "Village Blacksmith," and of town pumps, watering troughs, and village greens:

> Then contented with my State,
> Let me envy not the great;
> Since true pleasures may be seen,
> On a cheerful village green.[2]

Moreover, children learned that village and country life surpassed that in cities. As a rule, McGuffey simply ignored urban ways or used them as examples of corruption. The story, "Mysterious Stranger," described the unhappiness of a man from another planet when he learned that city pleasures in our world were accompanied with the penalty of death. Still another story told of "Old Tom Smith," the drunkard, whose downfall came from city life. Through a clerkship in a city store, he became acquainted with bad company. Instead of spending his evenings reading, he went to theatres, balls, and suppers. Drinking and card playing followed next, and soon thereafter his saintly mother had to pay large gambling debts for him. Although his mother and wife grieved themselves to death over his city vices, nothing could stop his drinking. The story ended with reception of the news that he had received a ten-year prison sentence for stealing.[3] Village boys often misbehaved in McGuffey's stories but they seldom fell prey to major vices.

McGuffey's emphasis on rural and village life pleased an agrarian age. His environmental picture squared with physical facts, and people knew just enough of the outside world to share his doubts about cities. His Readers thus gained strength by applying the eternal verities to a simple culture, uncomplicated by urban and industrial problems. This very strength, however, became a source of weakness as village and farm gave way to city and factory.

McGuffey ideals retreated slowly. Rural America believed in a classless society, which helped enforce still other pressures toward con-

---

[2] *Third Reader*, 201–202.
[3] See *Sixth Reader*, 206–211, 398–400, and *Third Reader*, 118–120.

formity. In the 1830's Tocqueville commented on the tyranny of the majority in making Americans conform to a common pattern. Although disagreeing with Tocqueville's analysis, James Bryce said much the same in the 1880's. According to him, American public opinion was not stated along class lines; it applied to all. In Bryce's estimation, Americans believed that common sense resided in the minds of the majority, with a consequent "fatalism of the multitude" evident in much of American life. Ed Howe commented that city people would behave better if they knew one another as well as did villagers who heard gossip about their sins on the way home from committing them,[4] thus implying that conformity was even greater in small towns.

Perhaps also an emphasis on the immediately useful and the practical contributed to the survival of current moral values. An Iowa lawyer who spent his youth in a small town commented that most pioneers were of the earth, earthy. They knew practical things—weather, rains, common plants and animals, good livestock. But they were not philosophers.[5] Whatever the explanation, small-town beliefs changed slowly, and this characteristic gave village life an impression of stability and permanence.

The God-centered, small-town code emphasized man's immortality. School and home both paid obeisance to God's plan and God's laws, for everything fell within His master plan. From McGuffey's Readers the pupil learned that Jesus was above Plato, Socrates, and all the philosophers, for He was a God.[6] Evidences of His power and wisdom existed on every hand. McGuffey proved this with simple stories. Washington's father, for instance, secretly planted seeds in a design which spelled out George's name when they sprouted. Although George was surprised, he refused to accept his father's suggestion that chance explained the phenomenon. His father now admitted that he had planted the seeds to teach George a lesson, and urged the boy to look around him at God's planning on every hand. And thus, said McGuffey, driving home his point as usual, from that day George never doubted the existence of a God who was the creator and owner of all things.[7]

Even the problem of evil in a universe governed by divine law was explained to school boys through simple stories. Everything happened for the best and every object had a purpose in the great plan of things. When one of two boys caught in a thunderstorm remarked that he hated the evil lightning, the other explained that lightning was necessary to purify the air of bad vapors, a greater good thus offsetting a lesser evil.[8] Understanding would always clarify the appearance of evil. An observant boy asked his father to help him cut down thorn bushes and thistles which were snagging wool from the sides of passing sheep. Since parents in McGuffey's Readers were always wiser than children, the boy profited by taking his father's advice to wait until morning. In doing so, he discovered that birds

[4] Edgar W. Howe, *Plain People* (New York, 1929), 305.
[5] Roger S. Galer, "Recollections of Busy Years," *Iowa Journal of History and Politics*, XLII (January, 1944), 3–72.
[6] *Fifth Reader*, 280–282.
[7] *Fourth Reader*, 82–83.
[8] *Ibid.*, 180–183.

used the wool to build their nests, and that God indeed was wise and good and had made everything for the best.[9]

A former resident of Hillsboro, Iowa, described the operation of this philosophy in his childhood days. Belief in God was universal. People wondered why certain things occurred, chiefly the deaths of children and very good people, but no one doubted God's existence and His fatherly care. If a death occurred, the Lord willed it. The Lord sent afflictions to punish sin and disbelief. The Lord could be prevailed upon to help His people out of difficulties. If the corn needed rain, the churches set a day of prayer. If success accompanied this, it had been the proper thing to do; if intercession failed, the people had not prayed with sufficient faith. The heavenly books were balanced daily by an omniscient bookkeeper who recorded every act. The idea of universal and impersonal law was displeasing. These people wisely turned to something warmer, something more directly personal in which man played the central part. He participated in a drama which included sky and earth, which began with Adam, and which would end only when the heavens were rolled up as a scroll.[10]

McGuffey taught that society depended on religion. Christianity was conducive to national prosperity. It raised the poor from want, brought rich and poor together on a common level for an hour of prayer, and promoted good order and harmony. Self-respect and elevation of character, softness and civility of manners came from religious teaching. Christianity strengthened the family circle as a source of instruction, comfort, and happiness.[11] Moreover,

> If you can induce a community to doubt the genuineness and authenticity of the Scriptures; to question the reality and obligations of religion; to hesitate, undeciding, whether there be any such thing as virtue or vice; whether there be an eternal state of retribution beyond the grave; or whether there exists any such being as God, you have broken down the barriers of moral virtue, and hoisted the floodgates of immorality and crime.[12]

Insofar as school books are concerned, small-town Mid-America now reads of miracles of science. God, church, and even human death are generally ignored. Separation of church and state and a desire to shield children from morbid thoughts help explain this marked change. Perhaps, however, it would not have occurred had science not become the god of so many people, for gods are too important to be omitted in formal education of the young.

In the second half of the nineteenth century grade schools commonly opened the day with brief devotional exercises. Lessons also had a religious

[9] *Third Reader*, 139–142.
[10] Galer, "Recollections of Busy Years."
[11] *Fifth Reader*, 306–307.
[12] *Sixth Reader*, 421–423.

slant. McGuffey's *First Reader* pictured a little girl kneeling in prayer and asking God to protect her from sin.[13] A poem in the *Second Reader* stressed the blessings of immortality:

> A little child who loves to pray,
> And read his Bible too,
> Shall rise above the sky one day,
> And sing as angels do;
> Shall live in Heaven, that world above,
> Where all is joy, and peace, and love.[14]

These simple stories and poems in public-school readers document the tremendous shift in faith between the nineteenth and twentieth centuries, from a man-centered and God-centered universe on the one hand to an impersonal and science-centered universe on the other.

McGuffey also stressed the need for public schools. "We must educate!" Literary as well as religious institutions must keep pace with the headlong rush of western settlement. If the Middle Border expected to preserve republican institutions and universal suffrage, both *head* and *heart* must be trained.[15] McGuffey thus urged pupils to feverish activity:

> Haste thee, school boy, haste away,
> While thy youth is bright and gay;
> Seek the place with knowledge blest;
> It will guide to endless rest;
> Haste thee, school boy, haste away,
> While thy youth is bright and gay.[16]

Newspapers expressed the same ideas.[17] Parents supposedly could do nothing finer for their children than to educate them.[18] Although children often attended school only irregularly and quit at an early age, and less than half the adult population were formal church members,[19] citizens generally believed that churches and schools made communities "decent

---

[13] *First Reader*, 26.

[14] *Second Reader*, 81.

[15] *Fifth Reader*, 150–153.

[16] *Third Reader*, 21–22.

[17] See, for example, article on value of schools in Algona, Iowa, *The Upper Des Moines*, March 7, 1867, and a similar article in Gallatin, Missouri, *North Missourian*, March 10, 1893.

[18] Comment on removal of H. C. Callison from Jamesport to Gallatin, in Gallatin, Missouri, *North Missourian*, September 1, 1893.

[19] For the state of Illinois as a whole in 1900, for instance, only 46.6 per cent of adults were church members. United States Bureau of the Census, *Religious Bodies, 1906* (Washington, 1910), I, 305–308.

places" in which to live.[20] Even real-estate promotion—the most absorbing interest of all—stressed the presence of churches and schools as selling points.

McGuffey ranked family life with church and school as a third major conservator of ideals. Families were like a bundle of twigs; the strength of all far surpassed that of the individual:

> We are all here!
> Father, Mother,
> Sister, Brother,
> All who hold each other dear.[21]

McGuffey stressed love of brother and sister in a nature poem which Theodore Roosevelt later was to criticize for its ignorance of birds:

> Birds in their little nests agree;
> And 'tis a shameful sight,
> When children of one family
> Fall out, and chide, and fight.[22]

Idealization of motherhood and the mother's central position in family life was a frequent theme. One poem referred to the mother's voice:

> It always makes me happy, too,
> To hear its gentle tone;
> I know it is the voice of love
> From a heart that is my own.[23]

Mutual interdependence was illustrated in simple stories. In one, grandfather sat in his easy chair before the fire, smoking his pipe. The family dog reclined nearby, and grandmother was busy at her spinning wheel. A granddaughter sat on the man's knee. As he thought about the death of the child's mother, tears rolled down his cheeks. Although the innocent child had not yet realized her loss, she was already repaying her grandparents for their care by catching the flies which buzzed around grandpa's head.[24]

McGuffey stressed complete obedience to parental direction and parental ideals in return for the love and care lavished on younger members of the family. The poem "Casabianca" told of a boy burning to death on the deck of a naval vessel in obedience to his father's order to await his return, which was prevented by the father's death during the

[20] Edward O. Moe and Carl C. Taylor, *Culture of a Contemporary Rural Community: Irwin, Iowa, Rural Life Studies* No. 5 (Washington, 1942), 61.
[21] *Sixth Reader*, 167–168.
[22] *Second Reader*, 151–152.
[23] *Ibid.*, 101–103.
[24] *Fifth Reader*, 51–52.

naval battle then under way. While such Spartan obedience may seem unduly severe to modern-day parents, it obviously was better to die than to suffer the intense remorse of a daughter who returned to her mother's grave in the village cemetery thirteen years after the funeral. Grief overwhelmed her at the memory of how unwillingly she had brought a glass of water at her mother's request the night of the latter's death. True, she had planned to ask forgiveness the following morning, but her mother was then cold in death.[25] "Meddlesome Matty" received her just deserts in McGuffey's stories, as did a group of curious boys who applied to a rich old squire's advertisement for a youth to wait on him at table. To test the applicants, he filled his reception room with appealing items. The first boy could not resist eating a luscious-appearing cherry, only to find it filled with cayenne pepper, and others received equally just rewards for their curiosity. The one applicant who sat in the room for twenty minutes without yielding to temptation got the job, and ultimately a legacy from the rich old squire.[26] Obedience paid off in many ways in McGuffey's stories, as the disobedient little fish learned after being pulled from the water on a hook:

> And as he faint and fainter grew,
> With hollow voice he cried,
> Dear mother, had I minded you,
> I need not thus have died.[27]

At company dinners, McGuffey-trained parents made children eat at the second table and also expected them to be seen and not heard. Elders were always addressed as "Mr." and "Mrs." by properly reared children. At the same time, parents wanted their offspring to have every advantage of religion and education, if they really had taken the McGuffey lessons to heart.

CULTURAL PATTERNS

Church, school, and home thus furnished education for *heart* and *mind*, a process which involved the teaching of an extensive code of morality. Without doubt, this fitted best the needs and desires of a pious, church-going, middle-class society. For such people, the McGuffey code was both adequate and right. In their estimation, it underlay decent society in this world and salvation in the next. Midwestern ideals did not come solely from this one middle-class group, however. Although it dominated education and fought hard to enforce its convictions, it was never able to establish conformity on the part of all citizens.

At least four additional sources competed with and modified the dominant middle-class code. The first can be loosely identified as upper

---

[25] *Fourth Reader*, 172–174, 239–241.
[26] *Fifth Reader*, 65–69.
[27] *Second Reader*, 84–85.

class in nature, although its ramifications were broader than simple class structure. Virtually everywhere on the Middle Border were families which held substantial or respectable places in society without bowing to the McGuffey code. Episcopalians like Benjamin F. Mackall of Moorhead, Minnesota, and Daniel M. Storer of Shakopee, Minnesota, danced and played cards and ignored the gloomy restrictions which dominated so many of their contemporaries. Even good Presbyterians and Methodists who read more than church and secular newspapers often slighted McGuffey's code. In 1865 Helen Clift Shroyer of New Castle, Indiana, and her friends played euchre and seven-up without the slightest sense of guilt; and she and her fiancé accompanied others to a dance in a neighboring town which lasted so late that they reached home at five in the morning. Her wedding trip included visits to the Chicago theatre. Oyster suppers, cards, dances, popcorn parties, visits to ice cream parlors, and Sunday afternoon buggy rides appealed to her. She dodged funerals if at all possible and ignored many of the common commercial entertainments. The "Mysterious Man," a sleight-of-hand performer, was passed by on the grounds that she was too tired to attend, a lame excuse for one of her energy. She was critical of a temperance lecture which she made herself attend, and was bored in Brother Norris' Sunday School class because she thought he could not teach "worth a cent." The Sunday reading of the *Atlantic Monthly*, which she and her husband enjoyed, may have taken the bloom from Brother Norris' penetrating remarks on the scriptures.[28] The families of Edgar Lee Masters and Thomas Hart Benton were neither pious nor active church members, and both taught their children a set of standards which deviated from McGuffey's code. Zona Gale's father, a self-educated railroad engineer, taught her that the spirit of man is God, and that no other God exists. From him she obtained other convictions, like pacifism, which ran counter to dominant middle-class beliefs.[29] Such families generally dared not flaunt their heresies in the face of local society, especially since they relied on local people for their livelihood, but they did maintain a measure of individuality.

Catholics represented still another departure from the dominant code. In their views on education, Sabbath recreation, and intoxicants, they clashed with middle-class Protestant sentiments. Although McGuffey opposed religious intolerance, anti-Catholic feeling existed in midwestern country towns. Don Marquis, himself the product of a small Illinois town, pictures this in his novel, *Sons of the Puritans*. Aunt Matilda, guardian of the dominant small-town code, becomes alarmed when she learns that a Catholic has been entertaining village youngsters with stories. She suspects him of showing them beads, speaking in Latin, and even of exhibiting idols, with an invitation to fall down and worship them. Aunt Matilda

---

[28] Kate Milner Rabb, "A Hoosier Listening Post," feature section of Indianapolis *Star*, March 14 to May 24, 1935. During this period the column carried the Shroyer diary which may also be found in a folder of clippings from the column, Indiana State Library, Indianapolis.

[29] August Derleth, *Still Small Voice: The Biography of Zona Gale* (New York, 1940), 27–28.

belongs to the group that circulates rumors about collections of firearms in Catholic churches.[30] Bromfield's novel, *The Farm*, in large measure the story of his family's life in Ohio, recounts the anti-Catholic sentiment which a youngster in his family heard in livery stables, police stations, and other gathering places. Copies of a paper, *The Menace*, containing vivid accounts of rapes committed by Catholic priests and of illegitimate children born to Catholic nuns, passed from hand to hand. Secret passages supposedly connected homes of priests with neighboring convents so they could visit nuns at their convenience.[31] An occasional minister condemned Catholicism from the pulpit. In a Thanksgiving Day sermon in 1869 at Centreville, Michigan, a Methodist preacher boasted that infidel France and Catholic Mexico had been incapable of reaching the same high civilization then prevalent in Protestant America. Three generations locally, he said, had been sufficient to stamp out Romanism in family life.[32] Similarly, a Baptist preacher preparing for a revival meeting at Gallatin, Missouri, in 1893, claimed that Protestants modelled themselves on Christ while Catholics worshipped lesser figures.[33]

Although many immigrants were Catholics, it is well to note that still another cultural influence in small towns came from foreign immigration. Immigrants could not know all the shadings of the dominant, moralistic code followed by middle-class Protestants. A considerable number of German Lutherans and Catholics at Monroe, Wisconsin, in the late 1860's and early 1870's, organized a local Turnverein and carried on an active social program in Turner's Hall. Masked balls, beer drinking, and uniformed acrobatic groups of young Germans performing on the bars and trapeze conflicted with local ideas of proper behavior. People got along, to the credit of all groups, but "Christians" sniffed nonetheless. In December, 1869, the Monroe editor reported that the Turners had decided to close their bar on Sunday nights in favor of a "Lyceum Concert." Older and wiser heads had persuaded the younger people to make the change. Perhaps a Turner's idea of God was different from that of a "genuine" Christian, said the editor. If the Turners thought God liked conviviality, a good glass of lager beer, or even a comic song, the community might indulge them so long as they closed their bar on Sunday.[34]

Lastly, every community had a group of inhabitants who simply ignored the middle-class code of respectability and religious observance. They drank and fought and caroused and "cussed," or they hunted on Sunday, shunned the churches, and pursued their simple pleasures without yielding to community pressure to lead a "better" life. Here, then, was the cultural pattern—a dominant middle-class Protestant group given to religion and stern morality; an upper-class group of "respectable" peo-

---

[30] Don Marquis, *Sons of the Puritans* (New York, 1939), 30–33.

[31] Louis Bromfield, *The Farm* (New York, 1935), 157–162.

[32] Centreville, Michigan, *St. Joseph County Republican*, November 27, 1869.

[33] Gallatin, Missouri, *North Missourian*, April 14, 1893.

[34] See accounts in Monroe, Wisconsin, *Monroe Sentinel*, January 13, 27, February 3, March 3, April 7, May 5, and December 8, 29, 1869, for activities of the group and comments by the editor of the local paper.

ple who failed to see any necessary connection between pleasure and sin; Catholics; foreigners; and a "lower" class, which ignored the dominant code except perhaps for temporary allegiance following revival meetings. In spite of latent antagonisms, villagers lived close together and could not avoid influencing one another. It was a rare boy indeed who grew to manhood solely as the product of one cultural layer.

Outstanding interpreters of small-town culture have recognized this diversity of beliefs. Americans chuckle at the exploits of Huckleberry Finn, son of the town drunkard, who was free to swear, smoke, swim and go barefooted, and who ran away from riches when they came his way simply because he refused to conform to local standards of respectability. Mark Twain grew up in small midwestern towns and he knew from experience the conflicting cultural patterns within such communities. When Van Wyck Brooks later wrote *The Ordeal of Mark Twain*,[35] in which he presented Mark as wanting to rebel against a sex-warped and barren culture, he ignored the many cultural differences illustrated in Twain's own small-town characters. Bernard De Voto has pointed out the dangerous oversimplification in Brooks' thesis and the many strands running through midwestern culture.[36] In the so-called "battle of the village" which novelists fought in the early twentieth century, some, like Zona Gale, emphasized sweetness and light, and others, like Sinclair Lewis, concentrated on the drab and monotonous aspects of town life. In such novels, emphasis became distortion instead of insight, and they inevitably fell below the level of realism which Twain achieved.

MIDDLE-CLASS IDEALS

The dominant, middle-class code of McGuffey and his followers held that life was a serious business. In selections like Longfellow's "Psalm of Life" readers were urged to make the most of their opportunities:

> Tell me not in mournful numbers,
> Life is but an empty dream!
>
> .   .   .   .   .
>
> Life is real! Life is earnest!
>
> .   .   .   .   .
>
> Footprints on the sands of time.
>
> .   .   .   .   .
>
> Let us, then, be up and doing,
>   With a heart for any fate;
> Still achieving, still pursuing,
>   Learn to labor and to wait.[37]

---

[35] Van Wyck Brooks, *The Ordeal of Mark Twain* (New York, 1920).
[36] Bernard De Voto, *Mark Twain's America* (Boston, 1932).
[37] *Sixth Reader*, 212.

Even the ancients were cited to the same effect. Hercules turned away
from the siren called "Pleasure" to follow a maiden whose path to happiness involved both pain and labor.[38] In this selection, and others like
"Hugh Idle and Mr. Toil," [39] McGuffey stressed the virtues of labor.
Youngsters who took him seriously could not indulge in leisurely enjoyment of wealth later on without a sense of guilt. Moreover, perseverance
was highly recommended:

> Once or twice though you should fail,
>   Try, Try, Again;
> If you would at last prevail,
>   Try, Try, Again;
> If we strive, 'tis no disgrace,
> Though we may not win the race;
> What should you do in that case?
>   Try, Try, Again.[40]

Truth, honesty, and courage belonged to the cluster of desirable
traits. Washington's father so loved truth that nailing George in a coffin
and following him to the grave would have been less painful than hearing
a lie from the boy's lips. When George cut down the cherry tree, he man-
fully told his father "I can't tell a *lie*, father. You know I can't tell a *lie*."
And his father in turn joyfully cried, "Come to my arms, my dearest
boy. . . ." Common people could be equally noble. Susan's widowed
mother made the family living by taking in washing, and Susan helped by
making deliveries. On one occasion, Farmer Thompson gave her two bills
in payment by mistake. She was severely tempted. The additional money
would mean a new coat for mother, and little sister could have the old one
to wear to Sunday School. Little brother could have a new pair of shoes.
In spite of such desperate need, Susan corrected the mistake, and, sobbing
with anguish, refused a shilling's reward on the grounds that she did not
want to be paid for honesty. In this case, she received only a lightened
heart, but McGuffey's heroines usually gained financially as well. Mc-
Guffey also stressed courage, even at the risk of ridicule. A boy who
snowballed the schoolhouse to avoid the taunts of others, when he knew
the act was wrong, was pictured as lacking in true courage.[41]

Contentment, modesty, and kindness were praised. One story told of
Jupiter permitting unhappy people to exchange burdens with others.
One man discarded his modesty instead of his ignorance; another his
memory rather than his crimes. An old man threw off his gout in favor of
a male heir, only to obtain an undutiful son discarded by an angry father.
All begged Jupiter to restore their old afflictions. Patience stood by as
they resumed their old troubles and automatically reduced their loads by a

---

[38] *Ibid.*, 215–217.
[39] *Fourth Reader*, 231–236.
[40] *Ibid.*, 95–96.
[41] See *Third Reader*, 233–236, 110–113, 144–148.

third. The moral was plain, according to McGuffey. One should never repine over his own problems or envy another, since no man could rightly judge his neighbor's misfortune.[42] A beauty who tossed her glove into a ring with lions to prove her lover's devotion, only to have him throw it in her face after regaining it, showed the silliness of vanity.[43] A poem about Mary's lamb demonstrated the rewards for kindness to animals. When it followed her to school one day, and the children marvelled at its affection, the teacher commented:

> And you each gentle animal
> To you, for life may bind,
> And make it follow at your call,
> If you are always *kind*.[44]

Greed, revenge, and selfishness toward others were castigated in stories which made plain the moral involved. "The Tricky Boy," for instance, was mean and given to teasing others. When a tired little girl asked help in shifting a jug of milk to her head in order to rest her weary arms, he purposely let it fall to the ground and break. He thought it was fun to see her cry until he slipped on the ground, made slick by the spilled milk, and was laid up for three months with a broken leg.[45]

While McGuffey's code has been ridiculed for its emphasis on material rewards for virtue and unremitting labor—and a hasty reading of his stories may seem to bear this out—he offered a nicely balanced philosophy in which life's purpose and rewards transcended material gains. In his own life and in his Readers, McGuffey preached against the foolishness of material ambition alone, to which so many of his pupils turned:

> Praise—when the ear has grown too dull to hear;
> Gold—when the senses it should please are dead;
> Wreaths—when the hair they cover has grown gray,
> Fame—when the heart it should have thrill'd is numb.[46]

Newspapers and preachers supported McGuffey's scheme of values. In 1870, the Centreville, Michigan, paper published a letter addressed to "My Dear Obadiah," urging young men to attend church, to act and dress modestly, to be ambitious, and to abhor drinking, smoking, and chewing. A companion letter to "My Dear Dorinda" encouraged girls to be sober and thoughtful in preparation for marriage and motherhood. Many were interested only in clothes, and their vocabulary was studded with vapid expressions like, "I thought I should die," "O my," "What are you going

[42] *Ibid.*, 215–217.
[43] *Ibid.*, 335–336.
[44] *Second Reader*, 99–101.
[45] *Third Reader*, 80–81.
[46] *Sixth Reader*, 217–218.

to wear," "O ain't that pretty," "Now you're real mean," "You think you're smart, don't you," and "Well I don't care, there now." The writer asked what such girls could do in the kitchen or sick room.[47] A Chatfield, Minnesota, sermon on the "Fast Young Man" in 1896 pictured various types—"the Dude," "the Softie," "the Lazy," "the Dissipate." Young men, said the preacher, should adopt habits of personal cleanliness, avoid bad company, retire early at night, and practice modesty.[48]

Protestant pulpit and press also generally supported McGuffey's views on Sabbath observance. At Monroe, Wisconsin, in 1896, the local Presbyterian preacher asked bicycle riders to discontinue the practice of visiting neighboring towns in groups on Sunday. Another local preacher used the bicycle problem as a springboard for discussing the relation of Sabbath observance to morals as a whole. Granting that times had changed and that the Sabbath was made for man, he insisted that people still must square their actions with their consciences. In developing this theme, he offered a number of observations paralleling McGuffey's ideals. Gambling at church affairs was as evil as gambling in saloons. Card playing wasted time that could be better employed. A man should feel just as free to encircle the waist of his neighbor's wife in a round dance as he would on the way home from prayer meeting. And there was no more harm in a bicycle "spin" on Sunday than in a drive with horse and carriage; less, as a matter of fact, if the horse was tired. People winked at bigger sins on weekdays, liquor drinking for example.[49]

McGuffey firmly believed in private property and in its blessings to society. He quoted Blackstone to prove that necessity begat property and recourse was had to civil society to insure it. Private property had enabled a part of society to provide subsistence for all. It had insured leisure to cultivate the mind, invent useful arts, and to promote science. Simple stories again drove home the lesson. Although a little chimney sweep wanted more than anything else a beautiful, tune-playing watch which he saw in a lady's boudoir, he did not touch it because of his aversion to stealing. Fortunately for him, the lady saw him resist the temptation and took him as her ward. Education and success naturally followed. If he had stolen the watch, said McGuffey, he would have gone to jail. One could not steal the smallest thing without sin, and children should remember that God's eye saw all that transpired.[50]

McGuffey also recognized an obligation of the rich to aid the unfortunate. "Grateful Julian" set the standard. Beyond old rags for clothing and a straw pallet, he possessed nothing but a rabbit which he dearly loved. When he fell ill, a rich and good man took him in and cured his sickness. In return, Julian wished to present the rabbit to his benefactor, an act which so touched the latter that he sent the boy to school. Julian naturally grew up into a bright and honest lad.[51] Moreover, people were

[47] Centreville, Michigan, *St. Joseph County Republican*, January 15 and 22, 1870.
[48] Chatfield, Minnesota, *Chatfield Democrat*, September 17, 1896.
[49] Monroe, Wisconsin, *Monroe Sentinel*, June 3, 1896.
[50] *Sixth Reader*, 246–250; *Second Reader*, 115–118.
[51] *Third Reader*, 203–206.

expected to give according to their means, as illustrated in a poem called "The Philosopher's Scales":

> A long row of alms-houses, amply endow'd
> By a well-esteem'd Pharisee, busy and proud,
> Next loaded one scale; while the other was prest
> By those mites the poor widow dropp'd into the chest;
> Up flew the endowment, not weighing an ounce,
> And down, down the farthing-worth came with a bounce.[52]

Apart from illness and misfortune, no man needed to be poor. As one McGuffey story put the matter, all could find employment and there was no place for idlers and vagrants. Of course, one should be frugal, as the famous story of the string-saving boy proved, and labor was essential to success:

> Shall birds, and bees, and ants, be wise,
>   While I my moments waste?
> O let me with the morning rise,
>   And to my duty haste.[53]

Henry, the orphan boy, illustrated the fruits of rugged individualism. In need of a new grammar book, he shoveled snow to earn the price, thus proving "Where There's a Will, There is a Way." [54]

Newspapers elaborated the same theme. In 1867 the editor of the Algona, Iowa, paper replied sharply to a letter from a local citizen who objected to raising money for foreign missions when Algona had poor and destitute families of its own. The editor doubted if any Algonans were too poor to deny themselves at least one luxury, like owning a worthless cur, smoking or chewing at a cost of twenty-five to fifty dollars a year, or the inordinate use of tea or coffee. A man had recently told a local storekeeper a pitiful tale of hard times and no job, and had been given a sack of flour on credit. Having obtained this, he immediately produced twenty-five cents in cash to buy tobacco. With that style of poverty the editor had no sympathy. Furthermore, he had no sympathy with thievery, since any healthy man could "earn a living in this land of plenty." [55]

Preachers and newspaper editors agreed with McGuffey that individuals could rise in the world through their own efforts. A Centreville, Michigan, preacher, in 1869 affirmed that his community had no rich, no poor, no ignorant citizens save as each individual's own vice or virtue, own energy, or indolence had made him so.[56] When former Senator John J. Ingalls of Kansas expressed similar sentiments in 1893, the editor of the

---

[52] *Sixth Reader*, 205–206.
[53] See *Fourth Reader*, 111–112, 63–65; *First Reader*, 51.
[54] *Fourth Reader*, 31–32.
[55] Algona, Iowa, *The Upper Des Moines*, January 10 and February 28, 1867.
[56] Centreville, Michigan, *St. Joseph County Republican*, November 27, 1869.

Gallatin, Missouri, paper devoted virtually a whole column to summarizing his remarks. According to Ingalls, all men were self-made; even chance and circumstance were made by men and not the other way round. He who was born poor was fortunate. Future leaders of thought, business, and society would not come from the gilded youth of 1893 but from ambitious sons of farmers and laborers.[57]

Near the turn of the century, Markham's famous poem, "The Man with the Hoe," disturbed defenders of the old order because it seemingly condemned the economic system for injuring the common man. Businessmen offered prizes for poetical rebuttals, and William Jennings Bryan lectured on the implications of the poem. Small-town Mid-America was also disturbed. A "goodly contingent" of Brookfield, Missouri, businessmen gathered at the local Congregational church in the fall of 1899 to hear the pastor discuss the poem. According to him, the idea that the hoe could debase mankind was utterly un-American, degenerate, and unpatriotic. The man with the hoe was the man with opportunity; one needed only to keep an eye on the individual who refused to grasp its handle. Our mightiest leaders had been the products of lives of toil with the hoe, axe, crucible, mallet, and saw.[58]

According to McGuffey, the inferior animals made no mistakes and no improvements; man made both.[59] People were inclined to agree, although they accepted progress as so natural as to need no proof or analysis. And, of course, American standards were the measuring sticks. When John E. Young summarized world events in his diary at the close of 1868, he concluded that China was making rapid progress toward civilization and political greatness. American influence was given as the reason. Political revolution in Japan, moreover, gave hope that civilization and human progress would find a lodgment there. Even Abyssinia had been compelled to bow before the prowess of English civilization and Christianity.[60]

Progress was most generally interpreted as growth in material things. When the historian of Kossuth County, Iowa, came to the subject of progress, he followed a very common pattern in telling the story in terms of *growth*—growth of population, of property values, of roads, of the butter and cream industry.[61] Although the editor of a Kossuth County paper was inclined to agree with such measurements, he expressed some doubts in an article published in 1896. After pointing out the great growth in population, fine homes, wealth, and railroads in the short interval since Algona's first New Year's celebration in 1859, he raised the question of whether people locally were any happier. How much, he asked, had such externals added to the zest for life of those pioneers still present? [62] Even

[57] Gallatin, Missouri, *North Missourian*, May 26, 1893.

[58] Brookfield, Missouri, *Brookfield Gazette*, September 2, 1899.

[59] *Fifth Reader*, 88–90.

[60] Entry, December 31, 1868, John E. Young Diaries, 1843–1904, Illinois Historical Society Library, Springfield.

[61] Benjamin F. Reed, *History of Kossuth County, Iowa* (Chicago, 1913), II, Chapter 27, "Some Evidences of Progress."

[62] Algona, Iowa, *The Upper Des Moines*, January 1, 1896.

town boosters could be sentimental about the good old days, but sentiment was not allowed to interfere with the constant itch for bigness, growth, and numbers—in short, with progress.

MAJOR AND MINOR SINS

McGuffey also introduced his young readers to the major moralistic theme of the dominant, middle-class group, the dangers of liquor and its associated evils. In a story called "Touch Not—Taste Not—Handle Not" he described the terrible economic, physical, and moral consequences of drinking. Still other stories told of "intemperate husbands," who abused their first-born sons and brought their wives to a sorrowful death, and of the "venomous worm" which was more deadly than the rattlesnake or the copperhead. In an account filled with suspense, McGuffey described this terrible creature which bit only the human race, and then identified it as the "*Worm of the Still.*" [63] Gambling was also bad, for it grew on one at an insatiable rate and ultimately led to other evils, such as drinking, cheating, and murder.[64] While not condemned outright, dancing obviously found hospitable allies in liquor and cards, and the serious-minded-and-aspiring youngster was taught to avoid all three.

This cluster of moral convictions fascinated later novelists like Don Marquis, who pictured the saloon and church as concrete symbols of the age-old conflict of light and darkness, of evil and good. Church and saloon offered escape and refuge.[65] The swinging doors of a saloon gave sanctuary from too much virtue; the double portals of a church opened avenues to goodness. Neither church nor saloon could win total victory in the eternal struggle of good versus evil.

The Middle West was not unique in supporting both church and saloon. McGuffey himself came from a moralistic, middle-class background farther to the East, and only through his fear that savagery would destroy civilization on the Middle Border frontier did he express sentiments peculiar to that area. Although the battle of church-versus-saloon perhaps was more intense on the Middle Border, the struggle itself was nationwide.

The conflict left no room for halfway measures on either side. Men generally drank to excess or were teetotalers. In this battle of extremes drunkenness often led to disaster. The warden of the Indiana state prison in 1859 reported that 446 of the 556 inmates had been addicted to drink.[66] Newspapers and diarists constantly referred to tragedies resulting from intoxication. John E. Young of the little town of Athens, Illinois, recorded the death of a local physician in 1893 from an overdose of morphine following a drunken spree; the serious injury to a local citizen, who fell off the railroad cars while on a "tare" in Springfield on the Fourth of July in 1894; the loss of an arm by "old man Hess," who fell under a train at the

[63] *Fifth Reader,* 83–85, 155–160, 192–193.
[64] *Ibid.,* 204–208.
[65] Don Marquis, *Sons of the Puritans.*
[66] Logan Esarey, *A History of Indiana from 1850 to 1920* (Bloomington, 1935), 589.

local depot while on a Christmas drunk in 1895; and drunken antics at local saloons during the Christmas season of 1896.[67] Such widespread evidence fired the opponents of liquor to greater efforts in behalf of total prohibition, and this in turn encouraged still heavier drinking by those who dared to transgress.

Dancing, cards, and smoking also continued in spite of moral opposition. William Allen White's father and mother occasionally played euchre and seven-up, but when White caught his son doing the same with other boys in the haymow, he set up a table on the front porch and made them play in full view of citizens passing on the street. That was sufficient to cure his son of the habit for years to come.[68] Chewing and smoking by men were tolerated within limits, but many thought of them as dirty, expensive, and conducive to still greater evils. An exchange item labelled "Boys Beware" in a Michigan paper in 1869 warned youngsters against chewing tobacco, smoking cigars, drinking, and playing cards or billiards. Such habits cost money, led to stealing, and were filthy in nature.[69]

Cigarettes increased greatly in popularity near the turn of the century. Youngsters liked the early cigarette brands like Duke's Cameo and Sweet Caporals. Each packet of the latter contained a picture of an "opera star" dressed in tights, of which Lillian Russell was the favorite. Smokers who preferred Sweet Caporals could assemble a whole collection of twenty-four near-to-nude beauties.[70] In the 1890's papers began to publish material from the National Cigarette Association explaining the evil effects of smoking. According to Dr. David Starr Jordan, president of Stanford University, boys who smoked cigarettes were like wormy apples and very few ever got to college. While other boys pushed ahead, they had need of the undertaker and the sexton. Still, said Dr. Jordan, philosophically, this speeded up the race for the survival of the fittest.[71] One country paper in 1893 mentioned a cigarette "fiend" who, on his way to the World's Fair, missed his train in Brookfield while trying to purchase a nickel's worth of "coffin nails." [72]

The word "sex" was too horrible a thing for McGuffey to bandy about. Others might frighten pubescent youngsters with the dire consequences of "impure thoughts," but McGuffey seemingly preferred to believe that Christian children would concentrate on school books and their duties to parents. McGuffey said that marriage and a family gave men the necessary stimulus to succeed, and that marriage and motherhood constituted the natural and most honored vocation for women.[73]

This attitude harmonized nicely with prevailing opinion on the Middle Border. Since all women were expected to marry, spinsters had no place in society. They could work as domestics for others or live with more fortunate married relatives, but no woman was supposed to have become an "old

[67] John E. Young Diaries 1843–1904, Illinois Historical Society Library.

[68] William Allen White, *Autobiography* (New York, 1946), 52.

[69] Centreville, Michigan, *St. Joseph County Republican*, April 10, 1869.

[70] Fred L. Holmes, *Side Roads Excursions into Wisconsin's Past* (Madison, 1949), 59.

[71] Greencastle, Indiana, *Star-Press*, March 3 and July 28, 1894.

[72] Gallatin, Missouri, *North Missourian*, November 3, 1893.

[73] See, for example, *Fifth Reader*, 169–170, and *Sixth Reader*, 76.

maid" by choice.[74] If no husband was available, a woman could save her pride by pretending that her lover had died on the eve of their marriage and that she had been unable thereafter to think of caring for another man. Idealized love appealed to that sentimental age, partially because it helped conceal the grim practicality surrounding so much of the marriage relationship.

Although circumscribed, the wife's position was important. She prided herself on being a good cook and housekeeper. Company dinners with lavish quantities of food demonstrated her ability as a cook and her husband's success as a "good provider." While guests crammed themselves with food, she bustled about the table to see that all were properly served, and not until the last guest had finished did she permit herself to eat. As an angel of mercy to neighbors in distress and an avenging instrument of gossip, she maintained her family's influence in society and church affairs. She was economical of her husband's worldly goods, condemned the vanities of rouge and the sin of cigarettes, and got her washing on the line at an early hour on Monday morning. Most of all, she sought "advantages" for her children, and operated as a matchmaker in behalf of her marriageable daughters. In carrying out these functions she personified the traits of the successful middle-class housewife.

Marriage itself involved a combination of Rabelaisian humor and prudery. The Christmas season rivalled June for weddings, perhaps because routine activities slackened between Christmas and New Year's. Charivaris, infares, and joshing often marked the occasion. When William Allen White's parents returned from their honeymoon, they found that every chamber pot in their home had been gaily decorated by friends in honor of the occasion. Similarly, the editor of the Gallatin, Missouri, paper honored the marriage of a respectable couple in 1865 with the comment that he was glad to see them obeying the Apostle Paul's injunction that it was better to marry than to burn.[75]

In marriage, as in most aspects of life, the puritanical streak was uppermost. When Tocqueville visited America in the 1830's he was surprised to see how freely unchaperoned young girls went places with men. In his opinion, this very freedom explained in part why American women made excellent wives in a practical sense. At the same time, he felt sure that mothers had to warn girls of the dangers in unrestricted association with men, and he wondered if this did not invigorate judgment at the expense of imagination.[76] A midwestern paper put the matter more bluntly in 1898 in a story headed "Where is Papa?" In this case, an unfortunate girl had been deserted by her lover, and the editor urged mothers to warn their daughters against the falsity of men's promises. Girls should be told that

[74] See Zona Gale, *Miss Lulu Bett* (New York, 1920) for an excellent treatment of the plight of the unmarried female, and Rose Wilder Lane, *Old Home Town* (New York, 1935), for a shrewd but sympathetic account of the life of the small-town woman.

[75] Gallatin, Missouri, *North Missourian*, February 23, 1865.

[76] Alexis de Tocqueville, *Democracy in America*, edited by Henry Steele Commager (New York, 1947), 393.

shame could not be covered up no matter how long one lived or how good one became in later life. A woman's entire life could not atone for such a sin.[77]

Mothers apparently needed little urging to instruct their daughters in matters vital to maintaining their purity before marriage. Unfortunately, advice and information seems to have gone no further. Young girls and old maids were excluded from matronly discussions of delicate matters. In watching their elders at home and in society, girls must have concluded that virtue and prudery were synonymous. Married people in small towns carefully avoided any appearance of undue interest in the opposite sex. Social intercourse was stilted and formal, and men and women sat apart at social gatherings to prevent any threat of gossip. Parents avoided displays of affection toward one another in front of their children, and widowed people waited at least a year to remarry in order to escape community censure.

"Sex-warped" attitudes were common enough on the Middle Border. Both Sherwood Anderson and Edgar Lee Masters were obsessed with sex. Both engaged in a series of tawdry sexual alliances, and both had trouble living a normal married life. Although few others wrote equally frank autobiographies, these men were not unique. Still other Midwesterners, seemingly repelled by the sexual crudity which they observed, turned to an impossibly idealized love. The tragedy played out in Ed Howe's *Story of a Country Town* rests basically on Jo Erring's ridiculous and impossible idealization of the gentle and innocent Mateel. Howe's own boyhood was marred by his father's desertion of the family for another woman, and Howe's own marriage in later years came to grief. Idealized love and sex-obsession alike owed something to the puritanical code which permeated much of the Middle Border. But before one joins with Van Wyck Brooks in calling this culture "sex-warped," he must explain the happy marriages which are spelled out in the writings and autobiographies of other men like Garland, Quick, and White. Midwestern culture was complex, composed of several layers, and out of this came markedly different men. . . .

UNCO-OPERATIVE SINNERS

McGuffey and his followers liked to speak of the simple virtues of the village green. A rigorous moral code, closely knit communities in which sinners could easily be exposed, and devoted guardians like the W.C.T.U. supposedly created an ideal environment in which to rear the young. All this, however, ignores a large body of contrary evidence which reduces much of the bucolic theme of rural and small-town purity to the status of folklore. Less than half of the people maintained church membership.[78]

[77] Gallatin, Missouri, *North Missourian*, August 26, 1898.

[78] In 1900 the figures were: Michigan, 40.5%; Ohio, 42%; Iowa, 35.2%; Indiana, 37.4%; Wisconsin, 48.35%; and Missouri, 38.5%, for example. Figures compiled from U. S. Bureau of the Census, *Religious Bodies, 1906*, Part I (Washington, 1910), 308–372.

Many unaffiliated individuals, like the Quick family, were respectable citizens, but virtually every community also had ne'er-do-wells or submarginal families who lived by intermittent day labor. Transient day laborers, bums, and wandering horse traders also invaded small towns at various periods of the year. Boys and girls engaged freely in unsupervised play at school and in outbuildings of family homes. Actually, the environment was both good and bad, as a large body of evidence clearly indicates.

The autobiographies and other published works of Floyd Dell, Edgar Lee Masters, and Sherwood Anderson describe an appalling amount of moral laxity in small towns. A series of slovenly hired girls in his parents' home introduced Masters to sex at an early age. Moreover, the two "Shetland Ponies," as they were widely known, who provided gossip in Sherwood Anderson's boyhood town, had rivals in virtually every midwestern village. One was the daughter of a ne'er-do-well who travelled about exhibiting a stuffed whale, and the other had a drunken tailor for a father. One of them became interested in Sherwood, and asked her confederate to bring him to a rendezvous in the recesses of a rail fence at the edge of town. She had hung her little white pants on a rail and was enticing Sherwood to intimacy at the moment when a barrage of stones was thrown by a young man who, learning of the rendezvous, had followed the couple. Sherwood immediately took off in a wild flight of dismay, yelling as he ran, "Get your pants, Lily. Get your pants, Lily." [79]

Small-town oral tradition contains similar episodes, differing only in details, and the writings of well-balanced, moral men confirm the pattern. William Allen White early acquired a knowledge of basic Anglo-Saxon four-letter words which were scribbled on sidewalks and school toilets. One summer day he and his friends discovered a covered wagon in a wooded camping place near town where strange girls were meeting local men: in his words, "And the knowledge of good and evil came to us, even as to the Pair in the Garden." On another occasion he and his friends discovered the Sunday School Superintendent and a visiting teacher in the woods cooling their toes in the water and rapidly returning to nature. When the boys yelled from a concealed vantage point, the couple rushed hurriedly away. The youngsters were even more astonished, however, when the Superintendent returned to the spot with his wife. Only later in life did White understand the purpose in this. It prevented a divorce when the story circulated in town since the wife naturally believed that she was the woman in question. White's father permitted him to sell cigars and listen to stories by travelling salesmen in the family hotel. As he saw it, there was little to teach a youngster who

> had grown up in a pioneer town around the slaughterhouse and in
> the livery stable, who had roamed through the romantic woods
> where the peripatetic strumpets made their camps, who had picked
> up his sex education from Saxon words chalked on sidewalks and
> barns, who had taken his Rabelaisian poetry from the walls of
> backhouses, and who had seen saloons spew out their back door

[79] *Sherwood Anderson's Memoirs* (New York, 1942), 63–64.

their indigestible drunkards, swarming with flies, to furnish amusement and devilment for the entertainment of little boys, as it was
in the beginning of civilization.[80]

Anderson and Masters succumbed to the erotic appeal of such influences; White and Quick continued to place girls on a pedestal and to honor
chastity in womankind. White knew a boy from an Ohio boarding school
with quite a different point of view, and Quick discerned more immediately than did his elders the purpose behind the very embarrassing but
seemingly innocent questioning carried on by a young hellion in his own
home town who had served a period in a reform school. According to
Quick,

> Rural simplicity was supposed to make for a virtuous life. We had
> this delusion in our family. I have often wondered what city boy
> ever had more evil associates than did I out there on the prairie.
> . . . The simple innocence of the Deserted Village was absent. . . .
> I went with these boys, played with them, and knew them for
> what they were; but so far as I can see I took little harm from
> them. They seemed to be mere phenomena, like the weather, in-
> teresting but nothing to imitate.[81]

"Social purity" of *thought* was only a myth everywhere on the Middle Border; in practice it varied from individual to individual.

Prudery and frankness went hand in hand. There is truth in the legend
that refined women spoke of "lower extremities," while the less refined
used the word "limbs," and only those of no standing spoke of "legs." On
the other hand, an advertisement of Velpeau's French Female Pills in the
Monroe, Wisconsin, paper in 1869 would not be accepted today by village
editors. According to the descriptive material, the pills had been kept off
the American market until recently because of the ease with which they
caused abortion. Pregnant married ladies were warned to avoid them because they invariably caused a miscarriage. Customers could obtain them
by mail in packages sealed against the eyes of the curious and they were
guaranteed to be entirely safe to take.[82]

Undesirable transients and a rough local element caused trouble everywhere. Itinerant field hands were especially bothersome during the harvest
season. Hamlin Garland had to deal with them while operating his father's
farm near Osage, Iowa, in the 1870's. They reminded him of a flight of
unclean birds. To these former soldiers, errant sons of poor farmers, and
unsuccessful mechanics from older states a "girl" was the most desired
thing in the world, to be enjoyed without remorse. They furnished local
boys with smutty information from South Clark Street in Chicago and the

80 William Allen White, *Autobiography*, 40, 46, 67. Quotations on pages 40 and 67.
81 Herbert Quick, *One Man's Life* [Indianapolis, 1925], 147–150.
82 Monroe, Wisconsin, *Monroe Sentinel*, January 6, 1869. See also advertisement of
   "pessaric remedies" in Chatfield, Minnesota, *Chatfield Democrat*, January 5, 1867.

river front in St. Louis. On rainy days and Saturday nights they fought and caroused with local riffraff in country towns. In Garland's words:

> Saturday night in town! How it all comes back to me! I am a timid visitor in the little frontier village. It is sunset. A whiskey-crazed farmhand is walking bare footed up and down the middle of the road defying the world.—From a corner of the street I watch with tense interest another lithe, pock-marked bully menacing with cat-like action a cowering young farmer in a long linen coat. The crowd jeers at him for his cowardice—a burst of shouting is heard. A trampling follows and forth from the door of a saloon bulges a throng of drunken, steaming, reeling, cursing ruffians followed by brave Jim McCarty, the city marshal, with an offender under each hand. . . .
>
> We are on the way home. Only two of my crew are with me. The others are roaring from one drinking place to another, having a "good time." The air is soothingly clean and sweet after the tumult and the reek of the town.[83]

When a heavy Sunday-night rain stopped harvesting on a Monday in 1876 near Chatfield, Minnesota, nine fights occurred, and hands were "drunk, fighting, raising h—l generally." Some Chatfield residents had participated, and the local paper warned them that order would be maintained, even if it meant a policeman on every corner.[84] Garland's description of such men and their activities applied widely over the Middle West except for a shortage of "brave" Jim McCartys. Constables generally lacked his fortitude and strength, and when a town started boiling over they often failed to meet the crisis.

Nor was the problem limited simply to the harvest season. During one week in December, 1879, the marshal at Mendon, Michigan, accommodated twenty-eight tramps overnight in the village lockup, a part of the immense army, according to a local citizen, which was willing to live by begging and petty thievery.[85] In September, 1897, Centreville, Michigan, had a number of hoboes on its streets daily. They were described as umbrella menders, chimney sweeps, tinkers, and the blind, deaf, lame, lazy, and crazy. The local editor warned that while they seemed harmless, they usually were "whiskey suckers," and would bear watching. Housewives were warned not to leave their washing on the line unguarded.[86]

Local rowdies seem to have been awed only slightly by the better classes. At Athens, Illinois, in the 1890's, the rougher element stole ice cream intended for church socials and slashed harness on teams tied to hitching racks at local churches. At times, officers were called out to

---

[83] Hamlin Garland, *A Son of the Middle Border* (New York, 1920), 175–176.

[84] Chatfield, Minnesota, *Chatfield Democrat*, August 19, 1876.

[85] Report of Mendon correspondent in Centreville, Michigan, *St. Joseph County Republican*, December 13, 1879.

[86] Centreville, Michigan, *St. Joseph County Republican*, September 10, 1897.

handle rough individuals intent on disrupting revival services. A local group of gamblers and petty thieves engaged in a gun fight with the city marshal and tortured an individual in his isolated home in hopes of learning where his money was hidden.[87]

The activities of this class can be traced in the newspaper files of any midwestern town. Though Gallatin, Missouri, was very proud of its city park in the 1890's, ladies stayed away to avoid the vulgar and profane language being used by male loafers. On Saturday nights, when the "Honey Creekers" tried to "take the town," women remained at home as no section of the business district was immune. At times, the local editor lectured readers on the low respect shown for law and order. According to him, an especially brutal murder aroused only mild resentment. Howling mobs of men and boys surrounded the town marshal in an effort to keep him from taking reluctant drunks to the calaboose. Crap-shooting games and "young blades" intent on injuring school property added to the problem of law enforcement. When "smart" boys pelted a disorderly house near the Windsor hotel one of the women returned the insult with gun fire. Although she left town before arrests could be made, two remaining "soiled doves" had to be brought into court before they would agree to depart. Travelling "crap sharks" had no trouble locating gamblers in Gallatin and neighboring towns.[88]

Twentieth-century cities surpass country towns in crimes against property, but they differ little in crimes of violence. Murder, rape, and manslaughter are sufficiently common in smaller communities to deny them any claim to special purity,[89] and small-town newspaper records indicate that such communities never were better in curbing crimes of violence.[90]

---

[87] John E. Young Diaries, 1843–1904, entries October 24, 1894, March 27, 1896, March 2, 1898, and March 18, 1900.

[88] Gallatin, Missouri, *North Missourian*, June 2, August 4, and December 29, 1893; March 11, 18, and July 29, 1898.

[89] George B. Vold, "Crime in City and Country Areas," *The Annals of the American Academy of Political and Social Science*, CCXVII (September, 1941), 38–45.

[90] As early as 1900 F. W. Blackmar of the University of Kansas published an article questioning the purity of the village green. Blackmar emphasized the weaknesses leading to "social degeneration" in smaller communities. Village police forces were inadequate to cope with local problems. Gangs of idle village boys loafed on street corners, shot craps and played cards, were guilty of profane language and indecent remarks on Main Street, and engaged in long, leisurely conversations on smutty subjects. Blackmar's article pioneered a sociological trend toward a more realistic appraisal of village morals. F. W. Blackmar, "Social Degeneration in Towns and Rural Districts," *Proceedings of the National Conference of Charities and Correction*, XXVII (1900), 115–124.

"The Fashionable Diseases": Women's Complaints and Their Treatment in Nineteenth-Century America

ANN DOUGLAS

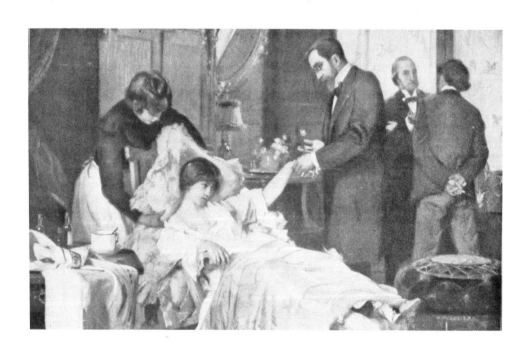

Rarely in history has the female role been as clearly defined as in Victorian America, when women were expected to dedicate their lives to "the cult of true womanhood" or "the cult of domesticity."

Before the nineteenth century, most women worked alongside their husbands in agricultural pursuits or domestic manufacture. With the growth of cities, however, and the rise of the middle class, women lost their traditional economic function and were admonished to withdraw behind the domestic curtain. There they were to practice the virtues of piety, purity, submissiveness, and domesticity as described in Barbara Welter's seminal essay, "The Cult of True Womanhood." Their station in life was determined by the achievements and social status of their husbands, and women were expected to maintain the home as a refuge to which their husbands could retreat from the hurly-burly of nineteenth-century business dealings. Increasingly, women became the primary child-rearers until the children were old enough to leave home.

The conventions that fixed this burden upon women did not imply that women were inferior. On the contrary, women were considered superior and were expected to serve as the guardians of faith and morals. But this strict dichotomization of sex roles was a much more effective tool for male dominance than any theory of superiority or inferiority could have been. The principal assumption of this dichotomy was that men and women were to occupy different spheres in society. The male sphere was public life; the female, private life—a position derived from religious teachings, tradition, and biology.

For Victorian women, anatomy was indeed destiny. Women were regarded as biologically destined for familial duties. They bore the children and nursed them, and it seemed perfectly logical that women should continue caring for their offspring as long as necessary. For middle-class women, the years of childbearing and rearing took up nearly a lifetime.

As the medical profession began to mature in the nineteenth century, the care and treatment of women became a growing concern. Many Victorian women suffered from a variety of physical and nervous disorders that engaged the interest of doctors. Early in the century, most female illnesses were treated by the "heroic" method, which required massive doses of such dangerous substances as mercury, lead, or opium. Needless to say, the cure was often worse than the disease.

As gynecological specialization developed in the middle of the century, less drastic and somewhat more effective methods of treatment developed. Almost all female illnesses were attributed to some kind of uterine disorder. Doctors decided that, since the uterus was the particularly distinctive female organ, peculiarly female disorders must originate in or around the uterus. Another source of such disorders identified by medical practitioners of the day was deviation from the prescribed female role. Rarely did it occur to doctors that societal constraints could have been the source of the trouble.

Ann Douglas, of Columbia University, describes the treatment of female diseases during this period in the article reprinted here. Whether or not she is correct in her assumption that many attitudes of incipient gynecologists were a result of their fear of the sexual power of women, her description of the diagnosis and treatment of female illness is to the point.

Biological determinism continues to influence the treatment of female disorders, and doctors have added to their arsenal the teachings of Freudian psychology. Even though today the uterus is rarely regarded as the primary source of female illness, it is still commonly believed that women are particularly susceptible to certain emotional disorders that manifest themselves in organic symptoms. As a result, women are often placed in a dependent patient situation (as in psychotherapy) when a more appropriate diagnosis might require a direct treatment of the manifest symptoms.

Historians of nineteenth-century American culture and society have become increasingly aware that many of the medical theories and practices of the period fall within their province rather than within that of the scientist. Furthermore, the consensus of historical opinion seems to be that nineteenth-century treatments of mental illness, "nervous" conditions, and sexual difficulties, although telling little about scientific advancement, are particularly sensitive indicators of cultural attitudes. Historians Huber and Meyer, for example, have considered the "mind cure" movement of the late nineteenth and early twentieth centuries not as incipient psychoanalysis, but as an expression of contemporary conflict-laden ideas of success and achievement. Rothman has based his recent study of development of the asylum in the Jacksonian period on the stated assumption that "the march of science cannot by itself explain the transformation in the American treatment of the insane." He proceeds to analyze the asylum and the methods it adopted as the result of the tensions and ideas of Jacksonian society.[1]

[1] See Richard Huber, *The American Idea of Success* (New York, 1971), 124–186; Donald Meyer, *The Positive Thinkers: A Study of the American Quest for Health, Wealth, and Personal Power* (New York, 1965); David Rothman, *The Discovery of the Asylum: Social Order and Disorder in the New Republic* (Boston, 1971), xvi. For another treatment of insanity in the same period, see Norman Dain, *Concepts of Insanity in the United States 1789–1865* (New Brunswick, N.J., 1964).

"'The Fashionable Diseases': Women's Complaints and Their Treatment in Nineteenth-Century America" by Ann Douglas. From *Journal of Interdisciplinary History* 4 (Summer 1973): 25–52.

Such an approach is clearly dictated in the consideration of nine-teenth-century diagnosis and treatment of American women's nervous and sexual diseases.[2] The historian reading through the health books and medical manuals of the day dealing with the topic is confronted at once with a combination of scientific imprecision and emotionally charged conviction which demands interpretation.

Books written in the period between 1840 and 1900 consistently, if questionably, assert that a large number, even the majority of middle-class American women, were in some sense ill. Catharine Esther Beecher, daughter of the famous minister Lyman Beecher and a pioneer in women's education and hygiene, took as her chief concern in later life "the *health of women and children*" which, she wrote in 1866, had become "a matter of alarming interest" to all. In *Physiology and Calisthenics* she had already warned her readers that "there is a delicacy of constitution and an increase of disease, both among mature women and young girls, that is most alarming, and such as was never known in any former period." In *Letters to the People on Health and Happiness* she attempted to back up her apocalyptic rumblings with statistics. She had asked all of the numerous women she knew in cities and towns across the United States to make a list of the ten women each knew best, and rate their health as "perfectly healthy," "well," "delicate," "sick," "invalid," and so on. Her report, which covered hundreds of middle-class women, was as "alarming" as Beecher could have desired. Milwaukee, Wisconsin, provides a typical example:

> Milwaukee, Wisc. Mrs. A. frequent sick headaches. Mrs. B. very feeble. Mrs. S. well, except chills. Mrs. L. poor health constantly. Mrs. D. subject to frequent headaches. Mrs. B. very poor health. Mrs. C. consumption. Mrs. A. pelvic displacements and weakness. Mrs. H. pelvic disorders and a cough. Mrs. B. always sick. Do not know one healthy woman in the place.[3]

The accuracy of Beecher's findings is clearly open to question. How representative of other American women were her friends? How bad did a headache have to be to qualify a woman for ill health? And what woman in 1855 wanted to admit to so crude a state as robust vitality? Heroines of the sentimental fiction so popular with the women in the middle ranks of society whose health concerned Beecher were more often

[2] G. J. Barker-Benfield has given consideration to these medical practices from a cultural point of view in an unpublished paper entitled "The Spermatic Economy: A Nineteenth Century View of Sexuality" delivered at the Organization of American Historians meeting, April 15, 1971, at New Orleans. His primary focus is on masculine sexuality, however, while mine is on feminine sexuality. For a more general, and somewhat superficial survey of American sex mores and roles in the nineteenth century, see Milton Rugoff, *Prudery and Passion* (New York, 1971).

[3] Catharine E. Beecher, "The American People Starved and Poisoned," *Harper's New Monthly Magazine*, XXXII (1866), 771; *Physiology and Calisthenics for Schools and Families* (New York, 1856), 164; *Letters to the People on Health and Happiness* (New York, 1855), 124. Her findings were still being referred to in 1870. See the popular manual, Edward B. Foote, *Plain Home Talk* (New York, 1880), 451.

than not bearing up under a burden of sickness that would have incapacitated any less noble being. Indeed, as commentators on American society at the time emphasized, ill health in women had become positively fashionable and was exploited by its victims and practitioners as an advertisement of genteel sensibility and an escape from the too pressing demands of bedroom and kitchen.[4]

If the reliability of Beecher's statistics is shaky, their significance, on which this essay will focus, is not. Although American women of the eighteenth century may have been more sickly than their supposedly frail nineteenth-century descendants, they did not talk of themselves as sick; they did not define themselves through sickness, and their society apparently minimized rather than maximized their ill health, whatever its actual extent. As Meyer has argued, "attention" to a problem in a given period is as telling to the cultural historian as its actual "incidence," which may be almost impossible to determine.[5] Beecher's statistics at least reveal that a sizable number of American women wanted or needed to consider themselves ill.

Equally important, the self-diagnosis of these women was confirmed, even encouraged, by their society. Literary observers of the American scene like Cooper and Hawthorne were appalled at the delicate health of American women.[6] The doctors who specialized in women's diseases were equally gloomy and a good deal more verbose on the subject. Alcott, a noted Boston physician and author of several books on women's health, had estimated that one half of American women suffered from the "real disease" of nervousness. When Clarke of the Harvard Medical School published his controversial *Sex in Education*, he saw the ill health of middle- and upper-class American women as so pervasive that he pessimistically concluded they would soon be unable to reproduce at all. "It requires no prophet to foretell that the wives who are to be mothers in our republic must be drawn from trans-atlantic homes," he announced.[7]

---

[4] For a popular satire on the subject, see Augustus Hopper, *A Fashionable Sufferer: or Chapters from Life's Comedy* (Boston, 1883). There is an interesting chapter on the subject in Page Smith, *Daughters of the Promised Land: Women in American History* (Boston, 1970), 131–140. Wendell Phillips' wife was a typical example of a long-suffering but equally long-lived victim of nervous complaints. See Irving H. Bartlett, *Wendell Phillips: Brahmin Radical* (Boston, 1961), 79. One could multiply examples almost endlessly of women of this period who never expected to live through the next year and survived into their eighties and nineties. Still this evidence, like all the evidence in this area, is ambiguous. There are many diseases and ailments which, in the absence of sufficient medical knowhow, can become chronic and make their victim's life a torment without ending it.

[5] Meyer, *The Positive Thinkers*, 30.

[6] See James Fenimore Cooper (ed. Robert E. Spiller), *Gleanings in Europe* (New York, 1930), II, 92–97; Nathaniel Hawthorne, *Our Old Home*, in *The Complete Works of Nathaniel Hawthorne* (Boston, 1898), VII, 66–68, 390–391.

[7] William A. Alcott, *The Young Woman's Book of Health* (Boston, 1950), 17; Edward H. Clarke, *Sex in Education: or a Fair Chance for Girls* (Boston, 1878), 63. For the history of similar arguments, see Willystine Goodsell, *The Education of Women: Its Social Background and Problems* (New York, 1923). In 1868, Dr. F. Saunders wrote a book quite frankly pleading with middle-class American women to have more children. See *About Women, Love, and Marriage* (New York, 1868).

Beecher not only emphasized that many American women in the middle and upper ranks of society were sick, but she also implied that they were ill precisely *because they were women*. Most of the ailments that she records—pelvic disorders, sick headaches, general nervousness—were regarded as symptoms of "female complaints," nervous disorders thought to be linked with the malfunctioning of the feminine sexual organs.

This is not to imply that men could not and did not display similar symptoms. Napheys, for example, in 1878, noted peevishness, listlessness, pallor, and headaches in men and boys who practiced the "secret vice" of masturbation. Beard found men and women suffering from what he termed "American nervousness."[8] No doctor implied that signs of nervous disorder were apparent only in women in nineteenth-century America, and the historian should not overlook this evidence. The fact remains, nonetheless, that to some extent the *diagnosis*, and to a greater extent the *treatment* by doctors of these symptoms in women, was different from their interpretation of the same signs in men. This difference was inevitable, because medical analysis of a woman began and ended with consideration of an organ unique to her, namely her uterus. Here, supposedly, lay the cause and the cure of many of her physical ailments. As a result of this special focus, medical reactions to female nervous complaints are indicative of nineteenth-century American attitudes not only toward disease and sexuality in general but, more significantly, toward feminine sexual identity in particular.

Doctors in America throughout the nineteenth century directed their attention to the womb in a way that seems decidedly unscientific and even obsessive to a modern observer. Popular manuals on women's health neglected discussion of widespread and fatal diseases like breast cancer and consumption and concentrated on every type of menstrual and uterine disorder conceivable.[9] Hubbard, a professor from New Haven, addressing a medical society in 1870, explained that it seemed "as if the Almighty, in creating the female sex, *had taken the uterus and built up a woman around it*."[10] And the uterus, so essential to womankind, was apparently a highly perilous possession. Dewees, professor of midwifery at the University of Pennsylvania in the early part of the nineteenth century, stated in his standard work on the diseases of females that woman was subject to twice the sicknesses that affected man just because she has a womb. Her uterus exercises a "paramount power" over her physical and moral system, and its sway is "no less whimsical than potent." Further-

[8] See George H. Napheys, *The Transmission of Life: Counsels on the Nature and Hygiene of the Masculine Function* (Philadelphia, 1889), 71 ff. This was a standard analysis and countless supporting sources could be cited. One of particular interest is *Satan and Society By a Physician* (Cincinnati, 1872). See also George Beard, *American Nervousness* (New York, 1881).

[9] See, for example, Alcott, *The Young Woman's Book of Health;* Frederick Hollick, *The Marriage Guide or Natural History of Generation* (New York, 1860); George H. Napheys, *The Physical Life of Woman: Advice to the Maiden, Wife and Mother* (Philadelphia, 1880).

[10] Quoted in M. L. Holbrook, *Parturition Without Pain: A Code of Directions for Escaping from the Primal Curse* (New York, 1875), 15.

more, "she is constantly liable to irregularities in her menstrua, and menaced severely by their consequences." [11] It was these highly contagious irregularities in her womb's workings which were thought to produce the headaches, nervousness, and feebleness detailed by Beecher. Byford, professor of gynecology in the 1860s at The University of Chicago, was moved to exclaim in his monograph on the uterus, "It is almost a pity that a woman has a womb."

Rather complacently viewing the havoc that their natural biological disadvantages wreaked on women, these doctors detailed the symptoms of a typical case of (uterine-caused) nervous prostration. Its victims, like the women on whose health Beecher reported, according to Byford, would usually lose weight: They would frequently show a peevish irritability and suffer every kind of nervous disorder ranging from hysterical fits of crying and insomnia to constipation, indigestion, headaches, and backaches.[12] Since many of the practitioners of the first half of the nineteenth century traced all of these problems to disorders of the uterus, they consequently tried to cure them through what came to be called "local treatment," remedies specifically directed at the womb. This meant that not only the woman suffering from *prolapsus uteri* as the result of childbearing or the lady with cancer of the uterus or any menstrual difficulty, but also the girl suffering from backache and an irritable disposition with no discernible problem in her uterus might well be subjected to local treatment in the period 1830–1860.

"Local treatment" could mean manual adjustment by a doctor of a slipped uterus, a problem all too current in an age of poor midwifery, and the insertion of various pessaries for its support. It was more frequently used to designate a course of local medication for everything from cancer to cantankerousness. This treatment had four stages, although not every case went through all four: a manual investigation, "leeching," "injections," and "cauterization." Dewees and Bennet, a famous English gynecologist widely read in America, both advocated placing the leeches right on the vulva or the neck of the uterus, although Bennet cautioned the doctor to count them as they dropped off when satiated, lest he "lose" some. Bennet had known adventurous leeches to advance into the cervical cavity of the uterus itself, and he noted: "I think I have scarcely ever seen more acute pain than that experienced by several of my patients under these circumstances." [13] Less distressing to a twentieth-century mind, but perhaps even more senseless, were the "injections" into the

---

[11] William P. Dewees, *A Treatise on the Diseases of Females* (Philadelphia, 1843), 17, 14. For a discussion of attitudes toward menstruation in the period, see Elaine and English Showalter, "Victorian Women and Menstruation," *Victorian Studies,* XIV (1970), 83–89.

[12] William H. Byford, *A Treatise on the Chronic Inflammation and Displacements of the Unimpregnated Uterus* (Philadelphia, 1864), 22–41. For a similar discussion of symptoms, see S. Weir Mitchell, *Doctor and Patient* (Philadelphia, 1888), 25–27. and *Fat and Blood and How to Make Them* (Philadelphia, 1877), 35.

[13] James Henry Bennet, *A Practical Treatise on Inflammation of the Uterus, Its Cervix and Appendages and on Its Connection with Other Uterine Diseases* (Philadelphia, 1864), 237.

uterus advocated by these doctors. The uterus became a kind of catch-all, or what one exasperated doctor referred to as a "Chinese toy shop": Water, milk and water, linseed tea, and "decoction of marshmellow . . . tepid or cold" found their way inside nervous women patients.[14] The final step, performed at this time, one must remember, with no anesthetic but a little opium or alcohol, was cauterization, either through the application of nitrate of silver, or, in cases of more severe infection, through the use of the much stronger hydrate of potassa, or even the "actual cautery," a "white-hot iron" instrument.[15] The principle here is medically understandable and even sound: to drive out one infection by creating a greater inflammation, and thus provoking the blood cells to activity great enough to heal both irritations. But the treatment was used, it must be remembered, even when there was no uterine infection, and it was subject to great abuses in itself as its best practitioners realized. "It is an easy matter," Byford noted, "to do violence to the mucous membrane by a very little rudeness of management." In a successful case, the uterus was left "raw and bleeding" and the patient in severe pain for several days; in an unsuccessful one, severe hemorrhage and terrible pain might result.[16] It should be noted that the cauterization process, whether by chemicals or by the iron, had to be repeated several times at intervals of a few days.[17]

In the 1870s and 1880s, this form of treatment was largely dropped. Austin, in his book *Perils of American Women*, came out against local treatment and dismissed cauterization as a relic of the barbaric past of a decade ago:

> Thus it happened that thousands of women have been doomed to undergo the nitrate-of-silver treatment—their mental agony and physical torture were accounted nothing—in cases where soap and water and a gentle placebo would have been amply sufficient.[18]

Austin had his own panacea for women's nervous diseases, however. He was a devoted believer in the Philadelphia doctor S. Weir Mitchell and his famous "rest cure."

Firmly opposed to the cauterization school, Mitchell evolved a method of his own, which, in his own words, was "a combination of entire rest and of excessive feeding, made possible by passive exercise obtained through steady use of massage and electricity."[19] When he said

[14] *Ibid.*, 224.
[15] *Ibid.*, 255; Byford, *A Treatise on the Chronic Inflammation*, 152.
[16] *Ibid.*, 103, 117, 158, 164.
[17] Bennet, *A Practical Treatise on Inflammation of the Uterus*, 244.
[18] G. L. Austin, *Perils of American Women: or, A Doctor's Talk with Maiden, Wife, and Mother* (Boston, 1883), 198, 158–160. See also Monfort B. Allen and Amelia C. McGregor, *The Glory of Woman, or Love, Marriage, and Maternity* (Philadelphia, 1896), 241.
[19] Mitchell, *Fat and Blood*, 7. This cure, since it did not focus directly on the uterus, could be used on men as well as women, but rarely was. Significantly, in twenty-four case histories described by Mitchell in an account of his method, only one involved was a male. Furthermore, this man was suffering from consumption rather than a nervous complaint. See *Fat and Blood*, 93.

"entire rest," he meant it. For some six weeks, the patient was removed from her home, and allowed to see no one except the doctor and a hired nurse. Confined to her bed flat on her back, she was permitted neither to read, nor, in some cases, even to rise to urinate. The massage treatment which covered the whole body lasted an hour daily. Becoming progressively more vigorous, it was designed to counteract the debilitating effects of such a prolonged stay in bed. Meanwhile the patient was expected to eat steadily, and gain weight daily. Mitchell's claims to have cured menstrual disorders and every kind of "nervous" ailment met with widespread acceptance. He was the best known and most successful woman's doctor of his generation.

Both the local treatment and the rest cure look to a modern viewer at best like very imperfect forms of medical treatment for complex problems. The first was always painful and often fruitless; the second was frequently tedious and occasionally irrelevant. Both, as we will see, could exacerbate rather than diminish the nervous state they were designed to cure. One's first temptation is to dismiss them as the products of an unscientific age, and there is ample evidence to support such an attitude.

Before the Civil War the American doctor was quite simply ignorant, and even his post-Civil War successor did not receive the training expected of a doctor today. Few medical schools before 1860 required more than two years of attendance; almost none provided clinical experience for their fledgling physicians.[20] Furthermore, gynecology at this period was perhaps the weakest link in the already weak armor of the nineteenth-century doctor's medical knowledge. Lectures on "midwifery" and the sexual organs, as Elizabeth Blackwell was to learn, usually provided a professor more opportunity for dirty jokes than for the dissemination of knowledge.[21] J. Marion Sims, a pioneer in gynecological surgery, frequently lamented the frightening ignorance which seemed especially to attend doctors on the subject of women's ailments. He wrote feelingly about one lady who had long suffered from internal problems and from the cures designed to relieve them:

> The leeching, the physicking, the blistering, the anodynes, the baths, the mountain excursions, the sea-bathing and sea voyages that this poor patient suffered and endured for years are almost incredible![22]

He restored her to health by a simple operation.

Doctors had some excuse for their ignorance of woman's internal organs, although little for their pretended knowledge. Ladies were expected, even by their doctors, to object to "local examination," to prefer

[20] See J. Marion Sims, *The Story of My Life* (New York, 1884).
[21] Elizabeth Blackwell, *Pioneer Work in Opening the Medical Profession to Women* (New York, 1895), 257–259.
[22] Quoted in Seale Harris, *Woman's Surgeon: The Life Story of J. Marion Sims* (New York, 1950), 181.

modesty to health, and many of them did.[23] The French physician, Médéric Louis Elie Moreau de St. Méry, had commented on the unwillingness of Philadelphia women in the late eighteenth century to undergo even crucially necessary medical scrutiny, and Dewees, in the same city at the start of the next century, recounted several tales of women who put themselves in the hands of quacks rather than endure this ordeal. Bennet, the London authority, crusaded against the "absolutely criminal" delicacy of doctors who respected such fears in female patients.[24] He rightly attributed the birth of gynecology as a science to the increased possibility of uterine examination because of the use of the speculum and gradually changing attitudes.

Yet the ignorance of American doctors and the difficulties in the way of overcoming it certainly cannot explain the *forms* of the treatments they devised for nervous women. To understand these, one must cease to regard these fledgling gynecological techniques as part of a developing science and scrutinize them as part and parcel of a fully formed culture, and, as such, sharing in all the biases and assumptions about women which that culture possessed. This in no way suggests a failure of concern or good will on the part of nineteenth-century American doctors. Undeniably, the majority of these physicians were anxious to aid their female patients. J. Marion Sims, who devoted his life to the intelligent relief of woman's diseases is only an illustrious example of what was surely a numerous class. Yet it seems equally undeniable that a complicated if unacknowledged psychological warfare was being waged between the doctors and their patients. Even the best-intentioned practitioner was forced into a role in part hostile to his woman patients simply by the misconceptions he was trained to hold. Until well after the Civil War, for example, physicians in America, as in Europe, arguing by analogy with the animal world, maintained that woman's fertile period was right before and after menstruation.[25] Hence the nineteenth-century American woman, perhaps in ill health and eager to practice a semirespectable form of birth control, conscientiously slept with her spouse squarely in the middle of her menstrual cycle.

Given the presumably disastrous results action on this belief must have produced, one must turn from the world of science to the realm of culture to explain its surprising tenacity, and the equal persistence with which treatments like cauterization and the rest cure kept their

---

23 Charles D. Meigs, a conservative gynecologist of Philadelphia, wrote in 1848 that he "rejoiced" at the difficulty of making local examinations since it was "an evidence of a high and worthy grade of moral feeling" in American women (quoted in Harvey Graham, *Eternal Eve: The History of Gynecology and Obstetrics* [New York, 1951], 495).

24 Dewees, *A Treatise on the Diseases of Females*, 224–225, 242–243; Bennet, *A Practical Treatise on Inflammation of the Uterus*, 19. Another widely used foreign authority made the same point. J. W. von Scanzoni (trans. Augustus K. Gardner), *A Practical Treatise on the Diseases of the Sexual Organs of Women* (New York, 1861), 37–38. See also Byford, *A Treatise on the Chronic Inflammation*, 98.

25 Graham, *Eternal Eve*, 451. For an example, see Napheys, *The Transmission of Life*, 190–191.

hold in the medical world. Physicians both of the cauterist school and of the rest-cure school brought certain unexplored but pervasive presuppositions to their work. They assumed, as already mentioned, that women were physically dominated by their wombs. They held, moreover, even less carefully scrutinized beliefs about the social and psychological nature of femininity and its role and responsibilities in their society, beliefs which colored their attitude toward the illness of their female patients.

The first point to be noted is the element of distrust, even of condemnation lurking behind their diagnoses. Physicians tended to stress a certain moral depravity inherent in feminine nervous disorders and to waver significantly between labeling it a result and analyzing it as the cause of the physical symptoms involved. The patient, according to Byford's experience, may become "a changed woman"—irritable, indecisive, lacking in will power, morose, jealous. She is likely to show "a guarded cunning, a deceitful and perverted consciousness"; indeed, she may commit "acts of a depraved and indecent nature," and neglect her "duty in all the relations of life." [26]

In part, Byford was indirectly expressing his doubts as to whether or not his patients were truly sick. Such doubts were widely shared. Dixon, in *Woman and Her Diseases*, cautioned the physician always to pay "profound attention" to what he delicately called "moral circumstances." These moral causes were often, he warned, not of a nature "calculated to move our sympathy," and he was all too aware that women were cunning enough to "pretend hysteric attacks, in order to excite sympathy and obtain some desired end." [27] Even more important, of course, was the doctor's unspoken guess at the *reason* behind this calculated exploitation of illness. Who can doubt that, in an age when sex and childbirth involved very real threats to the health and life of women, some women would use the pretext of being "delicate" as a way not only of escaping household labor but also of closing the bedroom door while avoiding the guilt consequent upon a more flagrant defiance of their "duties"? Harriet Beecher Stowe understood the process and dramatized it at its worst in her portrait of Mrs. St. Clair (in *Uncle Tom's Cabin*) lying on her sofa, shirking responsibility and demanding attention. And Stowe herself, who suffered the burden of relative poverty and of a weak and dependent but

---

[26] Byford, *A Treatise on the Chronic Inflammation*, 22–41. Mitchell also testified to this pattern of moral degradation, *Fat and Blood*, 27, 28. One should add here that condemnation disguised as diagnosis and punishment offered as cure were hardly unique to medical treatment of women in this period. Napheys hints at "surgical operations" to curb masturbation in men and advocates blisterings and "infibulation" (*Transmission of Life*, 80–83). Rugoff discusses various painful contraptions used to prevent nocturnal emission (*Prudery and Passion*, 53). I am simply trying to show how two particular courses of punitive medicine reflected and supported culturally induced ideas about female sexual identity.

[27] Edward H. Dixon, *Woman and Her Diseases from the Cradle to the Grave* (New York, 1857), 134, 140.

potent husband, took periodic refuge from him and their numerous off-spring in those havens of escape, the health establishments.[28]

Clearly, in the case of a woman like Stowe, however, we do not have the simple problem of a woman failing to live up to her sexual and domestic responsibilities as we do in the case of her own fictional creation, Mrs. St. Clair. It is rather that her responsibilities, despite all her histrionic and martyred posturings about them, were genuinely more than she could handle: They were almost killing her. Doctors of the period were intermittently and partially aware of the frustrations inherent in the middle-class woman's lot. Alexander Combe, the Scottish phrenologist so influential in America, attributed the high level of insanity in women of this class to the monotony of their lives.[29] In 1834, Dr. Alcott of Boston advocated that ladies be trained as nurses because "these are individuals who need some employment, for the sake even of the emolument; but more especially to save them from ennui, and disgust, and misery—sometimes from speedy or more protracted suicide." [30] Professional work, however, was hardly a socially acceptable escape from a lady's situation, but sickness, that very nervous condition brought on by the frustrations of her life, was.

Yet, many doctors, despite the apparent conscious understanding shown in the analysis of Combe and Alcott, in practice tended unconsciously to see the neuralgic ailments of their female patients as a threatening and culpable shirking of their duties as wives and mothers, and to look upon those duties as the cure, not the cause, of the illness. Self-sacrifice and altruism on a spiritual level, and childbearing and housework on a more practical one, constituted healthy femininity in the eyes of most nineteenth-century Americans. Dr. Clarke of Harvard, who believed that girls of the 1870s were ill because they were quite literally destroying their wombs and their childbearing potential by presuming to pursue a course of higher education intended by nature only for the male sex, was very much a spokesman for the doctors of his generation.

One finds an underlying logic running through popular books by physicians on women's diseases to the effect that ladies get sick *because* they are unfeminine—in other words, sexually aggressive, intellectually ambitious, and defective in proper womanly submission and selflessness. Bad health habits were often put forth by doctors and others as causes of nervous complaints. But these, consisting as they did of improper diet, light reading, late hours, tight lacing, and inadequate clothing, were

---

[28] For a discussion of Stowe's marital problems and responsibilities, see the following biographies: Joanna Johnston, *Runaway to Heaven: The Story of Harriet Beecher Stowe* (New York, 1963) and Forrest Wilson, *Crusader in Crinoline: The Life of Harriet Beecher Stowe* (Philadelphia, 1941). Also of value is Edmund Wilson, *Patriotic Gore: Studies in the Literature of the American Civil War* (New York, 1966), 3–58.

[29] "Insanity: From Combe's Work on Mental Derangement," *Ladies' Magazine*, VIII (1835), 461–463.

[30] W. A. Alcott, "Female Attendance on the Sick," *Ladies' Magazine*, VII (1834), 302.

in themselves a badge of the "fashionable" and flirtatious female, only a step removed in popular imagination from the infamous one. Byford believed that "the influence of lascivious books" and frequent "indulgence" in intercourse would precipitate neuralgia.[31] Significantly, in Mitchell's fiction, the sick woman is almost invariably the closest thing he has to a villainess and she is often intelligent and usually predatory to an extreme. In *Roland Blake*, published in 1886, Octapia Darnell, an invalid, is branded by her name. Octapuslike, she uses her sickness like tentacles to try to squeeze the life out of her innocent young cousin, Olivia Wynne. Although we see her in genuine nervous spasms, Mitchell never shows her seized by a convulsion where it would be inconvenient to her purposes, nor does he let us forget that when she needs physical strength to accomplish her will, she always summons it. Again, the heroine of *Constance Trescott* (1905), his last and best novel, is driven by a demonic will to possess utterly where she loves and to revenge totally where she hates. Rather predictably she turns to invalidism at the book's close to gain her ends.

It is not that Mitchell totally condemns these women. Instead, he understands them, and adopts a tone of pitying patronage toward them. He thinks they are genuinely sick, but he believes, as did Clarke, that the root of their sickness was their failure to be women, to sacrifice themselves for others, and to perform their feminine duties. Typically, Octapia Darnell has a brief period of improvement when a "recent need to think of others had beneficently taken her outside of the slowly narrowing circle of self-care and self-contemplation, and, by relieving her of some of the morbid habits of disease, had greatly bettered her physical condition." [32] The truth is that Mitchell does not even need to blame or punish her: In his view, nature has conveniently done that job for him.

Mitchell's analysis, then, one standard with doctors in the nineteenth century, served an important psychological purpose, whatever its medical validity. The doctor, on some unacknowledged level, feared his female patient. Could he so emphasize the diseased potency of woman's unique and mysterious organ, the womb, if he did not worry that his sex, the constant companion of hers, was in some way menaced? How comfortable Mitchell must have felt, when, addressing a graduating Radcliffe class, he expressed his clearly faint hope "that no wreck from these shores will be drifted into my dockyard." [33] They might begin as his competitors, but, despite it—in fact, because of it—they would end as his patients.

Mitchell and his peers could indeed afford to pity the fair sex, even perhaps to "cure" them. Yet the consequent "cures" bore unmistakable signs of their culturally determined origin, for they made a woman's womb very much a liability. Since her disease was unconsciously viewed as a symptom of a failure in femininity, its remedy was designed both as a punishment and an agent of regeneration, for it forced her to acknowl-

---

[31] Byford, *A Treatise on the Chronic Inflammation*, 15.

[32] S. Weir Mitchell, *Roland Blake* (Boston, 1886), 254.

[33] Anna Robeson Burr (ed.), *Weir Mitchell: His Life and Letters* (New York, 1929), 374. Mitchell makes the same point in *Doctor and Patient*, 13.

edge her womanhood and made her totally dependent on the professional prowess of her male doctor. The cauterizer, with his injections, leeches, and hot irons seems suggestive of a veiled but aggressively hostile male sexuality and superiority, and the rest-cure expert carried this spirit to a sophisticated culmination.

Mitchell's treatment depended in actuality not so much on the techniques of rest and overfeeding, as on the commanding personality and charismatic will of the physician. "A slight, pale lad of no physical strength" by his own description, he moved as a young man in the shadow of his dominating, joyous, strong doctor-father.[34] To be the strong, healing male in a world of ailing, dependent women had obvious charms for him. "Electric with fascination" for women as his granddaughter saw him, he acknowledged that he played the "despot" in the sickroom, and boasted of reducing patients to the docility of children.[35] Doctors had always preferred to keep women in ignorance, and Mitchell was no exception. In a characteristically urbane and aphoristic remark, he said, "Wise women choose their doctors and trust them. The wisest ask the fewest questions." [36] But he wanted to be more than trusted: He wished to be revered, even adored, and he succeeded. The totality of the power he could acquire is revealed in a letter he received from a sick woman who positively grovels before him as she rhapsodizes on his potency:

> Whilst laid by the heels in a country-house with an attack of grippe, also an invalid from gastric affection, the weary eyes of a sick woman fall upon your face in the *Century* of this month—a thrill passed through me—at last I saw the true physician![37]

It is clear, moreover, that Mitchell encouraged this worshiping attitude as an important element in his "cure." A doctor, in his view, if he had the proper mesmeric powers of will, could become almost god-like.[38] Women doctors would always be inferior to male physicians, he believed, precisely because they could not exercise such tyranny: They were unable to "obtain the needed control over those of their own sex." [39] Mitchell here skated on the edge of a theory of primitive healing through mesmeric sexual powers.[40] Furthermore, his treatment was designed to make his female patients take his view of the doctor's role. They were

---

[34] Burr, *Weir Mitchell*, 37. The best recent biography is Ernest Earnest, *S. Weir Mitchell: Novelist and Physician* (Philadelphia, 1950).

[35] Mitchell, *Fat and Blood*, 48.

[36] Mitchell, *Doctor and Patient*, 48.

[37] Quoted in Burr, *Weir Mitchell*, 290.

[38] There are striking similarities between Mitchell's conception of his role, and that of Freudian psychiatrists. See Earnest, *Weir Mitchell*, 250.

[39] Mitchell, *Fat and Blood*, 39.

[40] He tried hypnosis in his practice, though with little success. See Earnest, *Weir Mitchell*, 229. Robert Herrick was to dramatize this aspect of the physician's role in *The Healer* (New York, 1911) and in *Together* (New York, 1909).

allowed to see no one but him, and to talk of their ills and problems to no one else. As doctor he became the only spot of energy, the only source of *life*, during the enforced repose of a cure process.

Undoubtedly, if Mitchell were aware of what he was doing, he would have felt it justifiable and even merciful. He was curing his patients—by restoring them to their femininity or, in other words, by subordinating them to an enlightened but dictatorial male will. His admirers delighted to tell how, when a strangely recalcitrant patient refused to rise from bed after Mitchell had decreed that her rest cure was over, Mitchell threatened to move into bed with her if she did not get up, and even started to undress. When he got to his pants, she got up. Although the story may well be apocryphal, its spirit is not. Not surprisingly, the lady in question was fleeing the fact where she embraced the shadow, for symbolically, Mitchell, like his cauterizing predecessor, played the role of possessor, even impregnator, in the cure process. Dominated, overfed often to the point of obesity, caressed and (quite literally) vibrating, were not his patients being returned to health—to womanhood? [41] The only other time that the Victorian lady took to her bed and got fat was, in fact, before delivery. J. Marion Sims had noted that his colleagues were erroneously wont to lament about a sick woman: "If she could only have a child, it would cure her." [42] Although he was a generation later, Mitchell was not so different from the doctors Sims opposed who looked to pregnancy for the cure of all feminine ills.

Here one senses a clue to the pertinacity with which doctors told women anxious to avoid pregnancy that they should sleep with their husbands only during what we now know as their most fertile period. In a sense, the practices and writings of the medical profession provide the other half of the picture of ideal womanhood presented in the sentimental literature of the day. Woman was at her holiest, according to the genteel novels and poetry of Victorian America, as a mother. Pregnancy itself, however, was avoided by the authors of such works as completely as the act of impregnation. The medical manual took on the role of frankness disowned by its more discreet companion. All the logic of contemporary medical lore adds up to the lesson that women were at their most feminine when they were pregnant. Pregnant, they were visible emblems of masculine potency.

It is impossible to determine how many nineteenth-century middle-class American women went to doctors, just as it is difficult to tell how real their much-advertised ailments were. Reluctant as American women apparently were to undergo local examination, many of them presumably stayed home and suffered with no medical aid except that provided by earlier versions of Lydia Pinkham's patent medicine. Others trusted to the hydropathic remedies provided at numerous water-cures or used homeopathic drugs, both of which represented forms of protest against current

[41] For examples of these weight gains, see Mitchell, *Fat and Blood*, 80–94. One 5′ 8″ woman went from 118 lbs. to 169 lbs.

[42] Quoted in Harris, *Woman's Surgeon*, 181.

medical practices.[43] Furthermore, the majority of women suffering from uterine and/or nervous disorders who underwent a form of local treatment or, later, the rest cure, were presumably in real distress and glad of whatever help their physician could offer.[44] Some, however, were undoubtedly using prescribed treatments for their own purposes. According to numerous masculine and feminine observers, many women grew positively addicted to local treatment as others did later to the rest cure, but, not surprisingly, these women have not left any direct confessions to posterity.[45]

What we do have record of is a masked but almost hysterical paranoia among a small group of feminist hygiene experts and lady doctors, a paranoia stemming from their exaggerated but astute perception of the unconscious purposes underlying the attitudes and practices of doctors with women patients. In their excited view, current medical treatment was patently not science, for which they professed respect, but a part of their male-dominated culture, for which they had both fear and contempt. They saw it as a form of rape, designed to keep woman prostrate, a perpetual patient dependent on a doctor's supposed professional expertise.

No one expressed this attitude better than did two Beecher women, Catharine Esther Beecher, who crusaded against local treatment, and her grandniece Charlotte Perkins Gilman, who protested against Mitchell's rest cure a generation later. Each of them wrote a work dedicated to exposing what they felt were the unstated motives of physicians treating women patients. In *Letters to the People on Health and Happiness*, Beecher described with heavy-handed irony the ineffectuality of the string of "talented, highly-educated and celebrated" doctors who had tried to cure her own severe nervous ailments (115).[46] She consumed sulphur and iron, she let one doctor sever the "wounded nerves from their centres," she let another cover her spine with "tartar emetic pustules," she subjected herself to "animal magnetism" and the water cure, but all to no purpose.

Beecher does not admit to having personally undergone local treatment, but when she discusses it, her tone changes from the condescending

---

[43] Both the homeopathic school, with its distrust of drugs and violent remedies, and the hydropathic school with its reliance on the efficacy of water, advocated relatively mild treatments for women's ailments. For examples, see John A. Tarbell, *Homeopathy Simplified: or Domestic Practice Made Easy* (Boston, 1859), 214–218; R. T. Trall, *The Hydropathic Encyclopedia: A System of Hydropathy and Hygiene* (New York, 1852), II, 285–296. It must also be added, however, that such doctors were outside the higher echelons of American medicine. Furthermore, it is striking how many women turned to such doctors as a result of bad experiences at the hands of more orthodox doctors. In other words, it seems likely that the lady at the water-cure had also sampled other forms of treatment.

[44] Angelina Grimké, for instance, a famous abolitionist and speaker for women's rights, suffered terribly from *prolapsus uteri*. See Gerda Lerner, *The Grimké Sisters from South Carolina* (Boston, 1967), 288–292.

[45] See Austin, *Perils of American Women*, 94–95.

[46] All page references will be to the edition already cited.

playfulness she uses to devastate such methods as the "tartar emetic pustules" to one of outraged horror. Doctors playing professional games with pustules had kept her sick perhaps, but they had left her with her honor. Local treatment, roughly equivalent to rape according to Beecher, seldom allowed a lady to retain that valuable possession. It is "performed," she explains, "with bolted doors and curtained windows, and with no one present but patient and operator," by doctors who have all too often "freely advocated the doctrine that there was no true marriage but the union of persons who were in love." Predictably, these immoral practitioners were said to have "lost all reverence for the Bible." With his "interesting" female patients, such a physician "naturally," in Beecher's gloomy view, tries "to lead them to adopt *his views of truth and right*" on moral matters. "Then he daily has all the opportunities indicated [through local examination]. Does anyone need more than to hear these facts to know what the not unfrequent results must be?" she ominously concludes (136). By the time she is through with this subject, she is calling the female patients "victims" and lamenting their "entire helplessness" (137). She refers the reader to an appended letter from a woman doctor, Mrs. R. B. Gleason of the Elmira Water Cure in New York, who solemnly testifies that manual replacement for *prolapsus uteri* was "in most cases totally needless, and in many decidedly injurious" (6★). After such evidence, Beecher can hardly avoid "the painful inquiry": "how can a woman *ever know* to whom she may safely entrust herself. . . in such painful and peculiar circumstances?" (138).

Gilman, a brilliant theorist and critic on women's role in American society, went through periods of nervous prostration strikingly similar to those of her aged relative.[47] She sampled the fruits of medical wisdom a few decades later, undergoing Mitchell's rest cure. She expressed the result in a story entitled "The Yellow Wall Paper," published in 1890, and designed to convince Mitchell "of the error of his ways." [48]

The story concerns a married woman, the mother of a young child, suffering from "nervous" disorders, and clearly laboring under disguised but immense (and justifiable) hostility for both her spouse and her offspring. Her husband, John, who is a doctor, is ostensibly overseeing her cure, but is in reality intent with sadistic ignorance on destroying her body and soul. John, apparently modeled on Mitchell himself, confines his wife to a country house, which to her seems "haunted," remote from friends or neighbors. Presumably hoping to force her back to her feminine and maternal functions, he symbolically makes her sleep in an old nursery. With its barred windows, rings attached to the wall, bed nailed to the floor, and disturbing and torn yellow wallpaper, this nursery all too significantly and frighteningly resembles a cell for the insane. Treating her

[47] See her own account in her autobiography, *The Living of Charlotte Perkins Gilman* (New York, 1935), 90 ff. She may have felt her similarities to Beecher since she named her daughter after her.

[48] All page references will be to Charlotte Perkins Gilman, "The Yellow Wall Paper," in William Dean Howells (ed.), *The Great Modern American Short Stories* (New York, 1920), 320–337; Gilman, *Living of Charlotte Perkins Gilman*, 121.

like a pet, the doctor alternates condescending tenderness ("Then he took me in his arms and called me a blessed little goose" [323]) with threats of punishment ("John says if I don't pick up faster he shall send me to Weir Mitchell in the fall" [326]). Since John "never was nervous in his life" (323), and is a doctor "of high standing" (320) to boot, he can "laugh" at her fears because he "knows there is no *reason* to suffer, and that satisfies him" (323). Complacently smug in his masculine insensitivity and his professional superiority, he is totally obtuse about the nature of her suffering and its possible cure. An early-day "mad housewife," she has been so browbeaten by his calm assumption of superiority that she can only timidly air the frightening truth:

> John is a physician, and *perhaps*—(I would not say it to a living soul, of course, but this is dead paper and a great relief to my mind)—*perhaps* that is one reason I do not get well faster [320].

He has left her with only one recourse, and she takes it. Slowly but steadily, she goes mad, thus dramatically pointing up the results of his "cure." At the story's close, she is creeping on hands and knees with insane persistence around the walls of her chamber. In a symbolic moment, her husband, suspicious about her behavior, breaks down the door she has finally locked against him. His act is the essence of his "cure" and her "problem"; like Catharine Beecher, Gilman sees the doctor "treating" his patient as violating her. But this patient is finally beyond feeling. When John faints away in shock at her state, their roles have been reversed: *He* has become the woman, the nervous, susceptible, sickly patient, and she wonders with a kind of calm, self-centered vindictiveness fully equal to his former arrogance: "Now why should that man have fainted? But he did, and right across my path by the wall, so that I had to creep over him every time!" (337). She has won, because she can ignore him now as completely as he ignored her, but she has won at the cost of becoming what he subconsciously sought to make her—a creeping creature, an animal and an automaton.

Beecher's *Letters* and Gilman's story are both intended to convey a nightmare vision of sick women dependent on male doctors who use their professional superiority as a method to prolong their patients' sickness and, consequently, the supremacy of their own sex. Both writers also hint, however, at a possible escape for such feminine victims. Beecher, according to her account, was finally cured by a timely tip from a *woman* physician, Dr. Elizabeth Blackwell. Gilman's heroine knows what her cure should be—work and intellectual stimulation—although she is too cowed and powerless to insist on it. Both Gilman and Beecher simply in writing their works, are implying that the untutored common sense of two women can outdo the professionally trained brains of those male doctors who labored in vain to cure them. Both are thus in essence urging that a woman should be independent, that *she be her own physician*, so that the real business of healing can get under way.[49]

[49] The demand for women doctors could be quite explicit. See Julia Ward Howe (ed.), *A Reply to Dr. E. H. Clarke's 'Sex in Education'* (Boston, 1874), 158.

After all, Beecher and Gilman realized, there might be two possible ways of looking at the much-advertised problem of the increasingly bad health of middle-class American women. Doctors like Clarke and Mitchell liked to think that the fault lay with the women themselves, who were neglecting their homes and pursuing such an unfeminine goal as higher education. Women like Beecher and Gilman, shrewdly reversing the charge, queried whether the blame might not belong to the men who were supposed to cure them and to the professional training which was supposed to enable them to do it. Harriot Hunt, one of the most impressive of the early women doctors in America, put the challenge succinctly: "Man, man alone has had the care of *us* [women], and I would ask how *our health stands now*. Does it do credit to *his* skill?" [50] Hunt is clearly aware that what had been a condemnation of women (the charge of ill health) could be used as a powerful weapon in their defense. The women doctors who began to appear on the American scene in the 1850s saw women's diseases as a *result* of submission, and promoted independence from masculine domination, whether professional or sexual, as their cure for feminine ailments.[51]

In dealing with these pioneer women doctors and their theories, one is at once aware that here, too, the issues are inevitably cultural rather than scientific. Their primary aim, often an unconscious one, was to free ailing women from male control. On the one hand, this desire could and did further scientific advancement, for their distrust of the male doctor made them eager to reject aspects of medical practice that were in fact unscientific, if not harmful. Their paranoid fear that the male doctor was degrading his female patient paradoxically led them to some sound conclusions about the worthlessness of many drugs and the necessity of sanitation and preventive medicine. On the other hand, the same fear also made them, on occasion, throw out the baby with the bath water. Their hostility to the male doctor too often became a hostility to any scientific practice which appeared to their oversensitive consciousness as an invasion of the patient's privacy. Gynecological surgery, for example, which, despite undoubted abuse, represented a significant step in medical treatment of women, was often rejected by these early pioneers. Yet one must keep in mind that what is unwitting stupidity from a scientific point of view can be (albeit equally unwitting) shrewdness from a social or political point of view. These women bypassed science in large part because they had a goal quite distinct from its advancement: namely, the advancement of their sex.

Nowhere is this aim clearer than in the work of Hunt, a well-known, if home-trained, Boston practitioner and the most outspoken of the first generation of women doctors. Her autobiography, *Glances and Glimpses*

---

[50] Harriot K. Hunt, *Glances and Glimpses: or Fifty Years Social, Including Twenty Years Professional Life* (Boston, 1856), 414.

[51] For the history of women doctors in America, see Kate Campbell-Hurd, *Medical Women in America: A Short History of the Pioneer Medical Women of America and of a Few of Their Colleagues in England* (Fort Pierce Beach, Fla., 1933); Esther Pohl Lovejoy, *Women Doctors of the World* (New York, 1957).

(1856), published when she was forty-one, is clearly oversimplified, one-sided, and sentimentalized, but one must keep in mind that she was writing not a scientific report, nor even a history, but rather a special kind of mythologized propaganda, a scenario for a sexual revolution.

The ritualized drama begins with Hunt's explanation of why she chose medicine for a career—her stunned realization of the profound ignorance of the male doctors treating feminine diseases (81).[52] Her ailing sister was put through a course of remedies somewhat similar to the one Beecher tried, and she, and Harriot, came away having "lost all confidence in medicine" (85). The male practitioner here emerges as one of the villains of Hunt's piece. According to her testimony, he usually made his living by creating false dependencies in his female patients, by keeping them ignorant and totally reliant on his shortsighted or even harmful remedies (32, 89). Indeed, Hunt insinuates, his professional training led him actually to want his patients to be sick so that he would have something to do with all the games he had learned.

Professional exploitation by the doctor of his female patient was a mask, in Hunt's opinion, for a deeper and more humiliating sexual exploitation. Like Catharine Beecher, Hunt was publicly and loudly aghast at local examinations. They were *"too often unnecessary"* (271) and their moral effects were terrible. Many medical men, in her view, were skeptics, who lived "sensually" (177), and contaminated their patients. At this point, Hunt's scenario grows both alarmist and lurid. A woman once forced to submit to local examination, Hunt reveals, was well on the road to ruin: She felt "disgraced, and a don't careativeness [*sic*] and sort of sullen desperation" settled on her (184). Yet this fantasized sexual violation was dreadful, according to Hunt, not so much because of the moral degradation involved as because of the patient's loss of control and her consequent dependence on the doctor's will. In describing a physician who took advantage of a patient and left her with an illegitimate child, she explains significantly: His "will overmastered the weaker will of his patient" (376).

The doctor's was not the only malevolent will pitted against his woman patient's will in Hunt's story. The villainous physicians who kept women sick were only collaborating with the villainous husbands who had caused their illnesses in the first place. In her favorite role as minister-doctor, she collected many of what she called the "heart-histories" of her women patients, and publicized them as evidence that women's "physical maladies" stemmed from "concealed sorrows" (139), often at the "sins" of their spouses (159).[53] Hunt never married, but she was always ready with sympathy for those who had. One married patient after another

---

[52] All page references will be to Hunt, *Glances and Glimpses*. For similar motivation in another woman doctor see Helen MacKnight Doyle, *A Child Went Forth* (New York, 1934), 15–18.

[53] There was some medical truth underlying this apparently sentimental declaration. Aside from subjecting women to the perils of childbirth, men not infrequently unwittingly gave them syphilis. See Elizabeth Blackwell, *Essays in Medical Sociology* (London, 1902), I, 90–91.

apparently confided to her: "I thank heaven, my dear doctor, that you are a woman; for now I can tell you the truth about my health. It is not my body that is sick but my heart" (120).

Hunt's vision, so filled with villains and victims, has a savior to offer as well. This heroine is of course Hunt herself, as a woman doctor and simply as a woman. As a doctor, she dramatically renounced "medical science" as "full of unnecessary details," but without "a soul . . . a huge, unwieldy body—distorted, deformed, inconsistent and complicated" (121). Medicine was generally "worse than useless" (371), she remarked; moreover, it did not meet her "perception of the dignity of the human body." She did not enter "the medical life through physics, but through metaphysics" (127). She was only too eager to announce her disavowal of "science," because she considered her disrespect precisely her strongest claim to respect. Flaunting her anti-professionalism like a medal of honor, she loved to proclaim herself an eclectic, as indeed she was, the "disciple of no medical sect" (171), but the sworn servant of her sex.[54]

Hunt's treatment consisted of telling her patients to throw away their medicines, begin a diary, and think of their mothers (401). The last item of this prescription is not simply the pure sentimentalism that it might appear. Hunt was symbolically turning her patients' thoughts to an acceptable but potent emblem of *female strength*.[55] It was from this source that she expected her patients to find their cure—not in the arms of their husbands, nor under the hands of the male doctor. The medicine that she gave her patients as a sure antidote to the wares peddled by her masculine colleagues was the example of her own ample and self-sufficient womanhood. Could they forget their mothers with Hunt before them?

[54] Anti-professionalism in women doctors had another complex side which mainly lies outside the scope of this article. Women had been active medical practitioners in America as midwives until the time of the Revolution. Then licenses, obtainable only in the newly opened medical schools, which did not take women, began to be required. So, in effect, professional requirements had spelled the demise of the woman physician in the late eighteenth century. Hence, the mistrust felt for such training by her nineteenth-century feminine successor was not surprising. Unquestionably, late eighteenth-century and early nineteenth-century American doctors had welcomed and even pushed for this change (see Victor Robinson, *White-Caps: The Story of Nursing* [Philadelphia, 1946], 137), although a few regretted it (see A. Curtis, *Lectures on Midwifery and the Forms of Disease Peculiar to Women and Children* [Columbus, Ohio, 1841], 9). On the whole question of women and the professions in this period, see Gerda Lerner, "The Lady and the Mill-Girl: Changes in the Status of Women in the Age of Jackson," *Mid-Continent American Studies Journal*, X (1969), 5–15.

[55] American society throughout this period agreed on the importance and potency of motherhood. In part this was a simple rationale of the fact that, since the American father was at work, the American mother was raising the children. See Anne L. Kuhn, *The Mother's Role in Childhood Education* (New Haven, 1947); Bernard Wishy, *The Child and the Republic: The Dawn of Modern American Child Nurture* (Philadelphia, 1968), 24–29. Contemporary paeans to motherhood are legion, but see Jabez Burns, *Mothers of the Wise and Good* (Boston, 1950); Margaret C. Conklin, *Memoirs of the Mother and Wife of Washington* (Auburn, N.Y., 1851).

Hunt was an ardent and proclaimed feminist and suffragist, but other women pioneers in medicine who did not share, or did not avow such sympathies, were almost without exception part of her crusade.[56] The most famous of these was Elizabeth Blackwell, usually considered the first woman doctor in America. In her girlhood an avowed admirer of the fiercely virginal goddess Diana, Blackwell always loved to project an almost monstrous force as woman's natural dowry.[57] Yet she was clearly drawn to such fantasies precisely because of her deep-seated perception and fear of the dependent role women usually played. With paradoxical logic, she explained that precisely *because* she was very "susceptible" to men and perpetually in love, she had determined never to marry. Not initially attracted to medicine, she deliberately chose it as a potentially "strong barrier between me and all ordinary marriage. I must have something to engross my thoughts, some object in life which will fulfill this vacuum and prevent this sad wearing away of the heart." [58]

Professionally, despite her soft-spoken, conciliating manner, she fought the code of the male medical establishment which in her view victimized women as surely as did matrimony. During medical school, she

[56] I have picked the two most famous of the early women doctors in America, but most of the others fall into similar patterns. All of them devoted themselves professionally almost exclusively to women, few of them married, and most met determined opposition from the majority of their male colleagues, in some cases amounting to what Elizabeth Blackwell called "medical starvation" (unpublished letter of Jan. 23, 1855, to Emily Blackwell in Blackwell Collection, Radcliffe Archives, Cambridge, Mass.). For works on and by the other three most famous women doctors of the period, Emily Blackwell, Mary Putnam Jacobi, and Maria Zakrewska, see the Blackwell Collection; Ruth Putnam (ed.), *Life and Letters of Mary Putnam Jacobi* (New York, 1925); *Mary Putnam Jacobi, M.D.: A Pathfinder in Medicine: With Selections from Her Writings* (New York, 1925); Rhoda Truax, *The Doctors Jacobi* (Boston, 1952); and the Jacobi papers, also at Radcliffe.

Jacobi was one of the most brilliant doctors of her day, and her monograph, *The Question of Rest for Women During Menstruation* (New York, 1877), an answer to Clarke, won the Harvard Boylston Medical Prize. For Zakrewska's autobiography, see Caroline H. Dall (ed.), *A Practical Illustration of Woman's Right to Labor: or A Letter from Marie E. Zakrewska, M.D.* (Boston, 1860); Agnes C. Victor (ed.), *A Woman's Quest: The Life of Marie E. Zakrewska, M.D.* (New York, 1924). Also of great interest, although falling outside of professional ranks, were Lydia Folger Fowler and Mary Gove Nichols. See Frederick C. Waite, "Dr. Lydia Folger Fowler: The Second Woman to Receive the Degree of Doctor in the United States," *Annals of Medical History*, IV (1932), 290–297; T. L. Nichols and Mary S. Gove Nichols, *Marriage: Its History, Character and Results* (New York, 1854); Mary S. Gove Nichols, *Mary Lyndon, or Revelations of a Life: An Autobiography* (New York, 1855); Helen Beal Woodward, *The Bold Women* (New York, 1953), 149–180.

[57] Ishbel Ross, *Child of Destiny: The First Life Story of the First Woman Doctor* (New York, 1949), 43.

[58] Blackwell, *Pioneer Work*, 28, 32. She consistently opposed the marriages of the male members of her large family; the women all stayed single. See Elinor Rice Hays, *Those Extraordinary Blackwells: The Story of a Journey to a Better World* (New York, 1967), 155. Zakrewska felt the same way. See *A Woman's Quest*, 193.

was shocked at the "horrible exposure" of women to male physicians, finding it "indecent for any poor woman to be subjected to such a torture." [59] In her later years, when local treatment was less common, Blackwell crusaded against its medical descendant, ovariotomy, or as she called it with characteristic dramatic flair, "the castration of women." Estimating that 1 of every 250 women in Europe had been "castrated," she collected newspaper clippings which supported her belief that young doctors were performing this operation needlessly on unsuspecting women just to obtain professional practice. [60]

The validity of Blackwell's fears is hard to estimate. Many reputable people shared them. Yet Dr. Maria Zakrewska lamented the fact that women had come to her Boston hospital insisting that their ovaries be removed as a birth control device. [61] Nonetheless, in Blackwell's eyes, male doctors were performing a kind of "vivisection"—a practice that she violently opposed in any form—on their female patients. [62] Ovariotomies for her simply dramatized the anti-woman bias of much of modern science. If man were going to dedicate himself to cold-blooded experimentation, would not woman be his ultimate subject? Consequently, despite her fine mind and excellent training, Blackwell, an incipient Christian Scientist, obstinately opposed not just the usual run of drugs and medication, but vaccination and "all medical methods which introduce any degree of morbid matter into the blood of the human system." [63] All such practices were "especially antagonistic to women." [64] Blackwell's medical short-sightedness seems ludicrous, perhaps culpable, but it furthered her underlying and non-medical goals.

To distrust science was to distrust masculinity, and to create an apparent immediate and desperate need for women doctors. She saw these projected new physicians, moreover, as undercover agents in enemy territory. Her advice to them reads a bit like a lesson in subversion. Proud that she had determined early in her career to "*commit heresy* with intelligence" to escape the perils of professionalized medicine, she declared that women doctors should not countenance practices like ovariotomies, vaccination, and vivisection. [65] In a crucial essay entitled "The Influence of Women in the Profession of Medicine" (1889), she urged women medical students, unfortunately, like all of their sex, trained to "accept

[59] Blackwell, *Pioneer Work*, 72.

[60] "Increase of Operations," undated paper in the Blackwell Collection. See also Elizabeth Blackwell, *Essays in Medical Sociology* (London, 1902), II, 120.

[61] Letter of March 21, 1891, in the Blackwell Collection.

[62] See Blackwell, *Essays*, II, 119 ff. Anti-vivisection had many passionate feminine adherents, medical and lay. Elizabeth Stuart Phelps, a popular writer and feminist of Blackwell's era, devoted much of her later work to the cause. See especially *Though Life Do Us Part* (Boston, 1908), 54–55, where she explicitly links male cruelty in vivisection with male cruelty in marriage, and *Trixy* (Boston, 1904) in which a girl refuses to marry a vivisectionist.

[63] See Blackwell, *Pioneer Work*, 178, 157, 240. See also Blackwell, *Essays*, II, 69 ff.

[64] Blackwell, *Essays*, II, 26. Jacobi seems to be making a similar point about the male intellect in "The Mad Scientist," in *Stories and Sketches* (New York, 1907).

[65] Blackwell, *Pioneer Work*, 173.

the government and instruction of men as final" (20), to exercise a "mild skepticism" (21).[66] Their task was quite simply to revamp the whole medical profession, for, as she explained, "methods and conclusions formed by one half the race only must necessarily require revision as the other half of humanity rises into conscious responsibility" (20). They had a sure guide in this apparently momentous undertaking: Nothing that revolted their "moral sense as earnest women" could be scientifically true, and no "logical sophistry" (30) could make it so. In a letter to a medical colleague, she echoes Emerson as she anticipates a day when women will plant themselves firmly "on the God-given force of their maternal nature" and oppose the male intellect in its too restless search for scientific truth.[67]

Blackwell was very clever. Male doctors had indirectly told their women patients that their procreative femininity was their dearest treasure. Coining that treasure into current cash, Blackwell pointed to her sacred maternal nature as justification for a revolt against the ways of the male doctor. For the woman physician of Blackwell's vision, womanhood was hardly a liability, and very much a weapon. She was no subordinate, but an aggressive censor of the masculine world.[68] Blackwell herself was only too ready. Calling herself a "Christian physiologist," she fought prostitution, masturbation, and obscene literature in addition to various medical abuses. It was in these crusades that her underlying anti-male bias most dramatically expressed itself. With so many of her feminine peers, she liked to see male sexuality, like male science, as one more method used by men to debase women to their own level by seducing them, and to keep them dependent by forcing them into parasitism. Blackwell's target in the anti-prostitution campaign organized by the Purity Alliance was not the prostitute, but her exploiter.[69] "Male lust must be restrained in order to check female obscenity"[70] was the telling slogan Blackwell issued in one of her many essays on the subject. It is not too much to say that the paid whore whom Blackwell wished to regenerate was simply another version of the female patient corrupted by immoral medical practices whom Beecher and Hunt had sought to redeem.

It is telling that Blackwell, like most of the first generation of women doctors, chose hygiene, or preventive medicine, as her chosen field, and she made great contributions there, despite her distrust of vaccination. There can be no doubt, furthermore, that she and her feminine colleagues contributed significantly to improve treatment of women's and children's

[66] All page references for this essay are to Blackwell, *Essays*, II.

[67] Undated letter to Dr. McNutt in the Blackwell Collection.

[68] Blackwell nowhere makes this more clear than in *The Human Element in Sex: Being a Medical Enquiry Into the Relation of Sexual Physiology to Christian Morality* (London, 1884).

[69] A good introduction to the spirit and work of the Purity Alliance is Aaron M. Powell (ed.), *The National Purity Congress: Its Papers, Addresses, Portraits* (New York, 1896).

[70] *Wrong and Right Methods of Dealing with Social Evil as Shown by English Parliamentary Evidence* (New York, n.d.), 41. See also "The Purchase of Women: The Great Economic Blunder" in Blackwell, *Essays*, I, 133–174.

diseases.[71] But they also answered a different and more subtle need strongly felt by some members of their sex. If the woman patient dependent on the male doctor had seemed to feminists like Beecher and Gilman emblematic of the most degrading elements in woman's relation to man in nineteenth-century America, the woman doctor, able to take care of herself and cure the world's ills, appeared to them not only as a beacon of hope but as an avenger of the wrongs of all those prostrate women, whether victimized in an office or in their own homes.

Elizabeth Stuart Phelps, an immensely popular post-Civil War authoress who knew personally every variety of nervous disorder in its most acute form, celebrated this revengeful angel in *Dr. Zay* (1882), a novel about a woman doctor.[72] Dr. Zay's first name rather appropriately is Atalanta. Totally self-confident, direct, brilliant, and rather unpoetic although womanly, she exudes the independence and the self-sufficiency that Elizabeth Blackwell and Harriot Hunt had so longed to see in their sex. Like them, she has devoted herself to relieving the sufferings of women and, a Christian physiologist of the first order, she even brings off shotgun weddings as part of her healing mission. The novel centers around her relationship with her only male patient—a young man named Waldo Yorke, poetic and unmotivated, although attractive and personally charming. He falls deeply in love with her, and Phelps devotes most of the plot to the resulting role-reversal which apparently fascinates her. Convalescent and ironically suffering from "nervous strain" (69), Yorke needs Dr. Zay, but she, in splendid health, "leaned against her own physical strength, as another woman might lean upon a man's" (110).[73]

By a further twist of irony, a twist clearly delightful to Phelps herself, Dr. Zay, out of her superfluous strength and in her off-hours, can provide salvation for man in the shape of Yorke, but he has nothing to offer her except the so-called feminine gifts of devotion and sexual attractiveness. The circle of revenge is complete, for Phelps is implying through Atalanta that the truly diseased sex is not woman, woman with her radiant maternal strength, but man, man with his barren professional pretenses and sexual excess. And so the last act of mercy Phelps' rather sadistic angel performs is to consent to enter the marriage relation with a sex she has demonstrated so clearly to be the inferior of her own.

Phelps' superwoman Dr. Zay is clearly the exaggerated product of wish-fulfillment fantasies on the part of a lifelong invalid and feminist, but she forcefully symbolizes what some women wanted women doctors to

[71] See Campbell-Hurd, *Medical Women in America*, and Robinson, *White-Caps*.

[72] For her own account see *Chapters from a Life* (Boston, 1897), 228–242. Her most important fictional accounts of illness are "Shut In" in *Fourteen to One* (Boston, 1891), 66–99, about an invalid's recovery, and *Walled In* (New York, 1907), about the relationship between a nurse and a male patient.

[73] All page references are to Elizabeth Stuart Phelps, *Dr. Zay* (Boston, 1886). I owe much of my thinking on Phelps to Christine Stansell's "Elizabeth Stuart Phelps: A Study in Female Rebellion," *Massachusetts Review*, XIII (1972), 239–256. For other contemporary fictional works on women doctors, see William Dean Howells, *Dr. Breen's Practice* (Boston, 1881), and Sarah Orne Jewett, *A Country Doctor* (Boston, c. 1884).

prove to them. With this novel, the drama of women and medicine in nineteenth-century America has in a sense reached its extreme dénouement. Unlike the male and female physicians who preceded (and succeeded) her, Phelps makes no pretense of interest in medicine as science. Her only concern is with medicine as a weapon in a social and political struggle for power between the sexes. In *Dr. Zay*, Phelps has seized upon the cultural assumptions underlying contemporary male doctors' treatments of women's diseases in order triumphantly to reverse them. Dr. Zay's example is meant to testify that, far from being the constitutionally diseased and dependent creature that Dewees and Byford saw, woman could be self-reliant. In Phelps' vision, woman need not be a prisoner in her own sick body, awaiting the coming of her deliverer, man, but a healer herself, the support of her sex, and by caring for its members, the donor to them of a new kind of self-esteem.

Mudsills and Bottom Rails: Blacks and Poor Whites in the South

C. VANN WOODWARD

There seems to be no end to the study of Afro-Americanism. Both the focus and the substance of these studies shift with changes in scholarly approaches and alterations in the relationship between the races. At least three areas of black life in American history are undergoing revision at this time. All three are concerned with the concept of the culture, or way of life, of black people.

First, and perhaps most significant, are the studies of slavery. Rather than viewing slavery as simply a dehumanizing process aimed at keeping the slaves subjugated, scholars are now investigating the positive aspects of slave culture—not the positive aspects of slavery as an institution, but the adaptation made to that institution by the Africans and their descendants. As a result, scholars are presenting studies that are concerned with family life, religious belief and practice, education, and work experiences other than simple field labor. Such studies enable us to see, then, that even in a system as oppressive to mind and body as slavery was, men, women, and children did go on living and making the best of things, even under difficult circumstances.

A second area that has undergone special scrutiny recently is the study of urban black life. While studies of the urban black are not new (W. E. B. DuBois' **The Philadelphia Negro** was published in 1899), contemporary examinations of black ghetto culture are influenced by a different perspective. Deriving their methodology from urban anthropology, these studies seek to identify and evaluate the adaptive qualities of the ghetto blacks, much as the new historical studies have done with the slaves.

A third area being reconsidered is the life of black people in the late nineteenth century. The primary focus here is on family life and work experience. One purpose of these studies is to counteract the notion that after freedom black people were reduced to poverty and consequently ended up completely demoralized because of segregation and discrimination. Some of this research leads to the conclusion that there was a relatively high level of working-class family stability, a level that compares favorably with nonblack families in the same economic circumstances. This is not to deny the debilitating impact of poverty, but only to remind us of the resiliency of the human spirit.

The selection reprinted here, by C. Vann Woodward, of Yale University, was one of the early attempts of modern scholarship to evaluate seriously the changes in the economic status of blacks after Reconstruction.

From the first days of emancipation, the masses of ex-slaves were less interested in politics than in gaining some degree of economic independence in order to support their family life. Their attempts to become farm owners came to little, however, and the great majority ended Reconstruction as tenant farmers and sharecroppers who remained bound to the land through debt to the landowners. Those who tried to escape the new system of economic bondage were faced with a return to forced labor through the convict-lien system, by which the South further exploited primarily black labor.

The economic difficulties in which blacks found themselves put a great strain on the other institutions of their culture. But they found in their families, their churches, and their schools (insofar as they were permitted to attend school) sources of strength and hope by means of which they sought to ride out their years of deprivation.

Also, in the postwar years, poor whites began to drift from the fields and hills of the South into the newly developed mill towns. But industry offered them merely a new type of misery, for owners kept wages at a minimum and responded to signs of labor unrest by threatening to replace white laborers with blacks.

It is one of the tragedies of American history that poor whites and blacks were never able to join together in order to force Southern capitalism to institute some form of industrial democracy. With few exceptions, poor whites through the years not only have refused to work with blacks for common goals but have sought the blacks' subordination, with the result that both labor groups have been deprived of important allies in their struggle for economic justice.

If Reconstruction ever set the bottom rail on top, it was not for long and never securely. Redemption seemed to leave little doubt that the bottom rail was again on the bottom—whatever its temporary dislocation. It remained for the New South to find what Reconstruction had failed to find: the measure of the emancipated slave's freedom and a definition of free labor, both black and white; for the white worker's place in the New Order would be vitally conditioned by the place assigned the free black worker.

Much discussion about the Negro's civil rights, his political significance, his social status, and his aspirations can be shortened and simplified by a clear understanding of the economic status assigned him in the New Order. Emancipation and Reconstruction had done little to change that picture. The lives of the overwhelming majority of Negroes were still circumscribed by the farm and plantation. The same was true of the white people, but the Negroes, with few exceptions, were farmers without land. Questionnaires from the census of 1880 revealed that in thirty-three coun-

"Mudsills and Bottom Rails: Blacks and Poor Whites in the South." From *Origins of the New South, 1877–1913*, by C. Vann Woodward, pp. 205–34. Reprinted by permission of Louisiana State University Press, copyright 1951, © 1971.

ties of Georgia where Negro population was thick, "not more than one in one hundred" Negro farmers owned land; the same proportion was reported from seventeen black Mississippi counties; twelve others reported not one in twenty, and many not one in fifty. From Tennessee as a whole the report was that only "a very small part of the Negroes own land or even the houses in which they live"; also from Louisiana and Alabama came reports of "very few" owners.[1]

More specific information is provided for one state by the report of the Comptroller General of Georgia for the year ending October 1, 1880. Of a total of some $88,000,000 in land value, the Negroes, who made up nearly half the state's population, owned around $1,500,000. Of a total of some $23,000,000 in value put upon cattle and farm animals, the Negroes owned about $2,000,000, and of some $3,200,000 in agricultural tools, the Negroes reported a little more than $163,000.[2] It is pretty clear that as a rule the Negro farmer not only worked the white man's land but worked it with a white man's plow drawn by a white man's mule. In the next two decades the race's landholdings improved slightly, but in 1900 black Georgians had taxable titles to only one twenty-fifth of the land; only 14 per cent of the Negro farmers owned their farms, and in 1910 only 13 per cent.[3] In the South as a whole, by 1900, 75.3 per cent of the Negro farmers were croppers or tenants.[4]

The landless Negro farmers, like the landless whites, worked either for wages or for shares, under any of several arrangements. When the Alabama planter furnished tools, animals, and feed, as well as the land, his share was one half of all crops; when he furnished only the land he took one fourth of the cotton and one third of the corn. There were numerous variations, including the "two-day system," on Edisto Island, where the tenant worked two days of the week for the landlord in the feudal manner.[5] The impression of uniformity in the labor system that replaced slavery would seem to have been exaggerated. As late as 1881 it was reported that in Alabama "you can hardly find any two farmers in a community who are carrying on their business alike," and frequently one planter might use several methods at once: "To one he rents, to another he gives a contract for working on shares, to another he pays wages in money, and with another he swaps work, and so *ad infinitum*." Whatever system was used "there follows the same failure, or partial failure." [6]

The share system called forth especially severe criticism from all sides as being "ruinous to the soil" and "a disgrace to farming." A large proportion of landlords preferred and used the wage system. From Tennessee

---

[1] *Tenth Census, 1880*, V, *Cotton Production*, "Mississippi," 154–55, "Tennessee," 104–05, "Louisiana," 83–84; VI, *Cotton Production*, "Georgia," 172–73.

[2] Quoted in [Glenn W.] Rainey ["The Negro and the Independent Movement in Georgia" (manuscript in possession of its author)], Chap. I.

[3] [Robert P.] Brooks [*The Agrarian Revolution in Georgia, 1865–1912* (Madison, 1914)], 44, 122.

[4] United States Census Bureau, *Negro Population in the United States, 1790–1915* (Washington, 1918), 571–72.

[5] *Tenth Census, 1880*, V, *Cotton Production* 60–66; VI, *Cotton Production*, 154–55.

[6] Montgomery *Advertiser*, August 12, 1881.

in 1880 it was reported that "advocates for shares and wages are about equally divided in number." Census reports of wages paid for labor in cotton production in 1880 make no distinction between white and black workers, and there probably was little difference. Prevalent monthly wages for a man's work "from sun to sun" were $8.00 to $14.00 in Alabama; $8.00 to $15.00 in Arkansas; $6.00 to $10.00 in Florida; $5.00 to $10.00 in Georgia ($4.00 to $6.00 per month for women); $6.00 to $15.00 in Louisiana; $8.00 to $12.00 in Mississippi, South Carolina, and Tennessee; $8.00 to $15.00 in Texas. Daily wages were usually 50 cents with board, or 75 cents without. A year's wages for a man in the central cotton belt of Georgia were $60.00 to $100.00; in Tennessee they were $100.00 to $125.00. Both yearly and monthly wages included rations.[7] In 1888 it was estimated by an authority that "the regular allowance of an ordinary hand is 12 pounds of bacon and 5 pecks of meal by the month," which "would cost him twenty-three dollars in the course of twelve months." [8]

It should be noted that the year 1880, for which the wage rates are quoted, was a relatively "good" year for cotton prices. When the price fell to half that in the nineties the wages could not have been nearly so high. If a yield of only three to six bales per hand could be expected, as estimated in Arkansas in 1880, the product of a year's labor would likely bring little more than $100.00 on the market in the middle nineties. Working on shares, the cropper at that rate received about $50.00 for his year's work. Neither he nor his landlord was likely to see or handle any cash, since both were in all probability deeply enmeshed in the toils of the crop lien. They received instead meager supplies at the prices demanded of credit customers.

The tides of Negro migration that had set in during Reconstruction, as the first and most characteristic expression of freedom, continued to move in the same general directions for some years after Redemption. These movements were of three kinds: from the country to the towns; from the poorer lands to the delta, bottom, and richer lands; and from the older states to the newer states of the Southwest. Intermittent complaint and a few laws against "enticing" labor persisted through the eighties. With one striking exception, however, the Negro migrations were largely from one part of the South to another. The great exodus northward did not begin until a half century after freedom.[9]

A census survey of the relation of land and labor in the cotton state of Alabama in 1880 revealed that the Negroes were most thickly concentrated upon the most fertile soil in the state, and the whites, upon the

---

[7] *Tenth Census, 1880,* V, *Cotton Production,* "Arkansas," 104–05; "Louisiana," 83–84; "Mississippi," 154–55; "Tennessee," 104–05; "Texas," 160–61; VI, *Cotton Production,* "Alabama," 154–55; "Florida," 70–71; "Georgia," 172–73; "South Carolina," 60–66.

[8] Philip A. Bruce, *The Plantation Negro as a Freeman* (New York, 1889), 200–01.

[9] The exception was the "Exodus" of 1879. This has been treated by . . . [E. Merton] Coulter [*The South During Reconstruction, 1865–1877,* in *A History of the South,* VIII (Baton Rouge, 1947)], 100–01. On Negro migration, see [Vernon L.] Wharton [*The Negro in Mississippi, 1865–1890,* in the *James Sprunt Studies in History and Political Science,* XXVIII (Chapel Hill, 1947)], 106–24.

poorest soil; that the most fertile land, where the sharecropping system was most prevalent, yielded the least product, and was rapidly being exhausted; that poorer lands under cultivation by owners produced greater yield per capita and per acre; and that the white farmer was rapidly gaining on the black in the proportion of cotton produced.[10]

In spite of these facts, there was an almost universal preference among Black-Belt landlords for Negro tenants and workers. "White labor is totally unsuited to our methods, our manners, and our accommodations," declared an Alabama planter in 1888. "No other laborer [than the Negro] of whom I have any knowledge, would be as cheerful, or so contented on four pounds of meat and a peck of meal a week, in a little log cabin 14 x 16 feet, with cracks in it large enough to afford free passage to a large sized cat." [11] "Give me the nigger every time," echoed a Mississippi planter. "The nigger will never 'strike' as long as you give him plenty to eat and half clothe him: He will live on less and do more hard work, when properly managed, than any other class, or race of people. As Arp truthfully says 'we can boss him' and that is what we southern folks like." [12]

The writer who estimated the cash value of freedom for the Negro thirty years after emancipation at a little less than one dollar a year to the individual [13] overstated his point, though not so grossly as it might seem. At least such expensive luxuries as civil liberties and political franchises were beyond his reach. He knew very well that immediate, daily necessities came first—land, mules, plows, food, and clothes, all of which had to be got from a white man who oftener than not had too little himself.

In the working out of a new code of civil rights and social status for the freedman—in the definition of the Negro's "place"—Reconstruction had been only an interruption, the importance of which varied from state to state, but which was nowhere decisive. The transition from slavery to caste as a system of controlling race relations went forward gradually and tediously. Slavery had been vastly more than a labor system, and the gap that its removal left in manners, mores, and ritual of behavior could not be filled overnight. The so-called "Black Codes" were soon overthrown, as were the laws imported by the Carpetbaggers. Redemption and Hayes's policy of *laissez faire* left the code to be worked out by Southern white men. It has already been pointed out that there was no unity of opinion among them concerning the Negro's political rights. There also existed a roughly comparable division with reference to his civil rights.

Hampton, Lamar, Nicholls, and Redeemers of that type gave their solemn pledges in the Compromise of 1877 to protect the Negro in all his rights. They were probably guilty of less hypocrisy than has been charged. The class they represented had little to fear from the Negro and at the same time considerable to gain for the conservative cause by estab-

[10] *Tenth Census, 1880,* VI, *Cotton Production,* "Alabama," 64.
[11] A. W. S. Anderson, in *Proceedings of the Third Semi-Annual Session of the Alabama State Agricultural Society* (Montgomery, 1888), 93–95.
[12] Quoted in Wharton, *Negro in Mississippi,* 121.
[13] [Walter G.] Cooper [*The Piedmont Region* . . . (Atlanta, 1895)], 77.

lishing themselves in a paternalistic relationship as his protector and
champion against the upland and lower-class whites. This would better
enable them to control his vote (against the same white element), not to
mention his labor. In 1877 J. L. M. Curry listened to a debate of the Virginia Assembly in Jefferson's neoclassic capitol. "A negro member," he
recorded with evident satisfaction in his diary, "said that he and his race
relied for the protection of their rights & liberties, not on the 'poor white
trash' but on the 'well-raised' gentlemen." [14] Black-Belt white men were
casual about their daily intimacy and easy personal relations with Negroes,
an attitude that made upland Southerners uncomfortable and shocked
Northerners, even Radical Carpetbaggers. So long as this old leadership
retained strong influence, the racial code was considerably less severe than
it later became.

In the early years of freedom saloons in Mississippi usually served
both whites and blacks at the same bar; many public eating places, "using
separate tables, served both races in the same room"; public parks and
buildings were still open to both to a great extent; and segregation in
common carriers was not at all strict. [15] The most common type of discrimination on railways was the exclusion of Negroes from the first-class,
or "ladies'" car. The races were accustomed to sharing the second-class
coach. In 1877, however, a South Carolinian wrote that Negroes were
"permitted to, and frequently do ride in first-class railway and street railway cars" in his state. This had caused trouble at first but was "now so
common as hardly to provoke remark." [16] In 1885 George W. Cable, who
was sensitive regarding discrimination, reported that in South Carolina
Negroes "ride in the first class cars as a right" and "their presence excites
no comment," while "in Virginia they may ride exactly as white people
do and in the same cars." [17] Even the ante-bellum practice of using a common cemetery continued for many years. White papers occasionally
"mistered" Negro politicians, if they were "good" politicians, and a Richmond paper affirmed in 1886 that "nobody here objects to sitting in
political conventions with negroes. Nobody here objects to serving on
juries with negroes." [18] Even the Tillman legislation of 1891 defeated a
Jim Crow bill for railway cars.

From the beginning, however, concessions to the harsher code and
developing phobias of the hillbillies of the white counties had to be made.
There were South Carolinians in numbers who did not share the Charles-

---

[14] Diary of J. L. M. Curry, January 13, 1877, in [The Jabez L. M. Curry Papers (Division of Manuscripts, Library of Congress)].

[15] Wharton, *Negro in Mississippi*, 232. The evolution of "caste as a method of social
control" is admirably worked out by this author.

[16] Belton O'Neall Townsend, "South Carolina Society," in *Atlantic Monthly*,
XXXIX (1877), 676. Commenting in 1879 on the "perfect equality" of races in
Southern tramcars, a member of Parliament wrote: "I was, I confess, surprised to
see how completely this is the case; even an English Radical is a little taken aback
at first." Sir George Campbell, *White and Black* . . . (New York, 1879), 195.

[17] [George W.] Cable [*The Silent South* (New York, 1885)], 85–86. Cable was
quoting the Charleston *News and Courier* with regard to South Carolina. The
observation on Virginia custom is his own.

[18] Richmond *Dispatch*, October 13, 1886.

ton *News and Courier*'s feeling that it was "a great deal pleasanter to travel with respectable and well-behaved colored people than with unmannerly and ruffianly white men."

It is one of the paradoxes of Southern history that political democracy for the white man and racial discrimination for the black were often products of the same dynamics. As the Negroes invaded the new mining and industrial towns of the uplands in greater numbers, and the hill-country whites were driven into more frequent and closer association with them, and as the two races were brought into rivalry for subsistence wages in the cotton fields, mines, and wharves, the lower-class white man's demand for Jim Crow laws became more insistent. It took a lot of ritual and Jim Crow to bolster the creed of white supremacy in the bosom of a white man working for a black man's wages. The Negro pretty well understood these forces, and his grasp of them was one reason for his growing alliance with the most conservative and politically reactionary class of whites against the insurgent white democracy. A North Carolina Negro wrote: "The best people of the South do not demand this separate car business . . . and, when they do, it is only to cater to those of their race who, in order to get a big man's smile, will elevate them [*sic*] to place and power." He believed that "this whole thing is but a pandering to the lower instincts of the worst class of whites in the South." [19]

The barriers of racial discrimination mounted in direct ratio with the tide of political democracy among whites. In fact, an increase of Jim Crow laws upon the statute books of a state is almost an accurate index of the decline of the reactionary regimes of the Redeemers and triumph of white democratic movements. Take, for example, the law requiring separate accommodations for the races in trains, said to be "the most typical Southern law." No state [20] enacted such a law for more than twenty years after 1865. Yet in the five years beginning in 1887 one after another adopted some variation of the law: Florida in 1887, Mississippi in 1888, Texas in 1889, Louisiana in 1890, Alabama, Arkansas, Kentucky, and Georgia in 1891. These were the years when the Farmers' Alliance was first making itself felt in the legislatures of these states. Mississippi, in 1888, was the first state to adopt a law providing for the separation of the races in railway stations, and Georgia, in 1891, the first to adopt the law for streetcars. [21] These laws, though significant in themselves, were often only enactments of codes already in practice. Whether by state law or local law, or by the more pervasive coercion of sovereign white opinion, "the Negro's place" was gradually defined—in the courts, schools, and libraries,

---

[19] Editorial, *Southland* (Salisbury, N.C.), I (1890), 166–67.

[20] The Tennessee legislature passed an act in 1875 abrogating the common law and releasing common carriers and other public servants from serving anyone they chose not to serve. A Federal circuit court declared this unconstitutional in 1880. An act of 1881 required separate first-class accommodations for Negroes, but left the two races unsegregated in second-class coaches. Stanley J. Folmsbee, "The Origin of the First 'Jim Crow' Law," in *Journal of Southern History*, XV (1949), 235–47.

[21] Franklin Johnson, *Development of State Legislation Concerning the Free Negro* (New York, 1919), 15, 54, 62–207; Gilbert T. Stephenson, *Race Distinctions in American Law* (New York, 1910), 216–17.

in parks, theaters, hotels, and residential districts, in hospitals, insane asylums—everywhere, including on sidewalks and in cemeteries. When complete, the new codes of White Supremacy were vastly more complex than the ante-bellum slave codes or the Black Codes of 1865–1866, and, if anything, they were stronger and more rigidly enforced.

Among the institutions of the Old Order that strained to meet the needs of the New, none proved more hopelessly inadequate than the old penitentiaries. The state was suddenly called upon to take over the plantation's penal functions at a time when crime was enormously increasing. The strain was too great. One after another of the states adopted the expedient of leasing the convicts to private corporations or individuals. In Louisiana the convict-lease system had an ante-bellum origin; in the other Southern states it was introduced by the provisional or military governments and retained by the Carpetbaggers and Redeemers.

For a number of reasons the lease system took firm roots in the New Order and grew to greater proportions. For one thing, it fitted perfectly the program of retrenchment, for under it the penitentiary not only ceased to be a heavy burden on the taxpayer but became a source of revenue to the state—sometimes a very lucrative source. The system also fitted conveniently the needs occasioned by the new criminal codes of the Redemption regimes, which piled up heavy penalties for petty offenses against property, while at the same time they weakened the protection afforded the Negro in the courts. The so-called "pig law" of Mississippi defined the theft of any property over ten dollars in value, or any cattle or swine of whatever value, as grand larceny, with a sentence up to five years. After its adoption the number of state convicts increased from 272 in 1874 to 1,072 by the end of 1877. The number in Georgia increased from 432 in 1872 to 1,441 in 1877. Additional convictions meant additional revenue instead of additional taxes. The system quickly became a large-scale and sinister business. Leases of ten, twenty, and thirty years were granted by legislatures to powerful politicians, Northern syndicates, mining corporations, and individual planters. Laws limiting hours of labor and types of work for convicts were nonexistent in some states and negligible in others, and in two states protective laws were later removed or modified. Responsibility of lessees for the health and lives of convicts was extremely loose. Some states had no inspectors and in others inspection was highly perfunctory if not corrupt. Where the law permitted, the large lessees subleased convicts in small or large gangs for short periods, thus rendering responsibility to the state even more fictitious and protection of the state's prisoners all but impossible. County prisons in many cases adopted the system and in Alabama had twice as many convicts leased as the state. The South's "penitentiaries" were great rolling cages that followed construction camps and railroad building, hastily built stockades deep in forest or swamp or mining fields, or windowless log forts in turpentine flats.[22]

---

[22] *Report of the United States Commissioner of Labor, 1886, Convict Labor* (Washington, 1887), especially pp. 72–79. For a dispassionate account by a warden, see J. C. Powell, *The American Siberia; or, Fourteen Years' Experience in a Southern Convict Camp* (London, 1891), *passim;* Wharton, *Negro in Mississippi,* 237–40.

The degradation and brutality produced by this system would be incredible but for the amount of evidence from official sources. A report of the inspectors of the Alabama penitentiary revealed that the prisons were packed with several times the number of convicts they could reasonably hold.

> They are as filthy, as a rule, as dirt could make them, and both prisons and prisoners were infested with vermin. The bedding was totally unfit for use. . . . [It was found] that convicts were excessively and sometimes cruelly punished; that they were poorly clothed and fed; that the sick were neglected, insomuch as no hospitals had been provided, [and] that they were confined with the well convicts.[23]

A grand-jury investigation of the penitentiary hospital in Mississippi reported that inmates were

> all bearing on their persons marks of the most inhuman and brutal treatments. Most of them have their backs cut in great wales, scars and blisters, some with the skin peeling off in pieces as the result of severe beatings. . . . They were lying there dying, some of them on bare boards, so poor and emaciated that their bones almost came through their skin, many complaining for want of food. . . . We actually saw live vermin crawling over their faces, and the little bedding and clothing they have is in tatters and stiff with filth.[24]

In mining camps of Arkansas and Alabama convicts were worked through the winter without shoes, standing in water much of the time. In both states the task system was used, whereby a squad of three was compelled to mine a certain amount of coal per day on penalty of a severe flogging for the whole squad. Convicts in the turpentine camps of Florida, with "stride-chains" and "waist-chains" riveted on their bodies, were compelled to work at a trot. "They kept this gait up all day long, from tree to tree," reported the warden.[25] The average annual death rate among Negro convicts in Mississippi from 1880 to 1885 was almost 11 per cent, for white convicts about half that, and in 1887 the general average was 16 per cent. The death rate among the prisoners of Arkansas was reported in 1881 to be 25 per cent annually. An indication of what was called "moral conditions" is provided in a report of the Committee on the Penitentiary of the Georgia Legislature: "We find in some of the camps men and women chained together and occupying the same sleeping bunks. The result is that there are now in the Penitentiary twenty-five bastard children, ranging from three months to five years of age, and many of the women

[23] *Biennial Report of the Inspectors of the Alabama Penitentiary from September 30, 1880, to September 30, 1882* (Montgomery, 1882), *passim*.
[24] Jackson *Clarion*, July 13, 1887.
[25] Little Rock *Daily Gazette*, March 24, 27, 1888; Powell, *American Siberia*, 22.

are now far advanced in pregnancy." [26] For the Southern convict-lease system a modern scholar can "find parallel only in the persecutions of the Middle Ages or in the prison camps of Nazi Germany." [27]

The lease system was under bitter attack, especially from the various independent parties, and repeated attempts were made to abolish or reform it. Julia Tutwiler of Alabama was a moving spirit in the reform movement. Almost everywhere, however, the reformers were opposed by vested interests within the Redemption party—sometimes by the foremost leaders of that party. Senator Brown of Georgia was guaranteed by his twenty-year lease "three hundred able-bodied, long-term men" to work in his Dade Coal Mines, for which he paid the state about eight cents per hand per day.[28] Senator Gordon was also a member of a firm leasing convicts. Colonel Colyar, leader of one wing of the Redemption party in Tennessee, leased that state's prisoners at $101,000 a year for the Tennessee Coal and Iron Company. Control over these Southern state "slaves" was the foundation of several large fortunes, and in one case, of a great political dynasty. Robert McKee, who was in a position to know all the workings of the system, wrote that the state warden of Alabama, John H. Bankhead, "grew rich in a few years on $2,000 a year," and manipulated the legislature at will. "The 'penitentiary ring' is a power in the party," he wrote privately, "and it is a corrupt power. One of the State officers is a lessee of convicts, and has a brother who is a deputy warden." [29] Former Secretary of State Rufus K. Boyd believed that the convict-lease ring was "as unscrupulous as any radical in the days of their power. . . . Are we all thieves? What is it leading to? Who can submit to these things patiently?" [30] Yet the party continued to submit.

The convict-lease system did greater violence to the moral authority of the Redeemers than did anything else. For it was upon the tradition of paternalism that the Redeemer regimes claimed authority to settle the race problem and "deal with the Negro."

The abandonment of the Negro by his Northern champions after the Compromise of 1877 was as quixotic as their previous crusade in his behalf had been romantic and unrealistic. The *Nation* thought the government should "have nothing more to do with him," and Godkin could not see how the Negro could ever "be worked into a system of government for which you and I would have much respect." [31] The New York *Tribune*, with a logic all its own, stated that the Negroes, after having

[26] Georgia *House Journal*, 1879, Pt. I, 386–91.
[27] Fletcher M. Green, "Some Aspects of the Southern Convict Lease System in the Southern States," in Fletcher M. Green (ed.), *Essays in Southern History Presented to Joseph Gregoire de Roulhac Hamilton . . .* (Chapel Hill, 1949), 122.
[28] Georgia *House Journal*, 1879, Pt. I, 386–91.
[29] Robert McKee to Boyd, February 3, 1882, in [Robert McKee Papers (Alabama Department of Archives and History, Montgomery)].
[30] Boyd to McKee, February 26, 1883; also Morgan to McKee, March 15, 1882; McKee to Thomas R. Roulhac, February 25, 1883, *ibid.*
[31] *Nation*, XXIV (1877), 202; Edwin L. Godkin, quoted by [Paul H.] Buck [*The Road to Reunion, 1865–1900* (Boston, 1937)], 295.

been given "ample opportunity to develop their own latent capacities," had only succeeded in proving that "as a race they are idle, ignorant, and vicious." [32]

The Supreme Court's decision in October, 1883, declaring the Civil Rights Act unconstitutional was only the juristic fulfillment of the Compromise of 1877, and was, in fact, handed down by Justice Joseph P. Bradley, Grant's appointee, who had been a member of the Electoral Commission of 1877. "The calm with which the country receives the news," observed the editor of the New York *Evening Post*, "shows how completely the extravagant expectations . . . of the war have died out." [33] A Republican who held repudiated bonds of South Carolina wrote from New York that the Civil Rights decision came "as a just retribution to the colored people for their infamous conduct" in assisting in the repudiation of the bonds; "if they expect the people of the North to fight their battles for them they can wait until doomsday," he added.[34]

It has already been pointed out that the wing of the Republican party that raised the loudest outcry against Hayes's policy of deserting the Negro promptly abandoned him itself as soon as it came to power under Garfield and Arthur and threw support to white Republicans in alliance with any white independent organization available. Repeated warnings from the South that the Negro voters were "getting demoralized," that they would "make terms with their adversaries," and that the Republican party was "losing its hold on the younger generation" were ignored.[35]

Political leaders of his own race furnished guidance of doubtful value to the Negro in his political quandary. For one thing the average cottonfield Negro voter had little more in common with the outstanding Negro politicians of the South than he had with the corporation lawyers who ran the Republican party in the North. Former Senator Blanche K. Bruce of Mississippi owned "a handsome plantation of 1,000 acres," which he operated as absentee landlord, much as had his predecessor, Senator Jefferson Davis.[36] Former Congressman James T. Rapier of Alabama was "the possessor of extensive landed interests" in that state in which he employed more than a hundred people. Former Congressmen Josiah T. Walls of Florida and John R. Lynch of Mississippi were reported to be "proprietors of vast acres under cultivation and employers of large numbers of men," [37] and Norris Wright Cuney, Negro boss in Galveston, Texas, was the employer of some five hundred stevedores.[38] Former Senator Bruce

[32] New York *Tribune*, April 7, 1877.

[33] New York *Evening Post*, October 16, 1883.

[34] Letter, *ibid.*, October 20, 1883.

[35] A. J. Willard, Columbia, S.C., to J. Hendrix McLane, [?] 12, 1882; James E. Richardson to Chandler, September 14, 1884, in [William E. Chandler Papers (Division of Manuscripts, Library of Congress)]; David M. Key to Hayes, December 31, 1882, in [Rutherford B. Hayes Papers (Hayes Memorial Library, Fremont, Ohio)].

[36] Washington *Bee* (Negro paper), July 21, 1883.

[37] Huntsville *Gazette* (Negro paper), February 11, 1882.

[38] Maud Cuney-Hare, *Norris Wright Cuney* (New York, 1913), 42.

was quoted in 1883 as saying that his party represented "the brains, the wealth, the intelligence" of the land, and that "the moneyed interests of this country would be seriously affected" by a Republican defeat.[39]

The more successful of the Negro politicians were maintained in some Federal office "of high-sounding titles and little importance" in Washington. At home they often came to an understanding with Democratic leaders of the Black Belt called "fusion," which served the interests of both by diminishing the power of the white counties in the white man's party and the authority of white leaders in the black man's party. The confusion in which this policy resulted for the average Negro voter may be imagined from the nature of the instruction Lynch gave Mississippi Republicans at a meeting in 1883. It made no difference whether the county machines decided "to fuse with the Independents instead of the Democrats, or with the Democrats instead of the Independents, or to make straight [Republican] party nomination instead of fusing with either"; it was the duty of all good party men, whatever the decision, to follow the machine, "although they may honestly believe the decision to be unwise."[40] Such instructions would not have sounded unfamiliar to followers of the white man's party.

Soon after the war Negroes began to break up into differentiated social and economic classes that eventually reproduced on a rough scale the stratified white society. Enough of a Negro middle class had emerged in the eighties to reflect faithfully the New-South romanticism of the white middle class, with its gospel of progress and wealth. A Negro paper named the *New South* made its appearance in Charleston. It warned the race against "following the *ignis fatuus* of politics," and urged the gospel of "real progress"—money-making.[41] The class of 1886 at Tuskegee adopted the motto "There is Room at the Top,"[42] and freshman W. E. B. Du Bois found his classmates at Fisk in 1885 of the same blithe turn of mind.[43] No American success story could match the Master of Tuskegee's *Up from Slavery!*

Another considerable Negro element saw nothing better than to take refuge under the paternalism of the old masters, who offered some protection against the extreme race doctrines of the upland whites and sometimes more tangible rewards than the Republican bosses. Cleveland's administration and its Southern lieutenants encouraged this tendency among Negroes. The *Nation*, a Cleveland supporter, rejoiced that "thousands of them" had discovered "that their true interests are bound up with the interests of their old masters."[44]

Although the majority of the Negro masses remained Republican or potentially Republican voters, suspicion and criticism of the party of

---

[39] New York *Globe* (Negro paper), February 24, 1883.
[40] Quoted in New York *Globe*, October 20, 1883.
[41] Quoted in *Nation*, XLVIII (1889), 461.
[42] *Southern Letter* (Tuskegee), V (July, 1888), 3.
[43] W. E. Burghardt Du Bois, *Dusk of Dawn: An Essay Toward an Autobiography of a Race Concept* (New York, 1940), 25–27.
[44] *Nation*, XLI (1885), 369.

liberation were on the increase during the eighties. The Compromise of 1877 was described as "disillusioning"; the Civil Rights decision as "infamous," a "baptism in ice water"; Chandler's politics as "fatuous" and "degrading." There was also a growing tendency to look upon Republican tariff, railroad, and financial legislation more critically. "The colored people are consumers," said the chairman of a Colored People's Convention in Richmond. "The Republicans have deserted them and undertaken to protect the capitalist and manufacturer of the North." [45] "Neither of these parties," wrote a Negro editor, "cares a tinker snap for the poor man. They are run in the interest of capital, monopoly and repression." [46] The defeat of the Blair bill was a bitter disappointment. Professor J. C. Price, editor of a Negro journal in Salisbury, North Carolina, pointed out that "the Republican party was committed to the enactment of national legislation for the education of the masses," yet the Blair bill had been "voted down and owed its death in the Senate to Republican opposition." Under the circumstances the Negro was not impressed by the Lodge bill to re-enact Reconstruction election laws, and was more disillusioned when it was defeated. "He is beginning to distinguish between real friendship and demagoguery." [47]

In the meanwhile, the movement to make the party "respectable" was gaining ground among "Lily-white" Republicans in the South. A party leader, addressing the Lincoln Club of Arkansas on the problem of attracting "persons who have heretofore acted with the Democratic party," announced that he was seeking "a way by which they could act with the Republican party without being dominated over by the negro." [48] The Republican White League of Texas believed that "the union is only safe in the hands of the Anglo-Saxon race, and that a Republican party in Texas to merit the respect of mankind must be in the hands of that race." [49] A New England traveler was grieved to report to the "kinsmen and friends of John Brown, Wendell Phillips, and William Lloyd Garrison" the words of a Southern white Republican who said, "I will not vote to make a negro my ruler. . . . I was a white man before I was a Republican." [50] Even the Northern churches in the South, stoutest proponents of the missionary phase of Northern policy, had drawn the color line by the end of the eighties.[51]

Not long after the inauguration of President Benjamin Harrison in 1889, the Negro press began to accuse him of throwing his support to the Lily-white faction of his party in the South and of not giving the Negroes

[45] Richmond *Dispatch*, April 16, 1890.

[46] New York *Globe*, April 5, 1884. See also, *ibid.*, October 13, 20, 27, 1883; May 3, 1884.

[47] *Southland*, I (1890), 162–63.

[48] Little Rock *Daily Gazette*, July 22, 1888.

[49] Dallas *Morning News*, June 9, 1892.

[50] Charles H. Levermore, "Impressions of a Yankee Visitor in the South," in *New England Magazine*, N.S., III (1890–1891), 315.

[51] [Hunter D.] Farish [*The Circuit Rider Dismounts: A Social History of Southern Methodism, 1865–1900* (Richmond, 1938)], 214–15.

their fair reward in patronage. The protest soon became bitterly critical.
In January, 1890, delegates from twenty-one states met at Chicago and
organized the National Afro-American League. Professor Price was
elected president and T. Thomas Fortune, who was easily the foremost
Negro editor of his day, was chosen secretary. In a militant speech Fortune said of the old parties that "none of them cares a fig for the Afro-
American" and that "another party may rise to finish the uncompleted
work" of liberation.[52] Inspired by the Chicago meeting, which established
numerous branch leagues, other Negro conventions were held. In Raleigh
a "Negroes' 'Declaration of Independence'" was proclaimed, declaring
that "the white Republicans have been traitors to us," and the Negroes,
"the backbone of the Republican party, got nothing" in the way of
patronage.[53] Joseph T. Wilson, chairman of a Negro convention in Richmond, protested that his race had been "treated as orphan children, ap-
prenticed to the rice-, cotton-, and tobacco-growers in the South." As
for the Negro's political plight, "The Republican party does not know
what to do with us and the Democratic party wants to get rid of us, and
we are at sea without sail or anchor drifting with the tide."[54] Five such
conventions were held in 1890, and all of them were said to have "declared their disaffection with existing political parties."[55] The black man
was beginning to feel toward his party much the same as the Southern
white man was feeling toward his—that his vote was taken for granted and
his needs were ignored.

By 1890 a million Negroes were reported to have joined the Colored
Farmers' Alliance. At their annual convention, held at the same time and
place as the convention of the white Alliance, the black farmers took a
more radical position than their white brethren, substantially affirming the
single-tax philosophy that "land is not property; can never be made property. . . . The land belongs to the sovereign people." They also leaned
even more toward political independence. Their leader reminded them:
"You are a race of farmers, seven-eighths of the colored people being
engaged in agriculture," and there was "little hope of the reformation of
either of the existing political parties."[56]

As the Populist rift in the ranks of white solidarity approached, the
Negro race was more prepared for insurgency than at any time since
enfranchisement. Leaders shrewdly calculated their opportunities. For
some it was the chance to "teach the White Republicans a lesson"; for
others, to strike a blow against "our old, ancient and constant enemy—
the Democracy"; for still others, an experiment in joint action with white
Southerners on a platform of agrarian radicalism. The general temper
was perhaps best expressed in the slogan offered by one Negro: "Let the

[52] New York *Age*, January 25, 1890.
[53] Richmond *Dispatch*, April 16, 1890.
[54] *Ibid*.
[55] *National Economist*, IV (1890), 234–35.
[56] *Ibid*.

vote be divided; it will be appreciated by the party who succeeds to power." [57]

The appeal that the proslavery argument had for the poorer class of whites had been grounded on the fear of being leveled, economically as well as socially, with a mass of liberated Negroes. Social leveling after emancipation was scotched by sundry expedients, but the menace of economic leveling still remained. The rituals and laws that exempted the white worker from the penalties of caste did not exempt him from competition with black labor, nor did they carry assurance that the penalties of black labor might not be extended to white.

The propagandists of the New-South order, in advertising the famed cheap labor of their region, were not meticulous in distinguishing between the color of their wares. If they stressed the "large body of strong, hearty, active, docile and easily contented negro laborers" who conformed to "the apostolic maxim of being 'contented with their wages,' and [having] no disposition to 'strike,'" they claimed the same virtues for the "hardy native Anglo-Saxon stock." The pledge of the *Manufacturers' Record*, for example, that "long hours of labor and moderate wages will continue to be the rule for many years to come," amounted almost to a clause of security in the promissory note by which the New South got capital to set up business. Additional security was not lacking. "The white laboring classes here," wrote an Alabama booster, "are separated from the Negroes, working all day side by side with them, by an innate consciousness of race superiority. This sentiment dignifies the character of white labor. It excites a sentiment of sympathy and equality on their part with the classes above them, and in this way becomes a wholesome social leaven." [58]

It was an entirely safe assumption that for a long time to come race consciousness would divide, more than class consciousness would unite, Southern labor. Fifty strikes against the employment of Negro labor in the period from 1882 to 1900 testify to white labor's determination to draw a color line of its own. It is clear that in its effort to relegate to the Negro the less desirable, unskilled jobs, and to exclude him entirely from some industries, white labor did not always have the co-operation of white employers.[59]

In the cotton mills, at least, racial solidarity between employer and employee held fairly firm. By a combination of pressures and prejudices,

[57] See opinions of several Negro leaders under the title "Will a Division Solve the Problem?" in *Southland*, I (1890), 222–44; also Huntsville *Gazette*, March 29, 1890; November 21, 1891.

[58] John W. Dubose, *The Mineral Wealth of Alabama and Birmingham Illustrated* (Birmingham, 1886), 109.

[59] Charles H. Wesley, *Negro Labor in the United States, 1850–1925; A Study in American Economic History* (New York, 1927), 235–38.

a tacit understanding was reached that the cotton-mill villages were reserved for whites only. Probably no class of Southerners responded to the
vision of the New South more hopefully than those who almost overnight left the old farm for the new factory. The cotton-mill millennium
had been proclaimed as the salvation of "the necessitous masses of the
poor whites." One enthusiastic promoter promised that "for the operative
it would be Elysium itself." Historians have placed the "philanthropic
incentive," undoubtedly present in some cases, high in the list of motives
behind the whole mill campaign.

The transition from cotton field to cotton mill was not nearly so
drastic as that which accompanied the change from primitive agriculture
to modern factory in England and New England. For one thing, the mill
families usually moved directly from farm to factory, and usually came
from the vicinity of the mill. For another, the ex-farmer mill hand found
himself in a mill community made up almost entirely of ex-farmers, where
a foreigner, a Northerner, or even a city-bred Southerner was a curiosity.
As late as 1907 a study revealed that 75.8 per cent of the women and children in Southern cotton mills had spent their childhood on the farm, and
the 20.2 per cent who came from villages usually came from mill villages.[60]

The company-owned shanties into which they moved differed little
from the planter- or merchant-owned shanties they had evacuated, except that the arrangement of the houses was a reversion to the "quarters"
of the ante-bellum plantation instead of the dispersed cropper system. As
pictured by an investigator in Georgia in 1890, "rows of loosely built,
weather-stained frame houses, all of the same ugly pattern and buttressed
by clumsy chimneys," lined a dusty road. "No porch, no doorstep even,
admits to these barrack-like quarters." Outside in the bald, hard-packed
earth was planted, like some forlorn standard, the inevitable martin pole
with its pendant gourds. Inside were heaped the miserable belongings that
had furnished the cropper's cabin: "a shackling bed, tricked out in gaudy
patchwork, a few defunct 'split-bottom' chairs, a rickety table, and a
jumble of battered crockery," and on the walls the same string of red
peppers, gourd dipper, and bellows. In certain mill villages of Georgia
in 1890 not a watch or clock was to be found. "Life is regulated by the
sun and the factory bell"—just as it had once been by the sun and farm
bell. The seasons in the vocabulary of the cracker proletariat were still
"hog-killin'," "cotton-choppin'," and " 'tween crops." The church was
still the focus of social life, and the mill family was almost as migratory as
the cropper family. The whole of this rustic industrialism moved to a
rural rhythm.[61]

[60] [Elizabeth H.] Davidson, *Child Labor Legislation in the Southern Textile States*
[Chapel Hill, 1939], 7–8; [Holland] Thompson [*From the Cotton Field to the Cotton Mill; A Study of the Industrial Transition in North Carolina* (New York,
1906)], 109–10; [Broadus] Mitchell [*The Rise of Cotton Mills in the South*, in
Johns Hopkins University *Studies in Historical and Political Science*, XXXIX, No.
2 (Baltimore, 1921)], 173–86.
[61] Clare de Graffenried, "The Georgia Cracker in the Cotton Mill," in *Century
Magazine*, N.S., XIX (1891), 487–88.

Mill-village paternalism was cut from the same pattern of poverty and makeshift necessity that had served for plantation and crop-lien paternalism. In place of the country supply store that advanced goods against a crop lien there was the company store that advanced them against wages, and since the weaver was as rarely able to add and multiply as was the plowman, accounts were highly informal. Mill-village workers were sometimes little further advanced toward a money economy than were cotton croppers, and payday might bring word from the company store that the family had not "paid out" that week. Pay was often scrip, good only at the company store, or redeemable in cash at intervals. Company-owned houses were usually provided at low rent and sometimes rent free. "Lint-head" fealty often carried with it certain feudal privileges like those of gathering wood from company lands and pasturing cows on company fields. The unincorporated company town, in which everything was owned by the mill corporation, was the most completely paternalistic. Here company schools and company churches were frequently subsidized by the corporation, which of course controlled employment of preacher and teacher.[62] In the smaller mills the relationship between owner and employees was highly personal and intimate, with a large degree of dependency on the part of the workers. "Not only are relations more friendly and intimate than at the North," found a Northern writer, "but there is conspicuous freedom from the spirit of drive and despotism. Even New England superintendents and overseers in their Southern mills soon glide into prevailing *laissez-faire* or else leave in despair." [63]

After all allowance has been made for the manna of paternalism, the "family wage," and the greater purchasing power of money in the South, the wages of Southern textile workers remained miserably low. The very fact that the wages of the head of a family combined with those of the other adult members were inadequate to support dependents makes the "family wage" a curious apology for the system. Wages of adult male workers of North Carolina in the nineties were 40 to 50 cents a day. Men constituted a minority of the workers, about 35 per cent in the four leading textile states in 1890; women, 40 per cent; and children between the ages of ten and fifteen years, 25 per cent. The wages of children, who entered into degrading competition with their parents, varied considerably, but there is record of mills in North Carolina that paid 10 and 12 cents a day for child labor.[64] The work week averaged about seventy hours for men, women, and children. Wages were slow to improve, and did not keep pace with mounting capitalization and profits. Adult male spinners in representative mills of North Carolina who had received $2.53 a week in 1885 were getting $2.52 in 1895, and adult female spinners in Alabama got $2.76 a week in the former and $2.38 in the latter year.[65] Hourly wages for adult male spinners in the South Atlantic states were

[62] Mitchell, *Rise of the Cotton Mills*, 225–26.
[63] De Graffenried, "Georgia Cracker in the Cotton Mill," *loc. cit.*, 487.
[64] Davidson, *Child Labor Legislation in the Southern Textile States*, 8, 16.
[65] *Eleventh Annual Report of the Commissioner of Labor, 1895–96* (Washington, 1897), 184, 235.

not quite 3 cents in 1890, only 2.3 cents in 1895, and a little over 3 cents
in 1900; for female spinners in the same section the rate declined from
about 4.5 cents an hour in 1890 to 4 cents in 1900.[66] Yet with these wages
and conditions, there seems to have been no trouble in filling the company
houses to overflowing. Few workers ever returned to farming permanently, and strikes were almost unheard of.

The glimpses one gets of life among this sunbonneted, wool-hatted
proletariat raise doubts about the sense of *noblesse oblige* and the "philanthropic incentives" with which their employers have been credited. If
paternalism sheltered them from the most ruthless winds of industrial
conflict, it was a paternalism that could send its ten-year-old children off
to the mills at dawn and see them come home with a lantern at night. It
could watch its daughters come to marriageable age with "a dull heavy
eye, yellow, blotched complexion, dead-looking hair," its "unmarried
women of thirty . . . wrinkled, bent, and haggard," while the lot of them
approached old age as illiterate as Negro field hands.[67] If white solidarity
between employees and employer was to save the white worker from the
living standard of the Negro, the results in the cotton mills were not very
reassuring.

The extent to which labor in other industries shared in the prosperity
of the New South is indicated by the level of wages maintained. In few
industries or crafts did wages rise appreciably, and in many they were
actually reduced. In the tobacco industry of the South Atlantic states, for
example, cigar makers got 26 cents an hour in 1890 and 25 cents in 1900,
while stemmers' wages remained at about 10 cents; in representative
leather industries of the same states tanners remained on 11-cent wages,
while in the South Central states their wages fell from 12.75 cents in 1890
to 11.5 cents in 1900; compositors' wages in the printing industry advanced from about 24 cents to nearly 26 cents in the South Atlantic states
over the decade, from 28 cents to 29 cents in the South Central states;
machinists did little better than hold their own in this period; bricklayers'
wages declined from 45 cents to 43 cents in the South Central states and
rose from 35 cents to about 37 cents in the South Atlantic states; carpenters in the former section got nearly 26 cents in 1890 and over 27 cents in
1900, while in the latter section their wages were raised from about 24
cents to about 26 cents; and wages of unskilled labor in the building trades
varied from 8 cents to 12 cents an hour in the nineties.[68]

To a large extent the expanding industrialization of the New South
was based upon the labor of women and children who were driven into
the mills and shops to supplement the low wages earned by their men. In
several states they were being drawn into industry much more rapidly
than men. In representative establishments studied in Alabama the number

[66] *Nineteenth Annual Report of the Commissioner of Labor, 1904* (Washington,
1905), 385.
[67] De Graffenried, "Georgia Cracker in the Cotton Mill," *loc. cit.,* 489–93, 495;
Davidson, *Child Labor Legislation in the Southern Textile States,* 12–13.
[68] *Nineteenth Annual Report of the Commissioner of Labor, 1904,* 374, 403, 417,
430–31, 461, 465.

of men increased 31 per cent between 1885 and 1895; that of women increased 75 per cent; girls under eighteen, 158 per cent; and boys under eighteen, 81 per cent. The increases over the same period in Kentucky were 3 per cent for men, 70 per cent for women, 65 per cent for girls, and 76 per cent for boys.[69] Of the 400,586 male children between the ages of ten and fourteen gainfully employed in the United States in 1890, the two census divisions of the Southern states accounted for 256,502, and of the 202,427 girls of that age at work they listed 130,546. The great majority in each case were employed in agriculture, fisheries, and mining.[70] Thousands of women who went to work in the cities lived on subsistence wages. In Charleston shops, where the average weekly earnings for women were $4.22, were "well-born, well-educated girl[s] side by side in the least attractive pursuits with the 'cracker.'" In Richmond, where women's wages averaged $3.93 a week, there was an "almost universal pallor and sallowness of countenance" among working women. In Atlanta "great illiteracy exists among the working girls. Their moral condition also leaves much to be desired. The cost of living is comparatively high."[71]

In spite of the contributions of women and children, the working family in the South seemed less able to own a house than that of any other section. Of the eighteen cities in the whole country with a percentage of home tenancy above 80, eleven were in the South. Birmingham, with 89.84 per cent of tenancy, had the highest rate in the United States; the percentage in Norfolk was 85.62, and in Macon, 84.66. In the South Atlantic states as a whole, over 75 per cent of home dwellers were tenants.[72] Interlarded with the long, shady boulevards of the "best sections" of Nashville, Norfolk, Macon, Memphis, and Montgomery were alleys lined with one- and two-room shanties of colored domestics. In the "worst sections" of every city sprawled the jungle of a darktown with its own business streets and uproarious, crime-infested "amusement" streets. Beyond, in suburban squalor and isolation, were the gaunt barracks of white industrial workers, huddled around the factories.

Conditions of public health and sanitation under which the urban working classes lived cannot be grasped from general descriptions, since health improvements and safeguards were highly discriminatory within the cities. Richmond justly boasted in 1887 of her relatively high expenditures for municipal improvements, of being "the best-paved city of her population in the Union," and of the splendor of Broad, Main, and Cary streets, "yearly improved by elegant houses built for merchants and manufacturers." Yet in 1888 the United States Commissioner of Labor blamed "bad drainage of the city, bad drinking water, and unsanitary homes" for the appalling conditions of health among the working girls of Richmond.[73] New Orleans, with a long start over her sisters, easily

[69] United States Bureau of Labor Bulletin No. 10 (Washington, 1897), 242.

[70] Eleventh Census, 1890, Compendium, Pt. III, 460–62.

[71] Fourth Annual Report of the Commissioner of Labor, 1888 (Washington, 1889), 13, 16, 24, 68.

[72] Eleventh Census, 1890, Farms and Homes, 29.

[73] Fourth Annual Report of the Commissioner of Labor, 1888, 24.

achieved pre-eminence among unsanitary cities by the filth and squalor of her slums. The president of the State Board of Health of Louisiana reported in 1881 that "the gutters of the 472 miles of dirt streets are in foul condition, being at various points choked up with garbage, filth and mud, and consequently may be regarded simply as receptacles for putrid matters and stagnant waters. The street crossings are in like manner more or less obstructed with filth and black, stinking mud." [74]

"We have awakened, or are fast awakening, from our dream," commented a Southern editor. "We have pauperism, crime, ignorance, discontent in as large a measure as a people need. Every question that has knocked at European doors for solution will in turn knock at ours." [75] When work relief was offered at twenty cents a week by private charity in Alexandria, Virginia, "poor women were more than glad to get the work, and came from far and near, and many had to be sent away disappointed every week." [76] In New Orleans "a multitude of people, white and black alike," lived on a dole of thirteen cents a day in the nineties. [77]

Labor in the Southern textile mills, largely unorganized, has claimed a disproportionate share of the attention of scholars. The result has been a neglect of the history of labor in other industries and in the crafts, as well as an encouragement of the impression that no labor movement existed in the region at this period.

A study of the labor movement in the largest Southern city concludes that "the South, to judge by New Orleans, had craft labor movements smaller but similar to those in Northern cities," and that they were growing in power and influence in the eighties and nineties. [78] It was a period of testing unknown strength and challenging tentatively the Old-South labor philosophy of the New-South doctrinaires and their pledge to Northern investors that long hours, low wages, and docile labor were assured.

However appealing white Southern labor found the doctrine of White Supremacy, it realized pretty early that "in nearly all the trades, the rates of compensation for the whites is [sic] governed more or less by the rates at which the blacks can be hired," and that the final appeal in a strike was "the Southern employer's ability to hold the great mass of negro mechanics *in terrorem* over the heads of the white." [79] Agreement upon the nature of their central problem did not bring agreement upon the proper means of dealing with it. Two possible but contradictory policies could be used: eliminate the Negro as a competitor by excluding

[74] *Annual Report of the Board of Health of the State of Louisiana . . . for the Year 1881* (New Orleans, 1881), 5–6. See also [Roger W.] Shugg [*Origins of Class Struggle in Louisiana; A Social History of White Farmers and Laborers During Slavery and After, 1840–1875* (University, La., 1939)], 282–89.

[75] New Orleans *Times*, September 13, 1881.

[76] New York *Tribune*, February 10, 1881.

[77] Shugg, *Origins of Class Struggle in Louisiana*, 297.

[78] Roger W. Shugg, "The New Orleans General Strike of 1892," in *Louisiana Historical Quarterly*, XXI (1938), 559.

[79] [Philip A.] Bruce [*The Rise of the New South* (Philadelphia, 1905)], 164–65.

him from the skilled trades either as an apprentice or a worker, or take
him in as an organized worker committed to the defense of a common
standard of wages. Southern labor wavered between these antithetical
policies from the seventies into the nineties, sometimes adopting one,
sometimes the other.

The rising aristocracy of labor, the railway brotherhoods, drew a
strict color line. On the other hand, the Brotherhood of Carpenters and
Joiners claimed fourteen Negro locals in the South in 1886. The coopers',
the cigar makers', the bricklayers', the steel workers', and the carpenters'
unions had by the eighties adopted the practice of "issuing . . . separate
charters to Negro craftsmen wherever existing locals debarred them." The
federations of deck workers in the cotton ports of New Orleans, Savan-
nah, and Galveston overrode race barriers and admitted, equally, white
and black longshoremen, draymen, yardmen, cotton classers, and screw-
men. Especially successful were the efforts to organize the Negroes in
New Orleans. The Central Trades and Labor Assembly of that city was
said "to have done more to break the color line in New Orleans than any
other thing . . . since emancipation of the slaves." [80]

Much of this temporary "era of good feeling" between black and
white workingmen has been credited to the guidance of the Knights of
Labor. The Knights' doctrine of interracial solidarity and democratic
idealism makes the history of the order of particular significance for the
central problem of Southern labor. The history of the Knights also
confutes the legend of the Southern worker's indifference to unionism.
As soon as the national organization of the Knights was established in
1878 it dispatched 15 organizers to the South. A quickening of Southern
interest was evident in 1884, and by 1886 there were in ten states 21,208
members attached to the Southern District assembly and perhaps 10,000
more members of locals attached to national trade assemblies or directly
to the General Assembly of the Knights. An incomplete list places 487
locals in the South in 1888, but there were many more. Concentrated
around such cities as Birmingham, Knoxville, Louisville, New Orleans, and
Richmond, locals were also scattered over rural areas and embraced cotton hands and sugar workers, black as well as white. The national convention of the Knights in 1886, the year of their greatest strength, met in
Richmond and was attended by delegates of both races from many parts
of the South. The convention heard reports that "colored people of the
South are flocking to us" and that "rapid strides" have been made in the
South.[81]

The Knights were involved in numerous strikes in the South during
the latter years of the eighties. These conflicts broke out in the coal
mines of Alabama and Tennessee, in the cotton mills of Augusta, Georgia,

[80] Sterling D. Spero and Abram L. Harris, *The Black Worker: The Negro and the
Labor Movement* (New York, 1931), 22, 43–44; Wesley, *Negro Labor in the
United States*, 236–37, 255.
[81] Frederic Myers, "The Knights of Labor in the South," in *Southern Economic
Journal* (Chapel Hill), VI (1939–1940), 479–85. One official asserted that the order
had 100,000 members in five Southern states, but this was an exaggerated claim.

and Cottondale, Alabama, among the sugar workers of Louisiana and the lumber workers in Alabama. The Knights' greatest strike victory, that against the Missouri Pacific system and Jay Gould in 1885, was won in considerable part in the shops of Texas and Arkansas. The Southwestern strike of 1886, which marked the climax and greatest failure of the order, broke out in Texas, and some of its most violent phases occurred there. The Knights experimented with co-operative enterprises of various kinds, though on no such scale as did the Farmers' Alliance. The order figured conspicuously in the politics of several cities. In 1886 the Workingman's Reform party, backed by the Knights, elected two blacksmiths, a cobbler, and a tanner to the city council of Richmond, and took control of nearly all departments of the government. In 1887 the Knights claimed that they had elected a congressman and eleven of the fifteen city council members in Lynchburg, a majority of the city and county officers in Macon, and several officers in Mobile. The following year they asserted that they had elected the mayors of Jacksonville, Vicksburg, and Anniston. The mayor of Anniston was a carpenter, and the council included two molders, a brickmaker, a butcher, a watchmaker, and a shoemaker. Their reforms were mild enough, but their experimental defiance of the color line was bitterly attacked in the Southern press. Under these burdens and the additional ones of lost strikes, the Knights passed into a decline in the South as in the nation. Co-operation with the Farmers' Alliance gave the order a decided agrarian color by the end of the eighties.[82]

A second peak of activity in the Southern labor movement came in 1892. It therefore coincided with the outburst of the Populist revolt and, like it, was symptomatic of popular discontent with the New Order of the Redeemers. It may be illustrated by two unrelated outbreaks of contrasting character—the general strike in New Orleans and the violent insurrection of Tennessee coal miners against the employment of convict labor.

The general strike in New Orleans, which followed the Homestead strike in Pennsylvania and preceded the Pullman strike in Chicago, has been described as "the first general strike in American history to enlist both skilled and unskilled labor, black and white, and to paralyze the life of a great city." It came as "the climax of the strongest labor movement in the South."[83] New Orleans was about as well unionized as any city in the country when the American Federation of Labor began a successful drive early in 1892 that added thirty new chartered associations, thus bringing the total up to ninety-five. A new unity was achieved in the Workingmen's Amalgamated Council, a centralized but democratically elected body made up of two delegates from each of the forty-nine unions affiliated with the A. F. of L. The New Orleans Board of Trade, an organization of the merchants of the city, was as determined to main-

---

[82] *Ibid.*, 485–87. Frank W. Taussig, "The South-Western Strike of 1886" in *Quarterly Journal of Economics* (Boston, Cambridge), I (1886–1887), 184–222; Dallas *Daily News*, March 2–April 23, 1886; Richmond *Dispatch*, May 18, July 2, September 30, October 3, 1886; Jackson *Clarion*, November 9, 1887; *National Economist*, II (1889), 221; *Tradesman*, XIV (May 15, 1886), 23.

[83] Shugg, "New Orleans General Strike of 1892," *loc. cit.*, 547.

tain traditional prerogatives of hiring and firing as the labor council was to establish the right of collective bargaining.

Inspired by a victory of the city streetcar drivers that put an end to a sixteen-hour day and gained a closed-shop agreement, the so-called "Triple Alliance," consisting of the unions of the teamsters, scalesmen, and packers (which included Negro members), struck for a ten-hour day, overtime pay, and the preferential closed shop. The Workingmen's Amalgamated Council appointed a committee of five workers, including a Negro, to conduct the strike. The Board of Trade refused to recognize the unions or to deal with them in any way. The workers' committee first threatened, and finally, on November 8, called a general strike in support of the unions of unskilled workers. Forty-two union locals, with over 20,000 members, who with their families made up nearly half of the population of the city, stopped work. Each union on strike demanded recognition and a closed shop. Business came to a virtual standstill; bank clearings were cut in half. The employers openly declared that it was "a war to the knife" and that they would resort to extreme measures, including violence. Yet in spite of the hysteria kept up by the newspapers, the importation of strikebreakers, and the threat of military intervention, the strikers refrained from violence and there was no bloodshed. On the third day of the strike the governor of the state came to the aid of the capitalists with a proclamation that, in effect, set up martial law and implied that the militia would be called unless the strike was ended. The labor committee, never very aggressive, accepted a compromise which, though gaining the original demands of the Triple Alliance concerning hours and wages, forfeited the fight for collective bargaining and the closed shop. The Board of Trade, confident that labor, like the Negro, had been put in its "place," boasted that New Orleans was an open-shop city, and that the old philosophy of labor had been vindicated.[84]

The second labor struggle was fought upon a more primitive level, for the most elemental rights, and fought with savage violence. Competition with convict labor leased by corporations had been a long-standing and often-voiced grievance of labor all over the South. As a conservative paper stated the case in Alabama, "Employers of convicts pay so little for their labor that it makes it next to impossible for those who give work to free labor to compete with them in any line of business. As a result, the price paid for labor is based upon the price paid convicts." [85]

In 1883 the Tennessee Coal, Iron, and Railroad Company leased the Tennessee penitentiary containing some 1,300 convicts. Thomas Collier Platt, the New York Republican leader, was president of the company and Colonel Colyar, the Tennessee Democratic leader, was general counsel. "For some years after we began the convict labor system," said Colyar, "we found that we were right in calculating that free laborers would be loath to enter upon strikes when they saw that the company was amply provided with convict labor." [86]

[84] *Ibid.*, 547–59. New Orleans *Times-Democrat*, October 25, November 4–11, 1892.
[85] Fort Payne (Ala.) *Herald*, quoted in Birmingham *Age-Herald*, August 8, 1889.
[86] Nashville *Daily American*, August 23, 1892.

Tennessee labor protested, and the legislature occasionally investigated, once reporting that the branch prisons were "hell holes of rage, cruelty, despair and vice." But nothing was done. In 1891, the miners of Briceville, Anderson County, were presented by the Tennessee Coal Mine Company with an "iron-clad" contract relinquishing employees' rights to a check weigher, agreeing to "scrip" pay, and pledging no strikes. When they turned down the contract the company ordered convicts to tear down their houses and build stockades for the convicts who were to replace free labor. The evicted miners then marched in force on the stockades and, without bloodshed, compelled guards, officers, and convicts to board a train for Knoxville. Governor John P. Buchanan, with three companies of militia, promptly returned the convicts to the stockades. A few days later more than a thousand armed miners packed the guards and convicts off to Knoxville a second time, and those of another company along with them, again without bloodshed. Only after the governor had promised to call a special session of the legislature were the miners pacified. Labor demonstrations in Chattanooga, Memphis, Nashville, and other towns demanded an end to convict labor and sent aid to the miners. Kentucky and Alabama labor, afflicted with the same evil, also became aroused. The Tennessee state convention of the Farmers' Alliance, which the governor attended, demanded the repeal of the convict-lease law. In spite of the official position of the Alliance, the fact that there were fifty-four Alliance members of the legislature, and that Governor Buchanan owed his election to the order, the special session of the legislature took no satisfactory action. After a futile appeal to the courts, the miners took the law into their own hands. On the night of October 31, 1891, they forcibly freed the convicts of the Tennessee Coal Mine Company, allowed them all to escape, and burned down the stockades. They repeated the same tactics later at two other mining companies, releasing in all some five hundred convicts. The mine operators of the area then employed free labor, gave up the "iron-clad" contract, and granted a check weigher.[87]

The insurrections of the following year made those of 1891 seem tame by comparison. The Tennessee struggles involved more men and deeper issues than the contemporary Homestead strike, but they got little attention then or later. These insurrections broke out in Middle Tennessee at the mines of the Tennessee Coal and Iron Company, which had put its free labor on half time and employed 360 convicts full time. Miners overcame the Tracy City guards, burned the stockades, and shipped the convicts to Nashville. Inspired by this example, miners of one of the Tennessee Coal, Iron, and Railroad Company mines in Anderson County, at which convict labor had been reinstated, burned the stockades, renewed their war, and laid seige to Fort Anderson, which was occupied by militia and civil guards paid jointly by the company and the state to guard the convicts. Although the miners killed a few of the troops sent to relieve

---

[87] A. C. Hutson, Jr., "The Coal Miners' Insurrection of 1891 in Anderson County, Tennessee," in East Tennessee Historical Society's *Publications* (Knoxville), No. 7 (1935), 105–15. Nashville *Daily American*, July 17–21, August, 13, 1891.

the besieged fort, the convicts were again reinstated. The final insurrection spelled the doom of the convict lease, however, for the following year the system was abolished by the legislature.[88]

By their actions the Tennessee miners, the New Orleans trade unions, and workers in the mines and foundries of Alabama, Georgia, and Virginia gave notice in 1892 that Southern labor was not going to accept the Old-South labor philosophy of the New-South leaders—not without a fight, anyway. The militancy of Southern labor also gave notice to the insurgent Southern farmer that he might seek recruits for the Populist revolt in the mines and factories as well as in the fields.

[88] A. C. Hutson, Jr., "The Overthrow of the Convict Lease System in Tennessee," in East Tennessee Historical Society's *Publications*, No. 8 (1936), 82–103; Nashville *Daily American*, August 15–23, 1892, Memphis *Appeal-Avalanche*, January 3, 7, March 1, 1892.

The Social Insulation of the Traditional Elite

E. DIGBY BALTZELL

The myth of equality has had a powerful influence in shaping American attitudes. Beginning in the colonial period and continuing until today, foreign visitors as well as native writers have commented on what they have perceived as the high degree of social mobility available to Americans as a result of the basic equality of opportunity that is their birthright. Of course, many of these same writers have also pointed out that certain elements of the population were left out of the equality scheme by definition, for example, women and non-whites. But the myth persisted, even among those denied access to its rewards.

At least one group of Americans, however, knew better—the wealthy traditional elite (which did assimilate newcomers, but slowly). From the colonial period to the Civil War, many wealthy citizens of WASP ancestry believed they had a special place in society. Their wealth and traditions insulated them from the entrepreneurial clamor of the Jacksonian period, and they maintained a castelike existence in the cities of the Eastern seaboard.

After the Civil War, however, traditions and family connections were no longer sufficient to maintain the exclusivity of the caste structure. The route to riches had shifted, and holders of the new wealth aspired to the life-style previously available primarily to the WASP elite. The homogeneous quality of upper-class existence began to break down under the onslaught of rapid economic growth and the extraordinary financial success of an increasing number of non-WASP families.

Initially, the traditional elite had supported open immigration from Eastern and Southern European countries in order to insure an overabundance of common laborers that would tend to keep wages down, but as participants in this new immigration began to rise in economic status, and in some cases to become actually wealthy, the elite began to reconsider their position. Although they were unable to restrict immigration until well into the twentieth century, they were able to take steps soon after the Civil War to insulate themselves from the society of wealthy non-WASPs.

E. Digby Baltzell, a sociologist at the University of Pennsylvania, has taken as his field of study the traditional elite of the Eastern seaboard. After publishing a book on the upper-class families of Philadelphia, he enlarged his focus to consider the exclusionary tactics of the WASP elite through the last hundred years. In the chapter reprinted below, he focuses on the anti-Semitic practices of the traditional families and enumerates the various devices by which the traditional upper class insulated itself socially from non-WASP wealth. Several features of the social life of the upper class taken so much for granted today have their origin in this period. Exclusive prep schools, college societies, restricted suburbs, summer resorts, and city clubs were founded in order to enable the traditional elite to protect what they saw as their caste privileges. Consequently, the excluded wealthy families formed their own parallel network of social organizations that were designed to reflect the class, if not the caste, prerogatives of upper-class existence.

We are still in power, after a fashion. Our sway over what we call society is undisputed. We keep the Jew far away, and the anti-Jew feeling is quite rabid.

HENRY ADAMS

The Civil War was fought, by a nation rapidly becoming centralized economically, in order to preserve the political Union. Although the Union was preserved and slavery abolished, the postwar Republic was faced with the enormously complex and morally cancerous problem of caste, as far as the formally free Negroes were concerned. The solution to this problem has now become the central one of our own age. But the more immediate effect of the Civil War was that, in the North at least, the nation realized the fabulous potential of industrial power. The Pennsylvania Railroad, for instance, began to cut back operations at the beginning of the war, only to realize a tremendous boom during the remainder of the conflict (total revenue in 1860: $5,933 million; in 1865: $19,533 million). But the profits of the war were nothing compared to those of the fabulous postwar years. Between 1870 and 1900, the national wealth quadrupled (rising from $30,400 million to $126,700 million and doubled again by 1914—reaching $254,200 million).[1]

During this same period, wealth became increasingly centralized in the hands of a few. In 1891, *Forum* magazine published an article, "The Coming Billionaire," which estimated that there were 120 men in the nation worth over $10 million. The next year, the *New York Times* published a list of 4,047 millionaires, and the Census Bureau estimated that 9 per cent of the nation's families owned 71 per cent of the wealth. By 1910 there were more millionaires in the United States Senate alone than there were in the whole nation before the Civil War. This new inequality was dramatized by the fact that, in 1900, according to Frederick Lewis Allen, the former immigrant lad Andrew Carnegie had an *income* of between $15

[1] Here I have followed Richard Hofstadter, *The Age of Reform*. New York: Vintage Books, 1960, Chap. IV.

"The Social Defense of Caste" (Editor's title: "The Social Insulation of the Traditional Elite"). From *The Protestant Establishment*, by E. Digby Baltzell, pp. 109–42. Copyright © 1964 by E. Digby Baltzell. Reprinted by permission of Random House, Inc.

and $30 million (the income tax had been declared unconstitutional in a test case in 1895), while the average unskilled worker in the North received less than $460 a year in wages—in the South the figure was less than $300. It is no wonder that the production of pig iron rather than poetry, and the quest for status rather than salvation, now took hold of the minds of even the most patrician descendants of Puritan divines.

This inequality of wealth was accompanied by an increasing centralization of business power, as the nation changed, in the half century after Appomattox, from a rural-communal to an urban-corporate society. President Eliot of Harvard, in a speech before the fraternity of Phi Beta Kappa in 1888, noted this new corporate dominance when he pointed out that, while the Pennsylvania Railroad had gross receipts of $115 million and employed over 100,000 men in that year, the Commonwealth of Massachusetts had gross receipts of only $7 million and employed no more than 6,000 persons.[2] And this corporate economy was further centralized financially in Wall Street. The capital required to launch the United States Steel Corporation, for example, would at that time have covered the costs of all the functions of the federal government for almost two years. J. P. Morgan and his associates, who put this great corporate empire together in 1901, held some three hundred directorships in over one hundred corporations with resources estimated at over $22 billion. This industrial age, in which the railroads spanned the continent and Wall Street interests controlled mines in the Rockies, timber in the Northwest, and coal in Pennsylvania and West Virginia, brought about a national economy and the emergence of a national mind.

And the prosperity of this new urban-corporate world was largely built upon the blood and sweat of the men, and the tears of their women, who came to this country in such large numbers from the peasant villages of Southern and Eastern Europe. Whereas most of the older immigrants from Northern and Western Europe had come to a rural America where they were able to assimilate more easily, the majority of these newer arrivals huddled together in the urban slums and ghettos which were characteristic of the lower levels of the commercial economy which America had now become.

Except for the captains of industry, whose money-centered minds continued to welcome and encourage immigration because they believed it kept wages down and retarded unionization, most old-stock Americans were frankly appalled at the growing evils of industrialization, immigration and urbanization. As we have seen, the closing decades of the nineteenth century were marked by labor unrest and violence; many men, like Henry Adams, developed a violent nativism and anti-Semitism; others, following the lead of Jane Addams, discovered the slums and went to work to alleviate the evils of prostitution, disease, crime, political bossism and grinding poverty; both Midwestern Populism and the Eastern, patrician-led Progressive movement were part of the general protest and were, in turn, infused with varying degrees of nativism; and even organized labor,

[2] Charles William Eliot, *American Contributions to Civilization*. New York: The Century Company, 1897, pp. 85–86.

many of whose members were of recent immigrant origin, was by no means devoid of nativist sentiment.

In so many ways, nativism was part of a more generalized anti-urban and anti-capitalist mood. Unfortunately, anti-Semitism is often allied with an antipathy toward the city and the money-power. Thus the first mass manifestations of anti-Semitism in America came out of the Midwest among the Populist leaders and their followers. In the campaign of 1896, for example, William Jennings Bryan was accused of anti-Semitism and had to explain to the Jewish Democrats of Chicago that in denouncing the policies of Wall Street and the Rothschilds, he and his silver friends were "not attacking a race but greed and avarice which know no race or religion." [3] And the danger that the Populist, isolationist and anti-Wall Street sentiment in the Middle West might at any time revert to anti-Semitism continued. As we shall see in a later chapter, Henry Ford, a multimillionaire with the traditional Populist mistrust of the money-power, was notoriously anti-Semitic for a time in the early 1920's.

Nativism was also a part of a status revolution at the elite level of leadership on the Eastern Seaboard. "The newly rich, the grandiosely or corruptly rich, the masters of the great corporations," wrote Richard Hofstadter, "were bypassing the men of the Mugwump type—the old gentry, the merchants of long standing, the small manufacturers, the established professional men, the civic leaders of an earlier era. In scores of cities and hundreds of towns, particularly in the East but also in the nation at large, the old-family, college-educated class that had deep ancestral roots in local communities and often owned family businesses, that had traditions of political leadership, belonged to the patriotic societies and the best clubs, staffed the government boards of philanthropic and cultural institutions, and led the movements for civic betterment, were being overshadowed and edged aside in making basic political and economic decisions. . . . They were less important and they knew it." [4]

Many members of this class, of old-stock prestige and waning power, eventually allied themselves with the Progressive movement. Many also, like Henry Adams, withdrew almost entirely from the world of power. The "decent people," as Edith Wharton once put it, increasingly "fell back on sport and culture." And this sport and culture was now to be reinforced by a series of fashionable and patrician protective associations which, in turn, systematically and subtly institutionalized the exclusion of Jews.

The turning point came in the 1880's, when a number of symbolic events forecast the nature of the American upper class in the twentieth century. Thus, when President Eliot of Harvard built his summer cottage at Northeast Harbor, Maine, in 1881, the exclusive summer resort trend was well under way; the founding of *The* Country Club at Brookline, Massachusetts, in 1882, marked the beginning of the country-club trend; the founding of the Sons of the Revolution, in 1883, symbolized the birth of the genealogical fad and the patrician scramble for old-stock roots; Endicott Peabody's founding of Groton School, in 1884, in order to rear

---

[3] Richard Hofstadter, *op. cit.*, p. 80.
[4] *Ibid.*, p. 137.

young gentlemen in the tradition of British public schools (and incidentally to protect them from the increasing heterogeneity of the public school system) was an important symbol of both upper-class exclusiveness and patrician Anglophilia; and finally, the Social Register, a convenient index of this new associational aristocracy, was first issued toward the end of this transitional decade in 1887 (the publisher also handled much of the literature of the American Protective Association, which was active in the nativist movement at that time).

The Right Reverend Phillips Brooks—the favorite clergyman among Philadelphia's Victorian gentry, who was called to Boston's Trinity Church in 1869, the year Grant entered the White House and Eliot accepted the presidency at Harvard—was one of the most sensitive barometers of the brahmin mind. Thus, although he himself had graduated from the Boston Latin School along with other patricians and plebeian gentlemen of his generation, he first suggested the idea of Groton to young Peabody in the eighties and joined the Sons of the Revolution in 1891, because, as he said at the time, "it is well to go in for the assertion that our dear land at least used to be American." [5]

ANCESTRAL ASSOCIATIONS AND THE QUEST
FOR OLD-STOCK ROOTS

The idea of caste dies hard, even in a democratic land such as ours. Our first and most exclusive ancestral association, the Society of the Cincinnati, was formed in 1783, just before the Continental Army disbanded. Its membership was limited to Washington's officers and, in accord with the rural traditions of primogeniture, was to be passed on to the oldest sons in succeeding generations. The society's name reflects the ancient tradition of gentlemen-farmers, from Cincinnatus to Cromwell, Washington and Franklin Roosevelt, who have served their country in times of need. Just as the founding of the Society of Cincinnati reflected the rural values of the gentleman and his mistrust of grasping city ways, it was quite natural that the new wave of ancestral associations which came into being at the end of the nineteenth century was a reaction to the rise of the city with its accompanying heterogeneity and conflict. As Wallace Evan Davies, in *Patriotism on Parade*, put it:

"The great Upheaval," the Haymarket Riot, the campaigns of Henry George, and the writings of Edward Bellamy crowded the last half of the eighties. The nineties produced such proofs of unrest as the Populist Revolt, the Homestead Strike with the attempted assassination of Henry Clay Frick, the Panic of 1893, the Pullman Strike, Coxey's Army, and, finally, the Bryan campaign of 1896. Throughout all this the conservative and propertied classes watched apprehensively the black cloud of anarchism, a menace as produc-

[5] Barbara Miller Solomon, *Ancestors and Immigrants: A Changing New England.* Cambridge, Mass.: Harvard University Press, 1956, p. 87.

tive of alarm and hysteria as bolshevism and communism in later
generations.[6]

These old-stock patriots, desperately seeking hereditary and historical
roots in a rapidly changing world, flocked to the standards of such newly
founded societies as the Sons of the Revolution (1883), the Colonial Dames
(1890), the Daughters of the American Revolution (1890), Daughters of
the Cincinnati (1894), the Society of Mayflower Descendants (1894), the
Aryan Order of St. George or the Holy Roman Empire in the Colonies of
America (1892), and the Baronial Order of Runnymede (1897). It is no
wonder that genealogists, both amateur and professional, rapidly came
into vogue. Several urban newspapers established genealogical departments;
the Lenox Library in New York purchased one of its largest genealogical
collections, in 1896, setting aside a room "for the convenience of the large
number of researchers after family history"; the *Library Journal* carried
articles on how to help the public in ancestor hunting; and, as of 1900, the
Patriotic Review listed seventy patriotic, hereditary and historical associations, exactly *half* of which had been founded during the preceding decade
alone.

This whole movement was, of course, intimately bound up with anti-
immigrant and anti-Semitic sentiments. Thus a leader of the D.A.R. saw
a real danger in "our being absorbed by the different nationalities among
us," and a president-general of the Sons of the American Revolution reported that: "Not until the state of civilization reached the point where
we had a great many foreigners in our land . . . were our patriotic societies successful." [7] The Daughters of the American Revolution was indeed extremely successful. Founded in 1890, it had 397 chapters in 38
states by 1897. That the anti-immigrant reaction was most prevalent in the
urban East, however, was attested to by the fact that the Daughters made
slow headway in the West and South and had a vast majority of its chapters in New York and Massachusetts.

But, as Franklin Roosevelt once said, "we are all descendants of immigrants." While old-stock Americans were forming rather exclusive associations based on their descent from Colonial immigrants, newer Americans were also attempting to establish their own historical roots. Such
organizations as the Scotch-Irish Society (1889), the Pennsylvania-German
Society (1891), the American Jewish Historical Society (1894), and the
American Irish Historical Society (1898) were concerned to establish ethnic recognition through ancestral achievement. "The Americanism of all
Irishmen and Jews," writes Edward N. Saveth, "was enhanced because of
the handful of Irishmen and Jews who may have stood by Washington
in a moment of crisis." [8]

[6] Wallace E. Davies, *Patriotism on Parade: The Story of Veterans' and Hereditary
Organizations in America, 1783–1900*. Cambridge, Mass.: Harvard University Press,
1956.

[7] *Ibid.*, p. 48.

[8] Edward N. Saveth, *American Historians and European Immigrants, 1875–1925*. New
York: Columbia University Press, 1948, p. 194.

The genealogically minded patrician has remained a part of the American scene down through the years. The front page of any contemporary copy of the Social Register, for instance, lists a series of clubs, universities and ancestral associations, with proper abbreviations attached, in order that each family may be identified by its members' affiliations. A recent Philadelphia Social Register listed an even dozen such societies, and a venerable old gentleman of great prestige (if little power) was listed in a later page as follows:

> Rittenhouse,   Wm.   Penn—Ul.Ph.Myf.Cc.Wt.Rv.Ll.Fw.P'83 . . .
>   Union League

It was indeed plain to see (after a bit of research on page 1) that this old gentleman was nicely placed as far as his ancestral, college and club affiliations were concerned. He belonged to the Union League (Ul) and Philadelphia clubs (Ph), had graduated in 1883 from Princeton University (P'83), and was apparently devoting himself to some sort of patriotic ancestor worship in his declining years, as suggested by his ancestral association memberships: Mayflower Descendants (Myf); Society of Cincinnati (Cc); Society of the War of 1812 (Wt); Sons of the Revolution (Rv); Military Order of the Loyal Legion (Ll); and the Military Order of Foreign Wars (Fw). And, as the final entry shows, he was living at the Union League.

THE SUMMER RESORT AND THE QUEST
FOR HOMOGENEITY

Americans have always longed for grass roots. In a society of cement, the resort movement in America paralleled the genealogical escape to the past. The physiological and physical ugliness of the city streets gradually drove those who could afford it back to nature and the wide-open spaces. Men like Owen Wister, Theodore Roosevelt and Madison Grant went out to the West, and the more timid, or socially minded, souls sought refuge at some exclusive summer resort. In spite of the efforts of men like Frederick Law Olmstead and Madison Grant to bring rural beauty into the heart of the city (Olmstead built some fifteen city parks from coast to coast, Central Park in New York City being the most well known), first the artists and writers, then the gentry, and finally the millionaires were seeking the beauty of nature and the simple life among the "natives" of coastal or mountain communities along the Eastern Seaboard. President Eliot and his sons spent the summers during the seventies camping in tents before building the first summer cottage in Northeast Harbor, Maine, in 1881.[9] Charles Francis Adams, Jr., saw his native Quincy succumb to industrialism and the Irish (the Knights of Labor gained control of the

---

[9] Henry James, *Charles W. Eliot*. Vol. I. Boston: Houghton Mifflin Company, 1940, p. 344.

Adams "race-place" in 1887), gave up his job with the Union Pacific in 1890, and finally escaped to the simple life at Lincoln, Massachusetts, in 1893.

The summer resort increased in popularity after the Civil War and went through its period of most rapid growth between 1880 and the First War. Long Branch, New Jersey, summer capital of presidents from Grant to Arthur, was filled with proper Philadelphians and New Yorkers. Further south, Cape May—where Jay Cooke, financier of the Civil War, spent every summer—was the most fashionable Philadelphia summer resort until well into the twentieth century. Boston's best retreated to the simple life at Nahant. Others went to the Berkshires, where large "cottages," large families and large incomes supported the simple life for many years (Lenox boasted thirty-five of these cottages as of 1880, and seventy-five by 1900).[10] Between 1890 and the First War, Bar Harbor became one of America's most stylish resorts. By 1894, the year Joseph Pulitzer built the resort's first hundred-thousand-dollar "cottage," Morgan and Standard Oil partners were the leaders of the community (when a Vanderbilt bought a cottage in 1922, it was the first to change hands in fifteen years; within the next three years, forty-seven such cottages changed hands). Less fashionable, but no less genteel, Northeast Harbor grew at the same time. Anticipating modern sociology, President Eliot made a study of the community in 1890. Among other things, he found that, as of 1881, non-resident summer people owned less than one-fifth of the local real property; only eight years later, in 1889, they owned over half (and total property values had almost doubled).[11]

Just as the white man, symbolized by the British gentleman, was roaming round the world in search of raw materials for his factories at Manchester, Liverpool or Leeds, so America's urban gentry and capitalists, at the turn of the century, were imperialists seeking solace for their souls among the "natives" of Lenox, Bar Harbor or Kennebunkport. Here they were able to forget the ugliness of the urban melting pot as they dwelt among solid Yankees (Ethan Frome), many of whom possessed more homogeneous, Colonial-stock roots than themselves. And these rustic "types" kept up their boats, taught their children the ways of the sea, caught their lobsters, served them in the stores along the village streets, and became temporary servants and gardeners on their rustic estates. But although most old-time resorters were patronizingly proficient with the "Down East" accent, and appreciated the fact that the "natives" were their "own kind" racially, sometimes the idyllic harmony was somewhat superficial, at least as far as the more sensitive "natives" were concerned. Hence the following anecdote circulating among the "natives" at Bar Harbor: "They emptied the pool the other day," reported one typical "type" to another. "Why?" asked his friend. "Oh, one of the natives fell in."

But the simple life was, nevertheless, often touching and always relax-

---

[10] Cleveland Amory, *Last Resorts*. New York: Harper & Brothers, 1952, p. 21.
[11] Henry James, *op. cit.,* p. 111.

ing. All one's kind were there together and the older virtues of communal life were abroad; Easter-Christmas-Wedding Christians usually went to church every Sunday; millionaires' wives did their own shopping in the village, and walking, boating and picnicking brought a renewed appreciation of nature. And perhaps most important of all, one knew who one's daughter was seeing, at least during the summer months when convenient alliances for life were often consummated.

When J. P. Morgan observed that "you can do business with anyone, but only sail with a gentleman," he was reflecting the fact that a secure sense of homogeneity is the essence of resort life. It is no wonder that anti-Semitism, of the gentlemanly, exclusionary sort, probably reached its most panicky heights there. Thus one of the first examples of upper-class anti-Semitism in America occurred, in the 1870's, when a prominent New York banker, Joseph Seligman, was rudely excluded from the Grand Union Hotel in Saratoga Springs. This came as a shock to the American people and was given wide publicity because it was something new at that time. Henry Ward Beecher, a personal friend of the Seligmans, reacted with a sermon from his famous pulpit at Plymouth Church: "What have the Jews," he said, "of which they need be ashamed, in a Christian Republic where all men are declared to be free and equal? . . . Is it that they are excessively industrious? Let the Yankee cast the first stone. Is it that they are inordinately keen on bargaining? Have they ever stolen ten millions of dollars at a pinch from a city? Are our courts bailing out Jews, or compromising with Jews? Are there Jews lying in our jails, and waiting for mercy. . . . You cannot find one criminal Jew in the whole catalogue. . . ." [12]

The Seligman incident was followed by a battle at Saratoga Springs. Immediately afterwards, several new hotels were built there by Jews, and by the end of the century half the population was Jewish; as a result, it is said that one non-Jewish establishment boldly advertised its policies with a sign: "No Jews and Dogs Admitted Here." At the same time, other prominent German Jews were running into embarrassing situations elsewhere. In the 1890's, Nathan Straus, brother of a member of Theodore Roosevelt's Cabinet and a leading merchant and civic leader himself, was turned down at a leading hotel in Lakewood, New Jersey, a most fashionable winter resort at that time. He promptly built a hotel next door, twice as big and for Jews only. And the resort rapidly became Jewish, as kosher establishments multiplied on all sides.

Even the well-integrated and cultivated members of Philadelphia's German-Jewish community eventually had to bow to the trend. As late as the eighties and nineties, for instance, leading Jewish families were listed in the Philadelphia Blue Book as summering at fashionable Cape May, along with the city's best gentile families. But this did not continue, and many prominent Philadelphia Jews became founding families at Long Branch, Asbury Park, Spring Lake or Atlantic City, where the first resort

[12] Quoted in Carey McWilliams, *A Mask for Privilege.* Boston: Little, Brown & Company, 1948, p. 6.

synagogues were established during the nineties: Long Branch (1890), Atlantic City (1893), and Asbury Park (1896).[13]

As the East European Jews rapidly rose to middle-class status, resort-hotel exclusiveness produced a running battle along the Jersey coast and up in the Catskills. One resort after another changed from an all-gentile to an all-Jewish community. Atlantic City, for example, first became a fashionable gentile resort in the nineties. By the end of the First War, however, it had become a predominantly Jewish resort, at least in the summer months (the first modern, fireproof hotel was built there in 1902; there were a thousand such hotels by 1930). According to Edmund Wilson, it was while visiting Atlantic City in the winter of 1919 that John Jay Chapman first became anti-Semitic. "They are uncritical," he wrote to a friend after watching the boardwalk crowd of vacationing Jews. "Life is a simple matter for them: a bank account and a larder. . . . They strike me as an inferior race. . . . These people don't know anything. They have no religion, no customs except eating and drinking." [14]

Just before the First World War, resort establishments began to advertise their discriminatory policies in the newspapers. The situation became so embarrassing that New York State passed a law, in 1913, forbidding places of public accommodation to advertise their unwillingness to admit persons because of race, creed or color.

Although the high tide of formal resort society has declined in recent years, the rigid exclusion of Jews has largely continued. As Cleveland Amory has put it:

> Certain aspects of the narrowness of the old-line resort society have continued, not the least of which is the question of anti-Semitism. Although certain Jewish families, notably the Pulitzers, the Belmonts and the Goulds have played their part in resort Society—and Otto Kahn, Henry Seligman, Jules Bache and Frederick Lewison have cut sizeable figures—the general record of resort intolerance is an extraordinary one; it reached perhaps its lowest point when Palm Beach's Bath and Tennis Club sent out a letter asking members not to bring into the club guests of Jewish extraction. Among those who received this letter was Bernard Baruch, then a member of the club and a man whose father, Dr. Simon Baruch, pioneered the Saratoga Spa. Several of Baruch's friends advised him to make an issue of the affair; instead, he quietly resigned. "No one," he says today, "has had this thing practiced against him more than I have. But I don't let it bother me. I always remember what Bob Fitzsimmons said to me—he wanted to make me a champion, you know—'You've got to learn to take it before you can give it out.' " [15]

[13] E. Digby Baltzell, *Philadelphia Gentlemen*. Glencoe, Ill.: The Free Press, 1958, p. 285.

[14] Edmund Wilson, *A Piece of My Mind*. New York: Doubleday Anchor Books, 1958, p. 97.

[15] Cleveland Amory, *op. cit.*, p. 48.

THE SUBURBAN TREND, THE COUNTRY CLUB
AND THE COUNTRY DAY SCHOOL

The resort and the suburb are both a product of the same desire for homogeneity and a nostalgic yearning for the simplicities of small-town life. Just as, today, white families of diverse ethnic origins and newly won middle-class status are busily escaping from the increasingly Negro composition of our cities, so the Protestant upper class first began to flee the ugliness of the urban melting pot at the turn of the century. In Philadelphia, for instance, the majority of the Victorian gentry lived in the city, around fashionable Rittenhouse Square, as of 1890; by 1914, the majority had moved out to the suburbs along the Main Line or in Chestnut Hill. And this same pattern was followed in other cities.

In many ways Pierre Lorillard was the Victorian aristocrat's William Levitt. Just as Levittown is now the most famous example of a planned community symbolizing the post World War II suburban trend among the middle classes, so Tuxedo Park, New York, established on a site of some 600,000 acres inherited by Pierre Lorillard in 1886, was once the acme of upper-class suburban exclusiveness. According to Cleveland Amory, the Lorillards possessed a foolproof formula for business success which, in turn, was exactly reversed when they came to promoting upper-class exclusiveness. He lists their contrasting formulas as follows:

For Business Success:
    1) Find out what the public wants, then produce the best of its kind.
    2) Advertise the product so that everybody will know it is available.
    3) Distribute it everywhere so that everybody can get it.
    4) Keep making the product better so that more people will like it.

For Snob Success:
    1) Find out who the leaders of Society are and produce the best place for them to live in.
    2) Tell nobody else about it so that nobody else will know it's available.
    3) Keep it a private club so that other people, even if they do hear about it, can't get in.
    4) Keep the place exactly as it was in the beginning so that other people, even if they do hear about it and somehow do manage to get in, won't ever like it anyway.[16]

At Tuxedo Park, Lorillard produced almost a caricature of the Victorian millionaire's mania for exclusiveness. In less than a year, he surrounded seven thousand acres with an eight-foot fence, graded some thirty miles of road, built a complete sewage and water system, a gate house

[16] *Ibid.*, p. 83.

which looked like "a frontispiece of an English novel," a clubhouse staffed
with imported English servants, and "twenty-two casement dormered
English turreted cottages." On Memorial Day, 1886, special trains brought
seven hundred highly selected guests from New York to witness the
Park's opening.

Tuxedo was a complete triumph. The physical surroundings, the
architecture and the social organization were perfectly in tune with the
patrician mind of that day. In addition to the English cottages and the
clubhouse, there were "two blocks of stores, a score of stables, four lawn-
tennis courts, a bowling alley, a swimming tank, a boathouse, an icehouse,
a dam, a trout pond and a hatchery. . . . The members sported the club
badge which, designed to be worn as a pin, was an oakleaf of solid gold;
club governors had acorns attached to their oakleafs and later all Tuxedo-
ites were to wear ties, hatbands, socks, etc., in the club colors of green and
gold. . . . No one who was not a member of the club was allowed to buy
property."

Tuxedo Park was perhaps a somewhat exaggerated example of an
ideal. It certainly would have suggested the conformity of a Chinese commune to many aristocrats seeking real privacy (in the eighties at Nahant,
for example, Henry Cabot Lodge built a high fence between his place and
his brother-in-law's next door). The upper-class suburban trend as a
whole, nevertheless, was motivated by similar, if less rigid, desires for
homogeneity. Unlike Tuxedo, however, the country club and the country
day school, rather than the neighborhood *per se*, were the main fortresses
of exclusiveness. Thus the beginning of a real suburban trend can conveniently be dated from the founding of *The* Country Club, at Brookline,
Massachusetts, in 1882. In the next few decades similar clubs sprang up
like mushrooms and became a vital part of the American upper-class way
of life. Henry James, an expert on Society both here and abroad, found
them "a deeply significant American symbol" at the turn of the century,
and an English commentator on our mores wrote:

> There are also all over England clubs especially devoted to par-
> ticular objects, golf clubs, yacht clubs, and so forth. In these the
> members are drawn together by their interest in a common pursuit,
> and are forced into some kind of acquaintanceship. But these are
> very different in spirit and intention from the American country
> club. It exists as a kind of center of the social life of the neighbor-
> hood. Sport is encouraged by these clubs for the sake of general
> sociability. In England sociability is a by-product of an interest
> in sport.[17]

This English commentator was, of course, implying that the real function of the American country club was not sport but social exclusion. And
throughout the twentieth century the country club has remained, by and

[17] George Birmingham, "The American at Home and in His Club," in *America in
Perspective*, edited by Henry Steele Commager. New York: New American Library, 1947, p. 175.

large and with a minority of exceptions, rigidly exclusive of Jews. In response to this discrimination, elite Jews have formed clubs of their own.[18] When many wealthy German Jews in Philadelphia first moved to the suburbs, as we have seen, the famous merchant Ellis Gimbel and a group of his friends founded one of the first Jewish country clubs in the nation, in 1906.[19] After the Second War, when many Jewish families began to move out on the city's Main Line, another elite club, largely composed of East European Jews, was opened.

If the country club is the root of family exclusiveness, the suburban day school provides an isolated environment for the younger generation. Thus a necessary part of the suburban trend was the founding of such well-known schools as the Chestnut Hill Academy (1895) and Haverford School (1884) in two of Philadelphia's most exclusive suburbs; the Gilman School (1897) in a Baltimore suburb; the Browne and Nichols School (1883) in Cambridge, Massachusetts; the Morristown School (1898), the Tuxedo Park School (1900), and the Hackley School (1899) in Tarrytown, to take care of New York suburbia.[20] While not as rigidly exclusive as the country club as far as Jews are concerned, these schools have been, of course, overwhelmingly proper and Protestant down through the years. Few Jews sought admission before the Second War, and since then some form of quota system has often been applied (this is especially true of the suburban schools run by the Quakers in Philadelphia, largely because of their extremely liberal policies of ethnic, racial and religious tolerance).

The greatest monuments are often erected after an era's period of greatest achievement. Versailles was completed after the great age of Louis XIV, the finest Gothic cathedrals after the height of the Catholic synthesis, and the neoclassic plantation mansions after the South had begun to decline. As we shall see below, upper-class suburban homogeneity and exclusiveness are rapidly vanishing characteristics of our postwar era. And when the upper class reigned supreme in its suburban glory (1890–1940), discriminatory practices were genteel and subtle when compared, for example, with the methods of modern automobile magnates in Detroit. The grosser, Grosse Pointe methods, however, will serve to illustrate (in the manner of our discussion of Tuxedo Park) the anti-Semitic and anti-ethnic values of suburban upper class, especially at the height of its attempted escape from the motley urban melting pot. As a somewhat tragic, and slightly ludicrous, monument to the mind of a fading era, the following paragraphs from *Time* magazine must be reproduced in full:

> Detroit's oldest and richest suburban area is the five-community section east of the city collectively called Grosse Pointe (pop. 50,000). Set back from the winding, tree-shaded streets are fine,

[18] John Higham, *Social Discrimination Against Jews in America, 1830–1930*. Publication of the American Jewish Historical Society, Vol. XLVII, No. 1, September 1957, 13.

[19] Mr. Gimbel had only recently been "blackballed" by the Union League Club in the city.

[20] Porter Sargent, *Private Schools*. Boston: Porter Sargent, 1950.

solid colonial or brick mansions, occupied by some of Detroit's oldest (pre-automobile age) upper class, and by others who made the
grade in business and professional life. Grosse Pointe is representative of dozens of wealthy residential areas in the U. S. where privacy, unhurried tranquility, and unsullied property values are respected. But last week, Grosse Pointe was in the throes of a rude,
untranquil exposé of its methods of maintaining tranquility.

The trouble burst with the public revelation, during a court
squabble between one property owner and his neighbor, that the
Grosse Point Property Owners Association (973 families) and local real estate brokers had set up a rigid system for screening families who want to buy or build homes in Grosse Pointe. Unlike
similar communities, where neighborly solidarity is based on an un-
written gentleman's agreement, Grosse Pointe's screening system
is based on a written questionnaire, filled out by a private investigator on behalf of Grosse Point's "owner vigilantes."

The three-page questionnaire, scaled on the basis of "points"
(highest score: 100), grades would-be home owners on such qualities as descent, way of life (American?), occupation (Typical of
his own race?), swarthiness (Very? Medium? Slightly? Not at
all?), accent (Pronounced? Medium? Slight? None?), name (Typically American?), repute, education, dress (Neat or Slovenly? Conservative or Flashy?), status of occupation (sufficient eminence may
offset poor grades in other respects). Religion is not scored, but
weighted in the balance by a three-man Grosse Pointe screening
committee. All prospects are handicapped on an ethnic and racial
basis: Jews, for example, must score a minimum of 85 points,
Italians 75, Greeks 65, Poles 55; Negroes and Orientals do not
count.[21]

On reading this questionnaire, one could not fail to see that these
Detroit tycoons were, after all, only reflecting their training in the methodology of modern social science. One might prefer the less-amoral world of
William James, who once said: "In God's eyes the difference of social
position, of intellect, of culture, of cleanliness, of dress, which different
men exhibit . . . must be so small as to practically vanish." But in our age,
when the social scientist is deified, several generations of young Americans
have now been scientifically shown that men no longer seek status "in
God's eyes." Instead they are asked to read all sorts of status-ranking studies, often backed by authoritative "tests of significance," which show how
one is placed in society by one's cleanliness, dress, and drinking mores.
How, one may ask, can one expect these suburbanites, most of whom have
been educated in this modern tradition, not to use these methods for their
own convenience.

[21] *Time*, April 25, 1960. [Reprinted by permission from *Time*, The Weekly News-
Magazine; Copyright Time Inc.]

THE NEW ENGLAND BOARDING SCHOOL

The growth in importance of the New England boarding school as an upper-class institution coincided with the American plutocracy's search for ancestral, suburban and resort-rural roots. At the time of Groton's founding in 1884, for example, these schools were rapidly becoming a vital factor in the creation of a national upper class, with more or less homogeneous values and behavior patterns. In an ever more centralized, complex and mobile age, the sons of the new and old rich, from Boston and New York to Chicago and San Francisco, were educated together in the secluded halls of Groton and St. Paul's, Exeter and Andover, and some seventy other, approximately similar, schools. While Exeter and Andover were ancient institutions, having been founded in the eighteenth century, and while St. Paul's had been in existence since before the Civil War, the boarding school movement went through its period of most rapid growth in the course of the half century after 1880. Exeter's enrollment increased from some 200 boys in 1880, to over 400 by 1905. The enrollment reached 600 for the first time in 1920, rose to 700 in the 1930's, and has remained below 800 ever since. St. Paul's went through its period of most rapid growth in the two decades before 1900 (the school graduated about 45 boys per year in the 1870's and rose to 100 per year by 1900, where it has remained ever since).

It is interesting in connection with the growth of a national upper class that the founding of many prominent schools coincided with the "trust-founding" and "trust-busting" era. Thus the following schools were founded within a decade of the formation of the United States Steel Corporation, in 1901:

> The Taft School in Watertown, Connecticut, was founded by Horace Dutton Taft, a brother of President Taft, in 1890; the Hotchkiss School, Lakeville, Connecticut, was founded and endowed by Maria Hotchkiss, widow of the inventor of the famous machine-gun, in 1892; St. George's School, Newport, Rhode Island, which has a million-dollar Gothic chapel built by John Nicholas Brown, was founded in 1896; in the same year, Choate School, whose benefactors and friends include such prominent businessmen as Andrew Mellon and Owen D. Young, was founded by Judge William G. Choate, at Wallingford, Connecticut; while the elder Morgan was forming his steel company in New York and Pittsburgh in 1901, seven Proper Bostonians, including Francis Lowell, W. Cameron Forbes; and Henry Lee Higginson, were founding Middlesex School, near Concord, Massachusetts; Deerfield, which had been a local academy since 1797, was reorganized as a modern boarding school by its great headmaster, Frank L. Boydon, in 1902; and finally, Father Sill of the Order of the Holy Cross, founded Kent School in 1906.[22]

22 E. Digby Baltzell, *op. cit.*, p. 302.

While the vast majority of the students at these schools were old-stock Protestants throughout the first part of the twentieth century at least, it would be inaccurate to suppose that the schools' admission policies rigidly excluded Catholics or even Jews. Few Catholics and fewer Jews applied (Henry Morgenthau attended Exeter. As he never referred to the fact, even in his *Who's Who* biography, he probably had a pretty lonely time there). As a matter of historical fact, these schools were largely preoccupied, during the first three decades of this century, with assimilating the sons of America's newly rich Protestant tycoons, many of whom were somewhat spoiled in the style of the late William Randolph Hearst, who had been asked to leave St. Paul's.

On the whole . . . , these schools have continued to assimilate the sons of the newly rich down through the years. John F. Kennedy, for example, was graduated from Choate School in the thirties, after spending a year at Canterbury. In this connection, it was a measure of the increasingly affluent status of American Catholics that the nation's two leading Catholic boarding schools, Portsmouth Priory and Canterbury, were founded in 1926 and 1915 respectively.

THE COLLEGE CAMPUS IN THE GILDED AGE: GOLD COAST AND SLUM

The excluding mania of the Gilded Age was of course reflected on the campuses of the nation, especially in the older colleges in the East. In his book, *Academic Procession,* Ernest Earnest begins his chapter entitled "The Golden Age and the Gilded Cage" as follows:

> It is ironic that the most fruitful period in American higher education sowed the seeds of three of the greatest evils: commercialized athletics, domination by the business community, and a caste system symbolized by the Gold Coast. . . . A smaller percentage of students came to prepare for the ministry, law, and teaching; they came to prepare for entrance into the business community, especially that part of it concerned with big business and finance. And it was the sons of big business, finance, and corporation law who dominated the life of the campus in the older Eastern colleges. To an amazing degree the pattern set by Harvard, Yale and Princeton after 1880 became that of colleges all over the country. The clubs, the social organization, the athletics—even the clothes and the slang—of "the big three" were copied by college youth throughout the nation. In its totality the system which flowered between 1880 and World War I reflected the ideals of the social class which dominated the period.[23]

---

[23] Ernest Earnest, *Academic Procession.* New York: Bobbs-Merrill Company, Inc., 1953.

It is indeed appropriate that Yale's William Graham Sumner added the term "mores" to the sociological jargon, for the snobbish mass mores of the campuses of the Gilded Age were nowhere more binding than at New Haven. In the nineties, Yale became the first football factory and led the national trend toward anti-intellectualism and social snobbishness. Between 1883 and 1901, Yale plowed through nine undefeated seasons, piled up seven hundred points to its opponents' zero in the famous season of 1888, and produced Walter Camp, who picked the first All-American eleven and who produced Amos Alonzo Stagg, who, in turn, taught Knute Rockne everything he knew about football. By the turn of the century, "We toil not, neither do we agitate, but we play football" became the campus slogan. And cheating and the use of purchased papers almost became the rule among the golden boys of Yale, most of whom lived in "The Hutch," an expensive privately owned dormitory where the swells patronized private tailors, ruined expensive suits in pranks, sprees and rioting, ordered fine cigars by the hundred-lot, and looked down on those poorer boys who had gone to public high schools. The Yale Class Book of 1900, appropriately enough, published the answer to the following question: Have you ever used a trot? Yes: 264, No: 15. At the same time, in a survey covering three floors of a dormitory, it was found that not a single student wrote his own themes. They bought them, of course. After all, this sort of menial labor was only for the "drips," "grinds," "fruits," "meatballs," and "black men" of minority ethnic origins and a public school education. But at least one gilded son was somewhat horrified at the mores of Old Eli in those good old days before mass democracy had polluted gentlemenly education. A member of the class of 1879, this young gentleman asked an instructor in history to recommend some outside reading. The reply was "Young man, if you think you came to Yale with the idea of reading you will find out your mistake very soon." [24]

This anti-intellectual crowd of leading Yale men was composed primarily of boarding school graduates who began to dominate campus life at this time. Owen Johnson, graduate of Lawrenceville and Yale (1900), wrote about this generation in his best seller, *Stover at Yale*.[25] Stover soon learned that the way to success at Yale meant following the mores established by the cliques from Andover, Exeter, Hotchkiss, Groton and St. Paul's: "We've got a corking lot in the house—Best of the Andover crowd." Even in the famous senior societies, caste replaced the traditional aristocracy of merit. Thus a committee headed by Professor Irving Fisher found that, whereas twenty-six of the thirty-four class valedictorians had been tapped by the senior societies between 1861 and 1894, after 1893 not a single one had been considered.[26]

By the turn of the century, the College of New Jersey which had only recently changed its name to Princeton was far more homogeneously upper class than Yale. "The Christian tradition, the exclusiveness of the

24 *Ibid.*, p. 232.
25 *Ibid.*, p. 208.
26 *Ibid.*, p. 230.

upper-class clubs, and the prejudices of the students," wrote Edwin E. Slosson in *Great American Universities* in 1910, "kept away many Jews, although not all—there are eleven in the Freshman class. Anti-Semitic feeling seemed to me to be more dominant at Princeton than at any of the other universities I visited. 'If the Jews once get in,' I was told, 'they would ruin Princeton as they have Columbia and Pennsylvania.' " [27]

Football mania and the snobberies fostered by the eating-club system gradually dominated campus life at Princeton. Thus in 1906, Woodrow Wilson, convinced that the side shows were swallowing up the circus, made his famous report to the trustees on the need for abolishing the clubs. Although many misunderstood his purpose at the time, Wilson actually desired to make Princeton an even more homogeneous body of gentlemen-scholars. His preceptorial and quadrangle plans envisioned a series of small and intimate groups of students and faculty members pursuing knowledge without the disruptive class divisions fostered by the existing club system. Wilson was defeated in his drive for reform (partly because of his tactlessness) and was eventually banished to the White House, where he would be less of a threat to the system so dear to the hearts of many powerful trustees.

One should not dismiss Princeton's idea of homogeneity without mentioning one of its real and extremely important advantages. Princeton is one of the few American universities where an honor system is still in force, and presumably works. In this connection, Edwin E. Slosson's observations on the system as it worked in 1910 should be quoted in full:

> At Harvard I saw a crowd of students going into a large hall, and following them in, I found I could not get out, that no one was allowed to leave the examination room for twenty minutes. The students were insulated, the carefully protected papers distributed, and guards walked up and down the aisles with their eyes rolling like the search lights of a steamer in a fog. Nothing like this at Princeton; the students are on their honor not to cheat, and they do not, or but rarely. Each entering class is instructed by the Seniors into the Princeton code of honor, which requires any student seeing another receiving or giving assistance on examination to report him for a trial by his peers of the student body. . . . I do not think the plan would be practicable in the long run with a very large and heterogeneous collection of students. It is probable that Princeton will lose this with some other fine features of its student life as the university grows and becomes more cosmopolitan. The semi-monastic seclusion of the country village cannot be long maintained.[28]

In contrast to Princeton, and even Yale, Harvard has always been guided by the ideal of diversity. A large and heterogeneous student body,

[27] Edwin E. Slosson, *Great American Universities*. New York: The Macmillan Company, 1910, p. 105.
[28] *Ibid.*, p. 106.

however, is always in danger of developing class divisions. Like his friend Woodrow Wilson, A. Lawrence Lowell was disturbed by this trend at Harvard at the turn of the century. In a letter to President Eliot, written in 1902, he mentioned the "tendency of wealthy students to live in private dormitories outside the yard" and the "great danger of a snobbish separation of the students on lines of wealth." [29] In a committee report of the same year, he noted how one of the finest dormitories was becoming known as "Little Jerusalem" because of the fact that some Jews lived there.

Samuel Eliot Morison, in his history of Harvard, shows how the college gradually became two worlds—the "Yard" and the "Gold Coast"—as Boston society, the private schools, the club system and the private dormitories took over social life at the turn of the century.[30] "In the eighties," he writes, "when the supply of eligible young men in Boston was decreased by the westward movement, the Boston mammas suddenly became aware that Harvard contained many appetizing young gentlemen from New York, Philadelphia, and elsewhere. One met them in the summer at Newport, Beverly, or Bar Harbor; naturally one invited them to Mr. Papanti's or Mr. Foster's 'Friday Evenings' when they entered College, to the 'Saturday Evening Sociables' sophomore year, and to coming-out balls thereafter." [31] These favored men were, at the same time, living along Mount Auburn Street in privately run and often expensive halls, and eating at the few final clubs which only took in some 10 to 15 per cent of each class. Closely integrated with the clubs and Boston Society were the private preparatory schools. Until about 1870, according to Morison, Boston Latin School graduates still had a privileged position at Harvard, but "during the period 1870–90 the proportion of freshmen entering from public high schools fell from 38 to 23 per cent." About 1890 the Episcopal Church schools and a few others took over. "Since 1890 it has been almost necessary for a Harvard student with social ambition to enter from the 'right' sort of school and be popular there, to room on the 'Gold Coast' and be accepted by Boston society his freshman year, in order to be on the right side of the social chasm . . . conversely, a lad of Mayflower or Porcellian ancestry who entered from a high school was as much 'out of it' as a ghetto Jew." [32]

During most of Harvard's history, according to Morison, a solid core of middle-class New Englanders had been able to absorb most of the students into a cohesive college life which was dominated by a basic curriculum taken by all students. The increasing size of the classes (100 in the 1860's to over 600 by the time Franklin Roosevelt graduated in 1904), the elective system which sent men off to specialize in all directions, and the increasing ethnic heterogeneity of the student body, paved the way for exclusiveness and stratification. By 1893, for example, there were enough Irish Catholics in the Yard to support the St. Paul's Catholic Club, which

[29] Ernest Earnest, *op. cit.*, p. 216.
[30] Samuel Eliot Morison, *Three Centuries of Harvard, 1636–1936*. Cambridge, Mass.: Harvard University Press, 1937.
[31] *Ibid.*, p. 416.
[32] *Ibid.*, p. 422.

acquired Newman House in 1912. The situation was similar with the Jews. "The first German Jews who came were easily absorbed into the social pattern; but at the turn of the century the bright Russian and Polish lads from the Boston public schools began to arrive. There were enough of them in 1906 to form the Menorah Society, and in another fifteen years Harvard had her 'Jewish problem.' "[33]

The "Jewish problem" at Harvard will be discussed below. Here it is enough to emphasize the fact that it grew out of the general development of caste in America at the turn of the century. And this new type of caste system was supported by all kinds of associations, from the suburban country club to the fraternities and clubs on the campuses of the nation. Not only were two worlds now firmly established at Harvard and Yale and to a lesser extent at Princeton; at other less influential state universities and small colleges, fraternities dominated campus life.

Although fraternities grew up on the American campus before the Civil War, they expanded tremendously in the postwar period. By the late 1880's, for instance, the five hundred undergraduates at the University of Wisconsin were stratified by a fraternity system which included no less than thirteen houses.[34] As class consciousness increased, campus mores of course became more rigidly anti-Semitic and often anti-Catholic. Bernard Baruch, who entered the College of the City of New York in 1884 (as he was only fourteen at the time, his mother would not let him go away to Yale, which was his preference), felt the full weight of campus anti-Semitism. Although he was extremely popular among the small group of less than four hundred undergraduates, and although he was elected president of the class in his senior year, young Baruch was never taken into a fraternity at C.C.N.Y. "The Greek-letter societies or fraternities," he wrote years later in his autobiography, "played an important part at the college. Although many Jews made their mark at the college, the line was drawn against them by these societies. Each year my name would be proposed and a row would ensue over my nomination, but I never was elected. It may be worth noting, particularly for those who regard the South as less tolerant than the North, that my brother Herman was readily admitted to a fraternity while he attended the University of Virginia." [35] In response to the "Anglo-Saxon-Only" mores which accompanied the fraternity boom in the eighties and nineties, the first Jewish fraternity in America was founded at Columbia, in 1898.

The campus mores were, of course, modeled after the adult world which the students in the Gilded Age were preparing to face. For the large corporations, banks and powerful law firms—in the big-city centers of national power—increasingly began to select their future leaders, not on the basis of ability alone, but largely on the basis of their fashionable university and club or fraternity affiliations. "The graduate of a small college or a Western university," writes Ernest Earnest, "might aspire to a judge-

[33] *Ibid.*, p. 417.
[34] Ernest Earnest, *op. cit.*, p. 207.
[35] Bernard M. Baruch, *Baruch: My Own Story.* New York: Pocket Books, Inc., 1958, p. 54.

ship or bank presidency in the smaller cities and towns; he might get to Congress, become a physician or college professor. Particularly west of the Alleghenies he might become a governor or senator. But he was unlikely to be taken into the inner social and financial circles of Boston, New York or Philadelphia." [36] In the first half of the twentieth century, five of our eight Presidents were graduates of Harvard, Yale, Princeton and Amherst. A sixth came from Stanford, "the Western Harvard," where the social system most resembled that in the East.

THE METROPOLITAN MEN'S CLUB:
STRONGHOLD OF PATRICIAN POWER

When the gilded youths at Harvard, Yale and Princeton finally left the protected world of the "Gold Coast" to seek their fortunes in the Wall streets and executive suites of the nation, they usually joined one or another exclusive men's club. Here they dined with others of their kind, helped each other to secure jobs and promotions, and made friends with influential older members who might some day be of help to them in their paths to the top. Proper club affiliation was, after all, the final and most important stage in an exclusive socializing process. As a character in a novel about Harvard, published in 1901, put it: "Bertie knew who his classmates in college were going to be at the age of five. They're the same chaps he's been going to school with and to kid dancing classes . . . it's part of the routine. After they get out of college they'll all go abroad for a few months in groups of three or four, and when they get back they'll be taken into the same club (their names will have been on the waiting list some twenty-odd years) . . . and see one another every day for the rest of their lives." [37] But, by the century's turn, the metropolitan club was gradually becoming more than a congenial gathering-place for similarly bred gentlemen.

British and American gentlemen, especially after the urban bourgeoisie replaced the provincial aristocracy, soon realized that the club was an ideal instrument for the gentlemanly control of social, political and economic power. For generations in England, top decisions in the City and at Whitehall have often been made along Pall Mall, where conservatives gathered at the Carlton and liberals at the Reform. But perhaps the best illustration of the role of the club in the making of gentlemen, and its use as an instrument of power, was a "gentlemanly agreement" which was made in the late nineteenth century at the frontiers of empire. And it is indeed symbolic and prophetic that it should have been made in racialist South Africa by the great Cecil Rhodes, that most rabid of racialists who dreamed of forming a Nordic secret society, organized like Loyola's, and devoted to world domination. The club served Rhodes well on his way to wealth.[38]

[36] Ernest Earnest, *op. cit.*, p. 218.

[37] *Ibid.*, p. 217.

[38] See Hannah Arendt, *The Origins of Totalitarianism*. New York: Harcourt, Brace and Company, 1951, p. 203. And S. Gertude Millin, *Cecil Rhodes*. London: Harper & Brothers, 1933, pp. 99–100.

The exploitation of Africa became a full-fledged imperialist enterprise only after Cecil Rhodes dispossessed the Jews. Rhodes' most important competitor in the fight for control of the Kimberley diamond mines was Barney Barnato, son of a Whitechapel shopkeeper, who was possessed by a passionate desire to make his pile and, above all, to become a gentleman. Both Rhodes and Barnato were eighteen years of age when they arrived in Kimberley in the early seventies. By 1885 Rhodes was worth fifty thousand pounds a year, but Barnato was richer. At that time Rhodes began his "subtle" and persistent dealings with Barnato in order to gain control of de Beers. Nearly every day he had him to lunch or dinner at the "unattainable," at least for Barnato, Kimberley Club (he even persuaded the club to alter its rules which limited the entertainment of nonmembers to once-a-month). At last, Barnato agreed to sell out to Rhodes for a fabulous fortune, membership in the Kimberley Club, and a secure place among the gentlemanly imperialists. While Rhodes had perhaps used his club and his race with an ungentlemanly lack of subtlety, "no American trust, no trust in the world, had such power over any commodity as Rhodes now had over diamonds." But in the end, his dream that "between two and three thousand Nordic gentlemen in the prime of life and mathematically selected" should run the world became the very respectable Rhodes Scholarship Association, which supported selected members of all "Nordic Races," such as Germans, Scandinavians and Americans, during a brief stay in the civilizing atmosphere of Oxford University (the "Nordic" criterion for selection has since been abandoned). In the meantime, his friend Barney Barnato, soon after realizing his dream of becoming both a millionaire and a gentleman, drowned himself in the depths of the sea.

Many such dreams of corporate and financial empire-building have been consummated within the halls of America's more exclusive clubs. The greatest financial imperialist of them all, J. Pierpont Morgan, belonged to no less than nineteen clubs in this country and along Pall Mall. One of his dreams was realized on the night of December 12, 1900, in the course of a private dinner at the University Club in New York. Carnegie's man, Charles M. Schwab, was the guest of honor and the steel trust was planned that night.

In the 1900's the metropolitan club became far more important than the country club, the private school and college, or the exclusive neighborhood as the crucial variable in the recruitment of America's new corporate aristocracy. Family position and prestige, built up as a result of several generations of leadership and service in some provincial city or town, were gradually replaced by an aristocracy by ballot, in the hierarchy of metropolitan clubdom. In New York, for example, this process can be illustrated by the club affiliations of successive generations of Rockefellers: John D. Rockefeller belonged to the Union League; John D., Jr., to the University Club; and John D. III to the Knickerbocker. Thus is a business aristocracy recruited.

And this associational, rather than familistic, process was certainly democratic, except for one thing. That is the fact that, almost without exception, every club in America now developed a castelike policy toward the Jews. They were excluded, as a people or race, regardless of their per-

sonal qualities such as education, taste or manners. It is important, moreover, to stress the fact that this caste line was only drawn at the end of the
nineteenth century, when, as we have seen, the members of the upper class
were setting themselves apart in other ways. Joseph Seligman's experience
at Saratoga Springs was part of a general trend which came to a head again
when Jesse Seligman, one of the founders of New York's Union League,
resigned from the club in 1893, when his son was blackballed because he
was a Jew. Apparently this sort of anti-Semitism was not yet a norm when
the club was founded during the Civil War.

Nor was it the norm among the more exclusive clubs in other cities.
The Philadelphia Club, the oldest and one of the most patrician in America,
was founded in 1834, but did not adhere to any anti-Semitic policy until
late in the century. During the Civil War, for instance, Joseph Gratz, of
an old German-Jewish family and a leader in his synagogue, was president
of the club. The membership also included representatives of several other
prominent families of Jewish origin. Yet no other member of the Gratz
family has been taken into the Philadelphia Club since the nineties, a period
when countless embarrassing incidents all over America paralleled the
Seligman incident at the Union League.[39] The University Club of Cincinnati finally broke up, in 1896, over the admission of a prominent member
of the Jewish community. Elsewhere, prominent, cultivated and powerful
Jews were asked to resign, or were forced to do so by their sense of pride,
because of incidents involving their families or friends who were refused
membership solely because of their Jewish origins. Gentlemanly anti-
Semitism even invaded the aristocratic South. As late as the 1870's one of
the more fashionable men's clubs in Richmond, the Westmoreland, had
members as well as an elected president of Jewish origins. But today all the
top clubs in the city follow a policy of rigid exclusiveness as far as Jews
are concerned. This is the case even though the elite Jewish community in
Richmond, as in Philadelphia, has always been a stable one with a solid core
of old families whose members exhibit none of the aggressive, *parvenu*
traits given as a reason for the anti-Semitic policies of clubs in New York,
Chicago or Los Angeles.

Yet the inclusion of cultivated Jews within the halls of the Philadelphia or Westmoreland clubs in an earlier day was characteristic of a
provincial and familistic age when the men's club was really social, and
membership was based on congeniality rather than, as it has increasingly
become, on an organized effort to retain social power within a castelike
social stratum. George Apley, whose values were the product of a rapidly
departing era, threatened to resign from his beloved Boston Club when he
thought it was being used, somewhat in the style of Cecil Rhodes, as an
agency for the consolidation of business power. At a time when his club-
mates Moore and Field were apparently violating his gentlemanly code in
seeking the admission of their business associate Ransome, Apley wrote the
admissions committee as follows:

[39] As a matter of "subtle" fact, there were no "Jewish" members of the Gratz family
left in the city by this time.

> I wish to make it clear that it is not because of Ransome personally that I move to oppose him.
>
> Rather, I move to oppose the motive which actuates Messrs. Moore and Field in putting this man up for membership. They are not doing so because of family connections, nor because of disinterested friendship, but rather because of business reasons. It is, perhaps, too well known for me to mention it that Mr. Ransome has been instrumental in bringing a very large amount of New York business to the banking house of Moore and Fields. This I do not think is reason enough to admit Mr. Ransome to the Province Club, a club which exists for social and not for business purposes.[40]

Today many other clubs like Apley's Province, but unlike Pittsburgh's Duquesne, are fighting the intrusion of business affairs into a club life supposedly devoted to the purely social life among gentlemen. "A year or two ago," wrote Osborn Elliott in 1959, "members of San Francisco's sedate Pacific Union Club (known affectionately as the P.U.) received notices advising them that briefcases should not be opened, nor business papers displayed, within the confines of the old club building atop Nob Hill." [41] At about the same time, patrician New Yorkers were shocked at a *Fortune* article which reported that "at the Metropolitan or the Union League or the University . . . you might do a $10,000 deal, but you'd use the Knickerbocker or the Union or the Racquet for $100,000, and then for $1 million you'd have to move on to the Brook or the Links." [42]

In this chapter I have shown how a series of newly created upper-class institutions produced an associationally insulated national upper class in metropolitan America. I have stressed their rise in a particular time in our history and attempted to show how they were part of a more general status, economic and urban revolution which, in turn, was reflected in the Populist and Progressive movements. All this is important as a background for understanding the present situation, primarily because it shows that upper-class nativism in general and anti-Semitism in particular were a product of a particular cultural epoch and, more important, had not always been characteristic of polite society to anywhere near the same extent. This being the case, it may well be true, on the other hand, that new social and cultural situations may teach new duties and produce new upper-class mores and values. As a measure of the success of these caste-creating associations, the following remarks made by the late H. G. Wells after a visit to this country soon after the turn of the century are interesting.

> In the lower levels of the American community there pours perpetually a vast torrent of strangers, speaking alien tongues, inspired by alien traditions, for the most part illiterate peasants and working-people. They come in at the bottom: that must be insisted

[40] John P. Marquand, *The Late George Apley*. New York: The Modern Library, 1940, p. 189.
[41] Osborn Elliott, *Men at the Top*. New York: Harper & Brothers, 1959, p. 163.
[42] *Ibid.*, p. 164.

upon. . . . The older American population is being floated up on the top of this influx, a sterile aristocracy above a racially different and astonishingly fecund proletariat. . . .

Yet there are moments in which I could have imagined there were no immigrants at all. All the time, except for one distinctive evening, I seem to have been talking to English-speaking men, now and then, but less frequently, to an Americanized German. In the clubs there are no immigrants. There are not even Jews, as there are in London clubs. One goes about the wide streets of Boston, one meets all sorts of Boston people, one visits the State-House; it's all the authentic English-speaking America. Fifth Avenue, too, is America without a touch of foreign-born; and Washington. You go a hundred yards south of the pretty Boston Common, and, behold! you are in a polyglot slum! You go a block or so east of Fifth Avenue and you are in a vaster, more Yiddish Whitechapel.[43]

At this point, it should be emphasized that it was (and still is) primarily the patrician without power, the clubmen and resorters and the functionless genteel who, as Edith Wharton wrote, "fall back on sport and culture." It was these gentlemen with time on their hands who took the lead in creating the "anti-everything" world which Henry Adams called "Society." So often, for example, it was the men of inherited means, many of them bachelors like Madison Grant, who served on club admission committees, led the dancing assemblies and had their summers free to run the yacht, tennis and bathing clubs at Newport or Bar Harbor. And these leisurely patricians were, in turn, supported by the new men, and especially their socially ambitious wives, who had just made their fortunes and were seeking social security for their children. In all status revolutions, indeed, resentment festers with the greatest intensity among the new rich, the new poor, and the functionless genteel. And these gentlemen of resentment responded to the status revolution at the turn of the century by successfully creating, as H. G. Wells so clearly saw, two worlds: the patrician and Protestant rich, and the rest.

[43] H. G. Wells, *The Future in America*. New York: Harper & Brothers, 1906, p. 134.

Suggestions for Further Reading

Few general works try to cover this period from the perspective of everyday life. One popular and entertaining work that attempts this view is J. C. Furnas, *The Americans: A Social History of the United States, 1587–1914* * (New York, 1969), available in a two-volume paperback edition. Other works that present some coverage of everyday life during the Gilded Age are Ray Ginger, *Age of Excess: The United States from 1877–1914* * (New York, 1965); Henry F. May, *Protestant Churches and Industrial America* * (New York, 1949); and Thomas Cochran and William Miller, *The Age of Enterprise: A Social History of Industrial America* * (New York, 1961). For a view of the closing decade, see Larzer Ziff, *The American 1890's: Life and Times of a Lost Generation* * (New York, 1966). Tamara Hareven has edited a useful collection of essays in *Anonymous Americans: Explorations in Nineteenth Century Social History* * (Englewood Cliffs, N.J., 1971). Fictional treatments of the period that are revealing are Mark Twain and Charles Warner, *The Gilded Age* * (New York, 1874), and two works by William Dean Howells, *The Rise of Silas Lapham* * (Boston, 1884) and *The Hazard of New Fortunes* * (New York, 1889).

For material on everyday life on the Middle Border and Great Plains, see Robert Dykstra, *The Cattle Towns* * (New York, 1968); Merle Curti, *The Making of an American Community: A Case Study of Democracy in a Frontier County* * (Stanford, 1959); and Everett Dick, *The Sod-House Frontier, 1854–1890: A Social History of the Northern Plains from the Creation of Kansas and Nebraska to the Admission of the Dakotas* (New York, 1937). Developments in agriculture are covered in Fred A. Shannon, *The Farmer's Last Frontier, Agriculture, 1860–1897* * (New York, 1945). Ruth Miller Elson has analyzed the books used in the schools in *Guardians of Tradition: American Schoolbooks of the Nineteenth Century* * (Lincoln, Neb., 1964). The role of popular literature in shaping values throughout American history is explored in Russell Nye, *The Unembarrassed Muse: Popular Arts in America* * (New York, 1970). Fiction provides an excellent source of information about life in the Midwest. Classic works of American literature on this subject are Mark Twain, *Life on the Mississippi* * (Boston, 1883), *Huckleberry Finn* * (New York, 1885), *Tom Sawyer* * (Hartford, Conn., 1892); Sherwood Anderson, *Winesburg, Ohio* * (New York, 1919); Sinclair Lewis, *Main Street* * (New York, 1920); and, most sympathetically, Willa Cather, *My Antonia* * (Boston, 1926); and Hamlin Garland's autobiographical *A Son of the Middle Border* (New York, 1918).

* Available in paperback edition.

The standard history of medical practice in the United States, badly in need of updating, is Richard Shryock, *The Development of Modern Medicine* (Philadelphia, 1936; rev. and enl. ed., 1947). See also William G. Rothstein, *American Physicians in the Nineteenth Century* (Baltimore, 1972). In *The Physician and Sexuality in Victorian America** (Champaign, Ill., 1974), John S. Haller and Robin M. Haller have provided a lively and thorough study of medical attitudes and practice. Ben Barker-Benfield's *The Horrors of the Half-Known Life: Male Attitudes Toward Women and Sexuality in Nineteenth Century America** (New York, 1976) is a controversial attempt to explore a complex subject. For further studies of women and doctors, see Barbara Ehrenreich and Deirdre English, *Complaints and Disorders: The Sexual Politics of Sickness** (Old Westbury, N.Y., 1973), and the relevant essays in Lois Banner and Mary Hartman, eds., *Clio's Consciousness Raised** (New York, 1974). Two important new books dealing, at least peripherally, with this area are James C. Mohr, *Abortion in America: The Origins and Evolution of National Policy* (New York, 1978), and James Reed, *From Private Vice to Public Virtue: The Birth Control Movement and American Society Since 1830* (New York, 1978).

The revisionist works on slave culture include John Blassingame, *The Slave Community: Plantation Life in the Ante-Bellum South** (New York, 1972); Gerald Mullin, *Flight and Rebellion: Slave Resistance in Eighteenth Century Virginia** (New York, 1972); and Eugene Genovese, *Roll, Jordan, Roll** (New York, 1974). The best studies of modern urban black life are Ulf Hannerz, *Soulside** (New York, 1969); Elliot Liebow, *Tally's Corner** (Boston, 1967); and Kenneth Clark, *Dark Ghetto: Dilemmas of Social Power** (New York, 1965).

Important works on black life in the late nineteenth century are Herbert G. Gutman, *The Black Family in Slavery and Freedom, 1750–1825** (New York, 1976); Nell Irvin Painter, *Exodusters: Black Migration to Kansas After Reconstruction* (New York, 1977); and Howard N. Rabinowitz, *Race Relations in the Urban South, 1865–1890* (New York, 1978). A rich source for this period and the early twentieth century is *All God's Dangers: A Life of Nate Shaw** (New York, 1974), by Theodore Rosengarten.

For a study of the Philadelphia elite, see E. Digby Baltzell, *Philadelphia Gentleman: The Making of a National Upper Class** (Glencoe, Ill., 1958). Glimpses of the life-style of the wealthy are found in Stewart Holbrook, *The Age of the Moguls* (Garden City, N.Y., 1953), and Stephen Birmingham, *The Right People: A Portrait of America's Social Establishment* (Boston, 1968). A contemporary critical analysis is Thorstein Veblen, *The Theory of the Leisure Class** (New York, 1899), and a recent critique is C. Wright Mills, *The Power Elite** (New York, 1956). William G. Domhoff has probed the upper class of today in *The Higher Circles: The Governing Class in America** (New York, 1971) and

*The Bohemian Grove and Other Retreats: A Study in Ruling Class Cohesiveness** (New York, 1975). Popular treatments of non-Anglo-Saxon wealth are found in Stephen Birmingham, *Our Crowd: The Great Jewish Families of New York** (New York, 1967), *The Grandees: America's Sephardic Elite** (New York, 1971), and *Real Lace: America's Irish Rich** (New York, 1973). Higher education is scrutinized in Richard Hofstadter and Walter P. Metzger, *The Development of Academic Freedom in the United States** (New York, 1955), available in a two-volume paperback edition.

1900–1930
The Early Twentieth Century

The Family, Feminism, and Sex
at the Turn of the Century

DAVID M. KENNEDY

Although recent historical research has clearly demonstrated that the nuclear family structure (parents and children) has existed widely in England and the United States since at least the seventeenth century, changing social and economic conditions led the late Victorians to assume it was a product of their own times. They were led, then, to believe that the problems of family life were caused by the emergence of a new family structure rather than by the changing environment. The growth of the industrial city, the separation of home and workplace, the shift in the role of children from units of production to units of consumption all led middle-class Americans to change certain generally accepted standards of family life. Perhaps the most widely noted of these changes was the reduced birthrate. While immigrants were continuing to have large families, many old-stock Americans were limiting the size of their families to two or three children. The implication seemed clear, and Theodore Roosevelt pronounced the words for it—"race suicide." To Roosevelt and others like him, the traditional stock that had made this nation great was about to be overrun by the children of the foreign born.

What was not seen at the time is what since has been called the process of stratification diffusion—a process that made the birthrate a function of social mobility. As the immigrants began to move up the social scale, they sought the advantages of a small family for themselves and their offspring, and their birthrate dropped. For example, Russian Jewish immigrants had the largest birthrate among the immigrant groups in the early twentieth century, but, by 1970, their descendants had the lowest birthrate among American ethnic groups.

The changing life-style of the middle-class family led to a changed role for the women in these families. Or perhaps it was the other way around—the changing role of women led to a new family life-style. But to traditionalists at the time, the relationship was clear —the women's new attitude attacked the basic structure of the family and led not only to race suicide but also to an increase in the divorce rate.

One outcome of the changing role of middle-class women was the turn-of-the-century feminist movement, which is well known for its espousal of suffrage and equal opportunities in education and employment for women. Another, but less well known, development is only now being seriously studied—the changing viewpoint toward the erotic, or sex. It was evident around the turn of the century that more women, and men as well, were marrying for reasons of personal satisfaction, although few talked about the erotic dimension of their choice. Only with the advent of Freudian terminology and the writings of sex-

ologists such as Havelock Ellis did people begin to discuss openly the
role of sex in human relations.

In his book on the career of Margaret Sanger and the birth
control movement in the United States, David Kennedy, of Stanford
University, includes a chapter, reprinted here, that summarizes the
background of the movement. Kennedy, in placing Sanger's work in
perspective, briefly discusses many of the controversies referred to
above. Much of the opposition to the birth control movement couched
its objections in the language of "the nature of woman" and, in some
cases, religion. But, clearly, concern with the race-suicide notion was
paramount. The closing of the immigrant stream in the 1920s reduced somewhat the furor over race suicide.

The nineteenth-century American considered the family, as Henry James
put it, "the original germ-cell which lies at the base of all that we call
society." That view drew support from the findings of American social
scientists, who, in their Germanic search for the origins of all institutions,
repeatedly demonstrated the initial formation of society in the microcosm
of the family. And the sacredness of the idea of the family had more than
an evolutionary derivation. In a country plagued by the divisive effects of
civil war, territorial expansion, and the birth of modern industrialism, men
put a high premium on the forces working for order and cohesion. The
family, they thought, was such a force. Its significance, therefore, was
less personal than social. The happiness of its members was well and good,
but as James pointed out, "the true sanctity of marriage inheres at bottom
in its social uses: It is the sole nursery of the social sentiment in the human
bosom." [1] Since the family was both germ cell and nursery, any attempts
to tamper with it contradicted nature and threatened the entire moral
order. As a woman writer said in 1873: "Whatever tends to deteriorate
the marriage relation and consequently the home, tends to deteriorate the
whole machinery of life, whether social or political." [2]

By the beginning of the twentieth century, the very forces against
which the home had been deemed the most effective defense appeared to
many to be undermining the home itself. Critics blamed especially the
recrudescence of primitive individualism, as evidenced by growing divorce rates, for the destruction of the traditional family. Several observers

[1] Henry James, "Is Marriage Holy?" *Atlantic Monthly*, March 1870, p. 363.
[2] Abba Goold Woolson, *Woman in American Society* (Boston: Roberts Brothers, 1873), p. 82.

"The Nineteenth-Century Heritage: The Family, Feminism, and Sex" (Editor's title: "The Family, Feminism, and Sex at the Turn of the Century"). From *Birth Control in America: The Career of Margaret Sanger* by David M. Kennedy (New Haven: Yale University Press, 1970), pp. 36–69.

saw that ruinous spirit best typified in the dramas of Henrik Ibsen, whose philosophy was described as "bold and uncompromising selfishness." Many Americans agreed with the literary critic Chauncey Hawkins that in the face of such egotism, "the family, that institution which we have long regarded as the unit of civilization, the foundation of the state," could not long survive.[3]

The alarm had little substance. The nineteenth-century family, which the Victorians regarded as a contemporary embodiment of the primeval social unit, was in fact a relatively modern institution. As the French historian Phillipe Ariés has convincingly shown, the concept of the family did not emerge until the late Renaissance, and then only among the upper classes. The apparent disintegration of the family which the late Victorians decried in fact represented its adjustment to new living conditions brought about by urbanization and industrialization. But those processes by no means spelled the death of the family.[4]

As Americans moved increasingly to cities in the nineteenth century, old patterns of family life had to change. Separated in most instances from the protective and preceptive influences of kin groups and village culture, men and women newly arrived in American cities began family life without precedents and with only vague prospects. As the sociologist Arthur W. Calhoun commented, America was the first civilization that in any large way experimented with "placing the entire burden of securing the success of marriage and the family life upon the characters and capacities of two persons. . . . American marriage is a union of two people and not an alliance between two families." In that new atomistic union, marital partners took on new roles and marriage itself assumed new character and functions. On the farm, the family had been an integral producing unit. In the city, families no longer worked together. The factory or the office kept the father away from the home most of the day. The urban economy forced the housewife out of the agricultural producing unit and, by emphasizing pecuniary rewards, tended to devalue household labor. Moreover, industry itself usurped many of the functions the housewife had once been accustomed to performing. "The machine," wrote E. A. Ross, "has captured most of the domestic processes." Thus the urban home by the early twentieth century had lost nearly all its economic cogency.[5]

[3] Chauncey J. Hawkins, *Will the Home Survive? A Study of Tendencies in Modern Literature* (New York: Thomas Whittaker, 1907), pp. 7, 56.

[4] Philippe Ariés, *Centuries of Childhood* (New York: Alfred A. Knopf, 1962); Christopher Lasch, "Divorce and the Family in America," *Atlantic*, November 1966, pp. 57–61; see also William L. O'Neill, *Divorce in the Progressive Era* (New Haven: Yale University Press, 1967).

[5] Arthur W. Calhoun, *A Social History of the American Family*, vol. 3, *Since the Civil War* (Cleveland: Arthur H. Clark, 1919), p. 169; E. A. Ross, "The Significance of Increasing Divorce," *Century Magazine*, May 1909, p. 151; see also Robert W. Smuts, *Women and Work in America* (New York: Columbia University Press, 1959).

As industry deprived the family of many of its economic functions, the state took over many of its welfare functions by enacting laws creating compulsory education, maternal health programs, and juvenile court systems. Social critics from John Spargo to Theodore Roosevelt endorsed the Socialist idea of the state as an "over-parent" which should provide schools, housing, sanitation, and recreation in the crowded cities. "If this be Socialism," Roosevelt said, "make the most of it!" Thus with little dissent, the state substituted its services for the old self-sufficiency of the family.[6]

Paradoxically, many of the same critics who blamed "individualism" for the destruction of the Victorian family also observed a "new solidarity of the state" being built "at the expense of the old solidarity of the family." Somehow, the individualism that destroyed one institution was supposed to give birth to the collectivism that strengthened another.[7] The confusion reflected the Victorian failure to recognize the transformation of the family not as a collapse but as an adjustment. The family did not retreat before new social forces. Indeed, the late nineteenth century saw a continuation of the strengthening of the notion of the family, especially among the middle and upper classes. As Ariés has remarked, "the whole evolution of our contemporary manners is unintelligible if one neglects this astonishing growth of the concept of the family. It is not individualism which has triumphed, but the family."[8]

But in that triumph the family took on a new vital center. "The old economic framework of the family has largely fallen away," noted E. A. Ross in 1909, "leaving more of the strain on the personal tie." Ross did not mean that husbands and wives had never before loved each other or that personal relations had not always figured importantly in marriage. But when urban industrialism displaced economic partnership from the matrix of marriage, such factors as congeniality and affection assumed greater importance. "Essentially," said George Elliott Howard, a sociologist who wrote frequently on the divorce problem, "the family society is becoming a psychic fact." The family, in other words, had taken on increased, rather than diminished, emotional significance. Husbands now had to be more than mere providers. And wives, having lost the role of economic partner, had to assume several new ones. "In the old days," commented a woman in 1907, "a married woman was supposed to be a frump and a bore and a physical wreck. Now you are supposed to keep up intellectually, to look young and well and be fresh and bright and entertaining." Rising divorce rates signaled more than the ease of separa-

---

[6] John Spargo, *Socialism and Motherhood* (New York: B. W. Huebsch, 1914); Theodore Roosevelt, *The Foes of Our Own Household* (New York: George H. Doran, 1917), p. 183.

[7] George Elliott Howard, "Changed Ideals and Status of the Family and the Public Activities of Women," *Annals of the American Academy of Political and Social Science* 56 (November 1914): 29.

[8] Ariés, *Centuries of Childhood*, p. 406.

tion in a free and rich society. They also bespoke the difficulty of adjustment to the intensified emotional demands of family life.[9]

The new industrial economy also demanded a new work discipline
which denied emotion and encouraged exclusively cognitive behavior in
the interests of production. That compartmentalization of experience
made the home the exclusive arena for the play of emotion. And the
growth of the family's emotional exclusiveness made the home an increasingly private place. As the urban family became less self-sufficient, therefore, it simultaneously grew more committed to self-determination. Ariés
has shown that "in the 18th century, the family began to hold society at
a distance, to push it back beyond a steadily extending zone of private
life." Nineteenth-century industrialism quickened that development, and
by 1906 an American sociologist frankly acknowledged "the manifest
conflict of interests between the individual family and the community at
large." That conflict was most marked, the writer said, when the family
refused to produce enough children for the service of the state.[10]

A new attitude toward childhood, along with the development of
the family as a "psychic fact" and as a progressively more private institution, completed the list of characteristics that distinguished the modern
family. Again, as Ariés has demonstrated, "the concept of the family,
which thus emerges in the 16th and 17th centuries, is inseparable from
the concept of childhood." Before the sixteenth century, children were
considered "little adults," who were loved, to be sure, but whose primary
value to the producing family was economic. After that time, in line with
the general restructuring of the family, children took on a greater emotional value. Moreover, childhood came increasingly to be regarded as a
special age of life, and the child as a special being with his own distinctive
qualities. Foremost among those qualities was the child's capacity for
formation and development. When that quality was recognized, as Christopher Lasch has said, "child-rearing ceased to be simply one of many
activities and became the central concern—one is tempted to say the central obsession—of family life." The late nineteenth century made that
concern explicit, as in the novelist Margaret Deland's proclamation of
"the right of children *not* to be born." When parents, she said, "unable
to support a child in physical and moral and intellectual well-being, bring
such a child into the world . . . they are socially criminal." And when
Charlotte Perkins Gilman said in 1911 that the duty of the family was to
ensure children "an ever longer period of immaturity," by extending their
education as long as possible, she was acknowledging the new status of
the child not as an economic asset, but as an economic liability. In that
way the oft-noted shift from a producing to a consuming psychology
affected even the affairs of the family. Parents no longer produced chil-

[9] Ross, "Increasing Divorce," p. 151; Howard, "Changed Ideals," p. 29; Lydia K.
Commander, *The American Idea* (New York: A. S. Barnes, 1907), p. 182.

[10] Ariés, *Centuries of Childhood*, p. 398; American Sociological Society, *Papers and
Proceedings* 1 (1906): 53. See also Kenneth Keniston, *The Uncommitted: Alienated
Youth in American Society* (New York: Harcourt, Brace and World, 1965), pp.
241–81.

dren in the greatest quantity possible. They had fewer children in order to provide each with a better quality of upbringing.[11]

The shrinking size of the American family—especially among the genteel classes—caused at least as much alarm at the turn of the century as did the growing divorce rate. Benjamin Franklin had predicted in 1755 that the abundance of the New World would cause the American people to double their numbers every twenty years. At that rate, there should have been nearly 130 million Americans by 1900; in fact, there were scarcely 76 million. In Franklin's day, families commonly had eight or ten children. By 1900, the average number of children per family was closer to three. The birthrate of American women had been falling steadily since at least 1820. While 1,000 mothers in 1800 had 1,300 children under five years of age, the same number of mothers in 1900 had fewer than 700 such children. The trend indicated, said Theodore Roosevelt, that the American people were committing "race suicide." With that utterance in 1903, Roosevelt minted the phrase which for the next forty years was a frequent rallying cry for the opponents of birth control.[12]

President Roosevelt, in his annual message to Congress in 1905, described the transformation of family life "as one of the greatest sociological phenomena of our time; it is a social question of the first importance, of far greater importance than any merely political or economic question can be." Yet much of Roosevelt's concern for the condition of the family proceeded from his political assumptions. In his view, the family should be the servant of the state; it should provide children to build national strength. Germany dominated Europe, Roosevelt wrote, because she had won "the warfare of the cradle . . . during the nineteenth century." If America aspired to ascendancy in world affairs, American parents must breed larger families.[13]

The race suicide alarm, however, fed more on ethnocentric fears than on nationalist ambition. Though Roosevelt complained because American population statistics did not keep pace with his jingoistic appetite, he considered the "worst evil" to be the greater infertility of "the old native American stock, especially in the North East," as compared with the immigrant population. In 1902 R. R. Kuczynski demonstrated what everyone had suspected for a long time—that the immigrant birthrate was 70 to 80 percent higher than the native birthrate. Worse, Kuczynski concluded, it was "probable that the native population cannot hold its own. It seems to be dying out." In a study a few years later, the United States Immigration Commission found that "the rate of childbearing on the part

---

11 Ariés, *Centuries of Childhood*, p. 353; Lasch, "Divorce and the Family," p. 59; Margaret Deland, "The Change in the Feminine Ideal," *Atlantic Monthly*, March 1910, p. 291; Charlotte Perkins Gilman, *The Man-Made World, or, Our Androcentric Culture* (New York: Charlton, 1911), p. 27.

12 *Historical Statistics of the United States* (Washington: Government Printing Office, 1961), pp. 23, 24, 180, 181; T. Roosevelt, *Foes*, p. 257.

13 *Messages and Papers of the Presidents* 16 (New York: Bureau of National Literature, n.d.): 6984; Theodore Roosevelt, "Race Decadence," *Outlook*, April 8, 1911, p. 765.

of women of foreign parentage is nearly twice as great as that of native American women." But significantly, the Immigration Commission reported another phenomenon: the average number of childern borne by the second generation immigrant woman "was invariably smaller than the average for the first generation." Clearly, then, the determinants of fertility were not solely ethnic; they apparently had a great deal to do with economic status and the amorphous notion of class.[14]

That perception added to ethnocentric fears the alarming prospect that not simply native Americans but in particular the upper classes, the highest products of evolution and natural selection, were failing to reproduce themselves. President Charles W. Eliot of Harvard confirmed the worst suspicions in 1902 when he reported that a typical group of Harvard graduates fell 28 percent short of replenishing its number. A later study revealed that only 75 percent of late nineteenth-century Harvard graduates married; of these, nearly a quarter had childless marriages, and the rest averaged scarcely two children per marriage. Yale graduates did little better. That was "gloomy enough," the report concluded, but it called the birthrate among college women "the most pathetic spectacle of all." In the average Wellesley class, for example, only one-half the graduates married, and those who did invariably had small families. A New York newspaper reporter in 1907 found only fifteen children in sixteen of the highest-rent residential blocks in New York. It seemed that the very class upon which many in the Progressive generation pinned their hopes for an orderly future was disappearing.[15]

Commentators cited a myriad of causes for the decline in the upper-class birthrate, ranging from the spread of venereal disease, to "physiological infertility" induced by "the high voltage of American civilization," to the inevitable consequences of spiritual degeneracy. But more disinterested observers recognized that the decline in the birthrate was voluntary. One writer noted that "outside our immigrant class, and a few native-born families scattered here and there, women have learned the art of preventing pregnancy."[16] Charles Knowlton's handbook of contraceptive techniques, *Fruits of Philosophy*, had only a small underground circulation in this country after its publication in 1832; but the declining birthrate indicated that the practices he described—probably vaginal douching in particular—were increasingly employed in certain social

[14] Theodore Roosevelt to Cecil Arthur Spring Rice, August 11, 1899, in *The Letters of Theodore Roosevelt*, Elting E. Morison, ed., 8 vols. (Cambridge: Harvard University Press, 1951–54), 2:1053; R. R. Kuczynski, "The Fecundity of the Native and Foreign Born Population in Massachusetts," *Quarterly Journal of Economics* 16 (1902): 141–86; U.S., Congress, Senate, *Report of the United States Immigration Commission*, 61st Cong., 2d sess. (Washington: Government Printing Office, 1911), 28:753, 749.

[15] *Annual Reports of the President and the Treasurer of Harvard College, 1901–02* (Cambridge: Harvard University, 1903), pp. 31–32; John C. Phillips, "A Study of the Birth-Rate in Harvard and Yale Graduates," *Harvard Graduates Magazine*, September, 1916, p. 25; Commander, *American Idea*, p. 198.

[16] Edward L. Thorndike, "The Decrease in the Size of American Families," *Popular Science Monthly* 63 (May 1903): 64–70.

classes. A doctor, as early as 1867, said that "there is scarcely a young lady in New England—and probably it is so throughout the land—whose marriage can be announced in the paper, without her being insulted within a week by receiving through the mail a printed circular, offering information and instrumentalities, and all needed facilities, by which the laws of heaven in regard to the increase of the human family may be thwarted." Anthony Comstock corroborated that statement in 1880 when he reported the confiscation, over the preceding seven years, of 64,094 "articles for immoral use, of rubber, etc.," and 700 pounds of "lead moulds for making Obscene Matter." Despite scanty official medical attention, by the late 1800s certain sections of the public were well supplied with contraceptive information and devices. There was "hardly a single middle-class family" among his clients, said a doctor in 1906, that did not expect him to implement their "desire to prevent conception." [17] As Lydia Commander said in 1907, among the upper classes some kind of contraceptive knowledge was "practically universal." [18]

But the availability of that knowledge did not in itself cause the general restriction in the size of native middle- and upper-class families. Many Americans manifested the modern consideration for the welfare of the child when they decided to limit their offspring to as many as could be "given the necessary education to fit them for the best in life." [19] But that idea, though pervasively "modern" in its concern for children, took firmest hold among the middle class; and in its emphasis on the "best in life" it reflected more than enlightened theories of child-rearing. It also revealed an increasing concern for social mobility and the development of a middle-class definition of an acceptable standard of living. The *Nation*, in 1903, noted the apparent paradox that in America, contrary to all Malthusian predictions, the population was beginning to shrink in the face of an increasing food supply. But the paradox was easily explained, said the *Nation*: Malthus "did not, perhaps, give sufficient weight to the fact that the means of subsistence is a relative term, varying from age to age, and having different meanings to different peoples." [20] Similarly, Lydia Commander argued that the instinct of reproduction was subordinate to the instinct of self-preservation, which had taken on a new meaning in America. "The full dinnerpail," she said, did not mark the limits of the American's ambition. "It is only the bare beginning of his needs." [21] An article in the *North American Review* in 1903, by "Pater-

17 Arthur W. Calhoun, *Social History of the American Family*, 3:228, 239; Anthony Comstock, *Frauds Exposed* (New York: J. Howard Brown, 1880), p. 435. Anthony Comstock, by his own account, also confiscated 202,679 "obscene pictures and photos," 4,185 "boxes of pills, powders, etc., used by abortionists," and 26 "obscene pictures, framed on walls of saloons"; see also E. A. Ross, "Western Civilization and the Birth Rate," American Sociological Society, *Papers and Proceedings* 1 (1907): 29–54; and Hawkins, *Will the Home Survive?* p. 12.

18 Commander, *American Idea*, pp. 89–92.

19 Hawkins, *Will the Home Survive?* p. 12.

20 "The Question of the Birth Rate," *Nation*, June 11, 1903, p. 469.

21 Commander, *American Idea*, p. 96.

familias," frankly stated that the modern family limited its size in order to enjoy a certain "style of living." The author's "social position" was "very dear" to him, he said, and it would be threatened by additional children. Furthermore, more children would make a household drudge of his wife. Therefore he intended to have no more. "I presume," he said, "there are those who will think that this is an ignoble statement. But it is not only true, but it is true of about every family of which I have any personal acquaintance." [22]

The article by Paterfamilias elicited extensive comment in 1903, and though few disputed the accuracy of its thesis about the motives behind family limitation, many saw in those motives, as Theodore Roosevelt put it, "frightful and fundamental immorality." What Paterfamilias had defended as dedication to his "style of living," Roosevelt called submission "to coldness, to selfishness, to love of ease, to shrinking from risk, to an utter and pitiful failure in sense of perspective." [23]

Many observers agreed with Roosevelt that a new and destructive slavishness to the self was strangling the American family, but they went beyond his criticism when they branded the feminist movement as the principal vehicle of that egotism. In the simultaneous rise of the emancipated woman and decline of the family, they saw the fulfillment of a dark prophecy. Herbert Spencer had proclaimed in the mid-nineteenth century the iron biological law of antagonism between "Individuation and Genesis." Every higher degree of evolution, he said, was followed by a "lower degree of race-multiplication." As the New Woman, therefore, evolved to a greater individualism and self-sufficiency, she lost her capacity for reproduction. Specifically, Spencer said, "the overtaxing of their brains" through too much mental effort had "a serious reaction on the physique" of women and resulted in a "diminution of reproductive power." Spencer thus lent the prestige of evolutionary science to the argument that the women's movement bore a heavy responsibility for the shrinking family. In fact, Spencer provided only one of many points of contact between the criticisms of the modern family and the criticisms of the New Woman. From the time in the late nineteenth century when the condition of the family became a topic of general public discussion, it was rarely mentioned apart from the "woman question." [24]

Edward Alsworth Ross ascribed both the liberation of women and the transformation of the family to a "transition process in social evolu-

---

[22] Paterfamilias, "'Race Suicide' and Common Sense," *North American Review* 176 (1903): 897. The phenomenon of lower fertility associated with social mobility and class standing was by no means peculiarly American. The French demographer Jacques Bertillon found that as the Frenchman advanced from "prolétaire" to "propriétaire," he limited the size of his family. Bertillon concluded that "l'aisance entrain la stérilité." *La Depopulation de la France* (Paris: Felix Alcan, 1911). See also J. A. Banks, *Prosperity and Parenthood* (London: Routledge and Kegan Paul, 1954).

[23] T. Roosevelt, "Race Decadence," p. 764.

[24] Herbert Spencer, *The Principles of Biology*, 2 vols. (New York: D. Appleton, 1898–99), 2:430, 512–13.

tion." At the heart of that process, said Ross, was a new sense of individuality which provided women with "a point of view of their own"
and replaced the patriarchal with the "democratic" family. Though the
process sometimes produced an "exaggerated self-will," Ross contended
that it was rare and not to be held responsible for divorce and smaller
families.[25]

But the individualism Ross thought salutary, conservative defenders
of the family continued to damn as rank selfishness. They especially indicted women. A symposium in the *North American Review* in 1889
blamed women's self-indulgent romanticism for the divorce rate. Twenty
years later Anna B. Rogers confidently explained "why American marriages fail": because women had become devoted to "the latter-day cult
of individualism; the worship of the brazen calf of Self." [26]

Feminists admitted their role in changing the family, but they had a
different explanation of their motives. In the feminists' view, the women's
movement was redressing an ancient historical grievance. Social scientists
such as Lewis Henry Morgan and Lester Ward, they said, had shown that
the original family was a matriarchal institution. Somewhere along the
line men had subverted that order and robbed women of their status and
independence. As Thorstein Veblen wrote, the masculine ideal of marriage was "in point of derivation, a predatory institution." It rested, said
Veblen, on the mechanisms of ownership, coercion, and control. More
than anything else, the feminists objected to the coercion to which they
said all married women were expected to submit. In that protest they but
shared a general antipathy to authority deeply seated in American traditions. Henry James, in 1870, touched on that tradition when he said
that marriage came into "dishonor" when it was not "*freely* honored, or
honored exclusively for its own sake." Prevailing opinion, on the other
hand, regarded marriage as "properly honored when it is enforced by
some external sanction." That element of force, said James, had made
marriage "the hotbed of fraud, adultery, and cruelty." It could only become "holy" when it rested not on constraint but on the sentiments of
its members.[27]

The acrimony of the debate on the transformation of the family
and the role of women in that process often obscured the common assumptions from which both sides argued. Conservatives wished to preserve the sanctity of the home, while reformers wanted to restore it to an
ancient dignity. Practically everyone agreed on the paramount importance of the family in human life. Both advocates and adversaries of easier
divorce invoked the sacredness of the marital relation in support of their

25 Ross, "Significance of Increasing Divorce," pp. 151–52.
26 "Are Women to Blame?" *North American Review* 148 (1889): 622–42; Anna B.
   Rogers, *Why American Marriages Fail* (Boston: Houghton Mifflin, 1909), p. 16.
27 Lewis Henry Morgan, *Ancient Society* (Cambridge: Harvard University Press,
   Belknap Press, 1964; first published, 1877); Lester Ward, *Pure Sociology* (New
   York: Macmillan, 1914), Ch. 14; Thorstein Veblen, "The Barbarian Status of
   Women," *American Journal of Sociology* 4 (1899): 503–14; Henry James, letter
   to the editor, *Nation*, June 9, 1870, p. 366.

respective cases. Partisans of women's suffrage and education justified their causes with reference to the improvement of the home fully as often as their opponents warned of its destruction. There were really no radical opinions about the family. Even the Socialist critics of marriage wanted only those changes that would "make it possible for every mother to devote herself to the care of her children." [28] From that goal, virtually no one dissented. For all the noise surrounding the transformation of the family in the late Victorian era, in the end the process simply strengthened the three distinctive characteristics that had been developing for two centuries. Beneath the confrontation of conservative and reformist views lay an undeniable consensus that the family had greater emotional importance than ever. With that growing importance had come the increasing privacy of the home. And within the segregated emotional center of the family, the child had come to be its greatest concern.

The divorce and race suicide alarm preoccupied, for a time, the debate on the "woman question," but that debate was an ancient one, and long after the height of the panic over the condition of the family had passed, Americans continued to disagree over the proper status of women. Indeed, that debate goes on, unresolved, in the present day. In the late nineteenth century, however, the age-old discussion of woman's place was just beginning to take on its modern urgency. No longer could that discussion be academic, as it had been earlier in the century: the New Woman was appearing on the scene and demanding to be taken seriously. The New Woman was in fact two different ladies, the self-sufficient working girl and the dependent, restless "parasite woman," the idle wife in a middle class with growing wealth and leisure. But each of these women was new, and each, in her own way, repudiated the nineteenth-century ideal of femininity.

The feminine ideal which the nineteenth century made an article of faith grew up as part of a reaction against older convictions of the sinfulness and depravity of humanity. That ideal was not so much Puritanical as it was anti-Puritan when it made woman symbolize the possibilities of perfection and benevolence. Man saw in woman, as Henry James said, "a diviner self than his own," and James himself enshrined such American goddesses as Daisy Miller and Milly Theale in the national imagination.[29]

The idealized American woman was above all incorruptibly innocent. James made Daisy Miller's unreflecting innocence the quality that most puzzled Europeans. That innocence, said the biographer and muck-raker Ida Tarbell, came easily to American girls who were "brought up

[28] Spargo, *Socialism and Motherhood*, p. 32.

[29] James, "Is Marriage Holy?" p. 364. For the development of the symbolic view of women, see Leslie Fiedler, *Love and Death in the American Novel* (New York: Criterion Books, 1960); William Wasserstrom, *Heiress of All the Ages: Sex and Sentiment in the Genteel Tradition* (Minneapolis: University of Minnesota Press, 1959); and Barbara Welter, "The Cult of True Womanhood," *American Quarterly* 18 (1966): 151–74.

as if wrongdoing were impossible to them." [30] Susan B. Anthony's mother had such a deeply bred fealty to the ideal of innocence that "before the birth of every child she was overwhelmed with embarrassment and humiliation, secluded herself from the outside world and would not speak of the expected little one." [31] High-minded men protected their wives and daughters from the outside world by making the home a citadel against threatening influences. Single-minded devotion to domestic duties, men preached, to "marriage and motherhood . . . the highest, indeed the only successful career for woman," was more than woman's duty; it was the only sure protection against the forces of corruption.[32]

A second characteristic of the feminine ideal was helplessness. In 1908 H. L. Mencken protested the "absurd" but nevertheless ubiquitous idea "that the civilization of a people is to be measured by the degree of dependence of its women." The idea of helplessness Veblen again traced to the predatory origins of marriage. But most Americans probably agreed with Theodore Roosevelt that "the woman has a harder time than the man, and must have, from the mere fact that she must bear and largely rear her children." Her dependence, in that view, proceeded from the "laws of nature," and it demanded of men, said Roosevelt, that they treat women with special respect, as they would treat "anything good and helpless." [33]

In a special way, the ideal American girl also embodied and symbolized goodness. Again, Henry James created the fictional archetype of the absolutely good woman in Milly Theale, the heroine of *The Wings of the Dove*. In Milly's unflinching purity of motive and action, James sought expression for an important part of the myth of the American woman. Milly's European acquaintances at first found her simply naïve; later, the terrible consistency of her conscience affected them all profoundly. "We shall never again be as we were," concluded Kate Croy after Milly's death, and she echoed James's own thoughts on the death of his cousin, Mary Temple. That death, he wrote, marked "the end of our youth." Somehow, James and other American men expressed their sense of lost youthful innocence, dependence, and goodness by creating an idealized picture of the American woman.[34]

Bronson Alcott pointed to another large component of the goodness the American woman was supposed to possess when he described his

30 Ida M. Tarbell, *The Business of Being a Woman* (New York: Macmillan, 1912), p. 179.

31 Ida Husted Harper, *The Life and Work of Susan B. Anthony* (Indianapolis: Bowen-Merrill, 1899), pp. 12–13.

32 Mary Roberts Coolidge, *Why Women Are So* (New York: Henry Holt, 1912), pp. 44–45.

33 H. L. Mencken, *The Philosophy of Friedrich Nietzsche* (Boston: Luce, 1908), p. 189; Veblen, "Barbarian Status of Women," pp. 504–07; Morison, *Letters of Theodore Roosevelt*, 2:904 (Roosevelt to Helen Kendrick Johnson, January 10, 1899), 3:520 (Roosevelt to Hamlin Garland, July 19, 1903).

34 Henry James, *Wings of the Dove* (New York: Dell, 1963), p. 512; Henry James, *Notes of a Son and Brother* (London: Macmillan, 1914), p. 47. See also Fiedler, *Love and Death in the American Novel*, and Wasserstrom, *Heiress of All the Ages*.

daughter as "duty's faithful child." [35] Louisa May Alcott earned that
paternal praise by eschewing marriage and personal happiness and tending her father without complaint until his dying day. To pious believers
in the feminine ideal, Miss Alcott revealed her true womanhood by that
self-abnegating devotion to the service of another. So central was the
belief in the generosity of the idealized woman that Americans found
any contrary suggestion blasphemous or incomprehensible. When Henrik
Ibsen's *Doll's House* opened in Boston in 1889, a reviewer remarked that
the "ending can never be liked by American audiences, who will be loath
to believe that a woman owes a higher duty to the development of her
own nature than to the young children she has brought into the world."
In New York, a reviewer confessed to "the difficulty an average audience
experiences to see what the playwright means—what he is driving at."
Another observer noted that when Americans came across a (rare)
woman like Nora Helmer, who resolved to "do her duty to herself," they
had "a dull trick of suspecting mental disease." [36] The nineteenth-century
woman, said Mary Roberts Coolidge, a perceptive and sympathetic critic
of the feminist movement, was raised to please men, not herself. Woman's
personality had come to resemble that of an actor, who, "like the woman,"
Mrs. Coolidge wrote, "makes his place in life chiefly by the cultivation
of manner and appearance. He, like her, depends for success upon pleasing rather than being admirable. The 'matinee idol' is an extreme example of character—or, rather, perversion of character—by the social
necessity of being charming and of trading in assumed emotions." [37]
Though "other-direction" has been called a characteristically twentieth-
century component of personality, American women obviously knew its
meaning well before 1900. So too, it could be argued, the "individualism"
so highly valued in the nineteenth century and ever since regarded as a
distinctive quality of American life in that epoch was apparently for men
only.

By the end of the century, however, feminists had mounted an active
revolt against the burden of assumed emotions. The picture of the idealized woman, they said, was false; and certainly that picture of American
women—as innocent, dependent, good, and selfless—had always fitted
masculine wishes better than it had the facts.

What men cherished as "innocence" was purchased at the price of
often disastrous ignorance. Charlotte Perkins Gilman indicted the belief
that innocence was a woman's chief charm. "What good does it do her?"
she asked. "Her whole life's success is made to depend on her marrying;
her health and happiness depends [*sic*] on her marrying the right man.
The more 'innocent' she is, the less she knows, the easier it is for the
wrong man to get her." Mary Roberts Coolidge noted ironically that
though marriage and motherhood constituted a woman's only permitted

[35] Thomas Beer, *The Mauve Decade* (Garden City, N.Y.: Garden City Publishing,
    1926), pp. 19–21.
[36] *New York Daily Tribune*, October 31, 1889, p. 6; *New York Times*, December
    22, 1889, p. 11; *Belford's Magazine*, April 1890, p. 772.
[37] Coolidge, *Why Women Are So*, p. 101.

career, "yet, nothing in her training had any direct relation to it, and the conventional standard of modesty required her to be wholly ignorant of its physical aspects." Certainly Susan B. Anthony learned little about the "physical aspects" of married life from a mother who took her confinement literally. An anonymous feminist in 1906 said that the average nineteenth-century girl "contemplated the sexual relation with the bitterest reluctance," because she had been "sedulously guarded from knowledge of the fundamental reasons of her being, cast suddenly and unprepared into marriage." Robert Latou Dickinson, probably America's most prominent gynecologist, corroborated those women's observations when he reported that his clinical practice had shown that "no single cause of mental strain in married women is as widespread as sex fears and maladjustments." He blamed the prevalence of those fears on the enforced sexual ignorance of women.[38]

The pathologic effects of the regimen of sheltered domesticity were not all psychological. The helplessness of the American woman—especially in the urban East and the upper-class South—owed at least as much to real physiological weakness as it did to compliance with a rigid moral ideal. "An American sculptor unhampered by the models of the past," said a woman writer in 1873, "would represent the Three Graces as lolling on sofa-cushions, with a bottle of salts in one hand and a fan in the other." To be ladylike, she said, was to be "lifeless, inane, and dawdling," and another woman later recalled a nineteenth-century rhyme which told that "the bride, *of course*, fainted, for, being acquainted with manners, she knew what was right." Robert Latou Dickinson insisted in the 1890s that the neurasthenic female was more than a caricature and that the causes of her condition were plain: lack of exercise and ridiculous standards of dress. "It is supposed to be sufficient exercise for the sister," he wrote, "to wave her handkerchief from the grand stand." Dickinson also suggested that the alleged "sexlessness" of American women owed at least in part to the relatively primitive state of gynecological medicine. Low-grade vaginal infections, later remedied routinely, could in the nineteenth century be an enduring and debilitating discomfort. And scores of other medical writers joined Dickinson in pointing out the harmful effects of the steel-ribbed corsets women wore to shrink their waists and expand their busts. The rigid "health waists" were especially damaging to working girls who leaned forward all day over a typewriter or a sewing machine. Still, in spite of almost daily evidence of the injury done to women by overdomestication and overdressing, the American male—whose house women kept and for whose eye they attired themselves—continued to pride himself on the manly protection he offered his delicate, dependent charges.[39]

38 Gilman, *Man-Made World*, p. 167; Coolidge, pp. 44–45. Elizabeth B. Wetmore, *The Secret Life* (New York: John Lane, 1906), p. 93; Robert Latou Dickinson, "Marital Maladjustment—The Business of Preventive Gynecology," *Long Island Medical Journal* 2 (1908)1: 1–5.
39 Woolson, *Woman in American Society*, p. 192; Deland, "Change in the Feminine Ideal," p. 293; R. L. Dickinson, "Simple and Practical Methods in Dress Reform,"

Similarly, the myth of the ideal woman sanctified her generosity and selflessness by piously glorifying the sacrifices she was expected cheerfully to make. Men impressed upon women, said Lydia Commander, the authoress of one of the most popular contemporary books on the family and feminism, "that it was a religious duty to suffer," especially to suffer the pains of childbirth and the exasperations of child-rearing. The duties of the American woman, said Theodore Roosevelt, exceeded those of the American fighting man and should receive far more adulation. Because of biology, he said, the woman "has a harder time than the man." A woman writer in 1916 perceived that in the nineteenth-century feminine ideal "the element of sacrifice is so obvious that it is even seized upon and treated as a virtue, an added glory for the crown of the wife and mother." [40]

Finally, the myth of the idealized American woman preserved her innocence and her goodness by denying her sexuality. In nineteenth-century fiction, said Thomas Beer, "the female principal is risen above romance and becomes an opalescent cloud, dripping odours which had nothing to do with the process of childbearing at all." The myth, therefore, not only kept women ignorant of what it simultaneously glorified as their chief honor and duty. It also insulated them from all passion and erotic desire. As Viola Klein has observed, in the whole Western world "during the nineteenth and at the beginning of the twentieth century it would have been not only scandalous to admit the existence of a strong sex urge in women, but it would have been contrary to all observation." H. L. Mencken called it a "good old sub-Potomac" idea that a woman "who loses her virtue is, *ipso facto*, a victim and not a criminal or *particeps criminis*, and that a 'lady,' by virtue of being a 'lady,' is necessarily a reluctant and helpless quarry in the hunt of love." But the idea held with nearly unassailable force above the Potomac as well. No genuinely passionate woman appeared in American fiction at least from the time of the Civil War to the naturalist outburst at the turn of the century. As late as 1908, Robert Latou Dickinson was urging the medical profession to tell nervous women patients there was no cause for alarm if they enjoyed sexual intercourse. And even such an otherwise perceptive man as E. A. Ross asserted confidently in 1906 that it was a "physiological fact that the sexual instinct is not only very much weaker in most women, but is altogether absent in a growing number of them." [41]

Gynecological Transactions 18 (1893): 411; R. L. Dickinson, "Bicycling for Women from the Standpoint of the Gynecologist," *American Journal of Obstetrics* 31 (1895): 25. See also Mark Sullivan, *Our Times*, vol. 1, *The Turn of the Century* (New York: Charles Scribner's Sons, 1926), pp. 385–95.

[40] Commander, *American Idea*, p. 235; Morison, *Letters of Theodore Roosevelt*, 3:520–21 (Roosevelt to Hamlin Garland, July 19, 1903); Jessie Taft, *The Woman Movement from the Point of View of Social Consciousness* (Chicago: University of Chicago Press, 1916), p. 55.

[41] Beer, *Mauve Decade*, p. 54; Viola Klein, *The Feminine Character* (New York: International Universities Press, 1949), p. 85; Mencken, *Philosophy of Friedrich Nietzsche*, p. 186; Dickinson, "Marital Maladjustment"; Ross, "Western Civilization and the Birth Rate," p. 51. See Steven Marcus, *The Other Victorians: A Study*

Feminists reacted against both the myth and the facts it so sancti-
moniously concealed but could not change. By the end of the nineteenth
century women were telling men that they wanted neither innocence
nor ignorance, dependence or disease, self-abnegation or sacrifice, goodness nor sexlessness. The New Woman, Leslie Fiedler has said, refused
to accept her prescribed function of "redemptive suffering," and with
that refusal she "threatened to upset the whole Sentimental Love Religion" in which the myth of the ideal woman was enshrined. Independence
became the religion of the New Woman, and Henrik Ibsen was one of
its chief prophets. Ibsen showed, said one of his American admirers in
1890, "the necessity of a new life . . . a life divested of the conventional
ideas of what is Woman's duty." In contrast to early feminist reformers
who had sought to restructure legal forms in order to give women control over their own property and persons, by the late nineteenth century
feminists more or less consciously sought to restructure the feminine
personality itself.[42]

Lydia Commander, describing the New Woman in 1907, noted the
"radical alteration in her personality. Under the old regime," she said,
"humility, self-sacrifice, and obedience were assiduously cultivated as the
highest of womanly virtues." But now, she concluded, "self-sacrifice . . .
is no longer in favor. Self-development is rapidly taking its place." For
many American feminists in the last quarter of the century, an encounter
with European ideas—in Ibsen, Friedrich Nietzsche, Henri Bergson, or
George Bernard Shaw—finally broke the long-standing tension of trying
to live up to the duties of the feminine ideal. After more than two generations of strictly legal progress, the women's movement began to turn
inward to search for a definition of a new feminine personality. Later,
the movement would again turn at least partly outward and justify itself
with claims of the benefits it could bestow on society. But for a season
its paramount concern was the development of a new sense of self. And
in that development, society, and society's expectations, could only be
enemies.[43]

The idea of antagonism between the feminine self and society coincided strikingly with a notion that underlay the very feminine ideal
against which the reformers protested: the idea of woman's victimization.
Men constantly regarded the innocent woman as a potential victim of sinister forces. They even sentimentalized the obviously corrupted woman,
as H. L. Mencken noted, as an unwitting gull of evil persons. When the
white slave panic reached its height around 1910, the image of the hapless
prostitute as a victim of poverty or lechery found ready acceptance and

---

of *Sexuality and Pornography in Mid-Nineteenth Century England* (New York:
Basic Books, 1964), pp. 28–32, for a most interesting discussion of a similar de-
sexualizing of women in nineteenth-century England; for more on the phenomenon in the United States, see Fiedler, *Love and Death in the American Novel*, and
Joseph Wood Krutch, *The Modern Temper* (New York: Harcourt, Brace, 1929).

[42] Fiedler, p. 221; Annie Nathan Meyer, letter to the editor, *Critic*, March 22, 1890, p.
148.

[43] Commander, *American Idea*, pp. 144–45.

frequent expression. And behind Theodore Roosevelt's idea that the woman achieved nobility by sacrifice stood the premise that biology—regrettably, but unavoidably—victimized women far more than it did men. A woman writer noted that society displayed its recognition of that victimization when it attempted to translate the experiences of women in marriage and motherhood "into a sort of fetish . . . exalted to the point where they are assumed to be a sufficient compensation for any and all sacrifices." [44]

But though the New Woman was not to be so easily compensated, she herself nevertheless appealed to society's sense of her victimization when she did demand compensation in the shape of legal, economic, and social reforms. When the suffragists first shifted from a "natural rights" to an "expediency" argument for the vote, says Aileen Kraditor, they insisted "that women needed the ballot for self-protection." In other words, they asked for political power to combat the forces that victimized them. Similarly, protective labor legislation first came into being "in the name of defenseless women and children." And Christopher Lasch has noted perceptively that "it was not the image of women as equals that inspired the reform of the divorce laws, but the image of women as victims." In her search for equality, says Lasch, by appealing to the idea of victimization, "woman depended on a sentimentalization of womanhood which eroded the idea of equality as easily as it promoted it." [45]

Both feminists and antifeminists spoke of woman's victimization in terms of her sex. As Aileen Kraditor notes, "the antis regarded each woman's vocation as determined not by her individual capacities or wishes but by her sex. Men were expected to have a variety of ambitions and capabilities, but all women were destined from birth to be full-time wives and mothers. To dispute this eternal truth was to challenge theology, biology, or sociology." [46] Feminists flirted occasionally with the idea that their distinctive sexual characteristics made them superior. That idea proceeded logically from the feminine myth which told women they were purer, more generous, and morally better than men. But more often women, in their quest for a new definition of self, resented what Elsie Clews Parsons, a prominent woman sociologist, called "the domination of personality by sex." When the feminists talked about sex, they did not intend the word as it is usually understood today. Today, "sex" has an erotic meaning. It generally connotes instinct, passion, emotion, stimulation, pleasure, often intercourse itself. But the nineteenth-century feminists used "sex" almost exclusively to denote gender. For them, "sex" indicated all the special feminine characteristics men used to differentiate and, said the feminists, to subjugate women. Charlotte Perkins Gilman

---

[44] Taft, *The Woman Movement*, p. 55. See also Illinois, General Assembly, Senate, Vice Committee, *Report* (Chicago: State of Illinois, 1916); and Prince A. Morrow, *Social Diseases and Marriage* (New York: Lea Brothers, 1904).

[45] Aileen Kraditor, *The Ideas of the Woman Suffrage Movement, 1890–1920* (New York: Columbia University Press, 1965), p. 54; Smuts, *Women and Work in America*, p. 107; Lasch, "Divorce and the Family," p. 59.

[46] Kraditor, p. 15.

repeatedly condemned what she called masculine oversexualization of the world; she was speaking not of pornography or lechery but of a caste system which kept women in their place. Men saw "nothing in the world *but* sex, either male or female," she argued, and in such an atmosphere neither men nor women could develop the truly human qualities common to each. "Our distinctions of sex," she said, "are carried to such a degree as to be disadvantageous to our progress as individuals and as a race." For women like Mrs. Gilman and Mrs. Parsons, the new feminine personality could only emerge when sex became "a factor, not an obsession." Then "relations between men and women will be primarily personal relations, secondarily sexual." That was the dominant feminist position, though some other feminist sympathizers, such as Ellen Key, and even, in his own way, Theodore Roosevelt, promoted the alternative view that women had a separate sexual identity but were nevertheless the equals of men. In any case, all the theories about the relation of feminine sex characteristics to personality manifested a conscious effort to define, or to redefine, woman's role.[47]

The redefinition of woman's role encountered entrenched but confused opposition. Antifeminists argued on the one hand that woman's God-given, natural role was so immutable that the suggestion of change was ludicrous, and on the other that her sacred maternal and connubial functions were so susceptible to corruption that she must be protected from the forces of change. But the antifeminists' confusion did not temper the strenuousness of their objections. Indeed, the strength of the objections indicated anxieties that only indirectly touched the question of economic and educational equality for women. Those anxieties primarily concerned the male's own social role and his sexual identity.

"The study of the changes in sexual attitudes is the very first step, the *sine qua non*, of all coherent historical research," writes Gordon Rattray Taylor, because sex lies at the heart of personality. Though Taylor somewhat overstates his case the fact nevertheless remains, as Phillipe Ariés has said, that "society's consciousness of its behaviour in relation to age and sex" is still an "unexplored subject," and the historical imagination is poorer for the lack.[48] While it is undoubtedly difficult to trace events in the innermost lives of men, it is more difficult to imagine that the developments that moved nineteenth-century American life worked no changes on sexuality. And at no time did the effects of those changes come closer to the surface than when the nineteenth-century man confronted the New Woman.

Sex has always been central to the human condition, but Steven Marcus has found that only in the nineteenth century "did there emerge

47 Elsie Clews Parsons, *Social Freedom* (New York: G. P. Putnam's Sons, 1915), pp. 29, 36; Gilman, *Man-Made World*, p. 154; Charlotte Perkins Gilman, *Women and Economics* (New York: Harper and Row, 1966; first published, 1898), p. 33.

48 G. Rattray Taylor, *Sex in History* (New York: Vanguard Press, 1954), p. 3; Ariés, *Centuries of Childhood*, p. 58.

as part of the general educated consciousness the formulation that it might
in fact be problematical—it is an idea that forms part of our inheritance."
Nineteenth-century Americans first met the modern problem of sex by
officially denying sexuality. In their minds, as William Wasserstrom has
said, "manliness signified a state of the soul which negated the claims of
the body; womanliness resulted when the body was eliminated." Lester
Ward complained that antagonism to the idea of sexuality was so pervasive that his fellow ethnologists even covered up the sex lives of former
ages in an attempt "to palliate the supposed humiliation involved in such
a state of things." [49]

In *Three Contributions to the Theory of Sex*, Freud noted that "the
most pronounced difference between the love life of antiquity and ours
lies in the fact that the ancients placed the emphasis on the impulse itself,
while we put it on the object. The ancients extolled the impulse and were
ready to ennoble through it even an inferior object, while we disparage
the activity of the impulse as such and only countenance it on account of
the merits of the object." [50] Only in that context did the oft-noted nineteenth-century ideal of sexlessness have meaning. The Victorian man
honored the ideal of sexlessness when he disparaged and even feared his
own sexual instinct and denied the existence of the instinct in women.
But, as the feminists often complained, he exaggerated sex—in the meaning of gender—when he emphasized and glorified the distinctly feminine
qualities of his sexual object.

On the occasion of a sex murder in New York in 1870, Henry James
and the editors of the *Nation* debated the nature of the problematic sexual instinct and its relation to marriage. Only in marriage, said James,
could men's "baser nature"—their sexuality—be adequately contained.
The purpose of wedlock, he said, "is to educate us out of our animal
beginnings." The *Nation*, though more extreme, agreed. Sex, it said, was
an "animal, brute passion, through which God, apparently in ignorance
of the laws of 'moral progress,' has provided for the perpetuation of the
species." But since "moral progress" was so desirable, some means had to
be devised to regulate sex, and that means, adopted in the infancy of the
race, was marriage. "The first object of marriage," said the *Nation*, "still
is to regulate [sex]." If the abstract entity, society, could somehow enun-
ciate that Pauline doctrine, the *Nation* went on, it would say: "To keep
down within [man] the animal love of change and attach him to his
home, I excite in his mind extravagant notions of his authority and of
the strength of the tie which unites his wife to him, and I confess that
from this *some* women do suffer a great deal; but I am sure the whole
female sex profits by it." In the *Nation*'s view, marriage, whatever its
cost to the individual, was essential to the social order. Henry James
hoped for a more spontaneous, humanitarian basis for marriage. But
though James and the *Nation* disagreed over the proper sources of marital

[49] Marcus, *The Other Victorians*, p. 2; Wasserstrom, *Heiress of All the Ages*, p. vii;
Ward, *Pure Sociology*, p. 340.
[50] Sigmund Freud, *Three Contributions to the Theory of Sex* (New York: Nervous
and Mental Disease Monographs, 1948), p. 14 n.

stability, they nevertheless shared a common appraisal of male sexuality as a bestial, egocentric, antisocial instinct that must somehow be regulated. And the *Nation*'s idea of marriage as the proper regulatory mechanism came closer than James's to the current popular view.[51]

Just as women were sentimentally venerated partly as compensation for their victimization, men, the *Nation* implied, were granted all the prerogatives of the patriarchal family to compensate for the difficulty with which they held their sexual instinct in check. In both cases, the denial of sexuality, in its modern sense of instinct, was closely tied to the nineteenth-century idea of sexual role. And in both cases, for themselves and for women, men defined the proper roles. Men saw themselves as patriarchal and authoritarian because they suppressed a sexual nature that was aggressive, even potentially brutal. And they saw woman as innocent, dependent, good, and generous because she was—ideally—sexless.

By the end of the nineteenth century, it was becoming increasingly difficult to contain real women within the myth of the feminine ideal. The emergence of the New Woman necessitated adjustments in man's role, and, less demonstrably but no less importantly, in his sexuality. Women entered the work force by the hundreds of thousands. Men showed their sensitivity to role when, often without economic logic, they allowed many newly emerging forms of employment to become exclusively women's. While women felt free to attempt almost any traditionally male job, men usually abandoned any occupation that became identified with women. G. Stanley Hall, the psychologist who brought Freud to Clark University, touched on that phenomenon in 1906 when he reported that several "independent statistical studies" showed that girls often held masculine "ideals," but that "boys almost never choose feminine ideals." In the transvaluation of sexual roles, the movement seemed to be all in one direction. Women took on traditionally masculine functions with apparently little stress; men, by contrast, feared the impairment of the very masculinity they had previously characterized as nearly beyond restraint. The "feminization" of education, Hall complained, rather than producing a desirable refinement in boys, instead unnaturally stifled their most virile traits—their "brutish elements." The fault with the women's movement, said Hall, lay in its exaggerated notion of sexual equality. The time had come, he insisted, for a "new movement . . . based upon sexual differences, not identities." He urged that course— which was in fact reactionary—not, as conservatives had previously done, for the sake of preserving a delicate femininity, but in defense of a beleaguered masculinity.[52]

Steven Marcus found in investigating the sex life of Victorian England that masculine fear of sexuality was ambivalent—men feared both impotence and potency, impulse and loss, attraction and repulsion. So too in America; ambivalence was built in. The furor over the changes

51 James, "Is Marriage Holy?" p. 364; "Society and Marriage," *Nation*, May 26, 1870, pp. 332–33.
52 G. Stanley Hall, "The Question of Co-Education," *Munsey's Magazine*, February 1906, pp. 588–92.

in men's and women's roles showed that while he had made the feminine principle symbolize goodness, the prospect of his "feminization" evoked profound anxieties in the nineteenth-century American man. And though he invested his sexual object with qualities which, according to Freud, should have justified the gratification of a supposedly despicable instinct, he often found that the glorified object, instead of elevating the instinct, precluded it. The figure of woman in American fiction, as Leslie Fiedler has said, became "refined to the point where copulation with her seems blasphemous." Further, however much the American man had denigrated his latent bestiality and bemoaned the difficulty of keeping it in check, that view of his sexual nature had lain at the heart of his self-image. By the 1890s it appeared that his purportedly primeval, almost irrepressible instinct was in fact propped up by an elaborate but fragile system of role definition based on exaggerated sexual differentiation. When women rebelled against that system, the illusion of man's aggressiveness—which seemed so indispensable to his sexual identity—grew more difficult to maintain. And in such laments as G. Stanley Hall's for the stifling of the "brutish elements," it became clear that the American man had feared more than the unleashing of his aggressive sexual instinct; he had also feared its loss.[53]

Male sexual ambivalence had underlain the notorious "double standard" against which feminists and moralists railed. "As a result of this double standard," said Dr. Prince Morrow, "society practically separates its women into two classes: from the one it demands chastity, the other is set apart for the gratification of the sexual caprices of its men. It thus proclaims the doctrine, immoral as it is unhygienic, that debauchery is a necessity for its men." [54] In either case, men made objects of women. Both the Fair Maiden and the Dark Lady served man's needs—one the needs of his conscience, the other the needs of his body. But the New Woman who came to self-consciousness toward the end of the century was no longer content to serve as a mere object. In a few years the double standard, and with it the traditional nineteenth-century idea of masculine sexuality, was under severe attack. It drew its heaviest fire in the hysteria about prostitution during the Progressive period.

The new form of male sexuality that began to emerge in the late nineteenth century was forced to abandon "full aggressive potency, demonic genitality," as Steven Marcus has said, because such a definition of personality was "permanently at odds with that elaborately developed life of the emotions which is our civilized heritage—and our burden." [55] That heritage proceeded primarily from the romantic movement of the late eighteenth and early nineteenth centuries. The feminists—indeed nearly all Progressives—spoke often about the "social consciousness" they wished to inaugurate. Under that regime, they thought, the self would no longer be the first referent for experience but would "appear and develop as the

---

[53] Marcus, *The Other Victorians*, p. 29; Fiedler, *Love and Death in the American Novel*, p. 276.

[54] Morrow, *Social Diseases and Marriage*, p. 342.

[55] Marcus, *The Other Victorians*, p. 180.

result of its relation to other selves." The new, socially conscious self would be the basic building unit in a society founded on cooperation and harmony rather than the pursuit of self-interest. That vision looked forward to the character style later called "other-directed." It also looked backward to the romantic philosophers' notion that sympathy should form the basis of all moral decision and human interaction.[56] Lester Ward considered it one of the nineteenth century's greatest tragedies that it had submerged the romantic heritage and allowed the "rational faculty" to outstrip the "moral sentiments." Even Spencer, he said, had recognized "that the abuse of women by men is due in the main to the feeble development of sympathy." But by the early twentieth century, said Elsie Clews Parsons, "sympathy and insight [were] called upon in measure undreamed of by the antique moralist whose sole anxiety is to preserve his reassuring social categories intact." And with the growth of the sympathetic faculty, men grew less able to objectify women. That did not mean that they afforded women full equality. But with sympathy the touchstone for sexual relationships, men no longer could entrap women so easily in myths and ignore their individual personalities.[57]

The romantic influence also modified that ambivalent fear of the emotions so evident in the nineteenth century. "There has been an increasing tendency," said Mary Roberts Coolidge, "to believe that imagination and intuition were effecting quite as much progress as the logical understanding." And, she implied, the system of masculine values was becoming "feminized" in a subtle way not usually perceived by the anti-feminists: modern psychologists were "placing higher value upon the very mental quality [intuition] which was not long ago held to establish woman's inferiority." In America, William James contributed much to the development of a new regard for sensibility and the validity of emotional experience. And the increasing emphasis on the emotions sanctioned a new sense of subjectivism. That subjectivism harked back to Emerson, but it grew especially strong in the late nineteenth century because it went hand in hand with the relativism engendered by new researches in the biological and social sciences. And with the liberation of women, the transformation of masculine sexuality, the destruction of the double standard, the sanctioning of emotional experience, and the encouragement of a new sense of subjectivism, the nineteenth century had set the scene for the revolution in morals of the twentieth.[58]

The new notion of morality shared the endemic contempt for formalism characteristic of the early twentieth century. The old morality, as exemplified by Theodore Roosevelt, had been founded on the concept of duty; and as Roosevelt said, "The doing of duty generally means pain,

[56] Taft, *The Woman Movement*, pp. 37–49.

[57] Ward, *Pure Sociology*, pp. 346–47; Parsons, *Social Freedom*, p. 32.

[58] Coolidge, *Why Women Are So*, p. 299; see also Henry May, *The End of American Innocence* (Chicago: Quadrangle Books, 1964); and for a good account of the elements of romanticism, see Walter Jackson Bate, *From Classic to Romantic: Premises of Taste in Eighteenth Century England* (New York: Harper and Row, 1961), especially Chs. 4 and 5.

hardship, self-mastery, self-denial." [59] But as the emotions grew less fear-some, they no longer needed to be so strenuously mastered and denied. As a sociologist said in 1908, "Virtue no longer consists in literal obedience to arbitrary standards set by community or church but rather in conduct consistent with the demands of a growing personality." [60] The new moral-ity no less than the old sprang from a sense of inwardness common to the Puritans, the proper Victorians, and the romantics; but the romantic ap-praisal of the inner self was by far the most sanguine. That optimistic view of the self, for example, revolutionized the function of the school, which had been one of the principal agencies of moral indoctrination. In the new view the school should no longer mold the child to make his behavior conform with rigid social rules. The popularity of the ideas of Maria Montessori and John Dewey reflected a new confidence in the goodness of the unfettered personality. Education should not discipline; it should liberate. And in its emphasis on the liberation of the individual personality, the new morality legitimized subjectiveness. Just as the family grew more and more private as it became increasingly an emotional center, so too did the new approval of emotionalism and subjectivism in the life of the individual reinforce the view that his conduct was his private concern.

The romantic ideas of sympathy, emotion, and subjectivism took more than one hundred years noticeably to affect sexual relationships. Nevertheless, by the early twentieth century the influence of those ideas could not be doubted. Then came Sigmund Freud. Freud did not so much start a revolution as rechannel one already in progress. William James and others in the nineteenth century had identified the inner self with the emotions. Freud superimposed on that view the idea that all emotion—indeed all psychic life—sprang from sexuality, and therefore that the self was defined by sexuality. Freud also provided the discussion of sex with a new, scientific vocabulary.

Unquestionably, Freud did much to further the liberation of sexual behavior, but in many ways Freud's influence was reactionary. For the old belief that woman was victimized by biology or by selfish men, Freud substituted the view that penis envy and a peculiar Oedipal situation made women the victims of their own psychic natures. The maternal impulse, according to the Freudians, proceeded not so much from biological and evolutionary laws as from inner psychological needs. That new thesis was scarcely less deterministic than the old. Thus Freud furnished scientific support for the old Victorian view that Nature victimized women and that they should seek compensation in wifehood and maternity. More-over, just as sympathy was beginning at last to inform sexual relation-ships, Freud reemphasized sexual differences and reinstated, in a new form, the old notion of necessary sexual inequality. For Freud, the essence of masculinity was action; of femininity, passiveness. The only currency of sexual interaction, therefore, must consist of power and domination.

[59] Morison, *Letters of Theodore Roosevelt*, 3:521 (Roosevelt to Hamlin Garland, July 19, 1903).
[60] American Sociological Society, *Papers and Proceedings* 3 (1908):171.

Finally, Freud's insistence that the primary component of the emotional life was sexual, irrational, and morally uncommitted both undermined the romantic confidence in the goodness of the emotions and made them seem more important than ever. Freud diverted a romantic revolution, or emotional revolution, at its very beginning and made it a sexual revolution. The sexual revolution, though carried forward under the banner of Freudian science, would continue to show its romantic beginnings. And the women's movement, with which the revolution, by whatever name, was intimately bound up, found in Freud a false liberation. Freudian ideas proved a diversion and an obstacle which women have not yet overcome.[61]

[61] See R. V. Sampson, *Equality and Power* (London: Heinemann Educational Books, 1965) and Hendrik M. Ruitenbeek, *Freud and America* (New York: Macmillan, 1966) for the influence of Freudian ideas.

Growing Up in the Ghetto

IRVING HOWE

In the early twentieth century, an American Jewish playwright coined a phrase that entered the common language as a description of American society's absorption of various immigrant streams. The United States was the "melting pot" of nations. Although some authorities, like the Dillingham Commission, questioned the validity of the melting-pot theory, for half a century this metaphor influenced the popular mind as a fulfillment of the promise of the founding fathers: **e pluribus unum** (out of many, one).

Up until the Civil War period, most voluntary immigrants had been rather easily assimilated into the dominant culture. The major exception among European immigrants had been the large numbers of Irish peasants who migrated during the 1840s and 1850s. Even the German Jews who had come to this country before the late nineteenth century had been largely absorbed. With the coming of the new immigrants from Southern and Eastern Europe in the late nineteenth and early twentieth centuries, however, the assimilation process shifted its intent. The new immigrants, Roman Catholic or Jewish for the most part, were not wanted in the dominant culture. Theories of racial superiority and social evolution were drawn on by the defenders of the traditional American way of life in order to demonstrate the danger these newcomers posed to the older values. As a result of their efforts, restrictive legislation was passed in the 1920s, virtually precluding further migration from the countries of the new immigration. Although the exclusion acts led to a surge of ethnic consciousness on the part of those excluded, the conventional wisdom about the immigration process came to be found in the melting-pot metaphor.

After the Second World War, however, it seemed to many that only the surface had been melted, producing an overlay of general cultural traits developed in the United States, while underneath remained a strong, distinctly traditional ethnic way of life that derived largely from old-world traditions. Beginning with the publication of **Beyond the Melting Pot** by Daniel P. Moynihan and Nathan Glazer in 1963, scholars began to reconsider the nature of ethnic survivals in American society. In the late 1960s, partly in response to the perceived gains of the civil rights and black militant movements of that decade, ethnic consciousness began to grow, and the children and grandchildren of the new immigration started to reevaluate their traditional cultures and to seek a more aggressive stance against an overall culture that they found chauvinistically denying the validity of ethnic pluralism.

The Eastern European Jews provide a special case in this ethnic history. The centuries-long religious and cultural oppression experienced by the Jewish people created in them an exceedingly strong sense of identity that survived intact the transfer to the United States. In addition, because discriminatory laws deprived Jews of access to certain kinds of work and career lines in Eastern Europe, they had learned to fill the interstices in the economic structure as peddlers, small shopkeepers, and artisans. These skills proved useful in America, since there were areas of great need in the rapidly expanding economy of the late nineteenth and early twentieth centuries. Like most of the new immigrants, Jews tended to form distinct communities and were, therefore, in a position to develop special markets for culture-specific items.

Jews provide a special case in another respect. Their relatively high level of literacy, or at least respect for literacy, found outlet and market in the growth of a literary culture, particularly on New York's Lower East Side. It also provided access to upward mobility through the educational process in the public schools. While most of the Jews of the immigrant generation found work in light industry, particularly in the garment business, many in the second generation moved into other areas of employment that proved to be upwardly mobile. In other immigrant groups, there was a greater tendency for children to follow in the line of work of their parents.

In a prize-winning memoir and history of the Jews of the Lower East Side, Irving Howe, of the City University of New York, has provided a richly textured and highly personalized account of an important American ethnic culture. His recounting of the problems and prospects of growing up in the ghetto, reprinted here, helps put in perspective certain cultural myths (for example, the bookishness of Jewish youth) and describes the awesome struggle of young immigrant women to free themselves to participate in the promise of American life.

The socio-economic rise of many of the descendants of this ghetto is one of America's great success stories. Many Jews have so successfully adopted the "American Dream" that some of their community leaders fear their distinctiveness may be lost through intermarriage and assimilation. In relation to Jewish immigration, then, perhaps the melting-pot metaphor was right, only expressed fifty years ahead of its time.

The streets were ours. Everyplace else—home, school, shop—belonged to the grownups. But the streets belonged to us. We would roam through the city tasting the delights of freedom, discovering possibilities far beyond the reach of our parents. The streets taught us the deceits of commerce, introduced us to the excitement of sex, schooled us in strategies of survival, and gave us our first clear idea of what life in America was really going to be like.

We might continue to love our parents and grind away at

school and college, but it was the streets that prepared the future. In the streets we were roughened by actuality, and even those of us who later became intellectuals or professionals kept something of our bruising gutter-worldliness, our hard and abrasive skepticism. You could see it in cab drivers and garment manufacturers, but also in writers and professors who had grown up as children of immigrant Jews.

The streets opened a fresh prospect of sociability. It was a prospect not always amiable or even free from terror, but it drew Jewish boys and girls like a magnet, offering them qualities in short supply at home: the charms of the spontaneous and unpredictable. In the streets a boy could encircle himself with the breath of immigrant life, declare his companionship with peddlers, storekeepers, soapboxers. No child raised in the immigrant quarter would lack for moral realism: just to walk through Hester Street was an education in the hardness of life. To go beyond Cherry Street on the south, where the Irish lived, or west of the Bowery, where the Italians were settling, was to explore the world of the gentiles—dangerous, since one risked a punch in the face, but tempting, since for an East Side boy the idea of *the others*, so steadily drilled into his mind by every agency of his culture, was bound to incite curiosity. Venturing into gentile streets became a strategy for testing the reality of the external world and for discovering that it was attractive in ways no Jewish voice had told him. An East Side boy needed to slip into those gentile streets on his own. He needed to make a foray and then pull back, so that his perception of the outer world would be his own, and not merely that of the old folks, not merely the received bias and visions of the Jews.

When he kept to the Jewish streets, the East Side boy felt at home, free and easy on his own turf. Even if not especially friendly or well mannered, people talked to one another. No one had much reason to suppose that the noisiest quarrel between peddler and purchaser, or parents and children, was anything but a peaceful ritual. Within the tight circle of the East Side, children found multiple routes for wandering, along one or another way:

*   *   *

•   Toward Canal Street, "suit-hunting avenue," as they called it, the stores bright with ties, *mezuzas*, hats, Hebrew books, *taleysim*, where you could jest with the hawkers, stare at the bowls shaped like hourglasses and filled with colored liquids which were kept in the drugstores, feast on windows, savor the territory.

*   *   *

•   Toward Hester or, a bit later, Orchard Street, pushcart territory: shawls, bananas, oilcloth, garlic, trousers, ill-favored fish, ready-to-wear spectacles. You could relax in the noise of familiars, enjoy a tournament of bargains, with every ritual of haggling, maneuver of voice, expertly known and shrewdly appraised. "After a light diet of kippered herring I would wander among the pushcarts for my dessert. I developed a knack for slipping bananas up my sleeve and dropping apples into my blouse while the peddler was busy filling some housewife's market bag. I used to pack a peach into my mouth with one snap of the jaws and look deeply offended when the peddler turned suspiciously upon me."

*   *   *

•   Toward Rutgers Square, with a stop in the summer to cool off at the Schiff Fountain, and then a prowl into the crammed adjacent streets: boys playing stickball or stoopball, and "on one corner the water hydrant turned on to clear the muck of the gutter. Half-naked children danced and shouted under the shower. . . . They pushed out the walls of their homes to the street." At night Rutgers Square changed colors, and it was fun to sidle along, watching the intellectuals as they strolled on East Broadway, and street speakers variously entertaining, some with little more than lung power, others artists in low-keyed enticement.

*   *   *

•   Toward the East River, in warm months, with a dive off the docks, where a blue film of oil from passing tugs coated the water "and a boy who didn't come out looking brown hadn't bathed." Once, after "washing away our sins in the water, we had to pass by gentile lumber yards, and the men there used to throw bricks at us. Then some of us got together and beat them up with sticks, and they never bothered us again."

*   *   *

•   Toward Allen Street, center of darkness and sin, "with its elevated structure whose trains avalanched between rows of houses and the sunlight never penetrated. I see the small shops, which somehow never achieved the dignity of selling anything new . . . a street which dealt in castoff merchandise. Even the pale children seemed old, secondhand."

*   *   *

These "ways," while hardly as elegant as more celebrated ones in modern literature, tracked discoveries into the familiar and the forbidden, into that which stamped one as a true son of the immigrants and that which made one a future apostate. Learning the lessons of cement, one lost whatever fragments of innocence remained. The apartments were crowded, the streets were crowded, yet for boys and girls growing up in the ghetto, the apartments signified a life too well worn, while the streets, despite their squalor, spoke of freedom. Freedom to break loose from those burdens that Jewish parents had come to cherish; freedom, if only for an hour or two, to be the "street bum" against whom fathers warned; freedom to live by the senses, a gift that had to be learned and fought for; freedom to sin. Cramped or denied, shushed or repressed, sexual yearnings broke out on the streets and were expressed through their grubby poetry, in hidden corners, black basements, glowering roofs: wherever the family was not.

To be poor is something that happens to one; to experience poverty is to gain an idea of what is happening. All the evidence we have suggests that the children of the East Side rarely felt deprived. They certainly knew that life was hard, but they assumed that, until they grew up and got a grip on things, it had to be hard. Only later, long after the proper occasion had passed, did self-pity enter their psyche. In the actual years of childhood, the streets spoke of risk, pleasure, novelty: the future—that great Jewish mania, the future.

Legends of retrospect, woven from a wish to make the past seem less rough and abrasive than it actually was, have transformed every Jewish boy into a miniature scholar haunting the Seward Park library and, before he was even out of knee pants, reading Marx and Tolstoy. The reality was different. Scholarly boys there certainly were; but more numerous by far were the street boys, tough and shrewd if not quite "bums," ready to muscle their way past competitors to earn half a dollar, quick to grasp the crude wisdom of the streets. Sammy Aaronson, who would rise to distinction as a fight manager, spent his boyhood as a street waif, sometimes sleeping in the Christopher Street public baths, sometimes at Label Katz's poolroom in Brownsville, sometimes riding the subways all night for a nickel. His family was the poorest of the poor, his mother worked as a junk peddler, their furniture often landed on the street after an eviction, but "there was nothing particularly tragic about that. . . . We didn't feel sorry for ourselves and nobody felt sorry for us." Harry Golden, whose youth was softer, assures us that he too was no Goody Two-shoes. "I played hooky and went to the movies. . . . I was unconscionably capable of forging a note the next day to explain my absence. 'My son Herschele was sick yesterday. (Mrs.) Anna Goldhurst.' Instinctively I knew 'Herschele' and the parentheses would lend absolute verisimilitude to my forgery." Eddie Cantor, before he began to appear in vaudeville skits in Chinatown, did come close to being a "bum." By the age of thirteen, he had "socked a teacher," lost a job through talking too much, perfected his game of pool, learned to hustle a few pennies by jigging and singing on a street corner, and taken up with an immigrant Russian girl, not Jewish, but with melancholy black eyes.

The streets were the home of play. Jewish boys became fanatics of baseball, their badge as Americans. In the narrow streets baseball was narrowed to stickball: a broomstick used as a bat, a rubber ball pitched on a bounce or sped into the catcher's glove, the ball hit high to fielders pinched into the other end of the street, with quarrels as to whether passers-by or wagons (later, cars) had hindered ("hindoo'd") the play. Or stoopball, with a rubber ball thrown smartly against the outer steps of a tenement—a game mostly for eleven-to-fourteen-year-olds.

> We'd go to play ball in Tompkins Park. If we couldn't afford a bat we'd bat a can around. The girls played jacks. We'd make a big circle and play marbles. The highly colored ones we called "immies," I couldn't tell my father I played ball, so my mother would

sneak out my baseball gear and put it in the candy store downstairs.
. . . Later, when I played semipro baseball I'd bring home five
dollars and give it to my mother.

Jewish boys were said to be terribly competitive at games, as if
already playing by adult norms: "You see it in the street where they
delight in 'spiking' tops, playing marbles 'for keeps,' and 'pussy cat,' in all
of which the sole idea is to win as an individual boy." The East Side
allowed no lingering in childhood; it thrust the ways of the world onto
its young. In their middle teens the boys turned clannish, forming "social
and athletic clubs," partly to imitate American models.

Girls had their own games, since "the separation of boys and girls so
rigidly carried out in the public schools also held for the street; boys
played with boys, girls with girls." Sophie Ruskay, who lived on Henry
Street, continues:

> Occasionally we girls might stand on the sidelines and watch the
> boys play their games, but usually our presence was ignored. . . .
> We knew it to be a boy's world, but we didn't seem to mind it too
> much. . . . Tagging after us sometimes were our little brothers
> and sisters whom we were supposed to mind, but that was no great
> hardship. We would toss them our bean-bags [to play with], little
> cloth containers filled with cherry pits. . . . Then we could pro-
> ceed to our game of potsy. Mama didn't like me to play potsy. She
> thought it "disgraceful" to mark up our sidewalk with chalk for
> our lines and boxes; besides, hopping on one foot and pushing the
> thick piece of tin, I managed to wear out a pair of shoes in a few
> weeks.
>
> Neither my friends nor I played much with dolls. Since fami-
> lies generally had at least one baby on hand, we girls had plenty of
> opportunity to shower upon the baby brothers or sisters the tend-
> erness that would otherwise have been diverted to dolls. Besides,
> dolls were expensive.
>
> Regardless of season, the favorite game of both boys and girls
> was "prisoner's base." We lined up on opposite sides of the curb,
> our numbers evenly divided, representing two enemy camps. One
> side turned its back to invite a surprise attack. Stealthily a contes-
> tant advanced and either safely reached the "enemy" and captured
> a "prisoner," or, if caught, "became a prisoner." When a sufficient
> number of prisoners had been taken, a tug of war followed to
> rescue them. Trucks and brewery wagons lumbered by. We looked
> upon them merely as an unnecessary interference.

The streets meant work. Children, like nine-year-old Marie Ganz,
went out to pick up bundles of sewing for her mother and was told they
could bring in "maybe five dollars a week if she's a good sewer." But the
full-time employment of children in shops and factories was rare on the
East Side, partly because there was not much for them in the "Jewish
industries," partly because the Jewish sense of family prompted fathers

to resist with every ounce of their being the idea of children as full-time workers.

By about 1905 most immigrant Jewish families were trying to keep their children in school until at least the age of fourteen; but almost all of them worked in the afternoons, evenings, weekends. Henry Klein, whose story is quite ordinary, peddled matches at the age of six and a bit later, with his ten-year-old brother Isadore, shined shoes at the Houston Street ferry. When he became experienced, he peddled with a professional named "Sammy" Cohen, working after school and earning twenty-five cents an hour extra when he taught English to his boss. He sold vegetables, fruit, fish; he hauled coal and wood from the Rheinfrank coalyard at the foot of East Third Street and ice from the Fifth Street dock. While attending high school and, later, City College, he spent weekends selling lozenges in Central Park, fearful of the police because he had no license and making his sister Estelle sit on the benches with boxes of lozenges hidden under her skirt. He would average about two dollars a day, on good days as much as three.

PARENTS AND CHILDREN

Between Jewish immigrant parents and the world of the streets there was a state of battle, not quite a declared war but far from a settled peace. To the older generations the streets enclosed dangers and lusts, shapeless enemies threatening all their plans for the young. The parents could not, nor did they really wish to, distinguish between their received sense of the gentile world and the streets to which their children fled. The older immigrants were too suspicious, too thoroughly under the sway of past humiliations, to believe there might really be some neutral ground, neither moral nor immoral, neither wholly purposive nor merely corrupting, for the years of adolescence. Immigrant parents feared the streets would lure their children from the Jewish path, would soften their will to succeed, would yield attractions of pleasure, idleness, and sexuality against which, they suspected, they were finally helpless.

"We push our children too much," wrote a Dr. Michael Cohen, who lived on the East Side. "After school they study music, go to Talmud Torah. Why sacrifice them on the altar of our ambition? Must we get *all* the medals and scholarships? Doctors will tell you about students with shattered nerves, brain fever. Most of them wear glasses. Three to five hours of studying a day, six months a year, are better than five to twelve hours a day for ten months a year." The *Forward* labored to explain to its readers:

> There is no question but that a piano in the front room is preferable to a boarder. It gives spiritual pleasure to exhausted workers. But in most cases the piano is not for pleasure but to make martyrs of little children, and make them mentally ill. A little girl comes home, does her homework, and then is forced to practice under the

supervision of her well-meaning father. He is never pleased with
her progress, and feels he is paying fifty cents a lesson for nothing.
The session ends with his yelling and her crying. These children
have not a single free minute for themselves. They have no time to
play.

The testimony we have on these matters comes from the sons and
daughters, hardly a word from the older people. What might *they* have
said? That they brought with them a bone knowledge of the centuries
and that being born a Jew meant to accept a life frugal in pleasures? Or
that, seeing opportunities for their children such as Jews had never
dreamed of, they felt it was necessary to drive them to the utmost?

The costs were high. "Alter, Alter," cried a mother, "what will become of you? You'll end up a street bum!" What had this poor Alter
done? He had been playing ball on the street. Later, when he broke a leg,
his mother came weeping to the hospital: "Alter, Alter, do you want to
kill me?" Trying to joke, he answered, "Wait, Mama, whose leg is
broken?" But as he realized later, "to the folks from the old country
sports always remained something utterly pagan." A good many Jewish
children would always suffer from a life excessively cerebral and in-
sufficiently physical; they would always be somewhat unnerved by the
challenge of the body and fearful before the demands of sports.

By their mid-teens, if not earlier, the children of the immigrants
began to shift the focus of their private lives from home to street. The
family remained a powerful presence, and the young could hardly have
envisaged its displacement had they not kept an unspoken sense of its
strength. But in their most intimate feelings they had completed a break
which in outer relations it would take several years to carry through. This
was, in part, no more than the usual rupture that marks the storms of
adolescence, but among the immigrant Jews it took a peculiarly sharp
form, a signal for a Kulturkampf between the generations.

The immediate occasions for battle were often matters of private experience. That sex could be coped with only through stealth and secrecy,
and in accordance with norms appropriated from the outer world—most
East Side boys and girls simply took this for granted. Sex was not merely
a pleasure to be snatched from the meagerness of days, it was the imaginative frontier of their lives, a sign of their intention to leave behind the
ways of their parents. Sex might begin as an embarrassed fumbling toward the life of the senses, but it soon acquired a cultural, even an
ideological aspect, becoming an essential part of the struggle to Ameri-
canize themselves. Day by day, the wish to be with one's girlfriend or
boyfriend, modest enough as a human desire, brought the most exasper-
ating problems. "On the East Side there was no privacy. Couples seized
their chance to be together when they found it; they embraced in hall-
ways, lay together on roofs. I passed them all with eyes averted."

In this tangle of relationships, the young could rarely avoid feelings
of embarrassment. One's mother spoke English, if she spoke it at all, with
a grating accent; one's father shuffled about in slippers and suspenders
when company came, hardly as gallant in manner or as nicely groomed

as he ought to be; and both mother and father knew little about those wonders of the classroom—Shakespeare, the Monroe Doctrine, quadratic equations—toward which, God knows, they were nevertheless sufficiently respectful. The sense of embarrassment derived from a half-acknowledged shame before the perceived failings of one's parents, and both embarrassment and shame mounted insofar as one began to acquire the tastes of the world. And then, still more painful, there followed a still greater shame at having felt ashamed about people whom one knew to be good.

> There never seemed any place to go. The thought of bringing my friends home was inconceivable, for I would have been as ashamed to show them to my parents as to show my parents to them. Besides, where would people sit in those cramped apartments? The worldly manner affected by some of my friends would have stirred flames of suspicion in the eyes of my father; the sullen immigrant kindliness of my parents would have struck my friends as all too familiar; and my own self-consciousness, which in regard to my parents led me into a maze of superfluous lies and trivial deceptions, made it difficult for me to believe in a life grounded in simple good faith. . . .
>
> So we walked the streets, never needing to tell one another why we chose this neutral setting for our escape at evening.

DELINQUENTS AND GANGS

When Alter's mother grew fearful that her son would end as a "street bum," she was not merely indulging a fantasy. All through the decades of immigration, the East Side and its replicas elsewhere in the country were harassed by outbreaks of juvenile crime and hooliganism, ranging in character from organized bands of pickpockets to young gangs half-social and half-delinquent. Crime had flourished in the Jewish immigrant quarters since the early 1880's . . . but the rise of a distinctive youth delinquency seems to have become especially troubling shortly after the turn of the century. The mounting congestion of the East Side drove more and more children into the streets, while the gradual improvement in economic conditions enabled them to acknowledge the extent of their desires.

By 1902, reported Louis Marshall, there were "upwards of 300 boys and girls of Jewish parentage" in the House of Refuge on Randall's Island, the New York Juvenile Asylum, and other municipal and non-Jewish institutions. By 1904 the children's courts, "which handle children under fifteen, are packed. Police courts are filled with boys over fifteen, second and third offenders who started at age thirteen-fourteen." The *Forward* printed discussions as to whether erring children should be driven out, as they sometimes were by enraged Orthodox fathers, or kept at home; its editors favored the latter course, "since if you let them out they will go to the dogs completely. They have aggressive natures; if they can't get to their sister's pocketbook for a few cents, they'll try to get the money by stealing. It is preferable that parents should suffer from a bad child."

In 1906 the head of the New York YMHA, Falk Younker, reported that "between 28 and 30 percent of all children brought to the children's court in New York are Jewish. There are three and a half times as many children among this number who are the children of recently arrived immigrants as there are of native born parents. Fifteen years ago Jewish prisoners were an unknown quantity." The main reason cited by Younker was blunt enough: "home life is unbearable."

So acute had the problem become by 1902–1903 that communal figures like Louis Marshall and Jacob Schiff—once relations with government were involved, German Jews still took the lead—started to apply pressure on municipal authorities. They proposed that Jewish children under sixteen committed for misdemeanors be sent, with a subvention from the city, to a reformatory organized by the Jewish community itself. A similar arrangement was already in effect within the Protestant and Catholic communities. Mayor Seth Low vetoed the necessary bill in 1902, but Marshall was a very stubborn man and he kept badgering city officials until the bill was passed a few years later. With a $110 annual contribution per child from the city, and a building fund of several hundred thousand dollars from wealthy donors, the Jewish Protectory Movement built the Hawthorne School, a reformatory in Hawthorne, New York, and supervised probationary work in the city. It tells us something about the magnitude of this problem that the Protectory Movement had to continue its work through and beyond the First World War.

In the gap between Jewish family and gentile world, the children of the immigrants improvised a variety of social forms on the streets. At one extreme were the good and earnest boys, future reformers and professionals, who organized the Social, Educational and Improvement Club of the late 1890's, built up a treasury averaging $11.50 in any given month, and listened to talks by "Mr. Ordway on his experience in the Arctic" (it seems, the secretary archly noted, that "he received a warm reception in a cold climate") and by Mr. Mosenthal on "the theory of our government." At the other extreme were the "tough" gangs, made up of boys from six to twenty years of age, popularly known as "grifters," or pickpockets. These gangs, devoted more to thievery than violence, were sometimes so successful that they could hire furnished rooms to shelter those bolder members living away from home. Their customary hangouts were street corners, alleyways, poolrooms. Crowded streetcars and parks were favorite arenas for "grifting." A frequent strategy would be to start a fake street fight between two of the older members and then, as a crowd collected, the younger ones would go through to pick pockets.

Members of these gangs would later graduate into the ranks of Jewish criminality, such figures as Arnold Rothstein and Legs Diamond becoming masters of their craft; but in any sober light, these formed only a small, marginal group. Far more characteristic were the gangs combining an urge toward social ritual and a staking of turf with occasional forays into petty lawbreaking. Rough schools of experience, these gangs were seldom as violent as those that would later spring up in American urban life. On the East Side they gave a certain structure to the interval between childhood and independence—half-illicit, half-fraternal agencies for a passage into adult life.

GIRLS IN THE GHETTO

For girls in the immigrant Jewish neighborhoods there were special problems, additional burdens. Both American and Jewish expectations pointed in a single direction—marriage and motherhood. But the position of the Jewish woman was rendered anomalous by the fact that, somehow, the Jewish tradition enforced a combination of social inferiority and business activity. Transported to America, this could not long survive.

In the earlier years of the migration, few Jewish women rebelled against the traditional patterns—life was too hard for such luxuries. Early union organizers repeatedly found, Lillian Wald reported, that a great obstacle to organization was "a fear of young women that it would be considered 'unladylike' and might even militate against their marriage." In the 1890's, after the Council of Jewish Women was started, with a membership drawing only slightly on immigrant women from eastern Europe, Rebecca Kohut "was sent on a series of speaking tours, and I frequently had to face hostile crowds" in Jewish neighborhoods. For "Jewish women were expected to stay at home. . . . To have opinions and to voice them was not regarded as good form even in the home."

A glimpse into the conditions under which immigrant shopgirls had to work is provided by Rose Schneiderman's sober account of her teen-age years:

> So I got a place in the factory of Hein & Fox. The hours were from 8 AM to 6 PM, and we made all sorts of linings—or, rather, we stitched in the linings—golf caps, yachting caps, etc. It was piece work, and we received from 3½ cents to 10 cents a dozen, according to the different grades. By working hard we could make an average of about $5 a week. We would have made more but we had to provide our own machines, which cost us $45. . . . We paid $5 down [for them] and $1 a month after that.
>
> I learned the business in about two months, and then made as much as the others, and was consequently doing quite well when the factory burned down, destroying all our machines—150 of them. This was very hard on the girls who had paid for their machines. It was not so bad for me, as I had only paid a little of what I owed.
>
> The bosses got $500,000 insurance, so I heard, but they never gave the girls a cent to help them bear their losses. I think they might have given them $10, anyway. . . .
>
> After I had been working as a cap maker for three years it began to dawn on me that we girls needed an organization.

It made all the difference, growing up in the ghetto, whether a girl had come with her parents from Europe or had been born here. The *Forward*, with its roving sociological eye, noted that

> When a grown girl emigrates to America, she becomes either a finisher or an operator. Girls who have grown up here do not work at these "greenhorn" trades. They become salesladies or

typists. A typist represents a compromise between a teacher and a finisher.

Salaries for typists are very low—some work for as little as three dollars a week. . . . But typists have more *yikhes* [status] than shopgirls; it helps them get a husband; they come in contact with a more refined class of people.

Typists therefore live in two different worlds: they work in a sunny, spacious office, they speak and hear only English, their superiors call them "Miss." And then they come home to dirty rooms and to parents who aren't always so courteous.

Other kinds of "refined" work were even less lucrative, department stores paying salesgirls in 1903–1904 only ten dollars a month to start with, and rarely more than five dollars a week when experienced. Librarians in those years started at three dollars a week, even though special training was required. The most desirable job for a Jewish girl, then as later, was felt to be in teaching, but this meant that she had to be supported in her schooling until she was at least eighteen or nineteen. Many families could not do that. Or, if they had to choose between keeping a son in college and sending a girl to high school, they would usually prefer the former, both for traditional and economic reasons.

Even Jewish girls who had come from Europe as children and were therefore likely to remain fixed in the progression from shopgirl to housewife found themselves inspired—or made restless—by American ideas. They came to value pleasure in the immediate moment; some were even drawn to the revolutionary thought that they had a right to an autonomous selfhood. Carving out a niche of privacy within the cluttered family apartment, they responded to the allure of style, the delicacies of manners, the promise of culture.

Hannah Chotzinoff, going out one evening to a ball at Pythagoras Hall,

> looked radiant in a pink silk shirtwaist and a long black satin skirt. . . . [How had] Hannah obtained her beautiful outfit? There never seemed to be an extra quarter around the house. . . . If the pink silk shirtwaist was an extravagance, Hannah took measures to preserve its freshness. She had tied a large white handkerchief around her waist, so arranged that it would protect the back of her shirtwaist from the perspiring right palms of her dance partners. . . . To [those who placed their hands above the handkerchief] Hannah said politely: "Lower, please."

Girls like Hannah were close to the small group of young immigrants who tried to model themselves on the styles of the late-nineteenth-century Russian intelligentsia. Tame enough by later standards but inspired by a genuine spiritual loftiness, the style of these young immigrants might be described as a subdued romanticism, a high-minded bohemianism. One of the topics in the air during these years was the double standard of morality. The Russian author Chernyshevsky had written a novel on the subject, and the book, though not new, was enjoying a vogue on the East Side. . . . It posed for its heroine and, by extension, to all women, the question of the acceptance or rejection of the hitherto unchallenged promiscuity of males. . . . It was earnestly debated in my own house, on the sidewalks, and on the benches by the Rutgers Square fountains. . . . The male arguments against a single standard appeared to lack force, and almost always capitulated to the sterner moral and spiritual convictions of the opposition.

Though snatches and echoes of such debates occasionally reached them, the double standard could hardly have been a major preoccupation of most immigrant shopgirls. Their lives were too hard for anything but the immediacy of need—especially those who, because they had come to America by themselves or had lost their parents through death, were now forced to live alone in hall bedrooms and support themselves over sewing machines. Lonely, vulnerable, exhausted, these girls were the lost souls of the immigrant Jewish world, rescued, if they were "lucky," by marriage or solaced by political involvement. In the years slightly before and after 1900, the Yiddish press carried reports of such girls taking their lives—"*genumen di gez*" ("took the gas") ran the headlines.

For the Jewish girl who had been born in America, or had come here at an age young enough so that she could learn to speak English reasonably well, there were other difficulties. Jewish boys faced the problem of how to define their lives with relation to Jewish origins and American environment, but Jewish girls faced the problem of whether they were to be allowed to define their lives at all. Feminism as a movement or ideology seems to have touched no more than a small number of Jewish girls, mostly those who had already been moved to rebellion by socialism. (The fiery socialist Rose Pastor became famous only after, or because, she married the millionaire Graham Stokes; the idea of a red Yiddish Cinderella made its claims on the popular imagination as the idea of a brilliant rebel girl could not.)

What stirred a number of young Jewish women to independence and self-assertion was not so much an explicit social ideology as their fervent relation to European culture, their eager reading of nineteenth-century Russian and English novels. One such young woman, Elizabeth Stern, recalls how her father

had come to look with growing distrust on my longing to know things; upon my books especially. . . . He discovered me with *Oliver Twist* bulging from the covers of my prayer book where, with trembling hands, I was trying to hide it. He flung the novel on top of the book case. He told me in his intense restrained angry voice that my English books, my desire for higher education, were making me an alien to my family, and that I must give up all dreams of continuing beyond the grammar school.

An intelligent woman who wished to be just toward her own memories, Elizabeth Stern remembered that her father later spoke in "a voice of rare tenderness" when he told her that "he wished me to grow up a pride to our people, quiet, modest. . . . I was to marry; I too could be another Rachel, another Rebecca." Her father "would joyfully sacrifice himself for any of his children, that they might follow the path he believes the ideal one. He could not see that I might have ideals different from those held by him."

When the moment came to decide whether Elizabeth would continue with her studies, her father kept repeating "impossible"—though all the poor girl wanted was to be allowed to enter high school! Finally her mother intervened with a memorable remark: "Let her go for a year. We don't want her to grow up and remember that we denied her life's happiness."

So it was with many other Jewish girls. Golda Meir, growing up in an immigrant home in Milwaukee, had to run away in order to assert her independence. Anzia Yezierska (1885–1970), for a time a well-known novelist, was locked in a struggle with her father that lasted for years. Her story, quite typical in its beginnings, turned at its end into an American legend:

She arrived in New York in 1901, sixteen years old. Her first job was as a servant in an Americanized Jewish family "so successful they were ashamed to remember their mother tongue." She scrubbed floors, scoured pots, washed clothes. At the end of a month she asked for her wages, and was turned out of doors: "Not a dollar for all my work." Her second job was in a Delancey Street sweatshop kept by "an old wrinkled woman that looked like a black witch." Anzia sewed buttons from sunup to sundown. One night she rebelled against working late and was thrown out: "I want no clock-watchers in my shop," said the old witch.

Her third job was in a factory where she learned a skill and, luxury of luxuries, "the whole evening was mine." She started to study English. "I could almost think with English words in my head. I burned to do something, be something. The dead work with my hands was killing me."

She began to write stories with heroines—Hannahs and Sophies—who were clearly projections of her own yearnings. They were not really good stories, but some streak of sincerity and desperation caught the fancy of a few editors and they were published in magazines. By now, she was no longer young—a woman in her mid-thirties, trying to make up for years of wasted youth.

A first novel, *Hungry Hearts*, won some critical praise. Like all her books, it was overwrought, ungainly, yet touching in its defenselessness. No woman from the immigrant Jewish world had ever before spoken with such helpless candor about her fantasies and desires. In one of her novels, *Salome of the Tenements*, a young immigrant girl named Sonia says of herself: "I am a Russian Jewess, a flame, a longing. A soul consumed with hunger for heights beyond reach. I am the ache of unvoiced dreams, the clamor of suppressed desires." Sonia meets and marries a

Yankee millionaire, the elegant Manning, and for a moment she thinks that she has won the world; but it all turns to dust, as in such novels it has to, and in the end what remains is the yearning of a Jewish girl, far more real than anything else in the book.

All the while, in the forefront of her imagination, loomed the figure of her father, a stern pietist who regarded her literary efforts with contempt. "While I was struggling, trying to write, I feared to go near him. I couldn't stand his condemnation of my lawless, godless, selfish existence." There were bitter quarrels. "He had gone on living his old life, demanding that his children follow his archaic rituals. And so I had rebelled . . . I was young. They were old."

Her first book published, Anzia confronted her father. "What is it I hear? You wrote a book about me? How could you write about someone you don't know?" Words of wrath flew back and forth, but Anzia, staring at her father in his prayer shawl and phylacteries, "was struck by the radiance that the evils of the world could not mar." He again threw up the fact that she had not married: "A woman alone, not a wife and not a mother, has no existence." They had no meeting ground but anger.

One morning a telegram was delivered to her room: ten thousand dollars for the movie rights to *Hungry Hearts!* She went to Hollywood, Yiddish accent and all; she wore expensive clothes, enjoyed the services of a secretary, met the "greats" of the movie world. But alas, not a word came out of her. The English she had worked so painfully to master ran dry.

Back home, defeated, she drifted through years of loneliness and poverty again. A few books published but little noticed: all with her fervent signature, pitiful in their transparency. At sixty-five, quite forgotten, she wrote an autobiography, *Red Ribbon on a White Horse*, summoning memories of the time when she had been a young immigrant woman locked in struggle with her father. By now she shared his view that the fame and money of her middle years had been mere delusion, and for the title of her book she chose a phrase from an old Jewish proverb: "Poverty becomes a wise man like a red ribbon on a white horse." In some groping, half-acknowledged way she had returned to the world of her fathers—a final reconciliation, of sorts.

The case of Anzia Yezierska was an extreme one, in that she had to confront, at their stiffest, the imperatives of both Jewish and American culture. Most Jewish girls of her day were neither wholly submissive nor wholly rebellious; within the bounds of the feminine role they found stratagems for cultivating their private interests and developing their private sensibilities. By 1914 a growing number of girls from East Side homes were going to high school and a small number to college; by the mid-twenties, about a generation later than the daughters of the German Jews, a good many girls from east European Jewish families had begun attending Hunter College and, in smaller numbers, Barnard.

A check of the graduating classes at Hunter—admittedly imprecise,

Year of Graduation	Number of Graduates	Estimated Jewish Graduates	Estimated East European Jewish Graduates
1906	156	43	13
1910	186	40	25
1912	155	36	25
1913	295	85	56
1914	273	102	66
1916	245	71	58

since it is difficult to know whether certain names are Jewish, let alone German-Jewish or east European–Jewish—confirms this trend.

If these figures are at all indicative, it would seem that by the years immediately before the First World War, the girls from east European Jewish families had become the majority within the graduating Jewish population at Hunter. Since there is no reason to suppose that the number of German-Jewish girls going to college declined, it would follow that at about the same time numbers of German-Jewish girls started going to private colleges like Barnard.

With eager if shy determination, the Jewish girls were redefining their lives. Elizabeth Stern, having won the battle for high school, found that she "wanted a room in which one simply sat. I had no clear idea of what I would do in it. But I had no room of my own yet. . . . Neighbors and relatives laughed in amusement at my wish." Like thousands of others, this young immigrant woman struck intuitively upon the demand that Virginia Woolf would voice in another setting: a room of one's own, a room with a view . . . .

JEWISH CHILDREN, AMERICAN SCHOOLS

For the New York school system, the pouring in of these immigrant Jews—as well as Italians, Germans, Poles, Slavs—seemed like an endless migraine. Language, curriculum, habits, manners, every department of the child's life and study had to be reconsidered. While the educational system was mostly in the hands of the Irish, there were a good number of German Jews among both administrators and teachers, and it was they, "progressive" in educational thought and eager to speed the assimilation of their east European cousins, who developed new educational strategies for the immigrants. Given the poor conditions—overcrowding in the schools, fear and suspicion among the immigrants, impatience and hostility among some teachers, and an invariably skimped budget (often worse during reform administrations than when Tammany dealt out the spoils)—a summary conclusion would be that the New York school system did rather well in helping immigrant children who wanted help, fairly well in helping those who needed help, and quite badly in helping those who resisted help.

In 1905, a peak year of immigration, the Jewish pupils on the East

Side were concentrated in thirty-eight elementary schools. These contained 65,000 students, of whom some 61,000, or almost 95 percent, were Jewish. Certain schools, like P.S. 75 on Norfolk Street, were totally Jewish. That condition which a half-century later would be called *de facto* segregation did not deeply trouble the Jewish immigrants—on the contrary, they found a certain comfort in sending their children to public schools overwhelmingly Jewish. Children who knew a little English served as translators for those who a week or two earlier had stepped off the boats. In the years between, say, 1900 and 1914 there were sporadic efforts by Jewish groups to pressure the Board of Education with regard to overcrowding of schools, released time for religious training, and the teaching of foreign languages; but we have no record of major objection to the racial homogeneity of a given school or district.

"The school personnel," writes a historian of New York education,

> considered it easier to teach English to a class in which all the youngsters spoke the same foreign language. . . . Only the social workers raised questions about the ethnic homogeneity of the schools. The assimilation of the immigrant would be retarded, they feared, and the learning of English impeded when the children used their native tongue everywhere but in the classroom. . . . But even the settlement house workers concentrated their fire on the methods of Americanization they saw [in the schools]. . . . They commented angrily on the gulf the teachers were creating between the foreign born parents and their native born children. Grace Abbott, Jane Addams, and Sophinisbe Breckenridge exhorted the schools to recognize the importance of foreign cultures.

From the immigrant spokesmen there were similar complaints, often furious in the Yiddish press and stiff even in the writings of so reasonable a man as David Blaustein. "Respect for age," he noted, "is certainly not an American characteristic, and this is an upsetting of all the immigrant's preconceived idea of society. . . . The children are imbued with the idea that all that is not American is something to be ashamed of. It is an unfortunate but indisputable fact that cheap and superficial qualities are the more likely to be assimilated."

But segregation of Jewish pupils failed to arouse any concerted protest among immigrant parents. It was a condition to which they had long been accustomed; it helped make the first years of settlement somewhat less frightening; and it also seemed, in its distinctive American form, a social springboard for plunging into the new world. The immigrants were prepared, indeed, eager, to have their children Americanized, even if with some psychic bullying, but they did not want to see themselves discarded in the process. As time went by, however, they came close to accepting even this fate as a price that had to be met.

Not without some dragging of feet—a mode of locomotion endemic to educational bodies—the Board of Education began to restructure the New York schools in order to "connect" with immigrant children. Good and even imaginative work was undertaken. Bilingualism in the schools was rejected out of hand: the authorities never saw it as a serious option, the immigrants would have been deeply suspicious of it. But an effort was made by such East Side superintendents as Gustave Straubenmuller, a specialist in teaching English to foreigners, and Julia Richman, an enthusiast for "progressive" education, to make their teachers sensitive to the special problems of Jewish pupils. One study of these problems, after listing the familiar virtues of Jewish students ("idealistic, thirst for knowledge," etc.), is candid enough to mention "other characteristics" that teachers might find disturbing: "occasional overdevelopment of mind at expense of body; keen intellectualism often leads toward impatience at slow progress; extremely radical; many years of isolation and segregation give rise to irritability and supersensitivity; little interest in physical sports; frank and openminded approach in intellectual matters, especially debatable questions."

Public school curriculums were revised to place a smaller stress on the memorizing of fixed materials (e.g., dates and names in American history) and a greater stress on what Julia Richman called "practical civics," study of the actual workings of American government and society. Schools and playgrounds were opened for afternoons, evenings, and weekends, to provide social centers for children and to lure them away from the streets. (Nothing could finally do that . . .) Emphasis was placed on manners, grooming, little courtesies, often annoying to immigrant pupils but which in later years they would be wryly grateful for. Miss Richman, ruling her school district with a stern hand, instituted a range of practical reforms, from regular eye examinations for children to the organization of parent groups.

The main problem, of course, was to teach children to read, write, and speak a new, a *second*, language. Good sense, even imaginative sympathy, is shown in a 1907 syllabus designed for special English classes for immigrant children:

> Spoken language is an imitative art—first teaching should be oral, have children speak.
> Teach children words by having them work with and describe objects.
> Words should be illustrated by means of pictures, toys, etc.
> Presentation of material should keep pace with the pupil's growth in power.
> A bright pupil should be seated next to one less bright, one should teach the other.
> In copying, the purpose is language, not penmanship.

Until 1903 immigrant children had been placed in classes together with much younger American-born children, and as the English of the immigrant pupils improved they were promoted into classes with children nearer their own age. But by 1903–1904 the Board decided, in accord with a plan developed by Straubenmuller, that this method no longer worked, since it tended to humiliate the immigrant children and slow down the

American ones. Special classes were therefore set up to teach pupils of foreign parentage whose intellectual condition was in advance of their ability to express themselves in English. Pupils would remain in these special classes for a period of four or five months and then, having gained the rudiments of English, be assigned to regular classes.

Of the 250 special classes organized in 1905, 100 were held on the East Side. Most were smaller in size than normal classes, containing 30 to 35 pupils rather than the usual 45 to 50. The peak year for these special classes was 1912, when 31,000 pupils attended them; after that, the number steadily declined.*

Once immigration came to a stop with the outbreak of the First World War, these problems, though still unsolved, seemed less acute. Yet as late as 1914 a law was enacted in New York stipulating that children under sixteen who left school would have to complete at least the sixth grade—indicating, it would seem, that a good number were still failing to get through grammar school. It is chastening to note that in 1910 only some 6,000 out of 191,000 Jewish pupils in New York were attending high school. One out of three pupils in New York was Jewish, but only one out of four high-school pupils was Jewish. Allowing for the probability that the proportion of Jewish children under high-school age was greater than among the rest of the population, these figures still suggest that the dropout rate among Jewish children at or before the end of grammar school was not significantly better than for the remaining two thirds of the school population taken as a whole. It was better, however, than for other immigrant segments such as the Irish and Italians. A 1908 study of laggard students in the New York schools showed that no simple correlations could be established between command of English and classroom performance: children of German-born parents did better than children of American-born parents, the latter better than children of Russian-born parents, and the latter better than the children of Irish-born

---

* To deal with varying abilities of the immigrant children, a complex system of special classes was elaborated in 1905–1906. "C" classes were held for immigrant pupils between eight and fourteen years old who could speak no English. After a few months of intensive work they were either sent to regular classes or shifted to a special "E" class. The "E" classes were for pupils over the normal age who were enabled to advance rapidly through a modified course of instruction that relaxed the usual demands with regard to English. Most children in "E" classes were between eleven and fifteen. Finally, "D" classes were organized for children approaching fourteen who had no prospects of finishing the eighth grade; they were given the bare elements of literacy so they could get working papers. Over the years, the "E" classes became the most numerous and important, while "D" classes were gradually eliminated.

This system worked with a certain rough effectiveness—best, as usual, for the best students. In a little while, however, it began to decline into an informal track system, especially in schools with the least sympathetic principals: slow pupils and those for whom English formed a hopeless barrier were allowed to linger, or waste, in the "E" classes. One East Side principal, Edwin Goldwasser of P.S. 20, complained about this trend in 1912 and proposed that "E" classes be abolished; he wanted immigrant children to be either transferred quickly from special to regular classes or directed toward entering the labor force in their mid-teens.

and Italian-born parents. The bulk of Jewish immigrant children, studies indicate, were not very different in their capacities or performances from the bulk of pupils from most other ethnic groups.

During the years between 1900 and 1914 the Board of Education published quantities of material on these matters, some of it notable for flashes of insight and sympathy in regard to immigrant children, but still more for honesty in grappling with problems of handicapped, ungifted, and recalcitrant children. Conscientious efforts were made to provide the rudiments of learning to immigrant children, within the financial constraints imposed by the city and the intellectual limits of a culture persuaded that a rigorous, even sandpapery Americanization was "good" for the newcomers. To read the reports of the school superintendents is to grow impatient with later sentimentalists who would have us suppose that all or most Jewish children burned with zeal for the life of the mind. Some did, seemingly more so than among other immigrant communities, and these comprised a layer of brilliant students who would be crucial for the future of the American Jews. What made the immigrant Jewish culture distinctive was the fierce attention and hopes it lavished upon this talented minority.

NOTES

"streets were ours": Irving Howe, unpublished memoir. "diet of kippered herring": Eddie Cantor, *My Life Is in Your Hands*, 1928, p. 21. "on one corner": Anzia Yezierska, *Red Ribbon on a White Horse*, 1950, p. 101. "boy . . . looking brown": Cantor, p. 31. "washing away our sins": Dr. Herman Welkowitz, interview, Hebrew Home for the Aged, New York, July 1970. Allen Street: Louis Waldman, *Labor Lawyer*, 1944, p. 27. Sammy Aaronson: Sammy Aaronson, *As High as My Heart*, 1957, p. 18. "I played hooky": Harry Golden, *The Right Time*, 1969, p. 49. close to being a bum: Cantor, pp. 47–62. "We'd go to play ball": Louis Green, interview, Hebrew Home for the Aged, New York, July 1970. Jewish boys competitive: Charles H. Warner, "Tendencies in East Side Boy's Clubs," USS [*University Settlement Society*] *Reports*, 1901, p. 43. "separation of boys and girls": Sophie Ruskay, *Horsecars and Cobblestones*, 1948, pp. 41–42. "maybe five dollars": Marie Ganz, *Rebels: Into Anarchy—and Out Again*, 1920, p. 56. Henry Klein's story: Henry Klein, *My Last Fifty Years*, 1935, p. 10.

Parents and Children

"We push our children": *For.* [*Jewish Daily Forward*], 20 January 1911. "piano in front room": *For.*, 6 July 1903. "Alter, Alter": Arthur Goldhaft, *The Golden Egg*, 1957, p. 122. East Side,

no privacy: Yezierska, p. 110. "There never seemed": Irving Howe,
"A Memoir of the Thirties," in *Steady Work*, 1966, p. 355.

Delinquents and Gangs

"upwards of 300 boys and girls": Louis Marshall to Nathaniel
Elsberg, 25 February 1902, in American Jewish Archives, Cincinnati. children's courts: *For.*, 18 April 1904. drive children out?:
For., 18 April 1904. Younker quote: "Jewish Delinquent Children,"
Charities, 26 May 1906. "Mr. Ordway": minutes, Social, Educational and Improvement Club. pickpockets: Frederick King, "Influences in Street Life," *USS Reports*, 1900, p. 31. Rough schools
of experience: *ibid.*

Girls in the Ghetto

"fear of young women": Lillian Wald, *The House on Henry
Street*, 1915, p. 203. Council of Jewish Women: Rebecca Kohut,
His Father's House, New Haven, 1938, p. 254. "So I got a place":
Rose Schneiderman, "A Cap Maker's Story," *Independent*, 27 April
1905, p. 936. "When a grown girl": *For.*, 8 September 1905. Han-
nah's blouse: Samuel Chotzinoff, *A Lost Paradise*, 1955, p. 173.
Chernyshevsky: *ibid.*, p. 83. One such young woman: Elizabeth
Stern, *My Mother and I*, 1917, pp. 84–87. Yezierska's jobs: Anzia
Yezierska, "America and I," *Scribner's*, February 1922. "I am a
Russian Jewess": Anzia Yezierska, *Salome of the Tenements*, 1923,
p. 65. "While I was struggling," "What is it I hear," "struck by the
radiance": Anzia Yezierska, *Red Ribbon on a White Horse*, 1950,
pp. 31, 93, 216. "wanted a room": Stern, pp. 99–100.

Jewish Children, American Schools

school figures, 1905: Charles Bernheimer, ed., *The Russian
Jew in the United States*, Philadelphia, 1905, p. 185. Jewish groups
vis-à-vis Board of Ed.: [Selma] Berrol, ["Immigrants at School,
1898–1914," dissertation, City University of New York, 1967] p. 52;
Tageblatt, 25 September 1908. historian of New York education:
Berrol, pp. 53–54. "Respect for age": David Blaustein, *Memoirs*, ed.
Miriam Blaustein, 1913, p. 61. "other characteristics," Jewish stu-
dents: David Snedden, *Civic Education*, Yonkers, N.Y., 1922, pp.
291–92. 1907 syllabus: Board of Superintendents, New York,
Syllabus for C Classes, 1907. C, D, E classes: Board of Superintend-
ents, New York, *Report*, 1912. study of laggard students, 1908: L. P.
Ayers, *Laggards in Our Schools*, 1909, pp. 106–107.

"Not Enough Pay": Lawrence, 1912

HENRY F. BEDFORD

When the textile mills of the eastern Massachusetts river towns were built in the first half of the nineteenth century, they were looked upon as models of industrial development. Totally planned economic systems, paternalistically managed, staffed with young American women, they augured a period of relatively peaceful economic expansion.

By the end of the nineteenth century, however, the mill towns were not as idyllic as they had appeared to be, at least to the proprietors. Of the variety of social changes that had affected industrial America, the coming of the new immigrants was perhaps the most widely noted. This new wave of largely unskilled settlers of diverse cultural backgrounds, combined with an increasing trend toward radicalism among labor, brought crisis after crisis to America's industrial towns and cities around the turn of the century.

Because of their high visibility and strange ways, the new immigrants seemed to present a real threat to traditional American institutions. The theory of race suicide that was propounded at this time was a manifestation of the fear that the new immigration created in the existing population. Both the basis of the fear and the reality of the threat can be appraised through an investigation of the immigration statistics covering this period.

There was a veritable tidal wave of immigrants between 1900 and 1915; nine and one-half million persons emigrated to the United States from southern and eastern Europe. That is almost equal to the total number of emigrants from the United Kingdom for the previous one hundred years. Most of the new immigrants poured into the country through the seaports of the Northeast, and most of them never left the cities of the Eastern seaboard. Those who did leave tended to settle in the new and old industrial cities of the East and the Great Lakes area. The massive concentration of immigrants in these cities gave them a greater visibility than would have occurred had they been more evenly dispersed among the general population. In spite of the vast number of immigrants during this period, however, a study carried out in the 1920s showed that 51 percent of the American people were descended from families who had lived here during colonial times. Also, further studies have demonstrated that in 1880 about 12 percent of the population was foreign-born and that, while the figure for the foreign-born rose to 15 percent at the height of the new immigration, by 1930 the percentage had receded to 12. It seems, then, that the fears of being overwhelmed by an alien horde were based more on xenophobia (fear of strangers) than on reality. As for race suicide, studies have indicated that between 1890 and 1930 the total number of children born to native whites more than doubled, while the number of children born of foreign or mixed parentage did not quite double. So "the race" did not die out but, rather, continued to dominate the country's life and institutions.

There were occasions, however, when new immigrants and labor radicals successfully combined to challenge the industrial hierarchy. Such a case occurred in Lawrence, Massachusetts, in 1912, and is the subject of the next selection, one of a series of essays on local history written by Henry F. Bedford, of the Phillips Exeter Academy. According to Bedford's account of the 1912 textile strike, the new immigrants were not so much interested in labor organizations as they were in relieving their economic distress. The International Workers of the World (IWW), perhaps America's most radical labor organization, assisted the Lawrence strikers in their campaign. But once the strike was settled the workers showed little inclination to join the union. The Wobblies (as the union members were called) were destroyed by the United States government during the First World War. Today the textile industry continues to be the most underorganized industry of the advanced industrial sector of the economy. The essay that follows gives some indication of the living conditions of the workers and the means by which the forces of society attempted to subdue the protests of textile workers.

T he looms stopped. An eerie stillness settled over the weaving room of the Everett Mill. News of the interruption reached the offices, where the staff was busy with the payroll for about 2000 employees. On an ordinary day, one man might have investigated. Thursday, January 11, 1912, was no ordinary day, and several officials, joined by an interpreter, made their way toward the weaving room. Through the interpreter, someone asked one of the weavers why she had shut down her machine. Using English instead of her usual Polish, the woman replied, "Not enough pay."

She was right on two counts: her envelope contained less money than she usually received, and, by most measures, even her usual wage was too low. One of the men explained that a new state law permitted women and children under eighteen to work no more than fifty-four weekly hours, two fewer than before. Surely, he went on, the weavers expected wages to fall in proportion. The woman heard him out, and repeated "Not enough pay."

The looms remained still. The managers concluded that a strike had begun and asked the idle weavers to leave the mill quietly. As they left, the weavers persuaded other workers to join them. When the mills closed

"'Not Enough Pay': Lawrence, 1912." From *Trouble Downtown: The Local Context of Twentieth-Century America* by Henry F. Bedford (New York: Harcourt Brace Jovanovich, 1978), pp. 9–45. © 1978 by Harcourt Brace Jovanovich, Inc. and reprinted with their permission.

on Thursday evening, a third of the looms lacked operators. On Friday morning, one in eight was in service. At noon on Saturday, the Everett Mill closed. That was only the beginning.

"AMERICA IN MICROCOSM"

"Lawrence, Massachusetts," one historian has written, "was America in microcosm" in the winter of 1912.[1] The mills that now seem dingy and brooding were new and throbbing then, symbols of the country's vigorous industrialization. The mixed accents and tongues that bubbled through tenements and factories illustrated the collision of "new" immigrants from southern and eastern Europe with northern Europeans who had arrived a generation or two earlier. In the city's suburbs and middle-class neighborhoods, concerned professional and business people worried about the potential political power of naturalized but unassimilated immigrants, about the exploitation of factory workers by corporate employers, about the social consequences of industrial and urban growth.

The strike held the nation's attention because other Americans had the same fears. The solidarity of Lawrence's ethnically diverse workers suggested the existence of social classes and the possibility of class warfare, developments that belied much national folklore. The glimpse of social and economic upheaval both enraged and terrified those with most to lose. Reformers understood, and to some extent shared, that reaction. But the strike also emphasized for them the necessity of enlightened change, the need for more tolerable working conditions and fairer wages. The apparent success of a radical labor union, which thrilled those opposed to capitalism, revealed to other Americans the weakness of ordinary labor organizations and the inadequacy of factory legislation already enacted. For a few months, Lawrence became a social laboratory, testing for a fascinated nation beliefs that had evolved in a simpler society.

Those beliefs were best expressed by people called progressives in the years before the First World War. The term "progressive" lacked precision and the "progressive movement" certainly was neither coherent nor unified. Indeed, most Americans subscribed to much of the progressive creed, which held that the American system, although fundamentally sound, could be improved through the careful effort of decent, disinterested people. Progressives tended to see most other Americans in their own image—as calm and reasonable citizens, more sympathetic to individualism and property rights than recent immigrants and laborers, less greedy and cynical than industrial oligarchs. It was a confident vision, sometimes condescending, but rarely arrogant or mean.

Nor was it entirely accurate. Industrialization seemed merely to alter the scale of things: factories replaced shops, cities grew from towns, proprietors became corporations, employees joined unions. But a qualitative change accompanied this change of scope. The tasks of city governments were not only greater than those of towns but were often entirely differ-

[1] Melvyn Dubofsky, *We Shall Be All* (New York: Quadrangle, 1974), p. 235.

ent tasks. Factories not only produced more shoes than had artisans, but converted shoemakers from craftsmen to unskilled "hands." Immigrants, who arrived in mounting numbers, differed in language, religion, tradition, and property from those who had come earlier.

Most progressives recognized the existence of social injustice, but they did not always correctly identify its causes. Often they explained social dislocation as the result of inefficiency or some local or individual "abuse," such as political corruption or monopolistic power. The most obvious evils were those closest to home—dishonest aldermen, noisome slums, high fares on streetcars. And the first line of defense was also local: better candidates, judicious pressure on landlords and employers, municipal regulation or even ownership of public services. The variety of the so-called progressive movement, and much of its vitality as well, reflected its origin in local circumstance. The smorgasbord of solutions reflected the diverse provisions of dozens of state constitutions and hundreds of municipal charters, as well as the interests of reformers themselves.

Two groups of Bay State reformers seemed rivals as often as allies. One was Yankee, patrician or middle-class, professional, Republican, Protestant, and personally tied to industry only through dividends. Cities and immigrants, as these progressives saw them, were part of the problem. The other progressive strain consisted of just the sort of people that made the first group apprehensive. City-dwellers, of Irish or more recent immigrant stock, Catholic, and often connected with labor unions and Democratic political machines, these urban liberals were developing a program that foreshadowed a half century of American reform.

Massachusetts reformers had enacted during the nineteenth century much of the legislation that engaged their counterparts elsewhere in the years before the First World War. The state's legislature established commissions to regulate railroads and public utilities, a bureau of labor statistics to permit informed industrial regulation, and incorporation laws that discouraged "trusts." Several Massachusetts communities experimented with municipal ownership of generating plants to supply power for street lights, and a few with municipal distribution of fuel and other consumer goods. The state had tried to restrict child labor as early as 1836, and subsequently provided for the inspection of factories to insure decent conditions and appropriate safety procedures. In 1874, ten hours became the legal working day for women and children; the maximum work week was reduced to fifty-eight hours, to fifty-six in 1910, and then to fifty-four, effective January 1, 1912.[2]

Ironically, that final reduction triggered the strike in Lawrence. Before 1912, most industrial managers had adjusted wages so that fewer hours had not caused thinner pay envelopes. The action was voluntary, because most judges agreed that states could not enact a minimum wage. In 1912, Lawrence's managers refused to discuss a compensatory raise, and anxious employees concluded that there would be none. On the first payday in January, then, the Polish weaver and her companions found "not

[2] Richard M. Abrams, *Conservatism in a Progressive Era* (Cambridge: Harvard University Press, 1964), *passim*, especially chapter 1.

enough pay." However pleasant the two weekly hours of additional leisure, she needed the money more.

After the strike began, in response to a resolution of the United States Senate, the Commissioner of Labor sent statisticians to Lawrence to find out where the money went. The strikers claimed their weekly wage averaged between $5 and $6, but Commissioner Charles P. Neill's careful figure was $8.76—about 15¢ or 16¢ an hour. The "full-time earnings of a large number of adult employees," Neill found, "are entirely inadequate to maintain a family." People apparently subsisted on bread (about 3¢ per loaf), beets and onions (a nickel per pound), potatoes (40¢ per peck), and cheap cuts of meat ("pork neck . . . 12¢"). Stew beef, eggs, and butter were luxuries.

The commissioner's investigators found that six families in ten took in lodgers to share the average $3 weekly rent; seven occupants in a four- or five-room flat seemed the usual census. Almost all of these dwellings had running water and toilets, but Lawrence's building code did not regulate lighting, ventilation, or the structural adequacy of a building. In the wooden tenements of central Lawrence, Commissioner Neill observed, "the fire risk both to life and property is very great." Even without a fatal fire, long hours, congested living, and inadequate diet shortened lives. Textile cities, like Lawrence, had a notoriously high incidence of pneumonia and tuberculosis, and a notoriously high rate of infant mortality. The mean age at death in Lawrence was fifteen.[3]

At fifteen, many of Lawrence's residents had been at work for a year, and some for more than that. The state required attendance at school to age fourteen, a well-meant provision that both parents and employers too often had an interest in evading. Family income was so low that the few dollars a child earned could make the difference between eating and hunger. An inquiring congressman asked a boy in 1912 whether he regretted his departure from school at the fourth grade and whether he wished the state had required him to attend until he was sixteen. Sure, the lad replied, and he continued with a question of his own: "but what would we eat?" At fifteen, his wages exceeded his father's; he was the oldest child and there were six others at home.[4]

Like most of Lawrence's inhabitants, the boy was the child of immigrants. Indeed most of the people in Massachusetts were either immigrants or the children of immigrants, though the foreign element in Lawrence was unusually large and diverse. Only 14 percent of the city's 85,000 inhabitants were native-born of native parents; almost half had been born abroad: nearly 8000 in Canada, most of whom spoke French as their

[3] The report of the Commissioner of Labor was published as U.S., Congress, Senate, *Report on Strike of Textile Workers in Lawrence, Mass. in 1912*, 62nd Cong., 2d sess., 1912, Senate Document 870. The references in these paragraphs may be found at pages 20, 486, and 27. See also Donald B. Cole, *Immigrant City* (Chapel Hill: University of North Carolina Press, 1963), p. 212.

[4] U.S., Congress, House, Committee on Rules, *The Strike at Lawrence, Mass., Hearings Before the Committee on Rules . . . 1912*, 62nd Cong., 2d sess., 1912, House Document 671, p. 153.

native tongue; about 6500 in Italy; 6000 in Ireland; more than 4000 in parts of the Russian Empire, including Poland; and about 2000, called Syrians in Lawrence, who had been born in the Turkish Empire.[5]

THE FIRST DAYS

Formal delegations of employees ordinarily met a frosty reception in the offices of the Lawrence mills. Lest courtesy be mistaken for recognition of a labor organization, management routinely refused to answer questions from groups with any resemblance to a union. Late in 1911, when workers tried to discover how the fifty-four-hour law would be implemented, local managers turned them aside or referred them to corporate headquarters in Boston, whence no answer was forthcoming either. Lawrence officials reassured an executive from Boston, who asked whether a proportional reduction in wages would cause trouble. "At worst," they reported, a strike would "probably be confined . . . in a single mill."

Management, Commissioner Neill observed later, had lost touch with the people on the payroll. Posting the new law in the mills, as the law itself required, hardly constituted informing the employees and might be deliberately evasive, since Polish- and Italian-speaking workers could not reasonably be expected to understand legal English. Answering the questions of representative employees could not, Neill thought, imply official recognition of a union; corporate refusal to talk with employees was a lame excuse for arrogance.[6]

William Madison Wood—behind his back people called him "Billy"—certainly thought he knew his employees. To be sure, he was the president of the American Woolen Company, the largest corporation in the business; as much as anyone, he was responsible for the mergers that built the hundred-million-dollar trust that owned the most important mills in Lawrence and employed several thousand people there. The orphaned son of a Portuguese sea cook, Wood himself had started in a New Bedford textile mill when he was eleven. He worked hard, attracted the paternal interest of his employer, and moved up, and eventually on, to Lawrence where he married the boss's daughter. Wood always maintained that the interests of capital and labor coincided, and not even radicals doubted his sincerity. He believed he deserved the confidence of his employees, that he knew what was best for them. The workers would soon realize, he remarked at the outset of the strike in 1912, that "justice [was] not on their side," and that their action was "hasty and ill-advised." He was, Wood said, as much a corporate employee as they were.

> . . . I am bound . . . to take proper care of the interests of 13,000 stockholders [and] . . . of some 25,000 employees. It is my duty to see that each side has a square deal. . . . I have consulted long and

[5] Cole, *Immigrant City*, p. 209.
[6] Senate Document 870, pp. 10–11.

> anxiously with the directors. . . . Reluctantly and regretfully we
> have come to the conclusion that it is impossible . . . to grant any
> increase in wages. . . . I ask you to have confidence in this state-
> ment and to return to your work. . . . [F]our times this company
> has increased your wages without your asking. . . . This proves
> that I have looked after your interests pretty well in the past. Why
> should I not have your confidence for the future? [7]

There was, Joe Ettor thought, an answer to that question in the first
sentence of the basic document of the Industrial Workers of the World
(IWW): "The working class and the employing class have nothing in
common." Like William Wood, Joe Ettor was the son of a working man;
like Wood, Ettor had started early to make his own way. He drifted
from Brooklyn to Chicago to San Francisco, where he learned a skilled
trade, survived the 1906 earthquake, and watched the great fire with his
friend the proletarian novelist Jack London. At seventeen Ettor sent his
nickel to Socialist party headquarters to purchase a red button; in 1907,
at twenty-two, he was in the logging camps of Oregon enrolling lumber-
jacks in the IWW. Soon he had a hand in the IWW's efforts to organize
workers in steel mills, shoe shops, and mining camps.

Joe Ettor could deliver the union's simple message in English, Italian,
Polish, Yiddish, and broken Hungarian. He told his audiences that one
industrial union of skilled and unskilled, male and female, immigrant and
native, was the only effective force against the united bosses. He called
industrial sabotage a legitimate weapon in that no-holds-barred struggle.
He damned private property as legal theft and the government as the
agent of the exploiting class. Not for Joe Ettor the moderate's search for
harmonious compromise; he had chosen the workers' side. The workers
in Lawrence never thought of him as the outsider Wood tried to paint
him when Ettor arrived in January 1912.

Organizing industrial workers was difficult because they had little
bargaining power. The nation's major labor union, the American Federation of Labor (AFL), concentrated on craftsmen whose skills gave them
an economic leverage that textile workers, for instance, lacked because
unskilled labor abounded. Still, the AFL chartered a textile affiliate, the
United Textile Workers (UTWU), and spent money, energy, and prestige in a futile drive in Lawrence, where in 1912 fewer than one in ten textile workers belonged to any labor organization. John Golden, president
of the UTWU, attributed his union's failure to the presence of "these
new people, unacquainted with our ways, unable to speak our language,"
who were willing to work for wages that would have outraged "English-
speaking people. . . ." He told the congressional committee investigating
the strike that "the Federal Government should seriously consider the
restricting of immigration," an ironic stance for one who had himself
immigrated about twenty years earlier. The workers in Lawrence displayed their own sense of irony in a booklet entitled *What John Golden*

---

[7] *Ibid.*, p. 40, see also John B. McPherson, *The Lawrence Strike of 1912* (Boston: The
Rockwell and Churchill Press, 1912), p. 15.

Has Done for the Textile Workers; bound inside the impressive cover
were several eloquent blank pages.[8]

Even without a union, the strike quickly spread beyond the Everett
Mill. Payday elsewhere in the city was Friday, January 12, and most
employees expected less money than usual and more trouble. The worried paymaster at the Washington Mill delayed his rounds when he heard
that knots of workers were collecting, talking instead of working. When
disorder began, he suggested that Frank Sherman at the Wood Mill ought
to secure the doors. Sherman moved too slowly. "Within three minutes,"
he said later, "I heard the most ungodly yelling and howling and blowing
of horns I ever heard. . . ." The paymaster, "scared white," reported
that the mob had come through the doors and overpowered the watch-
man. Sherman told the paymaster to lock up the cash and let the crowd
run its course until the police came. As they had done in the Washington
Mill, strikers shut down machinery, by throwing the switch, by slashing
the belt, or simply by pulling the operator into the throng that rushed
on. Untended machines ruined some unfinished fabric, and the unruly
crowds knocked over stacks of finished goods. Sherman waited until the
wave subsided; it lasted about thirty minutes.[9]

Sherman's tactics foreshadowed management's approach to the strike:
lock up the money, let the first spontaneous energy dissipate, send for
the police, and distribute thin pay envelopes. While employers sat tight,
disgruntled employees sought a method of converting the demonstration
to a strike. A few members of the IWW—in more or less good standing—
sent for Joe Ettor, who arrived on Saturday and used the weekend to
devise an organizational structure that raised money, sustained morale,
and kept the strikers united and the community on edge for almost two
months. Ettor used the threat of violence, and the city's fear of it, to
counter management's strategy of delay. He could not prevent every
thrown rock and fist, but even an unfriendly observer noted that Ettor
controlled the strikers "as completely as any general ever controlled his
disciplined troops." [10]

Ettor's device was a strike committee organized by ethnic group,
rather than by craft as the AFL would have done, or by mill or employer,
a pattern the owners preferred. Each group elected three representatives,
who typically assembled in the morning to receive reports ("The Syrians
are standing firm"; "there are a few scabs among the Jews.") and to
discuss plans. The representatives returned to their neighborhoods later
in the day to carry instructions and to encourage the faint-hearted. Ettor
presided, but the committee was not an arm of the IWW. It was the
strike, not the union, that was important.

On Sunday, the newly formed committee agreed on a set of demands. Fifty-six-hours' pay for fifty-four-hours' work was no longer

[8] House Document 671, p. 81; see also Henry F. Bedford, *The Socialists and the
Workers in Massachusetts, 1886–1912* (Amherst: University of Massachusetts Press,
1966), p. 248.
[9] House Document 671, pp. 439–40.
[10] McPherson, *Lawrence Strike,* p. 9.

enough. The strikers asked an immediate 15 percent increase in wages and double pay for overtime. In addition, they demanded abolition of the "premium system," a schedule of monthly bonuses employers used to speed up production. To protect their jobs, strikers wanted management's promise not to discharge anyone because of activity during the strike. Significantly, they did not insist on recognition of their union. The committee encouraged workers to gather at the gates of the mills on Monday morning to persuade (or intimidate) those who might want to return to work.

That was the sort of activity Mayor John Scanlon intended to prevent. He called the city's commissioners into session at 5:45 on Saturday morning to provide more policemen for the emergency. He warned strikers against violence, asked that they not congregate in the streets, and suggested that they start negotiations with management promptly. He probably could not have done more. Mayor Scanlon had taken office only two weeks before under a new city charter that replaced politicians with commissioners. The new officials were supposed to be experts, capable of providing services more efficiently and less expensively than corruptible politicians. Progressives around the country advocated the city commission form of government partly to avoid the ethnic politics to which Lawrence was especially susceptible. But ethnic representatives, as Joe Ettor recognized, at least had standing in their neighborhoods, which "experts" sometimes lacked. And the experts in Lawrence, like the politicians they succeeded, all seemed to be Irish anyhow.

Mayor Scanlon took another step on Sunday with an order that sent one company of militia to the armory. He asked for two more on Monday morning, when police met pickets on the bridges leading to the mills. The crowd surged up the bridges, and harried officials turned on the fire hoses. Strikers parried with hunks of ice, coal, and other handy trash. Panic mounted inside the mills as windows smashed. About thirty strikers braved the barricades and the water and attempted to shut down the mill. Soldiers and police reinforcements arrived, scattered the crowd, and arrested thirty-six strikers. The city's courts acted promptly: within hours of their arrest, twenty-four rioters had been sentenced to a year in jail, and those carrying weapons received two years.

The mayor's attempt to promote negotiations foundered when management refused to meet with mediators. The strike committee did assemble and outlined the demands strikers had approved the day before. But, William Wood said, employers had no counterproposals for workers who destroyed property and were "in no frame of mind to discuss conditions." The city's responsibility, Wood continued, was not to find a compromise, but to end "mob rule." Mayor Scanlon had already sent for more soldiers.[11]

Scanlon's request went to Governor Eugene Foss, whose preelection record had contained little to cheer advocates of industrial reform. Foss himself owned textile mills; his success as a businessman plus his ability to contribute heavily to Democratic campaigns combined to bring him a

[11] *New York Call*, January 16, 1912; Senate Document 870, pp. 37–38, 60.

slightly tainted nomination for governor in 1910. He won the election, reelection twice, and promised to run the state "along well established business lines."

Yet once in office Foss was not the stereotypical probusiness executive. Instead he compiled a progressive record of the urban liberal stripe. Although he vetoed bills that permitted picketing, he signed other labor legislation, including the fifty-four-hour law, which he did not like, and a first attempt to establish workman's compensation. He approved statutes that regulated railroad rates, monopolistic prices, and tenement housing. It was sober legislation, offering more to organized labor than unions had had before, and annoying "the interests" without undermining them. The Foss administration, in short, encouraged a somewhat more democratic and humane society, but did not fundamentally challenge the existing social order.[12]

The governor sent troops to Lawrence, and his secretary, Dudley Holman, as well. Foss wanted a first-hand report and, if possible, a resolution of the strike before events slipped out of control. Holman met late Monday night with Mayor Scanlon, police officials, and Colonel Leroy Sweetser, the officer in charge of the militia. Early the next morning, Holman prowled the mill district looking for Ettor, whose office seemed to be in the streets. Accompanied at first by Ettor's self-appointed bodyguards, who feared he might be arrested, the two men walked and talked in the subzero dawn. Holman reported the governor's hope that the state board of arbitration might be helpful. Ettor did not like the idea, but presented it to the strike committee, where a majority overruled him. Holman telephoned Foss to convey the strikers' willingness to take their case to the state agency.

The meeting never took place. The strikers sent the delegation they had promised. The state board of arbitration appeared. But several employers, including American Woolen, refused to send representatives. Consequently, Holman said, "the thing fell through." A committee of the Massachusetts legislature subsequently held an equally barren session in Lawrence. Two weeks later, Foss himself sought a way out of the impasse. He asked the workers to return to the mills for thirty days, and he asked the employers to keep weekly wages at the fifty-six-hour level. A month, Foss thought, should suffice for him to find a solution. He pledged his "best efforts" and expected "a settlement satisfactory to all parties." Nobody answered his letter.[13]

VICTORY!

The strike in Lawrence began about six weeks after James McNamara had ended a sensational trial by pleading guilty to blowing up the headquarters of the *Los Angeles Times* in the course of labor warfare in southern California. For some time after that explosion, any American

[12] Abrams, *Conservatism in a Progressive Era*, pp. 251–61.
[13] House Document 671, 347–48, 350; Senate Document 870, p. 44.

labor dispute inspired rumors of dynamite. Stories flashed through Lawrence and surfaced in the press—prematurely in one instance when a Boston newspaper described a cache police located about the time the headline appeared. Checking reports of three other bombs, Lawrence police raided a tenement in the Syrian district, where they found some explosives and arrested seven residents. More dynamite turned up in the cobbler shop in the Italian district Joe Ettor used as an address; the cobbler was arrested. But the police had trouble with the third batch they had heard about, which was supposed to be somewhere near the cemetery.

Who knew more about Lawrence's cemeteries than John Breen, the genial undertaker who had first told the police about the dynamite? Breen drew a map for the officers, who returned to the cemetery and found what they were looking for. It seemed a little strange that the explosives were wrapped in an undertaker's trade journal; it seemed even more strange when police discovered that only Breen, of all the city's undertakers, did not have that issue. The judge at the local police court, who without hesitation had sentenced "rioters" to a year, threw out the cases against the Syrians and the cobbler. Persons "interested in maintaining a reign of terror in this city," said Judge J. J. Mahoney, not the immigrant defendants in his courtroom, had planted the dynamite.

As a matter of fact—and of increasingly common knowledge—John Breen had. A local contractor, showing the effect of too much drink and perhaps of a troubled conscience as well, blurted to the prosecuting attorney that William Wood had had his hands on the dynamite. Or at least that was the story the prosecutor told to a grand jury. But the contractor sobered up and killed himself, and the indictment of Wood did not stick. Breen was convicted, fined, and recalled from the school committee, which was supposed to have been the first step toward succeeding his father as the city's Irish political boss.

The bungled dynamite plot was only one indication of rising tension as the days became weeks and neither side flinched. The strike committee improved its organization by adding alternates and designating substitutes to take over if leaders were arrested. A major effort to raise funds among radicals and labor groups brought in nearly $1000 each day to provide soup kitchens and living allowances for strikers and their families. Ettor designed new tactics to make picketing more effective and to harass the inexperienced militiamen. Parading pickets carried the American flag, taunted the soldiers to salute it, and then pushed through the formation that was supposed to be a barrier, shouting, "The American flag can go anywhere." Women—pregnant women if possible—marched in the first ranks of the strikers' demonstrations in order to make security forces think twice about nightsticks and bayonets. Other women, when arrested, refused to post bond or otherwise to expedite trial, and then nursed and cared for their children while in jail. When authorities forbade pickets to stop and talk with employees willing to return to work, Ettor marshaled 10,000 strikers who moved continuously through the mill district, thereby complying with the order and defeating its purpose. Pickets linked arms and swept singing through the streets four- or five-abreast.

When police or militia disrupted the columns, large groups, still singing and still with linked arms, moved from the streets to the stores. Nervous customers departed and nervous merchants protested. A congressman subsequently asked the acting chief of police why he had not arrested the leaders of these demonstrations. "There are no leaders in the streets," the bewildered chief replied.[14]

Monday, January 29, started badly when strikers stopped streetcars in order to keep passengers from reaching the mills. By seven in the morning, derailed cars, broken windows, and bruised patrons persuaded managers of the street railway company to shut the line down. The crowd, its anger momentarily dampened, flowed off singing radical songs. Several thousand jeering strikers paused in front of the residence of a priest who had urged his flock to return to work. People loudly discussed demolition of church and rectory, and then the throng moved along. When the bayonets of militiamen blocked further progress, Ettor tactfully diverted the demonstrators up a side street to avoid confrontation, for the mood of the city became increasingly ugly as the day wore on.

That afternoon strikers and police clashed in one of the residential neighborhoods. The jostling ended in shots, and a young striker named Annie LoPezzi died on the sidewalk. Strikers claimed a police officer fired the fatal shot; the police alleged that someone shooting at an officer had accidentally killed a bystander instead. Joe Ettor and Arturo Giovannitti, the radical editor and poet who had accompanied Ettor to Lawrence, were arrested the following day, charged with having incited an unknown killer. Both men had been in other parts of the city when the shooting took place, but they were denied bail and remained in prison for the next ten months.[15] The strike committee added a new demand to the list: Ettor and Giovannitti must be released.

Murder inspired a formal resolution from the city council asking the militia to restore order. Governor Foss raised the available force to 1300 men by sending twelve additional companies of infantry and two troops of cavalry to Lawrence. Colonel Sweetser forbade meetings, parades, picketing, and intimidation, and stationed his troops all over the city. The next day, a detachment responded to a report that a parade was forming in the Syrian section. Troops moved to disperse the band. John Ramy, a young musician, did not move quickly enough and died of a bayonet wound in the back. There was a perfunctory investigation that disclosed no names. A congressman later remarked sarcastically that he had missed in the account of Lawrence's chief of police "what sort of deadly weapon the boy had in his hand at the time he was killed." "I did not say he had a deadly weapon," the chief replied; "I said he had a musical instrument." [16]

[14] House Document 671, pp. 261ff, 292, 302; Philip S. Foner, *The Industrial Workers of the World* (New York: International Publishing Co., 1965), pp. 321–22.
[15] House Document 671, pp. 290–94; McPherson, *Lawrence Strike*, pp. 26–27; *New York Call*, January 29, 30, 1912.
[16] House Document 671, p. 296; Foner, *IWW*, p. 331; Senate Document 870, pp. 44–45.

Colonel Sweetser had made his point. The strikers stayed at home. So did many of those whom the strikers had been intimidating. Unions representing skilled workers decided they were on strike too. In the second month of the strike the number of employees actually present in the mills dipped to its lowest point. A reporter visited the Washington Mill, where the machinery hummed. But, he noted, "not a single operative was at work and not a single machine carried a spool of yarn." [17] His visit verified Big Bill Haywood's remark that "You can't weave cloth with bayonets."

Members of the IWW were often called "wobblies" and one-eyed William D. (Big Bill) Haywood had a national reputation as the wildest "wobbly" of them all. His foes, and some of his radical comrades, exaggerated Haywood's penchant for violence, but he was indeed a charismatic man with a genuine outrage about the exploitation of industrial workers and a demonstrated ability to inspire them. After Ettor's arrest, Haywood replaced him on the strike committee and assumed much of the responsibility for directing the strike. Together with Elizabeth Gurley Flynn, the twenty-two-year-old "red flame," and others of the union's hierarchy, he whipped up the spirit of workers on the scene and raised money outside the city for their support.

An Italian immigrant at a meeting in New York City did not have much money. But his family, he said, would welcome a child or two from a striker's family. Although one or two more mouths at his table would not make much difference, the absence of hungry babies might stiffen the resistance of wavering workers in Lawrence. That was how workers in the old country helped one another. Haywood and the strike committee liked the idea. *The Call*, a socialist daily in New York, made an appeal on behalf of "the little children of Lawrence," and volunteers appeared from all over the city.[18]

Other radicals in other places wanted their share of the heroic "little children." Emotional departures from the train station in Lawrence triggered one set of news releases, greetings at host cities another. Physicians examined the children and gave out statements about rickets and malnutrition. Observers remarked the shabby clothing children wore and the paradoxical fact that those who wove woolen cloth could not afford to wear it. Margaret Sanger, an idealistic young nurse whose experience in public health would make her the nation's foremost proponent of birth control, testified that only 4 of the 119 children she examined wore underwear.[19]

As the children moved out, the money rolled in, and the strike dragged on. The Lawrence city fathers, proud of their city, thought it deserved better than the publicity the "little children" generated, and decided to keep them at home. Colonel Sweetser informed the strike committee that he would not "permit the shipping off of little children

[17] *New York Times*, February 1, 1912.
[18] *New York Call*, February 8–11, 1912.
[19] *Ibid.*, February 12, 1912; House Document 671, pp. 232–33.

. . . unless I am satisfied that this is done with the consent of their parents." [20]

Within a few days, the strike committee announced that 150 children would, with the consent of their parents, accept invitations to visit Philadelphia for the duration of the strike. On the day of departure, almost two months after the walkout began, early arrivals at the depot noticed a company of militia parading in the street outside. Inside, an inordinate number of policemen fanned out through the station, clearing out loiterers and then assembling in two parallel ranks leading toward a door. Outside the door, the chief had parked an open truck he had borrowed from the militia. He approached the children, who had clustered in the waiting room, and told them of the city's readiness to supply charitable relief: "[I]f any of you make a . . . request for aid or assistance you will receive it." Only about 40 children, and fewer adults, had withstood the intimidating show of force, and they were not deterred by the chief's kind words. They declined to argue, waited for the train, and moved to board it when it was announced. The police diverted them to the truck, and thence to jail.

But not without an uproar. The radical press described beatings, blood, miscarriages, and weeping, bruised children in cells. The rhetoric was borrowed from Russian uprisings—Cossacks, tyranny, pogroms. Even Samuel Gompers, the president of the AFL and no supporter of the tactics of the IWW, grumbled that nobody would have detained the sons and daughters of millionaires. Judge Ben Lindsay, a reformer from Denver known as "the children's judge," noted that "those children will probably not miss the Constitution—they have missed so much else." The Attorney General of the United States said the authorities had made "a stupid blunder." Months later, the police chief was still bewildered. He had not seen any violence, he said; he was just enforcing the statute that prohibited parental neglect of children.[21]

One of the congressmen investigating the strike was delighted at last to have a statute to discuss. He tried to pin down the chief's superior, Lawrence's Commissioner of Public Safety: "Under what law of the State of Massachusetts were you acting in the matter?" The commissioner did not know "offhand." The congressman kept at it: "Did you know what the law was at the time?" The commissioner said somebody had looked it up. The congressman tried once more: Was there any applicable statute, he asked. "I think there is," was the best the commissioner could do. "Did you read that law?" the congressman inquired. "I did not read it; no sir," the commissioner replied. "I think not," the exasperated congressman remarked, and turned to another topic.[22]

Mill officials knew immediately that the scene at the station disgraced the one-sided law enforcement upon which they relied. They authorized a defensive statement denying responsibility for the city's effort to detain the children. "The manufacturers did not ask for this [action]; they were

[20] Senate Document 870, p. 51.
[21] *New York Call*, February 25, 29, 1912; House Document 671, pp. 303–09.
[22] House Document 671, p. 281.

not consulted about it; they were not informed of the contemplated action of the local authorities." [23] The owners knew they were in trouble; the struggle could no longer be kept in Lawrence where they had a chance to control it. The Senate would soon send Commissioner Neill's investigators to Lawrence; the Committee on Rules of the House of Representatives convened hearings on the strike. Congressional criticism of the industry's labor practices might undermine support for the textile schedules of the protective tariff.

And by the end of February, Governor Foss had had enough too. His disclaimer about events at the station echoed that of the mill owners: local authorities controlled the police; he had not been consulted; the militia was not involved. Indeed, Foss wrote the owners, it was time to send the militia home; he did not propose to have the military forces of Massachusetts used to break the strike. Both the governor and the owners knew that the militia's departure would leave discredited police officials responsible for law and order. Foss asked the state's attorney general to look into the incident at the depot to see whether any citizen's constitutional rights had been abridged. Foss then let the pressure build with the word that he was "disappointed" that management had not tried more diligently to settle the strike.[24]

In fact management had begun to seek a settlement, less because of political pressure than because of a flood of orders. On March 1, Wood met a delegation from the strike committee. American Woolen would raise wages 5 percent, he said, and similar notices appeared in the other mills. The strikers thought Wood's offer too little, too late, and too vague. Within a week, the delegation had another invitation. It would take time, Wood said, to spell out the new rates for each employee. The strikers replied that they could wait until the lists were prepared, even though some of the skilled employees had already accepted Wood's terms. On March 9, Wood clarified his offer another time, with a schedule that showed a raise up to 11 percent. The strikers waited again. Three days later, Wood gave in: the raise for the most poorly paid workers was more than 20 percent, and no one received less than 5; an additional 25 percent would be paid for overtime. Premiums would be calculated every two weeks instead of once a month. No worker would be penalized for participation in the strike. The strikers met on the Lawrence Common, cheered, sang, and accepted.[25]

One troubling loose end remained: Ettor and Giovannitti were still in jail. The employers promised to use their influence to achieve the prisoners' release, but Essex County's legal staff stubbornly did its duty. Spring became summer, and summer turned to fall. Haywood and Flynn went on to other struggles in other cities, where they occasionally took up a collection to help pay their comrades' legal expenses. Roland Sawyer, a socially conscious minister from Ware and the Socialist's party's candidate for governor against Eugene Foss, subordinated his political cam-

[23] McPherson, *Lawrence Strike*, pp. 37–38; *New York Call*, February 29, 1912.
[24] *New York Call*, February 9, 1912; Foner, *IWW*, p. 341.
[25] Senate Document 870, pp. 54–59.

paign to an effort to reach the jurors who might judge Ettor and Giovannitti. Sawyer made a batch of slides from his photographs of the strike, prepared a set of resolutions, and wrote an all-purpose speech, which he gave wherever he could find an audience.

Joe Ettor knew who his friends were. He sent Sawyer a warm note, thanking him for his public effort and private encouragement. Tell everybody for me, Ettor wrote, that "I am putting my time to good use reading and studying," that I "am enjoying my usual good health," that I "am not discouraged, [but] buoyant as ever." He was, Ettor claimed, guilty only of his *"loyalty to the working class."* If he were convicted, "and if the reward be death," he wrote, "I will part with life with a song on my lips." [26]

There was no need for that. The jury acquitted Ettor and Giovannitti and ended their months of imprisonment. The verdict came at Thanksgiving time, and there was indeed much to be thankful for. Textile workers elsewhere in New England received wage increases comparable to those in Lawrence, often without more than mentioning a strike. New windows and new belts made the mills as good as new, and the confidence of employers returned when membership in the IWW shrank as quickly as once it had grown. Civic boosters mounted a parade for "God and Country" to dramatize the transcience of radicalism and the permanence of conventional values, and to restore the city's morale and public reputation.

Anxiety about Lawrence's reputation stemmed from intense national interest in the strike. Social workers, labor leaders, journalists, politicians, and miscellaneous tourists swarmed to the city to see events at first-hand. Senator Miles Poindexter of Washington, barred by police from interviewing those arrested at the railway station, told reporters the city was a "concentration camp." William Allen White, whose Emporia, Kansas, newspaper had a national circulation, remarked that the immigrant strikers possessed a "clearer vision of what America stands for than did many of those who sneered at them." [27] When Congressman Victor Berger, a Socialist from Milwaukee, introduced a resolution authorizing a congressional investigation, he submitted a sheaf of supportive petitions. They came from labor organizations in Mattoon, Illinois, and Moundsville, West Virginia; from Bellingham, Washington, and Bellefontaine, Ohio; from the city council of Thief River Falls, Minnesota, and the Socialists of Jersey City; from reformers in Spokane, Washington, and Washington, D.C. [28]

The strike caught the nation's attention because it offered a glimpse of what might be the future—a sobering preview for progressive, middle-class Americans, a shocking one for conservatives, and an exhilarating one for radicals and factory workers. To be sure, Lawrence was a unique community, and conditions there did not obtain in every other industrial center. But conditions might rapidly change: if immigration were not

[26] Joe Ettor to Roland D. Sawyer, June 1912, ms in possession of author.
[27] *New York Call*, February 27, March 1, 1912.
[28] House Document 671, pp. 11–23.

restricted, if wealth were not more equitably distributed, if unions and bosses were not restrained—if somebody, in short, did not do something—any place might become a Lawrence in the none-too-distant future.

That was no pleasant prospect—for progressives, in many ways, least pleasant of all. Through reform, they had intended to enable Americans to avoid precisely the sort of class confrontation that had manifestly occurred in Lawrence. Progressives hoped to convince employers that justice and self-interest alike demanded decent wages and working conditions. And progressives believed that those concessions, whether coerced by legislation or freely offered by enlightened businessmen, ought to persuade employees that the American system worked. Progressives advocated reform because they believed the nation's institutions were fundamentally fair. The strike in Lawrence suggested that reformers might have to choose between their acceptance of social stability and their sympathy for the victims of social injustice.

Walter Weyl, a journalist and student of labor disputes, continued to postpone the choice. As he surveyed the strike for *The Outlook*, a progressive weekly that carried Theodore Roosevelt's name on the masthead, Weyl favored both the strikers and the militia—well-behaved lads, Weyl thought, who ought to have been playing ball. He condemned radical labor leaders, particularly Ettor and Haywood, and also "ruthless, immoral, ill-advised" employers for creating an explosive situation: "If out of this caldron of disillusion there should come a quick, hot flame of violence, it must be promptly extinguished. *Neither may we allow men, however wealthy or respectable, to scatter explosives on the ground.*"[29]

In condemning impartially all parties to an industrial dispute, progressives often unconsciously paraded their own purity of motive. The "best citizens" of Lawrence—"judges, ministers, . . . bankers, shopkeepers, and workingmen of character and reputation," *The Outlook* reported —had begun a disinterested search for compromise. These people, "who are viewed with confidence by all classes," the editorial continued, should urge "operators to return to work at once." [30] And that, presumably, would be that. In the public interest, workers and owners alike ought to defer to middle-class citizens. The proposition was not necessarily wrong, but it had no connection with the behavior of real people in Lawrence, Massachusetts, or much of anywhere else.

Yet the people who faced Eugene Foss were real enough, as were those during other industrial disputes who visited other progressive mayors, governors, and Presidents. In difficult circumstances, Foss struck a progressive balance with more skill than contemporaries saw: he sent troops to restore order and prepared to withdraw them when their presence enhanced unduly the bargaining power of the mill owners. In other circumstances, other progressive politicians had to find a similar balance between order and justice, between the rights of employees and

[29] The italics are Weyl's; the reference is not literally to dynamite, but to social explosives. Walter Weyl, "The Strikers at Lawrence," in *Outlook*, February 10, 1912, pp. 309, 312.

[30] *The Outlook*, February 17, 1912, pp. 352, 353, 358.

those of employers, between the need for governmental regulation and the tradition of individual liberty, between the protection of existing interests and the preservation of opportunity in the future.

That balance became increasingly elusive in the years before the First World War, and the optimistic faith of progressives increasingly difficult to sustain. In Lawrence, employers showed no shame about their un-awakened social consciences, and employees spurned progressive remedies in favor of unions and radicalism and solutions they designed themselves. Even progressive legislation, administered by progressive executives, had unpredictable, and sometimes unprogressive, results. Had the fifty-four-hour law improved life in Lawrence? If the commissioners enacted a new building code, would mill workers be able to secure better housing? If William Wood were converted to welfare capitalism, would the stock-holders of American Woolen indulge him? Did it all come down to restricting immigration, as labor leaders and patricians alike suggested, or to Prohibition, which became the crusade of Governor Foss? Was that the best the nation could do in the face of manifest injustice in Law-rence?

Walter Weyl kept coming back to a meeting in Mayor Scanlon's office. The visiting state legislators were seeking a middle ground and trying to impress the strikers with their good intentions and good will. Finally one of the strikers asked the legislators just how far they would go:

> If you find one party wrong, can your state force it to do right? . . . Would you arbitrate a question of life and death, and are the worst wages paid in these mills anything short of death? Do you investigate because conditions are bad, or because the workers broke loose and struck? Why did you not come before the strike? What can your state of Massachusetts do to make wrong right for the workingmen who are the bulk of your citizens?

That last one was the central question, Weyl thought. "What can the state do? What can we do to make wrong right for the people of our mills and factories?" [31] That was the question the strike had posed. And the nation had, as yet, no certain answer.

[31] Weyl, pp. 311–312.

Konklave in Kokomo

ROBERT COUGHLAN

Americans have always been enamored of secret societies. Since before the War of American Independence such organizations have been available for those seeking them. Most of these organizations were relatively harmless gatherings of men seeking to practice private peccadilloes as in the Hell Fire Club, or to escape humdrum religious belief as in the Rosicrucian and Freemason societies.

In the middle of the nineteenth century, however, the growing agitation against "foreign" influence in American life, primarily Roman Catholicism, led to a more ominous development. Indeed, a political party, the Know Nothings, grew out of a secret organization known as the Order of the Star Spangled Banner and had as its purpose the banning of foreigners from American political life.

During Reconstruction, the most famous of the secret societies was organized—the Ku Klux Klan. After a harmless beginning, the Klan took as its purpose the elimination of blacks and their white supporters and allies from political participation in the post-bellum South. Reconstruction and the first Klan died at about the same time. There was, in fact, no need for the Klan in the post-Reconstruction South because legal segregation forced the blacks into a subordinate caste system from which they only began to emerge after the Second World War.

That did not mean, however, that all threats to traditional society had been defeated. The new immigrants from Southern and Eastern Europe provided an even greater threat to "the American way of life" than did the blacks. After all, the new threat was from white men (albeit often swarthy in complexion) who followed alien dogmas. One medium for dealing with this problem proved to be the reborn Klan— whose white knights had become a legend that had grown through fiction and in fancy and had been fixed in celluloid with the production of D. W. Griffith's film classic "The Birth of a Nation."

A major factor in the growth of the second Klan was the social dislocation that came as a result of the First World War. The new Klan gave disgruntled native Americans a voice and an organization with which to try to turn back the clock. Interestingly, the new Klan had its greatest success, not in its old homeland, but in the transitional areas in the Border States and in the new industrial cities of the North and Midwest.

In the selection reprinted below, Robert Coughlan, magazine writer and editor, describes what the Klan meant in his home town of Kokomo, Indiana. Rather than discussing the violence and excesses of the Klan that have been adequately described elsewhere, Coughlan concentrates on the banality and unintentional humor of Klan ritual and practice. All the marks of the secret society are there: private language, secret signs, elaborate costume (the plain bed sheet was only for the rank and file), and complicated ritual. The author portrays the way in which charismatic leaders preyed on the simple prejudices of ordinary people in order to bind them together in a political movement that proved to be remarkably potent in the mid-1920s. Fortunately for American society, the new Klan fell apart in disillusionment with the revelation of immoral activities by the leadership. Having based the power of the Klan on the simple pieties and moralities of ordinary people, the leadership could not survive the moral revulsion of its members. Thus the second Klan died.

This does not mean that the sentiments expressed in the Ku Klux Klan have passed from the American scene. As a matter of fact, many private organizations today continue to bemoan the existence of alien elements in American life and spend a great deal of time espousing what is now usually called "one hundred percent Americanism." These organizations, along with many of the churches, formed the backbone of the anti-Communist hysteria of the post–Second World War era, and many of them continue to issue anti-Semitic, anti-Catholic, and, of course, anti-black propaganda.

1

On a hot July day in central Indiana—the kind of day when the heat shimmers off the tall green corn and even the bobwhites seek shade in the brush—a great crowd of oddly dressed people clustered around an open meadow. They were waiting for something; their faces, framed in white hoods, were expectant, and their eyes searched the bright blue sky. Suddenly they began to cheer. They had seen it: a speck that came from the south and grew into an airplane. As it came closer it glistened in the sunlight, and they could see that it was gilded all over. It circled the field slowly and seesawed in for a bumpy landing. A bulky man in a robe and hood of purple silk hoisted himself up from the rear cockpit. As he climbed to the ground, a new surge of applause filled the country air. White-robed figures bobbed up and down; parents hoisted their children up for a view. A small delegation of dignitaries filed out toward the airplane, stopping at a respectful distance.

The man in purple stepped forward.

"Kigy," he said.

"Itsub," they replied solemnly.

With the newcomer in the lead the column recrossed the field, pro-

"Konklave in Kokomo," by Robert Coughlan. From *The Aspirin Age*, edited by Isabel Leighton, pp. 105–29. Copyright © 1949 by Simon & Schuster, Inc. Reprinted by permission of Simon & Schuster, a Division of Gulf & Western Corporation.

ceeded along a lane carved through the multitude, and reached a platform decked out with flags and bunting. The man in purple mounted
the steps, walked forward to the rostrum, and held up his right hand to
hush the excited crowd.

"My worthy subjects, citizens of the Invisible Empire, Klansmen all,
greetings!

"I grieves me to be late. The President of the United States kept me
unduly long counseling upon vital matters of state. Only my plea that
this is the time and place of my coronation obtained for me surcease
·from his prayers for guidance." The crowd buzzed.

"Here in this uplifted hand, where all can see, I bear an official document addressed to the Grand Dragon, Hydras, Great Titans, Furies,
Giants, Kleagles, King Kleagles, Exalted Cyclops, Terrors, and All Citizens of the Invisible Empire of the Realm of Indiana. . . .

"It is signed by His Lordship, Hiram Wesley Evans, Imperial Wizard, and duly attested.

"It continues me officially in my exalted capacity as Grand Dragon
of the Invisible Empire for the Realm of Indiana. It so proclaims me by
Virtue of God's Unchanging Grace. So be it."

The Grand Dragon paused, inviting the cheers that thundered around
him. Then he launched into a speech. He urged his audience to fight
for "one hundred per cent Americanism" and to thwart "foreign elements" that he said were trying to control the country. As he finished
and stepped back, a coin came spinning through the air. Someone threw
another. Soon people were throwing rings, money, watch charms, anything bright and valuable. At last, when the tribute slackened, he motioned to his retainers to sweep up the treasure. Then he strode off to
a near-by pavilion to consult with his attendant Kleagles, Cyclopses, and
Titans.

2

That day, July 4, 1923, was a high-water mark in the extraordinary
career of David C. Stephenson, the object of these hysterics; and it was
certainly one of the greatest days in the history of that extraordinary
organization the Knights of the Ku Klux Klan. The occasion was a tri-
state Konklave of Klan members from Illinois, Ohio, and Indiana. The
place was Melfalfa Park, the meeting place, or Klavern, of the Klan chapter of Kokomo, Indiana, the host city. Actually, although planned as
a tri-state convention, it turned out to be the nearest thing to a rank-
and-file national convention the Klan ever had. Cars showed up from
almost every part of the country. The Klan's official estimate, which
probably was not far wrong in this case, was that two hundred thousand
members were there. Kokomo then had a population of about thirty
thousand, and naturally every facility of the town was swamped.

The Konklave was an important day in my life. I was nine years old,
with a small boy's interest in masquerades and brass bands. But I was

also a Catholic, the son of a Catholic who taught in the public schools and who consequently was the object of a good deal of Klan agitation. If anything worse was to come, the Konklave probably would bring it. Every week or so the papers had been reporting Klan atrocities in other parts of the country—whippings, lynchings, tar-and-feather parties—and my father and his family were logical game in our locality.

Nevertheless, in a spirit of curiosity and bravado, my father suggested after our holiday lunch that we drive out to Melfalfa Park, which lies west of the town, to see what was happening. My mother's nervous objections were overcome, and we all got into the family Chevrolet and set out for West Sycamore Road. We saw white-sheeted Klansmen everywhere. They were driving along the streets, walking about with their hoods thrown back, eating in restaurants—they had taken the town over. But it was not until we were well out toward Melfalfa Park that we could realize the size of the demonstration. The road was a creeping mass of cars. They were draped with flags and bunting, and some carried homemade signs with Klan slogans such as "America for the Americans," or "The Pope will sit in the White House when Hell freezes over." There were Klan traffic officials every few yards, on foot, on motorcycles, or on horseback, but they were having a hard time keeping the two lanes of cars untangled and moving, and the air was full of the noise of their police whistles and shouts. The traffic would congeal, grind ahead, stop again, while the Klan families sat steaming and fanning themselves in their cars. Most of them seemed to have made it a real family expedition: the cars were loaded with luggage, camping equipment, and children. Quite a few of the latter—even those too young to belong to the junior order of the Klan—were dressed in little Klan outfits, which did not save them from being smacked when their restiveness annoyed their hot and harassed parents. The less ardent or more philosophical Klansmen had given up and had established themselves, with their picnic baskets and souvenir pillows, in shady spots all along the road and far into the adjoining fields and woods. From his gilded airplane, D. C. Stephenson must have seen a landscape dappled for miles around with little knots of white.

Since there was no way of turning back we stayed with the procession, feeling increasingly conspicuous. Finally we came to the cross road whose left branch led past the entrance to Melfalfa. We turned right and started home.

So we missed seeing the Konklave close up. But the newspapers were full of it, and people who were there have been able to fill in the details for me. The program gave a good indication of what the Klan was all about, or thought it was about. The Konklave started in midmorning with an address by a minister, the Reverend Mr. Kern of Covington, Indiana. The Reverend Kern spent most of his time warning against the machinations of Catholics and foreigners in the United States. When he finished, a fifty-piece boys' band from Alliance, Ohio, played "America" and the crowd sang. Then a band from New Castle, Indiana, played the "Star-Spangled Banner" and the Reverend Everett Nixon of Kokomo gave the invocation. These preliminaries led up to a speech by Dr. Hiram Wesley Evans, the national leader of the Klan, who had come all the way from headquarters at Atlanta, Georgia. Dr. Evans commented gracefully on the fact that the center of Klan activities seemed to have shifted from Atlanta to Kokomo, and then talked on "Back to the Constitution." In his view, the Constitution was in peril from foreigners and "foreign influences," and he urged his audience to vote for Congressmen who would legislate "to the end that the nation may be rehabilitated by letting Americans be born into the American heritage." By the time Dr. Evans finished it was lunch time, and the Klan families spread their picnic cloths through the leafy acres of Melfalfa Park. Block-long cafeteria tables lined the banks of Wildcat Creek. From these, the women's auxiliary of the Klan dispensed five thousand cases of pop and near-beer, fifty-five thousand buns, twenty-five hundred pies, six tons of beef, and supplementary refreshments on the same scale.

It was after lunch, at about 2 P.M., when the crowd was full of food and patriotic ecstasy, that D. C. Stephenson made his dramatic descent from the sky.

The rest of the day, after Stephenson's speech, was given over to sports, band concerts, and general holiday frolic. That night there was a parade down Main Street in Kokomo. And while an outside observer might have found a good deal to be amused at in the antics of the Klan during the day, no one could have seen the parade that night without feelings of solemnity. There were thirty bands; but as usual in Klan parades there was no music, only the sound of drums. They rolled the slow, heavy tempo of the march from the far north end of town to Foster Park, a low meadow bordering Wildcat Creek where the Klan had put up a twenty-five-foot "fiery cross." There were three hundred mounted Klansmen interspersed in companies among the fifty thousand hooded men, women, and children on foot. The marchers moved in good order, and the measured tread of their feet, timed to the rumbling of the drums and accented by the off-beat clatter of the horses' hoofs, filled the night with an overpowering sound. Many of the marchers carried flaming torches, whose light threw grotesque shadows up and down Main Street. Flag bearers preceded every Den, or local Klan chapter. Usually they carried two Klan flags flanking an American flag, and the word would ripple down the rows of spectators lining the curbs, "Here comes the flag! Hats off for the flag!" Near the place where I was standing with my parents one man was slow with his hat and had it knocked off his head. He started to protest, thought better of it, and held his hat in his hand during the rest of the parade.

Finally the biggest flag I have ever seen came by. It must have been at least thirty feet long, since it took a dozen or more men on each side to support it, and it stretched almost from curb to curb. It sagged in the center under a great weight of coins and bills. As it passed us the bearers called out, "Throw in! Give to the hospital!" and most of the spectators did. This was a collection for the new "Klan hospital" that was to relieve white Protestant Kokomoans of the indignity of being born, being sick, and dying under the care of nuns, a necessity then since the Catholics supported the only hospital in town. It was announced afterward that the huge flag had collected fifty thousand dollars.

When the last of the marchers had filed into Foster Park the "fiery cross" was touched off. The Klansmen sang "The Old Rugged Cross," the Klan anthem, heard a few more speeches, and then dispersed, the hardier ones to drive back to Melfalfa Park to see a fireworks exhibition. Many of them were too spent, however, emotionally and physically, to make the trip. As we sat on our front porch after watching the parade, we could see the Klansmen of our neighborhood trickling home. Some still wore their regalia, too tired to bother with taking it off before they came into sight. Others carried little bundles of white: they were the ones who still made some pretense of secrecy about being members. One of the last to come down the street was old Mrs. Crousore, who lived a few doors away. Her white robe clung damply, and her hood was pushed back. As she climbed her steps and sank solidly into a rocking chair on her porch, we could hear her groan, "Oh, my God, my feet hurt!"

Mrs. Crousore spoke with such feeling that her words seemed to summarize the whole day. My parents adopted her comment as a family joke. July 4, 1923, became for us the day when Mrs. Crousore's feet hurt. But it was clear to me when I grew a little older that my parents needed the joke as much as Mrs. Crousore needed her rocking chair. There were wild rumors in the town in the months that followed: Father Pratt, the pastor at St. Patrick's Church, was on the list for tar-and-feathering; the church was going to be burned; the Klan was going to "call" on the Jewish merchants; it was going to "get" my father and Miss Kinney, another Catholic who taught in the public schools. Considering all the violent acts committed by the Klan elsewhere in the country, it seemed quite possible that any or all of these notions might mature into action.

As it turned out, none of them did. Six years later, in 1929, when the Klan was almost dead, vandals broke into St. Patrick's and defaced some of the statuary. Perhaps they were remnants of the Klan; perhaps they were only ordinary cranks. As for my family, nothing worse happened than that a few days after the Konklave I found a small cross painted in tar on one of our front steps—an ominous sign with no aftermath. I know of no explanation for the lack of violence, for Kokomo was one of the most "Klannish" towns in the United States. Perhaps the answer lay in the dead level typicalness of the town: a population overwhelmingly white Protestant, with small, well-assimilated numbers of Catholics, Jews, foreigners, and Negroes, and an economy nicely balanced between farming and industry. There were few genuine tensions in Kokomo in 1923, and hence little occasion for misdirected hate to flame into personal violence.

It may be asked why, then, did the town take so whole-heartedly to the Klan, which made a program of misdirected hate? And the answer to that may be, paradoxically enough, that the Klan supplied artificial tensions. Though artificial, and perhaps never quite really believed in, they were satisfying. They filled a need—a need for Kokomo and all the big and little towns that resembled it during the early 1920's.

3

In 1923, Kokomo, like the rest of the United States, was in a state of arrested emotion. It had gone whole-hog for war in 1917–18. My own earliest memories are mostly of parading soldiers, brass bands, peach pits thrown into collection stations on Main Street to be used "for gas masks," Liberty Bonds, jam-packed troop trains, the Kaiser hung in effigy, grotesque drawings of Huns in the old *Life*. But it was mostly a make-believe war, as it turned out, and by the time it was well started it was all over.

The emotions it had whipped up, however, were not over. As Charles W. Furgeson says in *Confusion of Tongues*: "We had indulged in wild and lascivious dreams. We had imagined ourselves in the act of intercourse with the Whore of the World. Then suddenly the war was over and the Whore vanished for a time and we were in a condition of *coitus interruptus*." To pursue the imagery, consummation was necessary. With the real enemy gone, a fresh one had to be found. Find an enemy: Catholics, Jews, Negroes, foreigners—but especially Catholics.

This seemingly strange transmutation was not really strange, considering the heritage of the times. Anti-foreignism has been a lively issue in American history since before the Republic. It became a major issue from the 1830's on, as mass migrations took place from Ireland, Germany, Scandinavia, Italy, Poland, Russia, and the Far East. Before immigration was finally curbed by the quota laws, many old-stock Americans in the South and Central West had been roused to an alarmed conviction that they were in danger of being overrun. The "foreigners" with their different ways and ideas were "ruining the country"; and hence anything "foreign" was "un-American" and a menace.

Another main stream in American history was anti-Catholicism, for the good and sufficient reason that a great many of the founding fathers had come to this continent to escape Catholic persecutions. This stream ran deep; and periodically it would emerge at the surface, as in the Know Nothing Party of the 1850's and the American Protective Association of the 1890's. It was submerged but still strong as this century began, and it came to a violent confluence in the 1920's with the parallel stream of anti-foreignism. The conscious or unconscious syllogism was: (1) foreigners are a menace, as demonstrated by the war, (2) the Catholic Church is run by a foreign Pope in a foreign city, (3) therefore the Catholic Church is a menace. Here was a suitable enemy—powerful, mysterious, international, aggressive.

To some extent, of course, the violence with which the jaws of this syllogism snapped shut was a result of parallel thinking in Washington. Wilson had been repudiated, and with him the League and the World Court, and internationalism had become a bad word. The great debates accompanying these events had stirred the country as it had not been stirred since the days preceding the Civil War, and things said then by the isolationists had been enough to frighten even normally sensible people. The exact sequence is a conundrum like that of the chicken and egg: whether the isolationist politicians led the people or

whether the people drove the isolationist politicians. The postwar disillusionment that swept all ranks, including the new generation of authors,
would seem to indicate the latter. Great men might have controlled the
tide, but they were not to be found in the administrations of Harding and
Coolidge.

There were other factors too: the deadly tedium of small-town life,
where any change was a relief; the nature of current Protestant theology,
rooted in Fundamentalism and hot with bigotry; and, not least, a native
American moralistic blood lust that is half historical determinism, and
half Freud. The Puritan morality that inspired *The Scarlet Letter* and the
hanging of witches spread across the country not far behind the moving
frontier; it gained new strength, in fact, in the revulsion against the excesses of frontier life. But Puritanism defies human nature, and human
nature, repressed, emerges in disguise. The fleshly appetites of the small
townsman, when confronted by the rigid moral standards of his social
environment, may be transformed into a fanatic persecution of those very
appetites. The Klan, which sanctified chastity and "clean living" and
brought violent punishment to sinners, was a perfect outlet for these
repressions. It is significant that the favored Klan method of dealing with
sexual transgressors was to strip them naked and whip them, an act of
sadism.

This sexual symbolism could, with not too much effort, be made
to dovetail with anti-foreignism and anti-Catholicism. Foreigners were
notoriously immoral, as proven by the stories the soldiers brought back
from wicked Paris. The Catholic Church, the "foreign church," must
condone such things; and besides, who knew *what* went on among the
priests and nuns! A staple in pornographic literature for at least one
hundred years had been the "revelations" of alleged ex-priests. The Klan
made use of these and other fables, such as the old and ever popular one
about the mummified bodies of newborn infants found under the floor
when a nunnery was torn down. Unhappily, Klan propagandists could
also find real ammunition by looking back far enough in history. The
Borgias were an endless mine of material, and their exploits came to be as
familiar to readers of the Klan press as the lives of soap-opera characters
are to modern housewives. Constant readers must, after a time, have begun
to think of them as The Typical Catholic Family of the Renaissance.

Thus the Catholic Church very easily assumed, in the minds of the
ignorant majority, the proportions of a vast, immoral, foreign conspiracy
against Protestant America, with no less a design than to put the Pope in
the White House. The Knights of Columbus were in reality a secret army
pledged to this aim. They kept their guns in the basements of Catholic
churches—which usually had high steeples and often were located on the
highest ground in town, so that guns fired from the belfries could dominate the streets. Not all Catholics were in on the plot: for example, the
Catholics you knew. These were well-meaning dupes whom one might
hope to save from their blindness. My parents were generally considered
to be among them. My mother's friend, Mrs. Wilson, would come often
and, in a high-strung and urgent manner, try to argue the thing out.
Against my mother's gentle insistences to the contrary, she would usually

end up by declaring, "Now I want to tell *you*, honey! As sure as you're born, the Pope is coming over here with his shirttail aflyin'!"

Mrs. Wilson was not a completely reliable witness, since she had also once had a vision of Jesus standing on the steps of the Baptist church. But the mass acceptance of this idea was shown one day at the little town of North Manchester, Indiana, when the rumor spread that the Pope was finally pulling into town on the south-bound from Chicago to take over. A mob formed and stormed the train. To their mixed disappointment and relief, all they found on the lone day coach was a traveling salesman who was able to give satisfactory evidence that he was not the Pope in disguise.

Kokomo first began to hear about the Klan in 1920. In 1921 the local Nathan Hale Den was established, and within two years the town had become so Klannish as to be given the honor of being host city for the tri-state Konklave. (Of course its name helped: the Klan loved alliterative K's.) Literally half the town belonged to the Klan when I was a boy. At its peak, which was from 1923 through 1925, the Nathan Hale Den had about five thousand members, out of an able-bodied adult population of ten thousand. With this strength, the Klan was able to dominate local politics. In 1924 it elected the mayor, a dapper character named Silcott E. "Silk" Spurgeon, a former clothing salesman, and swept the lists for city councilmen. It packed the police and fire departments with its own people, with the result that on parade nights the traffic patrolmen disappeared, and traffic control was taken over by sheeted figures whose size and shape resembled those of the vanished patrolmen. It ran the town openly and insolently.

As in most of the thousands of other towns where the Klan thrived, there was a strong undercurrent of opposition. But as in most towns, few men were brave enough to state their disapproval openly. The Klan first appealed to the ignorant, the slightly unbalanced, and the venal; but by the time the enlightened elements realized the danger, it was already on top of them. Once organized in strength, the Klan had an irresistible weapon in economic boycott. The anti-Klan merchant saw his trade fade away to the Klan store across the street, where the store window carried a "TWK" (Trade with Klansmen) sign. The non-Klan insurance salesman hadn't a chance against the fraternal advantage of one who doubled in the evenings as a Kladd, Nighthawk, or Fury. It takes great courage to sacrifice a life's work for a principle.

It also takes moral conviction—and it is difficult to arrive at such conviction when the pastor of one's own church openly or tacitly takes an opposite stand. Kokomo's ministers, like her merchants and insurance men, swung with the tide. Most of them, in fact, took little or no swinging, since they saw in the Klan what it professed to be: the militant arm of evangelical Protestantism. There were a few holdouts, but they remained silent; and their silence was filled by the loud exhortations of others such as the Reverend Everett Nixon, Klan chaplain and Klan-sponsored city councilman, and the Reverend P. E. Greenwalt, of the South Main Street Methodist Church, who whipped a homemade Klan flag from his pocket as he reached the climax of his baccalaureate sermon at the high-school graduation exercises. Other ministers, while less fanatic, were perhaps no less sure that the Klan was doing God's work. They found that it stimulated church attendance, with a consequent and agreeable rise in collections. They found their churches visited in rotation by a Klan "team" which would appear at the door unexpectedly, stride up the aisle with Klan and American flags flying, deposit a money offering at the foot of the pulpit, and silently depart. Generally, while this was going on, the ministers would find it in their consciences to ask the choir to sing "Onward, Christian Soldiers."

And so it went in Kokomo and in its equivalents all over the Middle West and South. The Klan made less headway in the big cities, with their strong foreign, Catholic, Negro, and Jewish populations, but from the middle-sized cities down to the country villages it soon had partial or full control of politics and commerce. Indianapolis, with a population of some two hundred thousand, was dominated almost as completely as Kokomo. D. C. Stephenson, the Grand Dragon, had his headquarters there, in a suite of offices in a downtown business building, and from there he ran the state government. "I am the law in Indiana," he said, and there was no doubt about it. He owned the legislature; he owned the Governor, a political hack named Ed Jackson; he owned most of the Representatives and both United States Senators. The Junior Senator was Arthur Robinson, a dark, thin-faced man with the eyes of a zealot and the instincts of a Torquemada. The Senior Senator was genial Jim Watson, who had his own powerful machine within the Republican party. Watson was the arch type of the cartoon politician: big, paunchy, profane, and opportunistic. He thought that he could control the Klan for his own ends, joined up, and shortly found himself swallowed by the new machine.

4

Stephenson in turn took his orders, after a fashion, from Atlanta, Georgia, where Dr. Evans presided over the Invisible Empire from a sumptuous Imperial Palace on fashionable Peachtree Road. Dr. Evans was a dentist by trade and an Imperial Wizard by usurpation. He had unhorsed the previous Wizard and founder, "Colonel" William Joseph Simmons, several months before the Kokomo Konklave. It was in Kokomo, incidentally, that Evans made his first Imperial appearance before a really large Klan audience, thus giving that event an extra significance for history, since it was during his Reign that the Klan was to have its greatest triumphs and sink finally almost to its nadir.

However, in understanding the place of the Klan in American life, Dr. Evans' significance is less than "Colonel" Simmons'. Evans was shrewd, aggressive, and a good administrator, but he stepped into a going concern. The concern existed because of Simmons. And it was going not through the efforts of either Evans or Simmons but those of an obscure couple named Edward Young Clark and Mrs. Elizabeth Tyler.

The tangled story of the Klans' twentieth-century rebirth opens officially in 1915, but stems back to a day in 1901 when Simmons was sitting
on a bench outside his home. The future Emperor at that time was a
preacher, but wasn't doing very well at it. As he sat gazing into the sky,
watching the wind drive masses of cumulus clouds along, he noticed an
interesting formation. As he watched, it split into two billowy lengths,
and these in turn broke up into smaller clouds that followed one another
in a procession across the sky. Simmons took the phenomenon as a sign
from God, and fell to his knees with a prayer.

A devotee of Southern history, Simmons was even more familiar
than most Southerners with the legends of the old Ku Klux Klan.
Founded in 1866 in Pulaski, Tennessee, by a group of young Confederate
troopers home from the war and with time heavy on their hands, it had
started out simply as a social club—a device, significantly enough, to re-
capture some of the lost wartime excitement and comradeship. The
young ex-soldiers picked their name from *Kuklos*, the Greek word for
"circle," which they transformed to Ku Klux, and framed a fantastic
ritual and nomenclature for their own amusement. The idea spread, and
as it spread it found a serious purpose in restoring the South to home rule.
Eventually the best manhood (and much of the worst) of the South took
part, with General Nathan Bedford Forrest as Imperial Wizard. Finally
it degenerated into mere terrorism, and General Forrest disbanded it in
1869, but not until the Carpetbaggers had been dispersed and the Klan
had become immortalized in Southern memory. It was the old Klan that
the convulsed mind of Reverend Simmons saw in the clouds.

Since he had been a boy, he later recalled, he had been dreaming of
organizing real Americans into an army of salvation. His cloudy vision
told him what form it should take. But it was not until 1915 that he felt
prepared for the great task. Meantime he carried on as a preacher, as
an instructor in history at Lanier University, a dubious little enterprise
that later became the official Klan university, and latterly as an itinerant
organizer for the Modern Woodmen of the World. Then, on Thanksgiving night, 1915, he led a troupe of sixteen followers up Stone Mountain near Atlanta and there, "on the top of a mountain at the midnight
hour while men braved the surging blasts of wild wintry mountain
winds and endured temperatures far below freezing [The temperature
was forty-five degrees.—R. C.], bathed in the sacred glow of the fiery
cross, the Invisible Empire was called from its slumber of half a century."

What Simmons called forth was not the old Klan, however, but a
greatly distorted image of it. For all its excesses, the original Klan had
some constructive purposes. Its prescript shows that it was devoted to
restoring Constitutional rights to white Southerners, to the protection
of Southern womanhood, and to the re-establishment of home rule. It
operated in secrecy for the good reason that its members would have been
shot or imprisoned by federal troops had they been found out.

The new Klan adopted the costume, the secrecy, and much of the
ritual of the old, but very little of the substance. Its purposes are indicated
in the Kloran, or book of rules and rituals:

1. Is the motive prompting your ambition to be a Klansman serious and unselfish?

2. Are you a native born, white, gentile American?

3. Are you absolutely opposed to and free of any allegiance of any nature to any cause, government, people, sect, or ruler that is foreign to the United States of America?

4. Do you believe in the tenets of the Christian religion?

5. Do you esteem the United States of America and its institutions above all other government, civil, political, or ecclesiastical, in the whole world?

6. Will you, without mental reservation, take a solemn oath to defend, preserve, and enforce same?

7. Do you believe in clannishness, and will you faithfully practice same toward Klansmen?

8. Do you believe in and will you faithfully strive for the eternal maintenance of white supremacy?

9. Will you faithfully obey our constitution and laws, and conform willingly to all our usages, requirements, and regulations?

10. Can you always be depended on?

Only in "white supremacy" did the aims of the old and new Klans coincide, aside from the banalities about unselfishness, patriotism, and dependability. By questions 2 and 3 Simmons excluded foreigners, Jews, and Catholics, all of whom had been accepted into the original Klan, and thereby set his course in an altogether new direction.

While appropriating much of the ritual of the original, Simmons also added some mumbo-jumbo of his own. The old plus the new enveloped his converts in a weird and unintelligible system of ceremonies, signs, signals, and words. The Klan had its own calendar, so that July 4, 1923, for example, became "The Dismal Day of the Weeping Week of the Hideous Month of the year of the Klan LVII." The local "dens" were governed by an "Exalted Cyclops," a "Klaliff," "Klokard," "Kludd," "Kligrapp," "Klabee," "Kladd," "Klagaro," "Klexter," "Klokann," and "Nighthawk," corresponding respectively to president, vice-president, lecturer, chaplain, secretary, treasurer, conductor, inner guard, outer guard, investigating committee, and proctor in charge of candidates. The Klansmen sang "klodes," held "klonvocations," swore blood oaths, burned crosses, muttered passwords ("Kotop," to which the reply was "Potok," both meaning nothing), and carried on "klonversations." The latter were an exchange of code words formed from the first letters of sentences.

Ayak	Are you a Klansman?
Akia	A Klansman I am.
Capowe	Countersign and password or written evidence.
Cygnar	Can you give number and realm?
No. 1 Atga	Number one Klan of Atlanta, Georgia.
Kigy	Klansman, I greet you.
Itsub	In the sacred, unfailing bond.

They would then *Klasp* left hands (Klan loyalty a Sacred Principle). If a known non-member approached at this fraternal moment, the one who spied him first would break off the klonversation with a warning, "*Sanbog*." (Strangers are near. Be on guard!)

Non-members were "aliens," and remained so until they were "baptized" as "citizens of the Invisible Empire," whereupon they received the "Mioak," or Mystical Insignia of a Klansman, a little red celluloid button bearing the inscrutable words "Kotop" and "Potok." Having taken the sacred oath, the new member was reminded by the Exalted Cyclops that "Mortal man cannot assume a more binding oath; character and courage alone will enable you to keep it. Always remember that to keep this oath means to you honor, happiness, and life; but to violate it means disgrace, dishonor, and *death*. May happiness, honor, and life be yours." The member's subsequent duties included absolute obedience to the Imperial Wizard, who was described in the Kloran as "The Emperor of the Invisible Empire, a wise man, a wonder worker, having power to charm and control."

Thus equipped, the Reverend Simmons set about creating his Empire. It was uphill work, however. Five years later he had enrolled only a few thousand subjects. The times, perhaps, were not quite right, but in addition the Emperor himself lacked two mundane qualities—executive ability and calculating greed. Both of these lacks were supplied in the spring of 1920, when he met Mr. Clark and Mrs. Tyler.

This couple were professional fund raisers and publicity agents whose accounts had included the Anti-Saloon League, Near East Relief, the Roosevelt Memorial Fund, and others of similar scope. Simmons' Ku Klux Klan was almost too small to be worth their attention, but they decided that it had possibilities. As Southerners, they saw in the anti-foreign, Catholic, Jewish, Negro provisions the raw material with which to appeal to four deep prejudices among other Southerners. After they took the project on Clark became King Kleagle, or second in command, and head of the promotion department, and Mrs. Tyler became his chief assistant. Simmons was left in the misty heights as Imperial Wizard and Emperor, where he was happy. Thereafter, between them, Clark and Mrs. Tyler systematized the appeals to racial and religious hatred and organized the sale of Klan memberships on a businesslike basis.

They divided the country into eight "domains," each headed by a Grand Goblin, and subdivided it into "realms," or states, each in charge of a Grand Dragon, such as Stephenson. The initiation fee was $10, of which $4 went to the Kleagle, or local solicitor, when he signed up a recruit, $1 to the King Kleagle, the state sales manager, 50 cents to the Grand Goblin, and $4.50 to Atlanta. Robes, which were made by the affiliated Gate City Manufacturing Company at a cost of $3.28, were sold for $6.50. Newspapers, magazines, Klorans, and other Klan printed matter was turned out at a substantial profit by the Searchlight Publishing Company, another Klan enterprise, and miscellaneous real estate was handled by the Clark Realty Company. The local Klaverns were supported by dues of a dollar a month, part of which was sent to the state organization. It was somewhat like a chain letter; almost everyone seemed guaranteed to make money.

Within a year and a half, this system had netted more than a hundred thousand members. It had also, according to the New York *World*, caused four killings, one mutilation, one branding with acid, forty-one floggings, twenty-seven tar-and-feather parties, five kidnapings, and forty-three threats and warnings to leave town. The *World's* exposé pricked Congress into an investigation in October, 1921. Emperor Simmons was called, but proved to be a slippery witness. The atrocities ascribed to the Klan were, he said, the work of imposters. The Klan did not permit violence, he assured the Congressmen, and cited instances wherein he had rebuked dens which disobeyed this rule by withdrawing their charters. The Klan was "purely a fraternal organization," dedicated to patriotism, brotherhood, and maintenance of law and order. Although circumstantial evidence was strong, the investigators could find no legal evidence that the Klan's national organization had caused the outrages or even approved of them, and the inquiry petered out.

However, the *World's* detective work did have one notable result. Shortly before the Congressional investigation got under way, the paper printed an account of how, two years before, Clark and Mrs. Tyler had been "arrested at midnight in their sleeping garments, in a notorious underworld resort at 185 South Pryor Street, Atlanta, run by Mrs. Tyler," and hauled off to jail, to be charged with "disorderly conduct" and possession of liquor. In the resultant furor Clark submitted his resignation to Simmons, which inspired Mrs. Tyler to issue a statement calling him "a weak-kneed quitter" and repudiating him. Simmons, who was well aware of what the couple had accomplished for the Klan, refused to take action against them. Instead, the propaganda department began to grind out denials, the *World* was branded as a "cowardly and infamous instrument of murder . . . against fair woman!" and the scandal was smoothed over.

But it left a scar. As the moral custodians of their communities, the rank-and-file Klansmen were deeply shocked by the story. Some of them were not convinced by the denials. Along with the evidence presented during the Congressional hearing, it gradually fermented into a basis for an insurgent movement within the ranks. This faction grew under the loving eye of Dr. Evans, who had deserted dentistry to become Grand Dragon of the Realm of Texas, and who had ambitions to the throne. In May, 1922, he became Kligrapp, or secretary, of the national organization, and from that vantage point accomplished a *coup d'état* the following Thanksgiving. With twelve of the fourteen members of the board of directors joining the cabal, he detached the Wizardship and all the real power from Simmons and took them himself, leaving Simmons only the cold comfort of a thousand dollars a month salary and a simple Emperorship. Simmons fought back energetically, and as a consequence, the following year, lost even this sop. "He Who Traversed the Realm of the Unknown, Wrested the Solemn Secret from the Grasp of Night, and Became the Sovereign Imperial Master of the Great Lost Mystery"—was out.

"I was in Gethsemane," Simmons wrote later, "and the gloom of its dense darkness entombed me; the cup which I drank surpassed bitterest gall, and my sweat was the sweat of blood; the hour of my crucifixion was at hand." He beckoned after his seduced flock: "Come unto ME all you who yearn and labor after Klankraft and I will give you rest. Take my program upon you and learn of me, for I am unselfish and true at heart. . . . I am the one custodian and sole Master of the sublime Mystery." But it was no use. Foxy Dr. Evans had stolen the show, and the ex-Emperor had to be content with a final cash settlement of ninety thousand dollars. He set about organizing a rival enterprise called the "Knights of the Flaming Sword," but was unsuccessful. In the mid-thirties he tried again with "The White Band," also a revival of a post-Civil War vigilante group, but had no better luck. He died in May, 1945, poor and disillusioned.

In spite of the shock of the Clark-Tyler case, the *World's* disclosures, and the Congressional investigation, the Klan continued to grow. It filled urgent needs in the contemporary psyche, and it was manifestly a good thing commercially. By the time Dr. Evans took over, it was adding thirty-five hundred members a day, and the national treasury was taking in forty-five thousand dollars a day. Within a year Evans could boast, probably with fair accuracy, of a membership of five million. Being in possession of that many adult voters, he and his henchmen naturally turned their thoughts to politics. Principles, they announced, were important to the Klan, not party labels; and accordingly the state and local organizations adopted whichever of the two major parties was stronger in its region. In the South, the Klan was Democratic, in the North, Republican. But since the Republicans were dominant nationally, both the arithmetic of membership and the ends of expediency dictated a stronger drive within that party. But 1924 was a poor year to interfere in Republican affairs. Calvin Coolidge was not only an extremely popular President, but represented in his person many of the parochial virtues that the Klan endorsed, and there was no point in contesting or even trying to bargain over his nomination. The Democratic convention was much more promising. The strongest candidate was Alfred E. Smith, Catholic, Tammany, wet, and a big-city product—in short, a symbol of everything the Klan was against. The Klan came out fighting for William Gibbs Mc-Adoo and managed to split and stalemate the whole proceedings. It finally lost, but it also prevented Smith's nomination; and after many angry hours and smoke-filled meetings John W. Davis, a J. P. Morgan lawyer, was served up as a compromise. The Harding scandals were fresh in the minds of everyone, and 1924 logically should have been a Democratic year, but Davis lost. Considering later events, it is easy to speculate that the Klan's battle in the 1924 Democratic convention was a decisive event in United States and world history.

For Dr. Evans and his Goblins and Dragons it was an encouraging show of strength, despite their failure to nominate their man. They looked forward to 1928. Then, suddenly, there was a disaster. D. C. Stephenson, the Grandest Dragon of the Empire, made a mistake.

5

"Steve"—as he was usually known—kept a bust of Napoleon on his desk. And like Napoleon, he knew what he wanted. He wanted money and women and power, and later on he wanted to be President of the United States. He got plenty of the first three, and he might have got the fourth. He was a prodigy; he was at the height of his career when he was thirty-three years old. But he looked ten years older, and he encouraged his followers to refer to him as "the old man." He had a fleshy, handsome face, with blond hair, thin eyebrows, a small mouth, and small, shrewd eyes. He could be as hearty as a country drummer, and as cold as a hangman. He preached righteousness, but he was oversexed and he drank too much. He was vain, but beyond vanity he had certainty. He could command; his orders were obeyed; he exuded power. He understood the average man.

Not much is known about his early life. He was born in 1891, evidently in Texas, and spent part of his youth in Oklahoma. He was a second lieutenant in World War I but saw no service overseas. He was married twice, but had divorced or abandoned both women by the time he moved to Evansville, Indiana, shortly after the war. There he began organizing veterans, and this took him into politics. In 1920 he entered the Democratic Congressional primary as a wet. Defeated by the Anti-Saloon League, he promptly became a dry Republican and at the same time joined the newly rising Ku Klux Klan. He became an organizer for the Klan. By 1922 he had succeeded so well that he was made organizer for the State of Indiana, and shortly afterward for twenty other states, mostly Midwestern. After a short period in Columbus, Ohio, he moved his offices to Indianapolis, and on July 4, 1923, at Kokomo he officially added the Grand Dragonship of Indiana to his portfolio. By that time he was well on his way to his first million dollars.

Within a year or so he had passed far beyond that goal. He branched out into the coal and gravel business, the tailoring business, and various other sidelines. He imported Florida real-estate salesmen and other high-pressure operators to carry Klankraft into the towns and up and down the country roads, and arranged a split with these sub-salesmen. In one eighteen-month period his personal income is estimated to have been between two and five millions. He owned one of the showplace homes of suburban Irvington, maintained a suite of rooms at a big hotel, kept a fleet of automobiles, a covey of bodyguards, and a yacht in Lake Michigan. He knew many women, and had a way with most of them.

One of the women he knew, but not very well, was Madge Oberholzer. She had a small job at the State House in the office of the State Superintendent of Public Instruction. She was not particularly attractive. Unmarried at twenty-eight, which in Indiana means ripe spinsterhood, she was a buxom 145 pounds, had a rather long nose, and wore her hair in an exaggerated upsweep that hung over her forehead. But for some reason Steve, whose taste usually ran to ripe beauties, was interested in Madge. He took her to several parties, and once, when the legislature was considering a bill that would have abolished her state job, he gallantly killed it for her.

On the night of March 15, 1925, Madge came home about ten o'clock from a date with another man. Steve had been telephoning, and when she called him back he told her he was going to Chicago and wanted her to come and see him on an important matter before he left. He would send Earl Gentry, one of his bodyguards, to escort her.

She found Steve drinking when she arrived at his home, and according to her later testimony he "forced" her to drink with him. Three drinks later he asked her to go along to Chicago. When she refused, Steve motioned to Gentry and Earl Klenck, another bodyguard, who produced guns; the three men then led her outside and into Steve's waiting car. They drove to the railroad station and boarded the midnight train to Chicago. Steve, Gentry, and Madge went into a drawing room. Gentry climbed into an upper berth and Steve shoved Madge into the lower. "After the train started," her testimony says, "Stephenson got in with me and attacked me. He held me so I could not move. I . . . do not remember all that happened. . . . He . . . mutilated me. . . ."

The next day in Hammond, Indiana, where Steve had the presence of mind to get off the train to avoid the Mann Act, Madge managed on a pretext to get hold of some bichloride-of-mercury tablets. She swallowed six of them. By the time Steve discovered what she had done she was deathly ill. Steve tried to get her to a hospital, then offered to marry her, and finally drove her back to Indianapolis. He kept her in a loft above his garage with the threat that she would stay there until she agreed to marriage. She still refused and finally he had her taken to her home, where she died several weeks later. Before her death she dictated the full story to the prosecuting attorney, William H. Remy, who was one of the few officials of Marion County that Steve did not control.

The case caused an unimaginable uproar. Steve, who had said, "I am the law," was calm and confident, but he took the precaution of having the trial venued to the little town of Noblesville. A quarrel with Evans had created factionalism in his Indianapolis stronghold, and he was afraid of being double-crossed there. But to his shock and dismay, the Noblesville jury found him guilty of murder in the second degree, and the judge sentenced him to life imprisonment.

To his further shock, Governor Ed Jackson refused to pardon him. The case had created such a bad smell that not only Jackson but nearly all of Steve's other political allies abandoned him. Steve threatened to bring out the "little black box" containing his records; when finally produced, the box's contents sent a Congressman, the Mayor of Indianapolis, the Sheriff of Marion County, and various other officials to jail. Jackson was indicted for bribery but was saved by the statute of limitations. But although Steve got his revenge, he did not get his liberty. He tried every kind of threat and legal dodge, but every one failed. Years later, when he had served enough time with good behavior to come up for parole, public feeling against him was still so strong that no governor would take the responsibility of releasing him. He stayed in prison, in effect a political prisoner.

Steve's crude mistake was a disaster for the Klan not only in Indiana but everywhere. His trial was a national sensation, and his conviction was a national indictment of the organization. It became too absurd and ironic for any Goblin or Dragon to proselytize in the name of morality. The Bible Belt might dismiss the Clark-Tyler episode as malicious gossip, but it could hardly dismiss the legal conviction of one who was probably the Klan's most powerful local leader. The Klan began to break up rapidly, leaving political chaos in its wake. In Indiana, the Democratic boss, Frank P. Baker, said, "We don't want the poisonous animal to crawl into our yard and die." The Republicans earnestly disclaimed any relationship with the Klan.

The Klan tried just as eagerly to disassociate itself from Stephenson. It had nominal grounds for doing so, since Steve's differences with Evans had caused him to be read out of the organization some months before. In reply, however, Steve had merely declared his independence of Atlanta and had carried on in his own Realm with no diminution of power. The general public knew and cared little about this internal squabble. The label of "Stephensonism" was applied to the Klan as a whole, and it stuck.

The Klan died hard, however. It took a new grip on life in 1927–28, with the nomination of Al Smith again in prospect, and the old cries of "Keep the Pope out of the White House!" were heard again. Although it could not prevent Smith's nomination this time, the new wave of religious prejudice it stirred up, and the backwash of intolerance it had created in the years before, were important factors in defeating Smith for the Presidency. Thereafter it subsided again, and by the end of the decade it had only a tiny fraction of its former strength. Here and there, during the next years, one heard of it: a whipping, a castration, a cross burning. The propaganda line changed with the times. During the thirties, emphasis switched from Catholics, Negroes, Jews, and foreigners to Communism and "labor agitators." It was an unrewarding strategy, for although it may have gained contributions from employers, especially in the South, it won back few members.

The crowning irony came in 1935 when the Imperial Palace, after passing through the hands of ten owners, was finally bought for $32,500 by the Savannah-Atlanta diocese of the Catholic Church as the site for a new cathedral. Two years later at the cathedral's consecration Dr. Evans, as a token of the spirit of tolerance of the "new Klan," posed in a friendly attitude with the Bishop G. P. A. O'Hara. This was too much for the remaining brothers. In 1939 there was another revolution from below, and Evans was disposed of in favor of Dr. James A. Colescott, a former veterinarian of Terre Haute, Indiana, and latterly Grand Dragon of the Realm of Ohio. In 1944, Dr. Colescott voluntarily returned to doctoring animals, which give him a better living, and the Klan was disbanded as a national organization. It survives under a system of state autonomy, but has no appreciable strength in any state with the possible exceptions of Georgia and Florida. There may be a few thousand members in the entire country.

6

And today, in Kokomo, the Klan is only an old memory. The Reverend Everett Nixon carried on for years as Secretary of the Melfalfa Park Association, trying to hold together the property and few believers. But he failed, and now the park is overgrown with brush, deserted and decayed, its sagging pavilion a meeting place for bats and owls. Steve, who had his greatest moment there, is still in the state penitentiary at Michigan City, still hoping. Not long ago he made his fortieth unsuccessful petition for freedom. The accounts of his triumphs and his trial are embalmed in the brittle files of the Kokomo *Tribune* and *Dispatch*, along with the Nell Brinkley Girl and ads for the Apperson Jackrabbit. It all seems a long time ago.

Yet it was only a generation ago—time for the children who marched in the big parade, and who were held on their fathers' shoulders to see Steve's dramatic landing near Melfalfa Park, to grow up and have small children of their own. Like its population, the town seems substantially changed, with its new store fronts, its better paving, and its night-time neon glow. But in many, deeper ways, both the people and the town are much the same. And 1949 is not unlike 1920.

In his book, *The Ku Klux Klan*, James Moffatt Mecklin observes:

What impresses the student of the Klan movement at every stage is the lack, on the part of the average American, of any real insight into its significance. Not man's innate depravity, not overt criminal acts, nor yet wicked attempts to subvert American institutions, but rather plain old-fashioned ignorance is the real enemy of the huge giant, the public, who is still the fumbling physician of our social ills.

When a new bogey appears on Main Street to take the place of the Pope, and a new organization arises to take the place of the Klan, one can only hope that the generation will turn out to be less ignorant than the old.

Suggestions for Further Reading

The classic description of American life in this period is Mark Sullivan, *Our Times, 1900–1925*, 6 vols. (New York, 1926–35). Other general treatments that consider various periods of the early twentieth century are Henry May, *The End of American Innocence: A Study of the First Years of Our Time, 1912–1917* * (New York, 1959); Walter Lord, *The Good Years* * (New York, 1960); and Gilman Ostrander, *American Civilization in the First Machine Age, 1890–1940* * (New York, 1970). J. C. Furnas has extended his popular history of American life with *Great Times: An Informal History of the United States, 1914–1929* (New York, 1974). The standard popular treatment of the 1920s is Frederick Lewis Allen, *Only Yesterday* * (New York, 1931). Two recent works that challenge Allen's interpretations are Paul Carter, *The Twenties in America** (New York, 1968), and John Braeman, Robert H. Bremner, and David Brody, eds., *Change and Continuity in Twentieth-Century America: The 1920's* (Columbus, Ohio, 1968). The novelist John Dos Passos' classic trilogy, *U.S.A.** (Boston, 1937), contains much valuable material on this period.

Two recent collections of historical essays that enable readers to see the newly developing methodologies in the field of family history are Michael Gordon, ed., *The American Family in Social-Historical Perspective*, 2nd ed.* (New York, 1978), and Theodore K. Rabb and Robert Rotberg, eds., *The Family in History: Interdisciplinary Essays* * (New York, 1974), a volume that was originally printed as an issue of the *Journal of Interdisciplinary History*. There is a great deal of useful material in the long-standard but seriously flawed Arthur W. Calhoun, *A Social History of the American Family*, 3 vols. (Cleveland, Ohio, 1919). Interesting but controversial insights are found in Philippe Ariès, *Centuries of Childhood** (New York, 1962). On feminism and the new role of women, see two works by William O'Neill, *Divorce in the Progressive Era** (New Haven, Conn., 1967) and *Everyone Was Brave: The Rise and Fall of Feminism in America** (Chicago, 1969), and Jane Sochen, *The New Woman: Feminism in Greenwich Village, 1910–1920** (New York, 1972). A good history of the feminist movement is Eleanor Flexner, *Century of Struggle: The Woman's Rights Movement in the United States** (Cambridge, Mass., 1959). See also Lois Banner, *Women in Modern America: A Brief History** (New York, 1974). Works by two important feminists are Charlotte Perkins Gilman, *Women and Economics** (Boston, 1898) and *The Home: Its Work and Its Influence** (New York, 1903), and Emma Goldman's autobiography, *Living My Life** (New York, 1931), available in a two-volume paperback edition. See also Richard Drinnon, *Rebel in*

* Available in paperback edition.

*Paradise: A Biography of Emma Goldman** (Chicago, 1961). The controversy over Margaret Sanger and the birth control movement in a single New England town is described by Kenneth Underwood in *Protestant and Catholic* (Boston, 1957). One approach to the race-suicide problem is found in Mark H. Haller, *Eugenics: Hereditarian Attitudes in American Thought* (New Brunswick, N.J., 1963).

On immigration, see Oscar Handlin, *The Uprooted*, rev. ed.* (Boston, 1973). The basic theoretical work on assimilation is Milton Gordon, *Assimilation in American Life** (New York, 1964). Other works dealing with the Jewish community are Moses Rischin, *The Promised City: New York's Jews, 1870–1914** (Cambridge, Mass., 1962); Arthur A. Cohen, *New York Jews and the Quest for Community: The Kehillah Experiment, 1908–1922* (New York, 1970); and a novel by Abraham Cahan, *The Rise of David Levinsky** (New York, 1917).

On the conditions of labor in the early twentieth century, see Harry Braverman, *Labor and Monopoly Capital: The Degradation of Work in the Twentieth Century** (New York, 1974); Milton Meltzer, *Bread—and Roses: The Struggle of American Labor, 1865–1915** (New York, 1977); and John Bodnar, *Immigration and Industrialization: Ethnicity in an American Mill Town, 1870–1940* (Pittsburgh, 1978). For the struggles of labor, see Bruno Ramirez, *When Workers Fight: The Politics of Industrial Relations in the Progressive Era, 1898–1916* (Westport, Conn., 1978). The standard work on the IWW is Melvyn Dubofsky, *We Shall Be All: A History of the Industrial Workers of the World** (New York, 1969). See also Gerard Rosenblum, *Immigrant Workers: Their Impact on American Labor Radicalism* (New York, 1973). Herbert G. Gutman's excellent labor essays have been collected in *Work, Culture and Society in Industrializing America** (New York, 1977).

The best book on the first Ku Klux Klan is Allen W. Trelease, *White Terror: The Ku Klux Klan Conspiracy and Southern Reconstruction** (New York, 1971). For information on the second Klan, see Kenneth Jackson, *The Ku Klux Klan in the City, 1915–1930** (New York, 1968), and Stanley Cohen, "The Failure of the Melting Pot," in *The Great Fear: Race in the Mind of America,** edited by Gary B. Nash and Richard Weiss (New York, 1970). John Higham describes the long tradition of anti-foreign agitation in *Strangers in the Land: Patterns of American Nativism, 1860–1925** (New Brunswick, N.J., 1955). Conservative Protestantism played an important role in the shaping of attitudes in this period. Two excellent books by William McLoughlin that give some insight into these attitudes are *Modern Revivalism: Charles Grandison Finney to Billy Graham* (New York, 1959) and *Billy Sunday Was His Real Name* (Chicago, 1955). See also Norman F. Furniss, *The Fundamentalist Controversy, 1918–1931* (New Haven, Conn., 1954). For the most significant religious confrontation of the period, see Ray Ginger, *Six Days or Forever: Tennessee v. John Scopes** (Boston, 1958).

1930–1950
Depression and War

What the Depression Did
to People

EDWARD ROBB ELLIS

After a period of relative affluence and optimism in the 1920s, the American economy crashed in a shambles in late 1929. Although the Great Depression of the 1930s is usually dated from the stock market crash of October 1929, prudent men might have foreseen the dangers as the rate of real investment began to drop and speculation increased. The widely noted Wall Street collapse and the subsequent failure of apparently stable economic institutions brought to the attention of the nation and the world that the affluence and optimism of the 1920s had been increasingly composed of hope (that is, speculation) and promises rather than of stable economic growth.

The economic downturn led to loss of hope and, so it seemed to some, a failure of nerve. It has been explained that loss of confidence in the business system was a major contributing factor in the spread of the depression. Whatever the causes—and these are still being debated—the bubble burst, and the country plunged into poverty and despair.

In writing the history of the 1930s, scholars have tended to concentrate on political developments. The election of Franklin Delano Roosevelt to the presidency and the advent of what he called the New Deal have captured the imagination of the historians of the period and have led to an overemphasis on the importance of the Roosevelt administration. While it is true that several important innovations in public welfare were adopted by the New Deal, these were applied only half-heartedly. And they did not end the depression, although they did ease its effects for some of the population. The end of the depression was brought about by the Second World War and the full employment that resulted from the United States establishing itself as the "arsenal of democracy."

What has often been slighted in the historical writing, then, is the impact of the depression on the lives of ordinary people. The best descriptions of the period have come from the pens of the creative writers of the decade; no later work is likely to surpass John Steinbeck's **The Grapes of Wrath** or James Agee and Walker Evans' **Let Us Now Praise Famous Men** as portraits of the despair of the 1930s. Today, however, there is a rising interest in the human cost of the depression, and many recent articles and books attempt to describe the suffering that afflicted so many during that decade.

One reason for the new interest in the depression is the advent of a new generation of historians who were very young or were not yet born in the 1930s and, therefore, have no memories of the period. The searing experiences of the older generation, who could recall the hunger and frustration of the times, led them to try to forget, not remember.

One who has tried to remember is Edward Robb Ellis, a former newspaperman and popular historian, who is the author of **A Nation in Torment,** a chapter of which is reprinted below. Ellis, who entered college in 1929, found that the crash wiped out the savings he had laid away for his education. After working his way through journalism school, he became that college graduate described in the selection below who took a job as a newspaper reporter for exactly nothing in salary.

Writing anecdotally and relying on a diary he kept in those years as well as memoirs of others like himself, Ellis describes the costs in human suffering paid by people across the United States. He juxtaposes the arrogant and stupid attitudes of the rich against the despair and hunger of the poor. There is an overriding sense of desperation in many of the statements found in this selection, and one wonders at the lack of success of alternative political movements that might have led to an easing of the burden of the depression for many.

The runaway economic consumerism of the post–Second World War era may have its source in the contrast between the affluence of the 1920s and the poverty of the 1930s. Many middle-class and would-be middle-class Americans were not able, because of the depression, to enjoy the fruits of the consumer society that had developed in the 1920s. As the economy took off again during the Second World War, these potential consumers took off with it, and it often seems as though they are attempting to ward off future terrors by surrounding themselves with as many material objects as possible.

The Depression smashed into the nation with such fury that men groped for superlatives to express its impact and meaning.

Edmund Wilson compared it to an earthquake. It was "like the explosion of a bomb dropped in the midst of society," according to the Social Science Research Council Committee on Studies in Social Aspects of the Depression.

Alfred E. Smith said the Depression was equivalent to war, while Supreme Court Justice Louis D. Brandeis and Bernard Baruch declared that it was worse than war. Philip La Follette, the governor of Wisconsin, said: "We are in the midst of the greatest domestic crisis since the Civil War." Governor Roosevelt agreed in these words: "Not since the dark days of the Sixties have the people of this state and nation faced problems as grave, situations as difficult, suffering as severe." A jobless textile worker told Louis Adamic: "I wish there would be war again." In a

"What the Depression Did to People." Reprinted by permission of Coward, McCann & Geoghegan, Inc. from *A Nation in Torment* by Edward Robb Ellis, pp. 229–54. Copyright © 1970 by Edward Robb Ellis.

war against a foreign enemy all Americans might at least have felt united by a common purpose, and production would have boomed.

Poor and rich alike felt anxious and helpless.

Steel magnate Charles M. Schwab, despite his millions and the security of his Manhattan palace, freely confessed: "I'm afraid. Every man is afraid." J. David Stern, a wealthy newspaper publisher, became so terrified that he later wrote in his autobiography: "I sat in my back office, trying to figure out what to do. To be explicit, I sat in my private bathroom. My bowels were loose from fear." Calvin Coolidge dolorously told a friend: "I can see nothing to give ground for hope."

Herbert C. Pell, a rich man with a country estate near Governor Roosevelt's, said the country was doomed unless it could free itself from the rich, who have "shown no realization that what you call free enterprise means anything but greed." Marriner Eccles, a banker and economist who had *not* lost his fortune, wrote that "I awoke to find myself at the bottom of a pit without any known means of scaling its sheer sides." According to Dwight W. Morrow, a Morgan associate, diplomat and Senator: "Most of my friends think the world is coming to an end— that is, the world as we know it." Reinhold Niebuhr, the learned and liberal clergyman, said that rich "men and women speculated in drawing-rooms on the best kind of poison as a means to oblivion from the horrors of revolution."

In Youngstown, Ohio, a friend of Mayor Joseph L. Heffernan stood beside the mayor's desk and said: "My wife is frantic. After working at the steel mill for twenty-five years I've lost my job and I'm too old to get other work. If you can't do something for me, I'm going to kill myself." Governor Gifford Pinchot of Pennsylvania got a letter from a jobless man who said: "I cannot stand it any longer." Gan Kolski, an unemployed Polish artist from Greenwich Village, leaped to his death from the George Washington Bridge, leaving this note: "To All: If you cannot hear the cry of starving millions, listen to the dead, brothers. Your economic system is dead."

An architect, Hugh Ferriss, stood on the parapet of a tall building in Manhattan and thought to himself that the nearby skyscrapers seemed like monuments to the rugged individualism of the past. Thomas Wolfe wrote: "I believe that we are lost here in America, but I believe we shall be found." Democratic Senator Thomas Gore of Oklahoma called the Depression an economic disease. Henry Ford, on the other hand, said the Depression was "a wholesome thing in general."

*   *   *

Obviously, the essence of a depression is widespread unemployment. In one of the most fatuous remarks on record, Calvin Coolidge said: "The final solution of unemployment is work." He might have added that water is wet. Senator Robert Wagner of New York called unemployment inexcusable.

A decade before the Crash the British statesman David Lloyd George had said: "Unemployment, with its injustice for the man who seeks and thirsts for employment, who begs for labour, and cannot get it, and who is punished for failure he is not responsible for by the starvation of his children—that torture is something that private enterprise ought to remedy for its own sake." Winston Churchill now used the same key word, "torture," in a similar comment: "This problem of unemployment is the most torturing that can be presented to a civilized society."

Before Roosevelt became President and named Frances Perkins his secretary of labor, she was so pessimistic that she said publicly it might take a quarter century to solve the unemployment problem. A Pennsylvania commission studied 31,159 workless men and then reported that the typical unemployed man was thirty-six years old, native-born, physically fit and with a good previous work record. This finding contradicted Henry Ford's belief that the unemployed did not want to work.

However, the Pennsylvania study was *not* typical of the unemployed across the entire nation. Negroes and aliens were the last hired and the first fired. Young men and women were graduated from high schools and colleges into a world without jobs. Mississippi's demagogic governor and sometime senator, Theodore G. Bilbo, vowed the unemployment problem could be solved by shipping 12,000,000 American blacks to Africa. The United Spanish War Veterans, for their part, urged the deportation of 10,000,000 aliens—or nearly 6,000,000 more than the actual number of aliens in the United States. Some noncitizens, unable to find work here, voluntarily returned to their homelands. With the deepening of the Depression, immigration dropped until something strange happened in the Year 1932: More than three times as many persons left this country as entered it. No longer was America the Promised Land.

* * *

The Depression changed people's values and thus changed society.

The Chamber of Commerce syndrome of the Twenties became a mockery in the Thirties. Business leaders lost their prestige, for now it had become apparent to all Americans that these big shots did not know what they were talking about when they said again and again and again that everything would be all right if it were just left to them. Worship of big business was succeeded by greater concern for human values. The optimism of the speculative decade was replaced by the pessimism of the hungry decade, by anguished interest in the problem of having enough food on the table.

People eager to make a big killing in the stock market had paid scant attention to politics, but now they wondered about their elected representatives and the kind of political system that could permit such a catastrophe to happen. Indifference gave way to political and social consciousness. Dorothy Parker, the sophisticate and wit, cried: "There is no longer I. There is WE. The day of the individual is dead." Quentin N. Burdick, who became a Senator from North Dakota, said long after the Depression: "I guess I acquired a social conscience during those bad days, and ever since I've had the desire to work toward bettering the living conditions of the people." Sylvia Porter, who developed into a financial columnist, said that while at Hunter College she switched from English to economics because of "an overwhelming curiosity to know why everything was crashing around me and why people were losing their jobs."

People lost their houses and apartments.

Franklin D. Roosevelt said: "One of the major disasters of the continued depression was the loss of hundreds of thousands of homes each year from foreclosure. The annual average loss of urban homes by foreclosure in the United States in normal times was 78,000. By 1932 this had increased to 273,000. By the middle of 1933, foreclosures had advanced to more than 1,000 a day."

In New York City, which had more apartments than private houses, there were almost 200,000 evictions in the year 1931. During the first three weeks of the following year there were more than 60,000 other evictions. One judge handled, or tried to handle, 425 eviction cases in a single day! On February 2, 1932, the New York *Times* described the eviction of three families in the Bronx:

> Probably because of the cold, the crowd numbered only about 1,000, although in unruliness it equalled the throng of 4,000 that stormed the police in the first disorder of a similar nature on January 22. On Thursday a dozen more families are to be evicted unless they pay back rents.
>
> Inspector Joseph Leonary deployed a force of fifty detectives and mounted and foot patrolmen through the street as Marshal Louis Novick led ten furniture movers into the building. Their appearance was the signal for a great clamor. Women shrieked from the windows, the different sections of the crowd hissed and booed and shouted invectives. Fighting began simultaneously in the house and in the street. The marshal's men were rushed on the stairs and only got to work after the policemen had driven the tenants back into their apartments.

In that part of New York City known as Sunnyside, Queens, many homeowners were unable to meet mortgage payments and were soon ordered to vacate. Eviction notices were met with collective action, the residents barricading their doors with sandbags and barbed wire, flinging pepper and flour at sheriffs who tried to force their way inside. However, it was a losing battle; more than 60 percent of Sunnyside's householders lost their homes through foreclosure.

Harlem Negroes invented a new way to get enough money to pay their rent. This, as it came to be called, was the house-rent party. A family would announce that on Saturday night or Thursday night they would welcome anyone and everyone to their home for an evening of fun. Sometimes they would print and distribute cards such as this: "There'll be plenty of pig feet/And lots of gin;/Jus' ring the bell/An' come on in." Saturday night, of course, is the usual time for partying, while Thursday was chosen because this was the only free night for sleep-in black domestics who worked for white people. Admission to a house-rent party cost 15 cents, but more money could be spent inside. A festive mood was established by placing a red bulb in a light socket, by serving food consisting of chitterlings and pigs' feet and by setting out a jug of corn liquor. These parties often went on until daybreak, and the next day the landlord got his rent. The innovation spread to black ghettos in other big cities across the land, and some white people began imitating the Negroes.

In Chicago a crowd of Negroes gathered in front of the door of a tenement house to prevent the landlord's agent from evicting a neighborhood family, and they continued to stand there hour after hour, singing hymns. A Chicago municipal employee named James D. O'Reilly saw his home auctioned off because he had failed to pay $34 in city taxes at the very time the city owed him $850 in unpaid salary.

A social worker described one pathetic event: "Mrs. Green left her five small children alone one morning while she went to have her grocery order filled. While she was away the constable arrived and padlocked her house with the children inside. When she came back she heard the six-weeks-old baby crying. She did not dare to touch the padlock for fear of being arrested, but she found a window open and climbed in and nursed the baby and then climbed out and appealed to the police to let her children out."

In widespread areas of Philadelphia no rent was paid at all. In this City of Brotherly Love evictions were exceedingly common—as many as 1,300 a month. Children, who saw their parents' distress, made a game of evictions. In a day-care center they piled all the doll furniture in first one corner and then another. One tot explained to a teacher: "We ain't got no money for the rent, so we's moved into a new house. Then we got the constable on us, so we's movin' again."

In millions of apartments, tension mounted and tempers flared toward the end of each month, when the rent was due. Robert Bendiner, in his book *Just Around the Corner*, wrote about conditions in New York City:

> Evictions and frequent moves to take advantage of the apartment market were as common in middle-income Washington Heights as in the poor areas of town, and apartment hopping became rather a way of life. My own family moved six times in seven years. . . . Crises occurred monthly, and several times we were saved from eviction by pawning leftover valuables or by my mother's rich talent for cajoling landlords. On one more than routinely desperate occasion she resorted to the extreme device of having one of us enlarge a hole in the bathroom ceiling and then irately demanding repairs before another dollar of rent should be forthcoming.

In moving from one place to another, some families left their furniture behind because it had been bought on the installment plan and they were unable to meet further payments. Time-payment furniture firms owned warehouses that became crammed with tables and chairs and other items reclaimed from families without money. Whenever a marshal, sheriff or constable evicted a family from a house or apartment, the landlord would simply dump the furniture on the sidewalk. If the installment company failed to pick it up, each article would soon be carried away by needy neighbors.

What happened to people after they were dispossessed? Many doubled up with relatives—or even tripled up, until ten or twelve people were crammed into three or four rooms. Human beings are like porcupines: they like to huddle close enough to feel one another's warmth, but they dislike getting so close that the quills begin pricking. Now, in teeming proximity to one another, the quills pricked, and relatives quarreled bitterly.

*   *   *

The Depression strained the family structure and sometimes shattered it. Well-integrated families closed ranks in the face of this common danger and became ever more monolithic. Loosely knit families, on the other hand, fell apart when the pressures on them became too great.

After a man lost his job, he would trudge from factory to factory, office to office, seeking other employment, but after weeks of repeated rejections he would lose heart, mutely denounce himself as a poor provider, shed his self-respect and stay at home. Here he found himself unwelcome and underfoot, the target of puzzled glances from his children and hostile looks from his wife. In the early part of the Depression some women simply could not understand that jobs were unavailable; instead, they felt there was something wrong with their men. In Philadelphia one unemployed man begged a social worker: "Have you anybody you can send around to tell my wife you have no job to give me? She thinks I don't want to work."

The idle man found himself a displaced person in the household, which is woman's domain, and in nameless guilt he crept about uneasily, always finding himself in the way. He got on his wife's nerves and she on his, until tension broke in endless wrangles. If the man tried to help by washing dishes and making beds, he lost status in the eyes of the rest of the family.

The Depression castrated some men by dethroning them from their position as the breadwinner and the head of the family. Ashamed, confused and resentful, they became sexually impotent. In Western culture a man tends to think of himself in terms of the work he does, this self-identity being what Jung calls his persona. Man does. Woman is. To rob a man of his work was to rob him of his idea of himself, leaving him empty and without much reason for living. The displacement of the man as the head of the family and the way some women moved in to fill this vacuum were described sensitively by John Steinbeck in his novel *The Grapes of Wrath*. This great book tells the story of the flight of the Joad family from the dust bowl of Oklahoma to the green valleys of California:

> "We got nothin', now," Pa said. "Comin' a long time—no work, no crops. What we gonna do then? How we gonna git stuff to eat? . . . Git so I hate to think. Go diggin' back to a ol' time to keep from thinkin'. Seems like our life's over an' done."

>"No, it ain't," Ma smiled. "It ain't, Pa. An' that's one more thing a woman knows. I noticed that. Man, he lives in jerks—baby born an' a man dies, an' that's a jerk—gets a farm an' loses his farm, an' that's a jerk. Woman, it's all one flow, like a stream, little eddies, little waterfalls, but the river, it goes right on. Woman looks at it like that. We ain't gonna die out. People is goin' on—changin' a little maybe, but goin' right on."

Some adolescent girls felt their fathers' agony and tried to comfort them with lavish expressions of love, much to the embarrassment of the man and the uneasiness of his wife. This did emotional damage to father, mother and the young girl, whose fixation on her father retarded her normal interest in boys her own age.

Strife between parents, together with the realization that it cost money to marry and have babies, resulted in a decision by many young people to postpone their weddings. One young man joined the Communist Party and swore he never would marry or have children under "the present system." Unable to repress their human needs, however, young men and women made love secretly and guiltily, regarding pregnancy as a disaster. Despite an increase in the sale of contraceptives, the abortion rate rose, and so did venereal disease. The birthrate dropped.

It has been estimated that the Depression postponed 800,000 marriages that would have occurred sooner if it had not been for hard times. Margaret Mead, the noted anthropologist, argued that there was nothing wrong about letting girls support their lovers so they could marry sooner. Surprisingly, there even was a decline in marriage among members of the *Social Register*. Liberals and feminists pointed out that half of all births were in families on relief or with incomes of less than $1,000 a year; they strongly advocated birth control. Who could afford babies when a sixty-one-piece layette cost all of $7.70? Gasps of horror arose when it was reported in Illinois that a sixteenth child had been born to a family on relief.

Housewives suffered as acutely as their husbands. Many had to send their kids to live with relatives or friends. Others took part-time jobs, while a few wives actually became temporary whores to earn enough money to keep the family going. Lacking money for streetcars and buses, without the means to buy clothes to keep them looking attractive, they remained cooped up in their homes until their nerves screamed and they had nervous breakdowns.

All too often their men simply deserted them. A California woman said: "My husband went north about three months ago to try his luck. The first month he wrote pretty regularly. . . . For five weeks we have had no word from him. . . . Don't know where he is or what he is up to."

A young man who lived in the French Quarter of New Orleans was solicited by five prostitutes during a ten-block stroll, each woman asking only 50 cents. In Houston a relief worker, curious about how the people were getting along, was approached by one girl after another. For the benefit of an insistent streetwalker, the man turned his pockets inside out to prove that he had no money. Looking at him ruefully, she said: "It doesn't cost much—only a dime!"

The close relationship between poverty and morals shocked Franklin D. Roosevelt, who told reporters about an investigator who went to southeastern Kentucky: "She got into one of those mining towns," Roosevelt said, "and started to walk up the alley. There was a group of miners sitting in front of the shacks, and they pulled down their caps over their faces. As soon as she caught sight of that she walked up and said, 'What are you pulling your caps down for?' They said, 'Oh, it is all right.' 'Why pull your caps down?' They said, 'It is sort of a custom because so many of the women have not got enough clothes to cover them.' "

*   *   *

The Depression made changes in the country's physical appearance.

Fewer pedestrians were to be seen on the streets since many men did not go to work and women shopped less frequently; for lack of warm clothing and fuel, many people stayed in bed most of the day during winter. The air became cleaner over industrial cities, for there was less smoke from factory chimneys. The downtown business districts of most cities had long rows of empty shops and offices. Trains were shorter, and only rarely did one see a Pullman car. However, gas stations multiplied because millions of Americans drove their battered family cars here and there in endless quest of work. In conflicting attempts to solve their problems, farmers moved into town while city folks moved into the country to build their own houses and grow their own food. More and more blacks were seen in northern cities as desperate Negroes fled from the hopeless South. Telephones were taken out of homes, and mail deliveries were lighter. Houses and stores, parks and fences sagged and lapsed into unpainted, flaked ugliness for want of money to make repairs.

In his novel called *You Can't Go Home Again*, Thomas Wolfe described a comfort station in front of New York City Hall:

> . . . One descended to this place down a steep flight of stairs from the street, and on bitter nights he would find the place crowded with homeless men who had sought refuge there. Some were those shambling hulks that one sees everywhere, in Paris as well as in New York. . . . But most of them were just flotsam of the general ruin of the time—honest, decent, middle-aged men with faces seamed by toil and want, and young men, many of them mere boys in their teens, with thick, unkempt hair. These were the wanderers from town to town, the riders of freight trains, the thumbers of rides on highways, the uprooted, unwanted male population of America. They drifted across the land and gathered in the big cities when winter came, hungry, defeated, empty, hopeless, restless, driven by they knew not what, always on the move, looking everywhere for work, for the bare crumbs to support their miserable lives, and finding neither work nor crumbs. Here in New

York, to this obscene meeting place, these derelicts came, drawn into a common stew of rest and warmth and a little surcease from their desperation.

Heywood Broun devoted a column to a description of a slum in San Antonio, Texas:

> . . . The Church of Guadalupe stands upon the fringe of what had been described to me as the most fearsome slum in all America. It covers four square miles. At first I thought that the extreme description might have been dictated by local pride. It was my notion to protest and say, "Why, we in New York City know worse than that." But after we had gone up the third back alley I had to confess defeat gracefully.
>
> You can see shacks as bad as these in several States, but I do not know of any place where they have been so ingeniously huddled together. This is flat, sprawling country, and there is much of it, and so it seems devilish that one crazy combination of old lumber and stray tin should be set as a flap upon the side of another equally discreditable. I did not quite comprehend the character of the alley until I discovered that what I took to be a toolhouse was a residence for a family of eleven people.
>
> And these are not squatter dwellings. People pay rent for them, just as if a few rickety boards and a leaky roof constituted a house. They even have evictions and go through the solemn and obscene farce of removing a bed and a frying pan as indication that the landlord's two-dollars-and-a-half rent has not been forthcoming. . . .
>
> Back at the Church of Guadalupe, the priest said, "I have other letters from those who fight federal housing because they like their rents." He tossed over an anonymous message, which read, "I could start a story that there is a priest who writes love letters to young girls and gives jewels to women of his congregation."
>
> "Doesn't this worry you?" one of us asked.
>
> "No," said the priest. "Last month we buried thirty-nine persons, mostly children, from this little church alone.
>
> "I am worried," he said, "about people starving to death."

Louis Adamic and his wife were living with her mother in New York City in January, 1932. Born in Yugoslavia, now a naturalized American, he was a writer, a tall young man with a look of eager curiosity in his eyes. One cold morning at seven forty-five the doorbell rang, and Adamic, thinking it was the postman, opened the front door. In his book called *My America*, he told what happened next.

There stood a girl of ten and a boy of eight. They had schoolbooks in their arms, and their clothing was patched and clean, but hardly warm enough for winter weather. In a voice strangely old for her age, the girl said: "Excuse me, mister, but we have no eats in our house and my mother she said I should take my brother before we go to school and ring a

doorbell in some house"—she swallowed heavily and took a deep breath—
"and ask you to give us . . . something . . . to eat."

"Come in," Adamic said. A strange sensation swept over him. He had
heard that kids were ringing doorbells and asking for food in the Bronx,
in Harlem and in Brooklyn, but he had not really believed it.

His wife and her mother gave the children some food. The girl ate
slowly. Her brother bolted his portion, quickly and greedily.

"He ate a banana yesterday afternoon," said his sister, "but it wasn't
ripe enough or somethin', and it made him sick and he didn't eat anything
since. He's always like this when he's hungry and we gotta ring doorbells."

"Do you often ring doorbells?"

"When we have no eats at home."

"What made you ring our bell?"

"I don't know," the girl answered. "I just did."

Her name was Mary, and her brother's name was Jimmie. They lived
in a poor neighborhood five blocks away.

Mary said: "We used to live on the fourth floor upstairs and we had
three rooms and a kitchen and bath, but now we have only one room
downstairs. In back."

"Why did you move downstairs?"

The boy winced.

"My father," said the girl. "He lost his job when the panic came.
That was two years ago. I was eight and Jimmie was six. My father he
tried to get work, but he couldn't, the depression was so bad. But he
called it the panic."

Adamic and the two women were astonished at her vocabulary:
"panic" . . . "depression."

"What kind of work did your father do?"

"Painter and paperhanger. Before things got so bad, he always had
jobs when his work was in season, and he was good to us—my mother
says so, too. Then, after he couldn't get any more jobs, he got mean and
he yelled at my mother. He couldn't sleep nights and he walked up and
down and talked, and sometimes he hollered and we couldn't sleep,
either."

"Was he a union man?"

"No, he didn't belong to no union."

"What did your father holler about?"

"He called my mother bad names."

At this point in the conversation, Adamic wrote, the little girl hesi-
tated, and her brother winced again. Then she continued: "Uh . . . he
was angry because my mother, before she married him, she was in love
with another man and almost married him. But my mother says it wasn't
my father's fault he acted mean like he did. He was mean because he
had no job and we had no money."

"Where's your father now?"

"We don't know. He went away four months ago, right after Labor
Day, and he never came back, so we had to move downstairs. The land-

lord didn't want to throw us out, so he told my mother to move in down-stairs."

Between sips of milk the girl said her mother did household work whenever she could find a job, but earned very little money this way. A charity organization had been giving her $2.85 a week, but lately it had stopped. Mary did not know why. Her mother had applied for home relief, but had not yet received anything from that source.

The boy stopped eating, turned to his sister and muttered: "You talk too much! I told you not to talk!"

The girl fell silent.

Adamic said: "It's really our fault, Jimmie. We're asking too many questions."

The little boy glared and said: "Yeah!"

* * *

In Detroit someone gave another little girl a nickel, which seemed like such a fortune to her that she agonized three full days about how best to spend it.

In Erie, Pennsylvania, a seven-year-old boy named Tom received a tiny yellow chick as an Easter present. Using some old chicken wire, he built a coop for his pet beneath the back step to the house and fed and tended it carefully. His father was an unemployed molder, and the family often ate nothing but beans. Time passed. Now the little chick had grown into a full-sized chicken. One day Tom's father announced that the boy's pet would have to be killed and served for Sunday dinner, since every-one was hungry. Tom screamed in horrified protest but was unable to prevent his father from taking his chicken into the backyard and chop-ping off its head. Later that day the family sat around the table feasting on fowl, while the boy hunched in his chair, sobbing.

There was another boy who never forgot a scene from his childhood days during the Depression. He lived in a small town in Iowa. Every so often a train would stop there for a few minutes, and a man would get out carrying bags of buttons. He would distribute these buttons to wait-ing farmers and their wives, collect the cards to which they had sewn other buttons, pay them a meager sum for their labor, get back into the train and depart. This trivial piecework provided them with the only income they could get.

* * *

President Hoover was foolish enough to let himself be photographed on the White House lawn feeding his dog. This picture did not sit well with Americans who were hungry, suffering from malnutrition or even starving to death. Several times Hoover denied that there was widespread undernourishment in the nation, but he depended on unreliable statistics. Comedian Groucho Marx, who was closer to the people, said he knew things were bad when "the pigeons started feeding the people in Central Park." However, it was no laughing matter.

In Oklahoma City a newspaper reporter was assigned to cover state relief headquarters. Walking into the building one morning, he ran into a young man he had met through his landlady. This fellow offered the reporter some candy. The reporter did not want the candy but accepted it lest he hurt the other's feelings. As they stood and chewed, a social worker approached them.

"We don't allow any eating in here," she said.

The reporter, who thought she was jesting, made a wisecrack.

"We don't allow any eating in here," she repeated sternly. "Some of these applicants haven't had any breakfast. We make it a rule among ourselves never to eat or to drink Cokes in front of them."

Ashamed of himself, the reporter mumbled an apology and slunk behind a beaver-board wall. He wanted to throw away the morsel of candy remaining in his hand but felt that this would be even more sinful with hungry people so near.

Arthur Brisbane, the rich columnist and editor, walked into a Manhattan restaurant and ordered two lamb chops. When he had finished the first one, he looked longingly at the second but was too full to eat it, too. After much thought he summoned a waiter.

"What happens if I don't eat this chop?" Brisbane asked. "Will you take it back?"

"No, sir. We can't do that, sir."

"But what will you do with it? Will it be thrown away?"

"Not at all, sir. We give the leftovers to poor people."

Brisbane sighed in relief, nodded approvingly, paid his check and left.

In 1933 the Children's Bureau reported that one out of every five children in the nation was not getting enough of the right things to eat. A teacher in a coal-mining town asked a little girl in her classroom whether she was ill. The child said: "No. I'm all right. I'm just hungry." The teacher urged her to go home and eat something. The girl said: "I can't. This is my sister's day to eat." In the House of Representatives, during a debate about appropriations for Indians living on reservations, a Congressman said that eleven cents a day was enough to feed an Indian child. A Senate subcommittee learned that the president of a textile firm had told his workers they should be able to live on six cents a day.

AFL President William Green said: "I warn the people who are exploiting the workers that they can only drive them so far before they will turn on them and destroy them. They are taking no account of the history of nations in which governments have been overturned. Revolutions grow out of the depths of hunger."

Sidney Hillman, president of the Amalgamated Clothing Workers of America, appeared at a Senate hearing in 1932 and was told that it was not yet time to give federal relief. Angrily, he cried: "I would ask by what standards are we to gauge that time! Must we have hundreds of thousands of people actually dead and dying from starvation? Must we have bread riots? What is necessary to convince them that there is a need for federal and speedy relief?"

The Communists took up the slogan: "Starve or fight!"

At the University of Pennsylvania a prim audience was shocked to hear Daniel Willard, president of the B & O Railroad, say: "While I do not like to say so, I would be less than candid if I did not say that in such circumstances I would steal before I would starve."

Obviously, less fortunate Americans agreed. Petty thievery soared. Children hung around grocery stores begging for food. Customers emerging from groceries had bundles snatched from their arms by hungry kids, who ran home with the food or ducked into alleys to gobble it as fast as they could. Small retail stores had their windows smashed and their display goods stolen. Grown men, in groups of two and three, walked into chain store markets, ordered all the food they could carry and then quietly walked out without paying for it. Chain store managers did not always report these incidents to the police for fear that publicity would encourage this sort of intimidation. For the same reason the newspapers engaged in a tacit conspiracy of silence.

However, newspapers did not mind reporting that in Manhattan a debutante supper for 600 guests at the Ritz-Carlton cost $4,750. On nearby Park Avenue, beggars were so numerous that a well-dressed man might be asked for money four or five times in a ten-block stroll. President Hoover not only denied that anyone was starving, but said: "The hoboes, for example, are better fed than they ever have been. One hobo in New York got ten meals in one day."

People of means thought up ways to protect themselves from panhandlers and from begging letters. Boston's mayor, James M. Curley, had a male secretary named Stan Wilcox, who was adept at brushing off approaches. Whenever a beggar asked if he had a quarter, Wilcox would reply: "Heavens, no! I wouldn't dream of taking a drink at this hour!" Alfred E. Smith received the following letter from Milwaukee: "This is unusual, but I am in need. Would you send me $2,500, as this is the amount I am in need of. I will give you as collateral my word of honor that I will repay you if possible. If not, let the good Lord repay you and he will also pay better interest."

Governor Gifford Pinchot of Pennsylvania flatly declared that starvation was widespread. Among the many pathetic letters he received was this one: "There are nine of us in the family. My father is out of work for a couple of months and we haven't got a thing eat [*sic*] in the house. Mother is getting $12 a month of the county. If mother don't get more help we will have to starve to death. I am a little girl 10 years old. I go to school every day. My other sister hain't got any shoes or clothes to wear to go to school. My mother goes in her bare feet and she crys every night that we don't have the help. I guess that is all, hoping to hear from you."

Bernard Baruch, who felt burdened by the thought of his wealth, got a desperate letter from his cousin, Fay Allen Des Portes, who lived in his home state of South Carolina. "The horrible part of the whole situation," she wrote to him, "is these poor starving people here in our midst. The banks can't let anyone have money, the merchants are all broke; the farmers can't let the poor Negroes on the farm have anything to eat. I don't know what is going to happen. I have about four hundred Negroes that are as absolutely dependent upon me as my two little boys, but I can't help them any more and God knows what is going to happen to them."

John L. Lewis, president of the United Mine Workers, once said to a group of mine operators: "Gentlemen, I speak to you for my people. I speak to you for the miners' families in the broad Ohio valley, the Pennsylvania mountains and the black West Virginia hills. There, the shanties lean over as if intoxicated by the smoke fumes of the mine dumps. But the more pretentious ones boast a porch, with the banisters broken here and there, presenting the aspect of a snaggle-toothed child. Some of the windows are wide open to flies, which can feast nearby on garbage and answer the family dinner call in double-quick time. But there is no dinner call. The little children are gathered around a bare table without anything to eat. Their mothers are saying, 'We want bread.' "

A writer named Jonathan Norton Leonard described the plight of Pennsylvania miners who had been put out of company villages after losing a strike: "Reporters from the more liberal metropolitan papers found thousands of them huddled on the mountainsides, crowded three or four families together in one-room shacks, living on dandelion and wild weed-roots. Half of them were sick, but no local doctor would care for the evicted strikers. All of them were hungry and many were dying of those providential diseases which enable welfare workers to claim that no one has starved."

In 1931 four New York City hospitals reported 95 deaths from starvation. Two years later the New York City Welfare Council said that 29 persons had died from starvation, more than 50 others had been treated for starvation, while an additional 110 individuals—most of them children—had perished of malnutrition. In one routine report the council gave this picture of the plight of one family in the Brownsville section of Brooklyn: "Family reported starving by neighbors. Investigator found five small children at home while mother was out looking for vegetables under pushcarts. Family had moved into one room. Father sleeping at Municipal Lodging House because he could get more to eat there than at home and frequently brought food home from there in pockets for children and wife. Only other food they had for weeks came from pushcarts."

A family of fourteen was on relief in Kewanee, Illinois, the hog-raising center of the Midwest. The family was given $3 worth of groceries a week, and of course this food soon ran out. After giving the last crumbs to the children, the adults would exist on nothing but hot water until they received their next grocery allotment.

In Chicago a committee investigated city garbage dumps and then reported: "Around the truck which was unloading garbage and other refuse were about 35 men, women and children. As soon as the truck pulled away from the pile all of them started digging with sticks, some with their hands, grabbing bits of food and vegetables."

Edmund Wilson described another Chicago scene: "A private incinerator at Thirty-fifth and La Salle Streets which disposes of garbage from restaurants and hotels, has been regularly visited by people, in groups of as many as twenty at a time, who pounce upon anything that looks edible before it is thrown into the furnace. The women complained to investigators that the men took unfair advantage by jumping on the truck before it was unloaded; but a code was eventually established which provided that different sets of people should come at different times every day, so that everybody would be given a chance."

A ballad called "Starvation Blues" was sung by some of the poor people of America during the Depression.

Prentice Murphy, director of the Children's Bureau of Philadelphia, told a Senate committee: "If the modern state is to rest upon a firm foundation, its citizens must not be allowed to starve. Some of them do. They do not die quickly. You can starve for a long time without dying."

Scientists agree that a person can starve a long time without dying, but this is what it is like to starve to death: After a few days without food the stomach cramps and bloats up. Later it shrinks in size. At first a starving child will cry and eat anything to ease hunger pains—stuffing his mouth with rags, clay, chalk, straw, twigs, berries and even poisonous weeds. Then, as the child weakens, his cries change to whimpers. He feels nauseated. All the fat is being burned from his body. This burning produces acidosis. The fruity odor of acetone can be smelled on the breath, and it also appears in the urine. When starvation reaches this point, nature becomes kinder. The child grows listless and sleepy. The bulging eyes are sad and dull. Now body proteins have been depleted, while the water and electrolyte balance has been destroyed. Degeneration of the vital organs, such as the liver and kidneys, proceeds in earnest. By this time the child lacks all resistance to diseases and may be killed by some infection.

*   *   *

John Steinbeck has told how he survived the early part of the Depression before he became a famous author. "I had two assets," he wrote. "My father owned a tiny three-room cottage in Pacific Grove in California, and he let me live in it without rent. That was the first safety. Pacific Grove is on the ocean. That was the second. People in inland cities or in the closed and shuttered industrial cemeteries had greater problems than I. Given the sea, a man must be very stupid to starve. That great reservoir is always available. I took a large part of my protein food from the ocean.

"Firewood to keep warm floated on the beach daily, needing only handsaw and ax. A small garden of black soil came with the cottage. In northern California you can raise vegetables of some kind all year long. I never peeled a potato without planting the skins. Kale, lettuce, chard, turnips, carrots and onions rotated in the little garden. In the tide pools of the bay, mussels were available and crabs and abalones and that shiny kelp called sea lettuce. With a line and pole, blue cod, rock cod, perch, sea trout, sculpin could be caught."

The sale of flower seeds shot up as Americans, tired of the ugliness of their lives, turned to the beauty of homegrown flowers. As might have been expected, there was widespread cultivation of vegetable gardens. Many did this on their own, while others received official encouragement. Big railroads rented garden plots for their workers. The United States Steel Corporation used social workers and faculty members of Indiana University to develop an extensive garden project for its workers in Gary, Indiana. In New York State, in the summer of 1933, jobless men and women were tending 65,000 gardens. The city of Detroit provided tools and seed for "thrift gardens" on empty lots, an idea which Mayor Frank Murphy said he had borrowed from Hazen S. Pingree. During the Panic of 1893 Pingree had been the mayor of Detroit, and confronted with a city of jobless men, he provided them with gardens to cultivate—"Pingree's Potato Patches"—receiving national attention.

Now, in the present emergency, Henry Ford ordered all his workmen to dig in vegetable gardens or be fired. Out of his imperious command there developed what the Scripps-Howard Washington *News* called 50,000 "shotgun gardens." Rough-grained Harry Bennett, chief of Ford's private police, supervised this vast project and kept a filing system on all Ford employees. If a man had no garden in his own backyard or on some neighborhood lot, he was assigned a patch of earth somewhere on Ford's 4,000 acres of farmland around Dearborn, Michigan. Each workman had to pay fifty cents to have his strip plowed.

More than one-third of the men employed in Ford's Dearborn plant lived 10 to 20 miles away, and some protested that since they did not own a car they would have to spend an extra two hours daily just traveling to and from their allotted patches. A Bennett henchman would snarl: "Why don't-cha buy a car? You're makin' 'em, ain't-cha?" Bone-weary workmen who simply couldn't muster the energy to toil on their garden plots soon were brought into line by Bennett's personal deputy, Norman Selby, the former boxer "Kid McCoy."

*   *   *

In the spring of 1932 the Community Council of Philadelphia ran out of private funds for the relief of needy families. Eleven days elapsed before this relief work could be resumed with public funds, and many families received no help during this interim. A study was made to find out what had happened when food orders stopped.

One woman borrowed 50 cents from a friend and bought stale bread at 3½ cents per loaf. Except for one or two meals, this was all she could serve her family throughout those eleven days.

A pregnant mother and her three children could afford only two meals a day. At eleven o'clock in the morning she would serve breakfast, which consisted of cocoa, bread and butter. This left everyone so hungry that the mother began advancing the time of their evening meal, which was just one can of soup.

Another woman scoured the docks, picking up vegetables that fell from produce wagons. Fish vendors sometimes gave her a fish at the end of the day. On two separate occasions her family went without food for a day and a half.

On the day the food orders stopped, one family ate nothing all day. At nine o'clock that night the mother went to a friend's house and begged for a loaf of bread. Later she got two days' work at 75 cents a day. With this pittance she bought a little meat. Then, adding vegetables picked up off the street, she made a stew which she cooked over and over again each day to prevent spoilage.

One family ate nothing but potatoes, rice, bread and coffee, and for one and a half days they were totally without food.

*   *   *

Hunting jackrabbits to feed the family became a way of life among farmers and ranchers. This gave birth to a Depression joke reported by John Steinbeck in *The Grapes of Wrath*. One man said to another: "Depression is over. I seen a jackrabbit, an' they wasn't nobody after him." The second man said: "That ain't the reason. Can't afford to kill jackrabbits no more. Catch'em and milk'em and turn'em loose. One you seen prob'ly gone dry."

Audie Murphy was born on a Texas farm five years before the Crash, the son of very poor parents. Almost as soon as he could walk, he began hunting game for the family. Since shells were expensive, every shot had to count. Aware of this, Audie Murphy developed into an expert marksman—so expert that when he was a GI during World War II, he killed 240 Nazis and emerged as the most decorated American soldier of the war.

Wheat growers, bankrupted by drought, talked about heading for Alaska to kill moose to fill their growling bellies. In the timberlands of the great Northwest some desperate men set forest fires so that they would be hired to extinguish them, while in big cities other men prayed for heavy snowfalls to provide them with shoveling jobs. When some Pittsburgh steel mills reopened briefly, the steelworkers called back to their jobs were too weak from hunger to be able to work.

At the age of eleven Cesar Chavez, who later won renown as a Mexican-American labor leader, fished and cut mustard greens to help keep his family from starving.

Charles H. Percy, who wound up a multimillionaire and a United States Senator, never forgot what it was like to be a poor boy in Chicago during the Depression: "I remember a great feeling of shame when the welfare truck pulled up to our house. And you talk about cheating! Once they delivered us 100 pounds of sugar by mistake. My father wanted to return it, but my mother said, 'God willed us to have it,' and she wouldn't give it up." She swapped some of the sugar for flour and helped tide the family over by baking cookies that little Chuck Percy peddled door to door.

Americans under the stress of the Depression behaved with a dignity that varied in terms of their religious backgrounds, their mental images of themselves and their rigidity or flexibility. Brittle people snapped, while the pliant bent and survived.

In Georgia a blind Negro refused all relief, harnessed himself to a plow like a mule and tilled the fields, day after day. In Pittsburgh a father with starving children stole a loaf of bread from a neighbor, was caught, hanged himself in shame. In Youngstown, Ohio, a father, mother and their four sons preferred to starve rather than accept charity. Before they died, their condition was discovered by a neighbor who happened to be a newspaper reporter. They were existing on fried flour and water.

Charles Wayne also lived in Youngstown. He had been a hot mill worker for the Republic Iron and Steel Company until he was laid off. For the next two years he was unable to get any kind of work. Now a fifty-seven-year-old man, workless, hopeless, unable to feed his wife and ten children, he climbed onto a bridge one morning. He took off his coat, folded it neatly, then jumped into the swirling Mahoning River below. Instinct caused him to swim a few strokes, but then he gave up and let himself drown. Later his wife sobbed to reporters: "We were about to lose our home and the gas and electric companies had threatened to shut off the service."

An elderly man receiving $15-a-week relief money for his large family went out each day, without being asked, to sweep the streets of his village. "I want to do something," he said, "in return for what I get." A graduate of the Harvard Law School, now old and almost deaf, gladly took a $15-a-week job as assistant caretaker at a small park.

Rather than accept charity, a New York dentist and his wife killed themselves with gas. He left this note: "The entire blame for this tragedy rests with the City of New York or whoever it is that allows free dental work in the hospital. We want to get out of the way before we are forced to accept relief money. The City of New York is not to touch our bodies. We have a horror of charity burial. We have put the last of our money in the hands of a friend who will turn it over to my brother."

John Steinbeck wrote: "Only illness frightened us. You have to have money to be sick—or did then. And dentistry also was out of the question, with the result that my teeth went badly to pieces. Without dough you couldn't have a tooth filled."

Shoes were a problem. Upon reaching home, poor people took off their shoes to save wear and tear. Middle-class people bought do-it-yourself shoe-repair kits. Those unable to afford the kits would resole their shoes with strips of rubber cut from old tires. Some wore ordinary rubbers over shoes with holes in their bottoms. A miner's son, Jack Conroy, told what a hole in a shoe could mean to a man walking the streets looking for work: "Maybe it starts with a little hole in the sole; and then the slush of the pavements oozes in, gumming sox and balling between your toes. Concrete whets Woolworth sox like a file, and if you turn the heel on top and tear a pasteboard inner sole, it won't help much. There are the tacks, too. You get to avoiding high places and curbstones because that jabs the point right into the heel. Soon the tack has calloused a furrowed hole, and you don't notice it unless you strike something unusually high or solid, or forget and walk flat-footed. You pass a thousand shoe-shops where a tack might be bent down, but you can't pull off a shoe and ask to have *that* done—for nothing."

Keeping clean was also a problem, since soap cost money. Steinbeck washed his linen with soap made from pork fat, wood ashes and salt, but it took a lot of sunning to get the smell out of sheets. As the sale of soap declined across the nation, its production was reduced. Procter & Gamble did not lay off its workers, as it might have done under the circumstances, but put them to work cutting grass, painting fences and repairing factories until soap production began to rise again.

Steinbeck wrote a short story called "Daughter" about a sharecropper who shot and killed his own daughter because he had no food to give her. This could not be shrugged off as mere fiction, for in Carlisle, Pennsylvania, a starving man named Elmo Noakes actually suffocated his three small daughters rather than see them starve.

*   *   *

The Depression scarred many young men and women who later became celebrities or who already were well known. Jack Dempsey, former heavyweight boxing champion of the world, became so strapped for money that at the age of thirty-six he got himself sufficiently back into shape to fight fifty-six exhibition bouts. Babe Ruth, always a big spender, tried to supplement his income by opening a haberdashery on Broadway but lost his own shirt after five months.

Clifford Odets wrote his first play while living on ten cents a day. Lillian Hellman, who later became a renowned playwright, earned $50 a week as a script reader for Metro-Goldwyn-Mayer. William Inge, who also won fame as a playwright, acted in tent shows during the Depression, long afterward recalling: "We actors considered ourselves fortunate if we earned five dollars a week. Sometimes the farmers of Kansas would bring in flour and meat as barter for admission to Saturday matinees."

Songwriter Frank Loesser learned from his parents that they had lost all their money. He took any job he could get, including screwing the tops on bottles of an insecticide. He also worked as a spotter for a chain of restaurants, getting seventy-five cents a day plus the cost of each meal for reporting on the food and service. Later he reminisced: "I used to eat twelve times a day. When you're poor, you're always hungry from walking around so much."

Danny Thomas performed in saloons, but finally even this kind of work came to an end. The chance of getting another job seemed so slim that he considered giving up show business. In desperation, he prayed to St. Jude, the patron saint of the hopeless, and the next day he landed a job in Chicago that proved to be the turning point of his career.

Ralph Bellamy almost starved to death in the basement of a Greenwich Village apartment. Cary Grant was working in Hollywood as an extra. Dana Andrews worked four years as a gas station attendant in Van Nuys, California. Robert Young was employed as a soda jerk, grease monkey and truck driver. Ray Milland, living on credit in Hollywood, was about to go to work in a garage when he landed a part in a movie called *Bolero*. In Chireno, Texas, a twelve-year-old girl named Lucille Ann Collier began dancing professionally to help the family finances; later she grew into a long-legged beauty and won fame under the name of Ann Miller. In the Bronx a four-year-old girl named Anna Maria Italiano sang for WPA men working on a nearby project; today she is known as Anne Bancroft.

Victor Mature set out for Hollywood in 1935 at the age of seventeen, with $40 in cash and a car loaded with candy and chewing gum. He drove for five days and slept in his automobile each night, and by the time he reached the film capital he was almost broke. To his father in Louisville he wired: ARRIVED HERE WITH 11 CENTS. His father, an Austrian scissors grinder who had taken up refrigerator selling, wired back: FORTY-THREE YEARS AGO I ARRIVED IN NEW YORK WITH FIVE CENTS. I COULD NOT EVEN SPEAK ENGLISH. YOU ARE SIX CENTS UP ON ME.

The effect of the Depression on Hollywood extras was told by Grover Jones to an amused courtroom in a trial concerning Metro-Goldwyn-Mayer. Jones, once an extra and then a scriptwriter, gave this entertaining testimony: "They wanted eighty Indians, and I got the job only because I knew how to put on what they called bolamania—burnt umber and raw umber mixed. But they made me a chief. That meant I didn't have to go naked. I could wear a suit, you see. And at that time I was convinced I was fairly smart. So there were now eighty-one Indians. I had never seen a camera during all those months, because I was always in the background, waiting over in back of the hill for the call to come over the hill on the horses to rescue the child. And I had never been on horses. So we sat on these horses, each confiding in the other, and none of them had ever been on horses, except we were all hungry. Finally the man said, 'Now look, when you hear shooting I want you all to come over the hills, and I want some of you to fall off the horses.' Well, in those days they paid three dollars extra for a man who would fall off a horse, because it is quite a stunt. So we waited until finally we got the call to come over the hill, and somebody shot a gun off—and eighty-one Indians fell off their horses."

*   *   *

There was nothing surprising about the fact that men would risk injury or death by falling off a horse to earn an extra $3 a day. People felt that if they could just live through the Depression, they could endure anything else life had to offer. To *endure* was the main thing. Many took pay cuts without a murmur. A young man just out of college with a Bachelor of Journalism degree accepted a job on a newspaper at exactly *nothing* per week; a month later he was grateful to be put on the payroll at $15. Graduate engineers worked as office boys. College graduates of various kinds ran elevators in department stores. Unemployed architects turned out jigsaw puzzles. One jobless draftsman, Alfred Butts, used his spare time to invent the game of Scrabble.

Young men who might have grown into greatness chose, instead, to seek the security of civil service jobs, becoming policemen, firemen, garbage collectors. Fewer sailors deserted from the Navy. Enlistments rose in all branches of the nation's military establishment. When Congress voted a 10 percent pay cut for all federal employees, President Hoover secretly asked the Senate to make an exception for soldiers and sailors, because he did not wish to rely on disgruntled troops in case of internal trouble.

Women and children toiled for almost nothing in the sweatshops of New York City, welfare workers reporting these grim examples:

• A woman crocheted hats for 40 cents a dozen and was able to make only two dozen per week.

• An apron girl, paid 2½ cents per apron, earned 20 cents a day.

• A slipper liner was paid 21 cents for every seventy-two pairs of slippers she lined, and if she turned out one slipper every forty-five seconds she could earn $1.05 in a nine-hour day.

• A girl got half a cent for each pair of pants she threaded and sponged, making $2.78 a week.

Connecticut's state commissioner of labor said that some sweatshops in that state paid girls between 60 cents and $1.10 for a fifty-five-hour week. In Pennsylvania men working in sawmills were paid 5 cents an hour, men in tile and brick manufacturing got 6 cents per hour, while construction workers earned 7½ cents an hour. In Detroit the Briggs Manufacturing Company paid men 10 cents and women 4 cents an hour, causing auto workers to chant: "If poison doesn't work, try Briggs!" Also in Detroit, the Hudson Motor Car Company called back a small-parts assembler and then kept her waiting three days for a half hour of work, forcing her to spend 60 cents in carfare to earn 28 cents.

Two Maine fishermen put out to sea at four o'clock one morning and did not return to port until five o'clock that afternoon. During this long day of toil they caught 200 pounds of hake and 80 pounds of haddock. They burned up eight gallons of gas at 19 cents a gallon and used 100 pounds of bait costing two cents a pound. For their catch they were paid one cent a pound for the hake and four cents a pound for the haddock. Thus they earned less than two cents an hour for their day's work.

Meantime, Henry Ford was declaring: "Many families were not so badly off as they thought; they needed guidance in the management of their resources and opportunities." Ford needed no guidance. He managed to transfer 41½ percent of stock in the Ford Motor Company to his son, Edsel, without paying a cent in inheritance or estate taxes.

*   *   *

Ford, who liked to boast that he always had to work, declared in 1930 that "the very poor are recruited almost solely from the people who refuse to think and therefore refuse to work diligently." Roger W. Babson, the statistician, pontificated two years later: "Better business will come when the unemployed change their attitude toward life." Most rich men were quick to moralize.

The concept of hard work was central to capitalism and the Protestant ethic. Americans had been raised on a diet of aphorisms praising work and self-reliance. Benjamin Franklin said: "God helps them that help themselves." The Bible insisted: "In the sweat of thy face shalt thou eat bread." Thomas Carlyle said: "All work, even cotton-spinning, is noble; work alone is noble." Elizabeth Barrett Browning wrote: "Whoever fears God, fears to sit at ease." It was either Bishop Richard Cumberland or George Whitefield (no one is sure) who first said: "Better to wear out than to rust out." Most Americans agreed, but now in these Depression times men did sit at home and rust, through no fault of their own, losing the fine edge of their skills.

Idle, dispirited, hungry, defeated, withdrawn, brooding—people began to feel that somehow they were to blame for everything, that somehow, somewhere, they had failed. Maybe the Depression was punishment for their sins. After all, Protestant Episcopal Bishop John P. Tyler attributed it to the lack of religion. Perhaps Christians, if they wished to be good Christians, should bow to fate by accepting Christ's words that "to everyone that hath shall be given; and from him that hath not, even that which he hath shall be taken from him." But some found it difficult to find comfort in a sermon preached by the Reverend William S. Blackshear, an Episcopalian clergyman, in the bleak year of 1932. Blackshear said in part: "Christ was happy to be at the banquets of the rich. It was at such a place that the woman broke the vial of costly ointment and anointed His feet. There were those who cried out for the improvident and rebuked the woman, saying that this should have been converted into cash and given to the poor. It was then that Christ spoke on the economic plan, 'The poor ye have always with you.' "

This kind of sermon, representing conservative Protestantism, offended liberal clergymen. Forced by the Depression to rethink their values, they began searching for a new theology. Some began with the premise that if the church were to serve any purpose or perform realistically, it had to divorce itself from economic and political values. This developing viewpoint was expressed with crystal clarity by H. Richard Niebuhr, a pastor and a brother of Reinhold Niebuhr. He wrote:

> The church is in bondage to capitalism. Capitalism in its contemporary form is more than a system of ownership and distribution of economic goods. It is a faith and a way of life. It is faith in wealth as the source of all life's blessings and as the savior of man from his deepest misery. It is the doctrine that man's most important activity is the production of economic goods and that all other things are dependent upon this. On the basis of this initial idolatry it develops a morality in which economic worth becomes the standard by which to measure all other values and the economic virtues take precedence over courage, temperance, wisdom and justice, over charity, humility and fidelity. Hence nature, love, life, truth, beauty and justice are exploited or made the servants of the high economic good. Everything, including the lives of workers, is made a utility, is desecrated and ultimately destroyed. . . .

Other dissenters noted the supremacy of capitalism over every other value in the fact that church property was exempt from taxation. State constitutions and special statutes declared that no real estate taxes could be levied on church-owned properties, such as the church building itself, parochial schools, parsonages, the parish house and cemeteries. Why? A Missouri Supreme Court decision said that "no argument is necessary to show that church purposes are public purposes."

But was this really true? The United States of America was a Christian nation nominally, but not legally. No single religion, sect or church was recognized as the established church. Although the phrase "separation of church and state" does not appear in the Constitution of the United States or in that of any state but Utah, the idea for which it stands is found in the constitutional provisions against religious tests and in the words of the First Amendment: "Congress shall make no law respecting an establishment of religion. . . ."

During the Depression some liberal Christians, agnostics, atheists and others fretted about the special status given churches and church property. A few scholars recalled that President Ulysses S. Grant had said: "I would suggest the taxation of all property equally, whether church or corporation, exempting only the last resting place of the dead, and possibly, with proper restrictions, church edifices." Dissenters objected on principle to the exemption of church property, regarded this as an indirect subsidy by the state to religion and pointed out that personal taxes might be less if churches bore their share of the tax burden.

They got nowhere. At the core of capitalism was the belief that God looked with favor on the rich. This idea had been expressed as long ago as 1732 by one of J. P. Morgan's ancestors, the Reverend Joseph Morgan, who sermonized: "Each man coveting to make himself rich, carries on the Publick Good: Thus God in His Wisdom and Mercy turns our wickedness to Publick Benefit. . . . A rich Man is a great friend of the Publick, while he aims at nothing but serving himself. God will have us live by helping one another; and since Love will not do it, Covetousness shall."

*   *   *

J. P. Morgan himself flatly told a Senate committee: "If you destroy the leisure class you destroy civilization." When reporters pressed for a definition of the leisure class, Morgan said it included all who could afford a maid. In 1931, according to *Fortune* magazine, there still were 1,000,000 families with servants. One wealthy family announced that it had solved its Depression problem by discharging fifteen of its twenty servants—although the family members showed no curiosity or concern about the fate of the unemployed fifteen.

John Jacob Astor came of age in 1933 and thereupon inherited about $4 million. Nonetheless, he dabbled at a job in a downtown Manhattan brokerage house. Before long he quit with the explanation: "I didn't finish until five o'clock and by the time I got uptown it was six. And then I had to get up early the next morning." At a later date Astor was employed briefly by a shipping firm, and when he quit this second job, he commented: "I have discovered that work interferes with leisure." He was a representative of that leisure class which Morgan felt must be maintained to save civilization.

When Dwight Morrow was running for governor of New Jersey, he said: "There is something about too much prosperity that ruins the fiber of the people. The men and women that built this country, that founded it, were people that were reared in adversity." Morrow made this statement and died before Adolf Hitler declared: "It was poverty that made me strong." Joseph P. Kennedy, a busy member of the leisure class, felt that the rich had to make some sacrifices. Writing about the Depression, Kennedy said: "I am not ashamed to record that in those days I felt and said I would be willing to part with half of what I had if I could be sure of keeping, under law and order, the other half."

One member of the enormously wealthy Du Pont family seems to have been out of touch with reality. An advertising agency wanted his company to sponsor a Sunday afternoon radio program, but this Du Pont rejected the idea, saying: "At three o'clock on Sunday afternoons everybody is playing polo."

Everybody except the millions of Americans gobbling the last morsel of food from their plates in the fear that it might be their last meal—a habit that persisted in some people down through the next three decades. As Sinclair Lewis commented in his novel *It Can't Happen Here*, people were so confused, insecure and frustrated that they hardly could do anything more permanent than shaving or eating breakfast. They were tortured with feelings of inadequacy and guilt.

A young Alabama school teacher with eight years of tenure was fired after the Wall Street Crash. Eager to work, willing to take any job however low in the social scale, she became a maid in a private home. However, upon learning that she would be expected to work seven days a week, getting room and board but no wages, she quit. Then she took a job in a convalescent home which paid her room and board and $3 a week, but soon the home closed for lack of funds. The gentle schoolteacher completely lost faith in herself, confessing to a caseworker: "If, with all the advantages I've had, I can't make a living, then I'm just no good, I guess!"

Forty experienced secretaries found work after being unemployed a year, but the first few days on the job they were unable to take dictation from their bosses without weeping from sheer nervousness. After seeking employment for a long time, a man finally landed a job and became so overwrought with joy that he died of excitement. A corporation executive was given the nasty chore of firing several hundred men. A kind and compassionate person, he insisted on talking to each of them personally and asking what plans each had for the future. In a few months the executive's hair had turned gray.

*   *   *

The Depression began to erode freedom.

Some Americans, a little more secure than others, asked harsh questions. How about fingerprinting everyone on relief? Was it proper for a man on relief to own a car—even if he needed it to try to find work? Wasn't it wrong to sell liquor to the head of a family on relief? Did anyone owning a life insurance policy deserve relief? Should reliefers be allowed to vote? Did they deserve citizenship?

In New Orleans a federal judge denied citizenship to four qualified persons because they were on relief and therefore, in the judge's words, "unable financially to contribute to the support of the government." In California another judge withheld citizenship from Jacob Hullen; in response to the judge's questions Hullen had said he believed in municipal or federal ownership of public utilities.

In New York City, one cold and rainy day, the police arrested 38 men who had taken shelter in the Pennsylvania Railroad's ferry terminal on Cortlandt Street. All were marched to the nearest police station. Fifteen of them, able to prove that they had a few nickels and dimes in their pockets, were released. The other 23 men, who did not have a cent on them, were led before a magistrate, who sentenced them to jail for vagrancy. Newspaper stories about this obvious injustice raised such a hullabaloo, however, that the 23 prisoners soon were freed.

Robert Morss Lovett, a professor of English literature at the University of Chicago, wrote in his autobiography:

> An example of the injustice meted out to foreign-born workers involved a Yugoslav named Perkovitch. When conditions were at their worst in 1932–33 the unemployed on the West Side [of Chicago] were in the habit of crossing the city to the South Side where food was sometimes available from bakeries, disposing of yesterday's bake, and where, at least, the garbage was more lavish.
>
> One morning these itinerants were picked up by the police and held at the station house on the absurd pretext that a revolution was planned. Perkovitch told me that he and about one hundred others were kept in the basement all day without food. Once a lieutenant with a bodyguard of patrolmen raged through the room, striking and kicking the men in an ecstasy of sadism. At six the prisoners were released with no charges.

Paul D. Peacher, the town marshal of Jonesboro, Arkansas, arrested a group of Negro men without cause and forced them to work on his farm. A federal grand jury indicted him under Title 18 of the Anti-Slavery Act of 1866 for "causing Negroes to be held as slaves" on a cotton plantation. This was the first case ever tried under the slavery statute. A county grand jury absolved Peacher, but the federal Department of Justice would not drop the case. Now the marshal was forced to stand trial—this time before a *federal* jury. Taking the witness chair in his own behalf, he denied that he had done anything wrong. However, the jury disagreed with him and found him guilty. Peacher was sentenced to two years in prison and fined $3,500. He appealed, lost his appeal, paid the fine and accepted a two-year probationary sentence.

Someone asked Eugene Talmadge, the governor of Georgia, what he would do about the millions of unemployed Americans. Talmadge snarled: "Let 'em starve!" It made him happy when the city fathers of Atlanta put unwanted nonresidents in chain gangs. When some textile workers went on strike in Georgia the governor had barbed-wire concentration camps built and threw pickets into them. Frank Hague, the mayor and ruthless boss of Jersey City, called for the erection in Alaska of a concentration camp for native "Reds."

Wise and temperate men worried about the growing loss of liberty in America, the land of the free and the home of the brave. George Boas, a professor of philosophy, sadly said: "It is taken for granted that democracy is bad and that it is dying." Will Durant, busy writing his many-volumed *Story of Civilization*, asked rhetorically: "Why is it that Democracy has fallen so rapidly from the high prestige which it had at the Armistice?"

Race Relations in
a Southern Town

HORTENSE POWDERMAKER

In the Southern United States prior to the end of the Civil War, the relationship between blacks, most of whom were slaves, and whites was carefully regulated by a complex of laws and customs based on the institution of slavery. After abolition, for a few years, race relations were in a relatively ambiguous state. C. Vann Woodward's **The Strange Career of Jim Crow,** revised for the third time in 1974, and the controversy this work has engendered have charted for us the formulation of a new pattern of Southern race relations that was substantially complete by the opening years of the twentieth century. The resulting system of segregation, or "Jim Crow," called for legally enforced separation of the races into a two-level caste system that permeated both public and private life in the South.

The public aspects of segregation, because of their basis in law and local ordinance, finally came under attack by the federal judiciary after years of litigation forced primarily by the National Association for the Advancement of Colored People. The decision of the United States Supreme Court in 1954 declaring school segregation unconstitutional rang the death knell for official racial discrimination in the public sphere. But it has been a long time dying. In the years after 1954, continued litigation brought many areas of segregation under public scrutiny, and as federal legislation was gradually enforced in the South and border regions, the long-standard structure of race relations began to crumble.

Less well known, but in many ways more dehumanizing, were the private patterns of racial discrimination throughout the South. Historians have been more interested in the larger, public institutions and their change over time. Sociologists, however, and particularly social and cultural anthropologists, have through the years been concerned with the more intimate relationships within communities and groups of all sorts. During the 1930s and 1940s, several excellent studies of black communities and race relations in the South were published. Perhaps the best of these is an anthropological study of Indianola, Mississippi, published in 1939 by Hortense Powdermaker, formerly of Queens College of the City University of New York. While the primary purpose of Powdermaker's work was to provide a social portrait of the black people in Indianola (called Cottonville in the study), she necessarily included a great deal of material on the relationship between the races. Few people who have not lived in the segregated South can understand the extent to which race relations formed a major topic of interest and concern for all involved, the dominant as well as the dominated. This same level of concern, however, is now being approached in urban centers, which have taken the place of the South as the major area of racial conflict.

It has often been said that the major difference between Northern and Southern white attitudes toward blacks in past times has
been that in the North black people were loved as a race and despised
as individuals, while in the South they were loved as individuals and
despised as a race. The practical application of this Southern attitude, however, was set within narrow limits. In the selection from
Powdermaker's book reprinted below, she explores these limitations
and delineates the ways in which the racial attitudes of whites work
themselves out in action. Her concern here is not with the segregation
of public institutions but with the refusal of whites to grant to blacks
the common respect of humanity. The constant interpersonal humiliation, and its ultimate form, lynching, rather than the better known
institutional discrimination is her subject in this section.

As the pattern of public segregation began to break down in recent years, a concomitant change often occurred in interpersonal relations. The "affection" based on hard and fast caste lines often was
lost as the caste lines became more permeable. But, at the same
time, a grudging acknowledgment of respect based on a common humanity began to develop. A major factor in the elimination of the kind
of discriminatory behavior described below has been the increasing
refusal of black Americans to accept such treatment. And, as far as
racial attitudes and patterns of racial relationships are concerned, the
nation now more nearly resembles the condition described by Malcolm
X: "The South begins at the Canadian border." For the first time in
American history, race relations now are being looked at from a national, rather than a regional, perspective.

What the white inhabitants of the Cottonville community think and
feel about the Negro finds expression whenever there is contact between
the two races. The more subtle manifestations of prevailing attitudes appear only after examination, but the cruder expressions are apparent to any
visitor who is not so familiar with them as to take them for granted. That
the local Whites do take them for granted so thoroughly as hardly to be
aware of them until they are commented upon or violated is an essential
feature of the social scene.

Any American visitor is prepared to find the well-known Jim Crow
arrangements of the railroad station with its separate waiting-rooms and
toilets. He will know that there are separate and inferior day coaches
reserved for the Negroes at the standard fares, and that they are not permitted to ride in Pullmans at any price. He will note that here, as in many

places up north, Negroes are not allowed to eat in white restaurants, but may patronize two or three small eating places run by and for colored people. The balcony of the one moving picture theater is reserved for them. Seats here are cheaper than those downstairs, and they may not buy the more expensive seats. There are separate schools and churches for Negroes, in buildings removed from the white neighborhood—either Across the Tracks or in the country. These divisions are absolute. No white person would attend a Negro institution or sit in the places reserved for Negroes, though presumably he could if he would. No Negro would be admitted to the institutions or places reserved for Whites.

Hardly less rigid are the social mechanisms which express the conviction that the two races are distinct and that one of them is distinctly inferior, and which confirm the well-known fact that in this section of our democracy the accepted order is analogous to, though not identical with, a caste system. These social mechanisms are familiar enough to American readers so that brief mention of a few will suffice to indicate their nature and their relation to factors already discussed. They take the form of prohibitions, injunctions, usages; they may be chiefly "social," or may carry economic and even legal consequences. They vary also in the significance attached to them, which is not always in proportion to their apparent magnitude.

A social prohibition to which great weight is attached is that which forbids addressing a Negro as "Mr.," "Mrs.," or "Miss." Just what the white person withholds in avoiding the use of these titles is suggested by those he is willing to employ. Ordinarily, a Negro is simply called by his first name, regardless of his age, attainments, or wealth, and often by Whites who may be less endowed in any of these respects. "Doctor" and "Professor" are readily granted to professional people, however. A teacher who has charge of a small one-room country school, and who himself has never been to high school, is regularly called Professor. A medical man will be addressed as "Doctor" by Whites who could not conceivably bring themselves to call him "Mister." It may not seem entirely inappropriate that members of a race considered inferior should more easily be accorded an indication of status achieved by effort than one which stands for respect and social parity acquired by birth. It is to be remembered, however, that special titles are used more easily and with less significance in the South than in the North, and that the general American attitude toward members of the learned professions is somewhat ambiguous.

It is quite in order for Whites to address Negroes by terms which imply relationship or affection. Women are called "Aunty" and men "Uncle" even when they are younger than the person speaking to them. On the other hand, Whites often say "Boy" or "Girl" to Negroes who are much older than themselves.

> A moderately prosperous man in his late fifties is a highly respected member of the Negro group. As presiding elder in his church on Sunday, wearing gloves and a neatly pressed suit, he presents a most dignified appearance. On Monday, going to work, he is stopped by a young white woman who is having tire trouble.

Both have lived in the same town all their lives and she knows his name very well. She addresses him only as "Boy," repeating the word sharply as she orders his moves in rendering her this unpaid service.

The prohibition against courtesy titles extends to the telephone. If a Negro puts in a long-distance call for "Mr. Smith" in a town fifty miles away, the operator, who can tell where the call comes from, will ask: "Is he colored?" On being told that he is, she replies: "Don't you say 'Mister' to me. He ain't 'Mister' to me."

To violate this strong taboo is to arouse the resentment, suspicion, fear, which attends the breaking of taboos or customs in any culture. If a Melanesian is asked what difference it would make if he failed to provide a feast for his dead maternal uncle, or if he broke the rule of exogamy, his attitude is one of complete bewilderment and strong fear at the mere suggestion. If a member of his community should actually commit such a breach, he would resent it as an invitation to general disaster. The exogamy rule is felt, inarticulately, to be an inherent and indispensable part of the Melanesian *status quo*, one of the balances which keep the culture revolving in orderly fashion. The title taboo is sensed as equally essential to the *status quo* in Mississippi. To question either is to question the whole system; to violate either is to violate, weaken, endanger, the entire *status quo*. In either case this is merely the background to the immediate reaction, which is seldom reasoned, and may be intensified by the secondary meanings which become attached to any social pattern.

The rule for forms of address is concerned also with what the Negro calls the White. The white person's name is never to be mentioned without some title of respect. It may be the first or the last name, depending on the degree of acquaintance. Military titles, traditionally accorded to Whites, are less frequently heard today, and the old-time "Massa" has given way to "Boss." If no other title is used, the Negro says "Ma'am" or "Sir." Among Whites and among Negroes, this is a matter of courtesy; but when a Negro is speaking to a white person it is compulsory. If he mails a package at the post office he must be very careful to observe this usage toward the clerk who is serving him. He must be equally careful in addressing the telephone operator.

A man who had lived in a large city for several years forgot the injunction when he was putting in a long-distance call. The operator repeated his number several times, each time asking if it was correct, and each time receiving the answer: "Yes." Finally in an ominous tone she said: "You'll say 'Yes, Ma'am' to me." The Negro canceled his call. Since then a kind of secret warfare has gone on. Whenever he uses the phone the operator asks a question that would ordinarily be answered with a "Ma'am," and he extricates himself by saying: "That's it," "That is correct," or some phrase that evades the difficulty. The operator continues her campaign, undaunted.

There often appears to be a relation between the insistence of the White upon observance of such a usage, and his own adjustment within his group.

> A woman who was disliked and resented by both races tried to get the Negroes to call her Miss Sylvia instead of Mrs. T. The Negro who spoke of this said: "Miss Sylvia is more like slavery times," and added scornfully that she guessed Mrs. T. didn't know other people have been born since slavery.

Closely connected with the title taboo is the term used when Whites talk among themselves about Negroes. "Nigger" is the term used almost universally. Its emotional tone varies according to the context of the situation and the individual using it. It ranges from contempt to affection, and its use is so prevalent and so much a part of the *mores*, that it may not necessarily be deeply charged. "Darky" is sometimes substituted for "nigger," and then the tone is practically always one of affection. When a white person is talking to a Negro, and wishes to use the third person, "nigger" is the common term. There are occasional exceptions. A sensitive and "good White" may substitute "your people." State and county officials in addressing Negro groups use this term, or "colored people," or "Negroes." The latter is the one to which the Whites show the most resistance, and several linguistic variations have occurred as a result, such as "niggra." Although all these terms occur in intra-Negro conversation, they always resent intensely "nigger" and "darky" when used by the Whites. "Negro" and "colored people" are the preferred terms. Among themselves, "darky" is heard rarely, but "nigger" is used frequently, and again its emotional tone varies. A colored person may call another "nigger" in either affection or anger, and the emotion connected with the term may be small or great. The term does not usually call forth resentment when used by a Negro, as it always does when used by a White.

The taboo against eating with a Negro is another which suggests analogies from different cultures. Eating with a person has strong symbolic value in many societies, and usually signifies social acceptance. White children may on special occasions eat with Negroes, but for colored and white adults to eat together under ordinary conditions is practically unheard of. If a white person in the country would for some reason ask for food at a Negro home, he would eat apart. Special circumstances may, however, constitute an exception to the rule: if a white man and a colored man went fishing, they might grill their fish over an open fire and eat together, in the open. Exceptions are extremely rare, and the taboo is extended to colored people who are not Negroes.

> A Chinese doctor who was participating in a public health study lived at one of the town's boarding houses. Several of the boarders objected to sitting at the same table with him. The woman who told about it added: "You know, we are so narrow down here."

The rule that a Negro should not enter the front door of a house is so taken for granted that many white people, when they go out for a short time, will lock the back door against thieves and leave the front door open. They assume that no colored person would go in the front way and, apparently, that no white person would steal. The visibility of the front entrance in the daytime lends a practical support to the assumption.

The front-door prohibition is far less important to some Whites than to others.

> "A poor-raised white person can work alongside of you," one Negro said, "and then if he gets a fortune, you can't come to the front door but have to go round to the back. But a rich-raised White don't care if you walk out of the front door."
>
> Two women, each of whom considers herself a typical Southerner, illustrate divergent attitudes. Both are members of the middle class, but they represent as much contrast as can be found within the limits of that comparatively homogeneous group. One belongs to the "best people" of the town; the other has recently acquired a small competence, after years of insecurity and strain. The son of the second woman happened to see the first woman's cook leave the house by the front door. "Do you allow your cook to go out that way?" he asked in surprise. His hostess replied that it didn't make any difference to her which door her cook used. The boy exclaimed that his mother would never allow anything like that; one day when their cook did try to go out the front way, his mother picked up a piece of wood from the fireplace and threw it at her.

Few cooks would attempt to leave by the front door, and still fewer mistresses would be indifferent to it. The amount of individual variation with regard to this prohibition, however, suggests that it is not one of those which carry the strongest symbolic force for the Whites.

In connection with shaking hands, it again appears that affection may be permissible where respect is denied. A colored mammy may kiss her charges, perhaps even on rare occasions after they have grown up. But colored people and white people do not as a rule shake hands in public. If a white educator addresses a group of Negro teachers, he might shake hands with them after his speech. On such occasions refreshments might also be served, but it would be lap service, with no question of sitting at the same table.

It is of course taken for granted that ordinary courtesies have no place between the two races. A white man thinks nothing of sitting while a colored woman stands, regardless of who she is. A highly educated woman who always stood in talking to the white man under whose direction she worked was frightened when on one occasion he invited her to sit.

Courtesies of the road are among those withheld. Negroes in Cottonville are very cautious drivers, and they have need to be, since white drivers customarily ignore the amenities toward a car driven by a colored person.

A white Northerner driving through the town with Negro passengers in the rumble seat of her car was startled to find other machines passing her without sounding their horns. It is simply assumed that the Negro will proceed with caution, keep to the side of the road, and not count on the right of way. The assumption is sound, since if there is an accident the Negro as a rule shoulders the penalty.

> A white lawyer driving at about fifty miles an hour came to a cross road. He saw another car coming but did not stop, figuring that the other would do so. He figured wrong, and there was a collision in which he was slightly bruised and his car was battered. A white bystander urged him to "just kill the nigger," since he couldn't collect any money for damages. "That's the only thing to do—just kill him." The lawyer said he would not kill him, but would take the case to court. When it came up, the Negro pleaded guilty and was fined $25, which he had to work out at the county work house, as he did not have the money. The white woman who told the story said it was good he pleaded guilty or "he'd have got worse." It might be unjust, she admitted, but "you have to treat the niggers that way; otherwise nobody knows what would happen." The lawyer received insurance for his car and nothing but satisfaction from the Negro's sentence.
>
> Exceptions happen to this rule also. One occurred when the mayor of the town happened to witness an accident in which the white man was unmistakably at fault. The white driver, not knowing this, had the Negro arraigned and brought before the mayor, who promptly dismissed the case. The Negroes' comment was that the mayor "is mighty fair for a southern man."

It is of course assumed that Negroes always wait until white people are served. In the case of an appointment, the Negro waits until all Whites have been taken care of, even if they come in after him. If someone comes in during an interview, he is expected to step aside and wait. He may also expect to be kept waiting even if nobody else is there. There are always and everywhere people ready to employ this popular device for putting others in their places and feeling that one is in his own place. Certain local Whites derive obvious satisfaction from being able to keep Negroes waiting as long as possible, and for no reason—especially the educated, prosperous, or "uppity" Negroes.

In the white stores, where Negroes do the bulk of their buying, they have to wait until the white clientele has been served. A Negro who has money for purchases is permitted to enter almost any store and buy, although certain ones cater to the colored trade and others do not. Even in the latter, however, the more distinguished individuals among the Negroes may expect to receive courteous treatment. The depression has wrought a definite change in the policy of most white shops toward the other race. Under stress of hard times, the shopkeepers made an effort to attract Negro trade as they had never done before. Negro customers were no longer kept waiting indefinitely for attention. In many cases they were permitted to try on garments rather than, as before, being required to buy shoes, gloves, hats, without first finding out whether they were the right size or shape. Once such concessions have been granted, they cannot easily be withdrawn.

The granting of the privilege of trying on garments before they are bought has an economic value for the Whites not directly involved in such a usage as, for example, the front-door prohibition. Economic implications are strong in several others among the mechanisms expressing white attitudes toward the Negro—notably the Jim Crow arrangements, which are also more official in their manner of enforcement. In the subtle gradation from social through economic to legal aspects, one comes finally to issues which seem of a different order, although they rest upon the same basis. The attitudes that prompt minor social taboos, prohibitions, injunctions, also underlie the disenfranchisement of the Negro, his exclusion from jury service, and his liability to lynching. These have been investigated throughout the deep South, and the reports and discussions published cover Mississippi. They will be touched upon here only in connection with the attitudes that surround them.

The device for withholding the franchise from Negroes in the community is very simple. In order to qualify as a voter, one must have paid one's taxes, including the two-dollar poll tax, and must be able to read and interpret a paragraph of the Constitution. This test is admittedly designed to prevent Negroes from voting; no white person in charge of it would admit that a Negro's interpretation was correct. Knowing this, the Negroes make no attempt to qualify. The Whites justify the prohibition on the ground that, since the Negroes are in the majority, the franchise would give them political control, which would spell disaster: a Negro might even be elected to office. It is assumed that the Negroes would all vote Republican, because that party freed the slaves. The Whites feel that any measure is justifiable that would prevent control by the Negroes or the Republicans, and that either eventuality might lead to the other. One reason for fearing the entrance of the Republican Party is the suspicion that it would give the Negro the vote in order to strengthen its following. The danger is not imminent, since the community is so strongly Democratic that no Republican primaries are held there.[1]

That no Negro should serve on a jury is as universally taken for granted by the Whites as that no Negro should vote. The two prohibitions are closely linked, and the fact that Negroes pay so small a percentage of the taxes is offered as partial justification for both.

Denial of legal rights guaranteed by the Constitution is more severe and more tangible in its effects than denial of social amenities. Most severe of all are the denials involved in lynching. Nevertheless, it too is a mode of behavior customary in certain situations, and is a direct product of the creed and attitudes which have been described. It differs from the other mechanisms in its spectacular nature, in the fact that it is a sporadic mani-

---

[1] The author's impression is that, if they had had the chance, most Negroes during the period of this survey would have voted the Democratic ticket because of their faith in the New Deal.

festation, and in the more limited and covert social sanction which supports it.

Very few white men except the Poor Whites would declare in favor of lynchings. Very few white men would actively try to halt one. There is a report from another community that a member of the aristocracy did once come out definitely against a lynching and succeeded in stopping it. A middle-class storekeeper, under rather special circumstances, did much the same thing in a case given earlier. The rarity of such an act is due chiefly to the danger of opposing a mob. In addition, many a White who deplores lynching yet feels it may serve a beneficent purpose. There are good and kind Christians who will explain that lynchings are terrible, but must happen once in a while in order to keep the Negro in his place.

It is generally assumed that lynching as a rule occurs because of an alleged sexual crime. This is not strictly true, but it is usually associated with the cry of rape. The alarm is calculated to set off a maximum of excitement. It awakens latent fears in connection with the Negro man and the white woman, against a background of guilt and fear related to the white man and the Negro woman. It brings out into the open the forbidden subject of sex. And in addition, it affords the Poor Whites their one opportunity to avenge themselves for the degradation and misery of their own position. A lynching is the one occasion when they can vent all their stored-up resentment without fear of the other Whites, but rather with their tacit consent.

Under proper stimulation, the consent becomes more than tacit. The following reports and editorials in a local paper concern an incident which took place in a near-by community during the course of this study.

> Crimes like the one that shocked this county last week call for the most severe and swift penalty that can be invoked. Our officers are doing their utmost to capture the guilty fiends, and when caught "may the Lord have mercy on their souls." The swiftest penalty that will be given them will be entirely too slow for the temper of the people at present.

> One of the most horrible crimes ever attempted in the county occurred about two miles west of M. Tuesday evening, when two negroes attempted to kill a young man . . . and after cutting his throat, stabbing him several times in the chest, and throwing him in the rear of the car, drove off toward a secluded place with the young lady. . . .
>
> After going some distance the young lady, with rare presence of mind, when they came near a house, told one of them to open the car door as she wanted to spit. When he opened the door she jerked the key out of the car and threw it away, and jumped out screaming. People who lived in the house came running and the negroes fled. When assistance came the wounded young man was taken . . . to the hospital . . . where his wounds were pronounced fatal, as his jugular vein was almost severed, besides the chest wounds.

The alarm was quickly sounded and posses rapidly assembled organized for the man hunt. . . . [The sheriff] was quickly on the scene with his deputies and hunted all Tuesday night but failed to capture them. The sheriff found out where they lived and arrested a brother of one of the fiends, who told all he knew of them. That they had come to his house with bloody clothes and changed the clothes and told him they had gotten into some trouble and had to run for it. They left and up to this time they have not been captured, although Sheriff L. is still on the trail. The bloody clothes were secured by the sheriff. It is a miracle that the young lady was unharmed and had the presence of mind to distract their attention while she threw the car key away.

We hope they will be speedily caught near the scene of their crime. We do not think the county jail has any room at present for such criminals, but we feel certain that the splendid citizens of C. and vicinity will properly place them should they get hold of them.

These newspaper accounts and comments were hardly calculated to act as a deterrent to the mob, made up mainly of Poor Whites. On the day after the attack, a group of these shabby men, their eyes burning, tramped up and down the road and through the woods, mingling their oaths with the barking of their dogs. The middle-class white men sitting in their offices or homes remarked that of course they did not approve of lynching, but that undoubtedly these Negroes would be lynched, and "what can you do when you have to deal with the primitive African type, the killer?" The Negroes in the neighborhood sat at home all day, afraid to go out. Those in a town thirty miles distant said that things must be getting better because a few years ago, if the mob had not found the men they wanted by this time, they would have lynched someone else.

The town in which the murder had been committed was quiet. The Negroes had escaped into another state. Nobody knew where they were. At last the mob broke up; the dogs were quiet. A few of the middle-class Whites murmured that perhaps the Negroes were after the man and not the girl; that maybe there was some real ground for their grudge against him. These were a few almost inaudible whispers. Most of the people said nothing. The eyes of the shabby men no longer gleamed with excitement. They had gone back to the dull routine of the sharecropper. The middle class sat back and reaffirmed that they did not believe in lynching.

Not all of them say so, however. A few openly condone it. Interestingly enough, of the group who answered the questionnaire, more young people than old said that lynching for rape is justifiable, and slightly more women than men. If any weight can be attached to this type of sampling, it must be assumed that, despite the more liberal and less emotional attitude of the younger generation in general, a "nigger-hunt" appeals to them more than to their parents. The vigor of youth may have something to do with this, and the type of imagery that would be evoked by the suggestion of a Negro raping a white woman. Perhaps also there is less interference by social and religious inhibitions. It is hardly to be supposed that when these Junior College students are middle-aged they will be more in favor of lynching than their parents are today. The differential between men and women could not be accepted as reliable in itself, but corresponds to the difference in attitudes generally expressed, and is not at odds with impressionistic evidence. It is to be remembered of course that none of the Whites who answered the questionnaire was of the class that takes an active part in this practice.

Of the social mechanisms described, lynching is the one that has the least consistent, the least whole-hearted, and certainly the least open sanction from the white group. It is also the one that has roused the most active protest from the North. If a Federal law is passed prohibiting it, change will be enforced from the outside. In any case, the pressure of outside opinion is a potent factor in its gradual decline. Furthermore, the attention drawn to the South by lynching tends to overflow onto mechanisms of racial discrimination that might otherwise be less noticed from the outside.

From the sketch of white attitudes and the social mechanisms that express them, it can readily be seen that the Negro carries a large load of the white man's prejudices and fears. All peoples in all cultures have both prejudice and fear; the forms they take are determined by the historical accidents that have shaped the culture and the way the culture impinges upon the individuals who participate in it. In a community such as this, where there are socially sanctioned channels for group fear and prejudice and a socially determined object for them, their effects become somewhat specialized. We shall be concerned chiefly with the effects on the Negroes, although it may be assumed that they are equally profound for the Whites, and would well repay investigation.

The Mexican Worker and the Great Depression

MARK REISLER

Americans of Mexican ancestry occupy a special place in our ethnic history. Unlike blacks and American Indians, the first Mexicans were neither brought here in chains nor conquered in battle; they became Americans by treaty. After the Mexican War (1846–48), the Treaty of Guadalupe Hidalgo transferred thousands of Mexicans and Indians from Mexican sovereignty to United States jurisdiction. The terms of the treaty provided for protection of their rights and claims, but, as is so often the case in matters of this sort, they found themselves deprived of promised land and resources by the Anglo population.

As the southwestern territories of the United States began to organize themselves for statehood, people of Mexican ancestry stood at a distinct disadvantage. They had three characteristics that automatically made them subject to discriminatory action by the dominant society: many were of mixed "racial" ancestry (Spanish and Indian), they were not white, and in religion they were overwhelmingly Roman Catholic. These features of the population delayed the acceptance of New Mexico as a state for fifty years.

As the settlement of the Southwest by people from the eastern states increased, so did the need for unskilled labor, both in agriculture and in construction. The primary source of that labor which was not supplied domestically was the northern states of Mexico. Immigrants poured across the border from Mexico to fill the demand for labor. They worked in the expanding agricultural lands in Texas and California, toiled in the mines of the West, provided the majority of laborers in railroad construction around the turn of the century, migrated farther northward into the sugar-beet fields of Colorado and Idaho, and supplied industrial workers in the expanding factory cities of the upper Midwest. Their traditional life-style and apparent acceptance of oppressive labor conditions made the Mexican immigrants seem like an ideal source of labor for the rapidly growing economy of the West in the early twentieth century.

After the upheavals of revolution in Mexico in the early part of this century, migration to the United States increased significantly, and more of the newcomers sought permanent residence here. Most of the work they found was temporary and low paying. Many joined the stream of migratory farm workers, a situation that left them deprived of any opportunity to become economically stable or politically influential. At the same time, many others found themselves among the ranks of the urban poor, segregated on the edges of the cities of the Southwest and West Coast, where they met with widespread social, economic, and political discrimination, particularly in Texas and Southern California.

246

As is the case with other minority groups today, the Mexican-Americans have formed protest organizations and political movements. In some areas with high concentrations of Mexicans, political control has been wrested from the "Anglos." The successes of Cesar Chavez and the United Farm Workers union movement among agricultural workers In California have inspired migrant workers throughout the United States to attempt to organize in order to combat some of the worst aspects of agricultural labor.

In a study of Mexican workers in the United States, Mark Reisler, of Virginia Commonwealth University, has impressively documented a story of backbreaking labor under discriminatory conditions. As one might expect, the Great Depression of the 1930s fell hardest on those most marginal to the economy. In the selection from Reisler's study reprinted here, the peculiar nature of the impact of the depression on Mexican-American workers is spelled out. Among other things they had to deal with was a moderately successful attempt to deport thousands of them (American citizens and noncitizens alike) to Mexico. But they continued to enter the United States, and today large numbers of Mexicans are crossing the border daily (both legally and illegally), in an attempt to establish for themselves a minimal standard of living.

A few days after the 1928 presidential election, *Mexico*, the Mexican community newspaper in Chicago, noted expectantly that "Herbert Hoover's accession to the Presidency according to the press, will herald a period of prosperity." It hoped that with Hoover in the White House the chronic unemployment problem of Mexican workers might be alleviated. "In this city," the paper declared,

> there is a multitude of men whose sole occupation is to walk the streets from day to day waiting for the uncertain time when someone might give them a nickel with which to buy a cup of coffee.
>
> If Hoover has the power to eliminate this suffering, his accession to the Presidency will be a blessing for our countrymen who have come here to barter their labor for an honest living.[1]

The Hoover years, however, proved to be far from a blessing for Mexican workers. The ill-fated president, who as food administrator

[1] *Mexico*, November 13, 1928, reel 62, Chicago Foreign Language Press Survey (CFLPS), Chicago Public Library.

"The Mexican Worker and the Great Depression." From *By the Sweat of Their Brow* by Mark Reisler (Westport, Conn.: Greenwood Press, 1976), pp. 227–57. Used with the permission of the publisher.

during World War I had eagerly recruited farm laborers from Mexico, presided over a nation confronted with economic collapse. Millions of Americans got some taste of the suffering that Mexican immigrants had always experienced. But if times were hard for Americans, they were even worse for Mexican workers.

Regardless of whether they labored in the fruit, vegetable, and cotton fields of the Southwest, on the beet farms of Colorado and Michigan, or in the factories of Chicago, the depression was disastrous for Mexican workers. In all areas of the nation, they faced acute problems of unemployment as financially strapped Americans began to compete with them for unskilled jobs. Surplus labor became so abundant in the early 1930s that growers, who had initially grumbled about possible crop losses resulting from the State Department's administrative restriction of Mexican immigration, soon ceased their complaints.[2] Local and, later, out-of-state labor flooded the southwestern farm labor market. At the same time crop production declined sharply. In the Imperial Valley, for example, carlot shipments of cantaloupes fell from 14,378 in 1929 to 6055 in 1935, and lettuce shipments fell from 12,608 to 6356 during the same period. In January 1933 California experienced a peak period of agricultural labor oversupply when there were an estimated 2.36 workers available for each farm job.[3]

In the Midwest many Mexican industrial and railroad workers lost their jobs. A lucky few were able to work two or three days a week on the tracks. Fending off starvation became a major problem.[4] To make matters worse, many states and municipalities during the early years of the depression passed legislation requiring that all laborers on public works projects be U.S. citizens. By 1931 California, Arizona, and Illinois had enacted such statutes. In Texas a law mandated that U.S. citizens receive preferential treatment for highway construction jobs. Although these measures applied to all aliens, in the Southwest they were designed to bar Mexicans from the unskilled construction jobs that they had held for well over a decade. As a result of this discriminatory legislation, contractors often refused to hire Mexicans for private construction jobs as well as public projects. In California social pressure and threats of vio-

[2] U.S., Congress, House, Committee on Immigration, *Hearings on Western Hemisphere Immigration*, 70th Cong., 1st sess., 1928, p. 36; American Consulate, Nuevo Laredo, to Secretary of State, April 30, 1929, State Department File 811.111 Mexico/214, Washington National Records Center (WNRC), Suitland, Maryland; Paul S. Taylor, *An American-Mexican Frontier* (Chapel Hill: University of North Carolina Press, 1934), p. 292.

[3] Paul S. Taylor and Edward J. Rowell, "Patterns of Agricultural Labor Management Within California," *Monthly Labor Review* 47 (November 1938): 988; "In Sunny California," *Nation* 138 (April 25, 1934): 460; Subcommittee of the Senate Committee on Education and Labor, *Hearings on Violations of Free Speech and Rights of Labor*, 76th Cong., 3d sess., 1940, pt. 47: 17305 (hereafter referred to as La Follette Committee Hearings).

[4] Norman D. Humphrey, "Employment Patterns of Mexicans in Detroit," *Monthly Labor Review* 61 (November 1945): 918–919; *El Nacional*, December 17, 1930, May 7, 14, 1932, and *La Defensa*, February 29, 1936, reel 62, CFLPS.

lence were reportedly used against employers who hired Mexicans rather than unemployed Americans.[5]

While no precise measurements of the financial resources of Mexicans in the United States during the depression were made, the local studies that do exist indicate that in all parts of the country the income of Mexican workers plummeted to abysmally low levels. A study of 775 migratory families in California in 1935, for example, revealed an average family annual income of $289. In that year, the California State Relief Administration estimated that a family of 4.5 persons required at least $780 a year to maintain even a "minimum subsistence" budget, which covered food, utilities, and rent but no incidentals. The actual average family income in the United States at the time was $1784 a year.[6] In Texas during the late 1930s, investigators learned that Mexican farm worker families earned incomes of between $278 and $500. Because children joined in the field work, larger families generally enjoyed higher incomes.[7] Other studies found that Mexican families laboring in the beet fields of Colorado and the Midwest averaged between $340 and $436 annually.[8] Most midwestern beet workers wintered in Texas and were transported north each spring by truck for a fee of $9.00 to $15.00 per capita. Contractors or independent truckers often crammed more than forty people onto unsafe, unlicensed vehicles, which were so overloaded that there was often no room to sit down. To avoid detection by the police, the trucks made the 1600-mile, five-day trip along back roads, stopping only for gas. Truckers refused to stop to allow workers to cook meals or use lavatory facilities.[9]

[5] Harold Fields, "Where Shall the Alien Work?" *Social Forces* 12 (December 1933): 213–214, 217; Robert N. McLean, "Good-bye, Vicente!" *Survey* 66 (May 1, 1931): 195; Robert N. McLean, "A Dike Against Mexicans," *New Republic* 59 (August 14, 1929): 335.

[6] California, State Relief Administration, *Migratory Labor in California*, (San Francisco, 1936), pp. 109, 123; U.S., Bureau of Labor Statistics, *Monthly Labor Review* 49 (July 1939): 69; U.S., Bureau of the Census, *Historical Statistics of the United States* (Washington, D.C., 1960), p. 166. The Heller Committee for Research in Social Economics at the University of California set a $972 "health and decency" budget for an average family.

[7] Selden Menefee, *Mexican Migratory Workers in South Texas*, (Washington, D.C.: Work Projects Administration, 1941), pp. xiv, 29–39; Amber A. Washburton et al., *The Work and Welfare of Children of Agricultural Laborers in Hidalgo County, Texas*, U.S. Children's Bureau, Publication 298 (1943), pp. 4–5, 15.

[8] Elizabeth S. Johnson, *Welfare of Families of Sugar-Beet Laborers*, U.S. Children's Bureau, Publication 247 (1939), pp. 3–5, 70–71; Carey McWilliams, *Ill Fares the Land* (Boston: Little, Brown, 1942), p. 118; Menefee, *Mexican Migratory Workers in South Texas*, pp. xiv, 22–24. In 1924 beet worker families in Colorado averaged $782. The nationwide average beet wage fell from $23 per acre in 1923 to $14 per acre in 1933. Between 1930 and 1933 beet wages fell about 40 percent, while prices to farmers fell 28 percent to 30 percent. Harry Schwartz, *Seasonal Farm Labor in the United States* (New York: Columbia University Press, 1945), p. 127.

[9] U. S., Senate, House, Select Committee to Investigate the Interstate Migration of Destitute Citizens, *Hearings on Interstate Migration*, 76th Cong., 1st sess., 1941, pt. 5: 1847–1849.

As bad as the trip to northern farms might have been, Mexican beet workers were better off than many of their brethren who remained in San Antonio. A study by Selden Menefee revealed that of all Mexican workers in the United States, those whose only income came from the shelling of pecans were the poorest. In the mid-1930s between 10,000 and 20,000 Mexicans in San Antonio received $.05 to $.06 for each pound of shelled pecans. The average worker could shell eight or nine pounds of cracked nuts per day. At that rate, whole families earned but $192 annually. Including pay from odd jobs and relief aid, Menefee found that the average family of Mexican pecan shellers had to eke out an existence on a total income of $251 per year, or about $.69 a day. Desperate Mexican workers accepted wages that were so low that it became profitable for pecan shelling companies to cut back on mechanization and to rely completely on hand labor. Passage of the New Deal's National Industrial Recovery Act in 1933 did nothing to improve the lot of workers. Companies in San Antonio refused to abide by an NRA code for the pecan shelling industry that fixed a $6.00 weekly minimum wage. The largest operator in San Antonio, Julius Seligmann, who founded the Southern Pecan Shelling Company in 1926 on a $50,000 investment and was grossing over $3 million by the mid-1930s, called the code "unreasonable, capricious, arbitrary, and confiscatory." But adherence to the NRA was voluntary, and the pecan shelling code became a dead letter. In late 1937 Mexican workers began to organize to protect their meager earnings under the auspices of the United Cannery, Agricultural, Packing and Allied Workers of America, a CIO affiliate. Early the following year, in response to a further wage cut, a spontaneous strike occurred. The union claimed that half of the 12,000 Mexicans employed as shellers that year joined the walkout. Local officials arrested 1000 pickets for unlawful assembly, disturbing the peace, and "blocking the sidewalk," and they fired bursts of tear gas on numerous occasions. Said Police Chief Owen Kilday: "I did not interfere with the strike. I interfered with a revolution." An arbitration board appointed by the governor of Texas finally settled the strike by setting the shelling wage at from $.055 to $.065 per pound. The settlement quickly became outdated, however, with the implementation of the Fair Labor Standards Act in October 1938. Rather than meet the $.25 per hour minimum wage mandated by the act, shelling companies in San Antonio laid off workers, shut their doors, and began installing machinery. The companies soon reopened but with new equipment, and they now employed fewer than 3000 laborers. With no alternative jobs available, the balance of the Mexican pecan shellers were faced with starvation. Scores of workers trudged several miles daily to the Salvation Army's breadline to obtain a loaf or two for their families.[10]

[10] Selden Menefee and Orin Cassmore, *The Pecan Shellers of San Antonio* (Washington, D.C.: Work Projects Administration, 1940), pp. 3–38; U.S., Bureau of Labor Statistics, "Working Conditions of Pecan Shellers," *Monthly Labor Review* 48 (March 1939): 549–550. By 1941 the shelling industry in San Antonio employed only 600 workers. Harold A. Shapiro, "The Pecan Shellers of San Antonio," *Southwestern Social Science Quarterly* 32 (March 1952): 242.

Incomes insufficient for subsistence and long periods of unemployment compelled many Mexican workers in both the Southwest and the Midwest to turn to municipal relief.[11] Dismayed local welfare officials, faced with skyrocketing relief rolls during the early years of the depression, hoped to alleviate their burden by deporting Mexican immigrants. They pressured the federal government to remove all indigent Mexicans from the country. Local officials, particularly those in Los Angeles, the most aggressive city to demand federal action, expected that several well-publicized deportations would provoke a mass exodus of Mexicans receiving relief.[12] The Hoover administration obliged by initiating a campaign to rid the nation of illegal aliens. Secretary of Labor William Doak dispatched a special supervisor to Los Angeles to direct a deportation campaign aimed at Mexicans.[13] Legal deportation, however, required a formal federal hearing and evidence of unlawful entry. The Immigration Bureau, explained Commissioner-General Harry Hull, was unable to carry out "wholesale deportations" of Mexicans on relief because they had "fallen into distress through inability to obtain employment" arising from depression conditions. The law mandated expulsion of only those individuals who had become public charges within five years of their arrival from causes "not affirmatively shown to have arisen subsequent to entry." [14] Thus the Immigration Bureau deported only a limited number of Mexicans through formal channels. But because local officials and the press played up the government's deportation efforts, the Los Angeles

[11] Johnson, *Welfare of Families of Sugar-Beet Laborers*, pp. 4–5, 80; Menefee and Cassmore, *Pecan Shellers of San Antonio*, p. xviii; McWilliams, *Ill Fares the Land*, p. 117; Faith Williams and Alice Hanson, *Money Disbursements of Wage Earners and Clerical Workers in Five Cities in the Pacific Region*, U.S. Bureau of Labor Statistics, Bulletin 639 (1939), p. 87; Faith Williams et al., *Money Disbursements of Wage Earners and Clerical Workers in Twelve Cities of the South*, U.S. Bureau of Labor Statistics, Bulletin 640 (1941), p. 121; Humphrey, "Employment Patterns," 919; Laurence Waters, "Transient Mexican Agricultural Laborer," *Southwestern Social Science Quarterly* 22 (June 1941): 61.

[12] Charles P. Visel, Coordinator of Los Angeles Citizens Committee on Unemployment Relief, to Secretary of Labor William M. Doak, March 19, 1931, Immigration Bureau File 55739/674, Record Group (RG) 85, National Archives (NA); Paul E. Kelly, East Chicago American Legion, to Secretary of Labor, March 4, 1932, U.S. Conciliation Service File 165-223B, RG 280, NA; Abraham Hoffman, "The Repatriation of Mexican Nationals from the United States During the Great Depression" (Ph.D. diss., University of California, Los Angeles, 1970), pp. 66–67. This dissertation has been published as *Unwanted Mexican Americans in the Great Depression*, Tucson: University of Arizona Press, 1974).

[13] W. F. Watkins to Robe Carl White, February 8, 1931, and Visel to Doak, March 19, 1931, Immigration Bureau File 55739/674, and William A. Whalen, District Director of Immigration, San Antonio, to Commissioner-General of Immigration, August 30, 1933, Immigration Bureau File 55739/674A, RG 85, NA; Hoffman, "Repatriation of Mexican Nationals," pp. 59–62, 78–86; Paul Taylor, "Mexicans North of the Rio Grande," *Survey* 66 (May 1, 1931): 205.

[14] Harry E. Hull to J. C. Brodie, March 23, 1933, Immigration Bureau File 55739/674, RG 85, NA.

district director of immigration noted that thousands of Mexicans "have been literally scared out of southern California." [15]

The federal government also did its best to cut off further Mexican immigration completely. As the economic outlook darkened, the State Department exercised its policy of administrative restriction with increasing severity and virtually squeezed the southern border shut. So effective was the policy of refusing visas to Mexican workers on the ground that they would become public charges that on September 9, 1930, the administration began to apply it to immigrants from throughout the world. In announcing his success in reducing overall immigration, President Hoover took special pains to point out how few aliens from Mexico had been admitted recently. Franklin Roosevelt continued Hoover's policy of administrative restriction after he assumed the presidency. So effective was the policy that the Immigration Bureau ceased calling for a Mexican quota. In 1933 Commissioner-General of Immigration D. W. MacCormick stated that "under present conditions" quota legislation would be "superfluous." [16]

Deportation scare tactics and the curtailment of fresh immigration from Mexico, however, did not alleviate the welfare problems of local authorities. They therefore devised a more expedient solution: the repatriation of Mexicans on relief rolls. In singing the praises of Mexican workers, growers had always stressed that perhaps the foremost advantage of Mexicans, compared to other groups, was their deportability. In times of economic decline, argued growers, the laborers could be returned to Mexico. With the advent of the depression, these predictions came true. In an attempt to reduce their welfare burden, localities began to pressure Mexicans into leaving the country. Without jobs, savings, or permanent housing, and sometimes fearing the racist hostility of unemployed whites, many Mexican workers fell victim to repatriation. Welfare authorities would grant Mexicans temporary relief on the promise that they would return willingly to Mexico at public expense. Relief agencies and private charities in such cities as East Chicago, Gary, Detroit, and St. Paul paid the railroad fares of several thousand back to Mexico. In the Chicago area, the steel companies that had stimulated Mexican migration to the Midwest in the 1920s now actively encouraged repatriation.[17] Los Angeles

[15] Walter E. Carr to Commissioner-General of Immigration, June 17, 1931, Immigration Bureau File 55739/674, RG 85, NA.
[16] Herbert Hoover, *The Memoirs of Herbert Hoover, the Great Depression* (New York: Macmillan, 1952), pp. 47–48; Ray L. Wilbur and Arthur M. Hyde, *The Hoover Policies* (New York: Charles Scribner's Sons, 1937), pp. 144–45; U.S., State Dept., *Press Releases*, September 8, 1930, pp. 176–177; Robert A. Divine, *American Immigration Policy, 1924–1952* (New Haven: Yale University Press, 1957), p. 89; U.S., Department of Labor, *Annual Report of the Secretary of Labor* (1933), pp. 46–47.
[17] Robert N. McLean, "The Mexican Return," *Nation* 135 (August 24, 1932): 165–166; Emory S. Bogardus, "Mexican Repatriates," *Sociology and Social Research* 18 (November-December 1933): 169–176; Julian Samora and Richard Lamanna, *Mexican-Americans in a Midwest Metropolis* (Los Angeles: University of California Graduate School of Business Administration, 1967), pp. 5–6; Norman D. Hum-

County carried out the most organized and largest of all the local repatriation programs. Beginning in 1931, trainloads of Mexicans, at the
rate of one a month through 1933, containing both aliens and citizens,
were transported south of the border. The cost of one shipment of about
6000 repatriates was $77,000; the yearly relief cost for these people would
have amounted to $425,000. Between 1931 and 1934 Los Angeles County
repatriated more than 13,000 Mexicans.[18]

Some workers and their families left the United States of their own
free will. Others were aided by Mexican consuls who encouraged the
idea of repatriation, but in many instances, particularly after 1931, coercion was applied.[19] As a result of these repatriation campaigns, the fear of
expulsion became firmly rooted in Mexican communities in the Southwest
for years to come. Anxiety about receiving relief attained such heights,
reported Agnes Hanna of the U.S. Children's Bureau, that many Mexicans
"are now afraid to accept hospital care; mothers attending the prenatal
clinics refuse to go to the hospital for confinement. . . ."[20] Precisely how
many Mexicans returned to Mexico during the depression and what percentage were pressured into departing is unknown. The federal government, which sanctioned the concept of "voluntary deportation" by local
agencies, kept no statistics on repatriations. Estimates range as high as
400,000. Southwestern officials were confident that if the need arose again,
the Mexican worker could easily be attracted back. Indeed, many repatriates attempted to return to the United States during the 1930s. Finding
that the Mexican government, despite its promises to set up agrarian
colonies for repatriates, did little to aid returnees financially and that their
American-born children often had problems adjusting to life in Mexico,
a good number of Mexican workers applied for visas to regain admittance.
Others tried to reenter the United States illegally. But as a result of the
State Department's rigorous visa policy and the border patrol's "utmost
vigilance," most repatriates were unable to return during the 1930s.[21]

phrey, "Migration and Settlement of Detroit Mexicans," *Economic Geography* 19
(October 1943):360–361; Minnesota, Governor's Interracial Commission, *The
Mexican in Minnesota* (August 15, 1948), pp. 9–10, 41; Neil Betten and Raymond
Mohl, "From Discrimination to Repatriation: Mexican Life in Gary, Indiana,
During the Great Depression," *Pacific Historical Review* 42 (August 1973): 379–
380.
[18] Carey McWilliams, "Getting Rid of the Mexican," *American Mercury* 28 (March
1933): 322–324; Hoffman, "Repatriation of Mexican Nationals," pp. 129–130, 170.
[19] *El Nacional*, May 14, 28, 1932, reel 63, CFLPS; John L. Zurbrick, Detroit District
Director of Immigration, to Commissioner-General of Immigration, October 20,
1932, Immigration Bureau File 55784/585, and W. A. Whalen, San Antonio District
Director of Immigration, to Commissioner-General of Immigration, August 30, 1933,
Immigration Bureau File 55739/674A, RG 85, NA; Hoffman, "Repatriation of
Mexican Nationals," pp. 130–148; Norman D. Humphrey, "Mexican Repatriation
from Michigan—Public Assistance in Historical Perspective," *Social Service Re-
view* 15 (September 1941): 505–509.
[20] Agnes K. Hanna, "Social Services on the Mexican Border," *National Conference of
Social Work Proceedings* (1935): 700–701.
[21] U.S., Department of Labor, *Annual Report of the Commissioner-General of
Immigration* (1931), p. 25; ibid. (1932), p. 18; ibid. (1933), p. 44; ibid. (1936), p. 97;

Although a large number of Mexicans returned to their homeland during the depression, the great majority remained in the United States. These workers, when they were lucky enough to find jobs, confronted ever-sinking wage levels. A careful examination of the situation in California agriculture provides a good indication of the conditions under which Mexicans labored during the 1930s. Focusing on California also allows an investigation of the Mexican worker's most intense and extensive effort to protect himself by means of unionization.

In 1928, a peak year for California agriculture, Mexican migrants averaged $.35 an hour. By 1933 wages had tumbled to $.14 an hour.[22] In the wake of falling crop prices and diminishing urban markets, California farmers suffered severe financial distress. Faced with such fixed obligations as land taxes, interest rates, and power and irrigation charges, growers sought to cut the one cost over which they had control—labor.[23] Since California growers were highly organized they could easily fix low wage rates prior to each picking season through regional associations like the San Joaquin Labor Bureau. In this way, California "factory agriculture" sought to exert its total control over labor.[24]

Against the combined power of large-scale California growers, the individual Mexican farm laborer stood helpless. Only through collective action could he hope to protect himself. Given the unskilled and seasonal nature of migratory labor, however, such collective action was almost impossible. Growers thought too that the Mexican's racial traits constituted an insurmountable obstacle to his organization. Employers were well satisfied with the isolation and seeming docility of the Mexican worker. The foreman of a cantaloupe farm expressed the prevailing predepression view:

> Mexicans are very satisfactory. They offer no disciplinary problem, but require constant supervision and driving. Mexican laborers do not possess initiative, but that's no criticism of them from our point

---

McWilliams, "Getting Rid of the Mexican," 323–324. The 400,000 estimate was made by Abraham Hoffman, author of the only important scholarly study of repatriation during the depression. It is based on Mexican government figures. Hoffman, "Repatriation of Mexican Nationals," pp. vii, 219–221. Only 27,000 legal Mexican immigrants entered the United States during the 1930s. Leo Grebler, *Mexican Immigration to the United States: The Record and Its Implications* (Los Angeles: University of California Graduate School of Business Administration, 1965), p. 28.

[22] California, State Relief Administration, *Migratory Labor in California* (San Francisco, 1936), p. 31.

[23] Paul Taylor and Clark Kerr, "Uprisings on the Farm," *Survey Graphic* 24 (January 1935): 21–22; U.S., Congress, House, Committee on Labor, *Labor Disputes Act*, 74th Cong., 1st sess., 1935, p. 349.

[24] *La Follette Committee Hearings*, pt. 47: 17217-17218, 17228; ibid., pt. 51 18593-18595, 18837; ibid., pt. 53: 19481. Carey McWilliams deals with the similarities between California agriculture and mass production industry in *Factories in the Field* (Boston: Little, Brown, 1939), pp. 265–266.

of view. They do with good grace what we tell them to do, and we
don't have to be too particular about the way we tell them.[25]

In an effort to defend themselves against arbitrary wage rates and
working conditions, Mexican workers did, however, take the initiative.
They attempted to form unions and thereby smashed the docility myth.
Even before experiencing the increased financial hardships of the depression, Mexican laborers had taken the first steps on the path toward organization. In late 1927 representatives from several Mexican *mutualistas* in
Los Angeles met and called upon their societies to establish a Mexican
trade union. They issued a resolution charging that Mexicans in the
United States lived in a "deplorable condition of abandonment and isolation . . . deprived of food, cooperation and mutual self-help." [26] Seeking
to remedy these conditions, Mexican workers soon formed local organizations throughout southern California. On March 23, 1928, delegates
officially organized the Confederation of Mexican Labor Unions (Confederación de Uniones de Obreras Mexicanas [CUOM]) and adopted a
constitution. The constitution, modeled after that of the Regional Confederation of Labor of Mexico (CROM), employed radical rhetoric, but
the objectives of the union, clearly reflecting its mutual-aid society roots,
centered upon gradual economic and social gains. The central committee
of the confederation took special pains to disavow any radical intent and
issued a manifesto stating its goals "so that it will not be supposed that
the movement in question is harmful. . . ." The committee recognized
"that the laboring Mexican has not come to this country to legislate, and
considers absurd [the] propagation of dissolvent doctrines which only
lead to the ruin of the worker [and are] much more a sin if he is a
foreigner." The union sought improved pay, the end of exploitation by
labor contractors, employment agencies, and commissary stores, and
regulation of emigration from Mexico by the Mexican government. It
also promised to conserve "our racial and patriotic principles" by building
schools and libraries, as well as to provide welfare and legal aid for indigent countrymen.[27]

The most active local union in California was the Imperial Valley
Workers' Union (La Unión de Trabajadores del Valle Imperial). Carlos
Ariza, former Mexican consul at Calexico, suggested its formation. He
hoped that it could protect the interests of Mexican nationals who consistently had appealed to his office for help in settling labor claims.

[25] Paul S. Taylor, *Mexican Labor in the United States: The Imperial Valley* (Berkeley: University of California Press, 1929), pp. 40–41.
[26] California, Governor C. C. Young's Mexican Fact-finding Committee, *Mexicans in
California* (San Francisco, 1930), p. 123 (hereafter referred to as *Governor Young
Report*).
[27] Ibid., pp. 123–136; Porter Chaffee, "Organization Efforts of Mexican Agricultural
Workers," Federal Writers Project, Oakland, c. 1938, unpublished manuscript in
Bancroft Library, pp. 5–15. Chaffee estimated that the total membership of the
confederation was 2000 to 3000 in May 1928 but that it fell to about 200 within
a year.

Mutual-aid societies in the nearby towns of El Centro and Brawley quickly acted upon Ariza's suggestion and organized a union in April 1928, which soon claimed more than 2700 members. The following month it issued a set of respectfully worded demands to the cantaloupe growers of the Imperial Valley. The demands included a raise in wages from $.135 a crate for cantaloupe picking to $.15 a crate, free picking sacks and ice for drinking water, lumber for sheds and outhouses, employer responsibility for accident indemnity, and the withholding of wages by growers rather than labor contractors.[28]

The union addressed its grievances to the chambers of commerce in El Centro and Brawley and requested their aid in negotiating with the growers. Dominated by growers, the chambers of commerce believed the union was weak and ignored the request. A strike ensued. According to Louis Bloch, who investigated the strike for the California Department of Industrial Relations, the union leadership did not plan the walkout; it was the result of spontaneous action by the rank and file. Employer reaction was predictable. "The growers became genuinely alarmed," reported Bloch.

> Heretofore they have been accustomed to considering the Mexican workers as bovine and tractable individuals, best adapted to the climatic conditions in the Imperial Valley and therefore the most desirable workers in the valley. The organization of a union of Mexican laborers seems to have evoked in the growers an ardent wish for its earliest demise.[29]

The growers did not sit idly by "wishing" for the union's demise. Rather, they prepared to escort it to the grave. The financial implications of a Mexican farm workers' union were clear, and the growers considered them intolerable. Two years earlier Dr. George Clements, manager of the Agriculture Division of the Los Angeles Chamber of Commerce, had warned:

> The Mexican laborer, if he only realized it, has California agriculture and industry in the hollow of his hand. . . . If he be unionized . . . California agriculture is at an end and with our agriculture will go our industry, commerce and prosperity.[30]

Growers acted quickly to forestall such a calamity. The county sheriff deputized over forty farm foremen and superintendents and began to arrest strikers by the dozens, charging them with vagrancy and dis-

---

[28] Chaffee, "Organization Efforts of Mexican Agricultural Workers," pp. 16–18; Taylor, *Mexican Labor in Imperial Valley*, pp. 45–51; Stuart Jamieson, *Labor Unionism in American Agriculture*, Bureau of Labor Statistics Bulletin 836 (1945), p. 77; *Governor Young Report*, pp. 137–139.

[29] *Governor Young Report*, pp. 138–140; Taylor, *Mexican Labor in Imperial Valley*, pp. 46–48.

[30] *La Follette Hearings*, pt. 53: 19671.

turbing the peace. Local courts set bail at the prohibitive sums of from $250 to $1000. Mexican pool halls, which served as informal places of assembly, and the union office were closed down by the sheriff, and workers were threatened with mass deportations if they participated in the strike movement. Sheriff Charles Gillett's "ardent enthusiasm for law enforcement" overwhelmed the union, and the strike was broken in a matter of days. Bloch's official report on the strike declared: "The sheriff's decisiveness in rounding up and incarcerating the actual and potential disturbers of the peace undoubtedly had the effect of stopping a movement which might have resulted in an effective general strike and in heavy losses to the growers." [31]

The behavior of growers and local law enforcement authorities in the cantaloupe strike set a pattern for future labor confrontations. Company officials, Sheriff Gillett, and the local press all charged that the strike was fomented by outside "Red" agitators from Mexico, and they predicted it would lead to a communist uprising. They presented no evidence whatsoever to corroborate this contention. The union's tactic of using the chamber of commerce as an intermediary, plus its mutual-aid society origins, make such a charge most dubious.[32] The Imperial Valley Workers' Union was, on the contrary, an indigenous and independent movement of Mexican immigrant laborers.

Although the strike was broken, labor achieved limited gains. The growers adamantly refused to recognize the union, but some granted a small wage increase and agreed to abide voluntarily by a "standard picking agreement" proposed by the California Department of Industrial Relations. This agreement ended some of the worst abuses of the contract labor system, including the withholding of wages. The Department of Industrial Relations hoped that these developments foreshadowed a period of labor peace.[33]

The following year, 1929, justified these hopes. The Imperial Valley Workers' Union, which had changed its name to the "more innocuous" Mexican Mutual Aid Society, entered into a temporary period of quiescence.[34] But labor calm was soon shattered by the advent of the depression. Reductions in crop prices led to even greater reductions in agricultural wage rates. Desperate workers' only possible protection against continual wage cuts by growers was collective action. As a result, the

[31] *Governor Young Report*, pp. 143–144; *Phoenix Republican* May 10, 1928, in House Immigration Committee File, 70A-F14.3, RG 233, NA. For a more detailed account of grower reaction to the strike, see Charles Wollenberg, "*Huelga*, 1928 Style: The Imperial Valley Cantaloupe Workers' Strike," *Pacific Historical Review* 38 (February 1969): 51–56.

[32] *Governor Young Report*, p. 146; Taylor, *Mexican Labor in Imperial Valley*, pp. 50–51; Charles T. Connell to H. L. Kerwin, June 2, 1928, U.S. Conciliation Service File 165-223B, RG 280, NA.

[33] *Governor Young Report*, pp. 148–150. According to Lloyd Fisher, the agreement was never widely observed. *The Harvest Labor Market in California*, (Cambridge: Harvard University Press, 1953), p. 38.

[34] Conrad Seiler, "Cantaloupes and Communists," *Nation* 131 (September 3, 1930): 244; Chaffee, "Organization Efforts of Mexican Agricultural Workers," pp. 18–19.

pace of unionization picked up after 1929 and accelerated rapidly after the start of the New Deal. California during the 1930s witnessed more than 140 agricultural strikes, over half of the national total, almost all concerning the issue of wages. Over 90 percent of the strikes took place subsequent to Franklin Roosevelt's inauguration as president, the greatest number occurring during his first year in office.[35]

If Mexican migrant laborers were going to engage in collective action, it was not going to be with the aid of organized labor. In 1935 Paul Scharrenberg, secretary of the California Federation of Labor, expressed in a *New York Times* interview an attitude that had long been held by the AFL toward migrants: "Only fanatics are willing to live in shacks or tents and get their heads broken in the interest of migratory laborers." [36] Such "fanatics" were left-wing organizers who recognized the leadership vacuum in the agricultural labor field and saw the opportunity of forging a consolidated mass union cutting across crop, skill, and ethnic divisions. In a series of proposals on agriculture in 1930, the *Communist* stressed the importance of the migrant laborer as a candidate for organization:

> The agricultural proletariat, so oppressed and inarticulate yet so necessary and important to the proletarian revolution in building a sound alliance between workers and poor farmers, must no longer be neglected by our Party. Every district must show progress . . . in establishing the Communist Party among the agrarian proletariat, and in aiding the revolutionary industrial union of the T.U.U.L.[37]

The proposed agricultural union was to be dedicated to complete racial equality, and special efforts were to be made to attract Mexican workers.[38] The party called for "a persistent drive . . . , the weight of work being placed to organize regular nuclei on highly capitalistic farms. . . ." [39]

A primary target of the agricultural arm of the Trade Union Unity League (TUUL) was California "factory agriculture." The Agricultural Workers' Industrial League (AWIL), as the communist-led farm workers' union was later officially called, first appeared in the Imperial Valley in early 1930 during a strike that had been initiated by the Mexican Mutual Aid Society. AWIL organizers gained control of the strike from the relatively inexperienced and conservative Mexican leaders. Radical organizers expanded the strike demands, which had originally centered upon wages, to include the abolition of the contract labor and piecework

---

[35] Jamieson, *Labor Unionism*, p. 17.

[36] *New York Times*, January 20, 1935. During the 1920s and 1930s neither the AFL nor the California Federation of Labor made any attempt to organize migratory agricultural workers. California, State Relief Administration, *Migratory Labor in California* (San Francisco, 1936), p. 70.

[37] *Communist* (February 1930): 119.

[38] Ibid. (March 1930): 284; Chaffee, "Organization Efforts of Mexican Agricultural Workers," p. 20.

[39] *Communist* (April 1930): 373.

systems and recognition of workers' "job committees." They also extended the strike to other ethnic groups.[40] The *Daily Worker* described the events as "the beginning of a mass rebellion by all the scores of thousands of bitterly exploited Mexican, Filipino, Hindu, Japanese, and Chinese agricultural laborers who slave for the big open-shop fruit growers and packers under conditions bordering closely on peonage." "The agricultural proletariat," the paper proclaimed, "is ripe and over-ripe for organization and struggle." [41] The hoped for "mass rebellion" quickly fizzled out. The strike failed due to repressive tactics by local authorities and the lack of enthusiasm of some Mexican workers for the intruding outsiders who had taken over their strike. Left-wing organizers charged the Mexican Mutual Aid Society with betraying workers and colluding with growers to undermine the AWIL.[42] Nine leaders of the AWIL, two of whom had Spanish surnames, were arrested and convicted under a California criminal-syndicalism statute that was a vestige of the Red Scare era.[43] Deprived of leadership, the AWIL was inactive for the next two years, which saw only small-scale, sporadic, local outbursts in reaction to depression wage reductions.[44]

The next major agricultural labor disturbance occurred in June 1933 at El Monte in the San Gabriel Valley. Mexican berry pickers struck against predominantly Japanese growers, many of whom leased their land in violation of the state's anti-Asian land laws. A local chapter of the Confederation of Mexican Labor Unions called the strike to protest a rapidly sinking wage rate. Pay was as low as $.09 to $.10 an hour; the union demanded an increase to $.25.[45] According to one commentator: "In El Monte . . . a system of virtual peonage prevailed." Housing provided by growers consisted of hovels constructed from chicken coops, boxes,

[40] Frank Spector, *The Story of the Imperial Valley* (New York: International Labor Defense, c. 1930), p. 18; Jamieson, *Labor Unionism*, pp. 81–85.

[41] *Daily Worker*, January 6, 7, 1930.

[42] Chaffee, "Organization Efforts of Mexican Agricultural Workers," p. 21; *Daily Worker*, January 19, 23, 1930; Spector, *Story of the Imperial Valley*, pp. 15–20; interview with H. Harvey, in Porter Chaffee, "A History of the Cannery and Agricultural Workers Industrial Union," Federal Writers Project, Oakland, c. 1938, unpublished manuscript, appendix, pp. xx–xxvii, Bancroft Library. Harvey and Spector were AWIL organizers.

[43] Spector, *Story of the Imperial Valley*, pp. 5–6, 26–27; Seiler, "Cantaloupes and Communists," 243. According to Seiler, California law defined criminal syndicalism as "any doctrine . . . advocating, teaching, or aiding and abetting the commission of crime, sabotage, or unlawful methods of terrorism as a means of accomplishing a change in industrial ownership or control, or effecting any political change."

[44] Jamieson, *Labor Unionism*, p. 84.

[45] Charles B. Spaulding, "The Mexican Strike at El Monte, California," *Sociology and Social Research* 18 (August 1934): 571–572. For a more recent study of the El Monte strike, see Ronald W. López, "The El Monte Berry Strike of 1933," *Aztlan* 1 (Spring 1970): 101–102. See also Charles Wollenberg, "Race and Class in Rural California: The El Monte Berry Strike of 1933," *California Historical Society Quarterly* 51 (Summer 1972): 155–164, which emphasizes the Mexican-Japanese ethnic conflict dimension of this strike.

and other "improvised materials." [46] Organizers from the Trade Union Unity League's farm affiliate, which had changed its name to the Cannery and Agricultural Workers' Industrial Union (C&AWIU) in 1931, entered upon the scene. Initially they cooperated with the Mexican union and successfully spread the labor conflict into nearby onion and celery fields, until it encompassed a total of 7000 workers. [47] Having little influence with local law enforcement authorities and fearing American resentment against them because of their employees' agitation, the Japanese growers offered to settle at $.20 an hour for berry picking. [48] Under the influence of the local Mexican consul who had served as a mediator, the Mexican union favored the offer. C&AWIU leaders, however, rejected the settlement because it did not apply to the other crops. They hoped to expand what had been a limited strike in one crop into a general movement in a large and diverse agricultural region. But once they obtained their objective—a wage increase—Mexican berry pickers spurned the C&AWIU and returned to the fields. Their union, which had adopted the name Confederación de Uniones de Campesinos y Obreros Mexicanos (CUCOM) and claimed more than 5000 members, signed an agreement with the Japanese Growers' Association, which included union recognition and the discharge of strikebreakers. [49] Dr. Clements of the Los Angeles Chamber of Commerce warned of the implications of the El Monte strike: "Knowing the Mexican pretty well, my opinion is that unless something is done, this local situation is dangerous in that it will spread throughout the state as a whole. . . . This is the most serious break of the Mexican workers here." [50]

Depression wage cuts created potential strike situations throughout 1933. [51] The C&AWIU hoped to take advantage of the discontent among cotton pickers in the San Joaquin Valley. Realizing that their failure to retain workers' support in El Monte was due to faulty grassroots organization as well as a refusal to compromise, C&AWIU organizers took special efforts to prepare for their confrontation with cotton growers. Led by Pat Chambers, whom Carey McWilliams described as a "small, quiet, soft-spoken man, but a person of great courage and genuine ability as a leader," and Caroline Decker, a woman in her early twenties, the union attempted to build a strong rank-and-file following. [52] Its motto was: "An ounce of organization is worth a ton of talk!" [53] Preharvest preparation included training Mexican organizers and establishing farm committees consisting of worker representatives. A controversy over

[46] Theodore Rodriguez and W. S. Fennell, "Agrarian Revolt in California," *Nation* 137 (September 6, 1933): 272.

[47] Jamieson, *Labor Unionism*, pp. 90–92.

[48] Spaulding, "Mexican Strike," 577.

[49] Jamieson, *Labor Unionism*, p. 92.

[50] *La Follette Committee Hearings*, pt. 53: 19695.

[51] Chaffee, "History of the C&AWIU," pp. ii–vii; House, Committee on Labor, *Labor Disputes Act*, pp. 360–63.

[52] McWilliams, *Factories in the Field*, p. 219; Irving Bernstein, *Turbulent Years* (Boston: Houghton Mifflin, 1970), p. 153.

[53] Chaffee, "History of the C&AWIU," pt. 3, p. 4.

wages set the stage for a strike. During the late 1920s, cotton pickers had earned up to $1.50 per hundredweight, but in 1932 the rate had dropped to $.40. Prior to the October 1933 harvest, the powerful San Joaquin Valley Agricultural Labor Bureau, representing cotton growers, fixed the standard wage at $.60 per hundredweight. The union, having failed to achieve its demanded pay rate of $1.00, called a strike. About 12,000 laborers, over 75 percent of whom were Mexican, left the fields for three weeks in the C&AWIU's largest and most effective strike. Covering six counties and over 100,000 acres, the San Joaquin Valley cotton walkout was probably the most extensive agricultural strike in American history.[54]

"The atmosphere of the valley," reported the *San Francisco Examiner* on October 9, 1933, "is that of a smouldering volcano." [55] Growers and county officials reacted swiftly against the strike, which jeopardized most of California's cotton crop. Farmers evicted laborers from housing on their land, and police prevented peaceful picketing while arresting dozens. A deputy sheriff admitted in an interview:

> We protect our farmers here in Kern County. They are our best people. They are always with us. They keep the country going. They put us in here and they can put us out again, so we serve them. But the Mexicans are trash. They have no standard of living. We herd them like pigs.[56]

The growers, claiming that outside radical agitators had misled a formerly contented Mexican work force, threatened their workers with deportation and violence. The *Corcoran News* on October 20 warned:

> Practically all of the striking cotton pickers are Mexicans, so this article is addressed to the people of that nationality. . . . You have been fools . . . trying to reach a goal that is not possible for you to reach, the right to dictate to American employers what they shall pay, whether they can pay it or not.
> . . . Most of you want to work and all of you should be at work. In fact many of you will have to go to work very soon or go back to your own country. . . .
> If the strike continues, it is more than likely that every last one of you will be gathered into one huge bull pen. . . . And what will a bull pen mean to you? Many of you don't know how the United States government can run a concentration camp. First of all every last one of you will be deloused. . . .

[54] Ibid., pp. 1–4, B; Jamieson, *Labor Unionism,* p. 100; telegram, E. H. Fitzgerald to H. L. Kerwin, October 16, 1933, Labor Department File, "Cotton Pickers Strike," box 54, RG 174, NA.

[55] Quoted in Chaffee, "History of the C&AWIU," p. 10.

[56] Paul S. Taylor and Clark Kerr, "Documentary History of the Strike of Cotton Pickers in California, 1933," in *La Follette Committee Hearings,* pt. 53: 19992. This is the best source on the cotton strike. It was written by Professor Taylor and one of his graduate students, Clark Kerr, shortly after the labor dispute although it was not published for several years. Taylor to author, November 2, 1972.

Do you want to face the bull pen? Do you want to be deported to Mexico?

That is what you face, and don't fool yourselves about it![57]

Growers surrounded and fired upon strikers holding meetings at Pixley
and Arvin, killing three. A *New York Times* story reported that "the
man who fired the first shot said he had heard a speaker refer dispar-
agingly to the American flag." [58]

Despite the violence the determination and morale of the strikers
grew. The growers persuaded the Mexican consul from Monterey to
intervene and attempt to form a Mexican union to rival the C&AWIU.
His efforts were unsuccessful, and the strike continued.[59] Deprived of
shelter, the workers established makeshift tent camps. The largest, located
at Corcoran, contained 4300 people without water or sanitation facilities.[60]
The hostile *Los Angeles Times*, after describing the miserable living conditions in the camp, charged: "Promiscuity is unlimited. Some things are
not for printing in a home-going newspaper." [61]

The strikers soon began to suffer food shortages and health problems. Local welfare authorities refused to extend them aid. Hospitals
denied admittance to strikers' wives who were about to deliver babies.
Nine infants at the Corcoran camp died of malnutrition.[62] As mass starvation approached, Governor James Rolph, acting on federal advice,
ordered the California Emergency Relief Administration to provide the
strikers with relief. This was the first time laborers of any kind ever received food from a federal agency during a strike.[63] The relief, however,
came with strings attached. A fact-finding committee established by the
governor and California NRA Administrator George Creel, who also
served as a mediator, recommended a compromise wage settlement of
$.75 per hundredweight. To encourage union acceptance of the compro-
mise, all relief was halted. After some hesitation, the union agreed, and

---

[57] Quoted in Taylor and Kerr, "Documentary History," pt. 53: 19970-19971. See also
  Ella Winter, "California's Little Hitlers," *New Republic* 77 (December 27, 1933);
  188–190.

[58] *New York Times*, October 22, 1933. C&AWIU leaders appealed to the president
  for protection. Telegram, C. H. Ernest to Franklin Roosevelt, October 9, 1933.
  Secretary of Labor Frances Perkins wired Governor Rolph that she was confident
  that he would take steps to prevent violence. Telegram, Perkins to James Rolph,
  Jr., October 9, 1933, Labor Department File, "Cotton Pickers Strike," box 34, RG
  174, NA.

[59] Jamieson, *Labor Unionism*, pp. 102–103.

[60] Miriam A. DeFord, "Blood Stained Cotton in California," *Nation* 137 (December
  20, 1933): 706.

[61] Quoted in McWilliams, *Factories in the Field*, p. 223.

[62] Chaffee, "History of the C&AWIU," pp. 29–37; "Labor and the N.R.A.," *New
  Republic* 77 (November 22, 1933): 48. The *New Republic* charged that the nine
  deaths resulted from the "efforts of growers and relief officials to starve the pickers
  into submission." Telegram, F. C. MacDonald, California State Labor Commissioner, to Frances Perkins, October 11, 1933, Labor Department File, "Cotton
  Pickers Strike," box 34, RG 174, NA.

[63] Taylor and Kerr "Documentary History," pt. 53: 19993-19995.

workers returned to the fields. State and federal officials also placed pressure on the growers through the influence of the Federal Intermediate Credit Bank.[64] The growers asserted that their acceptance of the settlement was made "in the interests of good American citizenship, law and order, and in order to forestall the spread of communism and radicalism. . . ." [65]

In spite of the relative success of the cotton strike, the C&AWIU could not maintain its Mexican following, which was never ideologically committed to the Communist party. Workers left the San Joaquin Valley after completing the harvest and migrated to work on other crops, leaving their union allegiance behind.[66] The extent of radical influence on the strikers was well evaluated by *New York Times* reporter Frederick Forbes:

> There is no doubt that, whether or not it originated with the Reds, communistic propagandists took advantage of the conflict. . . . On the other hand, it is certain that the great bulk of the migratory laborers are not able to distinguish between Marxism and Zoroastrianism. What they wanted was more money for their labor.[67]

Labor unrest returned to the Imperial Valley in late 1933. Wages for lettuce harvesting had dipped from between $.35 and $.50 an hour in 1929 to $.15 in 1933.[68] To increase their pay, Mexican workers began to organize. Although the benefits of early New Deal legislation, such as the NIRA and the AAA, did not apply to farm laborers, the vague notion that these programs were somehow supposed to help workers did serve to inspire migrant organization. A report on Imperial Valley labor developments asserted: "The Mexicans have heard of the N.R.A., they believe that the Federal Government is going to protect them and improve their economic status, but they do not know the N.R.A. does not apply to agricultural pursuits." [69] Encouraged by New Deal publicity,

[64] Ibid., pp. 19996–20005; *New York Times*, October 26, 1933; Chaffee, "History of the C&AWIU," pp. 45–59; clippings, box 15, George Creel Scrapbooks, Library of Congress. Creel's autobiography, *Rebel at Large* (New York: G. P. Putnam's Sons, 1947), sheds little light on the strike settlement.

[65] *Tulare County Times-Delta*, October 25, 1933, quoted in Taylor and Kerr, "Documentary History," pt. 53: 20006. Edson Abel, attorney for the California Farm Bureau Federation, charged that Creel had implied that the Intermediate Credit Bank would loan growers up to $1 million to help pay for increased picking costs but that this was never done. *Pacific Rural Press* (February 3, 1934): 89. Growers claimed to have lost $3 million as a result of the strike. Chaffee, "History of the C&AWIU," p. 60.

[66] Jamieson, *Labor Unionism*, p. 105; Taylor and Kerr, "Uprisings on the Farm," 22.

[67] *New York Times*, October 22, 1933.

[68] Jamieson, *Labor Unionism*, p. 108.

[69] J. L. Leonard, Will J. French, Simon J. Lubin, "Report to the National Labor Board by Special Commission," February 11, 1934, in *La Follette Committee Hearings*, pt. 54; 20048. The CUOM and the Los Angeles Confederación de Sociedades Mexicanas had both pledged to cooperate with the NRA. Pascual S. Rodrigues, General Secretary, Confederación de Uniones Obreras Mexicanas, to Campbell

laborers, with the encouragement of the local Mexican consul, revived the dormant Imperial Valley Workers' Union in October, 1933. Hoping to prevent an organization drive by the C&AWIU, growers agreed to negotiate with the Mexican union. The parties reached an accord setting the lettuce harvest wage rate at $.225 an hour, with a guaranteed five-hour minimum per day. If the market price of lettuce improved, negotiations for a wage increase were to commence after January 1, 1934. Two weeks after the initial agreement, the union charged that the growers were reneging on the five-hour minimum guarantee, and it called a one-day strike for November 13. Meetings between the parties, mediated by the Mexican consul at Calexico, proved fruitless. On January 2 the union demanded a $.35 an hour wage, which the growers flatly rejected. Having no success, Mexican union leaders turned to the C&AWIU organizers, who had been arriving in the area, for aid. The C&AWIU called a strike for January 8, to which 5000 workers, overwhelmingly Mexican, responded.[70]

The Imperial Valley strike of 1934 was marked by pervasive violence, vigilante activity, and violations of civil liberties. In the words of Carey McWilliams, the Imperial Valley situation was "the most striking illustration of farmer-Fascism in California. . . ."[71] At the outset of the strike, town, county, and state police, using tear gas, broke up a caravan of workers on the way from Brawley to El Centro to attend a union meeting. Eighty-seven arrests were made on such charges as vagrancy, trespass, disturbing the peace, and resisting arrest. Local courts set bail at levels ensuring that workers would be kept in jail. Three days later police teargassed an overcrowded meeting of strikers in Brawley.[72] Local authorities augmented their ranks with deputized growers and vigilantes, who joined in an antiradical witch-hunt to suppress the strike. The *Calexico Chronicle* on January 12, 1934, reported the "mobilization of the American Legion reserve—to keep down the rising tide of strike sentiment."[73] A *Los*

MacCulloch, October 12, 1933, National Labor Board, Los Angeles Region Files, "Agricultural Code," box 459, RG 25, NA (hereafter cited as NLB-LA); A. Gonzalez, Executive President, and J. C. Ballin, General Secretary, Confederación de Sociedades Mexicanas, to National Recovery Administration, September 9, 1933, NLB-LA Files, "Mexican Labor Code," box 461, RG 25, NA.

[70] Leonard, French, and Lubin, "Report," pp. 20043–44. Chaffee, "History of the C&AWIU," pt. 2, pp. 1–5; O. C. Heitman, California State Labor Department, to Campbell MacCulloch, Executive Secretary, Los Angeles Regional Labor Board, January 16, 1934, National Labor Board File 15–33, "Lettuce Growers," RG 25, WNRC.

[71] Carey McWilliams, "The Farmers Get Tough," *American Mercury* 33 (October 1934): 241. The Associated Farmers later dubbed McWilliams "Agricultural Pest No. 1 in California, outranking pear blight and boll weevil." McWilliams, *Ill Fares the Land*, p. 13.

[72] Leonard, French, and Lubin, "Report," p. 20044. The ACLU reported that the tear gassing precipitated the death of a twenty-two month old Mexican child. Chaffee, "History of the C&AWIU," pt. 2, p. 7.

[73] Quoted in Carey McWilliams, "The Farmers Get Tough," *American Mercury* 33 (October 1934): 244.

Angeles Times article on January 15 stated: "It's a secret, but the vigilantes are really Legionnaires, and do they have fun!" [74] In an editorial, the liberal Christian journal *World Tomorrow* protested the Imperial Valley developments with horror: "Civil government as we in the United States have understood it, no longer exists. . . . In noteworthy respects these goings-on reproduce what has been happening in Hitler's Germany." [75]

The American Civil Liberties Union endeavored to protect the rights of the workers. An attorney for that organization, A. L. Wirin, after being refused permission to hold a strikers' meeting by the sheriff of Imperial County, obtained a federal injunction restraining the local authorities from interfering with the meeting. On the evening of January 23, while on his way to lead the gathering in Brawley, Wirin was kidnapped by a mob, robbed, beaten, threatened with branding, driven twenty miles into the desert, relieved of his shoes, and dumped. [76] The *Brawley News* of January 25, 1934, commented on Wirin's abduction:

> Sentiment in the Imperial Valley today approves of the action taken . . . when vigilantes ordered leaders in the agitation which has been rife for the past two weeks to leave the county, and took somewhat radical steps to see that they did leave. [77]

In addition to using violence, growers sought to undermine the strike, which had spread to pea pickers, by establishing a rival to the C&AWIU. The Mexican consul at Calexico, Joaquin Terrazas, was pressured into organizing the Associación Mexicana del Valle Imperial. Terrazas hoped that a new Mexican union could cement "cordial and permanent relations between workers and growers" and also eliminate the "outside influence of agitators." [78] Incapable of attracting members on its own, the new organization became virtually a company union in the hands of growers, who refused to hire anyone who was not a member. [79] The C&AWIU,

[74] Ibid., p. 244. See also George H. Shoaf, "California's Reign of Terror," *Christian Century* 51 (February 28, 1934): 282–284.

[75] "Toward Fascism in California," *World Tomorrow* 17 (April 12, 1934): 173. *World Tomorrow* was founded by Norman Thomas. Its editors included Reinhold Niebuhr, A. J. Muste, and Paul Douglas.

[76] Chester Williams, "Imperial Valley Mob," *New Republic* 78 (February 21, 1934): 39–40.

[77] Quoted in Chester Williams, "Imperial Valley Prepares for War," *World Tomorrow* 17 (April 26, 1934): 201. Vigilantes, encouraged by some local officials, roamed the valley with impunity. Wirin's abduction was only the first of several similar incidents. Ellis O. Jones, "Kidnap Valley, California," *Nation* 138 (April 25, 1934): 468–470; Lew Levenson, "California Casualty List," *Nation* 139 (August 29, 1934): 243; *La Follette Committee Hearings*, pt. 55: 20158-21062.

[78] Telegram, Joaquin Terrazas to Campbell MacCulloch, February 15, 1934, and MacCulloch to Terrazas, February 15, 1934, National Labor Board File 15-37, RG 25, WNRC; Jamieson, *Labor Unionism*, p. 109; Taylor and Kerr, "Uprising on the Farm," 44.

[79] Pelham D. Glassford to Charles E. Wyzanski, Solicitor, Department of Labor, May 27, 1934, box 26, folder 2, Glassford Papers, Special Collections Department,

deprived of its arrested leaders, was unable to expand the strike into the cantaloupe fields and keep its momentum going. Gradually workers joined Terrazas' union and drifted back to their jobs.[80] Local officials completely crushed the strike on February 19, when, ostensibly under orders of the county health officer, the strikers' camp was burned to the ground. Its more than 2000 inhabitants fled from a barrage of tear gas. One baby died from the fumes.[81] Tensions remained high.

In response to this pervasive violence, Senator Robert Wagner, chairman of the National Labor Board, appointed a special commission to investigate the Imperial Valley events.[82] Appalled at conditions in the valley, the commission recommended that the federal government protect the civil liberties of both citizens and aliens and send Spanish-speaking representatives to aid workers in organizing so "that collective bargaining may be effective in matters of wages and conditions, both living and working, and that the right to strike and peacefully to picket shall be maintained." Also, the commission advised appointing a labor coordinator to settle disputes.[83] The National Labor Board, however, could do little. It lacked statutory powers of enforcement in labor disputes and, in the words of Arthur Schlesinger, Jr., "had become almost impotent" by 1934.[84] The board hoped that state authorities would move to quiet the situation. The special commission members, however, had no faith that the Rolph administration would undertake any constructive action in the

UCLA Research Library, microfilm. According to Glassford, the Asociación Mexicana was totally dominated by the growers. See also Helen D. Marston to MacCulloch, March 20, 1934, National Labor Board File 15-37, RG 25, WNRC; Williams, "Imperial Valley Prepares for War," 199.

[80] Jamieson, *Labor Unionism*, p. 109. C&AWIU appeals such as the following were ineffective: "We must organize all the workers regardless of race and nationality. The bosses try to defeat us both by terror and by splitting us on nationalistic lines. *Don't listen to the lies in the boss owned newspapers, or any other tool of the bosses especially the Mexican consul.*" *La Follette Committee Hearings*, pt. 55: 20314.

[81] J. L. Leonard to Simon Lubin, February 20, 1934, National Labor Board File 15-37, RG 25, WNRC; Chaffee, "History of the C&AWIU," pt. 2, pp. 29–37; McWilliams, *Factories in the Field*, pp. 224–225.

[82] "More Than Mob Terror," *New Republic* 78 (March 21, 1934): 148. The members of the commission were Professor J. L. Leonard of the University of Southern California and chairman of the Los Angeles Regional Labor Board, Simon Lubin, chief of the California State Bureau of Commerce, and Will J. French, former director of the California Department of Industrial Relations.

[83] Leonard, French, and Lubin, "Report," pp. 20043–20057. S. Parker Frisselle, president of the newly formed Associated Farmers of California, appointed another commission consisting of Dean C. B. Hutchinson of the University of California's College of Agriculture, W. C. Jacobsen of the California State Department of Agriculture, and John Phillips, a state assemblyman, to study the situation. This commission refuted the findings of the Leonard, French, and Lubin report and presented the growers' viewpoint. *La Follette Committee Hearings*, pt. 49: 17944–17945, pt. 54: 20053–20063.

[84] Arthur M. Schlesinger, Jr., *The Coming of the New Deal* (Cambridge, Mass.: Riverside Press, 1959), p. 149.

valley because state officials had consistently violated workers' civil liberties in the past. They were also distressed to learn that the federal government instituted only one of their recommendations: the appointment of a labor conciliator.[85] To this position, Labor Secretary Frances Perkins, with the concurrence of Secretary of Agriculture Henry Wallace and Senator Wagner, named General Pelham D. Glassford, who had gained fame for his judicious handling of the Bonus Army in 1932 before retiring to his farm in Arizona.[86]

Despite this appointment, it is clear that the Roosevelt administration did not intend to intervene strongly on behalf of labor. Rather, it tried to take as little action as possible. In asking Glassford to accept the post of conciliator, Acting Secretary of Labor Charles E. Wyzanski stated that the administration disagreed with many of the recommendations of the National Labor Board's special Imperial Valley commission. In particular, explained Wyzanski, "it seemed doubtful whether the Government ought to lend its efforts directly to the organization of labor unions or should deport aliens for joining left-wing trade unions or should send into a local dispute agents of the Department of Justice." The general's instructions were simply to serve as a "mediator and coordinator for those who have grievances or difficulties to adjust." He was to be available for talks with employers, employees, state officials, and members of the general public.[87]

Glassford's appointment was greeted with hostility by the C&AWIU, the growers, and state and local officials.[88] The feeling soon became mutual. After the C&AWIU attacked him as a deceiver and rich landowner, Glassford issued a broadside in Spanish addressed to "all Mexican Workers in Imperial Valley," which charged that the C&AWIU organizers were communists and "have no interest in the welfare of the workers. Their only object is to create dissension, destroy property and foment a strike." He cautioned workers not to "follow the advice of these vile agitators. To do so will bring destitution and hunger and will add nothing to the welfare of the workers." He advised farm workers against striking and offered his services to mediate grievances.[89] The general also

---

[85] Lubin to Leonard, February 14, 1934, National Labor Board File 15-37, RG 25, WNRC; Leonard, French, and Lubin to Wagner, March 6, 1934, NLB-LA File "J. L. Leonard," box 457, RG 25, NA; MacCulloch to National Labor Board, NLB-LA, "Administrative Files 'B,'" box 458, RG 25, NA.

[86] Telegram, Charles Wyzanski, Acting Secretary of Labor, to Pelham D. Glassford, March 26, 1934, box 26, folder 1, Glassford Papers. For a sketch of Glassford's colorful career, see Irving Bernstein, The Lean Years (Baltimore: Penguin Books, 1966), pp. 441–454 Roger Daniels, The Bonus March (Westport, Conn.: Greenwood Press, 1971).

[87] Wyzanski to Glassford, March 27, 1934, box 26, folder 2, Glassford Papers, reprinted in La Follette Committee Hearings, pt. 55: 20298. For the federal government's reluctance to act, see telegram, National Labor Board to J. L. Leonard, February 14, 1934, National Labor Board File 15-37, RG 25, WNRC.

[88] McWilliams, "Farmers Get Tough," 243.

[89] Copies of the broadside, dated April 30, 1934, are in box 26, folder 2, Glassford Papers; a translation is reprinted in La Follette Committee Hearings, pt. 55: 20315-20316. Wyzanski told Glassford not to play up the presence of communists in the

received no cooperation from growers and local officials. His phone was tapped, his mail tampered with, and his life threatened.[90] An angry General Glassford charged that in the Imperial Valley "leadership is absent and it is time Imperial County awakens to the fact that it is part of the United States." [91] As far as the growers and local authorities were concerned, the general asserted:

> After more than two months of observation, . . . it is my conviction that a group of growers have exploited a "communist" hysteria . . . for their own interests; that they have welcomed labor agitation, which they could brand as "Red," as a means of sustaining supremacy by mob rule, thereby preserving what is so essential to their profits—cheap labor; that they have succeeded in drawing into their conspiracy certain county officials who have become the principal tools of their machine.[92]

Upon concluding his investigation, Glassford issued a report to the Imperial County Board of Supervisors and the federal government. It stated that Mexican migrants lived in "poverty and squalor" and earned less than $400 a year. To ameliorate these conditions he recommended the establishment of a minimum wage, the standardization of contracts to prevent exploitation of workers, and government-encouraged repatriation of surplus labor.[93] No action was taken on these recommendations by local, state, or federal officials.

The San Joaquin and Imperial Valley strikes inspired growers to organize on a statewide basis to combat farm worker unionization.[94] With financial backing from the California business community, they formed a group called the Associated Farmers, which was dedicated to the eradication of left-wing organizers.[95] Capitalizing on labor turmoil in the

area because such publicity might embarrass federal officials like Harry Hopkins "who has the function of feeding a considerable number of alleged 'reds.' " Glassford-Wyzanski telephone conversation notes, April 16, 1934, box 26, folder 2, Glassford Papers.

[90] Conversation between Red Harrigan and Glassford, June 13, 1934, box 24, folder 1, Glassford Papers; MacCulloch to Glassford, April 20, 1934, National Labor Board File 15-37, RG 25, WNRC; MacCulloch to Mrs. B. M. Stern, National Labor Board, June 5, 1934, NLB-LA, box 458, RG 25, NA; Chaffee, "History of the C&AWIU," pt. 2, pp. 23–24; House, Committee on Labor, *Labor Disputes Act,* p. 48.

[91] Press Release, June 13, 1934, box 24, folder 1, Glassford Papers.

[92] *La Follette Committee Hearings,* pt. 55: 20304.

[93] Ibid., pp. 20302-20303.

[94] Clarke A. Chambers, *California Farm Organizations* (Berkeley: University of California Press, 1952), pp. 39–41; *La Follette Committee Hearings,* pt. 49: 17910-17915, 17923, 17945-17946.

[95] John Steinbeck, "Dubious Battle in California," *Nation* 143 (September 12, 1936): 302–303. Steinbeck charged that the Associated Farmers was backed by speculative landowners like A. J. Chandler, publisher of the *Los Angeles Times,* Herbert Hoover, and William Randolph Hearst, as well as the Bank of America. See also Herbert Klein and Carey McWilliams, "Cold Terror in California," *Nation* 141 (July 24, 1935): 97–98; Chaffee, "History of the C&AWIU," pt. 4, pp. 1–5.

city of San Francisco, the Associated Farmers helped fan the flames of red hysteria in California, which culminated in a raid upon C&AWIU headquarters in Sacramento in July 1934. Police arrested seventeen people, and eight, including Chambers and Decker, were convicted of criminal syndicalism. After two years' imprisonment, their conviction was reversed on appeal. The arrests, however, had removed the union's most able leaders.[96] In 1935 the moribund C&AWIU faded from the scene. It was officially dissolved from above when the Communist party adopted the Popular Front tactic of working within existing unions.[97]

A speaker at a Communist party convention in 1934 boasted: "As a result of these struggles the Cannery and Agricultural Workers' Industrial Union has definitely rooted itself in the masses of farm workers."[98] That this statement was wishful thinking is indicated by the actions of Mexican workers after the arrest of C&AWIU leaders. The migrants made no attempt to revive the radical union. Neither did they contentedly accept low wages once radical agitators left the fields, as growers had predicted.[99] Instead they turned to the independent Mexican organization that had carried on the El Monte strike, the CUCOM. Headed by Guillermo Velarde, Armando Flores, and Nicholas Avila, this organization was the most effective agricultural union in California during 1935 and 1936, leading several relatively successful, small-scale strikes. Growers branded the union's leadership communist, and it was subjected to severe repression by the Associated Farmers and the police.[100]

The survival of the CUCOM was threatened not only by outside opposition but also by New Deal welfare policy and changes occurring in the California labor market. During the early New Deal years, Mexicans benefited from the establishment of the Federal Emergency Relief Administration and the Civil Works Administration, which provided relief and jobs to the needy, citizens and noncitizens alike. This was true also of the Works Progress Administration when it began in 1935. In 1937, however, the WPA eliminated aliens—regardless of whether their spouses or children were native born—from eligibility, which caused hardship for thousands of Mexican workers throughout the country. In San Antonio, for example, the WPA allocated 1800 jobs for needy pecan

[96] McWilliams, *Factories in the Field*, p. 228; Chaffee, "History of the C&AWIU," pt. 4: 1–32. The convictions were overturned because the Supreme Court had declared Oregon's criminal-syndicalism statute, which was similar to that of California, unconstitutional.

[97] Chaffee, "History of the C&AWIU," pt. 4, p. 33; Alexander Morin, *The Organizability of Farm Labor in the United States* (Cambridge: Harvard University Press, 1952), p. 16.

[98] H. Puro, "Speech at the Eighth Convention of the Communist Party of the U.S.A.," *Communist* (June 1934): 571.

[99] *Pacific Rural Press* (April 21, 1934): 364.

[100] Jamieson, *Labor Unionism*, pp. 122–126; Frank Stokes, "Let the Mexicans Organize," *Nation* 143 (December 19, 1936): 731–732; Chaffee, "Organization Efforts of Mexican Agricultural Laborers," pp. 22–29; U. S., Department of Labor, *Annual Report of the Secretary of Labor* (1936), p. 28; Guillermo Velarde and Nicholas Avila to Towne Nylander, June 25, 1935, NLB-LA, "Petition to Japanese Growers' Association of Los Angeles," box 462, RG 25, NA.

shellers, but only 700 Mexicans could qualify because of the citizenship stipulation. In that city during the late 1930s, Mexicans employed in the private sector received lower wages than the WPA minimum. Unskilled construction laborers working for private firms averaged $6.02 weekly, while those hired by the WPA for similar work earned $8.54 per week. Thus, for alien Mexicans, the WPA citizenship requirement was a harsh blow indeed. At the same time stiffer state residency and administrative requirements also made it more difficult for Mexican workers to obtain relief during the second half of the 1930s.[101]

To compound difficulties, growers consistently criticized the relief given to migrants and worked to prevent it. The *Saturday Evening Post*, too, hammered away at the theme that idle Mexicans were "sitting pretty" in the United States at public expense.[102] Dr. George Clements, still representing the Los Angeles Chamber of Commerce, charged in 1935 that the California Relief Administration's dole had "dammed up" the "great reservoir" of Mexican labor that had always been available to farmers. "The Mexican on relief," declared Clements, "is being unionized and is being used to foment strikes among the still few loyal Mexican workers. The Mexican casual labor[er] is lost to the California farmer unless immediate action is taken to get him off relief." [103] Employers were quite successful in pressuring both county agencies and local WPA and FERA officials to cut off relief during harvest seasons, regardless of the actual availability of jobs.[104] California Governor Frank Merriam in 1937 issued a statement mandating that all healthy workers receiving public assistance "must help the state's harvest or get off the dole." [105] Thus, growers were able to rely on indigent workers to undermine agricultural unionization attempts.

In addition to the competition posed by workers forced off the relief rolls, those Mexican farm laborers who remained in the fields faced competition from a new labor source during the second half of the depression —dust bowl refugees. As a result of depressed farm conditions and devastating dust storms, massive numbers of rural Americans left their homes in Texas, Oklahoma, Arkansas, and Missouri and headed for California. Between 1935 and 1940 more than 350,000 adults entered California "in need of manual employment." [106] Arriving penniless, most became mi-

[101] R. Clyde White and Mary White, *Research Memorandum on Social Aspects of Relief Policies in the Depression* (New York: Social Science Research Council, 1937), pp. 73–74; Humphrey, "Employment Patterns," 921-922; McWilliams, *Ill Fares the Land*, pp. 119–121; Menefee, *Mexican Migratory Workers in South Texas*, pp. 45–46; Brown and Cassmore, *Migratory Cotton Pickers in Arizona*, p. xii; Menefee and Cassmore, *Pecan Shellers of San Antonio*, pp. 32, 40.

[102] *Pacific Rural Press* (March 21, 1936): 387; "Is Mexican Labor Cheap?" *Saturday Evening Post* 207 (July 21, 1934): 22.

[103] *La Follette Committee Hearings*, pt. 53: 19674-19675.

[104] Ibid., pt. 53: 19529-19530, 19709, pt. 51: 18603-18604, 18846, 18850-18851. See also Brown and Cassmore, *Migratory Cotton Pickers in Arizona*, pp. 61–63, and Waters, "Transient Mexican Agricultural Labor," 63.

[105] McWilliams, *Factories in the Field*, pp. 286–287.

[106] *La Follette Committee Hearings*, pt. 47: 17229-17230; Paul Taylor and Tom Vasey, "Drought Refugee and Labor Migration to California, June-December, 1935," *Monthly Labor Review* 42 (February 1936): 312–318.

grant farm workers and accepted any jobs they could find. Despite huge labor supplies, growers advertised attractive wages to stimulate further migration.[107] By the mid-1930s Mexicans were no longer the backbone of the California agricultural labor force. In 1936 an estimated 85 percent to 90 percent of the state's migratory labor supply consisted of white Americans as compared to less than 20 percent prior to the depression. The organization efforts of independent Mexican unions were doomed to failure as dust bowl migration created a chaotic surplus labor pool and thereby made unionization impossible.[108]

Mexican workers in all areas of the nation fared poorly during the Great Depression. Jobs evaporated, wages plummeted, and relief did little to ease distress. Thousands of Mexican families, including their American-born children, were badgered into leaving the country by the communities whose unskilled labor needs they had so economically met during the previous decades. Those Mexican workers who remained generally lived under conditions of extreme privation. In most locations Mexican workers faced the depression as isolated individuals, but in California Mexican farm laborers took collective action to protect their meager earnings. Most of their organizations were indigenous products of the Mexican community, cemented by bonds of nationality. Totally disfranchised in a hostile American environment and ignored by industrial unions, Mexicans were forced to fend for themselves. They joined their countrymen in independent strikes against exorbitant depression wage cuts. They accepted temporary left-wing leadership for pragmatic rather than ideological considerations. Growers and local residents, their livelihood dependent upon the crops jeopardized by strikes, reacted against workers with Red Scare tactics and gross violations of civil liberties.

The New Deal did little to help Mexican farm workers. Its major measures, such as the NIRA and the AAA, came to the aid of big business and big agriculture, the most powerful organized interests in the United States, while ignoring the plight of unorganized and politically weak groups. Even the Wagner Act, which gave a huge boost to the unionization of industrial laborers, did not include migratory agricultural workers under its provisions. Similarly, the Social Security Act failed to provide coverage for farm laborers. Nor did the New Deal make any special effort to advance the cause of racial minorities when it did try to help weaker groups. Its only migratory labor program, the Farm Security Administration, which was initiated largely as a response to the needs of white dust bowl refugees, was not established until 1937—too late to offer assistance to the thousands of Mexicans who had been replaced in the fields by Okies and Arkies. One piece of New Deal legislation, the Federal Sugar Act of 1937, which allowed the secretary of agriculture to set a minimum wage for beet workers, did prove slightly beneficial to Mexi-

---

[107] *La Follette Committee Hearings*, pt. 51: 18850, 18601-18602, pt. 53: 19564-19565. Growers in Arizona and Texas did the same. Brown and Cassmore, *Migratory Cotton Pickers in Arizona*, pp. iii–iv, xvii–xviii; Menefee, *Mexican Migratory Workers in South Texas*, pp. 31–32.

[108] *La Follette Committee Hearings*, pt. 53: 19696, pt. 47: 17259; Waters, "Transient Mexican Agricultural Labor," 51, 66; Walter J. Stein, *California and the Dust Bowl Migration* (Westport, Conn.: Greenwood Press, 1973), p. 42.

cans, who continued to dominate the midwestern and Colorado beet labor markets throughout the depression.[109]

In strike situations the Roosevelt administration showed little inclination to protect the political or economic security of Mexican workers. It refused to send in federal personnel at times of labor turmoil to prevent abuses by employers or local officials. Despite the need for rigorous organization for self-protection, Mexican unions were more ad hoc than permanent. They were, through no fault of their own, victims of flaws characteristic of all migrant organizations: financial and political impotence engendered by rootlessness. Fragile in themselves, staggered by grower repression, and unshielded by government, Mexican unions were finally overwhelmed by the flood of desperate American labor from the Great Plains. Those Mexican workers who found themselves squeezed from the fields went on to confront new challenges in the barrios of American cities.

[109] Menefee, *Mexican Migratory Workers in South Texas*, pp. 23–34; *Tolan Committee Hearings*, pt. 5: 1845–1847; Schwartz, *Seasonal Farm Labor in the United States*, pp. 118–120.

Social Welfare, the American Way

GEOFFREY PERRETT

In contemporary America the word "welfare" projects primarily negative connotations to society at large. People who receive "welfare" are seen by many as typically lazy, good-for-nothing, inferior examples of humanity. The fact that the overwhelming majority of those who partake of welfare are dependent children and most of the rest are physically disabled does not alter the popular image of the welfare recipient as a failure—one of those misfits who has not managed to fill his or her rightful place in society.

The idea of welfare was not always so limited. The preamble to the United States Constitution indicates that one purpose in forming that government was to "promote the general Welfare." Clearly this was intended to mean that the government was to concern itself in some way with the quality of life of those living under its aegis.

Until the twentieth century, the national government concerned itself little with issues of social welfare. Beginning with the Progressive era, however, such issues became increasingly urgent. For vast numbers of the population, industrialization and urbanism created conditions of life that were seen as both intolerable and eradicable from various reformers' points of view. The national government (regardless of the political party in control) nevertheless resisted any role for itself in promoting the general welfare other than to give away vast portions of the national resources to the already wealthy. If there was any ideology involved here, it was the notion that the country's economic resources were in better hands when managed by private interests and that the population at large would benefit thereby.

Unfortunately, or fortunately, depending on one's point of view in these matters, the United States government welfare policy fell afoul of the depression of the 1930s. As Presidents Hoover and Roosevelt tinkered with the economy in traditional ways to try to restore growth (or even stability), the general welfare sank to an unprecedented low. The economic policies of the New Deal struggled fitfully with problems of social welfare and provided a measure of relief for those people furthest down. The New Deal reforms also established for the first time certain minimal standards for particularly helpless sectors of the nation's population—the old, the dependent young, the physically handicapped—those who today have become the recipients of "welfare."

These programs, however, even when linked with public-works employment plans, did little to bring an end to the depression. Only the Second World War did that, and then only after four years of mobilization. It has become increasingly obvious in recent years that it was the war, not the depression, as had commonly been thought, that brought about a fundamental change in the American political economy. Perhaps the most persuasive argument along these lines is found in **Days of Sadness, Years of Triumph,** by Geoffrey Perrett.

In his introduction, Perrett indicates that among the social consequences of the war were "that enormous new groups of government beneficiaries came into existence; that barriers to social and economic equality which had stood for decades were either much reduced or entirely overthrown; that the old pyramidal class structure of the United States was cast onto the rubbish heap of history and a genuine middle-class nation came into existence; that access to higher education became genuinely democratic for the first time; that the modern civil rights movement began then; that the greatest gains in longevity occurred then; that the only basic redistribution of national income in American history occurred then; and that an entirely new role in the world was taken on" (p. 11).

The selection from Perrett's book that follows indicates how the government, in trying to deal with the social stresses brought about by mobilization for war, backed into a massive program of economic relief that helped bring about the fundamental change he describes. Never was this infusion of money and resources called welfare, and rarely did its recipients feel that it was other than earned and therefore deserved. It was at this point that "welfare" became attached to those who were largely outside the economy. And many who were the primary recipients of forms of government largess during and immediately after the war are those who today are the most antagonistic to people who depend on welfare for their basic sustenance. Perhaps a clearer understanding of the history of government economic policy in recent years would lead to more sympathy and concern for America's poor and disabled.

W e have seen how the war had ushered in a massive revival of conservative interests, especially of big business and the military. At their feet were strewn the corpses of most New Deal programs and ambitions. Whatever surplus energies the country possessed would evidently go into defeating the Axis, instead of reducing social inequities. There was also an inclination to consider war abnormal, a form of social pathology, which lent its fruits an aura of shaky impermanence. What hope then of real social change?

No one could fail to be conscious of the widespread social dislocations of wartime. Total war is itself a social crisis which regiments society while cutting people adrift from normal emotional and ethical moorings. More than 16,000,000 people were physically set in motion as they went off in search of jobs or loved ones. Most of these wartime migrants were women. Another 16,000,000, nearly all men, left their homes and went into the Army and Navy.

There was also a vague but pervasive idea that the revival of the economy had given everyone a job and made social reform unnecessary, even though there were still at least 20,000,000 people living on poverty-level incomes in the fall of 1943. Social welfare programs, like food stamps, were meanwhile being cut back. Yet here was the other side of the grand paradox of wartime: This was a period of massive social change, including a quantum leap in social welfare. It was hidden or at least heavily disguised, but it was nonetheless real and its effects were long-lasting, as this chapter—which treats of social problems, social welfare and social change—will show.

Generally speaking, social welfare is half the world of governmental responsibility (the other half being national defense). But it conveniently breaks into four interlocking parts: education, housing, health and social insurance. This latter comes down to programs of social security and direct relief for the distressed. In all four areas (only three of which are discussed here, education being treated separately) the war had the greatest consequences. But, as with so much else, we must first take a brief look at the years before the war—specifically at the New Deal's achievements and limitations—in order to comprehend the importance and the scope of what now occurred.

The question of how much desirable social change had been effected from 1933 to 1939 is endlessly debatable. The orthodox view of its admirers was expressed by Frederick Lewis Allen two decades ago: The New Deal "had repealed the Iron Law of Wages. We had brought about a virtually automatic redistribution of incomes from the well-to-do to the less well-to-do. . . . We had discovered a new frontier to open up: the purchasing power of the poor. That, it seems to me, is the essence of the Great American Discovery." (As we shall see, Allen was not only wrong, but far more wrong than he ever realized.)

A less starry-eyed but still sympathetic view of the New Deal's major accomplishments makes, at best, a short list: welfare as a right; Social Security provisions for the old, the disabled and the unemployed; a minimum wage for millions of workers; bank and stock market regulation; smashing the near monopoly on government of the propertied elements—usually WASP's—by bringing Negroes, workers and ethnic minorities into national politics; and forging the tools to avoid future depressions. But the limitations are obvious: Minimum wages are frequently more a ceiling than a floor; in 1939 there was one Negro in Congress; only a third of the nation was covered by Social Security; and who, even now, can guarantee there will never be another depression?

Yet many good things were done, and were done in a swirling environment of social experiment and innovation. The federal government directly subsidized thousands of artists, writers, actors and musicians. With federal money about 200 cooperative living projects were set up, over conservative grumbling that they were "soviets." The Solicitor

General, Robert Jackson, had affronted conservative sensibilities even further by demanding legal aid for the poor, a proposal called "socialized law" by the president of the American Bar Association, who attributed it to the workings of "Termites in the temple of justice."

The federal government had launched a modest school-lunch program in 1935 that less than ten years later was feeding 9,000,000 schoolchildren at least one hot meal each day. Federal and local authorities split the cost, and the PTA, the Junior League, the American Legion and others provided labor and equipment. There was no discrimination in the program, and in the poorest areas breakfast was often available, too.

Nor had the innovations ended when the war began. In November, 1939, the federal food stamp program had begun, to popular approval, On the first of January, 1940, the new Social Security System mailed out the first 900,000 old age pension checks. But no one believed that the Depression had been beaten; only the most fervent New Dealers thought it was about to be. When people were asked late in 1939, "Do young men have a better chance to get ahead now than they had thirty years ago?" by a margin of three to one they chose "30 years ago."

For despite the impassioned efforts of recent years, the foundations of pessimism were unshaken. In 1937 Roosevelt had seen one-third of a nation ill-clothed, ill-housed, ill-fed. Two years later the chairman of the New York city housing authority saw 40 percent. In terms of housing alone, it was possibly even higher, for half of U.S. housing was substandard, and Congress turned back a proposal for a major assault on the housing problem in 1939. Moreover, average weekly earnings in industry and agriculture were lower in 1939 than they had been in 1937.

More disheartening still was the pattern of income distribution. What redistribution occurred under the New Deal chiefly benefited the comfortable middle class and the very top income groups—that is, the top 5 percent. Middle-class families who held onto their homes and their regular incomes had, given the depressed prices of the 1930's, enjoyed a substantial increase in their standard of living. For them, the Depression was something to read about or look at from a distance. In the country as a whole income had been more fairly apportioned in 1918 than it was twenty years later:

Shares of National Income	1918	1929	1937
Lowest Fifth	6.8	5.4	3.6
Second Fifth	12.6	10.1	10.4
Third Fifth	14.6	14.4	15.7
Fourth Fifth	18.3	17.9	21.8
Highest Fifth	47.4	51.3	48.5

It may be asked, did not the system of relief to the unemployed make up in benefits what was lost in cash income? It seems a fair assumption that it did not and never could. For the answer to unemployment was not relief, but jobs.

Before the Depression, systematic succor was extended primarily to the "deserving poor"—the temporarily unemployed but responsible, hard-working family man; the physically handicapped, such as the blind; and survivors—that is, widows and orphans. This was relief rooted in private charity and local control, tracing directly back to the poor laws of Elizabethan England. Almost last among industrialized Western nations did the United States enact permanent social legislation based frankly on the principle of governmental responsibility to alleviate the sufferings regularly visited on those least able to bear them by the mysterious workings of business cycles which no one knew how to regulate.

But by 1939 a new system had been developed, holding out five kinds of relief: general relief—that is, cash allowances for food and other necessities; aid to dependent children; old age insurance; aid to the blind; and public works employment. In all, some 16,500,000 people were receiving some kind of relief in 1939, and the number was rising.

Most of these measures were simply prudent. For a Western nation, none of them was exceptional. But in the popular imagination the public works programs came, in later years, to dwarf the other relief programs. And it is true that the Works Progress Administration built thousands of useful schools, post offices, bridges and dams. The Civilian Conservation Corps planted 2 billion trees and saved millions of acres of land from destruction. But all this obscured two important facts. First, public works were not an innovation of the New Deal; in fact, more money was spent on public construction each year under Hoover than the New Deal public works projects approached except at their peak. This points to the second —that despite New Deal public works, the country was losing ground each year: America was physically running down, falling apart, decaying.

New Construction (in billions of dollars)	1929	1930	1933	1939
Public	2.39	2.75	1.00	2.44
Private	7.52	5.31	1.22	3.62

And the drop in private construction showed no prospect of being closed for many years, if ever.

The central problem, of massive unemployment, was so profound that not until mid-1943—after a year and a half of defense crisis and another year and a half of war production—was full employment achieved. If it took four years with these stimulants, it is reasonable to suppose that it would have taken much longer without them.

And no sooner had recovery seemed imminent than conservative elements were at work trying to lay the ghost of the New Deal. We have seen how throughout the war a large and powerful bloc in Congress forced the dismantling of New Deal agencies and programs with a zest born of bitterness.

The CCC was abolished at the end of 1941. Two years later Roosevelt gave the WPA what he lightly called "an honorable discharge." The National Youth Authority survived only as a vocational training program for war industries. The National Labor Relations Board was in a state of suspended animation. The Agricultural Adjustment Agency was a prize trophy of conservative interests. The Justice Department stopped its trust-busting attacks on monopolies. The SEC had merged into the Wall Street Establishment. Almost without exception New Deal agencies were dead, dying or under a cloud, including even the free lunch program. Selective Service had demonstrated that young men from homes where the diet was poor provided most of the physical rejects. But Congress slashed the subsidies for the school lunch program to the bone. It was pointless, as well as cruel, for free lunches had improved health standards, school attendance, learning and discipline. Hungry children have never made alert or orderly pupils. But conservatives argued that there was no longer a food surplus to go into these subsidized meals; that there were now plenty of jobs, and parents should be able to take care of children themselves; that free meals undermined the spirit of free enterprise.

Congressional conservatives were meantime dismantling the Home Owners Loan Corporation. When the HOLC had been established in 1933, foreclosures were running at a rate approaching 1,000 a day. Ten years later it was 58 percent liquidated, and with a loss rate of only 2 percent there was every likelihood that before much longer the HOLC would liquidate itself entirely, with no overall loss, perhaps with a small profit, to the taxpayers. As if to indicate that what was involved in the dismantling of the New Deal was more than ideology, the savings and loans associations and the banks forced the HOLC to wind up its business in short order. By putting the HOLC out of business, many thousands of weak loans were foreclosed, at a cost to the taxpayers of hundreds of millions of dollars. Then the sound loans were refinanced by the banks and others, at higher rates. With Congress' help a public agency was forced to commit suicide for private gain. Even the president of the New York Stock Exchange was willing to concede these days that "There is a conservative reaction in progress."

Conservatives were strong enough by now to easily turn aside any attempt to reintroduce overt social reform. In 1939 Roosevelt had created a National Resources Planning Board to make a long-range study of work relief and Social Security programs. Almost everyone had forgotten it, until late in 1942, when it issued its report. There was general anticipation that it would parallel Britain's Beveridge Report, which, when adopted, had committed that country's government to the creation of a postwar welfare state.

Using the NRPB report as a springboard, Roosevelt early in 1943 sent his recommendations to Congress. The second part of his proposals followed some weeks later. Together, they formed a whole that was both vast and vague. Rarely did he ask for anything specific. "The most striking characteristic of the reports," thought one political editor, "is their essential conservatism . . . specific suggestions will be controversial but none is revolutionary or even novel." As it proved, there was not even much controversy. It was simply too nebulous to encourage debate. It was, summarized Time, merely "480,000 words of foggy goodwill."

Even so, Congress disapproved both the NRPB reports and forced the NRPB itself out of existence. Business set up a postwar planning body of its own, the Committee for Economic Development. Jesse Jones, the

ultra-conservative Texas banker who was both head of the Reconstruction
Finance Corporation and Secretary of Commerce, kindly provided the
fledgling CED with free office space in the Department of Commerce
building in overcrowded Washington.

Liberals were thrown into angry despair over developments like this.
The accomplishments of a decade were, it seemed to them, being trampled
underfoot by the most predatory elements of an avowedly competitive
society. The *New Republic*'s literary editor, Malcolm Cowley, vented
sentiments known to millions when he publicly mourned "The End of the
New Deal" in mid-1943.

Roosevelt himself acknowledged that an era had ended. In 1932 the
nation had been gravely ill, so he had called in Dr. New Deal, he said.
The patient had since recovered, but still needed help, so he had called in
Dr. Win-the-War. A mock-serious obituary soon followed, announcing:
"Death Revealed. The New Deal, aged ten, after long illness; of malnu-
trition and desuetude."

Thus, the New Deal and its fate. In large part it explains why even
thirty years later there is a common assumption that social change and
social welfare advanced little or not at all during the war. But when we
turn to those specifics by which the social welfare of a nation are measured, a different picture emerges.

Conscription provided a rough yardstick for measuring the social
costs of the Depression. Nearly 15 percent of the nation—and that presumably the healthiest, most vigorous part—was examined for military
service. No census had examined so many so thoroughly.

By setting its minimum requirements low, the Army expected to keep
the rejection rate at about 20 percent. During the defense crisis period it
required only a minimum height of 5 feet, minimum weight of 105
pounds, correctable vision, half the natural teeth, no flat feet, no hernias,
no venereal disease. Not a very exacting set of physical requirements for a
rich, modern nation. But rejections were running as high as 70 percent in
some areas in 1941, and the overall rate was 50 percent. Bad teeth and
bad eyes were the two chief causes for rejection, and they could all too
often be traced to malnutrition. Beyond a commonality of diets deficient
in essential vitamins and minerals there was a more fundamental defi-
ciency responsible for this stunning rejection rate—an acute shortage of
basic medical care.

Providing adequate medical care was already difficult in a nation
devoted to commerce, and the Depression had been a tremendous setback.
For a decade the annual production of doctors had remained much the
same from one year to the next. The same was true of dentists. It was also
true of the number of hospital beds. Population had meanwhile increased
by 9,000,000. There were thus fewer medical services per person in 1939
than there had been in 1929. And even though federal public health
expenditures had doubled in that decade, they still came to only 22 cents
a person each year.

The introduction in 1940 of dried, bleached, ground grass to be added to wheat, rye or barley to produce a food fit for human consumption but rich in vitamins for only six cents a pound spoke of a need that literally gnawed at the flesh of millions.

Much of this distress was hidden away in rural areas and small towns. But the cities, where half the population now lived, were usually a menace to public health. They were filthy, pestilential and, for the most part, ugly. The smoke in industrial towns was frequently so thick that daytime traffic could navigate the gloom only with headlights on and all the streetlights blazing. Smog, a word just coming into use, took an economic toll estimated at $3 billion. Industrial urban areas each year labored under a new accumulation of as much as 1,000 tons of fresh soot per square mile. Women's stockings, whether nylon or silk, were commonly pitted and holed by particles of sulfuric acid cast out by smoke-belching chimneys.

The sum of these distresses—the shortage of doctors, dentists and hospitals, the inadequate public health programs, the malnutrition and hunger, the pestilential cities—added up to a staggering health problem. And all were aggravated by the commercialized character of American medicine. Most people wanted something very much like the national health schemes of Scandinavian countries. Most doctors took the position of the American Medical Association, which was characterized by the notion of every man for himself and a fat profit to the tradesman with medicine to sell.

Against the AMA the New Deal had offered only token opposition. A few small-scale federal programs provided health care to the utterly destitute. For the rest, it relied on a modest expansion of public health facilities and looked to the food stamp program to approach the problem obliquely by reducing both farm surpluses and hunger. By combating malnutrition, food stamps would make millions of people less susceptible to the infectious diseases associated with poverty.

Not surprisingly, works like *The Modern Home Medical Adviser* enjoyed a large and profitable sale from year to year. And after Pearl Harbor sales doubled. Patent medicines and home remedies were hoarded on a scale not seen since the end of the frontier. Many a family medicine chest bulged with arnica, eyewash, ipecac and milk of magnesia. Cough drop sales doubled before sugar rationing curtailed production. When German propagandists credited the Third Reich's military prowess to the vitamin-rich diet of its soldiers, a massive demand for synthetic vitamins was created overnight. Before the war ended, an entire mythology had developed, especially around Vitamin B, which was hailed as "The morale vitamin." Besides the large home consumption, employers handed vitamins out to their workers in the hope of raising production.

Hundreds of new community service hospitals and thousands of new clinics were spun off from the economic gains of the pre-Pearl Harbor defense boom. But these badly needed facilities no sooner opened than they began to lose their doctors. By 1943 almost every American community suffered an acute doctor shortage. One news story told of an Albuquerque housewife who was jubilant when a doctor came to her house six hours after she called him: "Good heavens! Imagine calling a doctor and getting him to come over the same day!" A third of the country's doctors were in uniform. And in poor communities tales were rife of babies being delivered by the father or by friends of the family.

At first, the young doctors in whom the military services were most interested effectively resisted appeals to their patriotism. Many had lucrative practices for the first time in their lives. Only after General Hershey threatened to draft them into the Army as private soldiers—promising to keep them at that rank for the duration—did the military acquire the doctors it needed.

By 1943, where there was one doctor for every 100 servicemen, there was one doctor for 3,500 civilians. Those physicians and surgeons tending the civilian population were old or ill or both. Anonymously and courageously many of these men and women literally, if sometimes with rusty skills, worked themselves to death.

The strains on the reduced supply of medical resources at times seemed likely to swamp them. Syphilis and gonorrhea affected 3,000,000 people a year in peacetime. It was predictable that the incidence of those diseases would reach epidemic proportions in wartime, and it did. The world's first hospital devoted exclusively to venereal disease was opened in Chicago in 1942.* Aggravating the epidemics of these and other infectious diseases was the decision to assign nearly all production of penicillin to the military.

Polio also increased spectacularly in wartime. In 1943 the incidence of this disease was twice the prewar rate, reaching epidemic proportions in some states. California alone suffered more than 1,000 cases in a matter of weeks that summer. In 1944 polio was still more virulent, reaping the largest harvest of victims—principally children—since 1916. And no one knew the cause, the means of transmission or the cure. An angry controversy swirled around an Australian physiotherapist named Sister Elizabeth Kenny, who had worked out a system of baths, massages and exercises that were clearly effective. But her theories of why and how her methods worked made little or no sense to doctors engaged in polio research.

Besides physical illness, the country had a staggering incidence of mental illness the dimensions of which were only just beginning to emerge. Psychiatric screening had been almost nonexistent in the First World War. It was far more rigorous this time, yet the rate of admissions to Army hospitals for neuropsychiatric diseases was twice as high. About one-fourth of the teen-agers examined for induction into the military were turned away for psychiatric reasons. And the overall rate of psychiatric rejections was nearly 20 percent, or about seven times the First World War rate.

There was, then, a critical national health problem, exacerbated by the war. Yet, as we shall see, just as matters seemed to reach a breaking point there was a startling reversal. Rather like a person who falls ill, grows more desperately ill yet is ultimately saved by timely, drastic measures, so did the U.S. go from being unhealthy to being very unhealthy

---

* It soon became a landmark for men in search of wayward women, presumably just cured.

to recovering (or as much so as a reasonable distribution of available resources allowed).

An important obstacle to recovery however was the AMA, especially in its ardent opposition to prepaid medical care. It brought lawsuits charging that health insurance plans were a restraint on trade and therefore illegal. The AMA vehemently attacked Blue Shield, a surgical insurance plan comparable to the Blue Cross hospitalization insurance plan begun in 1937. And leading the counterattack to the AMA was not the federal government or a liberal social reformer, but none other than that preeminent businessman-hero of the war, Henry J. Kaiser.

Probably the place where the health crisis was most acute and most immediate was in the war industries. War plants were burdened with 4-F's, dangerous machinery, unsanitary conditions. Many were located in squalid, overcrowded boom towns where the menace of epidemics was ever-present. But the more than 125,000 war workers employed by Kaiser were enrolled in a health plan which, for a few cents each day, provided every one of them and their families with excellent medical care. Alongside every Kaiser shipyard or assembly line there was invariably a modern hospital or clinic.

Other companies launched comparable plans, and the Farm Security Agency had operated a similar plan of its own in rural areas in the 1930's. But with Kaiser they were a passion. He waged a national publicity campaign for prepaid medical care for everyone. He argued endlessly that a healthy, worry-free work force was a positive aid to production and pointed to his shipyards as proof. Kaiser, however, was not simply a pragmatically minded businessman, but a social crusader with a business background. It was also said that he had a strong personal grievance against the medical establishment, that he believed his mother had died prematurely because she could not afford simple medical care.

Kaiser had been experimenting with health programs for years before the war began. His current system was thus ambitious, proved and potentially very popular. Each of the clinics and hospitals was staffed with a balanced team of specialists, carrying group medicine to new levels of practice. Preventive medicine was practiced, with vaccinations, inoculations and periodic physical checkups being provided at nominal charges. House calls were free. Ambulance service and outside consultants were provided at reasonable prices. By 1943 Kaiser was operating the biggest prepaid medical plan in the country. The AMA bitterly assailed it, calling it "contract medicine," and opened a private war on Kaiser's clinics.

Doctors who worked in them were threatened with expulsion from the association; to show its sincerity, one was expelled. Where doctors took up group practice on the Kaiser model, they found local hospitals closed to them. There were long legal battles. Local draft boards were pressured, sometimes with apparent success, into reclassifying and drafting Kaiser's doctors. There was a national publicity campaign charging that Kaiser was bribing doctors into mollycoddling his workers, the result of which was that wounded soldiers were going without medical attention.

Kaiser stubbornly refused to give ground. And the AMA was soundly defeated in the courts. The Justice Department brought its own antitrust suit against the AMA. The harassment of doctors in group practice resulted in the conviction of the AMA leadership for illegal conspiracy. So Kaiser's plan was saved. Beyond that, the AMA gave up the fight against health insurance. In the next few years Blue Cross and Blue Shield would enroll tens of millions of subscribers. It would still be true, as one writer said in 1943, that "The cost of complete medical care is outrageous. It is bearable only by the rich." Yet, thanks in large part to Kaiser's crusade, a major advance had nevertheless been scored.

The war had also brought a more rational, more effective, more just distribution of the country's medical resources. There were still 8,000,000 people receiving food stamps a year after Pearl Harbor, but the emphasis had shifted from simply feeding people to making sure that they had properly balanced diets. In war plants, when large numbers of women were employed, sanitary and safety conditions often improved dramatically: Hot meals were provided, heavy work was simplified or mechanized; women workers were given complete physical examinations at company expense. Dentists had recently discovered the decay-resisting properties of fluoride, and some towns were putting it into their drinking water.

In the boom towns the federal government financed the construction of new clinics and hospitals and found doctors and nurses to staff them. The experience of Seneca, Illinois, was typical of hundreds of boom towns. The U.S. Public Health Service set up a community health center. The local hospital was expanded with the aid of a government grant. A PHS nurse was assigned to the town and she supervised immunization drives, school health services, first-aid classes—none of which had ever been seen before in Seneca. Both of the town's prewar physicians had been drafted. Yet never had its citizens been so healthy.

A small revolution, in fact, had been worked in the nation's health even though nearly all its youngest, best-trained doctors were in uniform. In the state of Indiana, for example, public health had improved beyond all expectation. Typhoid fever, scarlet fever, tuberculosis, diphtheria and pneumonia dropped to unprecedentedly low levels. The typical diseases of infancy, such as measles and whooping cough, dropped off sharply. In the country at large, the war saw a drop in the death rate and a rise in the birthrate. People were eating more, and eating more sensibly. And the improvement in the health of children was so marked that their elders were amazed.

One of the reasons for the improvement in health was that some 16,000,000 men and many of their dependents were the beneficiaries of what was, in effect, a short-term program of socialized medicine. About half the men examined for induction needed immediate medical care. Nearly 2,000,000 were salvaged for military service at government expense. Military authorities put nutritionists to work ensuring that menus provided a balanced diet. Army doctors fitted millions with glasses, made the fat lose weight, built up the undernourished, performed minor corrective surgery. The Army Dental Corps had many of its stations working around the clock. At government expense tens of millions of teeth were saved; hundreds of thousands of dental plates and bridges were installed.

People were also better able to provide for themselves. During the Depression medical expenditures had dropped by a third. Most people were forced to cut back heavily on what they spent on doctors, dentists, health insurance and prescriptions. But now that they had money to spare, they were spending it freely on their health. Before the war ended, the amount spent on purchasing accident and health insurance was up 100 percent over the 1939 level.

Whereas the number of doctors and dentists had changed hardly at all during the Depression, the number graduated in 1944 was twice that of any prewar year. The number of hospital beds per 1,000 people increased only marginally during the 1930's; during the war it rose 50 percent. Federal, state and local government expenditures on health meanwhile went from several hundred million in 1939 to more than $1.1 billion in 1945. With these increased resources there also went, as we have seen, a fairer and more effective utilization.

The results were as astonishing as they were welcome. Life expectancy had altered hardly at all, for either race or both sexes, between 1932 and 1939. But in the six years from 1939 to 1945 there was an overall increase of three years. For blacks it was five years. At the same time, the death rate for infants under one year of age per 1,000 live births (which is a common index of public health standards and general economic conditions) was cut by more than a third, from 48 to 31 per 1,000. The 1942 overall death rate of 10.3 per 1,000 people was the lowest in the country's history.

Even the war's cost in combat dead and wounded could not blunt the great advance in America's physical health. Some 292,000 men were killed in battle; another 671,000 were wounded. It was a painful loss. The premature death of so many young men weighs heavily; the grief of their families and friends should never be discounted. Yet the effect on the overall death rate was small. They represented less than 5 percent of all the Americans who died between Pearl Harbor and the end of the war.*

Social insurance is nearly always thought of in terms of special programs set up by government in a direct and explicit attempt to relieve individual distress; unemployment compensation is a typical example. But in a country where central government is strong, yet centralized administration is weak, that view is too narrow to deal with the realities. By European standards American social policy has long been Victorian in its petty cruelties and structural inadequacies. Recent crises have done much to justify the critics. What has gone unappreciated is the fact that the American approach has, until recently, been possible because it has been better able to preclude distress than to alleviate it, and do we not all say that prevention is better than cure? And that was what occurred in the 1940's. It was done in a uniquely American way; it is probably unrepeatable. But for a generation it worked.

* I calculate that from December, 1941, to August, 1945, inclusive, some 5,231,000 deaths were recorded in the United States. For raw data see the 1947 edition of *Statistical Abstract of the U.S.*

Unemployment, the scourge of the thirties, was a thing of the past, the fear of the future. Jeff Davies, the president of Hoboes of America, Inc., filed his annual report with Indiana authorities in 1942 and reported that all 2,000,000 members were "off the road." Some were in uniform; more than half a million were in war industries. Those few who were still on the road or riding the rods were not hoboes, Davies sneered. "They're just bums."

In retirement towns like San Diego and Long Beach up to 40 percent of the retirees went back to work. The country was literally sweeping the streets for labor as urban police forces rounded up skid row denizens, screened them for useful skills and offered suspended sentences to those who would go to work. Midgets were employed as aircraft inspectors, being able to crawl inside wings and other cramped spaces. Deaf-mutes were employed in factory areas where machinery noise was intolerable to others. Handicapped workers generally were, for once, welcomed by employers. Ford, for instance, had a wartime work force 10 percent of which was blind, deaf or crippled.

Farmers no longer brutalized migrant workers. Instead, they welcomed them with open arms—when they could find them. Big-farm interests demanded unrestricted immigration of Mexican *braceros*, and nearly 200,000 Mexicans and West Indians were brought into the country.

Everywhere the shortage of labor made itself felt. A Manhattan restaurant chain posted signs reading, "Please be polite to our waitresses. They are harder to get than customers." A shortage of mailmen inspired the Post Office to start zoning and numbering the nation's cities. Child labor started to make a comeback, often with the explicit encouragement of conservative state governments which used the present emergency to set aside anti-child-labor laws. By the summer of 1943 nearly 3,000,000 youngsters aged twelve to seventeen were at work.

Even the pathetic Okies and Arkies chronicled by Steinbeck were no longer pariahs. Farmers sought them out and offered them living wages. But they were leaving the land at last, drifting into war industries. The Okies and other poor white migrants were still stock figures of contempt and derision. They were still taunted as being stupid, shiftless, ignorant and dirty. West Coast shipyard urinals were nicknamed "Okie drinking fountains." The Okies struck back by writing on lavatory walls:

> The miners came in '49
> The whores in '51
> And when they fucked each other
> They begot the Native Son.

Yet when all was said and done, the poor white migrants (of whom there had been more than 4,000,000 in 1939) were passing into the lower-middle and skilled working classes; they acquired new skills, new attitudes, bank accounts and permanent homes. They were becoming urbanized, sending their children to school, and year by year throughout the war their old life lost its hold on them.

But a cloud hung over the humming factories and fields. It preyed on people's minds even as they worked. For with war production at its peak, when asked what would be the principal problem of the postwar period, only 13 percent said a lasting peace, while 58 percent said jobs.* The National Resources Planning Board had projected postwar unemployment would reach 8,000,000 to 9,000,000. The Department of Labor predicted 12,000,000 to 15,000,000 unemployed. And by the summer of 1944, with some factories already cutting back, federal officials were forced to devise make-work expedients to maintain full employment. This was the pall that hung over all the social gains of wartime. But for the moment everyone who wanted a job could find one, and the immediate problem was not how to make a living but how to make living more pleasant.

Boom-town life, wretched before Pearl Harbor, often became still more miserable after it. By universal agreement the worst of everything could be found in Willow Run, Michigan, where most of the plant's 42,000 workers would rather commute 60 miles each day than live in the squalid camp of trailers and temporary shelters that had sprung up about it, complete with dysentery and periodic typhoid scares. Years afterward, when the question was raised of how war industries should be decentralized, one authority wrote: "Willow Run supplied some answers by demonstrating with impressive finality how not to do the job." But Willow Run exemplified wartime living at its worst, not its most typical.

Federal agencies had been working since 1940 to ease the miseries of boom-town life, and after Pearl Harbor the Community Facilities Act (popularly known as the Lanham Act, after its sponsor) provided an effective instrument. The Federal Works Agency was authorized to provide money for nursery schools, child-care centers, clinics, elementary- and secondary-school expansion, the construction of recreation facilities and almost anything else for which a war-created need could be shown. In this way, thousands of U.S. towns and villages got new schools, playgrounds, clinics, community centers, all completely paid for out of federal funds. The gain to each community and to the country as a whole was enormous. Many of those wartime creations are even now in daily use. Of all the countries at war only in America was there such as awesome rebuilding of physical plant while the war was still under way.

All this was improvised. It was treated and looked upon as something temporary and unimportant. Certainly it did not come within the ambit of explicitly planned social reform, and for that reason it was invisible to most liberal reformers. For all the credit attached to it, it may as well have been nonexistent. The advocates of planning loudly despaired that the country was edging its way willy-nilly into disaster.

What planning there was for the postwar world took for its object not something avowedly aimed at social welfare but the provision of veterans' benefits for 16,000,000 servicemen and their families. It was not thought of as a program of social welfare in the traditional mold. It was seen principally as a payment for services rendered.

Soldiers' bonuses had, in the course of three wars, become overwhelmingly unpopular. Roosevelt himself had vetoed two bonus acts.

---

* Interestingly, most workers thought *they* would still be working; other people would be laid off.

When he made his first public address after a six months' silence in 1943, he made provisions for veterans the subject of his speech. His proposals looked to providing education, improved hospitalization and rehabilitation programs, more generous pensions for the disabled and other measures to help veterans get ahead instead of just paying them off. Congress took a similar approach, as did most veterans' organizations.

The biggest of these, the American Legion, drew up its own plan and submitted it to Congress as an omnibus bill. It combined every one of the measures others had proposed, except for a bonus. The object of its bill, said the Legion, was the readjustment of the veterans to civilian life, calling its proposal "a bill of rights for G.I. Joe and G. I. Jane." Eighty Senators rushed to attach their names to it before it appeared on the floor, and most of the remaining sixteen complained that they had not been given a fair chance to do likewise.

The administration was not entirely blind to the potential of veterans' benefits in advancing social welfare. Some of Roosevelt's staff tried to link these benefits to the needs of the entire nation. But Roosevelt would not fight for them. A handful of New Dealers fought against the principle of veterans' exclusiveness, without the support of the White House. The Legion was therefore under no serious pressure to compromise, and its bill passed almost intact. Liberals mourned it as a great opportunity lost. Yet, as we shall see, the GI Bill still represented an unprecedented achievement.

Veterans were returning in large numbers long before the war ended. These first returnees were usually war-wounded or combat heroes, like Pittsburgh's "Commando" Kelly, credited with killing forty Germans at Salerno. He went to the White House to receive the Medal of Honor. His hometown honored him with a parade, and one excited citizen threw him a three-foot length of salami. But most of the homecomings were not like this. Many were touched with a bitter hostility.

Nasty incidents between civilians and returning veterans kept breaking out, especially in overcrowded trains, restaurants and buses. A soldier at Camp Shelby, Mississippi, wrote a poem called "Back Home," expressing sentiments commonly found around Army bases:

> Money and liquor and girls
> They are grabbing for all they are worth.
> Why do the swine get the pearls
> And the meek inherit the Earth?

Football hero and fighter pilot Tom Harmon returned to Detroit after being shot down in China and told the crowd that turned out to cheer his safe return that they made him ashamed. On their heads he wished the descent of enemy bombs.

Civilians were nervously defensive, squirming at any mention of relative sacrifices. "The fighters of course suffer far greater perils, pains and hardships" was a typical remark. It was a half-truth at best, for only one serviceman in ten was ever exposed to combat. For the rest, they were in no more danger than they would have been at home. With an overall death rate of 5 per 1,000 the military was a safer place to be than at home, where the death rate was more than twice as high and where the death and injury rates were higher still in war industries.

The frictions were also aggravated by the high proportion of neuropsychiatric cases among the men being discharged. These men should never had been inducted, but they were. Once they had been discharged, they were not always averse to hiding the reasons for their separations from duty and to creating fictitious combat records.

Readjustment, despite the aid of a grateful nation, often proved to be rocky. The last year of the war brought the ominous phenomenon of the veterans who turned to crime, frequently violent crime. Unable to settle down, troubled by physical or mental illness, they invariably pleaded when caught that America did not appreciate what they had done for it. Police and courts could not have been more sympathetic. A Chicago judge typically sentenced a veteran convicted of armed robbery and serious bodily harm to just six months in prison. Passing sentence, he said, "We will try to forget the crime you have committed and remember what you have done for your country." People were less worried at such leniency than they were at the prospect of what was in store if millions of the returning veterans took this man's path.

By the spring of 1944 a million veterans had returned to civilian life. Veterans often felt cut off from the security of military life; they found themselves adrift in a hostile, alien environment which was without obvious regularity, discipline, authority and predictability. They missed the comradeship of service life. All too often their friends and relatives seemed remote, stupid, lackadaisical inhabitants of a world they no longer knew as their own. Their old jobs seemed pointless and boring. Congress, thinking it was doing what the veterans wanted, required employers to restore these men to their former jobs. But 70 percent did not want them. Thanks to the GI Bill, they now had a good chance to prepare for better-paying, more interesting work. Or they could go into business for themselves backed by government-guaranteed loans.

More and more men were showing up on city streets short of a limb. Most were victims of industrial accidents, but unless an amputee was very old or very young, he was tacitly assumed to be a combat veteran. There were also persistent rumors that the military was hiding away hundreds, perhaps thousands, of multiple amputees, especially quadruple amputees, callously nicknamed "basket cases." In vain did military officials deny them. One man wrote to *Time*: "There is a whole ward of the ————— hospital devoted to these pitiful [basket] cases. They are brought in at night so the squeamish public will not know they exist." *

Most amputees were annoyed; not without cause. They endured the torments of prosthetics which had not been improved on since the Civil War. Plastics, fiber glass, lightweight alloys may as well not have existed so far as prosthetics manufacturers were concerned. An artificial arm, for example, weighed 10 pounds. These false limbs, besides being clumsy and uncomfortable, were very expensive. And the demand far exceeded

---

* There were, in truth, only two such cases in all: one caused by an accident, the other resulting from combat.

the supply. There were 17,000 military amputees. Industrial accidents in the war years produced over 100,000 more. Polio contributed its thousands of victims. Amputees were commonly simply given some money, then told to go and buy an artificial limb, if they could find one.

The Veterans Administration found this and a host of other sins laid at its door. Returning veterans waxed wrathful over what they considered the VA's heartless, bureaucratic approach to their problems. The medical care it provided was dismissed as being third-rate. VA officials pleaded that they were simply swamped: Their work load had increased 400 percent over the levels of the First World War, but their work force was no bigger. Angry Congressmen brushed the rejoinders aside and brandished letters from their constituents in VA hospitals: "I refused to eat the food because it wasn't fit for a dog." "Personally I would much rather be on Iwo Jima." It was a cause for national rejoicing when the head of the VA since 1920 was fired in 1945 and replaced by General Omar Bradley. For the country sincerely wanted to treat its returning veterans, if not as heroes, at least as men who had fought a just war with honor and courage.

America certainly did not let the veterans down. If anything, it turned them into a privileged group. But it was, when veterans' dependents were included, a group so large that it enhanced, and was enhanced by, a powerful wartime trend to the creation of a genuine middle-class democracy. It was one of the most remarkable and successful instances of social welfare without Socialism.

This war's veterans were provided for by legislation going back to 1940. Ever since then, more and more benefits had been added. By 1945 a grateful nation would help a veteran buy a home, set himself up in business, take up farming, go to college, learn a trade, finish high school or get a government job. Those in small business had access to a billion dollars' worth of surplus government property. Veterans and their families could be buried at government expense in government cemeteries. Millions of these families carried inexpensive, government-subsidized life insurance. To federal benefits, the states, municipalities and private organizations added their own. There was also a bonus—though it was never called that—which amounted to $1,300 and was supposed to ease the return to civilian life. Twenty-one states also gave their own bonuses, totaling $2.4 billion.

Though not explicitly a program of social welfare, the results were the same as if it had been. Veterans' benefits were a variety of Socialism that, counting the 16,000,000 veterans and their families, by 1950 embraced approximately one-third of the total population. The true nature of veterans' programs was occasionally acknowledged. The purpose of the loan program was said to be primarily to help veterans readjust by buying homes or businesses. But second, "to help overcome the national housing deficit," a deficit which by 1945 ran to millions of units. Ten years later some 4,300,000 home loans had been granted, with a face value of $33 billion. Veterans' loans accounted for 20 percent of all the new homes built in the decade after the war. Nearly 8,000,000 veterans went back to school or learned a trade or went to college under the GI Bill.

They represented an infusion of $14.5 billion in federal money into the nation's schools and colleges by 1955.

The total money cost of veterans' benefits cannot be computed precisely. But excluding insurance dividends, surplus property and intangibles such as Civil Service preference, $50 billion is a conservative minimum estimate. To date, the entire sum is probably twice that amount.

No status group of comparable size prospered as did veterans after the war. They did not, could not, see themselves as the recipients of welfare programs. To the largess spread before them they brought not the sullen, self-destroying agonies of welfare clients but the assertive, self-respecting attitudes of people whose claims are based on having earned, not simply deserved, what they received. It was a very middle-class program, all the more effective for the disguise that it wore. And now, in the professional and managerial ranks, the veterans of World War II are represented out of all proportion to their numbers in the total population. They have, on the average, three years more formal education than the average nonveteran of the same age. The GI Bill more than made up for the wartime deficits in training lawyers, doctors, engineers, teachers and other highly trained persons. Today war veterans make more money, are more likely to own their own homes, and their families are better fed and better educated than the nonveterans of their own age. They and their children are the bedrock of America's modern middle class.

It was with good reason that Roosevelt had included housing in his pithy summary of social distress when he saw a third of the nation ill-fed, ill-clothed, ill-housed. The administration had saved millions of homes from foreclosure through the HOLC. Rural electrification programs had brought light into millions of homes. The Farm Security Administration had striven valiantly to improve sanitation in rural homes. But throughout the New Deal years the government fought a losing battle with the housing problem.

During the twenties more than 7,000,000 new nonfarm dwellings were constructed; during the thirties construction fell by nearly two-thirds. Population grew while the existing housing stock deteriorated. Between 1932 and 1939 public agencies financed the construction of only 23,000 new homes. Just as war began in Europe, an administration request for $800,000,000 to make a serious assault on the problem of low-cost housing was rejected by Congress. It was a gloomy prospect indeed. About half the housing in the United States was in need of major repairs or was a menace to health, and there was an overall shortage of 4,000,000 to 5,000,000 units.

"The picture is one of barriers built up from every side," wrote a housing expert. "The housing industry in 1940 remained in the grip of ancient traditions. No trends visible in that year showed sufficient strength to promise any radical break from these traditions for perhaps another decade." Then "The impact of war speeded up the rate of industrial change. [It] brought about increased efficiency in the design of dwellings, in the use of materials in building dwellings, and in the building processes themselves. At the same time government orders permitted producers to by-pass many of the obstacles existing in the private market."

The results were evident before the war ended. From 1933 to 1939 roughly 1,500,000 new houses were built, few of them, as mentioned above, with public financing. In the next six years, to 1945, despite the wartime shortages of materials and labor nearly 3,000,000 houses were built; more than 600,000 of them were publicly financed, an increase of nearly thirty-fold. Wartime prosperity also saw the number of houses owned by those who lived in them jump from 15,000,000 in 1940 to 20,000,000 in 1945.

That prosperity, carrying over into the postwar era, fueled a housing boom that, in conjunction with the veterans' programs, saw the housing problem solved within another decade. Ironically, the United States was the only Allied country which did not have a set of housing policies for the postwar world to offer as an incentive to its people to endure the rigors of wartime. There was no overall housing plan. Yet it was the United States which was the first to solve its housing problem.

Women posed a special problem in wartime. They were supposed to be cosseted as tradition required. But they were also the country's largest labor reserve. Though employers were cool to the idea, sooner or later they would have to put women into war work if the Victory Program were to meet its targets. By the fall of 1943, with war production at its peak, 17,000,000 women made up a third of the total work force, and of those about 5,000,000 were in war industries. In some plants, particularly the airplane factories, women did most of the work while men did most of the supervising. The bombers and fighters which pounded Japanese and German cities were predominantly built by American women. Yet there was a lingering notion that they were unwilling to go into the factories. Unfavorable comparisons were drawn with the women of Russia and Britain. *Life* jeered:

AMERICAN WOMEN
Draft Them? Too Bad We Can't
Draft Their Grandmothers

But they were, in truth, working harder than they had ever worked, at home and elsewhere. They did heavier and more dangerous work than they had ever done. On jobs which did not require unusual muscular strength women proved to be more productive than men, *if* they were kept happy. Often enough that was difficult to do. For too many were trying to work full time and still run a home. One woman sarcastically replied to the question of why more women did not go into war work: "Because they don't have wives."

Industry was caught unprepared for this wartime influx of women workers. The telephone and insurance companies had, in recent years, been studying menstruation as a work problem. But industry had not. Rare was the factory manager who was prepared for tears, dermatitis, jewelry and child-care worries. Hastily they scraped up countermeasures. For the dermatitis, special creams were handed out. For the tears, sympathetic women counselors were hired. For the jewelry, there was an absolute ban. And for the children, there were full-time nurseries, at nominal cost. Clean, comfortable washrooms were installed. Lessons on diet, grooming and posture were offered. There were education and recreation programs. Cafeterias, rest periods, vitamin pills, periodic physical examinations, free inoculations—all followed women into the factories. The few plants which had offered these things before the war were considered radical; suddenly they were commonplace.

Employers were forced to make adjustments and grumbled endlessly about them, especially about the rest periods which most states began to require by law. Most of the changes, however, worked to the advantage of workers generally, for they usually resulted in safer, cleaner plants. Even then, war work was dangerous. One highly educated woman working in a munitions plant finished her stint with burned hands and a badly gashed face. Of the 10,000 workers in the plant where she worked, some 200 were injured on the average working day.

Women were also susceptible to fears that war work was harmful. It was widely believed that heavy work increased the chances of breast cancer. Rosie the Riveter was supposedly prone to a mysterious ailment called "Riveter's arm." There was also a new malady called "Riveter's ovaries," supposedly caused by excessive vibration. But the greatest barrier to counteracting the tears and absenteeism was not the fearful rumors but unequal treatment.

As one woman worker pointedly said, "No working woman (in whatever line of work) labors under the delusion that any woman is actually, either socially or economically, equal to men in the U.S. in 1944." It was federal government policy that women should be paid the same as men for doing the same work. But it was an open secret that the policy was never implemented except by accident or as a token. That was true even in the eight federally owned and operated shipyards. The highest pay for women working in these yards was $6.95 a day; for men, $22 a day. Most women earned the bare minimum, $4.65 a day. Sanitary conditions were often poor and the rest periods theoretical. And no matter how long or how hard they worked, the chances of women being promoted into the better, or better-paying, jobs were virtually nonexistent.

In vain did women war workers look to organized labor to help them. Of the 15,000,000 union members at the end of 1944 about 1 in 5 was a woman. But most union organizers and much of the leadership considered women a threat to the other four-fifths of the membership. Women had gone into war work in the earlier war, and by 1918 of every 1,000 workers in war plants 139 were women; those gains had not been reversed, so that in 1939 the figure was 135 per 1,000. With women now constituting a third of the war industry work force, male workers were apprehensive indeed. The country as a whole when asked if women should surrender their jobs to returning soldiers said yes by more than four to one. "Americans may no longer believe that a woman's place is in the home. But more important, we believe even less that a man's place is on the street without a job," concluded one observer. And most women agreed.

But as the war drew to a close, many women workers surrendered their jobs with the greatest reluctance. Their families had come to rely on the money they earned. A new sense of independence had taken root once they were earning money of their own. And the war had opened up all manner of opportunities, not just in the factories but throughout the economy. Even before the end of 1942 one journal observed, "There is hardly any job that women cannot get if they want them. . . ." Many a predominantly male bastion crumbled. By 1944 *Editor and Publisher* estimated that the 8,000 editors and reporters in uniform had been replaced by 8,000 women. Dozens of the smaller papers, in fact, were almost fully staffed by women. Nine of the country's major symphony orchestras each had ten or more women musicians. The New York Stock Exchange in 1943 hired the first female clerk in its history, turning half of Wall Street apoplectic.

The Army and Navy had likewise succumbed. When the Women's Auxiliary Army Corps was established in the summer of 1942 less than 500 officer openings brought 50,000 applications in a matter of days. The Navy established the WAVES—Women Accepted for Volunteer Emergency Service. The Marines, who had accepted female recruits in the First World War for clerical work, followed suit. But to them a marine was a marine, regardless of sex, and they steadfastly refused to give female marines a separate names, such as mariness, she-marine, femarine or marina, all of which were suggested by civilians.

The WAAC's (shortened to WAC's with the dropping of "Auxiliary" in 1943) were at first the very byword for military glamor. They completely overshadowed the elite paratroop division which was being formed at the same time. But the WAC was dogged by rumors of promiscuity. It was widely believed that thousands were illegitimately pregnant. The rumors kept interest high but enlistments low. Enlistments were further discouraged by the dull, dusty-looking uniform. The WAC hoped to have 150,000 women at its peak, but it never numbered more than 60,000.

All-women ROTC units were meanwhile set up at Smith and the University of New Hampshire. These provided officers for the WAC's and the WAVES. There were also more than 1,000 WASP's—Women's Auxiliary Service Pilots. They ferried planes, towed targets, flew weather observation flights and generally released male pilots for more dangerous work.

In all, more than 100,000 American women were in military uniform during the war. But some military men never became entirely reconciled to it. One marine officer, told that women were being posted to his camp, was said to have cursed, "Goddamn it all. First they send us dogs. Now it's women."

Other women were knitting for servicemen and rolling bandages for the Red Cross. Volunteer all-women fire brigades appeared in scores of small towns. An American Women's Volunteer Service came into existence, patterned after the British WVS. Its 260,000 members drove trucks, navigated for military convoys, made maps, chauffered Army and Navy officers, taught housewives what to do during an air raid and manned information centers for the Air Warning Service.

The American Legion's female auxiliary, with 2,500,000 members, snorted derisively at other women-come-latelies: "We see this emergency a little more clearly than the others. . . . We stand ready." And when 10,000 women doing volunteer war work showed up for a parade down Fifth Avenue in 1942, there were so many organizations represented, each with its own uniform, that no one managed to keep track of which was which.

Had the feminist movement been as strong at the beginning of this war as it had been in 1914 it could doubtless have scored great gains, as it had then. But the Depression had absorbed whatever energies people had for social protest, and feminism, though still alive, was not vibrant in 1939. Lacking its earlier leadership and organizational base, it could not capitalize on the wartime gains. There was nothing comparable to the impassioned movement of the pre-World War I suffragettes to press home the wartime opportunities and capitalize on the new importance of women, to turn a temporary advantage into permanent gain. Dorothy Thompson was demanding that the postwar world be reorganized on "feminine principles." Eleanor Roosevelt provided inspiration and example, as ever. But these were voices from the mountaintop. No one was working down below.

Thus are great opportunities lost. By 1944 there were a dozen women in the House and one in the Senate. More than 100 of the Democratic Party's county chairmen were women, compared with 12 in 1940. At both the nominating conventions that year more than 25 percent of the Republican and Democratic delegates were women. Usually they made up less than 10 percent. Both major parties incorporated into their platforms the Equal Rights Amendment that the National Woman's Party had been pressing for for years. But once the election was over and the men started to return from the war, the amendment was allowed to die a natural death.

Anyway, most women were currently less interested in equal rights than they were in the shortage of men. One mourned:

> Of all sad words of tongue or pen
> The saddest are these: there are no men.

Widows were told by the president of the Widows and Widowers Clubs that it was their duty "to keep love alert for the duration." She conceded that that was no easy task. For while "it used to be that a woman could get any man she liked, now she has to like any man she can get." The response to "Don't Sit Under the Apple Tree with Anyone Else but Me" was a song called "They're Either Too Young or Too Old," which plaintively concluded "I *can't* sit under the apple tree with anyone else but me."

Probably the most poignant sight in wartime America was the "strange, unorganized home-front battle being fought all over the U.S. by a vast, unorganized army of women. They are the wives, mothers, sweethearts or fiancees of servicemen. Their only plan of campaign is to follow their men." For many, perhaps most, the only married life they had ever known was built around suitcases, rented rooms, frequent good-byes, packed trains and buses, soaring prices and low, fixed incomes, missed connections, exorbitant rents and unscheduled changes in military orders.

These women more often than not were disheveled and careworn, dressed in mismatched odds and ends that happened to be handy when the time came to pack. On their coats they sported costume jewelry denoting which service their men were in. About one in five seemed to be pregnant at any given time. But they all refused to be deterred. These women seemed to mix easily, sharing whatever they had to make this nomadic life more bearable. Long before the war ended, they were the saddest and the most predictable feature of the crowded train stations and bus terminals in the great cities.

At one time or another almost all the women under forty were caught up in this migration. They were more self-aware, more self-reliant than their mothers had been. But above all, they were lonely. The tensions and separations of wartime had created in them one overwhelming desire: to settle down and have children. Very few by 1945 wanted anything else.

As with the Depression, a disproportionate share of war's social strains was shouldered by America's children and adolescents. Pearl Harbor was not a year past before there were hundreds of thousands of "eight-hour orphans" roaming the streets of the boom towns, latchkeys often tied to a string around their necks. Tens of thousands more children were locked inside automobiles in war-plant parking lots. Still others could be found in trailer camps chained to the family trailer by a length of chain, much like dogs. Unlicensed, unregulated nurseries sprang up. Tales of squalor, brutality and child molesting clung to many of these places, and not all the stories could be wrong.

Here was a national child welfare problem at its worst. But the chief manifestation of it was a staggering rise in juvenile delinquency. The delinquency usually involved vice or violence. Of the two, vice was the more obvious.

The bus depots of the larger cities and towns were crowded with teen-age girls variously called Victory Girls, Patriotutes, Cuddle Bunnies and Round-Heels. Hauled in by the police, they protested that they were performing a patriotic service, maintaining military morale. Some were as young as twelve years old. There are no unimpeachable figures, but it seems clear that vice by girls was more common than violence by boys.

Nor were servicemen the only recipients of adolescent favors. Federal housing projects spawned "wolf packs"—clubs for teen-agers where girls seeking admission paid their dues by copulating with every male member. One determined young initiate joined a club with ninety boys. A New York City court in 1943 tried and convicted a seventeen-year-old girl named Josephine Tencza for running a vice ring of thirty young hookers aged twelve to fifteen catering to a clientele of middle-aged men. Older, more established practitioners fiercely resented the competition. A San

Antonio social worker reported, "The girls are sore as all get-out. They say the young chippies who work for a beer and a sandwich are cramping their style." The head of Vassar's Child-Study Department was more sympathetic. To her, these young girls were really "war casualties."

Much of the problem could be traced to the fact that there was no explicit place in the war effort for youngsters below draft age. There was also the parental neglect attendant on the wartime disruptions of everyday life. And juvenile delinquency not only rose steadily during the war, but was growing uglier and more violent. There was a growing callousness that made it possible for twelve adolescents to rape a seventeen-year-old girl in a crowded movie house in the Bronx in 1943 without one of the patrons moving to interfere. In 1944 two girls aged eleven and thirteen cold-bloodedly planned and then carried out the ritual execution of a nine-year-old in a New York schoolyard during the morning recess. Again, no one interfered. These days schoolteachers in the city were terrified. They begged, then through their union demanded, that policemen be placed in the schools. La Guardia scoffed that they were exaggerating the dangers—until a teacher was tortured to death in her classroom.

It was this evident readiness to employ deadly force that was the most frightening feature of the youth gangs which sprang up during the war in most big cities. This was the first zip-gun generation. The gangs, organized on racial and ethnic lines, waged pitched battles in the streets with as many as a hundred participants to a side.

Younger children were showing an ominous propensity to vandalism. An El Paso movie house manager was confronted nightly by so many marijuana-smoking, rebellious young patrons that he literally armed himself to the teeth and patrolled his theater like a one-man army. After he had been thrown out of his own establishment several times, he dressed for work each night in a Sam Browne belt complete with a .38-caliber automatic and three clips of ammunition; a bone-breaking device called an "iron claw"; a blackjack; a pair of handcuffs; a shiny police-type badge; and, "on extra busy nights," a 24-inch police nightstick in one hand and a long, heavy flashlight in the other.

Zoot suits had meanwhile gone from being the fad of harmless jitterbuggers to being the uniform of young thugs organized in street gangs. Youth dances frequently ended up as free-for-alls. To the standard zoot suit accessories there had been added an ornate switchblade knife for boys and a whiskey flask shaped to fit inside a brassiere for girls.

Some communities tried to curb delinquency by simply imposing a curfew. Others tried more positive measures, such as "Teen Canteens." A few tried a combination of restraint and diversion. The High School Victory Corps also managed to siphon off some of the excessive youthful energies into parades, scrap drives, bond sales and physical education. But there were any number of cities with mayors like La Guardia, who cut the number of city-operated parks from 400 to 35 despite social workers' warnings that he was aggravating delinquency; opposed child-care programs ("The worst mother is better than the best nursery school"); and said, "Let the police deal with juvenile delinquency. There is no need for after-school programs to keep children off the streets."

Ironically, despite the current rise in youthful violence, the streets had become safer than ever and property was more secure. Adult crime rates dropped, and the big prisons holding the most dangerous prisoners—like San Quentin, Sing Sing and Folsom—lost up to half their inmates.

Gradually the rising tide of delinquency was turned as the initial hard-nosed attitudes proved futile. The era of physical fitness programs and scrap drives gave way to a new phase in which the rudiments of an adolescent subculture asserted themselves. Social recreation schemes meshed easily with the demand of adolescents to have something of their own. Social centers, glamorized as counterparts to servicemen's "canteens," were established in thousands of American communities in the last two years of the war. Dances, swimming parties, jam sessions, table tennis tournaments—every kind of recreation short of sexual intercourse or drinking was encouraged. Public and private money poured into these centers with names like "The Rec," "Coke Bar," "Club Victory" and "Teentown Night Club." Adults launched most of the centers; soft-drink manufacturers underwrote many of them. But everyday operation was predominantly exercised by the patrons, who were usually high school students.

The upshot was the creation of a new social phenomenon: the teenager. Before the war there had been children and adults. Now there was an entirely new category of social and individual identities that had sprung up between them. By the time the war ended, advertising, clothing styles, sociological surveys, scores of magazine articles and considerable parental interest revolved about this novel subculture. Where women's magazines had traditionally catered to the mature woman, the new need had spawned *Seventeen, Mademoiselle* and *Glamour.* The *Saturday Evening Post* waxed angry over the development of "Your generation" and "Our generation" and demanded to know, "Who Made Our Youngsters 'Generation' Conscious?" hinting darkly that it was another left-wing initiative.

It was, in truth, an extraordinary act of social regeneration. Yet among the nation's elders there was a profound pessimism. One sensitive woman reporter pitied the youngsters. They were too young to go into the Army, they had been generally left to fend for themselves, and the loftiest role they had been offered in the war effort was to collect junk. The famed sociologist Robert Lynd thought it was "a hell of a world for kids to be trying to grow up in." He prophesied a new Lost Generation. La Guardia grimly forecast such massive postwar unemployment that it might be the better part of wisdom not to train this violence-prone younger generation for anything but menial jobs. When the inevitable disappointment of high expectations set in, he said, they would turn on society and ravage it. And a noted psychiatrist predicted such an orgy of violence and wildness in the postwar world that it would make the Jazz Age look timid and introspective in comparison.

Yet there was also at least one authority who saw the war as being "far better for adolescents than Depression; for it does meet that one great need, the need of youth to count in the world of men, the need to belong, the need to serve."

NOTES

276 Wartime migrants: Henry S. Shryock, Jr., and Hope T. Eldridge, "Internal Migration in Peace and War," *American Sociological Review*, February, 1947.

276 Hard-core poverty in wartime: *New Republic*, November 1, 1943.

276 "Repeal the Iron Law of Wages": Frederick Lewis Allen, *The Big Change* (New York, 1952), p. 286. See p. 154, where he makes it quite clear that he believed this redistribution occurred during the Depression, not during the war years.

276 The new Deal's major accomplishments: William E. Leuchtenberg, *Franklin D. Roosevelt and the New Deal*, pp. 331–32.

277 Chances to get ahead: Cantril, p. 829.

277 Redistribution of income: Simon Kuznets, *Shares of Upper Income Groups in Income and Savings*, deals particularly with the top 5 percent. Table on income distribution in the interwar years: *Historical Statistics of the U.S., 1789–1945*.

278 Table on new construction: "National Income Supplement," *Survey of Current Business*, July, 1947.

279 Free meals and free enterprise: *Newsweek*, April 17, 1944.

279 "There is a conservative reaction in progress": *Satevepost*, May 29, 1943.

279 "The most striking characteristic": Ernest K. Lindley, *Newsweek*, March 22, 1943.

279 "Foggy goodwill": *Time*, March 22, 1943.

280 Malcolm Cowley: "The End of the New Deal," *New Republic*, May 31, 1943.

280 "Death Revealed": *Time*, January 3, 1944.

280 Draft rejection rates: *Ibid.*, October 23, 1941.

281 "Good heavens!": quoted in *New Republic*, May 10, 1943.

282 Army's neuropsychiatric problem: *Time*, December 6, 1943; *ibid.*, February 28, 1944.

283 Kaiser's mother: *Ibid.*, November 23, 1942.

283 Kaiser's medical plan: Paul de Kruif, *Kaiser Wakes the Doctors*.

284 "The cost of complete medical care": *Ibid.*, p. 36.

284 Seneca's health: Robert Havighurst and H. Gerthon Morgan, *The Social History of a War Boom Community*, pp. 282–88.

284 Indiana's health: Cavnes, p. 197.

284 Obvious good health of children: *Harper's*, February, 1944.

285 Spending on health insurance: "National Income Supplement," p. 42.

285 Hospital beds: *Historical Statistics of the U.S. 1789–1957*, pp. 34–35.

285 Public health expenditures: *Statistical Abstract of the U.S.*, 1947 edition, p. 236.

285 Longevity increases: *Historical Statistics*, p. 25.

285 Death rates: *Statistical Abstract*, 1948 edition, pp. 66, 79.

286 "They're just bums": quoted in Rosebery, p. 212.

286 Handicapped workers: *Time*, June 21, 1943.

286 "Please be polite to our waitresses": *Nation*, June 19, 1943.

286 "The miners came in '49": Katherine Archibald, *Wartime Shipyard: A Study in Social Disunity*. Miss Archibald euphemistically writes it "bunked together."

287 Opinion on the postwar period: Polls quoted in *Time*, October 11, 1943.

287 NRPB estimates: *Newsweek*, August 9, 1943.

287 Department of Labor estimates: *Nation*, November 23, 1943.

287 "Willow Run supplied some answers": Lowell J. Carr and James E. Stermer, *Willow Run*, p. 7; cf. William H. Jordy, "Fiasco at Willow Run," *Nation*, May 8, 1943.

288 "GI Joe and GI Jane": *NYT*, January 9, 1944.

288 The story of the GI Bill is told in David R. B. Ross, *Preparing for Ulysses*, pp. 118–24.

288 "Back Home": Quoted in *Life*, April 17, 1944.

288 Tom Harmon: *Ibid.*

288 "The fighters of course suffer more": Allan Nevins, in Goodman.

289 Military and civilian death rates: Shannon, p. 814.

289 "We will try to forget": *Newsweek*, May 7, 1945.

289 Veterans' grievances: cf. Arch Soutar, "Homecoming Isn't Easy," *Satevepost*, December 9, 1944; Charles G. Bolte, "The Veterans' Runaround," *Harper's*, April, 1945.

289 "There is a whole ward": Letter to *Time*, April 2, 1945.

290 Treatment of amputees: *Nation*, March 10, 1945, and *Time*, August 27, 1945.

290 "I refused to eat the food" and "Personally": *Newsweek*, April 16, 1945.

290 Veterans and their families: President's Commission on Veterans' Pensions, *Veterans Benefits in the United States*, pp. 63–77.

290 Veterans and the housing problem: *Ibid.*, p. 301.

291 Federal appropriations for veterans' benefits totaled $49 billion by 1957: *Historical Statistics of the U.S., 1789–1956*.

291 Representation of veterans and their dependents in the upper strata of society: Ross, p. 289.

291 GI Bill making up wartime educational deficits: *President's Commission*, p. 299.

291 Figures on housing construction and financing in the 1930's: U.S. Housing and Home Finance Agency, *Housing Statistics Handbook*, p. 2.

291 "The picture is one of barriers": Miles Colean, *American Housing*, p. 9.

292 Housing construction and homeownership from 1939 to 1945: *Housing Statistics Handbook*, p. 43.

292 AMERICAN WOMEN: *Life*, January 29, 1945.

293 The side effects of getting women into the factories: Elinor M. Herrick, "With Women at Work the Factory Changes," *NYT Magazine*, January 24, 1943; cf. A. G. Mezerik, "The Factory Manager Learns the Facts of Life," *Harper's*, September, 1943.

293 Dangers of factory work: Josephine von Miklos, *I Took a War Job*, p. 126.

293 "No working woman labors under the delusion": Elizabeth Hawes, "Do Women Workers Get an Even Break?": *NYT Magazine*, November 19, 1945.

293 The federal shipyards: Susan B. Anthony II, "Working at the Navy Yard," *New Republic*, May 1, 1944.

293 "America may no longer believe": Bruner, p. 215.

294 "There is hardly any job": *Time*, October 19, 1942.

294 Women in journalism: *Satevepost*, May 13, 1944.

294 New York Stock Exchange: *Time*, May 10, 1943.

294 "Goddam it all": Quoted in *Life*, March 15, 1943.

295 "We see this emergency a little more clearly": *Time*, January 26, 1942.

295 Dorothy Thompson: *Newsweek*, January 26, 1942.

295 Women at the conventions: *Ibid.*, June 19, 1944.

295 Widows and Widowers Clubs: Rosebery, pp. 102–3.

295 "Strange unorganized home-front battle": *Time*, August 30, 1943; cf. Elizabeth R. Valentine, "Odyssey of the Army Wife," *NYT Magazine*, March 5, 1944.

296 What women wanted: *Time*, February 26, 1945.

296 Children in the trailer camps and boom towns: Warner Olivier, "Eight Hour Orphans," *Satevepost*, October 10, 1942.

296 Vice more common than violence: *Newsweek*, March 6, 1944.

296 Wolf packs: *Ibid.*, May 8, 1944.

297 "The girls are sore as all get-out": *Time*, March 29, 1943.

297 "War casualties": *Ibid.*, October 5, 1942.

297 Rape in a movie house: *Ibid.*, April 12, 1943.

297 Murder of a nine-year-old: *Ibid.*, May 22, 1944.

297 Teen-age gangs: Eleanor Lake, "Trouble on the Street Corner," *Common Sense*, May, 1943; Bradford Chambers, "Boy Gangs of New York," *NYT Magazine*, December 10, 1944.

297 El Paso movie house manager: *Time*, November 22, 1943.

297 La Guardia: *New Republic*, February 22, 1943.

297 "The worst mother" and "Let the police deal with juvenile delinquency": Quoted in Elizabeth Hawes, *Why Women Cry*, p. 187.

298 Drop in prison population: *Newsweek*, September 13, 1943; cf. *Historical Statistics of the U.S., 1789–1945*.

298 "Who made our youngsters 'generation' conscious?": *Satevepost*, December 2, 1944.

298 The sympathetic woman reporter was Agnes Meyer of the Washington *Post*, whose *Journey Through Chaos* was one of the best narratives of social life in wartime.

298 "A hell of a world for kids": Quoted in *Time*, January 29, 1945.

298 La Guardia and the psychiatrist: *Ibid.*

298 "Far better for adolescents than Depression": Caroline B. Zachry, in *Adolescents in Wartime*, AAPSS, Vol. 236, November, 1944, p. 141.

Suggestions for Further Reading

William Manchester has provided an exhaustively detailed history of the years since 1932 in *The Glory and the Dream: A Narrative History of America, 1932–1972** (Boston, 1974). Frederick Lewis Allen followed his work on the 1920s, *Only Yesterday*, with a work on the 1930s, *Since Yesterday** (New York, 1940). Two popular histories of the depression that consist partly of recollections are Carolyn Bird, *The Invisible Scar** (New York, 1966), and Robert Bendiner, *Just Around the Corner: A Highly Selective History of the Thirties** (New York, 1967). David A. Shannon has edited a collection of documents detailing the social impact of the depression in *The Great Depression** (Englewood Cliffs, N.J., 1960). See also Milton Meltzer, *Brother, Can You Spare a Dime? The Great Depression, 1929–1933** (New York, 1969). A view of the American workingman during this period is given in Irving Bernstein, *The Lean Years: A History of the American Worker, 1920–1933** (Boston, 1961) and *The Turbulent Years: A History of American Labor, 1933–1941** (Boston, 1970).

The impact of the depression is measured in the essays collected by Bernard Sternsher in *Hitting Home: The Depression in Town and Country** (Chicago, 1970) and *The Negro in Depression and War: Prelude to Revolution** (Chicago, 1970). The long-term impact on children raised during the 1930s is analyzed in a unique longitudinal study by Glen H. Elder, Jr., *The Children of the Great Depression: Social Change in Life Experience** (Chicago, 1974). Robert and Helen Merrill Lynd returned to Muncie, Indiana, to measure the changes wrought by the depression, which they describe in *Middletown in Transition** (New York, 1937). An important demographic shift is outlined by Walter J. Stein in *California and the Dust Bowl Migration** (Westport, Conn., 1973). The classic statement on this westward migration is found, of course, in John Steinbeck, *The Grapes of Wrath** (New York, 1939). For the effects of the depression on Appalachia, see Harry M. Caudill, *Night Comes to the Cumberlands: A Biography of a Depressed Area** (Boston, 1963). Recollections of the depression have been compiled by Studs Terkel in *Hard Times: An Oral History of the Great Depression** (New York, 1970), also available in a two-disc, long-playing record album. Woody Guthrie's autobiography, *Bound for Glory** (New York, 1943), contains a great deal of material on growing up in the dust bowl and bumming around the country in the 1930s.

W. J. Cash, *The Mind of the South** (New York, 1941), is an impressionistic and insightful study of Southern life and culture. Among the studies of race relations in the South, the following were produced in the period of the 1930s and 1940s: John Dollard,

* Available in paperback edition.

Caste and Class in a Southern Town* (New Haven, Conn., 1937); Allison Davis, B. G. Gardner, and Mary R. Gardner, *Deep South: A Social Anthropological Study of Caste and Class** (Chicago, 1942); Allison Davis and John Dollard, *Children of Bondage** (Washington, 1940); Arthur F. Raper, *Preface to Peasantry** (Chapel Hill, N.C., 1934); and three works by Charles S. Johnson, *Shadow of the Plantation** (Chicago, 1934), *Growing Up in the Black Belt** (Washington, 1941), and *Patterns of Negro Segregation** (New York, 1943). A later community study is Hylan Lewis, *Blackways of Kent** (Chapel Hill, N.C., 1955). Sharecroppers are the subject of a recent study by Pete Daniel, *The Shadow of Slavery: Peonage in the South, 1901–1969** (Champaign-Urbana, Ill., 1972). Ernest J. Gaines' fictional *The Autobiography of Miss Jane Pittman** (New York, 1971), a narration of one woman's experiences, gives a sympathetic and brilliant portrait of black life from the end of the Civil War to the present. Autobiographical episodes about growing up in the depression South are found in Richard Wright, *Black Boy** (New York, 1945). Ralph Ellison, *Invisible Man** (New York, 1952), one of the best American novels of the century thus far, provides useful information about various facets of black life.

Still the best history of Mexican-Americans is Carey McWilliams, *North from Mexico: The Spanish-speaking People of the United States** (Philadelphia, 1949). Manuel Servín has edited a useful set of readings in *The Mexican-Americans: An Awakened Minority** (Beverly Hills, Calif., 1970; rev. ed. 1974). For expressions of the mood of Mexican-Americans, see Stan Steiner, *La Raza: The Mexican Americans** (New York, 1970). The Chavez movement is most fully treated in Ronald Taylor, *Chavez and the Farm Workers** (Boston, 1975). On the organization of migrant workers, the best source is Dick Meister and Anne Loftis, *A Long Time Coming: The Struggle to Unionize America's Farm Workers* (New York, 1977).

Aside from Perrett's study, the two best works on the domestic side of the Second World War are the colorful *Don't You Know There's a War On? American Home Front, 1941–1945** (New York, 1970), by Richard R. Lingeman, and the provocative *V Was for Victory: Politics and American Culture During World War II** (New York, 1976), by John Morton Blum.

1950–1975
Contemporary Society

The Quality of Suburban Life

HERBERT J. GANS

Although scholars have been writing for some time about the United States as an urban nation, as early as the 1920s, an important new demographic trend was noticed—the increasing growth of suburbs.

Before the advent of mass transportation facilities, the wealthy tended to live in the central city with the outlying areas being populated by the less wealthy and the poor. As the cities continued to grow, however, the older housing began to deteriorate, and the wealthy moved to newer, more fashionable urban neighborhoods, leaving the rundown areas to the working people and the poor. With the arrival of the first breakthrough in urban mass transit—the horse drawn streetcar—some of the more well-to-do citizens decided to abandon the older portions of the city altogether for new, culturally homogeneous settlements on the periphery called suburbs.

In the 1880s, a socialist critic had pointed out that "this modern fashionable suburbanism and exclusiveness is a real grievance to the working class. Had the rich continued to live among the masses, they would with their wealth and influence make our large towns pleasant places to live. . . ." What could not be seen at the time, of course, was the increased prosperity of the working classes that, along with the automobile, would make suburban living available to all except the poorest and most discriminated against among our citizens by the middle of the twentieth century.

By the 1920s, the rate of growth of the suburbs began to exceed that of the cities. The goal of almost every American family seemed to be the purchase of a single-family detached house in a suburban development. While many people moved to the suburbs to escape real or imagined perils in the city, most simply moved there because they found it a more congenial way of life.

Aided by federal legislation, suburban growth rocketed after the Second World War. Veterans Administration loans, Federal Housing Administration mortgage policy, and federally funded highway and road building all contributed to this development. In 1970, the census indicated that more people were living in suburbs—defined as the metropolitan area outside the central city—than in the cities themselves. By 1972, the number of jobs was about equal in both areas. Thus we are rapidly becoming, not an urban nation, but a suburban one.

In the late 1950s, social critics began to find in suburbia the source of many of the ills they saw plaguing American society. And what one sociologist called the myth of suburbia emerged. The fault, the myth ran, lay in the homogeneity of both the population and life-style in the typical suburb. This sameness led to a mass culture and the apparent ethic of conformity that so concerned the critics.

As serious scholarly studies of suburban communities began to appear, however, it became evident that, no matter how much the critics deplored the quality of life in the suburbs, the people who lived there liked it. Herbert J. Gans, of Columbia University, a sociologist who had previously studied an urban working-class community, decided to analyze suburban life firsthand. When the famous builder William Levitt began a new suburban development of lower-middle-class housing near Philadelphia, Gans moved into the community and remained there for two years. During that period, he explored the inhabitants' reasons for moving to the community and their attitudes after settling in. His book, **The Levittowners,** is a result of that study.

Gans' findings are most notable for their refutation of the suburban myth. With few exceptions, the people who moved to Levittown found there what they had expected to find, and consequently the level of satisfaction was quite high. In the selection from his book reprinted below, Gans discusses some of the questions raised by the critics about the relationship between suburban living and mass society. He describes the features of the life-style that have been scrutinized and found wanting by outsiders and reports that, rather than annoying the residents of the community, these very features make the community attractive. In closing, however, Gans notes that one segment of the population—the adolescent group—is generally dissatisfied with suburbia. He warns the residents of suburban communities that some steps should be taken to relieve teen-age discontent in order to prevent an increasingly dangerous generation gap, which might lead to undesirable consequences.

L eading with their assumption of homogeneity and conformity, many critics see the culture of communities like Levittown—those features transcending social life—as marked by sameness, dullness, and blandness. The image of sameness derives from the mass-produced housing, and also from the prevalence of a national and equally mass-produced culture of consumer goods which is extended to characterize the consumers themselves. Part of the critique is tinged with political fear that the national culture and the deleterious effects of conformity may sap the strength of local organizations, which will in turn break down the community social structures that act as barriers between the individual and the state. According to

"The Vitality of Community Culture" (Editor's title: "The Quality of Suburban Life"). From *The Levittowners: Ways of Life and Politics in a New Suburban Community,* by Herbert J. Gans, pp. 185–219. Copyright © 1967 by Herbert J. Gans. Reprinted by permission of Pantheon Books, a Division of Random House, Inc.

theorists of the mass society, the individual then becomes submissive and subject to demagoguery that can incite mass hysteria and mob action, destroying the checks and balances of a democratic society. This hypothesis, developed originally by Ortega y Gasset, the Spanish conservative philosopher who feared popular democracy, gained prominence during the 1930s when Hitler and Stalin systematically eliminated local organizations to forestall opposition to their plans. In America, this analysis has flowered with the increasing centralization of the federal government, but suburbia is considered particularly susceptible to the dangers of mass society because of the rootlessness and absence of community strength supposedly induced by the large number of Transients.[1] Other observers, less fearful of mass society, stress the blandness of suburban life, which, they fear, is producing dull and apathetic individuals.[2]

These charges are serious and, if accurate, would suggest that suburbia is a danger to American democracy and culture. Most of them, however, are either inaccurate or, when accurate, without the negative consequences attributed to them. Levittown is very much a local community; if anything, it neglects its ties to the larger society more than it should. It is not rootless, even with its Transients, and it is not dull, except to its teenagers. The critics' conclusions stem in part from the previously mentioned class and cultural differences between them and the suburbanites. What they see as blandness and apathy is really a result of the invisibility and home-centeredness of lower middle class culture, and what they consider dullness derives from their cosmopolitan standard for judging communities, which condemns those lacking urban facilities—ranging from museums to ethnic districts—that are favored by the upper middle class.

They also look at suburbia as outsiders, who approach the community with a "tourist" perspective. The tourist wants visual interest, cultural diversity, entertainment, esthetic pleasure, variety (preferably exotic), and emotional stimulation. The resident, on the other hand, wants a comfortable, convenient, and socially satisfying place to live—esthetically pleasing, to be sure, but first and foremost functional for his daily needs. Much of the critique of suburbia as community reflects the critics' disappointment that the new suburbs do not satisfy their particular tourist requirements; that they are not places for wandering, that they lack the charm of a medieval village, the excitement of a metropolis, or the architectural variety of an upper-income suburb. Even so, tourism cuts across all classes. A neighbor, returning from a trip to Niagara Falls, complained bitterly about commercialization, using much the same language as the critics do about suburbia. What he felt about the Falls, however, he did not feel about Levittown.

We are all tourists at one time or another, but most communities can serve both tourist and residential functions only with difficulty. For example, the crowding and nightlife that attract the tourist to Greenwich Village make it uncomfortable for the resident. Although the tourist perspec-

[1] See, e.g., Fromm, pp. 154–163; and Stein, Chaps. 9 and 12.
[2] This charge is made by Keats and, in more qualified and muted tones, by Riesman (1957).

tive is understandable, and even justifiable, it is not by itself a proper criterion for evaluating a community, especially a purely residential one like Levittown. It must be judged first by the quality of community life and culture it offers its residents; the needs of the tourist are secondary.

THE NATIONAL CULTURE AND THE COMMUNITY

To the outside observer, Levittown appears to be a community on which the national American culture has been imprinted so totally as to leave little room for local individuality. The houses express the current national residential style: pseudo-Colonial fronts borrowed from the eighteenth century glued on a variety of single-family house styles developed between the eighteenth and twentieth centuries, and hiding twentieth century interiors. Schools are contemporary, modular, one-story buildings that look like all other new schools. The shopping center is typical too, although the interior is more tastefully designed than most. It consists mainly of branches of large national chains, whose inventory is dominated by prepackaged national brands, and the small centers are no different. The old "Mom and Pop" grocery has been replaced by the "7 to 11" chain, which, as its name indicates, opens early and closes late, but sells only prepackaged goods so that each store can be serviced by a single cashier-clerk. Even the Jewish and Italian foods sold at the "delis" are cut from the loaf of a "pan-ethnic" culture that is now nationally distributed.

A large, partially preplanned residential development must almost inevitably depend on national organizations, since these are the only ones that can afford the initial capital investment and the unprofitable hiatus before the community is large enough to support them properly. This is as true of stores in a new shopping center—which sometimes wait years before they show a profit—as it is of churches and voluntary organizations. In addition, Levittown itself is in some ways a national brand, for the size of Levitt's operation in an industry of small entrepreneurs has made his communities a national symbol of low-price suburbia. This has helped to attract national organizations, as well as Transients who work for large national corporations. When they move into a new metropolitan area, they usually do not know where to find housing, and having heard of Levittown, are likely to look there first. The brand name "Levittown" makes the housing more trustworthy than a small subdivision constructed by an unknown local builder.

Although Levittown would thus seem to be, as much as any community in America, an example of Big Culture, this is only superficially true, for the quality of life in Levittown retains a strictly local and often antinational flavor, exploiting national bodies and resources for strictly local purposes whenever possible. To the visitor, the Levittown houses may look like all other pseudo-Colonial ones in South Jersey, but Levittowners can catalog the features that distinguish their houses from those in nearby subdivisions. The stores may be chains selling brand-name goods, but the managers become involved in local activities and enable local groups to hold bazaars and other fund-raising affairs, including bakesales which compete with store merchandise. The same patterns obtain in voluntary associations and churches. For example, the Boy Scouts are run by an intricate national bureaucracy which sets detailed rules for the activities of local troops. Since the organization must attract children, however, what actually goes on at troop meetings bears little resemblance to the rules, and the less the national office knows, the better for it and the troop leader.

The priority of local concerns is even more emphatic in government, for federal agencies and national party headquarters are viewed mainly as sources of funds and power to be used for local needs. A civil defense agency was set up in Levittown, not to satisfy national regulations, but because the county civil defense director was running for political office. The national program provided him an opportunity to distribute some funds to local communities, which in turn enhanced his political fortunes. Federal funds which came to Levittown for civil defense were used for local police and fire needs as much as possible within the limits of the law. Similarly, when the Township Committee in 1960 invited both Nixon and Kennedy to campaign in Levittown, its purpose was not to support the national candidates of the two parties but to gain publicity for Levittown.

Many Levittowners work in branch offices or factories of national corporations, and their reports about their work and their employers suggest that national directives are often viewed as outlandish and unreasonable, to be sabotaged in favor of local priorities. However much a national corporation may give the appearance of a well-run and thoroughly centralized monolith, in actual fact it is often a shaky aggregate of local baronies. The result is considerable skepticism among Levittowners about the effectiveness and power of national corporations, a skepticism easily extended to all national agencies.

Generally speaking, Levittowners do not take much interest in the national society, and rarely even see its influence on their lives. As long as they are employed, healthy, and able to achieve a reasonable proportion of their personal goals, they have no need for the federal government or any other national agency, and being locals, they do not concern themselves with the world outside their community. Indeed, they might better be described as *sublocals*, for they are home-oriented rather than community-oriented. Although the lower middle class is sometimes said to reject bigness, the Levittowners do not share this feeling. They do not scorn big supermarkets and national brands as do the critics, and although they do not see the big society very clearly, it appears to them as an inept octopus which can only cope with the community through force or bribery. It is opposed not because of its size, but because it is an outsider. When a national service club organized a branch in Levittown, one of the Levittowners said, "They are big and they can help us, but we don't have to follow national policy. . . . National headquarters is only a racket that takes your money." The cultural orientation toward localism is supported by more pressing sociological factors; if a local branch of a national association is to succeed, it must adapt itself to local priorities in order to attract members, and national headquarters must be opposed if it refuses to go along. The most disliked outsider is not the national society, however, but the cosmopolitan with his "Brookline values."

All this does not, of course, imply that the national society and culture are powerless in Levittown. When industrial giants set administered prices for consumer goods sold in the local shopping center, or when Detroit engineers the annual style change in its automobiles, the individual purchaser can only express his discontent by refusal to buy, and when it comes to necessities, he lacks even that choice. In Levittown, however, the discontent and the lack of choice are minimized, for most people have enough money to pay administered prices and enough freedom to choose among products. In fact, they find themselves well served by the corporations who sell them their housing, food, furnishings, and transportation. However, Levittowners are less concerned with "consumption" than the critics. They care less about the things they buy and are less interested in asserting individuality through consumer behavior, for they do not use consumption to express class values as much as the upper middle class does. They may not like mass-produced bread as well as the local bakery product they perhaps ate in childhood, but they do not make an issue of it, and do not feel themselves to be mass men simply because they buy a mass-produced item. Goods are just not important enough. Only when they become tourists are they "materialistic"—and traditional. One of my neighbors who was once stationed in Japan was not at all concerned about the national prepackaged brands sold in Levittown, but talked frequently about the commercialization of Japanese culture and the unattractive goods he found in the souvenir shops.

The Mass Media

For Levittowners, probably the most enduring—and certainly the most frequent—tie to the national culture is through the mass media. Yet even this is filtered through a variety of personal predispositions so that not many messages reach the receiver intact. Few people are dominated by the mass media; they provide escape from boredom, fill up brief intervals, and (perhaps most important) occupy the children while the adults go about their business.

The most frequently used mass medium is television, with newspapers, magazines, and paperback novels following in that order. In working class homes in Levittown as elsewhere, the TV set is likely to be on all the time, even when company comes, for as one Levittowner explained, "If conversation lags, people can watch or it gives you something to talk about." This statement suggests more the fears that working class people have about their social skills than their practice, for conversation does not often lag, at least among friends.

Middle class people, surer of their social skills, use television more selectively. The children watch when they have come in from play; after they are put to bed the adults may turn on the set, for television fills the hours between 9 P.M. and bedtime, when there is not enough of a block of time for other activities. A few favorite programs may get rapt attention, but I doubt that television supplanted conversation among either middle or working class Levittowners. There is no indication that television-viewing increased after people moved to Levittown, for no one mentioned it when interviewed about changes in spare-time activities. I suspect that viewing had actually decreased somewhat, at least during the time of my study, when gardening was still a time-consuming novelty for many people.

Television viewing is also a much less passive activity than the critics of the mass media suspect.[3] Routine serials and situation comedies evoke little response, although Levittowners are sensitive to anachronisms in the plots and skeptical of advertising claims.[4] Dramatic programs may provoke spirited—and quite personal—reactions. For example, one evening my neighbors and I watched an hour-long drama which depicted the tragic career of an introverted girl who wanted desperately to become a serious actress but was forced to work as a rock-and-roll dancer, and finally decided to give up show business. One neighbor missed the tragedy altogether, and thought the girl should have kept on trying to become an actress. The other neighbor fastened on—and approved of—the ending (in which the actress returned to her husband and to the family restaurant in which she had been "discovered") and wondered, rightly, whether it was possible to go back to a mundane life after the glamor of the entertainment world.

People do not necessarily know what they want from the media, but they know what they do not want and trust their ability to choose correctly. A discussion of television critics one night revealed that Levittowners read their judgments, but do not necessarily accept them. "The critics see so much that they cannot give us much advice," said one. "They are too different in their interests from the audience, and cannot be reviewers for it," said another.

Forty per cent of the people interviewed said they were reading new magazines since moving to Levittown; general-interest periodicals—*Life, Look, Reader's Digest, Time,* and the *Saturday Evening Post*—led the list. Only 9 of the 52 magazines were house-and-garden types such as *American Home* and *Better Homes and Gardens,* but then 88 per cent of the people were already reading these, at least in the year they moved to Levittown. Although not a single person said these magazines had helped in the decision to buy a home in Levittown, 57 per cent reported that they had gotten ideas from the magazines to try out in their houses, primarily on the use of space, furniture, and shrubbery arrangements, what to do about pictures and drapes, and how to build shelves and patios. The magazines provided help on functional rather than esthetic problems of fixing up the new house. People rarely copied something directly from the magazines, however. Most often, their reading gave them ideas which they then altered for their own use, sometimes after talking them over with the

[3] This cannot be surmised either from inferences about media content or from sociological surveys, but becomes quite evident when one watches TV with other people, as I did with my neighbors.

[4] I had observed the same reactions among the working class Bostonians I studied previously, although they were more interested in the performers than the Levittowners. Gans (1962a), Chap. 9.

neighbors. Similarly, people who adopted new furniture styles after moving to Levittown got their inspiration from their neighbors rather than from magazines, although all who changed styles (but only 53 per cent who did not) said they had obtained some hints for the house from the home and garden magazines.

The media also provide "ideas" for community activities, but these are altered by local considerations and priorities. For example, a few days after the Nixon-Kennedy television debates in 1960, candidates for township offices were asked to participate in a similar debate in Levittown. Everyone liked the idea, but after a few innocuous questions by out-of-town reporters, the debate turned into the traditional candidates' night, in which politicians from both parties baited their opponents from the audience with prepared questions. Sometimes, local organizations put on versions of TV quiz games, and honored retiring officers with a "This Is Your Life" presentation. A few clubs, especially Jewish ones, held "beatnik" parties, but since most Levittowners had never seen a beatnik, the inspiration for their costumes came from the mass media.

The impact of the media is most apparent among children; they are easily impressed by television commercials, and mothers must often fight off their demands on shopping trips. But the adults are seldom touched deeply; media content is always secondary to more personal experience. For example, people talked about articles on child-rearing they had seen in popular magazines, but treated them as topics of conversation rather than as possible guides for their own behavior. A neighbor who had read that "permissive" child-rearing was going out of style after thirty years had never even heard of it before, even though she had gone to college. I remember discussing Cuba with another neighbor, an Air Force officer, shortly after Castro confiscated American property there. Although he had been telling me endless and angry stories about being exploited by his superiors and about corruption among high-ranking officers, he could not see the similarity between his position and that of the Cuban peasant under Batista, and argued strenuously that Castro should be overthrown. His opinions reflected those of the media, but their content did not interest him enough to relate it to his own experiences. He did, however, feel that Castro had insulted the United States—and him personally—and the media helped him belong to the national society in this way. Indeed, the media are a message from that society, which, like all others, remains separate from the more immediate realities of self, family, home, and friends. These messages really touch only the people who feel isolated from local groups or who, like the cosmopolitans, pay close attention to the printed word and the screen image.

Levittown and the Mass Society

The Levittowners' local orientation will not prevent them from becoming submissive tools of totalitarian demagogues if, according to the critics of mass society, the community is too weak to defy the power of the state. Social scientists concerned about the danger of dictatorship have often claimed, with DeTocqueville, that the voluntary association is the prime bulwark against it. For example, Wilensky writes: "In the absence of effective mediating ties, of meaningful participation in voluntary associations, the population becomes vulnerable to mass behavior, more susceptible to personality appeals in politics, more ready for the demagogues who exploit fanatical faiths of nation and race." [5]

If Wilensky is correct, Levittowners should be invulnerable to mass behavior, for they have started about a hundred voluntary associations and 73 per cent of the two interview samples belong to at least one. Levittown should also be more immune than other communities, for about half of both interview samples reported more organizational participation than in the former residence. [6] The way they participate, however, has little consequence for their relation to the national society. The handful of leaders and really active people become familiar with the mechanics of organizational and municipal politics, but the rank-and-file members, coming to meetings mainly for social and service reasons, are rarely involved in these matters. Yet not even the active participants are exposed to national issues and questions, and they learn little about the ways of coping with the manipulatory techniques feared by the critics of mass society.

Nor does participation necessarily provide democratic experience. Organizations with active membership are likely to have democratic politics, but when the membership is passive, they are often run by an individual or a clique and there is little demand for democratic procedure. Nothing in the nature of the voluntary association would, however, preclude mob behavior and mass hysteria when the members demand it. The ad hoc groups that arose during the school budget fight and in the controversies over liquor, nonresident doctors, and fluoridation, often acted in near-hysterical ways. Admittedly, these were temporary organizations; permanent ones, conscious of their image, are more likely to refrain from such behavior and, like political parties, often avoid taking stands on controversial issues. They do inhibit mob action—or, rather, they refuse to be associated with it, forcing it into temporary organizations. Yet if the majority of a permanent group's membership is angry about an issue, it can act out that anger and even put its organizational strength behind hysteria. At the time of racial integration, a sizeable faction in one of the men's groups was contemplating quasi-violent protest, and was restrained as much by pressure from the churches, the builder, and some government officials as by cooler heads within the group.

Mob action and mass hysteria are usually produced by intense clashes of interest between citizens and government agencies, especially if government is not responsive to citizens' demands. If an issue is especially threatening and other avenues for coping with it are blocked, irrational action is often the only solution. Under such conditions, voluntary associations can do little to quell it, partly because they have no direct role in the government, but mainly because their impact on their membership is, in

[5] Wilensky, p. 237. See also Kornhauser, Chap. 3, and Lipset, pp. 66–67.
[6] Fifty-six per cent of the random sample and 44 per cent of the city sample reported more participation than previously.

Wilensky's terms, not meaningful enough to divert members from affiliating with violent protest groups. Even national officers of voluntary associations can rarely control irrational actions by local branches, especially since these rarely come to "national's" attention.

The other relationships of the individual Levittowners vis-à-vis the national society are so indirect that it would be hard to pinpoint where and how the two confront each other. It would be harder still to convince the average Levittowner, locally oriented as he is, to change his stance. Unlike the aristocrat or the intellectual, who was once able as an individual to influence the national society and still attempts to do so, the Levittowners come from a tradition—and from ancestors—too poor or too European even to conceive the possibility that they could affect their nation. And unlike the cosmopolitans of today, they have not yet learned that they ought to try. As a result, the Levittowner is not likely to act unless and until national issues impinge directly on his life. When this does happen, he is as frustrated as the cosmopolitan about how to be effective. All he can really do is voice his opinion at the ballot box, write letters to his congressman, or join protest groups. In times of crisis, none of these can change the situation quickly enough, and this of course exacerbates threat, hysteria, and the urge toward mob action or scapegoating.

The national society and the state have not impinged negatively on the average Levittowner, however; indeed, they have served him well, making him generally content with the status quo. The Congress is dominated by the localistic and other values of the white lower middle and working class population, and since the goods and services provided by the influential national corporations are designed largely for people like the Levittowners, they have little reason to question corporate behavior. The considerable similarity of interests between Levittowners and the nationally powerful agencies, private and public, makes it unnecessary for the Levittowners to concern themselves with the national society or to delude themselves about the sovereignty of the local community.[7]

What appears as apathy to the critics of suburban life is satisfaction with the way things are going, and what is interpreted as a "retreat" into localism and familism is just ahistorical thinking. Most lower middle and working class people have always been localistic and familistic; even during the Depression they joined unions only when personal economic difficulties gave them no other alternative, becoming inactive once these were resolved or when it was clear that political activity was fruitless.[8] Indeed, the alleged retreat is actually an advance, for the present generation, especially among working class people, is less isolated from the larger society than its parents, less suspicious, and more willing to believe

---

[7] In this respect, the Levittowners differed significantly from the residents of Springdale, a rural community in New York State, who developed a set of illusions to hide their dependence on state and national political and economic forces. See Vidich and Bensman.

[8] Part of the difficulty is that critics compare the present generation to the previous generation, that of the Depression, which was an unusual period in American history and no baseline for historical comparisons of any kind.

that it can participate in the community and the larger society. The belief is fragile and rarely exercised, but people like the Levittowners confront the national society more rationally than their ancestors did, and if the signs of progress are few, progress has nevertheless taken place. Whether there has been enough progress to prevent the emergence of dictatorship in a severe national crisis is hard to tell, but certainly the Levittowners and their community fit few of the prerequisites that would make them willing tools of totalitarian leaders today.

TRANSIENCE AND ROOTLESSNESS

Part of the fear of mass society theorists and suburban critics alike is the transience of the new suburban communities and the feelings of rootlessness that allegedly result. About 20 per cent of Levittown's first purchasers were Transients, who knew even when they came that their employers—national corporations or the armed services—would require them to move elsewhere some years hence. Their impermanency is reflected in residential turnover figures which showed that in 1964, 10 per cent of the houses were resold and another 5 per cent rented, and that annual turnover was likely to reach 20 per cent in the future.[9] Not all houses change hands that often, of course; a small proportion are sold and rented over and over again.[10] Much of the initial turnover resulted from job transfers—55 per cent in 1960, with another 10 per cent from job changes.[11]

Whether or not the 15 per cent turnover figure is "normal" is difficult to say. National estimates of mobility suggest that 20 per cent of the population moves annually, but this figure includes renters. Levittown's rate is probably high in comparison to older communities of home owners, fairly typical of newer ones, and low in comparison to apartment areas.[12]

[9] There is no secular trend in turnover, however, for between 1961 and 1964 the rate in the first neighborhood increased from 12 per cent to only 14 per cent, but the third and fourth neighborhoods both showed turnover rates of 19 per cent in 1964. Renting occurs primarily because the softness of the housing market makes it difficult for people to sell their houses without a considerable loss; they find it more profitable to rent them, with management turned over to the local realtors.

[10] According to a story in the October 21, 1957 issue of Long Island's *Newsday*, 27 per cent of the first 1800 families in Levittown, New York, were still living there ten year later.

[11] Another 10 per cent left because they were unhappy in the community; 7 per cent, for financial reasons; 5 per cent, because of an excessive journey to work; and 4 per cent, because of death, divorce, or other changes in the family. These figures were collected from real estate men and people selling their homes privately and may not be entirely reliable. Real estate men may not be told the real reasons for selling and private sellers may have been reluctant to mention financial problems. However, only about 1 per cent of the houses were foreclosed annually.

[12] In the mid-1950s, when Park Forest was seven years old, annual turnover of homes was 20 per cent. See Whyte (1956), p. 303. In Levittown, New York, a 1961 study reported an average annual rate of about 15 per cent. See Orzack and Sanders, p. 13. In Levittown, Pennsylvania, the rate varied from 12 to 15 per cent between 1952 and 1960. See Anderson and Settani. A study of a forty-year-old English new

Conventional standards of "normal" turnover are so old and communities like Levittown still so new on the American scene that it is impossible to determine a normal turnover rate. Indeed, the need to judge turnover stems from the assumption that it is undesirable; once there are sufficient data to test this assumption, the concept of normal turnover can perhaps be dismissed.

The crucial element in turnover is not its extent but the change in population composition and its consequences. If the departing Transients and Mobiles are replaced by Settlers, then turnover will of course be reduced. Early in the 1960s, the second buyers were, however, also Transients, who needed a house more quickly than the builder could supply it, as well as people of lower income (probably Settlers) who could not afford the down payment on a new house. If more of the latter come to Levittown over the years, the proportion of lower-status people in the community will increase, and there may be fears of status loss among those of higher status. Although such fears were rare during my time in the community, they existed on a few blocks and may account in part for the strong reactions to status-depriving governmental actions that I described earlier.

Despite the belief that Transients do not participate in community life, in Levittown they belonged to community organizations in considerably larger numbers than Settlers did, partly because of their higher status.[13] More of them also reported increased participation after moving to Levittown than did Settlers.[14] They were, however, likely to list fewer people with whom they visited frequently.[15] Their organizational activity is not surprising, for being used to transience, they are socially quite stable, usually gravitating to the same kinds of communities and joining the same kinds of organizations in them. In fact, their mobility has provided them with more organizational experience than other Levittowners have, enabling them to help found several groups in the community.

It has often been charged that modern transience and mobility deprive people of "roots." Because of the botanical analogy, the social conception of the word is difficult to define, but it generally refers to a variety of stable roles and relationships which are recognized by other residents.

---

town reported an annual rate of 10 per cent the first ten years, which has now dropped to 1 per cent. See Willmott (1963), p. 20. A study of 30,000 apartments in 519 buildings all over the country, conducted by the Institute of Real Estate Management and reported in the *New York Times* of November 10, 1963, showed an annual turnover of 28 per cent, and 35 per cent for garden apartments.

13 Eighty-four per cent of the Transients reported organizational membership at the time of the second interview, as compared to 86 per cent of the Mobiles and only 44 per cent of the Settlers. Sixty-two per cent of the Transients belonged to organizations other than the church, compared to only 25 per cent of the Settlers.

14 Seventy-five per cent of the Transients were more active than in their former residence, as compared to 60 per cent of the Settlers, and none of the Transients but 20 per cent of the Settlers said they were less active than before.

15 The mean number of couples named by Transients was 2.75; by Mobiles, 3.25; and by Settlers, 3.3. Nineteen per cent of the Transients said they had no friends in Levittown, as compared to 8 per cent of the Settlers.

Traditionally, these roles were often defined by one's ancestors as well. Such roots are hard to maintain today and few people can resist the temptation of social or occupational mobility that requires a physical move. This does not mean, however, that the feeling of rootedness has disappeared. One way in which Transients maintain it is to preserve the term "home" for the place in which they grew up. When Levittowners talk of "going home," they mean trips to visit parents. People whose parents have left the community in which they grew up may, however, feel homeless. I remember a discussion with a Levittowner who explained that he was going "home to Ohio" to visit his mother, and his wife said somewhat sadly, "My parents no longer live where I grew up, and I never lived with them where they live now. So I have only Sudberry Street in Levittown; I have no other home." Because they were Transients, she could not think of Levittown as home and, like many others, looked forward to the day when her husband's occupational transience would come to an end and they would settle down.

Such Transients obviously lack roots in an objective sense and may also have feelings of rootlessness. My impression is that these feelings are not intense or frequent. One way they are coped with is by moving to similar communities and putting down temporary roots; another, by joining organizations made up of fellow Transients.[16] Professionals who are transient often develop roots in their profession and its social groups. As Melvin Webber and others have argued, occupational or functional roots are replacing spatial roots for an ever increasing proportion of the population.[17] This kind of rootedness is easier for men to establish than for women, and wives, especially the wives of professionals, often suffer more from transience than their husbands. Some become attached to national voluntary associations—as men in nonprofessional occupations do—and develop roots within them. This is not entirely satisfactory, however, for it provides feelings of rootedness in only a single role, whereas spatial rootedness cuts across all roles, and rewards one for what one is rather than for what one does.

New communities like Levittown make it possible for residents, even Transients, to put down roots almost at once. People active in organizations become known quickly; thus they are able to feel part of the community. Despite Levittown's size, shopkeepers and local officials get to know people they see regularly, offering the feeling of being recognized to many. The ministers take special care to extend such recognition, and the churches appoint themselves to provide roots—and deliberately, for it attracts people to the church. Protestant denominations sought to define themselves as small-town churches with Colonial style buildings because these have been endowed with an image of rootedness.

Intergenerational rootedness is seldom found today in any suburban or urban community—or, for that matter, in most small towns—for it requires the kind of economic stability (and even stagnancy) characteristic only of depressed areas of the country. Moreover, the romanticizing of this type of rootedness ignores the fact that for many people it blocked

[16] Whyte (1956), p. 289.
[17] Webber.

progress, especially for low-status persons who were, by reason of residence and ancestry, permanently defined as "shiftless" or "good for nothing." Roots can strangle growth as well as encourage it.

Transience and mobility are something new in middle class American life, and like other innovations, they have been greeted by predictions of undesirable consequences, on family life, school performance, and mental health, for example. Interviews with school officials, doctors, and policemen indicated, however, that Transients appeared no more often as patients and police or school problems and delinquents than other Levittowners. Transience *can* create problems, but it has different effects for different people. For young men, a transfer usually includes a promotion or a raise; for older ones it may mean only another physical move or a transfer to a corporate "Siberia." If a Transient is attached to his home, but is asked to move by his company, he can say "no" only once or twice before being asked to resign or face relegation to the list of those who will not be promoted further. The move from one place to another is a pleasure for few families, but the emotional costs can easily be overestimated.[18] Because Transients move to and from similar types of communities, they have little difficulty adapting themselves to their new homes. In large corporations, they generally receive advice about where to look for housing, often going to areas already settled by colleagues who help them make the residential transition.

Frequent moving usually hurts other family members more than the breadwinner. Wives who had made good friends in Levittown were especially sad to go, and adolescents object strenuously to leaving their peers, so that parents generally try to settle down before their children enter high school. For wives and adolescents transience is essentially an involuntary move, which, like the forced relocation of slum dwellers under urban renewal, may result in depression and other deleterious effects.[19] Transience may also engender difficulties when problems of social mobility antedate or accompany it, as in the case of older corporate employees who must transfer without promotion, or suburbanites who move as a result of downward or extremely rapid upward social mobility.[20] Studies among children of Army personnel, who move more often than corporation Transients, have found that geographical mobility per se did not result in emotional disturbance,[21] except among children whose fathers had risen from working class origins to become officers.[22]

---

[18] Gutman, p. 180.

[19] See, e.g., Fried.

[20] Gordon, Gordon, and Gunther. This study did not distinguish between residential and social mobility, but its case studies of disturbed suburbanites suggest the deleterious effects of the latter.

[21] Pederson and Sullivan.

[22] This study—by Gabower—came to other conclusions, but a close reading of her data shows that the strains of the long and arduous climb required of an enlisted man in the Navy who becomes an officer were passed on to the children. Conversely, children from middle class homes, whose fathers had graduated from Annapolis, rarely suffered emotionally from geographical mobility. Teenagers of both groups suffered from moving, however.

These findings would suggest that transience has its most serious effects on people with identity problems. The individual who lacks a fairly firm sense of his identity will have difficulties in coping with the new experiences he encounters in moving. He will also suffer most severely from rootlessness, for he will be hindered in developing the relationships and reference groups that strengthen one's identity. This might explain why adolescents find moving so difficult. Transients without roots in their community of origin or their jobs must rely on their family members in moments of stress. Sometimes, the family becomes more cohesive as a result, but since stresses on one family member are likely to affect all others, the family is not always a reliable source of support. If identity problems are also present, the individual may have no place to turn, and then transience can produce the *anomie* that critics have found rampant in the suburbs. But such people are a small minority in Levittown.

THE VITALITY OF LEVITTOWN: THE ADULT VIEW

When the Levittowners were asked whether they considered their community dull, just 20 per cent of the random sample said yes, and of Philadelphians (who might have been expected to find it dull after living in a big city), only 14 per cent.[23] Many respondents were surprised at the very question, for they thought there was a great deal to do in the community, and all that was needed was a desire to participate. "It's up to you," was a common reaction. "If a person is not the friendly type or does not become active, it's their own fault." "I don't think it's dull here," explained another, "there are so many organizations to join." Some people noted that Levittown was short of urban amusements, but it did not bother them. A former Philadelphian pointed out: "If Levittown is compared to city living, there are no taverns or teenage hangout places. Then it is dull. But we never had any of this in our own neighborhood and it's even better here. . . . We are perfectly content here, I'm afraid. Social life is enough for us; we are becoming fuddy-duddy." Nostalgia for urban places was not common; most people felt like the one who said, "We like quiet things . . . visiting, sitting out front in summer, having people dropping by." And if Levittown seemed quiet to some, it did not to others. "This is the wildest place I've ever been. Every weekend a party, barbecues, picnics, and things like that. I really enjoy it." [24] The only people who thought Levittown was indeed dull were the socially isolated, and upper middle class people who had tasted the town's organizational life and found it wanting.

---

[23] The question read: "Some people have said that communities like Levittown are pretty dull, without any excitement or interesting things to do. How do you feel about that? Do you agree or disagree?"

[24] This respondent was describing the extremely active social life of the Jewish community. Even so, Jews (particularly the better educated) were more likely than non-Jews to agree that Levittown was dull. Jews also seem to be more interested in city amusements.

What Levittowners who enjoy their community are saying is that they find vitality in other people and organizational activities; the community is less important. That community may be dull by conventional standards (which define vitality by urban social mixture and cultural riches) but Levittowners reject these standards; they do not want or need that kind of vitality or excitement. Mothers get their share of it from the daily adventures of their children and the men get it at work. The threshold for excitement is low, and for many, excitement is identified with conflict, crisis, and deprivation. Most Levittowners grew up in the Depression, and remembering the hard times of their childhood, they want to protect themselves and their children from stress.

Another difference in values between critics and Levittowners is at play here. The Italians who lived in the center city working class neighborhood I studied before Levittown were bored by "the country"—in which they included the suburbs—and so are critics of suburbia, albeit for different reasons. Many working class city dwellers enjoy street life and urban eating or drinking places; upper middle class critics like crowds and cosmopolitanism. The lower middle class and the kinds of working class people that came to Levittown had no interest in either. Even previous urbanites had made little if any use of the cultural facilities valued by the cosmopolitan, and had no need for them in the suburbs. And as the struggles over the liquor issue suggest, they want none of the vitality sought by the working class urbanite, for they are just escaping corner bars and the disadvantages of aging urban areas. What they do want is a kind of interpersonal vitality along with privacy and peace and quiet.[25] Vicarious excitement is something else again. Television provides programmed and highly predictable excitement, but it can get boring. A fire or accident, a fight at a municipal or school board meeting, and marital strife or minor misbehavior among neighbors involve real people and known ones. The excitement they provide is also vicarious, but it is not programmed and is therefore more rewarding.

The Blandness of Lower Middle Class Culture

Levittown's criteria for vitality may spell dullness to the critic and the visitor, partly because much of community life is invisible. Lower middle class life does not take place either on the street or in meetings and

[25] Cosmopolitan friends often asked me if I did not find Levittown dull. As a participant-observer, I could not answer the question, for I was immersed in community life and strife and saw all of their vitality and excitement. Even the most routine event was interesting because I was trying to fit it into an overall picture of the community. As a resident, I enjoyed being with Levittowners, and the proportion of dull ones was certainly no higher than in academic or any other circles. Of course, Levittown lacked some of the urban facilities that I, as a city-lover, like to patronize. It was not dull, however—but then I would not make a public judgment about any community simply because it could not satisfy some of my personal preferences, particularly when the community seemed to satisfy the preferences of the majority of residents so well.

parties; it is home-centered and private. Once one penetrates behind the door, however, as does the participant-observer, people emerge as personalities and few are either dull or bland. But when all is said and done, something is different: less exuberance than is found in the working class, a more provincial outlook than in the upper middle class, and a somewhat greater concern with respectability than in either. In part, this is a function of religious background: being largely Protestant, the lower middle class is still affected by the Puritan ethos. It lacks the regular opportunity for confession that allows some Catholics to live somewhat more spiritedly, and has not adopted the sharp division into sacred and secular culture that reduces Jewish religiosity to observance of the High Holidays and permits Jews to express exuberance in their organizational, social, and cultural activities. But the difference is not entirely due to Puritanism, for "restrictive" lower middle class culture appears also among Catholics who have moved "up," especially German and Irish ones, and even among Italians and among some Jews who have risen from working class origins.

If "blandness" is the word for this quality, it stems from the transition in which the lower middle class finds itself between the familial life of the working class and the cosmopolitanism of the upper middle class. The working class person need conform only within the family circle and the peer group, but these are tolerant of his other activities. Believing that the outside world is unalterably hostile and that little is to be gained from its approval, he can indulge in boisterousness that provides catharsis from the tensions generated in the family and peer circles. The upper middle class person, on the other hand, is lodged firmly in the world outside the home. At times he may have trouble reconciling the demands of home and outside world, but he has a secure footing in both.

Lower middle class people seem to me to be caught in the middle. Those whose origins were in the working class are no longer tied so strongly to the extended family, but although they have gone out into the larger society, they are by no means at ease in it. They do not share the norms of the cosmopolitans, but, unlike the working class, they cannot ignore them. As a result, they find themselves in a situation in which every neighbor is a potential friend or enemy and every community issue a source of conflict, producing a restraining and even inhibiting influence on them. Others, lower middle class for generations, have had to move from a rural or small-town social structure. They too are caught in the middle, for now they must cope with a larger and more heterogeneous society, for which their cultural and religious traditions have not equipped them.

If left to themselves, lower middle class people do what they have always done: put their energies into home and family, seeking to make life as comfortable as possible, and supporting, broadening, and varying it with friends, neighbors, church, and a voluntary association. Because this way of life is much like that of the small-town society or the urban neighborhood in which they grew up, they are able to maintain their optimistic belief that Judeo-Christian morality is a reliable guide to behavior. This world view (if one can endow it with so philosophical a name) is best seen in the pictures that amateur painters exhibited at PTA meetings in Levittown: bright, cheerful landscapes, or portraits of children and pets painted in primary colors, reflecting the wish that the world be hopeful, humorous, and above all, simple. Most important, their paintings insisted that life can be happy.

Of course, life is not really like this, for almost everyone must live with some disappointment: an unruly child, a poor student, an unsatisfied husband, a bored wife, a bad job, a chronic illness, or financial worry. These realities are accepted because they cannot be avoided; it is the norms of the larger society which frustrate. Partly desired and partly rejected, they produce an ambivalence which appears to the outsider as the blandness of lower middle class life. This ambivalence can be illustrated by the way Levittown women reacted to my wife's paintings. Since her studio was at home, they had an opportunity to see her work and talk to her about being a painter. The working class Italians with whom we had lived in Boston previously knew, by and large, how to deal with her activity. Unacquainted with "art," they could shrug off her activity and her abstract expressionist style to admire colors they liked or forms that reminded them of something in their own experience. Not knowing what it all meant, and not having to know, they concluded that painting was a good thing because it kept her out of trouble, preventing boredom and potentially troublesome consequences such as drinking or extramarital affairs.

The lower middle class Levittowners could not cope with her paintings as easily. They did not like her abstract expressionist style any more than the working class women, but they knew it was "art" and so could not ignore it. They responded with anxiety, some hostility, and particularly with envy of her ability to be "creative." But even this response was overlaid with ambivalence. As teenagers they had learned that creativity was desirable, and many had had some cursory training in drawing, piano, or needlework. Once they had learned to be wives and mothers and had enough sociability, the urge for creativity returned—but not the opportunity.

For working class women, keeping the family together and the bills paid is a full-time job. Upper middle class women are convinced that life ought to be more than raising a family, but lower middle class ones are not that sure. They want to venture into nonfamilial roles, but not so intensively as to engender role conflict and anxiety. As a result, they search for easy creativity, activities that do not require, as Levittowners put it, "upsetting the family and household." Serious artistic activity is difficult under such conditions, yet a compromise solution such as needlework or painting-by-numbers is not entirely satisfactory either, because, however rewarding, people know it is not really art. One Levittowner I met expressed the ambivalence between the familial role and artistic aspirations in an especially tortured way. She explained that she was very sensitive to paintings, but confessed that whenever she visited museums, she would begin to think about her family. She resolved the ambivalence by rejecting paintings that made her "think too much about art." For most people, however, the ambivalence is less intense.

A similarly ambivalent pattern is evident in government involvement.

Many lower middle class people believe that the moral framework which governs their personal lives, the sort of relations they have with family members and friends, ought to govern organizational life and society as well. Any other type of behavior they call "politics," in and out of political life, and they try to avoid it as immoral. Working class people have the same perspective, but they are also realists and will exploit politics for their own ends, and upper middle class people believe in moral (reform) politics, but its norms are not borrowed from the family. Lower middle class citizens are once again caught between the standards of home and of the outside world, however, and the result is often political inaction. It is for them that politicians put on performances to show that their decisions are based on the standards of home and family and run election campaigns demonstrating the personal honesty of their candidates and the opposition candidates' immorality.

Of course, these are cultural propensities to act, and when personal interests are threatened, lower middle class people defend them as heartily as anyone else. Then, they identify their actions with morality—so much so that they lose sight of their self-interest and are easily hurt when others point out to them that they are selfishly motivated. Whereas working class people then become cynical, lower middle class people become hypocritical, often without being conscious of it. Blandness turns easily to bitterness, anger, and blind conflict—blind because every act of offense or self-defense is clothed in the terminology of personal morality.

What appears as blandness, then, to the outside observer is the outcome of conflict between self and society, and between what ought to be and what is. When and if a lower middle class person is secure, he appears bland, because he is not really willing to act within the larger society; when he is threatened, he is extremely angry, because his moral view of the world is upset. One target of his anger is the working class people who are less bothered by the moral dilemmas of the larger society; another is the upper middle class activists who keep pressuring him to translate morality into action and to take a stand on community issues.

Many of these cultural predispositions seem to occur more among lower middle class women than among their husbands. If the men are employed in a bureaucracy, as most are, their work involves them not only in the larger society but also in office or factory political struggles which leave them little time to think about the ambivalence between the standards of home and outside world. The women, however, caught in a role that keeps them at home, are forever trying to break out of its confines, only to confront ambivalent situations. They respond with inhibiting blandness; it is they who are most concerned with respectability. Indeed, living with neighbors employed in large bureaucracies, I was struck over and over again by the feeling that if the men were "organization men," they were so only by necessity, not by inclination, and that if they were left alone, they would gravitate toward untrammeled creativity and individualism. Their wives, on the other hand, defended what Whyte called the Social Ethic, rejecting extreme actions and skeptical opinions, and tried to get their men to toe the line of lower middle class morality. If anything, their inclinations drove them toward being "organization women." But then, they had the job of maintaining the family's status image on the block, and they spent their days in the near-anarchy created by small children. Perhaps they were simply escaping *into* the order of lower middle class norms, while the men were escaping *from* the order imposed by their bureaucratic work.

LEVITTOWN IS "ENDSVILLE": THE ADOLESCENT VIEW

The adult conception of Levittown's vitality is not shared by its adolescents. Many consider it a dull place to which they have been brought involuntarily by their parents. Often there is no place to go and nothing to do after school. Although most adolescents have no trouble in their student role, many are bored after school and some are angry, expressing that anger through thinly veiled hostility to adults and vandalism against adult property. Their relationship to the adults is fraught with tension, which discourages community attempts to solve what is defined as their recreational problem.

Essays which students in grades 6–12 wrote for me early in 1961 suggest that most children are satisfied with Levittown until adolescence.[26] Sixty-eight per cent of the sixth-graders liked Levittown, but only 45 per cent of the eighth-graders, 37 per cent of the tenth-graders, and 39 per cent of the twelfth-graders did. In comparison, 85 per cent of the adults responded positively to a similar question.[27] Likes and dislikes reflect the state of recreational and social opportunities. Girls make little use of recreational facilities until they become adolescents, and before the tenth grade, they like Levittown better than the boys. Dislikes revolve around "nothing to do." The sixth- and eighth-grade boys say there are not enough gyms, playing fields, or hills, and no transportation for getting to existing facilities. Both sexes complain about the lack of neighborhood stores and that the houses are too small, lack privacy, and are poorly built. By the twelfth grade, disenchantment with the existing facilities has set in; those who like Levittown stress the newness and friendliness of the community, but references to the pool, the shopping center, and the bowling alley are nega-

26 The students were asked what they liked and disliked about living in Levittown, and what they missed from their former residence. Since they were not asked to sign their names, and the questions were general, I believe the essays were honest responses. I purposely included no questions about the schools, and teachers were instructed not to give any guidance about how the questions should be answered. (One teacher did tell the children what to write, and these essays were not analyzed.) The data presented here are based on a sample of one sixth- and one eighth-grade class from each of the three elementary schools, and of all tenth- and twelfth-grade classes.

27 The data are not strictly comparable, for the adults were asked outright whether they liked or disliked living in Levittown, whereas the teenagers' attitudes were inferred from the tone of the essays.

tive.[28] As one twelfth-grader pointed out, "Either you have to pay a lot of money to go to the movies or the bowling alley, or you go to too many parties and that gets boring." Lack of facilities is reported most often by the older girls, for the boys at least have athletic programs put on by civic groups.[29]

But the commonest gripe is the shortage of ready transportation, which makes not only facilities but, more important, other teenagers inaccessible. One girl complained, "After school hours, you walk into an entirely different world. Everyone goes his own separate way, to start his homework, take a nap, or watch TV. That is the life of a vegetable, not a human being." A car, then, becomes in a way as essential to teenagers as to adults. Moreover, many small-town teenagers like to meet outside the community, for it is easier to "have fun" where one's parents and other known adults cannot disapprove. A high school senior who took a job to buy a car put it dramatically:

> I had no choice, it was either going to work or cracking up. I have another week of boring habits, then (when I get the car) I'll start living. I can get out of Levittown and go to other towns where I have many friends. . . . In plain words, a boy shouldn't live here if he is between the ages of 14–17. At this age he is using his adult mind, and that doesn't mean riding a bike or smoking his first cigarette. He wants to be big and popular and go out and live it up. I am just starting the life I want. I couldn't ask for more than being a senior in a brand new high school, with the best of students and teachers, and my car on its way.

Girls are less likely to have access to a car, and one explained, "We have to walk, and the streets wind, and cause you to walk two miles instead of one as the crow flies."

The adults have provided some facilities for teenage activities, but not always successfully. One problem is that "teenage" is an adult tag; adolescents grade themselves by age. Older ones refused to attend dances with the younger set, considering forced association with their juniors insulting.[30] Some adolescents also found the adult chaperones oppressive. At

---

[28] Twenty-eight per cent of the boys liked the community's newness; 18 per cent, the friendly people. Among the girls, 34 per cent liked the people; 20 per cent, Levittown's newness.

[29] Twenty-five per cent of the tenth-graders and 50 per cent of the twelfth-graders say there is nothing to do, and 25 per cent and 46 per cent, respectively, mention the lack of recreational facilities. Among the twelfth-grade girls, 56 per cent mention it.

[30] Similarly in the elementary schools, seventh- and eighth-graders complained about having to go to school with "immature" and "childish" students; when they were moved to the high school, the older students objected to their presence in the same terms.

first, the chaperones interfered openly by urging strangers to dance with each other in order to get everyone on the floor and to discourage intimate dancing among couples. When the teenagers protested, they stopped, but hovered uneasily in the background.[31]

Specifically, adolescent malcontent stems from two sources: Levittown was not designed for them, and adults are reluctant to provide the recreational facilities and gathering places they want. Like most suburban communities, Levittown was planned for families with young children. The bedrooms are too small to permit an adolescent to do anything but study or sleep; they lack the privacy and soundproofing to allow him to invite his friends over. Unfortunately, the community is equally inhospitable. Shopping centers are intended for car-owning adults, and in accord with the desire of property owners, are kept away from residential areas. Being new, Levittown lacks low-rent shopping areas which can afford to subsist on the marginal purchases made by adolescents. In 1961, a few luncheonettes in neighborhood shopping centers and a candy store and a bowling alley in the big center were the only places for adolescents to congregate.[32] Coming in droves, they overwhelmed those places and upset the merchants. Not only do teenagers occupy space without making significant purchases, but they also discourage adult customers. Merchants faced with high rent cannot subsist on teenage spending and complain to the police if teenagers "hang out" at their places. Street corners are off limits, too, for a clump of adolescents soon becomes noisy enough to provoke a call to the police. Eventually they feel hounded and even defined as juvenile delinquents. Said one twelfth-grade girl, "I feel like a hood to be getting chased by the police for absolutely nothing."

The schools were not designed for after-hours use, except for adults and for student activities which entertain adults, such as varsity athletics. The auditoriums were made available for dances, although when these began, the school administration promptly complained about scuffed floors and damaged fixtures. Only at the swimming pool are teenagers not in the way of adult priorities, and during the day, when adults are not using it, it is their major gathering place. But even here, smoking and noisy activities are prohibited.

The design deficiencies cannot be altered, and should not be if they are a problem only for teenagers, but there is no inherent reason why teenage facilities cannot be provided. However, adults disagree on what is needed and, indeed, on the desirability of facilities, for reasons partly

[31] There was also a dispute over programming: the adults wanted slow music and the traditional dances they knew best; the teenagers wanted the latest best-selling records and the newest dances. They signed petitions for the ouster of the man who chose the records, but the adults refused to accept the petitions, arguing that they would be followed by petitions to oust the school superintendent.

[32] Indeed, the existing teenage hangouts in little luncheonettes resulted from the lucky accident that the builder and the township planner were unable to regulate and limit the number of small shopping centers which sprang up on the edge of the community.

political, but fundamentally social and psychological. For one thing, adults are uncertain about how to treat teenagers; for another, they harbor a deep hostility toward them which is cultural and, at bottom, sexual in nature.

There are two adult views of the teenager, one permissive, the other restrictive. The former argues that a teenager is a responsible individual who should be allowed to run his own affairs with some adult help. The latter, subscribed to by the majority, considers him still a child who needs adult supervision and whose activities ought to be conducted by adult rules to integrate him into adult society. For example, when one of the community organizations set up teenage dances, there was some discussion about whether teenagers should run them. Not only was this idea rejected, but the adults then ran the dances on the basis of the "highest" standards.[33] Boys were required to wear ties and jackets, girls, dresses, on the assumption that this would encourage good behavior, whereas blue jeans, tee shirts, and sweaters somehow would not. The adults could not resist imposing their own norms of dress in exchange for providing dances.

The advocates of restriction also rejected the permissive point of view because they felt it wrong to give teenagers what they wanted. Believing that teenagers had it "too easy," they argued that "if you make them work for programs, they appreciate them more." Logically, they should, therefore, have let the teenagers set up their own activities, but their arguments were not guided by logic; they were, rather, rationalizations for their fear of teenagers. Although the "permissives" pointed out that teenagers might well set up stricter rules than adults, the "restrictives" feared catastrophes: fights, the "wrong crowd" taking over, pregnancies, and contraceptives found in or near the teenage facility. These fears accounted for the rules governing dances and inhibited the establishment of an adult-run teenage center, for the voluntary associations and the politicians were afraid that if violence or sexual activity occurred, they would be blamed for it.

The problem is twofold: restrictive adults want adolescents to be children preparing for adulthood, and are threatened by the teenage or youth culture they see around them. By now, adolescents are a cultural minority like any other, but whereas no Levittowners expect Italians to behave like Jews, most still expect teenagers to behave like children. They are supposed to participate in the family more than they do and, legally still under age, to subsume their own wishes to the adults'. The failure of teenagers to go along is blamed on the parents as well. If parents would only take more interest in their adolescent children, spend more time with them, be "pals" with them, and so on, then misbehavior—and even youth culture—would not develop. This argument is supported by the claim that delinquency is caused by broken homes or by both parents' holding full-time jobs.

Such views are espoused particularly by Catholics, who share tradi-

---

[33] At one point adult-run dances failed to attract teenagers, and a group of teenage leaders were delegated to run the dances themselves. This foundered because other teenagers disagreed with the rules and program set up by these leaders, and since only one opportunity for dancing was provided, they could express their disagreement only by nonattendance.

tional working class attitudes; the parochial school, with its emphasis on discipline to keep children out of trouble, is their embodiment. Even adult-devised programs are considered undesirable, for, as one Catholic working class father put it, "In summer, children should either work or be at home. Summer arts and crafts programs are a waste of time. My kid brought home dozens of pictures. What's he going to do with so many pictures?" The adolescents' social choices are also restricted. Adults active in youth programs frequently try to break up their groups, damning them as cliques or gangs, and even separating friends when athletic teams are chosen. Some teenagers react by minimizing contact with adults, pursuing their activities privately and becoming remarkably uncommunicative. In essence, they lead a separate life which frees them from undue parental control and gives an air of mystery to the teenager and his culture.

Among restrictive adults, the image of the teenager is of an irresponsible, parasitic individual, who attends school without studying, hangs out with his peers looking for fun and adventure, and gets into trouble—above all, over sex. There were rumors of teenage orgies in Levittown's school playgrounds, in shopping center parking lots, and on the remaining rural roads of the township. The most fantastic rumor had 44 girls in the senior class pregnant, with one boy singlehandedly responsible for six of them. Some inquiry on my part turned up the facts: two senior girls were pregnant and one of them was about to be married.

If the essays the students wrote for me have any validity, the gap between adult fantasy and adolescent reality is astonishing. Most teenagers do not even date; their social life takes place in groups. Judging by their comments about the friendliness of adult neighbors, they are quiet youngsters who get along well with adults and spend most of their time preparing themselves for adulthood. Needless to say, these essays would not have revealed delinquent activities of sex play. However, I doubt that more than 5 per cent of the older teenagers live up to anything like the adult image of them.

What, then, accounts for the discrepancy? For one thing, adults take little interest in their children's education; they want to be assured that their children are getting along in school, but not much more. The bond that might exist here is thus absent. Changes in education during the last two decades have been so great that even interested parents can do little to help their children with their school work. Consequently, adults focus on teenagers in their nonstudent roles, noting their absence from home, the intensity of their tie to friends and cliques, and their rebelliousness.

Second, there is the normal gap between the generations, enlarged by the recent flowering of youth culture, much of which is incomprehensible or unesthetic to adults. Despite the parents' belief that they should be responsible for their adolescents' behavior, they cannot participate in many joint activities or talk meaningfully with them about the experiences and problems of teenage life. This gap is exacerbated by a strange parental amnesia about their own—not so distant—adolescence. I recall a letter written by a twenty-one-year-old mother who wanted to help the Township Committee set up a delinquency prevention council because she was concerned about teenage misbehavior.

Third, there is enough teenage vandalism and delinquency to provide raw material for the adult image, although not enough to justify it. According to the police and the school superintendent, serious delinquency in Levittown was minimal; in 1961, about 50 adolescents accounted for most of it. Many were children from working class backgrounds who did poorly in school, or from disturbed middle class families. From 1959 to 1961, only 12 cases were serious enough to go to the county juvenile court, and some were repeaters. Vandalism is more prevalent. The first victim was the old Willingboro YMCA, which was wrecked twice before it was torn down. Schools have been defaced, windows broken, garbage thrown into the pools, flowerbeds destroyed, and bicycles "borrowed." The perpetrators are rarely caught, but those who are caught are teenagers, thus making it possible for adults to suspect all adolescents and maintain their image.

Finally, some adults seem to project their own desires for excitement and adventures onto the youngsters. For them, teenagers function locally as movie stars and beatniks do on the national scene—as exotic creatures reputed to live for sex and adventure. Manifestly, teenagers act as more prosaic entertainers: in varsity athletics, high school dramatic societies, and bands, but the girls are also expected to provide glamor. One of the first activities of the Junior Chamber of Commerce was a Miss Levittown contest, in which teenage girls competed for honors in evening gown, bathing suit, and talent contests—the "talent" usually involving love songs or covertly erotic dances. At such contests unattainable maidens show off their sexuality—often unconsciously—in order to win the nomination. Men in the audience comment *sotto voce* about the girls' attractiveness, wishing to sleep with them and speculating whether that privilege is available to the contest judges and boyfriends. From here, it is only a short step to the conviction that girls are promiscuous with their teenage friends, which heightens adult envy, fear, and the justification for restrictive measures. The sexual function of the teenager became apparent when the popularity of the Miss Levittown contest led to plans for a Mrs. Levittown contest. This plan was quickly dropped, however, for the idea of married women parading in bathing suits was thought to be in bad taste, especially by the women. Presumably, young mothers are potential sexual objects, whereas the teenagers are, like movie stars, unattainable, and can therefore serve as voyeuristic objects.

Although suburbia is often described as a hotbed of adultery in popular fiction, this is an urban fantasy. Levittown is quite monogamous, and I am convinced that most suburbs are more so than most cities.[34] The desire for sexual relations with attractive neighbors may be ever present, but when life is lived in a goldfish bowl, adultery is impossible to hide from the neighbors—even if there were motels in Levittown and baby-sitters could be found for both parties. Occasionally such episodes do take place,

[34] A comparison of urban and suburban marriages indicated that extramarital affairs occur principally in older and well-educated populations, and that place of residence is irrelevant. Ubell. For another observer's skepticism about suburban adultery, see Whyte (1956), pp. 355–357.

after which the people involved often run off together or leave the community. There are also periodic stories of more bizarre sexual escapades, usually about community leaders. In one such story, a local politician was driving down the dark roads of the township in a sports car with a naked young woman while his wife thought he was at a political meeting. If there was any roadside adultery, however, it remained unreported, for no cases ever appeared on the police blotters during the two years I saw them.[35] Similar stories made the rounds in Park Forest, the new town I studied in 1949, and one of them, which began after a party where some extramarital necking had taken place, soon reported the gathering as a wife-swapping orgy.

"The Juvenile Problem" and Its Solutions

The cultural differences between adults and adolescents have precipitated an undeclared and subconscious war between them, as pervasive as the class struggle, which prevents the adults from solving what they call "the juvenile problem." Indeed, putting it that way is part of the trouble, for much of the adult effort has been aimed at discouraging delinquency, providing recreational activities in the irrational belief that these could prevent it. Sports programs were supposed to exhaust the teenagers so that they would be too tired to get into trouble (harking back to the Victorian myth that a regimen of cold showers and sports would dampen sexual urges, although ironically, varsity athletes were also suspected of being stellar sexual performers); dances were to keep them off the street. When delinquency did not abate, a Youth Guidance Commission to deal with "the problem," and a Teenage Panel to punish delinquencies too minor for court actions, were set up. The police chief asked for a curfew to keep youngsters off the street at night, hoping to put pressure on parents to act as enforcing agents and to get his department out of the cross fire between teenagers, merchants, and home owners. Chasing the teenagers from shopping centers and street corners was useless, for having no other place to go they always returned the next night, particularly since they knew people would not swear out complaints against their neighbors' (or customers') children. The police chief also did not want "the kids to feel they are being bugged," for they would come to hate his men and create more trouble for them.[36] If he cracked down on them, they would retaliate; if he did not, the adults would accuse him of laxity. Although the curfew was strongly supported by parents who could not control their children, it was rejected as unenforceable.

Adult solutions to the juvenile problem were generally shaped by

---

[35] Since the blotter listed adolescent promiscuity, adult suicide attempts, and even drunkenness and family quarrels among community leaders, I assume it was not censored to exclude adultery.

[36] Actually, since the police usually sided with the merchants against the teenagers, the latter did feel "bugged."

other institutional goals which took priority over adolescent needs. The organizations which scheduled dances wanted to advertise themselves and their community service inclinations, even competing for the right to hold them, and the churches set up youth groups to bring the teenagers into the church. Indeed, those who decide on adolescent programs either have vested interests in keeping teenagers in a childlike status (parents and educators, for example) or are charged with the protection of adult interests (police and politicians). The primacy of adult priorities was brought out by a 1961 PTA panel on "How Is Our Community Meeting the Needs of the Adolescents?" With one exception the panelists (chosen to represent the various adults responsible for teenagers) ignored these needs, talking only about what teenagers should do for *them*. For example, the parent on the panel said, "The needs of adolescents should first be met in the home and young energies should be guided into the proper normal channels." The teacher suggested that "parents should never undermine the authority of the teacher. Parents should help maintain the authority of the school over the child, and the school will in turn help maintain the authority of the parent over the child." The minister urged parents to "encourage youth leadership responsibilities within the church," and the police chief explained "the importance of teaching adolescents their proper relationship to the law and officers of the law." [37]

Political incentives for a municipal or even a semipublic recreation program were also absent. Not only were prospective sponsors afraid they would be held responsible for teenage misbehavior occurring under their auspices, but in 1961 not many Levittowners had adolescent children and not all of them favored a public program. Middle class parents either had no problems with their youngsters or objected to the working class advocacy of municipal recreation, and some working class parents felt that once children had reached adolescence they were on their own. The eventual clients of the program, the adolescents, had no political influence whatsoever. They were too young to vote, and although they might have persuaded their parents to demand facilities for them, they probably suspected that what their parents wanted for them was more of what had already been provided.

In the end, then, the adults got used to the little delinquency and vandalism that took place, and the teenagers became sullen and unhappy, complaining, "This place is Endsville," and wishing their parents would move back to communities which had facilities for them or pressuring them for cars to go to neighboring towns.

The best summary of what is wrong—and what should be done—was stated concisely by a twelfth-grade essayist: "I think the adults should spend less time watching for us to do something wrong and help us raise money for a community center. We're not asking for it, we only want their help." If one begins with the assumption that adolescents are rational and responsible human beings whose major "problem" is that they have become a distinctive minority subculture, it is not too difficult to suggest

[37] "Panel Features Junior High P.T.A. Meeting," *Levittown Herald*, January 26, 1961.

programs. What else the teenagers want in the way of recreation can be readily inferred from their essays: besides the center, a range of inexpensive coffeehouses and soda shops and other meeting places, bowling alleys, amusement arcades, places for dancing, ice and roller skating rinks, garages for mechanically inclined car owners (all within walking or bicycling distance or accessible by public transportation), and enough of each so that the various age groups and separate cliques have facilities they can call their own. Since adolescents are well supplied with spending money, many of these facilities can be set up commercially. Others may need public support. It would, for example, be possible to provide some municipal subsidies to luncheonette operators who are willing to make their businesses into teenage social centers.[38]

Recreational and social facilities are not enough, however. Part of the adolescents' dissatisfaction with the community—as with adult society in general—is their functionlessness outside of school. American society really has no use for them other than as students, and condemns them to spend most of their spare time in recreational pursuits. They are trying to learn to be adults, but since the community and the larger society want them to be children, they learn adulthood only at school—and there imperfectly. Yet many tasks in the community now go unfilled because of lack of public funds, for example, clerical, data-gathering, and other functions at city hall; and tutoring children, coaching their sports, and leading their recreational programs. These are meaningful duties, and I suspect many adolescents could fill them, either on a voluntary or a nominal wage basis. Finally, teenagers want to learn to be themselves and do for themselves. It should be possible to give them facilities of their own—or even land on which they could build—and let them organize, construct, and run their own centers and work places.

Needless to say, such autonomy would come up against the very real political difficulties that faced the more modest programs suggested in Levittown, and would surely be rejected by the community.[39] The ideal solution, therefore, is to plan for teenage needs outside the local adult decision-making structure, and perhaps even outside the community. It might be possible to establish Teenage Authorities that would play the same interstitial role in the governmental structure as other authorities set up in connection with intercommunity and regional planning functions. Perhaps the most feasible approach is to develop commercially profitable facilities, to be set up either by teenagers or by a private entrepreneur who would need to be less sensitive to political considerations than a public agency. If and when the "juvenile problem" becomes more serious in the suburbs, federal funds may become available for facilities and for programs to create jobs, like those now being developed for urban teenagers. Most likely, this will only happen when "trouble" begins to mount.

[38] A combination neighborhood store and social center has been proposed in the plan for the new town of Columbia, Maryland.

[39] In 1966, no teenage centers had yet been established in Levittown, and campaigning politicians were still arguing about the wisdom of doing so.

REFERENCES

Anderson, Judith, and Settani, Nicholas. "Resales in Levittown, Pennsylvania, 1952–1960." Unpublished paper, Department of City Planning, University of Pennsylvania, 1961.

Fried, Marc. "Grieving for a Lost Home," in Leonard J. Duhl, ed., *The Urban Condition*. New York: Basic Books, 1963, pp. 151–171.

Fromm, Erich. *The Sane Society*. New York: Holt, Rinehart and Winston, 1955.

Gabower, Genevieve. *Behavior Problems of Children in Navy Officers' Families as Related to Social Conditions of Navy Life*. Washington: Catholic University of America Press, 1959.

Gans, Herbert J. *The Urban Villagers: Group and Class in the Life of Italian-Americans*. New York: Free Press of Glencoe, 1962(a).

Gordon, R., Gordon, K., and Gunther, M. *The Split Level Trap*. New York: Geis, 1961.

Gutman, Robert. "Population Mobility in the American Middle Class," in Leonard J. Duhl, ed., *The Urban Condition*. New York: Basic Books, 1963, pp. 172–183.

Keats, John. *The Crack in the Picture Window*. Boston: Houghton-Mifflin, 1956 (Ballantine Books paperback, 1957).

Kornhauser, William. *Politics of Mass Society*. New York: Free Press of Glencoe, 1959.

Lipset, S. M. *Political Man*. Garden City: Doubleday, 1960.

Orzack, Louis H., and Sanders, Irwin T. *A Social Profile of Levittown, New York*. Ann Arbor: University Microfilms, O. P. 13438, 1961.

Pederson, Frank A., and Sullivan, Eugene. "Effects of Geographical Mobility and Parent Personality Factors on Emotional Disorders in Children." Washington: Walter Reed General Hospital, 1963, mimeographed.

Riesman, David (with N. Glazer and R. Denney). *The Lonely Crowd*. New Haven: Yale University Press, 1950.

Stein, Maurice. *The Eclipse of Community*. Princeton: Princeton University Press, 1960.

Ubell, Earl. "Marriage in the Suburbs." *New York Herald-Tribune*, January 4–8, 1959.

Vidich, Arthur J., and Bensman, Joseph. *Small Town in Mass Society*. Princeton: Princeton University Press, 1958.

Webber, Melvin M. "Order in Diversity: Community Without Propinquity," in Lowdon Wingo, Jr., ed., *Cities and Space: The Future Use of Urban Land*. Baltimore: Johns Hopkins University Press, 1963, pp. 23–54.

Whyte, William H., Jr. *The Organization Man*. New York: Simon & Schuster, 1956.

Wilensky, Harold L. "Life Cycle, Work Situation and Participation in Formal Associations," in Robert W. Kleemeier, ed., *Aging and Leisure*. New York: Oxford University Press, 1961, pp. 213–242.

Willmott, Peter. *The Evolution of a Community*. London: Routledge & Kegan Paul, 1963.

The Counter-Culture

WILLIAM L. O'NEILL

If we use the term "culture" to refer to the way of life of a people, then American society from its very beginning has been made up of a variety of cultures. However, throughout our history a more or less prevailing culture has dominated or attempted to dominate competing or conflicting cultures. Over the years, attempts have been made to describe this dominant culture, and many studies have pointed out aspects of the culture that have had a tremendous success in creating certain attitudes, if not always in controlling behavior.

The idea of culture contains both attitudes and behavior, and the secret of successful studies of any culture derives from the ability of the scholar to ferret out the patterns of behavior that may, in fact, run counter to the overt attitudes of a group.

What interests us in the following selection, however, is not the conflict between attitude and behavior, but the conflict between the dominant culture and a deviant culture that has as its goal a deliberate attack on the dominant culture and an elimination of the gap between attitude and behavior—what the participants in this counter-culture call hypocrisy.

Ever since the founding of the Massachusetts Bay Colony, the body of New World society has contained deviant cultural elements. This description refers, not to such entirely foreign cultures as the American Indian or the African, but to those deviations from the dominant culture that were exhibited by the settlers themselves. The English settlers who danced with Indians around a Maypole at Merry Mount in the 1630s presented a challenge to the prevailing culture; such challenges persist to the present day. The dominant culture has usually had the power of public opinion or, when necessary, the power of police authority to subdue deviants in its midst. This power, however, is not always invoked. In the twentieth century, there has developed a tradition often referred to as "bohemian" culture, restricted almost entirely to a small number of artists, writers, and composers. These creative bohemians have not sought to foster their way of life —composed as it is of a freedom from what they call bourgeois morality—on the rest of America. They merely want to be left alone. And they usually are unless they become too flagrant in their violations of community norms.

In the 1960s, an extremely powerful challenge to the dominant culture came into being. The term counter-culture, rather than sub-culture, can correctly be applied to this movement because it saw itself as a frontal attack on what it called "straight" culture. It had a visionary purpose—to "turn on" the world. At the heart of the counter-culture was a contempt for all traditional forms of authority and, theoretically, an intent to replace them with the authority of in-

ner experience and interpersonal relationships. Since these new authorities were difficult to isolate and identify, much less obey, the
counter-culture's adherents turned to all sorts of gurus (spiritual leaders) in an attempt to find their way into the brave new world they
forecast.

In the chapter from his book on the 1960s reprinted below,
William O'Neill, of Rutgers University, describes many facets of the
counter-culture movement of the decade. He notes the critical importance of the mass media, which proved so influential in spreading the
new gospel as well as in denigrating it. O'Neill rightly points out that
the movement was not limited to the young but increasingly began to
attract older people to certain aspects of the freedom it espoused. In
his concluding paragraphs, the author, perhaps, renders too harsh a
judgment on the movement. A longer perspective will allow future
historians to evaluate more accurately the impact of this flashy and
furious attempt to find a more meaningful and more human life-style
in the midst of what many saw as an inhuman and materialistic
middle-class morality.

Counter-culture as a term appeared rather late in the decade. It largely
replaced the term "youth culture," which finally proved too limited.
When the sixties began, youth culture meant the way adolescents lived.
Its central institutions were the high school and the mass media. Its principal activities were consuming goods and enacting courtship rituals. Critics
and students of the youth culture were chiefly interested in the status and
value systems associated with it. As time went on, college enrollments increased to the point where colleges were nearly as influential as high
schools in shaping the young. The molders of youthful opinion got more
ambitious. Where once entertainers were content to amuse for profit,
many began seeing themselves as moral philosophers. Music especially became a medium of propaganda, identifying the young as a distinct force in
society with unique values and aspirations. This helped produce a kind of
ideological struggle between the young and their elders called the "generation gap." It was the first time in American history that social conflict was
understood to be a function of age. Yet the young were not all rebellious.
Most in fact retained confidence in the "system" and its norms. Many
older people joined the rebellion, whose progenitors were as often over
thirty (where the generation gap was supposed to begin) as under it. The
attack on accepted views and styles broadened so confusingly that "youth
culture" no longer described it adequately. Counter-culture was a sufficiently vague and elastic substitute. It meant all things to all men and em-

braced everything new from clothing to politics. Some viewed the counter-culture as mankind's best, maybe only, hope; others saw it as a portent of civilization's imminent ruin. Few recalled the modest roots from which it sprang.

Even in the 1950's and very early sixties, when people still worried about conformity and the silent generation, there were different drummers to whose beat millions would one day march. The bohemians of that era (called "beatniks" or "beats") were only a handful, but they practiced free love, took drugs, repudiated the straight world, and generally showed which way the wind was blowing. They were highly publicized, so when the bohemian impulse strengthened, dropouts knew what was expected of them. While the beats showed their contempt for social norms mostly in physical ways, others did so intellectually. Norman Mailer, in "The White Negro," held up the sensual, lawless hipster as a model of behavior under oppressive capitalism. He believed, according to "The Time of Her Time," that sexual orgasm was the pinnacle of human experience, perhaps also an approach to ultimate truth. Norman O. Brown's *Life Against Death*, a psychoanalytic interpretation of history, was an underground classic which argued that cognition subverted intuition. Brown called for a return to "polymorphous perversity," man's natural estate. The popularity of Zen Buddhism demonstrated that others wished to slip the bonds of Western rationalism; so, from a different angle, did the vogue for black humor.

The most prophetic black humorist was Joseph Heller, whose novel *Catch-22* came out in 1960. Though set in World War II the book was even more appropriate to the Indochinese war. Later Heller said, "That was the war I had in mind; a war fought without military provocation, a war in which the real enemy is no longer the other side, but someone allegedly on your side. The ridiculous war I felt lurking in the future when I wrote the book." *Catch-22* was actually written during the Cold War, and sold well in the early sixties because it attacked the perceptions on which that war, like the Indochinese war that it fathered, grew. At the time reviewers didn't know what to make of *Catch-22*. World War II had been, as everyone knew, an absolutely straightforward case of good versus evil. Yet to Heller there was little moral difference between combatants. In fact all his characters are insane, or carry normal attributes to insane lengths. They belong to a bomber squadron in the Mediterranean. Terrified of combat, most hope for ground duty and are free to request it, but: "There was only one catch and that was Catch-22, which specified that a concern for one's own safety in the face of dangers that were real and immediate was the process of a rational mind. Orr was crazy and could be grounded. All he had to do was ask; and as soon as he did, he would no longer be crazy and would have to fly more missions. Orr would be crazy to fly more missions and sane if he didn't, but if he was sane he had to fly them. If he flew them he was crazy and didn't have to; but if he didn't want to he was sane and had to."

The squadron's success depends more on having a perfect bomb pattern than hitting the target. Milo Minderbinder is the key man in the Theater, though only a lieutenant, because he embodies the profit motive. He puts the entire war on a paying basis and hires the squadron out impartially to both sides. At the end Yossarian, the novel's hero, resolves his dilemma by setting out for neutral Sweden in a rubber raft. This was what hundreds of real deserters and draft evaders would be doing soon. It was also a perfect symbol for the masses of dropouts who sought utopian alternatives to the straight world. One day there would be hundreds of thousands of Yossarians, paddling away from the crazed society in frail crafts of their own devising. *Catch-22* was not just black comedy, nor even chiefly an anti-war novel, but a metaphor that helped shape the moral vision of an era.[1]

Although children and adolescents watched a great deal of television in the sixties, it seemed at first to have little effect. Surveys were always showing that youngsters spent fifty-four hours a week or whatever in front of the tube, yet what they saw was so bland or predictable as to make little difference. The exceptions were news programs, documentaries, and dramatic specials. Few watched them. What did influence the young was popular music, folk music first and then rock. Large-scale enthusiasm for folk music began in 1958 when the Kingston Trio recorded a song, "Tom Dooley," that sold two million records. This opened the way for less slickly commercial performers. Some, like Pete Seeger, who had been singing since the depression, were veteran performers. Others, like Joan Baez, were newcomers. It was conventional for folk songs to tell a story. Hence the idiom had always lent itself to propaganda. Seeger possessed an enormous repertoire of message songs that had gotten him blacklisted by the mass media years before. Joan Baez cared more for the message than the music, and after a few years devoted herself mainly to peace work. The folk-music vogue was an early stage in the politicalization of youth, a forerunner of the counter-culture. This was hardly apparent at the time. Folk music was not seen as morally reprehensible in the manner of rock and roll. It was a familiar genre. Folk was gentle music for the most part, and even when sung in protest did not offend many. Malvina Reynolds' "What Have They Done to the Rain?" complained of radioactive fallout which all detested. Pete Seeger's anti-war song "Where Have All the Flowers Gone?" was a favorite with both pacifists and the troops in Vietnam.

Bob Dylan was different. Where most folk singers were either clean-cut or homey looking, Dylan had wild long hair. He resembled a poor white dropout of questionable morals. His songs were hard-driving, powerful, intense. It was hard to be neutral about them. "The Times They Are a-Changing" was perhaps the first song to exploit the generation gap. Dylan's life was as controversial as his ideology. Later he dropped politics

[1] Lenny Bruce was a more tragic harbinger of change. He was a successful night club comedian who created an obscene form of black comedy that involved more social criticism than humor. Bruce was first arrested for saying "motherfucker" on stage in 1962. Later he was busted for talking dirty about the Pope and many lesser offenses. He may have been insane. He died early from persecution and drug abuse, and then became an honored martyr in the anti-Establishment pantheon. He was one of the spiritual fathers of the yippies.

and got interested in rock music. At the Newport Jazz Festival in 1965 he was booed when he introduced a fusion of his own called "folk-rock." He went his own way after that, disowned by the politically minded but admired by a great cult following attracted as much, perhaps, by his independent life as by his music. He advanced the counter-culture in both ways and made money too. This also was an inspiration to those who came after him.

Another early expression, which coexisted with folk music, though quite unlike it, was the twist. Dance crazes were nothing new, but the twist was remarkable because it came to dominate social dancing. It used to be that dance fads were here today and gone tomorrow, while the two-step went on forever. Inexpert, that is to say most, social dancers had been loyal to it for generations. It played a key role in the traditional youth culture. Who could imagine a high school athletic event that did not end with couples clinging to one another on the dimly lit gym floor, while an amateur dance band plodded gamely on? When in 1961 the twist became popular, moralists were alarmed. It called for vigorous, exhibitionistic movements. Prurient men were reminded of the stripper's bumps and grinds. They felt the twist incited lust. Ministers denounced it. Yet in the twist (and its numerous descendants), bodies were not rubbed together as in the two-step, which had embarrassed millions of schoolboys. Millions more had suffered when through awkwardness they bumped or trod on others. The twist, by comparison, was easy and safe. No partner was bothered by the other's maladroitness. It aroused few passions. That was the practical reason for its success. But there was an ideological impulse behind it also. Amidst the noise and tumult each person danced alone, "doing his own thing," as would soon be said. But though alone, the dancer was surrounded by others doing their own thing in much the same manner. The twist celebrated both individuality and communality. This was to become a hallmark of the counter-culture, the right of everyone to be different in much the same way. The twist also foretold the dominance of rock, to which it was so well suited.

No group contributed more to the counter-culture than the Beatles, though, like folk music and the twist, their future significance was not at first apparent. Beatlemania began on October 13, 1963, when the quartet played at the London Palladium. The police, caught unawares, were hardly able to control the maddened throngs. On February 9, 1964, they appeared on U.S. television. The show received fifty thousand ticket requests for a theater that seated eight hundred. They were mobbed at the airport, besieged in their hotel, and adored everywhere. Even their soiled bed linen found a market. Their next recording, "Can't Buy Me Love," sold three million copies in advance of release, a new world's record. Their first movie, *A Hard Day's Night* (1964), was both a critical and a popular success. Some reviewers compared them with the Marx brothers. They became millionaires overnight. The Queen decorated them for helping ease the balance-of-payments deficit. By 1966 they were so rich that they could afford to give up live performances.

For a time the Beatles seemed just another pop phenomenon, Elvis Presley multiplied by four. Few thought their music very distinguished.

The reasons for its wide acceptance were hard to fathom. Most felt their showmanship was the key factor. They wore their hair longer than was fashionable, moved about a lot on stage, and avoided the class and racial identifications associated with earlier rock stars. Elvis had cultivated a proletarian image. Other rock stars had been black, or exploited the Negro rhythm-and-blues tradition. The Beatles were mostly working class in origin but sang with an American accent (like other English rock stars) and dressed in an elegant style, then popular in Britain, called "mod." The result was a deracinated, classless image of broad appeal.

The Beatles did not fade away as they were supposed to. Beatlemania continued for three years. Then the group went through several transformations that narrowed its audience to a smaller but intensely loyal cult following in the Dylan manner. The group became more self-consciously artistic. Their first long-playing record took one day to make and cost £400. "Sergeant Pepper's Lonely Hearts Club Band" took four months and cost £25,000. They were among the first to take advantage of new recording techniques that enabled multiple sound tracks to be played simultaneously. The Beatles learned new instruments and idioms too. The result was a complex music that attracted serious inquiry. Critics debated their contributions to musicology and argued over whether they were pathfinders or merely gifted entrepreneurs. In either case, they had come a long way aesthetically from their humble beginnings. Their music had a great effect on the young, so did their styles of life. They led the march of fashion away from mod and into the hairy, mustached, bearded, beaded, fringed, and embroidered costumes of the late sixties. For a time they followed the Maharishi, an Indian guru of some note. They married and divorced in progressively more striking ways. Some were arrested for smoking marijuana. In this too they were faithful to their clientele.

John Lennon went the farthest. He married Yoko Ono, best known as an author of happenings, and with her launched a bizarre campaign for world peace and goodness. Lennon returned his decoration to the Queen in protest against the human condition. Lennon and Ono hoped to visit America but were denied entry, which, to the bureaucratic mind, seemed a stroke for public order and morality. They staged a bed-in for peace all the same. They also formed a musical group of their own, the Plastic Ono Band, and circulated nude photographs and erotic drawings of themselves. This seemed an odd way to stop the war in Indochina, even to other Beatles. The group later broke up. By then they had made their mark, and, while strange, it was not a bad mark. Whatever lasting value their music may have, they set a good example to the young in most ways. Lennon's pacifism was nonviolent, even if wildly unorthodox. At a time when so many pacifists were imitating what they protested against, that was most desirable. They also worked hard at their respective arts and crafts, though others were dropping out and holding up laziness as a socially desirable trait. The Beatles showed that work was not merely an Establishment trick to keep the masses in subjection and the young out of trouble.

*   *   *

Beatlemania coincided with a more ominous development in the emerging counter-culture—the rise of the drug prophet Timothy Leary. He and Richard Alpert were scientific researchers at Harvard University who studied the effects of hallucinogenic drugs, notably a compound called LSD. As early as 1960 it was known that the two were propagandists as well as scientists. In 1961 the University Health Service made them promise not to use undergraduates in their experiments. Their violation of this pledge was the technical ground for firing them. A better one was that they had founded a drug cult. Earlier studies of LSD had failed, they said, because the researchers had not themselves taken the drug. In order to end this "authoritarian" practice, they "turned on" themselves. Their work was conducted in quarters designed to look like a bohemian residence instead of a laboratory. This was defended as a reconstruction of the natural environment in which social "acid-dropping" took place. They and many of their subjects became habitual users, not only of LSD but of marijuana and other drugs. They constructed an ideology of sorts around this practice. After they were fired the *Harvard Review* published an article of theirs praising the drug life: "Remember, man, a natural state is ecstatic wonder, ecstatic intuition, ecstatic accurate movement. Don't settle for less."

With some friends Leary and Alpert created the International Foundation for Internal Freedom (IF-IF) which published the *Psychedelic Review*. To advertise it a flyer was circulated that began, "Mescaline! Experimental Mysticism! Mushrooms! Ecstasy! LSD-25! Expansion of Consciousness! Phantastica! Transcendence! Hashish! Visionary Botany! Ololiuqui! Physiology of Religion! Internal Freedom! Morning Glory! Politics of the Nervous System!" Later the drug culture would generate a vast literature, but this was its essential message. The truth that made Western man free was only obtainable through hallucinogenic drugs. Truth was in the man, not the drug, yet the drug was necessary to uncover it. The natural state of man thus revealed was visionary, mystical, ecstatic. The heightened awareness stimulated by "consciousness-expanding" drugs brought undreamed-of sensual pleasures, according to Leary. Even better, drugs promoted peace, wisdom, and unity with the universe.

Alpert soon dropped from view. Leary went on to found his own sect, partly because once LSD was banned religious usage was the only ground left on which it could be defended, mostly because the drug cult *was* a religion. He wore long white robes and long blond hair. And he traveled about the country giving his liberating message (tune in, turn on, drop out) and having bizarre adventures. His personal following was never large, but drug use became commonplace among the young anyway. At advanced universities social smoking of marijuana was as acceptable as social drinking. More so, in a way, for it was better suited to the new ethic. One did not clutch one's solitary glass but shared one's "joint" with others. "Grass" made one gentle and pacific, not surly and hostile. As a forbidden pleasure it was all the more attractive to the thrill-seeking and the rebellious. And it helped further distinguish between the old world of grasping, combative, alcoholic adults and the turned-on, cooperative culture of the young. Leary was a bad prophet. Drug-based mystical religion was not the wave of the future. What the drug cult led to was a lot of dope-smoking and some hard drug-taking. When research suggested that LSD caused genetic damage, its use declined. But the effects of grass were hard to determine, so its consumption increased.

Sometimes "pot" smokers went on to other drugs—a deadly compound called "speed," and even heroin. These ruined many lives (though it was never clear that the lives were not already ruined to begin with). The popularity of drugs among the young induced panic in the old. States passed harsher and harsher laws that accomplished little. Campaigns against the drug traffic were launched periodically with similar results. When the flow of grass was interrupted, people turned to other drugs. Drug use seemed to go up either way. The generation gap widened. Young people thought marijuana less dangerous than alcohol, perhaps rightly. To proscribe the one and permit the other made no sense to them, except as still another example of adult hypocrisy and the hatred of youth. Leary had not meant all this to happen, but he was to blame for some of it all the same. No one did more to build the ideology that made pot-smoking a morally constructive act. But though a malign influence, no one deserved such legal persecution as he experienced before escaping to Algeria from a prison farm.

In Aldous Huxley's prophetic novel *Brave New World*, drug use was promoted by the state as a means of social control. During the sixties it remained a deviant practice and a source of great tension between the generations. Yet drugs did encourage conformity among the young. To "turn on and drop out" did not weaken the state. Quite the contrary, it drained off potentially subversive energies. The need for drugs gave society a lever should it ever decide to manipulate rather than repress users. Pharmacology and nervous strain had already combined to make many adult Americans dependent on drugs like alcohol and tranquilizers. Now the young were doing the same thing, if for different reasons. In a free country this meant only that individual problems increased. But should democracy fail, drug abuse among both the young and old was an instrument for control such as no dictator ever enjoyed. The young drug-takers thought to show contempt for a grasping, unfeeling society. In doing so they opened the door to a worse one. They scorned their elders for drinking and pill-taking, yet to outsiders their habits seemed little different, though ethically more pretentious. In both cases users were vulnerable and ineffective to the extent of their addiction. Of such ironies was the counter-culture built. . . .

The rebellion against traditional fashion went in two directions, though both were inspired by the young. The line of development just described emphasized brilliant or peculiar fabrics and designs. Here the emphasis was on costuming in a theatrical sense. People wore outfits that made them look like Mongols or cavaliers or whatever. These costumes, never cheap, were often very costly, though not more so than earlier styles. They were worn by others besides the young. What they owed to the emerging counter-culture was a certain freedom from constraint, and a degree of sensuality. Though the mini-skirt became a symbol of re-bellious youth, it was so popular that wearing it was not an ideological statement, even if Middle Americans often thought so.

The other direction clothing took was more directly related to counter-cultural patterns. This mode had two seemingly incompatible elements—surplus military garments and handcrafted ones. Army and navy surplus clothing was the first style to be adopted by young people look-ing for a separate identity. Socially conscious youths began wearing army and navy jackets, shirts, and bell-bottom trousers in the early sixties. This was not meant to show contempt for the military, for anti-war sentiment was then at a low ebb, but as a mark of ostentatious frugality in the high-consumption society. As these garments became more in demand, the price went up and more expensive commercial imitations appeared. Wear-ing them accordingly meant less, but a certain flavor of austere noncon-formity stuck to them all the same. They remained favorites of dissenting youths thereafter, even though worn by the merely fashionable too.

The hippies made handcrafted items popular. The implication here was that the wearer had made them, thus showing his independence and creativity. In the beginning this may often have been so. Soon, however, the market was so large and the people with skill and patience so limited that handcrafted items were commercially made and distributed, fre-quently by entrepreneurs among the young, sometimes through ordinary apparel channels. Bead shops and hippie boutiques became commonplace. Though their products were often quite costly, the vogue persisted among deviant youths anyway, partly because it was clear that whatever they wore would soon be imitated, partly because the message involved was too dear to abandon. Wearing beads, bangles, leather goods, fringes, color-ful vests, and what all showed sympathy for American Indians, who in-spired the most common designs, and fitted in with the popular back-to-nature ethic. When combined with military surplus garments they enabled the wearer to touch all the counter-cultural bases at once. Thus these fashions transmitted, however faintly, signals meaning peace, love, brother-hood, noble savagery, community, folk artistry, anti-capitalism and anti-militarism, and, later, revolutionary zeal.

This hippie *cum* military surplus mode also had a functional effect. It was a great leveler: when everyone wore the same bizarre costumes, every-one looked alike. Even better, it gave the ugly parity with the beautiful for the first time in modern history. Most of these costumes were pretty ghastly. A string of beads or an Indian headband did not redeem faded blue jeans and an army shirt. Long stringy hair or an untrimmed beard only aggravated the effect. Yet the young called such outfits beautiful. In effect, aesthetics were exchanged for ethics. Beauty was no longer related to ap-pearance but to morality. To have the proper spirit, though homely, was to be beautiful. This was a great relief for the poorly endowed and a point in the counter-culture's favor. Yet it enraged adults. Once the association between beads, beards, and military surplus goods on the one hand, and radicalism and dope on the other, was established, Middle America declared war on the counter-culture's physical trappings. School systems everywhere waged a relentless struggle against long hair. To dress this way in many places was a hostile act which invited reprisals. The style became a chief symbol of the generation gap, clung to fanatically by youngsters the more they were persecuted for it, as fiercely resisted by their elders. The progress of the generational struggle could almost be measured by the spread of these fashions.

No doubt older people would have resented the new styles in any case, but the way they emerged made them doubly offensive. They were introduced by young bohemians, mainly in New York and San Francisco, whose deviant attributes were highly publicized. New York hippies were concentrated in a section called the East Village. (Greenwich Village, the traditional bohemian refuge, had gotten too commercial and expensive.) By the mid-sixties a sizable community of radicals, dropouts, youthful vagrants, unrecognized avant-garde artists, and others were assembling there and a variety of cults beginning to flourish. One of the odder was called Kerista. It was a religio-sexual movement that planned to establish a colony in the Caribbean. "Utopia Tomorrow for Swingers," its publication, the *Kerista Speeler*, proclaimed. Kerista invoked a murky, perfectionist theology revolving around sexual love. Sometimes the members engaged in bisexual gropes to advance the pleasure principle. This sounded like more fun than it actually was, according to visitors.

The mainstream of East Village cultural life was more formally political and artistic. The many activities of Ed Sanders suggest the range of enterprises generated there. He was editor and publisher of *Fuck You: A Magazine of the Arts*. A typical editorial in it begins: "Time is NOW for TOTAL ASSAULT ON THE MARIJUANA LAWS. It is CLEAR to us that the cockroach theory of grass smoking has to be abandoned. IN THE OPEN! ALL THOSE WHO SUCK UP THE BENEVOLENT NARCOTIC CANNABIS, TEENSHUN!! FORWARD, WITH MIND DIALS POINTED: ASSAULT! We have the facts! Cannabis is a nonaddictive gentle peace drug! The marijuana legislations were pushed through in the 1930's by the agents and goonsquads of the jansensisto-manichean fuckhaters' conspiracy. Certainly after 30 years of the blight, it is time to rise up for a bleep blop bleep assault on the social screen. . . . But we can't wait forever you grass cadets to pull the takeover: grass-freak senators, labor leaders, presidents, etc.! The Goon Squads are few and we are many. We must spray our message into the million lobed American brain IMMEDIATELY!"

Sanders was also head of the East Village's most prominent rock group, The Fugs. They sang obscene songs of their own composition, and created equally obscene instruments for accompaniment (such as the erectophone, which appeared to be a long stick with bells on it). Among their better efforts were "What Are You Doing After the Orgy?" and the memorable "Kill for Peace." *The Fugs Song Book* described their music thusly:

The Fug-songs seem to spurt into five areas of concentration:

a) nouveau folk-freak
b) sex rock and roll
c) dope thrill chants
d) horny cunt-hunger blues
e) Total Assault on the Culture
   (anti-war/anti-creep/anti-repression)
. . . The meaning of the Fugs lies in the term BODY POETRY, to get
   at the frenzy of the thing, the grope-thing, The Body Poetry
   Formula is this:
The Head by the way of the Big Beat to the genitals
The Genitals by way of Operation Brain Thrill to the Body
   Poetry.

In his spare time Sanders made pornographic movies. His most epic work, *Mongolian Cluster Fuck!*, was described in *Fuck You* as a "short but searing non-socially redeeming porn flick featuring 100 of the lower east side's finest, with musical background by Algernon Charles Swinburne & THE FUGS." Though more versatile and creative than most, Sanders was typical of the East Village's alienated young artists. Tiny papers like *Fuck You* were springing up everywhere. All tried to be obscene, provocative, and, it was thought, liberating. They despised form, caring only for the higher morality and aesthetics it was their duty to advance. Some were more political (porno-political usually) than others. Collectively they were soon to be known as the "underground press."

Several cuts above the underground press were the flourishing little magazines. They were avant garde in the traditional sense and aimed, in their way, for greatness. By 1966 there were at least 250 of these (as against sixty or so in the 1920's). The better financed (*Outsider, Steppenwolf*) were tastefully composed and printed; others were crudely photo-offset (*Kayak, Eventorium Muse*). The *Insect Trust Gazette*, an annual experiment, once published an issue in which the original manuscripts were simply photographed and printed without reduction. About a third of the "littles" were mimeographed. There was even a little magazine for scientists, the *Worm-Runners' Digest*, edited by a droll researcher at the University of Michigan for people of like taste.

Older cultural rebels contributed to the ferment. George Brecht's musical composition "Ladder" went as follows: "Paint a single straight ladder white/Paint the bottom rung black/Distribute spectral colors on the rungs between." Even more to the point was "Laugh Piece" by John Lennon's future wife, Yoko Ono. It went "Keep laughing for a week." Nam June Paik composed a work known as "Young Penis Symphony." He was also an underground film producer and put on elaborate performances resembling the late happenings. One such was given at the Film-Makers Cinematheque using film, live music, and the cellist Charlotte Moorman. The audience saw short segments of a film by Robert Breer, alternating with views of Miss Moorman, silhouetted by backlighting behind the projection screen, playing short phrases of a Bach cello sonata. On completing each phrase she removed a garment. Another film clip would then be shown. This continued until she was lying on the floor, completely nude, playing her cello which was now atop her. Miss Moorman, "the Jeanne d'Arc of New Music," as she was called, appeared in other Paik compositions. She had been trained at the Juilliard School and was a member of Leopold Stokowski's American Symphony Orchestra.

As these few examples suggest, the East Village gained from its proximity to the New York avant garde. The mature counter-culture owed a lot to this relationship, but even in its early stages the East Village suffered from the influx of teenie-boppers and runaways who were to spoil both it and the Haight-Ashbury for serious cultural radicals. The people who were soon to be called hippies meant to build alternatives to the straight world. Against the hostile competitive, capitalistic values of bourgeois America they posed their own faith in nonviolence, love, and community. Drugs were important both as means to truth and advancers of the pleasure principle. The early hippies created institutions of sorts. Rock bands like the Jefferson Airplane, the Grateful Dead, Country Joe and the Fish flourished, as did communal societies, notably the Diggers. They were inspired by the seventeenth-century communists whose name they took. In practice they were a hip version of the Salvation Army.

Hippies lived together, in "tribes" or "families." Their golden rule was "Be nice to others, even when provoked, and they will be nice to you." In San Francisco their reservation was the Haight-Ashbury district near Golden Gate Park. They were much resented in the East Village by the natives, poor ethnics for the most part. In the Hashbury, on the other hand, they were welcome at first. Though peculiar, they were an improvement over the petty criminals they displaced. Even when freaked-out in public from drugs, a certain tolerance prevailed. After all, stepping over a drooling flower child on the street was better than getting mugged. Civic authorities were less open-minded. The drug traffic bothered them especially, and the Hashbury was loaded with "narks" (narcotics agents). Hunter S. Thompson wrote that "love is the password in the Haight-Ashbury, but paranoia is the style. Nobody wants to go to jail."

The fun-and-games era did not last long, perhaps only from 1965 to 1966. The hippie ethic was too fragile to withstand the combination of police surveillance and media exposure that soon afflicted it. The first hippies had a certain earnestness. But they were joined by masses of teen-age runaways. Nicholas von Hoffman observed that the Hashbury economy that began as a fraternal barter system quickly succumbed to the cash nexus. It became the first community in the world to revolve entirely around the buying and selling and taking of drugs. Marijuana and LSD were universal; less popular, but also commonplace, were LSD's more powerful relative STP, and amphetamines. "Speed kills" said the buttons and posters; speed freaks multiplied anyhow. To support themselves some hippies worked at casual labor or devised elaborate, usually unsuccessful schemes to make money out of hippie enterprises. Panhandling was popular, so was theft, disguised usually as communism.

Bohemians invariably deplore monogamy, and the hippies were no exception. As one member of the Jefferson Airplane put it "The stage is our bed and the audience is our broad. We're not entertaining, we're making love." Though committed to sexual freedom on principle, and often promiscuous in fact, the hippies were not really very sexy. Timothy Leary notwithstanding, drugs seemed to dampen the sexual urge. And the hippies were too passive in any case for strenuous sex play. Conversely, the most ardent free lovers, like those in the Sexual Freedom League, had little interest in drugs. Among hippies the combination of bad diets, dope, communal living, and the struggle to survive made for a restricted sex life. Of course the hippies were always glad of chances to shock the bourgeoisie, which made them seem more depraved than they were. Then too, people expected them to be sexually perverse, and the more public-spirited hippies tried to oblige. Like good troupers they hated to let the public down, though willing to put it on.

Hippie relations with black people were worse than might have been supposed. Hippies owed blacks a lot. Their jargon was derived from the ghetto. They admired blacks, as certain whites always have, for being more emotional, sensual, and uninhibited. But there were very few black hippies. Superspade, a beloved Negro drug pusher, was an exception. Most hippies were frightened of blacks. "Spades are programmed for hate" was the way many put it. The Hashbury was periodically swept by rumors of impending black attacks. Some hippies looked to the motorcycle outlaws to protect them from black rage. This was not without a certain logic. Outlaws hated blacks and loved to fight. But they played their role as hippie militiamen uneasily. In truth they were more likely to destroy a hippie than defend him.

In the end it was neither the bikers nor the blacks but the media that destroyed hippiedom. The publicity given the summer of love attracted countless thousands of disturbed youngsters to the Hashbury and the East Village in 1967. San Francisco was not burdened with the vast numbers originally expected. But many did come, bringing in their train psychotics, drug peddlers, and all sorts of criminals. Drug poisoning, hepatitis (from infected needles), and various diseases resulting from malnutrition and exposure thinned their ranks. Rapes, muggings, and assaults became commonplace. Hippies had little money, but they were irresistibly easy marks. Hippie girls were safe to assault. They reacted passively, and as many were drug users and runaways they could not go to the police.

So the violence mounted. On the West Coast one drug peddler was stabbed to death and his right forearm removed. Superspade's body was found hanging from a cliff top. He had been stabbed, shot, and trussed in a sleeping bag. On October 8 the nude bodies of Linda Rea Fitzpatrick, eighteen, and James Leroy "Groovy" Hutchinson, twenty-one, were discovered in an East Village boiler room. They had been murdered while high on LSD. Though pregnant, Miss Fitzpatrick had also been raped. That was how the summer of love ended. Two days earlier the death and funeral of hippie had been ritually observed in San Francisco's Buena Vista Park. But the killing of Linda and Groovy marked its real end. The Hashbury deteriorated rapidly thereafter. Bad publicity drove the tourists away, and the hippie boutiques that serviced them closed. Some local rock groups dissolved; others, like the Jefferson Airplane and even the Grateful

Dead, went commercial. The hippies and their institutions faded quietly away. The Hashbury regained something of its old character. The East Village, owing to its more diverse population and strategic location, changed less.

At its peak the hippie movement was the subject of much moralizing. Most often hippies were seen as degenerate and representative of all things godless and un-American. A minority accepted them as embodying a higher morality. The media viewed them as harmless, even amusing, freaks —which was probably closest to the truth. But before long it was clear that while the hippie movement was easily slain, the hippie style of life was not. Their habit of dressing up in costumes rather than outfits was widely imitated. So was their slang and their talk of peace, love, and beauty. The great popularity of ex-hippie rock groups was one sign of the cultural diffusion taking place, marijuana another. Weekend tripping spread to the suburbs. While the attempt to build parallel cultures on a large scale in places like the Hashbury failed, the hippies survived in many locales. Isolated farms, especially in New England and the Southwest, were particularly favored. And they thrived also on the fringes of colleges and universities, where the line between avant-garde student and alienated dropout was hard to draw. In tribes, families, and communes, the hippies lived on, despite considerable local harassment wherever they went.

Though few in number, hippies had a great effect on middle-class youth. Besides their sartorial influence, hippies made religion socially acceptable. Their interest in the supernatural was contagious. Some of the communes which sprang up in the late sixties were actually religious fellowships practicing a contemporary monasticism. One in western Massachusetts was called the Cathedral of the Spirit. Its forty members were led by a nineteen-year-old mystic who helped them prepare for the Second Coming and the new Aquarian Age when all men would be brothers. The Cathedral had rigid rules against alcohol, "sex without love," and, less typically, drugs. Members helped out neighboring farmers without pay, but the commune was essentially contemplative. Its sacred book was a fifty-seven-page typewritten manuscript composed by a middle-aged bus driver from Northfield, Massachusetts, which was thought to be divinely inspired. Another commune in Boston, called the Fort Hill Community, was more outward looking. Its sixty members hoped to spread their holy word through the mass media.

Some of the communes or brotherhoods sprang from traditional roots. In New York City a band of young Jews formed a Havurah (fellowship) to blend Jewish traditions with contemporary inspirations. They wanted to study subjects like "the prophetic mind; new forms of spirituality in the contemporary world; and readings from the Jewish mystical tradition." At the University of Massachusetts a hundred students celebrated Rosh Hashanah not in a synagogue but in a field where they danced and sang all night. Courses in religion multiplied. At Smith College the number of students taking them grew from 692 in 1954 to nearly 1,400 in 1969, though the student body remained constant at about 2,000. Columbia University had two hundred applicants for a graduate program in religion with only twenty openings.

Students saw traditional religion as a point of departure rather than a place for answers. Comparatively few joined the new fellowships, but large numbers were attracted to the concepts they embodied. Oriental theologies and the like grew more attractive, so did magic. At one Catholic university a coven of warlocks was discovered. They were given psychiatric attention (thereby missing a great chance. If only they had been exorcised instead, the Establishment would have shown its relevance). When a Canadian university gave the studentry a chance to recommend new courses they overwhelmingly asked for subjects like Zen, sorcery, and witchcraft. A work of classic Oriental magic, *I Ching*, or the *Book of Changes*, became popular. The best edition, a scholarly product of the Princeton University Press, used to sell a thousand copies a year. In 1968 fifty thousand copies were snapped up. Sometimes magic and mysticism were exploited more in fun than not. The Women's Liberation Movement had guerrilla theater troupes calling themselves WITCH (Women's International Terrorist Conspiracy from Hell). During the SDS sit-in at the University of Chicago they cursed the sociology department and put a hex on its chairman.

But there was a serious element to the vogue for magic. Teachers of philosophy and religion were struck by the anti-positivist, anti-science feelings of many students. Science was discredited as an agent of the military-industrial complex. It had failed to make life more attractive. Whole classes protested the epistemology of science as well as its intellectual dominion. Students believed the Establishment claimed to be rational, but showed that it was not. This supported one of the central truths of all religion, that man is more than a creature who reasons. Nor was it only the young who felt this way. Norman Mailer was something of a mystic, so was Timothy Leary. And the most ambitious academic effort to deal with these things, Theodore Roszak's *The Making of a Counter Culture*, ended with a strong appeal to faith. Like the alienated young, Roszak too rejected science and reason—"the myth of objective consciousness" as he called it. Instead of empiricism or the scientific method he wanted "the beauty of the fully illuminated personality" to be "our standard of truth." He liked magic as "a matter of communion with the forces of nature as if they were mindful, intentional presences." What he admired most in the New Left was its attempt, as he thought, to revive shamanism, to get back to the sanity and participatory democracy of prehistoric society. But he urged the left to give up its notion that violence and confrontation would change the world. What the left must do to influence the silent majority "was not simply to muster power against the misdeeds of society, but to transform the very sense men have of reality."

The anti-war movement was strongly affected by this new supernaturalism. On Moratorium Day in 1969 a University of Massachusetts student gave an emotional speech that brought the audience to its feet shouting, "The war is over." "He went into a dance, waving his arms," a campus minister said. "It was the essence of a revival meeting, where the audience makes a commitment to Christ at the end." The great peace demonstrations in 1969 were full of religious symbolism. In Boston 100,000 people gathered before a gigantic cross on the Common. In New York lighted candles were carried to the steps of St. Patrick's Cathedral. Candles were placed on the White House wall during the November mobilization. At other demonstrations the shofar, the ram's horn sounded by Jews at the beginning of each new year, was blown. Rock, the liturgical music of the young, was often played. So was folk music, which continued as a medium of moral expression after its popular decline.

. . . On its deepest level the counter-culture was the radical critique of Herbert Marcuse, Norman O. Brown, and even Paul Goodman. It also meant the New Left, communes and hippie farms, magic, hedonism, eroticism, and public nudity. And it included rock music, long hair, and miniskirts (or, alternatively, fatigue uniforms, used clothes, and the intentionally ugly or grotesque). Most attacks on the counter-culture were directed at its trivial aspects, pot and dress especially. Pot busts (police raids), often involving famous people or their children, became commonplace. The laws against pot were so punitive in some areas as to be almost unenforceable. Even President Nixon, spokesman for Middle American morality that he was, finally questioned them. Local fights against long hair, beards, and short skirts were beyond number. The American Civil Liberties Union began taking school systems to court for disciplining students on that account. New York City gave up trying to enforce dress codes. It was all the more difficult there as even the teachers were mod. At one school the principal ordered women teachers to wear smocks over their minis. They responded by buying mini-smocks.

Nor were athletics—the last bastion of orthodoxy, one might think— exempt, though coaches struggled to enforce yesterday's fashions. At Oregon State University one football player, the son of an Air Force officer, went hippie and dropped the sport. His coach said, "I recruited that boy thinking he was Jack Armstrong. I was wrong. He turned out to be a free-thinker." At the University of Pennsylvania a star defensive back showed up for summer practice with shoulder-length hair, sideburns down to the neck, beads, bells, thonged sandals, and a cloth sash round his waist. He was the only man on the team to bring a pet dog and a stereo set to the six-day camp. After a war of nerves culminating in an ultimatum from the coach, he grudgingly hacked a few inches off his mane. And so it went all over America.

Both sides in this struggle took fashion and style to be deadly serious matters, so political conflicts tended to become cultural wars. In the fall of 1969 the most important radical student group at New York University was called Transcendental Students. At a time when SDS could barely muster twenty-five members, five hundred or more belonged to TS. It began the previous semester when a group protesting overcrowding in the classroom staged a series of freak-outs in classrooms. This proved so attractive a custom that it was institutionalized. Rock, pot, and wine parties had obvious advantages over political action. The administration shrewdly made a former restaurant available to TS for a counter-cultural center. The students welcomed it as a haven for "guerrilla intellect" where the human spirit could breathe free. The administration saw it as just another recreational facility, which, of course, it was. And what dean would not rather have the kids singing out in a restaurant than locking him in his office? Sometimes culture and politics were united. When the $12 million center for the performing arts opened in Milwaukee, Wisconsin, on September 18, 1969, six hundred students disrupted the inaugural concert. They rubbed balloons, blew bubble pipes, threw rolls of toilet paper, and demanded that 20 per cent of the seats be given free to welfare recipients.

The greatest event in counter-cultural history was the Woodstock Festival in Bethel, New York. It was organized on the pattern of other large rock festivals. Big-name groups were invited for several days of continuous entertaining in the open. A large crowd was expected, but nothing like the 300,000 or 400,000 youngsters who actually showed up on August 15, 1969. Everything fell apart in consequence. Tickets could not be collected nor services provided. There wasn't enough food or water. The roads were blocked with abandoned autos, and no one could get in or out for hours at a time. Surprisingly, there were no riots or disasters. The promoters chartered a fleet of helicopters to evacuate casualties (mostly from bad drug trips) and bring in essential supplies. Despite the rain and congestion, a good time was had by all (except the boy killed when a tractor accidentally drove over his sleeping bag). No one had ever seen so large and ruly a gathering before. People stripped down, smoked pot, and turned on with nary a discouraging word, so legend has it. Afterward the young generally agreed that it was a beautiful experience proving their superior morality. People were nicer to each other than ever before. Even the police were impressed by the public's order (a result of their wisely deciding not to enforce the drug laws).

But the counter-culture had its bad moments in 1969 also. Haight-Ashbury continued to decay. It was now mainly a slum where criminals preyed on helpless drug freaks. Worse still was the Battle of Berkeley, which put both the straight culture and the counter-culture in the worst possible light, especially the former. The University of California owned a number of vacant lots south of the campus. The land had been cleared in anticipation of buildings it was unable to construct. One block lay vacant for so long that the street people—hippies, students, dropouts, and others—transformed it into a People's Park. Pressure was brought on the University by the local power structure to block its use, which was done. On May 15 some six thousand students and street people held a rally on campus, then advanced on the park. County sheriffs, highway patrolmen, and the Berkeley police met them with a hail of gunfire. One person died of buckshot wounds, another was blinded. Many more were shot though few arrested. Those who were arrested were handled so brutally that the circuit court enjoined the sheriff to have his men stop beating and abusing them. Disorders continued. Governor Reagan declared a state of emergency and brought in the National Guard. Five days later one of its helicopters sprayed gas over the campus, thus making the educational process at Berkeley even more trying than usual.

Of course the Establishment was most to blame for Vietnamizing the cultural war. But the meretricious aspects of the counter-culture were evident too. If the police were really "fascist pigs," as the street people said, why goad and defy them? And especially why harass the National Guardsmen who didn't want to be in Berkeley anyhow? This was hardly on the same order as murdering people with shotguns. Yet such behavior was stupid, pointless, and self-defeating, like so much else in the counter-culture. The silent majority was not won over. Nor was the People's Park saved. A year later the area was still fenced in. (Though vacant. The University, having pretended to want it as a recreational area, tried to make it one. But as the students thought it stained with innocent blood, they avoided it.)

The rock festival at Altamont that winter was another disaster. It was a free concert that climaxed the Rolling Stones' whirlwind tour of the U.S. They called it their gift to the fans. Actually it was a clever promotion. The Stones had been impressed with the moneymaking potential of Woodstock. While Woodstock cost the promoters a fortune, they stood to recoup their losses with a film of the event. This inspired the Stones to do a Woodstock themselves. At the last minute they obtained the use of Dick Carter's Altamont Raceway. It had been doing poorly and the owner thought the publicity would help business. Little was done to prepare the site. The police didn't have enough notice to bring in reserves, so the Stones hired a band of Hell's Angels as security guards (for $500 worth of beer). The Stones did their thing and the Angels did theirs.

The result was best captured by a *Rolling Stone* magazine photograph showing Mick Jagger looking properly aghast while Angels beat a young Negro to death on stage. A musician who tried to stop them was knocked unconscious, and he was lucky at that. Before the day was over many more were beaten, though no others fatally. Sometimes the beatings were for aesthetic reasons. One very fat man took off his clothes in the approved rock festival manner. This offended the Angels who set on him with pool cues. No one knows how many were clubbed that day. The death count came to four. Apart from Meredith Hunter, who was stabbed and kicked to death, they mostly died by accident. A car drove off the road into a clump of people and killed two. A man, apparently high on drugs, slid into an irrigation canal and drowned. The drug freak-outs were more numerous than at Woodstock. The medical care was less adequate. Not that the physicians on hand didn't try; they just lacked the support provided at Woodstock, whose promoters had spared no expense to avert disaster. Oddly enough the press, normally so eager to exploit the counter-culture, missed the point of Altamont. Early accounts followed the customary rock festival line, acclaiming it as yet another triumph of youth. In the East it received little attention of any kind.

It remained for *Rolling Stone*, the rock world's most authoritative journal, to tell the whole story of what it called the Altamont Death Festival. The violence was quite bad enough, but what especially bothered *Rolling Stone* was the commercial cynicism behind it. That huge gathering was assembled by the Stones to make a lucrative film on the cheap. They could have hired legitimate security guards, but it cost less to use the Angels. (At Woodstock unarmed civilians trained by the Hog Farm commune kept order.) They were too rushed for the careful planning that went into Woodstock, too callous (and greedy) to pour in the emergency resources that had saved the day there. And, appropriately, they faked the moviemaking too so as to have a documentary of the event they intended, not the one they got. *Rolling Stone* said that a cameraman was recording a fat, naked girl freaking out backstage when the director stopped him. "Don't shoot that. That's ugly. We only want beautiful things." The cameraman made the obvious response. "How can you possibly say that? Everything here is so ugly."

Rolling Stone thought the star system at fault. Once a band got as big as the Stones they experienced delusions of grandeur, "ego trips" in the argot. And with so much money to be made by high-pressure promotions, "the hype" became inevitable. Others agreed. The *Los Angeles Free Press*, biggest of the underground papers, ran a full-page caricature of Mick Jagger with an Adolf Hitler mustache, arm draped around a Hell's Angel, while long-haired kids gave them the Nazi salute. Ralph Gleason of the *San Francisco Chronicle* explained Altamont this way: "The name of the game is money, power, and ego, and money is first as it brings power. The Stones didn't do it for free, they did it for money, only the tab was paid in a different way. Whoever goes to the movie paid for the Altamont religious assembly."[2] Quite so. But why did so many others go along with the Stones? The Jefferson Airplane, and especially the Grateful Dead, reputedly the most socially conscious rock bands, participated. So did counter-culture folk heroes like Emmet Grogan of the Diggers. Here the gullibility—innocence, perhaps—of the deviant young was responsible. Because the rock bandits smoked pot and talked a revolutionary game, they were supposed to be different from other entertainers. Even though they made fortunes and spent them ostentatiously, their virtue was always presumed. What Altamont showed was that the difference between a rock king and a robber baron was about six inches of hair.[3]

If Altamont exposed one face of the counter-culture, the Manson family revealed another. Late in 1969 Sharon Tate, a pregnant movie actress, and four of her jet-set friends were ritually murdered in the expensive Bel-Air district of Los Angeles. Though apparently senseless, their deaths were thought related to the rootless, thrill-oriented life style of the Beautiful People. But on December 1 policemen began arresting obscure hippies. Their leader, Charles Manson, was an ex-convict and seemingly deranged. Susan Atkins, a member of his "family," gave several cloudy versions of

---

[2] Gleason was the best writer on popular music and the youth culture associated with it, which he once admired greatly. For an earlier assessment see his "Like a Rolling Stone," *American Scholar* (Autumn 1967).

[3] This is to criticize the singer, not the song. Whatever one might think of some performers, there is no doubt that rock itself was an exciting musical form. Adults rarely heard it because rock seldom was played on television, or even radio in most parts of the country. Rock artists appeared mainly in concerts and clubs, to which few over thirty went. Not knowing the music, there was little reason for them to buy the records that showed rock at its most complex and interesting. Like jazz, rock became more sophisticated with time and made greater demands on the artist's talent. Even more than jazz, rock produced an army of amateur and semi-professional players around the country. Though often making up in volume what they lacked in skill, their numbers alone guaranteed that rock would survive its exploiters.

what had happened. On the strength of them Manson was indicted for murder. Though his guilt remained unproven, the basic facts about his past seemed clear. He was a neglected child who became a juvenile delinquent. In 1960 he was convicted of forgery and spent seven years in the penitentiary. On his release he went to the Hashbury and acquired a harem of young girls. After floating through the hippie underground for a time, he left the Hashbury with his family of nine girls and five boys early in 1968. They ended up at Spahn's Ranch in the Santa Susana Mountains, north of the San Fernando Valley. The owner was old and blind. Manson terrified him. But the girls took care of him so he let the family stay on. They spent a year at the ranch before the police suspected them of stealing cars. Then they camped out in the desert until arrested.

Life with the Manson family was a combination of hippieism and paranoia. Manson subscribed to the usual counter-cultural values. Inhibitions, the Establishment, regular employment, and other straight virtues were bad. Free love, nature, dope, rock, and mysticism were good. He believed a race war was coming (predicted in Beatle songs) and armed his family in anticipation of it. Some of the cars they stole were modified for use in the desert, where he meant to make his last stand. And, naturally, he tried to break into the rock music business. One reason why he allegedly murdered Miss Tate and her friends was that they were in a house previously occupied by a man who had broken a promise to advance Manson's career. The Manson family was thought to have killed other people even more capriciously. Yet after his arrest most of the girls remained loyal to Manson. Young, largely middle class, they were still "hypnotized" or "enslaved" by him. Those not arrested continued to hope for a family reunion. Of course hippies were not murderers usually. But the repressed hostility, authoritarianism, perversity, and mindless paranoia that underlay much of the hippie ethic were never displayed more clearly. The folkways of the flower children tended toward extremes. At one end they were natural victims; at the other, natural victimizers. The Manson family were both at once.

Taken together the varieties of life among deviant youths showed the counter-culture to be disintegrating. What was disturbing about it was not so much the surface expression as its tendency to mirror the culture it supposedly rejected. The young condemned adult hypocrisy while matching its contradictions with their own. The old were materialistic, hung up on big cars and ranch houses. The young were equally devoted to motorcycles, stereo sets, and electric guitars. The old sought power and wealth. So did the young as rock musicians, political leaders, and frequently as salesmen of counter-cultural goods and services. What distinguished reactionary capitalists from their avant-garde opposite numbers was often no more than a lack of moral pretense. While condemning the adult world's addiction to violence, the young admired third-world revolutionaries, Black Panthers, and even motorcycle outlaws. The rhetoric of the young got progressively meaner and more hostile. This was not so bad as butchering Vietnamese, but it was not very encouraging either. And where hate led, violence followed.

Adults pointed these inconsistencies out often enough, with few good

results. Usable perceptions are always self-perceptions, which made the
Rolling Stone exposé of Altamont so valuable. This was a small but hopeful sign that the capacity for self-analysis was not totally submerged,
despite the flood of self-congratulatory pieties with which the deviant
young described themselves. The decline of the New Left was another.
Once a buoyant and promising thing, it became poisoned by hate, failure,
and romantic millennialism. Its diminished appeal offered hope of sobri-
ety's return. So did the surge of student interest in environmental issues
at the decade's end. These were not fake problems, like so many youthful
obsessions, but real ones. They would take the best efforts of many generations to overcome. No doubt the young would lose interest in them after
a while as usual. Still, it was better to save a forest or clean a river than to
vandalize a campus. No amount of youthful nagging was likely to make
adults give up their sinful ways. It was possible that the young and old
together, might salvage enough of the threatened environment to leave
posterity something of lasting value. The generations yet unborn were not
likely to care much whether ROTC was conducted on campus or off. But
they will remember this age, for better or worse, with every breath they
take.

One aspect of the counter-culture deserves special mention: its assumption that hedonism was inevitably anti-capitalist. As James Hitchcock
pointed out, the New Left identified capitalism with puritanism and deferred gratifications. But this was true of capitalism only with respect to
work. Where consumption was concerned, it urged people to gratify their
slightest wish. It exploited sex shamelessly to that end, limited only by law
and custom. When the taboos against nudity were removed, merchants
soon took advantage of their new freedom. Naked models, actors, even
waitresses were one result, pornographic flicks another. Who doubted that
if marijuana became legal the tobacco companies would soon put Mexican
gold in every vending machine? It was, after all, part of Aldous Huxley's
genius that he saw how sensual gratification could enslave men more effectively than Hitler ever could. Victorian inhibitions, the Protestant Ethic
itself were, though weakened, among the few remaining defenses against
the market economy that Americans possessed. To destroy them for freedom's sake would only make people more vulnerable to consumerism than
they already were. Which was not to say that sexual and other freedoms
were not good things in their own right. But there was no assurance that
behavioral liberty would not grow at the expense of political freedom. It
was one thing to say that sex promoted mental health, another to say it
advanced social justice. In confusing the two young deviants laid themselves open to what Herbert Marcuse called "repressive de-sublimation,"
the means by which the socio-economic order was made more attractive,
and hence more durable. Sex was no threat to the Establishment. Panicky
moralists found this hard to believe, so they kept trying to suppress it. But
the shrewder guardians of established relationships saw hedonism for what
it partially was, a valuable means of social control. What made this hard to
get across was that left and right agreed that sex was subversive. That was
why the Filthy Speech Movement arose, and why the John Birch Society
and its front groups divided a host of communities in the late sixties. They

insisted that sex education was a communist plot to fray the country's
moral fiber. They could hardly have been more wrong. As practiced in
most schools, sex education was anything but erotic. In fact, more students
were probably turned off sex than on to it by such courses. The Kremlin
was hardly less orthodox than the Birch Society on sexual matters, sexual
denial being thought a trait of all serious revolutionaries. But the sexual
propaganda of the young confirmed John Birchers in their delusions. As
elsewhere, the misconceptions of each side reinforced one another.

Still, the counter-culture's decline ought not to be celebrated prematurely. It outlasted the sixties. It had risen in the first place because of
the larger culture's defects. War, poverty, social and racial injustice were
widespread. The universities were less human than they might have been.
The regulation of sexual conduct led to endless persecutions of the innocent or the pathetic to no one's advantage. Young people had much to
complain of. Rebellious youth had thought to make things better. It was
hardly their fault that things got worse. They were, after all, products of
the society they meant to change, and marked by it as everyone was.
Vanity and ignorance made them think themselves free of the weaknesses
they saw so clearly in others. But adults were vain and ignorant too, and,
what's more, they had power as the young did not. When they erred, as
in Vietnam, millions suffered. The young hated being powerless, but
thanks to it they were spared the awful burden of guilt that adults bore.
They would have power soon enough, and no doubt use it just as badly.
In the meantime, though, people did well to keep them in perspective.

The dreary propaganda about youth's insurgent idealism continued
into the seventies. So did attempts to make them look clean-cut. American
society went on being obsessed with the young. But all popular manias are
seasonal. Each era has its own preoccupations. The young and their
counter-culture were a special feature of the 1960's and would probably
not be regarded in the old way for very long afterward. And, demo-
graphically speaking, youth itself was on the wane. The median age of
Americans had risen steadily in modern times, reaching a peak of thirty
years of age in 1952. The baby boom reversed this trend, like so many
others. In 1968 the median age was only 27.7 years. But as the birthrate fell
the median age began to rise. By 1975 it would be over twenty-eight. By
1990 it should be back up to thirty again, putting half the population
beyond the age of trust. Their disproportionate numbers was one reason
why youth was so prominent in the sixties. It was reasonable to suppose
they would become less so as their numbers declined in relation to older
people.

Common sense suggested that work and the pleasure principle would
both continue. Once life and work were thought to be guided by the same
principles. In the twentieth century they had started to divide, with one
set of rules for working and another for living. The complexities of a post-
industrial economy would probably maintain that distinction. The discipline of work would prevail on the job. The tendency to "swing" off it
would increase, and the dropout community too. The economy was already rich enough to support a substantial leisure class, as the hippies
demonstrated. The movement toward guaranteed incomes would make

idleness even more feasible. A large dependent population, in economic terms, was entirely practical—perhaps, given automation, even desirable. How utopian to have a society in which the decision to work was voluntary! Yet if economic growth continued and an effective welfare state was established, such a thing was not unimaginable, however repugnant to the Protestant Ethic. Perhaps that was what the unpleasant features of life in the sixties pointed toward. Later historians might think them merely the growing pains of this new order. A Brave New World indeed!

A further reason for taking this view was the rise of an adult counter-culture. Americans have always been attracted to cults and such. No enthusiasm, however bizarre, fails to gain some notice in so vast and restless a country. Crank scientists and religious eccentrics are especially welcomed. In the 1960's this was more true than ever, and there seemed to be more uniformity of belief among the cults than before. Perhaps also they were more respectable. The Esalen Institute in northern California was one of the most successful. It offered three-day seminars conducted by Dr. Frederick S. Perls, the founder of Gestalt therapy. When his book by that title was published in 1950 it won, as might have been expected, little attention. But in the sixties it flourished to the point where perhaps a hundred Gestalt therapists were in practice. As employed at Esalen, Gestalt therapy involved a series of individual encounters within a group context. Perls tried to cultivate moments of sudden insights that produced a strong awareness of the present moment. Unlike psychoanalysis, Gestalt therapy was directive. The therapist diagnosed the ailment and organized its cure in short bursts of intensive treatment. People were encouraged to act out dreams so as to discover their hidden message. The emphasis was on sensuality, spontaneity, and the reduction of language which was seen as more a barrier to understanding than a means of communication. There was much role-playing, aggression-releasing exercises, and "unstructured interaction." Esalen itself, with its hot sulphur baths where mixed nude bathing was encouraged, combined the features of a hip spa, a mental clinic, and a religious center. It brought social scientists and mystics together in common enterprises. By 1967 Esalen grossed a million dollars a year. Four thousand people attended its seminars. Twelve thousand used its branch in San Francisco.

Though Esalen was the most celebrated center of "Third Force Psychiatry," it was hardly alone. Encounter groups, T-groups, sensitivity groups all practiced variations of the same theme. So, in a more intense way, did Synanon. Synanon was founded in 1958 by an ex-alcoholic named Charles E. Dederich. It began as a way of reclaiming alcoholics, and especially drug addicts, through communal living and group therapy. It aimed to peel away the defenses that supported addiction. The cure was a drastic one and the Synanon ethic extremely authoritarian, as a treatment based not on clinical experience but actual street life would naturally be. Synanon's most popular feature was the Synanon game, a kind of encounter group open to outsiders. From its modest beginning Synanon expanded rapidly into a network of clinics and small businesses operated by members to support the therapeutic program. Already a corporation by the decade's end, Dederich expected it to become a mass movement in time. Others thought so too. Abraham Maslow of Brandeis University declared that "Synanon is now in the process of torpedoing the entire world of psychiatry and within ten years will completely replace psychiatry."

Esalen and Synanon got much publicity, but, though substantial efforts, they were only the tip of the iceberg. Beneath them were literally thousands of groups dedicated to better mental health through de-sublimation, often sponsored by businesses and universities. In a sense what they did was rationalize the counter-cultural ethic and bend it to fit the needs of middle-class adults. For some, expanding their consciousness meant little more than weekend tripping, with, or more commonly without, drugs. If most didn't give up work in the hippie manner, they became more relaxed about it. Some thought less about success and more about fun. Some found new satisfaction in their work, or else more satisfying work. The range of individual response was great, but the overall effect was to promote sensuality, and to diminish the Protestant Ethic. As with the counter-culture, an inflated propaganda accompanied these efforts. Ultimate truth, complete harmony with self, undreamed-of pleasures, and the like were supposed to result from conversion. De-sublimation did not mean license, of course. As the Haight-Ashbury showed, without self-denial there is self-destruction. The cults tried to develop more agreeable mechanisms to replace the fears and guilts undergirding the old morality. They wanted people to live more rich and immediate social lives, but they didn't propose to do away with restraint entirely. Mystic cults promoted self-discipline through various austere regimes. Psychiatric cults used the group as a control. One learned from his fellows what was appropriate to the liberated spirit.

The sensuality common to most of these groups was what the sexual revolution was all about. Properly speaking, of course, there was no sexual revolution. Easy divorce, relatively free access to contraceptives, and tolerated promiscuity were all well established by the 1920's. Insofar as the Kinsey and other reports are historically reliable, there had been little change since then in the rate of sexual deviance. What had changed was the attitude of many people toward it. In the 1960's deviance was not so much tolerated as applauded in many quarters. Before, college students having an affair used discretion. Later they were more likely to live together in well-advertised nonmarital bliss. Similarly, adults were not much more promiscuous in the sixties than in the forties or fifties, but they were more disposed to proclaim the merits of extra-marital sexuality. The sexualization of everyday life moved on. This was often desirable, or at least harmless, except for the frightening rise in the incidence of VD after the Pill made condoms seemingly obsolete.

Fornication, though illegal in most places, was not usually regarded as actionable. But there remained many laws against sexual behavior that were enforced, if erratically. Contraceptives were difficult to get in some places, especially for single women. Legal abortions were severely limited. Homosexuals were persecuted everywhere. Attempts to change these laws were part of the new moral permissiveness. Few legal reforms were actually secured in the sixties. Liberalized abortion laws were passed in Colorado and elsewhere to little effect. Abortions remained scarce and expensive. The overwhelming majority continued to be illegal. Contraceptive laws did not change much either, though in practice contraceptives became easier to get. Nor were the laws prohibiting homosexuality altered much. Here too, though, changes in practice eased conditions. The deliberate entrapment of homosexuals declined in some cities. Some police forces, as in San Francisco, made more of an effort to distinguish between harmless (as between consenting adults) and anti-social perversions.

More striking still was the willingness of sexual minorities to identify themselves. Male homosexuals were among the first to do so. In the Mattachine Society and later organizations they campaigned openly for an end to discriminatory laws and customs. The Daughters of Bilitis did the same for lesbians. Even the most exotic minorities, like the transvestites and transsexuals (men, usually, who wanted to change their sex surgically), became organized. Most of the groups were, their sexual customs excepted, quite straight. The creation of homosexual churches, like the Metropolitan Community Church of Los Angeles, testified to that. They hoped mainly to be treated the same as heterosexuals. But in the Gay Liberation Front the sexual underground produced its own New Left organization. Its birth apparently dated from the night of June 28, 1969, when police raided a gay bar in Greenwich Village called the Stonewall Inn. Homosexuals usually accepted arrest passively. But for some reason that night it was different. They fought back, and for a week afterward continued to agitate, ending with a public march of some one thousand people.

More sober homosexuals greeted this event with mixed emotions. They were astonished to find such spirit among the so-called street queens, the poorest and most trouble-prone homosexuals of all. But they didn't really dig the violence. As one leader of the Mattachine Society (a sort of gay NAACP) put it: "I mean, people did try to set fire to the bar, and one drag queen, much to the amazement of the mob, just pounded the hell out of a Tactical Patrol Force cop! I don't know if battering TPF men is really the answer to our problem." In any event, the Gay Liberation Front followed these events. Rather like a Homosexuals for a Democratic Society, the GLF participated in the next Hiroshima Day march that summer. It was the first time homosexuals ever participated in a peace action under their own colors. The "Pink Panthers" were mostly young, of course. But whether their movement flourished or, most probably, withered away, the mere fact of its existence said a lot about changing mores in America.

While it was difficult in 1969 to tell where the counter-culture would go, it was easy to see where it came from. Artists and bohemians had been demanding more freedom from social and artistic conventions for a long time. The romantic faith in nature, intuition, and spontaneity was equally old. What was striking about the sixties was that the revolt against discipline, even self-discipline, and authority spread so widely. Resistance to these tendencies largely collapsed in the arts. Soon the universities gave ground also. The rise of hedonism and the decline of work were obviously functions of increased prosperity, and also of effective merchandising. The consumer economy depended on advertising, which in turn leaned heavily on the pleasure principle. This had been true for fifty years at least, but not until television did it really work well. The generation that made the counter-culture was the first to be propagandized from infancy on behalf of the pleasure principle.

But though all of them were exposed to hucksterism, not all were convinced. Working-class youngsters especially soon learned that life was different from television. Limited incomes and uncertain futures put them in touch with reality earlier on. Middle-class children did not learn the facts of life until much later. Cushioned by higher family incomes, indulged in the same way as their peers on the screen, they were shocked to discover that the world was not what they had been taught it was. The pleasure orientation survived this discovery, the ideological packaging it came in often did not. All this had happened before, but in earlier years there was no large, institutionalized subculture for the alienated to turn to. In the sixties hippiedom provided one such, the universities another. The media publicized these alternatives and made famous the ideological leaders who promoted them. So the deviant young knew where to go for the answers they wanted, and how to behave when they got them. The media thus completed the cycle begun when they first turned youngsters to pleasure. That was done to encourage consumption. The message was still effective when young consumers rejected the products TV offered and discovered others more congenial to them.

Though much in the counter-culture was attractive and valuable, it was dangerous in three ways. First, self-indulgence led frequently to self-destruction. Second, the counter-culture increased social hostility. The generation gap was one example, but the class gap another. Working-class youngsters resented the counter-culture. They accepted adult values for the most part. They had to work whether they liked it or not. Beating up the long-haired and voting for George Wallace were only two ways they expressed these feelings. The counter-culture was geographical too. It flourished in cities and on campuses. Elsewhere, in Middle America especially, it was hated and feared. The result was a national division between the counter-culture and those adults who admired or tolerated it—upper-middle-class professionals and intellectuals in the Northeast particularly—and the silent majority of workers and Middle Americans who didn't. The tensions between these groups made solving social and political problems all the more difficult, and were, indeed, part of the problem.

Finally, the counter-culture was hell on standards. A handful of bohemians were no great threat to art and intellect. The problem was that a generation of students, the artists and intellectuals of the future, was infected with romanticism. Truth and beauty were in the eye of the beholder. They were discovered or created by the pure of heart. Formal education and training were not, therefore, merely redundant but dangerous for obstructing channels through which the spirit flowed. It was one thing for hippies to say this, romanticism being the natural religion of bohemia. It was quite another to hear it from graduate students. Those who did anguished over the future of scholarship, like the critics who worried that pop art meant the end of art. These fears were doubtlessly overdrawn, but the pace of cultural change was so fast in the sixties that they were hardly absurd.

Logic seemed everywhere to be giving way to intuition, and self-discipline to impulse. Romanticism had never worked well in the past. It seemed to be doing as badly in the present. The hippies went from flower power to death-tripping in a few years. The New Left took only a little longer to move from participatory democracy to demolition. The counter-cultural ethic remained as beguiling as ever in theory. In practice, like most utopian dreams, human nature tended to defeat it. At the decade's end, young believers looked forward to the Age of Aquarius. Sensible men knew there would be no Aquarian age. What they didn't know was the sort of legacy the counter-culture would leave behind. Some feared that the straight world would go on as before, others that it wouldn't.

Working Men and Women

LILLIAN BRESLOW RUBIN

Labor historians have been primarily concerned with men and industry. The long struggle of the worker in heavy industry to organize was finally ended during the mobilization for the Second World War. Although there continues to be conflict between unions and management over wages, conditions of work, and fringe benefits, both big business and big labor have come to agree that cooperation is a better tool than conflict in most labor disputes. Thus, if the economy does not deteriorate completely, continued improvement in wages and working conditions for organized industrial labor seems assured.

What is often not recognized, however, is the limited extent of union membership. The long-established and conservative craft unions, the newly arrived industrial unions, and the increasingly active white-collar and service unions still cover less than half of the American labor force. Women make up a disproportionate number of the unorganized workers, and most of these women are in the increasingly important service sector of the economy.

Recent legislation by the federal government prohibiting discrimination by gender in the labor market and the movement to amend the Constitution to grant equal rights to women in federal programs have focused national attention on working women. The history of women as a factor in the employed labor force began in the nineteenth century. Women had always worked, of course, in home, farm, and mill. But the same nineteenth-century urbanization that created the "cult of domesticity" for middle-class women forced working-class women (and their children) into the workplace so that their families could earn a survival income. Three nineteenth-century technological developments—the typewriter, the telephone, and the sewing machine —permitted women to enter the work force in unusually large numbers. It would be impossible to determine how many of them willingly exchanged boredom and drudgery in the home for boredom and drudgery in the office or telephone exchange.

Any attempt to sustain the notion that woman's sphere is limited to the home flies in the face of reality at all class levels. Today, over half of all women between the ages of eighteen and sixty-four are in the labor force. Four out of ten working women are mothers, and 36 percent of these have children under the age of six. The persistence of the traditional division of labor in the home requires many working women, particularly in families with limited income, to hold two full-time jobs—one in the workplace and one in the home.

In the economically precarious times in which we live, all families except the very wealthy are feeling the strains of trying to make ends meet. For working-class families the attempt to maintain a decent standard of living is particularly stressful. Lillian Breslow

Rubin, of the Institute for Scientific Analysis in San Francisco, has described working-class life in a remarkably perceptive and sympathetic fashion. Using interviewing techniques and applying her extensive knowledge of the scholarly literature on work and families, Rubin has created a masterpiece of social analysis.

There have been many studies in recent years that have described the attitudes of American workers toward their work. The boredom, alienation, and frustrations have been amply catalogued. What is new in Rubin's analysis of the work people do, as described in the chapter of her book reprinted here, is her account of the impact of work on domestic relations. What spillover does life on the job have on life in the home? What does it do to a man's image of himself if he has difficulty providing a good living for his household?

Perhaps the most important insights come in Rubin's description of what happens to the relationship between husband and wife when the wife goes to work. Even though most of the women interviewed worked only part-time, this apparent break with the traditional role differentiation of husband and wife often put an almost intolerable strain on the marriage. Not only was the authority of the husband threatened (an attitude the men described freely), but also the women experienced an exhilarating sense of independence when they had pay envelopes of their own, no matter how small. As increasing numbers of women continue to enter the work force, for whatever reasons, they are likely to continue to challenge male dominance both at home and in the workplace. If men fail to change their attitudes about the "proper" relationship between men and women, one can expect to see an increase in stressful family situations, which contribute heavily to the dis-ease of our society.

Tell me something about the work you do and how you feel about it.

For the men, whose definition of self is so closely tied to work, it's a mixed bag—a complex picture of struggle, of achievements and disappointments, of successes and failures. In their early work life, most move restlessly from job to job seeking not only higher wages and better working conditions, but some kind of work in which they can find meaning, purpose, and dignity:

> God, I hated that assembly line. *I hated it.* I used to fall asleep on the job standing up and still keep doing my work. There's nothing more boring and more repetitious in the world. On top of it, you

"Work and Its Meaning" (Editor's title: "Working Men and Women"). From *Worlds of Pain: Life in the Working-Class Family*, by Lillian Breslow Rubin (New York: Basic Books, 1976), chap. 9. © 1976 by Lillian Breslow Rubin, Basic Books, Inc., Publishers, New York.

don't feel human. The machine's running you, you're not running it.

> [*Thirty-three-year-old mechanic.*]

Thus, by the time they're twenty-five, their post-school work life averages almost eight years, and half have held as many as six, eight, or ten jobs.

Generally, they start out as laborers, operatives in an oil refinery, assembly-line workers in the local canneries, automobile or parts plants, warehousemen, janitors, or gas station attendants—jobs in which worker dissatisfaction is well documented. Some move on and up—into jobs that require more skill, jobs that still demand plenty of hard work, but which at least leave one with a sense of mastery and competence:

> I'm proud of what I've done with my life. I come from humble origins, and I never even finished school; but I've gotten someplace. I work hard, but it's good work. It's challenging and never routine. When I finish a day's work, I know I've accomplished something. I'm damned good at what I do, too. Even the boss knows it.
>
> [*Thirty-six-year-old steam fitter.*]

But the reality of the modern work world is that there are fewer and fewer jobs calling for such traditional skills. So most job changes don't mean moving up, but only moving on:[1]

> When I first started, I kept moving around. I kept looking for a job I'd like. You know, a job where it wouldn't make you tired just to get up in the morning and have to go to work. [*With a heavy sigh.*] It took me a number of years to discover that there's not much difference—a job's a job. So now I do what I have to do, and maybe I can get my family a little security.
>
> [*Twenty-seven-year-old mail sorter.*]

For some, the job changes are involuntary—due to lay-offs:

> When I first got out of high school, I had a series of jobs and a series of lay-offs. The jobs lasted from three weeks to three months.

---

[1] In his fine treatise on the nature of work in modern industrial society, Braverman (1974) argues that while short-term trends in rapidly growing industries may open the way for the advancement of a few, the lower skill requirements that characterize the largest majority of jobs mean that there are fewer and fewer opportunities to move into skilled work. This suggests even more serious limitations on upward mobility than the American society heretofore has known since, as Thernstrom (1972) persuasively argues, to the degree that upward mobility existed in the working class, it was *intra*stratum mobility—that is, men moving up within the class from less skilled to more skilled labor. If work itself has been and will continue to be stripped of skill requirements, then, as Braverman asserts, that avenue of upward mobility will be largely closed off. Cf., Aronowitz (1973) who also deals with this issue in his analysis of the forces that are shaping working-class consciousness in America.

Something always happened—like maybe the contract didn't come through—and since I was low man on the totem pole, I got laid off. A lot of times, the lay-offs lasted longer than the jobs.

. . . or industrial accidents—a common experience among men who work in factories, warehouses, and on construction sites:

I was working at the cannery about a week when my hand got caught in the belt. It got crushed, and I couldn't work for three months. When I got better, they wouldn't put me back on the job because they said I was accident-prone.

By the time they're thirty, about half are settled into jobs at which they've worked for five years. With luck, they'll stay at them for many more to come. Without it, like their fathers, they'll know the pain of periodic unemployment, the fear of their families doing without. For the other half—those still floating from job to job—the future may be even more problematic. Unprotected by seniority, with work histories that prospective employers are likely to view as chaotic and unstable, they can expect little security from the fluctuations and uncertainties of the labor market.

But all that tells us nothing about the quality of life on the job—what it feels like to go to work at *that* particular job for most of a lifetime—an experience that varies in blue-collar jobs just as it does in white-collar ones. For just as there are elite jobs in the white-collar work force, so they exist among blue-collar workers. Work that allows for freedom and autonomy on the job—these are the valued and high-status jobs, rare in either world. For the blue-collar worker, that means a job where he can combine skill with strength, where he can control the pace of his work and the order of the tasks to be done, and where successful performance requires his independent judgments. To working-class men holding such jobs—skilled construction workers, skilled mechanics, truck drivers—the world of work brings not only goods, but gratifications. The man who drives the long-distance rig feels like a free agent once he gets out on the road. It's true, there's a time recorder on the truck that clocks his stops. Still, compared to jobs he's had before in factories and warehouses, on this one, he's the guy who's in control. Sometimes the road's easy; sometimes it's tough. Always it requires his strength and skill; always he's master of the machine:

There's a good feeling when I'm out there on the road. There ain't nobody looking over your shoulder and watching what you're doing. When I worked in a warehouse, you'd be punching in and punching out, and bells ringing all the time. On those jobs, you're not thinking, you're just doing what they tell you. Sure, now I'm expected to bring her in on time, but a couple of hours one way or the other don't make no difference. And there ain't nobody but me to worry about how I get her there.

[*Twenty-eight-year-old trucker.*]

The skilled construction worker, too, finds challenge and reward in his work:

> I climb up on those beams every morning I'm working, and I like being way up there looking down at the world. It's a challenge up there, and the work's hardly ever routine. You have to pay attention and use your head, too, otherwise you can get into plenty of trouble in the kind of work I do. I'm a good man, and everybody on the job knows it.
>
> *[Thirty-one-year-old ironworker.]*

But most blue-collar men work at jobs that require less skill, that have less room for independent judgment—indeed, often expect that it will be suspended—and that leave their occupants with little freedom or autonomy. Such jobs have few intrinsic rewards and little status—either in the blue-collar world or the one outside—and offer few possibilities for experiencing oneself as a "good man." The men who hold these jobs often get through each day by doing their work and numbing themselves to the painful feelings of discontent—trying hard to avoid the question, "Is this what life is all about?" Unsuccessful in that struggle, one twenty-nine-year-old warehouseman burst out bitterly:

> A lot of times I hate to go down there. I'm cooped up and hemmed in. I feel like I'm enclosed in a building forty hours a week, sometimes more. It seems like all there is to life is to go down there and work, collect your pay check, pay your bills, and get further in debt. It doesn't seem like the circle ever ends. Everyday it's the same thing; every week it's the same thing; every month it's the same thing.

Some others respond with resignation:

> I guess you can't complain. You have to work to make a living, so what's the use.
>
> *[Twenty-six-year-old garage man.]*

. . . some with boredom:

> I've been in this business thirteen years and it bores me. It's enough.
>
> *[Thirty-five-year-old machine operator.]*

. . . some with alienation:

> The one thing I like is the hours. I work from seven to three-thirty in the afternoon so I get off early enough to have a lot of the day left.
>
> *[Twenty-eight-year-old assembly-line worker.]*

All, in fact, probably feel some combination of all these feelings. For the men in such jobs, bitterness, alienation, resignation, and boredom are the

defining features of the work experience. For them, work is something to
do, not to talk about. "What's there to talk about?"—not really a question
but an oft-repeated statement that says work is a requirement of life,
hours to be gotten through until you can go home.[2]

No big news this—at least not for readers of *The Wall Street Journal*
and *Fortune* magazine, both aimed at the leaders of the industrial world.
No big news either in the highest reaches of government where in 1972
the United States Senate sponsored a symposium on worker alienation.[3]
When absentee and turnover rates rise, when wildcat strikes occur with
increasing frequency—in short, when productivity falls off—the alienation
of workers becomes a focal concern for both industrial managers and
government. That concern increasingly is expressed both in the media
and in the work of industrial sociologists, psychologists, and labor relations experts who more and more talk of plans for "job enrichment," "job
enlargement," and "the humanization of work."

Despite the talk, however, the history of industrialization shows that
as industry has become more capital intensive, the thrust has been toward
technological developments which consistently routinize work and require less skill of the masses of workers. Today more than yesterday—

[2] This is, of course, not a new finding. Dubin (1956) long ago argued that work is
not a "central life interest" for most industrial workers. Chinoy (1955) studied
automobile workers and found that success and gratification were defined primarily
in non work-related terms. And Herzberg (1959) and Herzberg, et al. (1959) made
essentially the same observation that I make here—that is, that most blue-collar
workers are neither satisfied nor dissatisfied with their work. They do their jobs
because they must and try to think as little as possible about whether they're
happy, satisfied, or interested in their work.

Criticizing such work-satisfaction studies, Braverman (1974:28–29) argues that
the appropriate matter for concern ought not to be with how workers feel about
their jobs but with the nature of work itself. He charges that by the methods they
use (i.e., survey research) and the questions they ask "sociologists [are] measuring
not popular consciousness but their own." The sociologist, he asserts, shares with
management the conviction that the existing organization of the process of labor is
necessary and inevitable. "This leaves to sociology the function, which it shares
with personnel administration, of assaying not the nature of the work but the
degree of adjustment of the worker. Clearly, for industrial sociology the problem
does not appear with the degradation of work, but only with the overt signs of
dissatisfaction on the part of the worker."

[3] See U.S. Senate Committee on Labor and Public Welfare (1972) for the hearings
on SB 3916, a bill brought before the United States Senate whose purpose was: "To
provide for research for solutions to the problems of alienation among American
workers in all occupations and industries and technical assistance to those companies,
unions, State and local governments seeking to find ways to deal with the problem . . ." See also the U.S. Department of Health, Education, and Welfare report
entitled *Work in America* (1973). For other recent studies on the consequences of
alienation from work on life both on and off the job, see Levitan (1971); Meissner
(1971); Seashore and Barnowe (1972); Shepard (1970); Sheppard (1971); Sheppard and Herrick (1972). For a more radical view of the alienation of American
workers and their developing class consciousness, see Aronowitz (1973) and Braverman (1974).

because technology has now caught up with work in the office as well as the factory—most work continues to be steadily and systematically standardized and routinized; the skills of the vast majority of workers have been degraded. So profound is the trend that generally we are unaware that the meaning of "skill" itself has been degraded as well.[4] This, too, is no new phenomenon as even a casual glance at the historical record shows. For whether in 1875 or 1975, most of those concerned with the organization of work and with the qualities most desired in a work force talk not about skill but about "discipline" and "responsibility." [5] The difference in these hundred years in what is required of the mass of workers is one of degree not of kind. Advancing technology means that there is less need than before for skill, more for reliability—that means workers who appear punctually and regularly, who work hard, who don't sabotage the line, and who see their own interests as identical with the welfare of the company. These are the "skills" such capital-intensive industries need. And these are the skills toward which—today as yesterday —training programs of the unemployed and underemployed so often are directed.[6]

In fact, there is no argument among most students of work in America that most work—whether in the factory or in the office—requires less skill than before. Rather the argument is heard around the *meaning* of the trend in the lives of those affected by it. In the United States, at least, most analysts insist upon the inevitability of the process, arguing that where technology exists it will be used—as if it had a force or a life of its own; where it doesn't exist, it will be invented. Human beings, such

[4] See Aronowitz (1973) and Braverman (1974) for excellent recent discussions of this phenomenon and its consequences.

[5] See Blauner (1964:169) who comments that "the shift from skill to responsibility is the most important historical trend in the evolution of blue-collar work." For an historical analysis of continuity and change in the ideologies of management in the course of industrialization, see Bendix (1963). Bremer (1970) presents a documentary history of the early reform movements in America and their view of the poor and working classes. Threaded throughout, one finds expressions of concern about the unruliness of the masses and their consequent unfitness for the world of work. Even a casual examination of such early documents leaves the clear impression that one important—if not explicitly articulated—goal of the reformers was to turn the masses into docile and disciplined Americans who could be counted on to work every day in the factories for which they were destined. Cf., Bendix (1963) who shows that Sunday schools were introduced in eighteenth-century England as a means of governing the poor and training them for what was considered their appropriately subordinate place. In his outstanding analysis of the origins of early school reform in Massachusetts, Katz (1968) argues that this was precisely the function of the developing public-school system and compulsory attendance regulations.

[6] Punctuality, regularity, cleanliness, and orderliness have long been the focus of training for the industrial work world. Cf., Greer (1972) and Katz (1968) for excellent analyses of the historical function of the schools in providing this training. More recently, national manpower-training programs and state programs sponsored by the Human Resources Development Agency also have focused heavily on training the poor, the unemployed, and the underemployed in those traits.

people argue, must invent their future; that is one essential meaning of being "human." [7]

That argument, however, fails to grapple with the fact that only a tiny minority of us ever are involved in inventing our present, let alone our future. Ordinary women and men—which means almost all of us—struggle along with received truths as well as received ways of being and doing. For such people, at least one half of the waking hours of each day are spent in doing work that is dull, routine, deadening—in a word, alienating and alienated labor. True, these analysts would say. But for those people, there are substitute gratifications to be found in the private sphere of life—that is, the family—and in their leisure hours.

But again, that formulation fails to deal with the degree to which the parts of human life are interrelated—each interacting with and acting upon the other—so that such a separation is nearly impossible. In fact, any five-year-old child knows when "daddy has had a bad day" at work. He comes home tired, grumpy, withdrawn, and uncommunicative. He wants to be left alone; wife and children in that moment are small comfort. When *every* working day is a "bad day," the family may even feel like the enemy at times. But for them, he may well think, he could leave the hated job, do something where he could feel human again instead of like a robot.

Over a century ago, in the early stages of industrialization, Karl Marx spoke to the profoundly important human consequences of alienation from work—of work that doesn't permit the development of skill, of a sense of mastery, of an understanding of the totality of the *process* of production, of a connectedness with its *product*. Those issues are no less real today. The overt brutalization of industrial workers is no longer with us. But the intensification of technological developments has given rise to dehumanization and alienation in the work world on a scale far greater than anything known before.

For the working-class men I met, these issues, while unarticulated in this way, are nevertheless real. Most are in a constant struggle to make some order and continuity out of the fragments of their lives. Thus, they come home after work and plunge into projects that offer the possibility for feeling useful, competent, whole again—fixing the car or truck, remodeling the kitchen, building something for the kids.[8] Others—those

---

[7] See, for example, the publications of the Harvard University Program on Technology and Society established in 1964 by a grant from International Business Machines Corporation. Also Burke (1966); Theobald (1967); Torbert (1963). For a fine critique of the technology-as-progress view, see Ellul (1967).

[8] Discussing the trivialization of labor in modern capitalist society, Aronowitz (1973:130) comments on the same point:
> Under modern conditions, the self is only realized in the world of leisure, which now becomes the location for autonomy rather than work . . . That is why, with few exceptions, workers expect nothing intrinsically meaningful in their labor, and satisfy their desire for craftsmanship in the so-called "private realm." For example, tens of thousands of young people have become "car freaks." The automobile is invested with much more than reified status or power. It has become a

who seem already to have given up life and hope—collapse into a kind of numbed exhaustion from which they stir only to eat, drink, and watch television. Either way, the implications for family life are clear. Husbands and fathers are removed from active involvement—some because they are in a desperate struggle to retain some sense of their humanity, others because they have given it all up.

There are still a few who have fantasies of one day doing some other kind of work—owning a farm, a ranch, a small business are the most common of these dreams. No new phenomenon; for part of the American dream always has been to have a business of one's own. Rarely, however, are these dreams voiced spontaneously in the course of a discussion about work and their feelings about it. In that context, work tends to be seen as a given in life—more or less enjoyable, but ultimately unavoidable, thus not something to give much thought to. Only when the question itself has a dreamlike and unreal quality does it encourage and get a fantasy response:

Would you fantasy for a minute about what you'd do if you suddenly inherited a million dollars?[9]

----

vital means for the realization of the frustrated need to make a direct link with the totality of production for youth who are condemned to either the fragmented labor of the factory or the office or the truncated learning of the school.

[9] For three decades now, a popular question used in surveys seeking to determine work satisfaction asks the respondent whether he would continue to work if he had enough money to live comfortably without working. See, for example, Kaplan and Tausky (1972); Morse and Weiss (1955); Tausky (1969); Veroff and Feld (1970). The question I asked also was designed to tap attitudes about work. I chose the more ambiguous wording, however, in order that it might be more in the nature of a projective test which gives the respondent fewer cues toward which to direct an answer. The question, therefore, tapped not only attitudes toward work, but also gave me data on the issues that preoccupy the people in this study and their fantasied solutions.

In a challenge to attitude surveys and the traditional questions in work-satisfaction studies, Kaplan and Kruytbosch (1975) made a "behavioral test of the commitment to work" by studying lottery winners in New York and New Jersey. They found that while commitment to *work* was pervasive, commitment to one's *job* was not, and that the greater the amount of the winnings, the greater was the number of quits and job changes. The authors conclude:

The most significant finding of this study is that many people when given a real opportunity to choose between keeping their present jobs and quitting or changing, choose the latter. When the economic necessity to work is removed [in fact, not in fantasy], as in the case of the millionaires, eight out of ten quit their jobs . . . If there are lessons to be learned from this research it is that attitudinal questions about satisficing states are intriguing but not necessarily conducive to an accurate interpretation of social reality. Asking workers whether they are satisfied with the work they do and finding that most say they are is like asking a horse that has always been fed hay if he likes his diet. The opportunities for a change of work or diet are closed, unknown or impractical . . . But when people had a chance, they knew what to

Most working-class people—men and women—are stopped cold by the question. Most say at once, "I've never thought about it." One thirty-two-year-old man added in wonder:

> Most of my life I've been lucky to have ten dollars; thinking about a million—wow, that seems impossible.

When pushed to think of the question in terms of the work they'd like to do, slowly, thoughtfully, a few gave voice to their fantasies. But always the implicit understanding was there: both of us knew that *he knew* it was just a dream:

> Well, I guess if I had a million dollars, I'd buy me a cattle ranch in the mountains and go live in the country. I like to hunt and fish. I like the country. I like animals. And I'd sure like to be my own boss and to work when I want to work. Oh, I know I'd have to work hard on a ranch, but it would be *my* work, and it would be on *my* time, and with me deciding what needed doing and doing it.
>   [*Thirty-three-year-old delivery man.*]

> Like I said, my job is tedious. I'd actually be glad to quit it. I don't mean I'd quit work; nobody should ever do that. I might buy a goat farm and raise goats and pigs—just something where I could do something a person could care about. You know, something that was mine and that wasn't so tedious.
>   [*Twenty-nine-year-old postal clerk.*]

> I guess if I was going to have a fantasy about anything, it would be to have a little sporting-goods store in the neighborhood, a place where all the kids on the local teams could come to get outfitted. I would feel a lot of satisfaction to have a store like that, and I think it would be a terrific business to be in. But it's just a dream. I'll never get enough money together to do it, and you can be sure there's nobody going to leave me no thousand dollars, let alone a million.
>   [*Thirty-one-year-old night watchman.*]

One twenty-seven-year-old warehouseman, after talking at length about the business he hoped he'd have some day, took a mental step back from our conversation, observed himself thoughtfully and said:

> After all that talk, I really doubt I'll ever make any change. I'll probably stay where I am forever. Once you've been on the job seven years, look what you'd have to give up—good money, good benefits, seniority. What if I tried my own business and it didn't

---

do. They got out—not of *work* . . . but of their *jobs* which they viewed as dull, dirty and dead-end.

work? Then I'd have to come back and start all over again. No. I don't think I'll ever take that chance.

Paradoxically, then, the "good money, good benefits, seniority" that come with long tenure on the job also serve to limit his choices—to bind him to it, trading the dream for this stagnant stability. Perhaps, in the long run, that makes sense given the failure rate of small, independent businesses in America. In the immediate moment, there's pain and pathos when, at twenty-seven, he already knows his life choices largely are over.

Imagine the consequences to the shape and form of that human life. Imagine, too, an environment in which the same paucity of choices is the reality of most lives—no friends or relatives around who see a future with plenty of possibilities stretching before them; no one who expects very much because experience has taught them that such expectations end painfully. Such is the fertile field in which the fatalism, passivity, and resignation of the working class grow—qualities so often remarked upon by professional middle-class investigators. But it is not these qualities that are responsible for their humble social status. That is the illusion with which so many middle-class observers attempt to palliate their guilt about the inequalities in American life—inequalities that are at such odds with our most cherished ideological myth of egalitarianism. Rather it is their social status from which these qualities stem. No, these are not personal failings, nor are they outgrowths of character or personality deficiencies. They are, instead, realistic responses to the social context in which most working-class men, women, and children live, grow, and come to define themselves, their expectations, and their relationship to the world around them.

Would you fantasy for a minute about what you'd do if you suddenly inherited a million dollars?

For a few of the men, answering the fantasy question is easier; they know just what they would do. These are the half dozen who have some natural skill or talent in music or drawing and painting—talents that are untutored and undeveloped, talents discovered accidentally:

I don't know how I know how to draw. I just know how. I guess I've been doing it since I was a little kid but nobody paid it any mind.

"Nobody paid it any mind"—unthinkable that such childhood demonstration of artistic abilities would go without attention and nurturance in most modern middle-class families. At the very least, such a boy would be encouraged to use those capabilities to become an architect, an engineer. But when you're one of ten children in a family where survival is the principal preoccupation, it seems quite natural that no one pays "any mind" to a boy who draws. No surprise, either, if you grow up without a family at all:

I was about sixteen the first time I held a banjo in my hands, and I just played it. It was the same thing later, the first time I sat down at a piano. I just taught myself how to play. I've wondered before about how that happened, but I don't know. One thing I remember from when I was little was I was a quiet, unhappy kid. Every time I moved to a new foster home, I'd be scared all over again, and I got quieter and quieter. I think what kept me from being panicked out all the time was the music I had in my head. It was like it kept me company. I used to make up songs and sing them to myself. And I used to pretend I was playing music on a great big piano in front of a hundred people. [*Laughing.*] I thought that was a lot of people then.

For these men, without exception, some part of the million would be spent on training—perhaps on becoming professionals—in their particular creative endeavor.

Whether the men like their work or not, whether it offers more gratification or less, whether they have active fantasies about another way of life or they accept what is without allowing dreams to intrude upon reality, the work they do powerfully affects the quality of family life. What happens during the day on the job colors—if it doesn't actually dictate—what happens during the evening in the living room, perhaps later in the bedroom. And the size of the weekly pay check is importantly related to how men feel about themselves, their work, and their responsibilities. Probably men of all classes experience those responsibilities with heavy weariness at times, but they seem to be felt more keenly among the working class where the choices are narrower and the rewards slimmer.[10]

[10] For the last two decades, social scientists have argued about whether the work force has become increasingly proletarianized or increasingly middle class. Mills (1951), for example, argues for the increasing proletarianization of white-collar workers as their traditional status edge over blue-collarites disappears as office work requires less and less specialized skill and training. Wilensky (1964, 1966), one of the foremost proponents of the other side of the argument which rests on the diminution of observed lifestyle differences between the classes, developed the notion of the "middle mass" to reflect his view of the homogenization of the upper working class and the lower middle class. In recent years, Marxist theorists have developed a theory of the "new working class" which takes as its starting point the fact that not only are white-collar workers divorced from the means of production as are manual workers, but that they, too, have been systematically dispossessed of their skills, their status, their prestige, and their historical advantage in earnings over blue-collar workers. Aronowitz (1973); Braverman (1974); Smith (1974) persuasively develop and argue various facets of new working-class theory.

These provocative formulations, while pointing to some important core truths about the *process* of work in America, still leave us with some dilemmas about how to define class in this advanced industrial society, and about the differences in life situation between what traditionally has been known as the working class and the middle class. While it is patently absurd to hold tenaciously to these traditional distinctions, there still remains an important difference between the mass of hourly

Even before 1975 and early 1976, when the national unemployment rate consistently stood at more than 8 percent, and the California rate at 10 percent, the vision of the American worker supporting his family with ease and style was a palpable distortion, visible to any observer not blinded by the prevailing myth of his affluence. For just below that apparent affluence, working-class families have always lived with the gnawing fear of unemployment and underemployment—always aware that any cutback in overtime, any lay-off would send them over the edge into disaster. For most, it takes the combined incomes of wife and husband, plus a heavy load of overtime for him, just to stay even. In fact, even with those conditions met, few manage to keep up with all their bills:

> *Would you fantasy for a minute about what you'd do if you suddenly inherited a million dollars?*

After the first surprised silence, both women and men answer with a regularity that quickly becomes predictable. "I'd pay off my bills," is the first thought that comes to 70 percent; for another 25 percent, it is the second thought. To the remaining few who don't give this evidence of financial stress, I remarked:

> *Most people I've talked to say they'd pay off their bills, and I'm wondering why that doesn't occur to you?*

The answer is simple: they have no bills. These are the few families who buy only when they have cash in hand—a rare phenomenon in American life at any class level.

There is no issue in which the class differences are more striking, none which tells more about how differently families in the professional middle class experience financial pressures. For not one woman or man in the middle-class families talked about paying off their bills if they were suddenly to come into a large inheritance. It is not that such families don't have bills; indeed, they have very large ones—mortgages on expensive homes; cars, boats, vacations bought on credit; the bills from monthly charge accounts. Rather their failure to mention them stems from the relatively secure knowledge that annual incomes are high and climbing, and that professionals generally get hit last and least in the crunch of economic hard times.[11] In their mid-thirties, these professional men stand

---

workers and the mass of salaried workers in their vulnerability to economic fluctuations. Despite the fact that some white-collar occupations have been hard hit by the current recession, the burden of unemployment and underemployment still is carried most heavily by the hourly workers in the factories, the trades, and the service sector of the economy. In 1974, for example, the rate of unemployment among male professional and technical workers, age 25–44, was 1.5 percent compared to 5.3 percent for operatives and 4.5 percent for transport equipment operators (U.S. Department of Labor, *Handbook of Labor Statistics*, 1975).

[11] A recent article in the San Francisco *Chronicle* (December 25, 1975) reported the research of Eugene Hammel and Virginia Aldrich, who studied the job fate of 5,550 University of California, Berkeley, students who received the Ph.D. degree

on the lower rungs of their career ladders. Barring a national economic catastrophe, a long climb up with steadily increasing earnings is assured.

At the same age and stage of the life cycle, working-class men generally are at the top of their truncated career ladders. Increased earnings can be anticipated only insofar as union negotiations are successful or in routine cost-of-living increases, which at best keep them barely even with the inflationary spiral. Moreover, even in the event of economic disaster, most men in the professional middle class can count on holding jobs or getting them more readily than their less educated working-class brothers. Recall the depression of the 1930s when college graduates displaced those with only a high-school diploma behind the counters in major department stores and at the gas pumps.

> *Would you fantasy for a minute about what you'd do if you suddenly inherited a million dollars?*

Other interesting differences between the classes appear—differences that speak powerfully to their widely divergent early life experiences as well as to differences in their present life styles. Among the working-class families, for example, 34 percent said they would help their families:

> First of all, I'd fix up my parents and Bob's so that none of them would ever have to worry again. Then I'd buy my sister and brother-in-law a house.
> [*Thirty-year-old housewife.*]

> I'd be able to help my mother and father and set them up so they wouldn't have to worry about anything anymore.
> [*Twenty-seven-year-old carpenter's helper.*]

Almost identical words issuing from so many lips—"so they wouldn't have to worry anymore"—give testimony to the precariousness with which their parents and some of their siblings still live, to the continuing fragility of life in these families. Only one professional man exhibited a similar concern for his family—the only man from a working-class background. For the rest, there is no need to think about such things. Their parents can not only take care of themselves but usually can—and often do—help the children as well.

Finally, there are those—just over half and most often women—whose fantasies include buying some small services not now possible:

---

between 1967 and 1974. Expressing irritation at the press stories about Ph.D.'s who can't find work, Hammel said, "Sure, you can always find a taxi-driving physicist somewhere . . . but that just isn't typical." In fact, the research found that *at least* 97.6 percent of these women and men found work in their chosen fields, indicating an unemployment rate of "no higher than 2.4 percent and maybe as low as 1.1 percent." While it may be true that the job market is less favorable to professionals from less prestigious schools, it still is a far cry from the unemployment rate of, for example, automobile workers.

> I'd get the TV fixed. It's not working right, but right now, it's hard to take the money to have it fixed. There's so many bills that *have* to be paid right now.
>
> [*Thirty-six-year-old mother of four.*]

. . . getting some needed, but neglected, medical attention:

> I'd make sure the kids would have everything they needed. Then I'd go to the dentist and get me some teeth where I've got some missing.
>
> [*Twenty-nine-year-old father of two.*]

. . . or doing something special for the children—"special" usually defined in such a way as to highlight the scarcity of comforts that are taken for granted in most middle-class families:

> I think I'd buy each of the kids a dozen pair of shoes. Poor little things, they only have one pair of shoes at a time. They're lucky to get that. It's practically a holiday when we go out to buy shoes for one of the kids. They get so excited.
>
> [*Thirty-four-year-old mother of five.*]

> I'd spend a lot of it on giving the kids a good time. We hardly ever have anything extra to take them to Kiddieland or something like that. Once this year we did, and they were so happy and excited. It made both of us feel good to see them that way.
>
> [*Twenty-eight-year-old mother of three.*]

Under the pressures of these financial strains, 58 percent of the working-class wives work outside the home—most in part-time jobs.[12] Of those who stay at home, about two-thirds are happy to do so, considering the occupation of "housewife and mother" an important and gratifying job. Some are glad to work only in the home because jobs held earlier were experienced as dull and oppressive:

> I worked as a file clerk for Montgomery Ward's. I hated it. There was always somebody looking over your shoulder trying to catch you in mistakes. Besides, it was boring; you did the same thing all day long. Now I can stop when I don't feel like doing something and play with the children. We go for walks, or we work in the garden.

. . . some, because life outside seems frightening:

> No. I don't ever want to work again if I don't have to. It's really too hectic out there. Now when I'm home, I can go out to it when

---

[12] In 1973, the labor force participation of all married women (husbands present), regardless of class, with children under six was 32.7 percent; with children between six and seventeen, it was 50.1 percent. (U.S. Bureau of the Census, 1974).

> I want. I suppose it sounds like I'm hiding from something, or es-
> caping from it. But I'm not. It's just that sometimes it's overwhelm-
> ing.

. . . and some, just because they enjoy both the tasks and the freedom of
work in the home:

> I wouldn't work ever again if I didn't have to. I like staying home.
> I sew and take care of the house and kids. I go shopping. I'm my
> own boss. I like that. And I also like fixing up the house and
> making it look real nice. And I like cooking nice meals so Ralph is
> proud of me.

But few working-class wives are free to make the choice about working inside or outside the home depending only on their own desires. Most
often, economic pressures dictate what they will do, and *even those who
wish least to work outside the home probably will do so sometime in
their lives.* Thus, for any given family, the wife is likely to move in and
out of the labor force depending on the husband's job stability, on
whether his overtime expands or contracts, on the exigencies of family life
—a sick child, an aging parent.

The women I met work as beauticians, sales clerks, seamstresses,
cashiers, waitresses, office clerks, typists, occasionally as secretaries and
factory workers; and at a variety of odd jobs such as baby-sitters, school-
crossing guards, and the like. Their work hours range from a few hours
a week to a few—nine in all—who work full-time. Most—about three-
quarters—work three or four days a week regularly.

Their attitudes toward their work are varied, but most find the work
world a satisfying place—at least when compared to the world of the
housewife. Therefore, although many of these women are pushed into
the job market by economic necessity, they often stay in it for a variety
of other reasons.

An anomaly, a reader might say. After all, hasn't it already been said
that wives who hold jobs outside the home often are resentful because
they also bear most of the burden of the work inside the home? Yet both
are true. Women can feel angry and resentful because they are overbur-
dened when trying to do both jobs almost single-handedly, while at the
same time feeling that work outside the home provides satisfactions not
otherwise available. Like men, they take pride in doing a good job, in
feeling competent. They are glad to get some relief from the routines of
housewifery and mothering small children. They are pleased to earn some
money, to feel more independent, more as if they have some ability to
control their own lives. Thus, they ask no more—indeed, a good deal
less—than men do; the chance to do work that brings such rewards while
at the same time having someone to share some of the burdens of home
and family.

There is, perhaps, no greater testimony to the deadening and deadly
quality of the tasks of the housewife than the fact that so many women
find pleasure in working at jobs that by almost any definition would be

called alienated labor—low-status, low-paying, dead-end work made up of dull, routine tasks; work that often is considered too menial for men who are less educated than these women. Nor is there greater testimony to the efficacy of the socialization process. Bored and discontented with the never-ending routine of household work, they seek stimulation in work outside the home. But a lifetime of preparation for housewifery and motherhood makes it possible to find gratification in jobs that require the same qualities—service, submission, and the suppression of intellectual development.[13]

No accident either that these traits are the ideal complements for the needs of the economy for a cheap, supplemental labor pool that can be moved in and out of the labor force as the economy expands and contracts. Indeed, the sex-stereotyped family roles dovetail neatly with this requirement of our industrial economy. With each expansion, women are recruited into the labor force at the lowest levels. Because they are defined primarily in their family roles rather than as workers, they are glad to get whatever work is available. For the same reason, they are willing to work for wages considerably below those of men. When the economy contracts, women are expected to give up their jobs and to return quietly to the tasks of housewifery and mothering.[14] Should they resist, they are reminded with all the force that society can muster that they are derelict in their primary duties and that those they love most dearly will pay a heavy price for their selfishness.

Tell me something about the work you do and how you feel about it?

A thirty-one-year-old factory worker, mother of five children, replies:

> I really love going to work. I guess it's because it gets me away from home. It's not that I don't love my home; I do. But you get awfully tired of just keeping house and doing those housewifely things. Right now, I'm not working because I was laid off last month. I'm enjoying the lay-off because things get awfully hectic at work, but it's only a short time. I wouldn't like to be off for a long time. Anyhow, even now I'm not completely not working.

---

[13] The literature on the socialization of women to "femininity" is vast. For some recent analyses of particular interest, see Bardwick and Douvan (1971); Bem and Bem (1972); Broverman, et al. (1972); Brun-Gulbrandsen (1971); Chafetz (1974); Chodorow (1971, 1977 forthcoming); Freeman (1974); Oakley (1972); Shainess (1972); Weisstein (1971); Weitzman, et al. (1972). Hoffman (1972) and Horner (1972) are particularly interesting on the issue of achievement-related conflicts in women. In a study of urban natives in Alaska, Jones (1975) also argues that one reason why native women adapt more readily than men to low-status demeaning jobs is because the women are so well socialized to passivity and subordination.

[14] See Aronowitz (1973); Braverman (1974); Holter (1971); Sokoloff (1975); Zaretsky (1973) for discussion and analysis of the importance of women as a reserve labor force in the economy.

I've been waiting tables at a coffee shop downtown. I like the people down there, and it's better than not doing anything.

You know, when I was home, I was getting in real trouble. I had that old housewife's syndrome, where you either crawl in bed after the kids go to school or sit and watch TV by the hour. I was just dying of boredom and the more bored I got, the less and less I did. On top of it, I was getting fatter and fatter, too. I finally knew I had to do something about it, so I took this course in upholstery and got this job as an upholstery trimmer.

"It gets me away from home"—a major reason why working women of any class say they would continue to work even apart from financial necessity. For most, however, these feelings of wanting to flee from the boredom and drudgery of housewifery are ambivalently held as they struggle with their guilt about leaving young children in someone else's care.

For all women, the issues around being a "working mother" are complex, but there are some special ones among the working class that make it both harder and easier for women to leave their homes to work. It is harder because, historically, it has been a source of status in working-class communities for a woman to be able to say, "I don't *have* to work." Many men and women still feel keenly that it's his job to support the family, hers to stay home and take care of it.[15] For her to take a job outside the house would be, for such a family, tantamount to a public acknowledgment of his failure. Where such attitudes still are held strongly, sometimes the wife doesn't work even when it's necessary; sometimes she does. Either way, the choice is difficult and painful for both.

On the other hand, it's easier for the wives of working-class men to override their guilt about leaving the children because the financial necessity often is compelling. On one level, that economic reality is an unpleasant one. On another, it provides the sanction for leaving the home and makes it easier for working-class women to free themselves from the inner voices that charge, "You're self-indulgent," that cry, "What kind of mother are you?"—as this conversation with a twenty-five-year-old working mother of two shows:

How do you feel about working?

I enjoy it. It's good to get out of the house. Of course, I wouldn't want to work full-time; that would be being away from the kids too much.

Do you sometimes wish you could stay home with them more?

Yeah, I do.

---

[15] See Easton (1975, 1976) for a picture of the historical development of the woman's-place-is-in-the-home ideology and its relationship to the economic requirements of the burgeoning industrial society. Cf., also Lazerson (1975); Sokoloff (1975).

What do you think your life would look like if you could?

Actually, I don't know. I guess I'd get kind of bored. I don't mean that I don't enjoy the kids; I do. But you know what I mean. It's kind of boring being with them day after day. Sometimes I feel bad because I feel like that. It's like my mind battles with itself all the time—like, "Stay home" and "Go to work."

So you feel guilty because you want to work and, at the same time, you feel like it would be hard for you to stay home all the time?

Yeah, that's right. Does it sound crazy?

No, it doesn't. A lot of women feel that way. I remember feeling that way when my children were young.

You, too, huh? That's interesting. What did you do?

Sometimes I went to work, and sometimes I stayed home. That's the way a lot of women resolve that conflict. Do you think you'd keep on working even if you didn't need the money at all?

I think about that because Ed says I could stop now. He says we can make it on his salary and that he wants me home with the kids. I keep saying no, because we still need this or that. That's true, too. It would be really hard. I'm not so sure we could do it without my salary. Sometimes I think he's not sure either. I've got to admit it, though, I don't really want to stay home. I wouldn't mind working three days instead of four, but that's about all. I guess I really work because I enjoy it. I'm good at it, and I like that feeling. It's good to feel like you're competent.

So you find some real gratifications in your work. Do you also sometimes think life would be easier if you didn't work?

Sure, in some ways, but maybe not in others. Anyhow, who expects life to be easy? Maybe when I was a kid I thought about things like that, but not now.

Faced with such restlessness, women of any class live in a kind of unsteady oscillation between working and not working outside the home —each choice exacting its own costs, each conferring its own rewards. Another woman, thirty-two and with four children, chooses differently, at least for now:

Working is hard for me. When I work, I feel like I want to be doing a real good job, and I want to be absolutely responsible. Then, if the little one gets a cold, I feel like I should be home with her. That causes complications because whatever you do isn't right. You're either at work feeling like you should be home with your sick child, or you're at home feeling like you should be at work.

So right now, you're relieved at not having to go to work?

Yeah, but I miss it, too. The days go faster and they're more exciting when you work.

Do you think you'll go back to work, then?

Right now, we're sort of keeping up with the bills, so I probably won't. When we get behind a lot again, I guess I'll go back then.

Thus, the "work-not work" issue is a lively and complicated one for women—one whose consequences radiate throughout the marriage and around which important issues for both the individuals and the marital couple get played out. Even on the question of economic necessity, wives and husbands disagree in a significant minority of the families. For "necessity" is often a relative term, the definition ultimately resting on differences between wives and husbands on issues of value, lifestyle, sex-role definitions, and conjugal power. Thus, he says:

She doesn't have to work. We can get by. Maybe we'll have to take it easy on spending, but that's okay with me. It's worth it to have her home where she belongs.

She says:

My husband says I don't have to work, but if I don't, we'll never get anywhere. I guess it's a matter of pride with him. It makes him feel bad, like he's not supporting us good enough. I understand how he feels, but I also know that, no matter what he says, if I stop working, when the taxes on the house have to be paid, there wouldn't be any money if we didn't have my salary.

In fact, both are true. The family *could* lower its living standard—live in an apartment instead of a house; have less, do less. On his income of about $11,500, they undoubtedly could survive. But with all his brave words about not wanting his wife to work, he is not without ambivalence about the consequences. He is neither eager to give up the few comforts her salary supports nor to do what he'd have to do in order to try to maintain them. She says:

He talks about me not working, then right after I went back this time, he bought this big car. So now, I have to work or else who would make the payments?

He says:

If she stops working, I'd just get a second job so we could keep up this place and all the bills and stuff.

How do you feel about having to do that?

Well, I wouldn't exactly love it. Working two jobs with hardly any time off for yourself isn't my idea of how to enjoy life. But if I had to, I'd do it.

What about the payments on the car? Wouldn't they get to be a big problem if she didn't work?

Yeah, that's what she says. I guess she's right. I don't want her to work; but even if I worked at night, too, I don't know how much I could make. She's right about if I work two jobs then I wouldn't have time to do anything with the family and see the kids. That's no life for any of us, I guess.

The choices, then, for this family, as for so many others, are difficult and often emotionally costly. In a society where people in all classes are trapped in frenetic striving to acquire goods, where a man's sense of worth and his definition of his manhood rest heavily on his ability to provide those goods, it is difficult for him to acknowledge that the family really does need his wife's income to live as they both would like. Yet, just beneath the surface of his denial is understanding—understanding that he sometimes experiences with pain, sometimes masks with anger. His wife understands his feelings. "It's a matter of pride with him," she says. "It makes him feel bad, like he's not supporting us good enough," she says. But she also knows that he, like she, wants the things her earnings buy.

It should be clear by now that for most women there are compensations in working outside the home that go beyond the material ones—a sense of being a useful and valued member of society:

If you don't bring home a pay check, there's no gauge for whether you're a success or not a success. People pay you to work because you're doing something useful and you're good at it. But nobody pays a housewife because what difference does it make; nobody really cares.

[*Thirty-four-year-old typist.*]

. . . of being competent:

In my work at the salon, it's really like an ego trip. It feels good when people won't come in if you're not there. If I go away for two weeks, my customers will wait to have their hair done until I come back. I'm not always very secure, but when I think about

that, it always makes me feel good about myself, like I'm really
okay.

[*Thirty-one-year-old beautician.*]

. . . of feeling important:

I meet all kinds of interesting people at work, and they depend on
me to keep the place nice. When I don't go in sometimes, the place
gets to be a mess. Nobody sweeps up, and sometimes they don't
even call to have a machine fixed. It makes me feel good—you
know, important—when I come back and everybody is glad to see
me because they know everything will be nice again.

[*Twenty-nine-year-old manager*
of a self-service laundromat.]

. . . and of gaining a small measure of independence from their husbands:

I can't imagine not working. I like to get out of the house, and the
money makes me feel more independent. Some men are funny.
They think if you don't work, you ought to just be home every
day, like a drudge around the house, and that they can come home
and just say, "Do this," and "Do that," and "Why is that dish in
the sink?" When you work and make some money, it's different. It
makes me feel more equal to him. He can't just tell me what to do.

In fact, students of the family have produced a large literature on
intra-family power which shows that women who work outside the house
have more power inside the house.[16] Most of these studies rest on the
resource theory of marital power—a theory which uses the language of
economics to explain marital relations. Simply stated, resource theory
conceptualizes marriage as a set of exchange relations in which the balance
of power will be on the side of the partner who contributes the greater
resources to the marriage.[17] While not made explicit, the underlying

[16] For a comprehensive review of the literature on working mothers and family
power along with an extensive and up-to-date bibliography, see Hoffman and Nye
(1974). Chapter 7, written by Stephen J. Bahr is of particular interest. For a fine
critique of this literature and its unspoken assumptions, see Gillespie (1972).

[17] For an early and comprehensive statement, see Blood and Wolfe (1960). In a
more recent formulation, Scanzoni (1972:66–70) writes:

In simplified form, we may suggest that *the husband in modern society
exchanges his status for marital solidarity*. If we accept as given that
expressive satisfactions (companionship, physical affection, empathy) are
the obvious goals of modern marriage, and that the major latent goal is
status and economic well-being, then we may say that the latent goal
influences the attainment of the manifest goal. *Specifically, the greater
degree of the husband's integration into the opportunity system (the
more his education, the higher his job status, the greater his income),
the more fully and extensively is the interlocking network of marital
rights and duties performed in reciprocal fashion. The economic rewards*

assumption of this theory is that the material contributions of the husband are the "greater resource." The corollary, of course, is the implicit denigration and degradation of the functions which women traditionally perform in the household—not the least of them providing the life-support system, the comfort, and the respite from the outside world that enables men to go back into it each day.

So pervasive is the assumption of the greater importance of the male contribution to the family, that generations of social scientists have unthinkingly organized their research around this thesis. Unfortunately, however, it is not the social scientists alone who hold this view. For women as well too often accept these definitions of the value of their role in the family and do, in fact, feel more useful, more independent, more able to hold their own in a marital conflict when they are also working outside the home and contributing some share of the family income. Such is the impact of the social construction of reality[18]; for, as the old sociological axiom says: "If men define situations as real, they are real in their consequences."

Indeed, it is just this issue of her independence that is a source of conflict in some of the marriages where women work. Mostly, when women hold outside jobs, there is some sense of partnership in a joint enterprise—a sharing of the experience of two people working together for a common goal. But in well over one third of the families, husbands complain that their working wives "are getting too independent." Listen to this conversation with a thirty-three-year-old repairman:

> She just doesn't know how to be a real wife, you know, feminine and really womanly. She doesn't know how to give respect because she's too independent. She feels that she's a working woman and she puts in almost as many hours as I do and brings home a pay check, so there's no one person above the other. She doesn't want there to be a king in this household.

> *And you want to be a king?*

> No, I guess I don't really want to be a king. Well [*laughing*] who wouldn't want to be? But I know better. I just want to be recognized as an important individual. She needs to be more feminine. When she's able to come off more feminine than she is, then maybe we'll have something deeper in this marriage.

> *I'm not sure I know what you mean. Could you help me to understand what you want of her?*

---

he provides motivate the wife to respond positively to him, and her response to him in turn gives rise to a continuing cycle of rectitude and gratitude. [emphasis mine]

For other similar analyses, see Bahr (1972, 1974); Blood and Hamblin (1958); Heer (1958, 1962); Hoffman (1960).

[18] See Berger and Luckman (1967).

> Look, I believe every woman has the right to be an individual, but
> I just don't believe in it when it comes between two people. A man
> needs a feminine woman. When it comes to two people living to-
> gether, a man is supposed to be a man and a woman is supposed
> to be a woman.

> *But just what does that mean to you?*

> I'd like to feel like I wear the pants in the family. Once my decision
> is made, it should be made, and that's it. She should just carry it
> out. But it doesn't work that way around here. Because she's work-
> ing and making money, she thinks she can argue back whenever she
> feels like it.

Another man, one who has held eight jobs in his seven-year marriage,
speaks angrily:

> I think our biggest problem is her working. She started working
> and she started getting too independent. I never did want her to
> go to work, but she did anyway. I don't think I had the say-so that
> I should have.

> *It sounds as if you're feeling very much as if your authority has
> been challenged on this issue of her working.*

> You're damn right. I feel the man should do the work, and he
> should bring home the money. And when he's over working, he
> should sit down and rest for the rest of the day.

> *And you don't get to do that when she's working?*

> Yeah, I do it. But she's got a big mouth so it's always a big
> hassle and fight. I should have put my foot down a long time ago
> and forced her into doing things my way.

The women respond to these charges angrily and defensively. The men
are saying: be dependent, submissive, subordinate—mandates with which
all women are reared. But for most white working-class women—as for
many of their black sisters—there is a sharp disjunction between the
commandments of the culture and the imperatives of their experience.

The luxury of being able to depend on someone else is not to be
theirs. And often, they are as angry at their men for letting them down
as the men are at the women for not playing out their roles in the culturally approved ways. A thirty-two-year-old mother of two speaks:

> I wish I could be dependent on him like he says. But how can you
> depend on someone who does the things he does. He quits a job
> just because he gets mad. Or he does some dumb thing, so he gets

fired. If I didn't work, we wouldn't pay the rent, no matter what he says.

Another thirty-year-old mother of three says:

He complains that I don't trust him. Sure I don't. When I was pregnant last time and couldn't work, he went out with his friends and blew money around. I never know what he's going to do. By the time the baby came, we were broke, and I had to go back to work before she was three weeks old. It was that or welfare. Then he complains because I'm too independent. Where would we be if I wasn't?

Thus are both women and men stuck in a painful bind, each blaming the other for failures to meet cultural fantasies—fantasies that have little relation to their needs, their experiences, or the socio-economic realities of the world they live in. She isn't the dependent, helpless, frivolous child-woman because it would be ludicrously inappropriate, given her life experiences. He isn't the independent, masterful, all-powerful provider, not because he does "dumb" or irresponsible things, but because the burdens he carries are too great for all but a few of the most privileged—burdens that are especially difficult to bear in a highly competitive economic system that doesn't grant every man and woman the right to work at a self-supporting and self-respecting wage as a matter of course.

For those who hold to traditional notions that men are entitled to power and respect by virtue of their position as head of—and provider for—the family, a working wife may, in fact, be a threat. When, as is the case among the working-class families, a woman working part-time earns almost one fourth of the total family income, there is a shift in the power relations in the family—a shift which may be slight but with which, nevertheless, men of any class in this culture are likely to be uncomfortable. The fact that the professional middle-class men I met did not express these negative feelings about their wives working may be less related to their liberated attitudes about sex roles than to the fact that their wives' earnings comprise only 9 percent of the family income—a proportion so insignificant that it poses no threat to the traditional balance of power in the family.[19]

[19] At the time of this study, the range of income among working-class women was $400 to $8,000 annually. Median income for part-time workers was $2,900; for full-time workers (only nine in number), $6,000, with those women who worked full-time found in the lower family income levels. Assuming even that the income in a family where a woman works full-time was at the median of $12,300, that woman would be contributing very close to half the total family income. In contrast, median wages of part-time women workers in the professional middle-class families was $2,000, or 9 percent of family income. Only one wife in those families worked full-time. With earnings of $15,000 a year, she still contributed only 27 percent of the total family income which was $54,000.

The literature which compares class differences in family power is slim, indeed. Still, what exists supports the argument I make here. Bahr (1974) reviewed that

No surprise this, in a culture where "money talks" is a phrase embedded deep in the folklore. No surprise either that working-class men often feel forced into an arbitrary authoritarianism as they seek to uphold their authority in the family and to insist upon their entitlement to respect. Sadly, probably no one is more aware than they are that the person who must insist upon respect for his status already has lost it. That fact alone is enough to account for the seemingly arbitrary and angry demands they sometimes make upon wives and children. Add to that the fact that, unlike their professional counterparts, the family is usually the only place where working-class men have any chance of exercising authority, and their behavior—while often unpleasant—may no longer seem so unreasonable. Those realities of their husbands' lives also at least partly explain the apparent submissiveness of working-class wives who, understanding the source of their men's demands, often try to accede to them in a vain attempt to relieve their husbands' pain and restore their bruised egos.

Thus, in some families, husbands win the struggle to keep their wives from either working or going to school to prepare for a job. Sometimes the wife is compliant, as in this family:

> I want to go back to school, but he doesn't want me to. He thinks I should just stay home with the children. But you know, I just can't stay home with them forever. After all, what am I going to do when they get to junior high school?

> I always really wanted to be a teacher, and I thought now would be a good time to start. I could take classes while the children are in school and be home before they get back. I keep telling him that it wouldn't make any difference in the house. I'd still get all my work done. It wouldn't interfere with anything—not with the housework, or cooking the meals, or the kids, or anything. He wouldn't even know I was gone. By the time he'd get home, everything would be just like it always was.

> I don't know what he worries about. Just because I want to go to school doesn't mean I'm going to go out and do anything. I guess he just doesn't want me getting too independent. We know some couples where the wife works, and then they get into fights over who should keep her money or what to spend it on. I wouldn't do that, but I guess he really isn't sure.

---

literature and concluded that "Working-class wives gain more power through employment than middle-class wives." Cf., also Scanzoni (1972:66–70) who examines the tools for measuring family decision-making and shows that regardless of the methodology or the instrument used, "husbands are more powerful than wives in routine family decisions as well as in conflict resolution, and higher status husbands generally have the greatest amount of family authority." See also Note 17 above for a further statement of his argument.

That seems like a real issue between you. How do you resolve such a conflict?

I keep talking to him, but I'm not getting anywhere yet. I'll keep trying, and maybe in a few years, he'll see it my way. Sometimes I understand how he feels, but sometimes I get mad because it doesn't seem fair that he can tell me no. I say to him, "It's my life; why can't I do what I want." And he says, "It's my life, too, and I say no." Then I get mixed up and I don't know what to say, so I just wait, and I'll try to talk to him again sometime when he's in a good mood.

The husband:

I don't want her to work, and I don't want her to go to school. What for? She doesn't have to. She's got plenty to keep her busy right here.

You feel strongly about that. Could you say why?

Mostly because of the kids. I think a mother should stay home with the kids. I told her when we first got married that I'd earn the money and she'd take care of the kids. I've never run across a family yet where the husband and wife work where there wasn't a lot of arguments and where the kids seem to grow up differently.

I understand that right now all she wants is to go to school.

Yeah, for five years and then eventually do something I don't want her to do anyhow. I told her she can't. Anyhow, I don't think she'd go all the way with it. Becoming a teacher, I don't know how many years you'd have to go to college for that. She wouldn't be able to go through with it.

If that's so, wouldn't it be worth letting her try so that she could find out for herself either that she couldn't or didn't want to do it?

No, not really. It would cause arguments between us, and the kids would be growing up with baby-sitters, and stuff like that. No, she can't do it.

I wonder, how far do you think you'd be willing to hold this position? If it threatened your marriage, would you be willing to go along with her even if you don't like the idea?

No, I wouldn't. I'd say this is the way it's going to be; it's the way I want it. If I was to back down because I feel it's not worth risking what I've got, what good would it be? I wouldn't have that much. She wouldn't be the same girl I married, so what would I be giving up?

So far, the stress of this struggle is not evident in the marriage. The battle lines are drawn, but the rules of war in this household are those of gentlepeople.

In other families, the battle is far more devastating and the victory a pyrrhic one—as the story of this couple, married thirteen years and parents of four, shows. Before the first word is spoken, the senses give evidence of the chaos in which they live. The front yard is a weed-infested patch, the porch cluttered and unswept. Inside, the house is dirty and disordered. My hostess matches the house—unkempt and uncared for. When she starts to speak, however, I am surprised. For here is an extremely articulate woman—her eyes bright, her voice lively and energetic. With a wave of her hand, she apologizes:

> I know it's a mess, but somehow I just can't ever seem to get things organized. I know it doesn't look like it, but I really do work hard around here. It's just that I'm so disorganized that I never finish anything I start. So there's always a million things piled on top of one another.

She talks easily and brightly about one subject after the other. Finally, we get to the issue of work. Her voice flat, she says:

> No, I don't work. My husband doesn't like me to work. He thinks a wife ought to be home taking care of the children and her husband.

You sound as if you wish it were otherwise.

> [*Wistfully.*] Yes, I really enjoyed working. I used to work down at the bank and I really enjoyed it. I was the best girl in the office, too. You know, it's funny, but I'm very organized when I work. I guess you wouldn't believe it, would you, but my desk was as neat as a pin. There was never a paper out of place. I even used to be more organized around the house when I was working.

> Maybe it'll sound silly to you, but I still belong to the Business and Professional Women's Club here. When I get dressed to go to one of their meetings, it's the only time I feel like a whole individual. I'm not somebody's wife, or somebody's mother. I'm just Karen. I suppose that's why I liked working, too. When I'd be there, I could just be who I am—I mean, who I am inside me not just all those other things.

It seems as if you all pay a heavy price for your not working. Have you and your husband tried to reconcile that difference in some way that wouldn't be so costly to all of you?

We've tried, but we don't get anywhere. I understand his point, too. He wants me to be at home when he leaves and he wants me to be here when he comes home. It's because of his upbringing. He was sent from one foster home to another when he was growing up, and he has a pretty big thing about the family staying together and about mothers being home with their kids. I suppose I would, too, if my mother ran off and left me.

Here, then, we see expressed her yearnings for herself, her anger because she feels deprived of an important part of that self, and her insight into the source of her husband's unwillingness to compromise the issue. But while insight generates understanding, it does little to assuage the pain of deprivation she experiences every day of her life.

Her husband, a tall, thin man, with a shy, sensitive smile, also talks openly and easily, but with a great deal of bitterness about the state of the house:

I just don't understand. She works like a beaver around here and never gets anything done. [*Pointing to the litter of cans all over the kitchen.*] I don't know how to convince her that if you open a tin can, it's easier to put it right in the garbage instead of sticking it on the sink, then opening another one and putting it on top of the frig, then opening another one and putting it on the table. Eventually, you spend all your time cleaning up all the opened cans. I keep telling her, but I can't make a dent.

You sound very frustrated about that.

Sure, I hate to walk into the bathroom and try to shave with everything stacked up around me, or try to find a clean coffee cup, or try to find a place to sit down with junk all over everything, or to look in my drawer and not find any underwear for the fourth day in a row because it's still stacked up on a chair in the living room.

Karen says things were different around the house when she was working, that things were much more organized. Is that your recollection, too?

Oh yeah, when she's working, she's much better.

It sounds as if there might be a message in that for you. Don't you hear it?

Sure, I hear that message, but I'm a little stubborn myself. And from my background, I can't help wanting her home with my kids. Sometimes I think I'm nuts or something. I can't understand why a young woman who only wanted to get married can do such a poor job of being a housewife and such a good one at an occupation.

Since she does so much better a job at home when she's also working outside, maybe you could both get what you want if she felt free to do that.

[*Slamming his hand down on the table in anger.*] Dammit, no! A wife's got to learn to be number two. That's just the way it is, and that's what she better learn. She's not going to work. She's going to stay home and take care of the family like a wife's supposed to do.

And she does. But the wreckage of the struggle is strewn around the house, its fallout contaminating everything it touches—husband, wife, children, and the marriage.

Thus does work performed outside the house—the values associated with it and the stereotypic conceptions about who must do it—touch the core of life inside the house.[20] For the men, there is no real choice. Like it or not, they work—never seriously questioning how it came to be that way, why it must remain so. Despite the enormity of the burdens they carry, many men still feel they must do it alone if they are to fulfill their roles successfully. Often they cannot, as the soaring proportion of married women who work attests. For the working-class man, that often means yet another challenge to his already uncertain self-esteem—this time in the only place where he has been able to make his authority felt: the family. For his wife, it means yet another burden in the marriage—the need somehow to shore up her husband's bruised ego while maintaining some contact not only with her own desires but with family needs as well. For both wives and husbands, it means new adjustments, new ways of seeing themselves and their roles in the family—a transition that some make more successfully than others.

Who works? What kind of work do they do? Do they earn enough —either separately or together—to support the family in reasonable comfort? What are the objective conditions *and* the subjective experience of work? In the context of family life, these are the central questions around work and its meaning. The answers determine the quality not only of work but of leisure as well.

REFERENCES

Aronowitz, Stanley. *False Promises.* New York: McGraw-Hill, 1973.

Bahr, Stephen J. "Comment on 'The Study of Family Power Structures: A Review 1960–1969.'" *Journal of Marriage and the Family* 34 (1972): 239–243.

[20] See Terkel (1974) for some compelling vignettes about the ways in which a person's work life, the social value placed on a particular kind of work, and the internalization of that value affect off-work life. Also Sennett and Cobb (1973) for an analysis of these issues.

Bahr, Stephen J. "Effects on Family Power and Division of Labor in the Family." In *Working Mothers*, edited by Lois W. Hoffman and F. Ivan Nye. San Francisco: Jossey-Bass, 1974.

Bardwick, Judith M., and Elizabeth Douvan. "Ambivalence: The Socialization of Women." In *Woman in Sexist Society*, edited by Vivian Gornick and Barbara K. Moran. New York: Basic Books, 1971.

Bem, Sandra L., and Daryl J. Bem. "Training the Woman to Know Her Place." In *The Future of the Family*, edited by Louise Kapp Howe. New York: Simon and Schuster, 1972.

Bendix, Reinhard. *Work and Authority in Industry*. New York: Harper Torchbooks, 1963.

Berger, Peter L., and Thomas Luckman. *The Social Construction of Reality*. Garden City, N.Y.: Anchor Books, 1967.

Blauner, Robert. *Alienation and Freedom*. Chicago: University of Chicago Press, 1964.

Blood, Robert O., Jr., and Robert M. Hamblin. "The Effect of the Wife's Employment on the Family Power Structure." *Social Forces* 36 (1958): 347–352.

Blood, Robert O., Jr., and Donald M. Wolfe. *Husbands and Wives: The Dynamics of Married Living*. New York: Free Press, 1960.

Braverman, Harry. *Labor and Monopoly Capitalism: The Degradation of Work in the Twentieth Century*. New York: Monthly Review Press, 1974.

Bremer, Robert H., ed. *Children and Youth in America*, vols. 1 and 2. Cambridge, Mass.: Harvard University Press, 1970.

Broverman, Inge K., et al. "Sex-Role Stereotypes: A Current Appraisal." *Journal of Social Issues* 28 (1972): 59–78.

Brun-Gulbrandsen, Sverre. "Sex Roles and the Socialization Process." In *The Changing Roles of Men and Women*, edited by Edmund Dahlström. Boston: Beacon Press, 1971.

Burke, John, ed. *The New Technology and Human Values*. Belmont, Calif.: Wadsworth Publishing, 1966.

Chafetz, Janet Saltzman. *Masculine/Feminine or Human?* Itasca, Ill.: F. E. Peacock, 1974.

Chinoy, Eli. *Automobile Workers and the American Dream*. New York: Random House, 1955.

Chodorow, Nancy. "Being and Doing: A Cross-Cultural Examination of the Socialization of Males and Females." In *Woman in Sexist Society*, edited by Vivian Gornick and Barbara K. Moran. New York: Basic Books, 1971.

Chodorow, Nancy. *The Reproduction of Mothering: Family Structure and Feminine Personality*. Berkeley: University of California Press (forthcoming, 1977).

Dubin, Robert. "Industrial Workers' World: A Study of the Central Life Interests of Industrial Workers." *Social Problems* 3 (1956): 131–141.

Easton, Barbara Leslie. "Industrialization and Femininity: A Case Study of Nineteenth Century New England." *Social Problems* 23 (forthcoming, 1976).

Easton, Barbara Leslie. "Women, Religion, and the Family: Revivalism as an Indicator of Social Change in Early New England." Ph.D. dissertation, University of California, Berkeley, 1975.

Ellul, Jacques. *The Technological Society*. New York: Vintage Books, 1967.

Freeman, Jo. "The Social Construction of the Second Sex." In *Intimacy, Family, and Society*, edited by Arlene Skolnick and Jerome Skolnick. Boston: Little, Brown, 1974.

Gillespie, Dair. "Who Has the Power? The Marital Struggle." In *Family, Marriage, and the Struggle of the Sexes*, edited by Hans P. Dreitzel. New York: Macmillan, 1972.

Greer, Colin. *The Great School Legend*. New York: Basic Books, 1972.

Heer, David M. "Dominance and the Working Wife." *Social Forces* 36 (1958): 341–347.

Heer, David M. "Husband and Wife Perceptions of Family Power Structure." *Marriage and Family Living* 24 (1962): 65–77.

Herzberg, Frederich. *Work and the Nature of Man*. Cleveland: World Publishing, 1966.

Herzberg, Frederich, et al. *The Motivation to Work*. New York: John Wiley, 1959.

Hoffman, Lois Wladis. "Early Childhood Experiences and Women's Achievement Motives." *Journal of Social Issues* 28 (1972): 129–155.

Hoffman, Lois Wladis. "Effects of Employment of Mothers on Parental Power Relations and the Division of Household Tasks." *Marriage and Family Living* 22 (1960): 27–35.

Hoffman, Lois Wladis, and F. Ivan Nye. *Working Mothers*. San Francisco: Jossey-Bass, 1974.

Holter, Harriet. "Sex Roles and Social Change." *Acta Sociologica* 14 (1971): 2–12.

Horner, Matina S. "Toward an Understanding of Achievement-Related Conflicts." *Journal of Social Issues* 28 (1972): 157–175.

Jones, Dorothy. *Urban Native Men and Women: Differences in Their Work Adaptations*. Publication of I.S.E.G.R., University of Alaska, Fairbanks, Alaska, 1975.

Kaplan, H. Roy, and Carlos Kruytbosch. "Sudden Riches and Work Behavior: A Behavioral Test of the Commitment to Work." Delivered at the Seventieth Annual Meeting of the American Sociological Association, San Francisco, California, August 25–29, 1975.

Kaplan, H. Roy, and Curt Tausky. "Work and the Welfare Cadillac: The Function of and Commitment to Work Among the Hard-Core Unemployed." *Social Problems* 19 (1972): 469–483.

Katz, Michael B. *The Irony of Early School Reform: Educational Innovation in Mid-Nineteenth Century Massachusetts*. Cambridge, Mass.: Harvard University Press, 1968.

Lazerson, Marvin. "Social Change and American Families: Some Historical Speculations." Xerox, 1975.

Levitan, Sar A., ed. *Blue Collar Workers: A Symposium on Middle America*. New York: McGraw-Hill, 1971.

Meissner, Martin. "The Long Arm of the Job: A Study of Work and Leisure." *Industrial Relations* 10 (1971): 239–260.

Mills, C. Wright. *White Collar*. New York: Oxford University Press, 1951.

Morse, Nancy C., and Robert S. Weiss. "The Function and Meaning of Work and the Job." *American Sociological Review* 20 (1955): 191–198.

Oakley, Ann. *Sex, Gender and Society*. New York: Harper Colophon, 1972.

Scanzoni, John H. *Sexual Bargaining: Power Politics in the American Marriage*. Englewood Cliffs, N.J.: Prentice-Hall, 1972.

Seashore, Stanley E., and Thad J. Barnowe. "Demographic and Job Factors Associated with the 'Blue Collar Blues.'" Mimeo, 1972.

Sennett, Richard, and Jonathan Cobb. *The Hidden Injuries of Class*. New York: Vintage Books, 1973.

Shainess, Natalie. "Toward a New Feminine Psychology." *Notre Dame Journal of Education* 2 (1972): 293–299.

Shepard, Jon M. "Functional Specialization, Alienation, and Job Satisfaction." *Industrial and Labor Relations Review* 23 (1970): 207–219.

Sheppard, Harold L. "Discontented Blue Collar Workers—A Case Study." *Labor Review* 94 (1971): 25–32.

Sheppard, Harold L., and Neal Herrick. *Where Have All the Robots Gone?* New York: Free Press, 1972.

Smith, David N. *Who Rules the Universities? An Essay in Class Analysis*. New York: Monthly Review Press, 1974.

Sokoloff, Natalie J. "A Description and Analysis of the Economic Position of Women in American Society." Xerox, 1975.

Tausky, Curt. "Meanings of Work Among Blue Collar Men." *Pacific Sociological Review* 12 (1969): 49–55.

Terkel, Studs. *Working*. New York: Avon Books, 1974.

Theobald, Robert, ed. *Dialogue on Technology*. Indianapolis: Bobbs-Merrill, 1967.

Thernstrom, Stephan. *Poverty and Progress: Social Mobility in a Nineteenth-Century City*. New York: Atheneum, 1972.

Torbet, William R. *Being for the Most Part Puppets*. Cambridge, Mass.: Schenkman Publishing, 1973.

United States Bureau of the Census. *Statistical Abstract of the United States: 1974*. 95th ed. Washington, D.C.: U.S. Government Printing Office, 1974.

United States Department of Health, Education, and Welfare. *Work in America*. Cambridge, Mass.: M.I.T. Press, 1973.

United States Department of Labor, Bureau of Labor Statistics. *Handbook of Labor Statistics—1975*. Washington, D.C.: U.S. Government Printing Office, 1975.

United States Senate Committee on Labor and Public Welfare. *Worker Alienation*. Hearings, Subcommittee on Employment, Manpower, and Poverty, July 25–26. Washington, D.C.: U.S. Government Printing Office, 1972.

Veroff, Joseph, and Sheila Feld. *Marriage and Work in America*. New York: Van Nostrand Reinhold, 1970.

Weisstein, Naomi. "Kinder, Küche, Kirche: Psychology Constructs the Female." In *Sisterhood Is Powerful*, edited by Robin Morgan. New York: Vintage Books, 1970.

Weitzman, Lenore J., et al. "Sex-Role Socialization in Picture Books for Preschool Children." *American Journal of Sociology* 77 (1972): 1125–1150.

Wilensky, Harold L. "Class, Class Consciousness, and American Workers." In *Labor in a Changing America*, edited by William Haber. New York: Basic Books, 1966.

Wilensky, Harold L. "Mass Society and Mass Culture: Interdependence or Independence." *American Sociological Review* 29 (1964): 173–197.

Zaretsky, Eli. "Capitalism, the Family, and Personal Life: Parts I and II." *Socialist Revolution* 3 (1973): 69–126, 19–70.

The Tragedy of Old Age in America

ROBERT N. BUTLER

Many historians and social scientists have recently been trying to understand what they call the life cycle. In particular, studies of childhood, adolescence, and young adulthood have been published in an attempt to comprehend better the life experiences of ordinary people. Most history has been "made" by men in their middle years, and, as a result, traditional historical writing has focused on the public lives of these people, to the exclusion of almost everyone else. The new methodologies of demography, psychohistory, and structural anthropology have been applied with increasing skill, resulting in significant enlightenment about matters previously believed unimportant or at least obscure.

The most rapidly growing segment of the population has been almost entirely ignored, however, by life-cycle historians—the aged, those over sixty-five. Advances in the fields of public health, nutrition, and medical science have led to a dramatic increase in the elderly segment of the population. Death control has had a greater demographic impact on American society than has birth control.

In past times, old age was not seen as much of a problem because not many people lived to the age of sixty-five. Those who grew old with their faculties intact were often respected and looked up to, particularly if they remained in positions of power or in control of property. Old age itself was no guarantee of veneration, however, for the historical record is full of references to the elderly being treated with contempt and, if they were also poor or failing in health, often being locked away in institutions or simply cast out of society to die.

The unprecedented increase of the elderly population in contemporary America confronts society with a situation that baffles social planners and policy-makers alike, not to mention the old people themselves. About 75 percent of all Americans now reach the age of sixty-five, as compared to only 40 percent at the turn of the century. Of those born in 1960, 90 percent are expected to reach old age. And that old age will be more vigorous than was heretofore possible for most. The number of the elderly in the population increased by 18 percent between 1970 and 1977, while the overall population increase in the United States was only 5 percent. The sheer numbers are staggering.

But the difficulties faced by older people are intensified when income levels are considered. According to a report released in 1978 by the Senate Committee on Aging, the after-tax income of family heads over sixty-five averages $5,764 a year, compared to an average income of $10,728 for family heads under sixty-five. This means that vast numbers of the elderly live in situations characterized by extreme poverty. What is to be done?

While it is clear that government Social Security and private pension plans assist those who receive benefits from them, income from such plans is incapable of providing a decent standard of living for most of the recipients. Forced retirement, even of those fully capable of continuing to work at their normal pace, has contributed to the problem and has recently come under close scrutiny by politicians fully aware that the elderly vote in higher proportion than do the young. National organizations such as the Gray Panthers are engaged in mobilizing political support among this rapidly increasing constituency for issues that will be to their benefit. The most important project to be undertaken, however, is educational. Americans in all stages of the life cycle have to be taught the facts of the aging process, in the hope that a clearer understanding will help eliminate "ageism"—the fear and prejudice aimed at the old.

In the forefront of the educational mission is Robert N. Butler, a doctor who is director of the National Institute on Aging of the National Institutes of Health. His prize-winning book, **Why Survive? Being Old in America,** is already recognized as a classic statement that addresses itself to the broad range of issues facing the elderly. The first chapter of that book, reprinted here, undertakes to challenge several myths concerning the aging process and seeks to suggest several directions for further research and study.

W hat is it like to be old in the United States? What will our own lives be like when we are old? Americans find it difficult to think about old age until they are propelled into the midst of it by their own aging and that of relatives and friends. Aging is the neglected stepchild of the human life cycle. Though we have begun to examine the socially taboo subjects of dying and death, we have leaped over that long period of time preceding death known as old age. In truth, it is easier to manage the problem of death than the problem of living as an old person. Death is a dramatic, one-time crisis while old age is a day-by-day and year-by-year confrontation with powerful external and internal forces, a bittersweet coming to terms with one's own personality and one's life.

Those of us who are not old barricade ourselves from discussions of old age by declaring the subject morbid, boring or in poor taste. Optimism and euphemism are other common devices. People will speak of looking forward to their "retirement years." The elderly are described respectfully as "senior citizens," "golden agers," "our elders," and one hears of old people who are considered inspirations and examples of how to "age well" or "gracefully." There is the popularly accepted opinion that Social Security and pensions provide a comfortable and reliable flow of funds so the elderly have few financial worries. Medicare has lulled the population into reassuring itself that the once terrible financial burdens of late-life illnesses are now eradicated. Advertisements and travel folders show relaxed, happy, well-dressed older people enjoying recreation, travel and their grandchildren. If they are no longer living in the old family home, they are pictured as delighted residents of retirement communities with names like Leisure World and Sun City, with lots of grass, clean air and fun. This is the American ideal of the "golden years" toward which millions of citizens are expectantly toiling through their workdays.

But this is not the full story. A second theme runs through the popular view of old age. Our colloquialisms reveal a great deal: once you are old you are "fading fast," "over the hill," "out to pasture," "down the drain," "finished," "out of date," an "old crock," "fogy," "geezer," or "biddy." One hears children saying they are afraid to get old, middle-aged people declaring they want to die after they have passed their prime, and numbers of old people wishing they were dead.

What can we possibly conclude from these discrepant points of view? Our popular attitudes could be summed up as a combination of wishful thinking and stark terror. We base our feelings on primitive fears, prejudice and stereotypes rather than on knowledge and insight. In reality, the way one experiences old age is contingent upon physical health, personality, earlier-life experiences, the actual circumstances of late-life events (in what order they occur, how they occur, when they occur) and the social supports one receives: adequate finances, shelter, medical care, social roles, religious support, recreation. All of these are crucial and interconnected elements which together determine the quality of late life.

Old age is neither inherently miserable nor inherently sublime—like every stage of life it has problems, joys, fears and potentials. The process of aging and eventual death must ultimately be accepted as the natural progression of the life cycle, the old completing their prescribed life spans and making way for the young. Much that is unique in old age in fact derives from the reality of aging and the imminence of death. The old must clarify and find use for what they have attained in a lifetime of learning and adapting; they must conserve strength and resources where necessary and adjust creatively to those changes and losses that occur as part of the aging experience. The elderly have the potential for qualities of human reflection and observation which can only come from having lived an entire life span. There is a lifetime accumulation of personality and experience which is available to be used and enjoyed.

But what are an individual's chances for a "good" old age in America, with satisfying final years and a dignified death? Unfortunately, none too good. For many elderly Americans old age is a tragedy, a period of quiet despair, deprivation, desolation and muted rage. This can be a consequence of the kind of life a person has led in younger years and the problems in his or her relationships with others. There are also inevitable personal and physical losses to be sustained, some of which can become overwhelming and unbearable. All of this is the individual factor, the existential element. But old age is frequently a tragedy even when the early years have been fulfilling and people seemingly have everything going for them. Herein lies what I consider to be the genuine tragedy of old age in America—we have shaped a society which is extremely harsh to live in when one is old. The tragedy of old age is not the fact that each of us must grow old and die but that the process of doing so has been made unnecessarily and at times excruciatingly painful, humiliating, debilitating and isolating through insensitivity, ignorance and poverty. The potentials for satisfactions and even triumphs in late life are real and vastly underexplored. For the most part the elderly struggle to exist in an inhospitable world.

Are things *really that bad?* Let's begin by looking at the basic daily requirements for survival. Poverty or drastically lowered income and old age go hand in hand. People who are poor all their lives remain poor as they grow old. Most of us realize this. What we do not realize is that these poor are joined by multitudes of people who become poor only after growing older. When Social Security becomes the sole or primary income, it means subsistence-level styles for many, and recent increases do not keep up with soaring costs of living. Private pension plans often do not pay off, and pension payments that do come in are not tied to inflationary decreases in buying power. Savings can be wiped out by a single unexpected catastrophe. In January, 1971, half of the elderly, or over 10 million people, lived on less than $75 a week, or $10 per day. Most lived on far less. Even the relatively well-off are not assured of an income that will support them:

> Rose Anderson was 90 years old, wispy and frail. She lived in a room filled with yellowed newspapers, magazines and books; it was filthy. There were cockroaches. There was an ugly permeating stench. She was too weary to clean. She gave her energy to caring for her canary.
>
> She had been the wife of a prominent physician but she had the "misfortune" of living to a ripe old age and outliving both the $300,000 her husband had carefully provided for her and her only child, a son, who died at the age of 57 when she was 76. She had given over some of her money to support her daughter-in-law and grandchildren. But most of it went for her own extensive medical expenses. She ended up living on welfare.

It has been estimated that at least 30 percent of the elderly live in substandard housing. Many more must deprive themselves of essentials to keep their homes in repair:

> Seventy-three-year-old Emil Pines was picked up by the police wandering along Market Street in San Francisco. He was mentally confused and unable to remember his name and address. After a medical examination it was determined that he had not eaten for several days and was dehydrated. Food and liquids were immediately prescribed and shortly thereafter his mind cleared. He re-

membered that he had used his pension check to pay for emergency house repairs and had not had enough left for food that month.

The American dream promised older people that if they worked hard enough all their lives, things would turn out well for them. Today's elderly were brought up to believe in pride, self-reliance and independence. Many are tough, determined individuals who manage to survive against adversity. But even the tough ones reach a point where help should be available to them:

> Now 81, Joseph Bartlett could look back on a long and useful life. He was living in a dusty Oklahoma town where he had lived since leaving farming and becoming a barber. He had been present at the opening of Indian Territory to white settlers and during the later oil boom. He had lost his wife and his only son ten years before. Since he had been self-employed he had no Social Security and was forced to turn to welfare. He was without transportation in the rural village. There were no social services, and medical care was inaccessible. His close friends and family had died, and he was too proud to ask other townspeople for the help he needed. He admitted to living in pain for a number of years but declared he would never burden anyone—"I will make do for myself."

Age discrimination in employment is unrestrained, with arbitrary retirement practices and bias against hiring older people for available jobs. Social Security penalizes the old by reducing their income checks as soon as they earn more than $2,400 a year. Job-training programs don't want the elderly (or the middle-aged, for that matter), so there is no opportunity to learn new skills. Employers rarely make concessions for the possible physical limitations of otherwise valuable older employees, and instead they are fired, retired or forced to resign.

It is obvious that the old get sick more frequently and more severely than the young, and 86 percent have chronic health problems of varying degree. These health problems, while significant, are largely treatable and for the most part do not impair the capacity to work. Medicare pays for only 45 percent of older people's health expenses; the balance must come from their own incomes and savings, or from Medicaid, which requires a humiliating means test. A serious illness can mean instant poverty. Drugs prescribed outside of hospitals, hearing aids, glasses, dental care and podiatry are not covered at all under Medicare. There is prejudice against the old by doctors and other medical personnel who don't like to bother with them. Psychiatrists and mental-health personnel typically assume that the mental problems of the old are untreatable. Psychoanalysts, the elite of the psychiatric profession, rarely accept them as patients. Medical schools and other teaching institutions find them "uninteresting." Voluntary hospitals are well known for dumping the "Medicare patient" into municipal hospitals; municipal hospitals in turn funnel them into nursing homes, mental hospitals and chronic-disease institutions without the adequate diagnostic and treatment effort which might enable them to return home. Persons who do remain at home while in ill health have serious difficulties in getting social, medical and psychiatric services brought directly to them:

> Professor Frank Minkoff, a 70-year-old Russian immigrant with a university degree in engineering, was still teaching mathematics at an evening school. He was unmarried, the only member of his family in the United States, and lived in an apartment crammed with books. Suddenly he became confused and disoriented. He was frightened and refused to leave his room. Concerned neighbors quickly called a doctor, who expressed his unwillingness to make a home visit, saying, "There is nothing I can do. He needs to be in a nursing home or a mental institution." The neighbors were unconvinced, remembering Mr. M.'s earlier good functioning. They pleaded with the doctor and, under pressure, he angrily complied and visited the home. While there he again repeated his conviction that Mr. M. needed "custodial" care. Mr. M. was coherent enough to refuse, saying he would never voluntarily go to a nursing home or mental hospital. He did agree to be admitted to a medical hospital. Admission took place and studies resulted in the diagnosis "reversible brain syndrome due to acute viral infection." Mr. M. was successfully treated and released to his home in good condition in less than a week.

Many others are not so fortunate. Afflicted with reversible conditions of all kinds, they are frequently labeled "senile" and sent to institutions for the rest of their lives.

Problems large and small confront the elderly. They are easy targets for crime in the streets and in their homes. Because of loneliness, confusion, hearing and visual difficulties they are prime victims of dishonest door-to-door salesmen and fraudulent advertising, and buy defective hearing aids, dance lessons, useless "Medicare insurance supplements," and quack health remedies. Persons crippled by arthritis or strokes are yelled at by impatient bus drivers for their slowness in climbing on and off buses. Traffic lights turn red before they can get across the street. Revolving doors move too quickly. Subways usually have no elevators or escalators.

Old women fare worse than old men. Women have an average life expectancy of seven years longer than men and tend to marry men older than themselves; so two-thirds (six million) of all older women are widows.* When widowed they do not have the same social prerogatives as older men to date and marry those who are younger. As a result, they are likely to end up alone—an ironic turn of events when one remembers that most of them were raised from childhood to consider marriage the only acceptable state. The income levels of older working women are

* Twenty percent of American women are widows by 60, 50 percent by 65, 66⅔ percent by 75.

generally lower than those of men; many never worked outside the home until their children were grown and then only at unskilled, low-paying jobs. Others who worked all their lives typically received low wages, with lower Social Security and private retirement benefits as a result. Until 1973, housewives who were widowed received only 82.5 percent of their husbands' Social Security benefits even though they were full-time home-makers.

Black, Mexican-American and American Indian elderly all have a lower life expectancy than whites, due to their socioeconomic disadvan-tages. Although the life expectancy of 67.5 years for white men remained the same from 1960 to 1968, the life expectancy for black men *declined* a full year during that time (from 61.1 to 60.0). Blacks of all ages make up 11 percent of the total United States population, but they constitute only 7.8 percent of the elderly. The life expectancy for Mexican-Americans is estimated at 57 years, and for American Indians at 44 years. Most do not live long enough to be eligible for the benefits of Social Security and Medicare. Poverty is the norm. Scant attention is paid to their particular cultural interests and heritage.

Asian-American elderly (Chinese, Japanese, Korean, Filipino and Samoan) are victims of a public impression that they are independently cared for by their families and therefore do not need help. However, pat-terns of immigration by Asian-Americans to this country, the cultural barriers, language problems and discrimination they have faced have all taken a toll of their elderly and their families.* This is particularly true of older Chinese men, who were not allowed to bring their wives and families with them to the United States or to intermarry.

MYTHS AND STEREOTYPES ABOUT THE OLD

In addition to dealing with the difficulties of physical and economic survival, older people are affected by the multitude of myths and stereo-types surrounding old age:

> An older person thinks and moves slowly. He does not think as he used to or as creatively. He is bound to himself and to his past and can no longer change or grow. He can learn neither well nor swiftly and, even if he could, he would not wish to. Tied to his personal traditions and growing conservatism, he dislikes innova-tions and is not disposed to new ideas. Not only can he not move forward, he often moves backward. He enters a second childhood, caught up in increasing egocentricity and demanding more from his environment than he is willing to give to it. Sometimes he be-comes an intensification of himself, a caricature of a lifelong per-sonality. He becomes irritable and cantankerous, yet shallow and

* One recommendation of the 1971 White House Conference on Aging was for fully crediting toward Social Security and other benefits the accumulated time spent by Japanese-Americans in United States "relocation" camps during World War II.

enfeebled. He lives in his past; he is behind the times. He is aimless and wandering of mind, reminiscing and garrulous. Indeed, he is a study in decline, the picture of mental and physical failure. He has lost and cannot replace friends, spouse, job, status, power, influence, income. He is often stricken by diseases which, in turn, restrict his movement, his enjoyment of food, the pleasures of well-being. He has lost his desire and capacity for sex. His body shrinks, and so too does the flow of blood to his brain. His mind does not utilize oxygen and sugar at the same rate as formerly. Feeble, uninteresting, he awaits his death, a burden to society, to his family and to himself.

In its essentials, this view I have sketched approximates the picture of old age held by many Americans. As in all clichés, stereotypes and myths there are bits of truth. But many of the current views of old age represent confusions, misunderstandings or simply a lack of knowledge about old age. Others may be completely inaccurate or biased, reflecting prejudice or outright hostility. Certain prevalent myths need closer examination.

The Myth of "Aging"

The idea of chronological aging (measuring one's age by the number of years one has lived) is a kind of myth. It is clear that there are great differences in the rates of physiological, chronological, psychological and social aging within the person and from person to person. In fact, physiological indicators show a greater range from the mean in old age than in any other age group, and this is true of personality as well. Older people actually become more diverse rather than more similar with advancing years. There are extraordinarily "young" 80-year-olds as well as "old" 80-year-olds. Chronological age, therefore, is a convenient but imprecise indicator of physical, mental and emotional status. For the purposes of this book old age may be considered to commence at the conventionally accepted point of 65.

We do know that organic brain damage can create such extensive intellectual impairment that people of all types and personalities may become dull-eyed, blank-faced and unresponsive. Massive destruction of the brain and body has a "leveling" effect which can produce increasing homogeneity among the elderly. But most older people do not suffer impairment of this magnitude during the greater part of their later life.

The Myth of Unproductivity

Many believe the old to be unproductive. But in the absence of diseases and social adversities, old people tend to remain productive and actively involved in life. There are dazzling examples like octogenarians Georgia O'Keeffe continuing to paint and Pope John XXIII revitalizing his church, and septuagenarians Duke Ellington composing and working his hectic concert schedule and Golda Meir acting as her country's vigorous Prime Minister. Substantial numbers of people become unusually creative for the first time in old age, when exceptional and inborn talents may be discovered and expressed. What is most pertinent to our discussion here, however, is the fact that many old people continue to contribute usefully to their families and community in a variety of ways, including active employment. The 1971 Bureau of Labor Statistics figures show 1,780,000 people over 65 working full time and 1,257,000 part time. Since society and business practice do not encourage the continued employment of the elderly, it is obvious that many more would work if jobs were available.

When productive incapacity develops, it can be traced more directly to a variety of losses, diseases or circumstances than to that mysterious process called aging. Even then, in spite of the presence of severe handicaps, activity and involvement are often maintained.

The Myth of Disengagement

This is related to the previous myth and holds that older people prefer to disengage from life, to withdraw into themselves, choosing to live alone or perhaps only with their peers. Ironically, some gerontologists themselves hold these views. One study, *Growing Old: The Process of Disengagement*, presents the theory that mutual separation of the aged person from his society is a natural part of the aging experience. There is no evidence to support this generalization. Disengagement is only one of many patterns of reaction to old age.

The Myth of Inflexibility

The ability to change and adapt has little to do with one's age and more to do with one's lifelong character. But even this statement has to be qualified. One is not necessarily destined to maintain one's character in earlier life permanently. True, the endurance, the strength and the stability in human character structure are remarkable and protective. But most, if not all, people change and remain open to change throughout the course of life, right up to its termination. The old notion, whether ascribed to Pope Alexander VI or Sigmund Freud, that character is laid down in final form by the fifth year of life can be confidently refuted. Change is the hallmark of living. The notion that older people become less responsive to innovation and change because of age is not supported by scientific studies of healthy older people living in the community or by everyday observations and clinical psychiatric experience.

A related cliché is that political conservatism increases with age. If one's options are constricted by job discrimination, reduced or fixed income and runaway inflation, as older people's are, one may become conservative out of economic necessity rather than out of qualities innate in the psyche. Thus an older person may vote against the creation of better schools or an expansion of social services for tax reasons. His property—his home—may be his only equity, and his income is likely to be too low to weather increased taxes. A perfectly sensible self-interest rather than "conservatism" is at work here. Naturally, conservatives do exist among the elderly, but so do liberals, radicals and moderates. Once again diversity rather than homogeneity is the norm.

The Myth of "Senility"

The notion that old people are senile, showing forgetfulness, confusional episodes and reduced attention, is widely accepted. "Senility" is a popularized layman's term used by doctors and the public alike to categorize the behavior of the old. Some of what is called senile is the result of brain damage. But anxiety and depression are also frequently lumped within the same category of senility, even though they are treatable and often reversible. Old people, like young people, experience a full range of emotions, including anxiety, grief, depression and paranoid states. It is all too easy to blame age and brain damage when accounting for the mental problems and emotional concerns of later life.

Drug tranquilization is another frequent, misdiagnosed and potentially reversible cause of so-called senility. Malnutrition and unrecognized physical illnesses, such as congestive heart failure, may produce "senile behavior" by reducing the supply of blood, oxygen and food to the brain. Alcoholism, often associated with bereavement, is another cause. Because it has been so convenient to dismiss all these manifestations by lumping them together under an improper and inaccurate diagnostic label, the elderly often do not receive the benefits of decent diagnosis and treatment.

Actual irreversible brain damage,* of course, is not a myth, and two major conditions create mental disorders. One is cerebral arteriosclerosis (hardening of the arteries of the brain); the other, unfortunately referred to as senile brain disease, is due to a mysterious dissolution of brain cells. Such conditions account for some 50 percent of the cases of major mental disorders in old age, and the symptoms connected with these conditions are the ones that form the basis for what has come to be known as senility. But, as I wish to emphasize again, similar symptoms can be found in a number of other conditions which *are* reversible through proper treatment.

* Human beings react in varying ways to brain disease just as they do to other serious threats to their persons. They may become anxious, rigid, depressed and hypochondriacal. (Hypochondriasis comprises bodily symptoms or fear of diseases that are not due to physical changes but to emotional concerns. They are no less real simply because they do not have a physical origin.) These reactions can be ameliorated by sensitive, humane concern, talk and understanding even though the underlying physical process cannot be reversed. Therefore, even the irreversible brain syndromes require proper diagnosis and treatment of their emotional consequences.

The Myth of Serenity

In contrast to the previous myths, which view the elderly in a negative light, the myth of serenity portrays old age as a kind of adult fairyland. Now at last comes a time of relative peace and serenity when people can relax and enjoy the fruits of their labors after the storms of active life are over. Advertising slogans, television and romantic fiction foster the myth. Visions of carefree, cookie-baking grandmothers and rocking-chair grandfathers are cherished by younger generations. But, in fact, older persons experience more stresses than any other age group, and these stresses are often devastating. The strength of the aged to endure crisis is remarkable, and tranquility is an unlikely as well as inappropriate response under these circumstances. Depression, anxiety, psychosomatic illnesses, paranoia, garrulousness and irritability are some of the internal reactions to external stresses.

Depressive reactions are particularly widespread in late life. To the more blatant psychotic depressions and the depressions associated with organic brain diseases must be added the everyday depressions that stem from long physical illness or chronic discomfort, from grief, despair and loneliness, and from an inevitably lowered self-esteem that comes from diminished social and personal status.

Grief is a frequent companion of old age—grief for one's own losses and for the ultimate loss of one's self. Apathy and emptiness are a common sequel to the initial shock and sadness that come with the deaths of close friends and relatives. Physical disease and social isolation can follow bereavement.

Anxiety is another common feature. There is much to be anxious about; poverty, loneliness and illness head the list. Anxiety may manifest itself in many forms: rigid patterns of thinking and behaving, helplessness, manipulative behavior, restlessness and suspiciousness, sometimes to the point of paranoid states.*

Anger and even rage may be seen:

> Mary Mack, 73, left her doctor's office irritable, depressed and untreated. She was angry at the doctor's inattention. She charged that he simply regarded her as a complainer and did not take the necessary time to examine her carefully. She had received the same response from other doctors. Meanwhile her doctor entered the diagnosis in his file: hypochondriasis with chronic depression. No treatment was given. The prognosis was evidently considered hopeless.

---

* No less a thinker than Aristotle failed to distinguish between the intrinsic features of aging and the reaction of the elderly to their lives. He considered cowardice, resentment, vindictiveness and what he called "senile avarice" to be intrinsic to late life. Cicero took a warmer and more positive view of old age. He understood, for example, "If old men are morose, troubled, fretful and hard to please . . . these are faults of character and not of age." So he explained in his essay "*De Senectute.*"

John Barber, an elderly black man, spent all his life working hard at low wages for his employers. When he was retired he literally went on strike. He refused to do anything. He would sit all day on his front porch, using his family as the substitute victim of his years of pent-up anger. He had always been seen as mild mannered. Now he could afford to let himself go into rages and describe in vicious detail what he was going to do to people. A social worker viewing his behavior declared to his family that he was "psychotic." But Mr. Barber was not insane; he was angry.

AGEISM—THE PREJUDICE AGAINST THE ELDERLY

The stereotyping and myths surrounding old age can be explained in part by lack of knowledge and by insufficient contact with a wide variety of older people. But there is another powerful factor operating—a deep and profound prejudice against the elderly which is found to some degree in all of us. In thinking about how to describe this, I coined the word "ageism" † in 1968:

> Ageism can be seen as a process of systematic stereotyping of and discrimination against people because they are old, just as racism and sexism accomplish this with skin color and gender. Old people are categorized as senile, rigid in thought and manner, old-fashioned in morality and skills. . . . Ageism allows the younger generations to see older people as different from themselves; thus they subtly cease to identify with their elders as human beings.[4]

Ageism makes it easier to ignore the frequently poor social and economic plight of older people. We can avoid dealing with the reality that our productivity-minded society has little use for nonproducers—in this case those who have reached an arbitrarily defined retirement age. We

† I first publicly described my notion of ageism at the time of stormy opposition to the purchase of a high-rise in northwest Washington for public housing for the elderly.[1] . . . I also developed it in observing the social and economic impact of the extended life span.[2] Ageism is a broader concept than "gerontophobia," the classic fear of old age. Gerontophobia refers to a rarer "unreasonable fear and/or irrational hatred of older people whereas ageism is a much more comprehensive and useful concept." [3]

[1] Carl Bernstein, "Age and Race Fears Seen in Housing Opposition," *Washington Post*, March 7, 1969.
[2] Robert N. Butler, "The Effects of Medical and Health Progress on the Social and Economic Aspects of the Life Cycle," *Industrial Gerontology*, 2 (1969), pp. 1–9. Presented at National Institute of Industrial Gerontology, March 13, 1969.
[3] See Erdman Palmore, "Gerontophobia Versus Ageism," *The Gerontologist*, 12 (1972), p. 213.
[4] Robert N. Butler and Myrna I. Lewis, *Aging and Mental Health: Positive Psychosocial Approaches* (St. Louis: C. V. Mosby, 1973).

can also avoid, for a time at least, reminders of the personal reality of our own aging and death.

Ageism is manifested in a wide range of phenomena, both on individual and institutional levels—stereotypes and myths, outright disdain and dislike, or simply subtle avoidance of contact; discriminatory practices in housing, employment and services of all kinds; epithets, cartoons and jokes. At times ageism becomes an expedient method by which society promotes viewpoints about the aged in order to relieve itself of responsibility toward them. At other times ageism serves a highly personal objective, protecting younger (usually middle-aged) individuals—often at high emotional cost—from thinking about things they fear (aging, illness, death).

The media illustrate the extremes to which negative attitudes toward the old can lead:

> August 29, 1970
> Mr. Douglas J. Stewart in *The New Republic* (Vol. 163, No. 8-9) advocated that all persons lose their vote after retirement, or at the age of 70, or at 55 when moving to another state.

Mr. Stewart, 37 years old at the time, was an associate professor of classics at Brandeis University. Perhaps one should allow for the possibility that he was speaking tongue in cheek, implying that the old are already effectively disenfranchised. But there can be no doubt about the serious-mindedness of the following proposal:

From Livermore, California, in what was described as an imaginative Rand Corporation study, a report entitled "The Post Attack Population of the United States" [5] suggested methods the United States should initiate with regard to old people, chronic invalids, and the insane in the event of nuclear war. The famous think tank said survivors of a nuclear war "would be better off without . . . old and feeble members." The author, Ira S. Lowry, stated that after a nuclear war, policy makers would be presented with a difficult problem because "the working members of the society would insist on transferring some part of their personal advantages to members of their families who were not directly contributing to output." The report continues by saying,

> Policy makers would presumably have to draw the line somewhere, however, in making such concessions and those most likely to suffer are people with little or no productive potential; old people, chronic invalids and the insane. Old people suffer the special disadvantage of being easily identified as a group and, therefore, subject to categorical treatment. . . . In a literate community, the elderly do not even serve their prehistoric function as repositories of traditional wisdoms . . . the amount of care and

[5] Memorandum RM–5115–TAB, prepared for Technical Analysis Branch, United States Atomic Energy Commission, the Rand Corporation, Santa Monica, California, December, 1966.

attention necessary to sustain life increases with age. . . . In this sense, at least, a community under stress would be better off without its old and feeble members. . . .[6]

The easiest way to implement a morally repugnant but socially beneficial policy is by inaction. Under stress, the managers of post-attack society would most likely resolve their problems by failing to make any special provision for the special needs of the elderly, the insane, and the chronically ill. Instead of Medicare for persons under 65, for example, we might have Medicare for persons under 15. Instead of pensions, we might have family allowances. To be sure, the government would not be able—nor would it be likely to try—to prevent the relatives and friends of old people from helping them: but overall the share of the elderly in the national product would certainly drop.[7]

Lowry, an economist and demographer, was quoted in a telephone conversation to Roger Rapaport of the Washington *Star* as follows: "The AEC (Atomic Energy Commission) told me that they were very satisfied with the final product." Extreme though this may sound, the abandonment of older people in time of crises is obviously not unthinkable.

Ageism, like all prejudices, influences the self view and behavior of its victims. The elderly tend to adopt negative definitions of themselves and to perpetuate the very stereotypes directed against them, thereby reinforcing society's beliefs. As one older woman describes it:

> Part of the neglect [of old people] can be attributed to the attitudes of the senior citizen himself. Rather than face the fact that being old is just another stage in the external aging process and being thankful that he has been blessed to reach this pinnacle in life, he has chosen to contemplate his plight with resignation, and even in some instances with disgust and frustration. This defeatist attitude has been adopted by society in general. We are now trying to reverse this trend.[8]

The elderly's part in eliciting the kind of response which they receive from the young and from society at large is often a subtle but powerful factor in the public's generally disparaging views of them. They collaborate with their ostracizers. Some individuals act "senile"; others may deny their true feelings in an attempt to "age graciously" and obtain the approval which is otherwise denied them. Psychologist Margaret Thaler Singer observed similarities between the Rorschach test findings in members of a National Institute of Mental Health sample of aged volunteers

[6] *Ibid.*, p. 122.
[7] *Ibid.*, p. 123.
[8] Mrs. Mae B. Phillips, president, Senior Citizens Clearinghouse Committee, Washington, D.C. Hearings on Needs of Senior Citizens, D.C. City Council, October 15, 1968.

who were resigned in the face of aging and those in American GI prisoners of war who collaborated with their captors in Korea.

Other self-sabotaging behavior can be a refusal to identify oneself as elderly at all. One sees older persons who affect the dress and behavior patterns of the young, pretending like Peter Pan that they have never grown up. Older women can be seen engaging in sad, frantic attempts to appear young, as if this would ensure appreciation and acceptance in the eyes of others.

A significant minority of older people conceal their age from themselves as well as from others. In a study of 1,700 elderly persons, Taves and Hansen[9] found that one-sixth thought of themselves as old between the ages of 54 and 69, one-third between the ages of 70 and 79, and only 40 percent by age 80 and over. About one person in seven said they never thought of themselves as old.

In a study by Tuckman and Lorge [10] that queried over 1,000 persons from 20 to 80, those under 30 classified themselves as young, and of those between 30 and 60, most classified themselves as middle-aged. At age 60 only a small proportion classified themselves as old, and at age 80 slightly over half called themselves old. A small percentage of the 80-year-olds persisted in describing themselves as young.

Of course, considering oneself "young" is not simply a prejudice or a delusion.[11] Healthy older people do feel strong and vigorous, much as they did in their earlier days. The problem comes when this good feeling is called "youth" rather than "health," thus tying it to chronological age instead of to physical and mental well-being.

Lack of empathy is a further reaction by the elderly to their experiences in the larger culture. Out of emotional self-protection, many healthy, prosperous, well-educated old people feel no identification with or protectiveness toward the poor elderly. A lack of compassion is of course not unique to the aged, but it has a special irony here—with the advent of catastrophic illnesses or the exhaustion of resources that goes with a long life, they too run a high risk of finding themselves among the poor, facing similar indifference from their wealthier peers.

Older people are not always victims, passive and fated by their environment. They, too, initiate direct actions and stimulate responses. They may exploit their age and its accompanying challenges to gain something they want or need, perhaps to their own detriment (e.g., by demanding services from others and thus allowing their own skills to atrophy). Exploitation can backfire; excessive requests to others by an older person may be met at first, but as requests increase they are felt as demands—and may indeed be demands. Younger people who attempt to deal with a

[9] Marvin J. Taves and G. O. Hansen, "1,700 Elderly Citizens," in Arnold M. Rose (ed.), *Aging in Minnesota* (Minneapolis: University of Minnesota Press, 1963), pp. 73–181.
[10] Jacob Tuckman and Irving Lorge, "Classification of the Self as Young, Middle-aged or Old," *Geriatrics*, 9 (1954), pp. 534–36.
[11] See, for example, Talcott Parsons, "Age and Sex of the Social Structure of the United States," in *Essays in Sociological Theory* (Glencoe Illinois: Free Press, 1954), especially pp. 89–103.

demanding older person may find themselves going through successive cycles of rage, guilt and overprotectiveness without realizing they are being manipulated. In addition to his "age," the older person may exploit his diseases and his impairments, capitalizing upon his alleged helplessness. Invalids of all ages do this, but older people can more easily take on the appearance of frailty when others would not be allowed this behavior. Manipulation by older people is best recognized for what it is—a valuable clue that there is energy available which should be redirected toward greater benefit for themselves and others.

It must also be remembered that the old can have many prejudices against the young. These may be a result of their attractiveness, vigor and sexual prowess. Older people may be troubled by the extraordinary changes that they see in the world around them and blame the younger generation. They may be angry at the brevity of life and begrudge someone the fresh chance of living out a life span which they have already completed.

Angry and ambivalent feelings flow, too, between the old and the middle-aged, who are caught up in the problems unique to their age and position within the life cycle. The middle-aged bear the heaviest personal and social responsibilities since they are called upon to help support—individually and collectively—both ends of the life cycle: the nurture and education of their young and the financial, emotional and physical care of the old. Many have not been prepared for their heavy responsibilities and are surprised and overwhelmed by them. Frequently these responsibilities trap them in their careers or life styles until the children grow up or their parents die. A common reaction is anger at both the young and the old. The effects of financial pressures are seen primarily in the middle and lower economic classes. But the middle-aged of all classes are inclined to be ambivalent toward the young and old since both age groups remind them of their own waning youth. In addition—with reason—they fear technological or professional obsolescence as they see what has happened to their elders and feel the pressure of youth pushing its way toward their position in society. Furthermore, their responsibilities are likely to increase in the future as more and more of their parents and grandparents live longer life spans.

THE ELDERLY POPULATION EXPLOSION

There are now well over twenty million people over 65 years of age in the United States, comprising 10 percent of the population.* A population explosion of older people has been under way for a number of decades, and the elderly are now the fastest-growing group in the United States. Between 1960 and 1970 the aging increased by 21 percent, compared with an 18 percent increase among those under 65.

Older people have become a highly visible phenomenon only since

---

* Two of every ten Americans are now between 45 and 65. This is 20 percent of the population, or 42 million people.

the nineteenth century; before then relatively few people were long lived. In 1900 only three million, or 4 percent of the population, were 65 and older. Influenza, pneumonia, tuberculosis, typhoid and paratyphoid fever, diphtheria and scarlet fever were major killers, causing high death rates all along the life cycle. Increased life expectancy followed medical advances in the prevention and treatment of these diseases, as well as generally improved public-health measures, particularly in sanitation. Lowered rates of infant and maternal mortality enabled larger numbers of people to reach old age, and once there, new drugs and medical techniques allowed many old people to survive once-fatal illnesses.

The average life expectancy at the turn of the century was 47 years; now it is 70.4 years. A boy born today can expect to live to 66.8 years; a girl to age 74.3. Half of all older people (ten million) are over 73; 1,000,000 elderly are 85 and over; and the 1970 census reports 106,441 centenarians (over 100 years old).

Every day 1,000 people reach 65; each year 365,000. More than 70 percent of the 65-and-over age group in 1970 entered that category after 1959. With new medical discoveries, an improved health-care delivery system and the presently declining birth rate, it is possible that the elderly will make up 15 percent of the total population by the year 2000. Major medical advances in the control of cancer or heart and vascular diseases could increase the average life expectancy by ten or even fifteen years. Discovery of deterrents to the basic causes of aging would cause even more profound repercussions. The presence of so many elderly, and the potential of so many more, has been a puzzlement to gerontologists, public-health experts and demographers, who don't know whether to regard it as "the aging problem" or a human triumph over disease. What is clear is that it will result in enormous changes in every part of society.

Changes will therefore occur in our definition of the aging process itself. Much of what we think of as aging today is actually disease and illness, and not a part of fundamental physical aging. This includes many of the physical, mental and emotional conditions seen in older people. The major diseases of late life may become preventable or at least treatable. The mental depressions of late life and the acute brain syndromes are already treatable and reversible. The removal of pathogenic elements—excessive sun exposure and cigarette smoking (both are causes of skin wrinkles), air pollution and others—may slow down the physical appearances of deterioration. Even genetic traits responsible for such changes as graying and loss of hair may eventually be controllable. What is in the future if acute and chronic disease states are identified and largely eliminated, undesirable genetic traits mainly nullified and pathogenic environmental conditions alleviated? We should see for the first time that flow of human life from birth through death truly called aging. Aging refers to patterns of late-life changes which are eventually seen in all persons but which vary in rate and degree. Although human beings will never be able to live indefinitely, they can live much longer and more comfortably, mostly free from the violent ravages of disease, with perhaps a gradual and fairly predictable decline toward eventual death.

The physical health of the majority of the elderly is already better than is generally believed. Eighty-one percent of those over 65 are fully ambulatory and move about independently on their own. Ninety-five percent live in the community; at any one time only 5 percent are in nursing homes, chronic-disease hospitals and other institutions—a startling fact when one thinks of the popular image of the old "dumped" en masse into institutions by their families because they have become enfeebled.

Our view of who is old and when aging happens will also change. It is becoming more common to find retired people in their sixties and seventies who have living parents in the eighties and nineties. Sometimes it is the 80-year-old who is taking care of the 60-year-old! Chronological age is an inaccurate measure of how old one is because aging as we presently experience it occurs unevenly—one may be at very different "ages" at one and the same time in terms of mental capacity, physical health, endurance, creativity and emotions. Society has arbitrarily chosen ages 60–65 as the beginning of late life (borrowing the idea from Bismarck's social legislation in Germany in the 1880s) primarily for the purpose of determining a point for retirement and eligibility for services and financial entitlements for the elderly. This social definition has had its legitimate uses but also its abuses. Not everyone is ready to retire at 60 or 65. Older people do not appreciate the "social" definition of old age encroaching into every corner of their lives, rigidly stamping them with a uniform label regardless of condition or functioning. Gerontologists divide old age into early old age, 65 to 74 years, and advanced old age, 75 and above. A much more flexible view, which took actual capacities into account, would be more realistic.

STUDYING THE OLD

We have put precious little work and research into examining the last phase of life. What research has been done has concentrated primarily on studies of the 5 percent of elderly who are in institutions. The few research studies on the healthy aged living in the community have produced exciting new looks at the possibilities and problems of this age group.[12] But on the whole medicine and the behavioral sciences seem to have shared society's negative views of old age and have quite consistently presented *decline* as the key concept of late life, with *neglect* forming the major treatment technique and research response.

Why study the elderly? Why spend research money on old people when there are compelling priorities for other age groups, particularly the young? In the first place, life cannot be carved up into bits and pieces —what affects one age group affects another. To illustrate this on the biological level, it is well known that carcinoma in the breast of a woman has a much more fulminating malignant course if it occurs in young

[12] James E. Birren, Robert N. Butler, Samuel W. Greenhouse, Louis Sokoloff and Marion R. Yarrow, *Human Aging: A Biological and Behavioral Study*, U.S. Public Health Service Publication No. 986 (Washington, DC.: U.S. Government Printing Office, 1963, reprinted 1971, 1974).

women than in old. Leukemia, another form of cancer, tends to be more chronic in the old and more acute in the young. Diabetes is much more severe in childhood than in the aged. Why? Is there something we can learn about disease processes in the old that may help both them and those who are younger? Many of the diseases occurring in old age do not begin there. Arteriosclerosis, a major cause of much morbidity and mortality (affecting such major organs as the kidney, the heart and the brain), begins early in life. If we are to stop it, it must be studied, prevented and treated in its earliest phases. Stroke, typically thought of as occurring in late life, also kills the young in significant numbers.

In the psychological sphere, too, our understanding of emotions like grief can gain enormously from the study of the old, in whom grief occurs with such frequency and profundity. This is true of a whole variety of human reactions to stress, as well as to the normal events in late life. The natural history of human character and its disorders can only really be studied in the old. The degree to which change and improvement in mental diseases and emotional illnesses occur, the nature of survival characteristics, and successful modes of adaptation, among other matters, are natural subjects for study in those who have lived an entire life span.

Ultimately interest must focus on clarifying the complex, interwoven elements necessary to produce and support physical and mental health up to the very end of life rather than our present preoccupation with "curing" ills after they develop. Understanding what interferes with healthy development throughout the life cycle gives us a chance to prevent problems, instead of rushing frantically and often futilely to solve them after they occur. Life is a continuing process from birth until death and it seems strange that it so seldom occurs to us to study life as a whole.

Finally, from a philosophic view, a greater understanding and control over the diseases and difficulties of later life would hopefully make old age less frightening and more acceptable as a truly valuable last phase of life. The relief of human suffering has merit in itself, but it also releases human beings from the fears and defenses they build up around it.

WHOSE RESPONSIBILITY ARE THEY?

Are older Americans entitled to decent income, health, housing, transportation and opportunities for employment as well as to social status and participation in society? Who should see to it that they get them? Why can't they manage their lives themselves? The struggle to decide on the place of the old in a culture has been familiar throughout history. Cultural attitudes have ranged from veneration, protectiveness, and sentimentality to derogation, rejection, pity and abandonment. William Graham Sumner, in his *Folkways*, published in 1907, wrote in a section, "Mores of Respect or Contempt for the Aged":

> . . . [There are] two sets of mores as to the aged: (1) in one set of mores the teaching, and usages, inculcate conventional respect for the aged who are therefore arbitrarily preserved for their wisdom

and counsel, perhaps also sometimes out of affection and sympathy; (2) in the other set of mores the aged are regarded as societal burdens which waste the strength of the society, already inadequate for its tasks. Therefore, they are forced to die, either by their own hands or those of their relatives. It is very far from being true that the first of these policies is practiced higher up in civilization than those who practice the second. The people in lower civilizations profit more by the counsel from the aged than those in higher civilizations and are educated by this experience to respect and value the aged.

Older Americans of today—indeed the old people in any society—contributed to the growth of the society in which younger people live. One might assume that they would have a justifiable expectation of sharing in what is referred to as America's affluence. All of us, whatever our age, are now contributing taxes and services to our nation and are collectively preparing for our own old age. What will the future bring for us? Will anyone help us if we cannot adequately help ourselves?

There are people who believe that the responsibility for one's old age can and should be assumed by the individual alone. They hold that improvidence is the major cause of an impoverished old age and agree with the nineteenth-century Social Darwinist, Herbert Spencer:

> Pervading all nature we may see at work a stern discipline, which is a little cruel that it may be very kind. . . . The poverty of the incapable, the distresses that come upon the imprudent, the starvation of the idle, and the shouldering aside of the weak by the strong . . . are the decrees of a large, far-seeing benevolence. . . . Similarly, we must call spurious philanthropists who, to prevent a present misery, would entail greater misery upon future generations. All defenders of a poor-law must be classed among them. . . . Blind to the fact that under the natural order of things society is constantly excreting its unhealthy, imbecile, slow, vacillating, faithless members, those unthinking, though well-meaning, men advocate an interference which not only stops the purifying process but even increases the vitiation.[13]

Such a harsh view fails to take into account the life circumstances and historical conditions of today's older Americans. Americans born in the 1900s found themselves, in the prime of their earning years, trapped in the massive Depression of the 1930s. Many lost jobs, homes, savings and their morale.

By the 1960s, when they were retiring, inflation eroded their fixed incomes to an alarming degree. Economic forces, not improvidence, have placed today's elderly in their predicament.

The Depression of the 1930s convinced many rugged individualists that

[13] Herbert Spencer, *Social Statics, or The Conditions Essential to Human Happiness Specified,* 1851.

forces beyond the control of the individual could bring widespread devastation and poverty. A legislative landmark of Roosevelt's New Deal was the inauguration of Social Security in 1935, a consequence of many pressures that included the Townsend movement;* perhaps the final impetus came from the need to have the old retire in order to provide employment for the young. Thus, years after most Western European industrial nations had introduced it, the United States made its decision for the collective insurance-policy form of income maintenance for the disabled and retired. Eighty-five cents ($0.85) of every federal dollar now expended annually for programs for the elderly derive from Social Security trust funds to which we all contribute—as did the majority of the present elderly themselves in their working days.

Social Security, Medicare and federal housing programs have helped to gain for the elderly *some* income security, *some* health care and *some* housing. But the task has not been finished and the efforts do not match the needs. . . .

---

* A movement representing older persons and led by Dr. Francis Townsend, a retired physician.

Suggestions for Further Reading

A useful survey of the postwar years is found in Godfrey Hodgson, *America in Our Time: From World War II to Nixon, What Happened and Why** (Garden City, N.Y., 1976). The history of suburban development is found in Kenneth T. Jackson, "The Crabgrass Frontier: 150 Years of Suburban Growth in America," in *The Urban Experience: Themes in American History,** edited by Raymond A. Mohl and James F. Richardson (Belmont, Cal., 1973). For works by critics of suburban life, see John Keats, *The Crack in the Picture Window* (Boston, 1956); William H. Whyte, Jr., *The Organization Man** (New York, 1956); and R. Gordon, K. Gordon, and M. Gunther, *The Split-Level Trap* (New York, 1961). The suburban myth developed by the critics was challenged by Herbert J. Gans, *The Levittowners** (New York, 1967), and Bennett M. Berger, *Working Class Suburb** (Berkeley, Cal., 1960). See also J. Seeley, R. Sim, and E. Loosley, *Crestwood Heights** (New York, 1956), a study of a Canadian suburb. An interesting study illustrating the suburbanization of small towns is found in Arthur J. Vidich and Joseph Bensman, *Small Town in Mass Society** (Princeton, N.J., 1958). A recent attempt to evaluate suburban life was made by Samuel Kaplan in *The Dream Deferred: People, Politics and Planning in Suburbia** (New York, 1976).

The problems of adolescents in the 1950s and early 1960s are critically explored in Paul Goodman, *Growing Up Absurd** (New York, 1960), and in two works by educational sociologist Edgar Z. Friedenberg, *The Vanishing Adolescent** (Boston, 1959) and *Coming of Age in America** (New York, 1965). For an interesting contrast, compare James S. Coleman's two works on young people, *The Adolescent Society** (Glencoe, Ill., 1961) and *Youth: Transition to Adulthood** (Chicago, 1974).

A good place to begin studying the youth of the counter-culture years is in two works by Kenneth Keniston that deal with nonhippie youth, *The Uncommitted: Alienated Youth in American Society** (New York, 1965) and *Young Radicals** (New York, 1968). A historian, Theodore Roszak, has written a sympathetic exploration of the reasons for the growth of the counter-culture in *The Making of a Counter-Culture** (New York, 1969). Many of the books that describe the cultural developments of the late 1960s also advocate change. See, for example, Tom Wolfe, *The Electric Kool-Aid Acid Test** (New York, 1968); Charles Reich, *The Greening of America** (New York, 1960); and William Braden, *The Private Sea: LSD and the Search for God* (Chicago, 1967). Nicholas von Hoffman, a journalist, has explored the hippie phenomenon in *We Are the People Our Parents Warned Us Against**

* Available in paperback edition.

(Chicago, 1968). The adult counter-culture is described in Rasa Gustaitis, *Turning On** (New York, 1969). For events leading to the music explosion among the counter-culture, see the work of art historian Carl Belz, *The Story of Rock** (New York, 1968). Lawrence Veysey has written a fascinating history of communitarianism in America, including many counter-culture communes, in *The Communal Experience: Anarchist and Mystical Counter-Cultures in America* (New York, 1973). On the student political movement, see *SDS** (New York, 1973) by Kirkpatrick Sale. The impact of Eastern religions on the United States can be seen in Robert Ellwood, Jr., *Religious and Spiritual Groups in Modern America** (Englewood Cliffs, N.J., 1973), and Jacob Needleman, *The New Religions** (New York, 1970). Two science fiction works that had a great influence on the counter-culture are Robert Heinlein, *Stranger in a Strange Land** (New York, 1961), and Frank Herbert, *Dune** (Philadelphia, 1965).

Two recent books that evaluate the status of the American family in contrasting ways are Kenneth Keniston and the Carnegie Council on Children, *All Our Children: The American Family Under Pressure** (New York, 1977), and Mary Jo Bane, *Here to Stay: American Families in the Twentieth Century** (New York, 1976). The working-class family was insightfully examined directly by Mirra Komarovsky in *Blue Collar Marriage** (New York, 1964) and indirectly by Richard Sennett and Jonathan Cobb in *The Hidden Injuries of Class** (New York, 1973). An excellent collection of documents is found in *America's Working Women: A Documentary History—1600 to the Present** (New York, 1976), edited by Rosalyn Baxandall, Linda Gordon, and Susan Reverby. Ann Oakley's two books on housework are basic for an understanding of women in families: *The Sociology of Housework** (New York, 1975) and *Woman's Work: The Housewife, Past and Present** (New York, 1976).

The first attempt to survey the place of the aged in American history is David Hackett Fischer's *Growing Old in America** (New York, 1977). A useful collection of articles is found in Beth B. Hess, ed., *Growing Old in America** (New Brunswick, N.J., 1976). See also Zena Smith Blau, *Old Age in a Changing Society** (New York, 1973). The nursing-home scandal is exposed by Mary Adelaide Mendelson in *Tender Loving Greed** (New York, 1974). Attempts of old people to gain political influence are described in Henry J. Pratt's *The Gray Lobby* (Chicago, 1976). A prize-winning article on aging was published in *Newsweek* (Feb. 28, 1977) under the title "The Graying of America."

A	9
B	0
C	1
D	2
E	3
F	4
G	5
H	6
I	7
J	8